T0389115

PSYCHOLOGY LIBRARY EDITIONS:
CHILD DEVELOPMENT

Volume 16

PSYCHOLOGY OF EARLY CHILDHOOD

PSYCHOLOGY OF EARLY CHILDHOOD

Up to the Sixth Year of Age

WILLIAM STERN

Translated by
ANNA BARWELL

Routledge
Taylor & Francis Group

LONDON AND NEW YORK

English translation first published in 1924 by George Allen & Unwin Ltd.
Second edition, enlarged and completely revised in accordance with the sixth German edition, 1930

This edition first published in 2018
by Routledge
2 Park Square, Milton Park, Abingdon, Oxon OX14 4RN

and by Routledge
711 Third Avenue, New York, NY 10017

Routledge is an imprint of the Taylor & Francis Group, an informa business

British Library Cataloguing in Publication Data
A catalogue record for this book is available from the British Library

ISBN: 978-1-138-74142-3 (Set)
ISBN: 978-1-351-27384-8 (Set) (ebk)
ISBN: 978-1-138-08835-1 (Volume 16) (hbk)
ISBN: 978-1-315-10989-3 (Volume 16) (ebk)

Publisher's Note
The publisher has gone to great lengths to ensure the quality of this reprint but points out that some imperfections in the original copies may be apparent.

Disclaimer
The publisher has made every effort to trace copyright holders and would welcome correspondence from those they have been unable to trace.

PSYCHOLOGY OF EARLY CHILDHOOD
UP TO THE SIXTH YEAR OF AGE

BY

WILLIAM STERN

SUPPLEMENTED BY EXTRACTS FROM THE UNPUBLISHED
DIARIES OF CLARA STERN

TRANSLATED BY
ANNA BARWELL

LONDON: GEORGE ALLEN & UNWIN LTD
NEW YORK: HENRY HOLT AND COMPANY

ENGLISH TRANSLATION FIRST PUBLISHED IN 1924
SECOND IMPRESSION 1926
SECOND EDITION, ENLARGED AND COMPLETELY REVISED IN
ACCORDANCE WITH THE SIXTH GERMAN EDITION
(THIRD IMPRESSION), 1930

PRINTED IN GREAT BRITAIN BY
UNWIN BROTHERS LTD., WOKING

PREFACE TO THE SIXTH EDITION

THE second edition of 1921 was practically an unaltered reprint of the first. But when the necessity of a fresh edition again arose, I determined to revise the book; when once I had begun, this revision so far exceeded the limits I had originally fixed as to make not only a material change in the book but considerably to enlarge it as well. Advantage was taken of the fourth edition (1927) and of the present sixth edition to make further revision, in order to keep abreast of the most important advances in the field of child-psychology. Consequently the book has been greatly altered from its original form; not only is it wider in range but the bibliography is three times more extensive and the table of contents revised.

As regards its subject-matter, the principal changes are as follows:—

In the general theory of child-psychology the personal standpoint has been even more emphasized than before, whilst at the same time other psychological theories such as mental-psychology, form-psychology, psychoanalysis and individual-psychology have been exhaustively treated, criticized and discussed in contradistinction to the theory of personality.

In various places the psychological and pedagogic suppositions of the Montessori method have been criticized and discussed.

Much fuller treatment has been given to the experimental examination of young children for purposes of research and tests, since it is in this form of investigation that such marked advance has been made during the last fifteen years.

As opportunity arose, consideration has been given to the literature—still very scanty—dealing with young children of the proletariate.

Most of the chapters in Part VII [Enjoyment and Creative Activity] and Part IX [Effort—Emotion—Will], when not completely new, have been entirely revised.

The value of the book has been greatly increased by a couple of contributions most kindly put at my disposal by two scientific friends, and which appear as "supplements". The omission—often regretted—in our book of any representations of "expression"-movements in childhood has now been supplied by the contribution of Professor Kurt Lewin (Berlin). Professor Lewin had arranged for the taking of scientific moving photographs of children's gestures, and grouped together several series of particularly characteristic photos in four plates accompanied by explanatory notes for my fourth edition. In the present fifth and sixth editions Professor Heinz Werner (Hamburg) has contributed a short article on Magic in Early Childhood, for which he had confirmation in extensive material as yet unpublished. I take this opportunity of expressing my warm thanks to both these collaborators.

WILLIAM STERN

HAMBURG,
   June 27, 1928

PREFACE TO THE FIRST EDITION

It is just a generation since Wilhelm Preyer first put the psychology of early childhood on to a scientific basis. His book, *The Soul of the Child*, has already become an historic landmark; the progress in this fresh field of enquiry as regards the manifold presentation of new problems, keenness of observation, caution in deductions and in the application of new methods, has gone far beyond Preyer's achievement. But no fresh attempt at a systematic summary and review of what has been accomplished has been made in these thirty-two years, at any rate not in the German language.

Yet at this moment the need for such a review is urgent, and that for very diverse reasons. Of chief weight, perhaps, are those of science, for child-psychology itself, which for a long time consisted only of the collection of data and individual investigations, is badly in need of clearly marked boundaries as to the extent, value and significance of its discoveries. Then, too, general psychology ought to enter into a closer relationship with child-lore, for from this it obtains an insight into the genesis of those psychic functions whose structure and laws are the object of its investigations, whilst, on the other hand, general psychology gives to child-lore the scientific points of view, theories and aims without which child-study would be nothing but worthless dilettantism. Of late, too, historians have begun to take an interest in child-study, for they believe that the similarities between the early development of the individual and the intellectual growth of the race are extensive enough to open fresh paths for historical research.

Then, too, educational interests are not without weight. Cultured parents desire to find some expert psychological guidance for the observation of their young children. Their teachers, too, in play-centres and kindergartens demand a foundation of scientific child-knowledge on which to build, not only their educational methods, but above all the efforts at reform which are so distinctive a feature of to-day. Moreover, even those educationists who have to deal with older pupils are becoming more generally convinced that a knowledge of the earlier stages tends to a better understanding of the entire future development of the child.

The physician and teacher of defective children find in the psychology of the normal child a standard which helps them to a truer understanding of the abnormalities and deficiencies of those under their care.

And finally comes the need of a textbook. For some years now child-psychology has been introduced into Training Colleges, both for kindergartens and other schools, whether for men or women students, and into University Extension courses, as a very important subject of the curriculum.

I am fully conscious that the present book is only capable of satisfying some of the demands mentioned above. I have endeavoured to the utmost of my power to discuss the most essential sides of the child's psychic life as far as they develop up to his sixth year; that full equality of treatment cannot be achieved in this way is due to the present condition of this science, for in many directions such progress had been made by earlier investigations that a firm foundation existed for further superstructure, whilst in others it was essential to begin by clearing a road.

I did my utmost in my restricted area of observation to work out the interrelations with psychology in general. On the other hand I have refrained—with but few exceptions—from all pedagogic deductions, since it must be left to practical teachers themselves to translate theories and illustrations of child-knowledge into the rules and facts of the child's education. Nor was I any better qualified to discuss phylogenetic similarities with the stages of the child's development.

The chief source of my studies was—with the addition of literature and general psychological theory—the observation through many years of our own children Hilde, Gunther and Eva; so I hope I have escaped the failing of many another author, viz. that of offering a child-psychology founded on an arbitrary theory alone. My wife's diaries provided for our mutual work, as they had done for earlier individual investigation, a well of information which even now, in spite of constant use, is not nearly exhausted. In addition to these I have, from time to time, drawn illustrations from other children mentioned in psychological literature, especially from the careful records of their son kept by G. and E. Scupin.

It is true all the more detailed scientific child-study has, until the present time, only concerned itself with children of the upper classes, and this book is no less limited in its examples from the same source. It is, of course, probable that the main features of the child's psychic development share the same general character, but in details such as the relative time of development or the influence of certain conditions of environment, it is but reasonable to suppose that amongst the lower classes variations will be found which, so far, are but little known and which offer a wide and important field for future enquiry.

The notification of age is given in the now generally accepted form of completed years and months. Thus: ; 7 means at the age of 7 months, 3 ; 4 means at the age of 3 years and 4 months, and so on. The examples taken from my wife's diaries are marked by inverted commas, and in these passages "I" always signifies the mother.

WILLIAM STERN

Breslau,
April 6, 1914

CONTENTS

PART III

DEVELOPMENT OF SPEECH

PART IV

LOOKING AT PICTURES

B

PART VII

ENJOYMENT AND CREATIVE ACTIVITY

PART VIII

THOUGHT AND INTELLIGENCE

PART IX

IMPULSE—EMOTION—WILL—THE VARIOUS FORMS AND DIRECTIONS OF ENDEAVOUR

SUPPLEMENTS

PART I

GENERAL CONSIDERATIONS

CHAPTER I

THE AIM AND DEVELOPMENT OF CHILD-PSYCHOLOGY

1. Aim

THERE are two paths of progress in science and culture; the one starts from what is normal, ordinary, matter-of-course, and leads into the far distance, looking for what is strange and mysterious, diseased and exceptionally gifted; for unknown regions, marvellous forms of life, and curious spiritual phenomena.

The other has no such distant goal, and yet it brings us to discoveries of no less value. It traverses only what is quite near and apparently known to all, and suddenly shows it to us in a totally new light. This is the more toilsome path; for, if we are to believe Plato's dictum that wonder is the beginning of all search, of all enquiry, how difficult is it to arouse wonder once more in our daily surroundings, to perceive that the "self-evident" is anything but evident at all.

So it is not difficult to understand why the science of childhood or child-study is one of the latest shoots on the tree of human knowledge. It is true that, at every period of human civilization, we find care, education and instruction of the child, but it has been reserved for our own times to look upon the child himself as a problem; now we suddenly discover beside what deep mysteries and riddles we have wandered blind and deaf for thousands of years, and, at the same time, we recognize that an examination of those untouched problems will not only increase our knowledge but also add to our skill in education.

Child-knowledge in the widest sense of the word has to concern itself with all sides of the immature human being, with his physical and spiritual nature, with his relation to society, morality, law; and so there is an anthropology, physiology, a pathology and psychology, a sociology and criminology of the child. But in the very centre of all these scientific efforts stands the study of the child's psychic life, and the aim of the present book is to present a certain part of this by dealing with the normal psychic development in early childhood, i.e. in the period before school-age.

Such a limit is fixed, not only by considerations of space, but by reasons arising from the matter under treatment. For the entire youth of a human being falls quite naturally into three periods, each of six to seven years, and every one of these periods may be looked upon as a whole, complete in itself.

It is no accident that educational authorities of all times have fixed the seventh year as the beginning of school-life, and the fourteenth year as the end of general education, whilst the third period of youth is given up to study in continuation and high schools or to vocational training, but rather is it an instinctive feeling that, at these ages, development reaches a natural turning-point. The time-periods are marked physically by the change of teeth and by puberty. But it is in psychic directions that the differences are most marked. The distinguishing feature of the first period is its character of *play*. The human being develops his natural powers by play; by it the child, through his senses, comes to a realization of the world outside himself, gains control over his own movements, and learns to express and communicate his ideas in speech. In the middle of the second period (seventh to fourteenth year) comes the differentiation of work and play, the systematic development of the powers of memory (conscious learning), and the reaching, thereby, of the last stage of the elementary education of man. In the third period (fourteenth to twentieth year) the hitherto predominate receptivity and interest in outside things of the human soul is replaced by a turning-in upon itself; there comes an independence of the personality; what is learnt is now the object of inner consideration and further development; a free choice of interests and individual judgment exercise great influence on the attitude to life. And thus a separate treatment of each of these three periods is not only possible but requisite.

The student of the first period has to do with the child whose world is the nursery and the kindergarten, and the difference between the psychology of early childhood and the psychology of school-age is no less marked than that between first education and school pedagogics. The problems of the first period are, primarily, of a genetic order concerned with the gradual unfolding of the mental powers from their very earliest beginning, whilst in school-psychology, the all-important point of interest is the existent psychic condition at fixed stages of childhood. And this difference makes itself felt even in the methods of scientific research; in early childhood by far the most important point is the continuous observation of as many sides as possible of the individual child, whilst at school-age we have to combine a wide observation of the child with experimental testing of separate powers and with statistic results of examination of great numbers.

This demarcation between early childhood and school-age must, however, not be so much emphasized that the teacher who only has to deal with school-children should think he need not take any interest in early psychology, for nothing could be wider of the mark than this conclusion. The orchard-grower who desires good fruits must not confine his observation to the growth of the fruit alone, but he must be familiar with and follow the whole development of the trees even before the fruit is formed. So too the teacher. The understanding of the psychic phenomena which he sees in his school-children is, in great measure, dependent upon his knowledge of how they have come to pass, and what conditions have determined the rate of their development and their special individuality.

But these first stages of development are found in early childhood. Sometimes indeed certain individual points of development in infancy may prove to be of the utmost importance through successive stages of growth right up to adult life; moreover, separate powers exist in far greater simplicity and can be observed with much more ease and control than in the older child, so that the study of these first stages has an incalculable educational value for every one who makes it his task to penetrate into the intricacies of the psychic life of school-age.

.   .   .   .   .

We will now attempt to give a short résumé of the work done in child-psychology up to the present time, and, in so doing, follow first the main-trend development and then two remarkable off-shoots, viz. psychoanalysis and the Montessori movement.

2. Development of Child-Psychology to 1914

The real founders of a psychology of early childhood were neither pedagogues nor psychologists by profession. It is true great educationists of earlier times—Comenius, Rousseau, Pestalozzi and others—had plainly asserted that educational principles should be deduced from child-nature, but all they could say about this child-nature was the sum of occasional experiences, keen intuitions and a wide range of preconceived ideas; they did not dream of scientific research. And when, in the nineteenth century, Herbart and his followers laid stress on the fact that pedagogy ought to be founded on the science of psychology, they meant, as a rule, general psychology, which was rooted in systematic logic and in the observation of adults—generally the investigator's own observation of himself; the conclusion which lay so close at hand of beginning a psychological study of the child was, as yet, not apparent.

Froebel has undoubtedly been one of those older pedagogues with the widest knowledge of child-nature. With deep intuition he has not only found a number of "occupations" for children which are at once psychologically suitable and of educational value for this early age, but he has taken up a standpoint in his theoretical arguments and reasons whose value—thanks to the "personalistic" turn in psychology—we are only now beginning to value at its true worth.[1] If Froebel has not exercised a direct influence on purely scientific research work amongst children, this is due to the fundamental attitude which he and his followers adopted of concentrating entirely on the practical education of young children.

It was medical men, rather, who were the first to make an earnest effort to tackle our problems. They were, indeed, the only investigators whose profession required them to study the child on his first stages of life's journey; as students of natural science, they were familiar with those vast, new questions arising from the problem of development. So, at an early date, we find physicians writing on this subject, but in too isolated a fashion to be productive of much result: Tiedemann's *Consideration of the Development of Psychic Qualities in Children* (as early as 1787!); B. Sigismund's *The Child and The World* (1856); Kussmaul's *Enquiry into the Psychic Life of the New-*

[1] Cf. especially Muchow IV.

born Child (1859). But, then, in 1882, Wilhelm Preyer brought out his *Soul of the Child*, a book which may be considered as the real foundation of modern child-psychology. For the first time a child—an only child, too, the author's son—was made the object of systematic observation—observation that began with the moment of birth and continued, day by day, until the end of the third year. As a physiologist, Preyer gave an important place in his study to the child's physical powers, especially to the development of muscular movements. Still, he was no less the first to record the early stages of the really psychic powers of speech, the sense of space, of memory, of voluntary action, etc. It was no matter for surprise that the deductions he drew from his observations were often wrong and, above all, too intellectual—we needed a full ten years' apprenticeship before we reached a certain degree of surety in the interpretation of these vague and ambiguous psychic expressions of a primitive kind.

Preyer found numerous imitators, strangely enough not so much in his native land as in others. America, above all, was flooded with descriptive records of little children; of these, by far the most comprehensive are the studies of Miss Shinn, but the records of Moore, Major, Chamberlain are deserving of mention. In France we find the works of Pérey, Egger and, lately, Cramaussel, in Bulgaria of Gheorgov. In various non-German countries, too, relatively early attempts were made at more summarized and generalized characterizations of early childhood, attempts that took up a not very clearly defined position between a scientific and popular presentation of the subject. They have all been translated into German, although, with the exception of the first two named, such translation seems scarcely justified. These books are written by Sully (English), Compayré (French), Tracy (American), Paola Lombroso (Italian), and Sikorski (Russian).

It is only since the beginning of the present century that the work has been taken up again in Germany with a pronounced scientific leaning, and has much benefited by the fact that psychologists (Ament, Meumann, Stumpf, and the author of this book), who, before, had only studied special sides of the question, have now taken up the work as a whole; philosophers, educationists and others have also joined them (Dyroff, Dix, etc.)

Nearly all the investigations named above have the one point in common, that they are limited to the first three years of childhood. This is partly due to the very nature of the observation itself. All investigations into the history of development —even in quite other fields—always show a great preference for the earliest stages; investigators always like to put their hands, if possible, on the first link of the chain to be followed. Besides, with the child's increasing years, it becomes increasingly difficult to exercise a more or less complete control over all the influences to which he is subjected, a control which allows the observer to distinguish how far the facts noted are due to inborn capabilities or are the result of outside causes. Also— as even Preyer emphasized—man, in the first three years of his life, accomplishes a mental development which, in range and extent, is scarcely less than the development of the whole of his after-life.

Partly, too, doubtless, Preyer set an example which has been only too slavishly followed; perhaps also the patience required for continuous note-taking would not last beyond three years. This is the more regrettable, as the next three years—also bringing with them a mighty quota of development—are likewise very little known as regards their psychological history.

For this reason the personal investigations of the author and his wife have been carried on to the sixth year and even beyond, as were those recently published by Herr Scupin and his wife.

These older investigators of child-psychology differ widely in arrangement and treatment of the subject in hand. Some follow Preyer also in observing the child's early development in every direction, but the majority confine themselves to individual treatment of some single psychic function, usually giving strong preference to the development of the sense of observation and of speech. There is, too, quite as much variety in the number of children under observation; many writers are content to give an individual presentation—psychography—of the one child observed by them, whilst others try, by comparison with observations gathered from other quarters, to arrive at more universal conclusions regarding the psychic nature of the child. In our own monographs on speech and memory in childhood the subjects are treated both from a psychographical and psychological point of view, but in separate sections. The most advisable course seems to deal with the subject both from a psychographical and a psychological point of view, keeping each, however, in its separate division.

In addition to the literature named above, which is exclusively confined to the earliest years of life, mention must be made of some German writings on the psychology of youth which treat of early childhood as well as of other ages. Such are the works of K. Groos and Dyroff, and the popular little books of Ament and Gaupp. Ament has also earned our gratitude by a very complete bibliography—with a short descriptive index—brought up to the year 1903.

3. The Development of Child-Psychology since 1914

The present book, whose aim and method are explained in the preface to the first edition, first appeared in the year 1914.

The attempt thus made to bring about a closer union between child-study and theoretical psychology brought forth good fruit in succeeding years, in the work of various psychologists. On the one hand, certain new theories were applied to explain psychic phenomena in the child, and, on the other, observations of such phenomena were accepted at their full value as indubitable proofs of new psychological ideas. These theories—however diverse in detail—have one point in common, viz. that they are all opposed to any explanation of psychological phenomena based on sensualistic or "association" theories.

Theories of the older school had referred the beginning of the child's psychic life to the reception of sense-impressions and to the union of sensations and their effects into perceptual forms (due to association-mechanism).

The present book had already opposed to this view the theory of "personality," i.e. the conviction that the independent unity of personal life is the starting-point and continuous cause of all psychic development. Meantime the critical view of personality, in its general application to man, has been systematically treated by me.[1]

Of late, too, special schools, of value in their consideration of child-psychology, seem more or less plainly to be in conformity with the "personality" theory.

Thought-psychology, taking its rise in Külpe's Wurzburg

[1] In my books *Human Personality* and *Wertphilosophie* (Vols. II and III).

school of thought, has proved that real thought-activity is not derived from sensational, perceptual and associative processes, but has its own original nature and is distinguished by a principle of consciously directed activity. These views, at first drawn from adult observation, had already been used by Karl Groos (and in the present book) in explanation of facts in child-psychology; but the fundamental treatment of the new theory as applied to the problem of mental development was first found in Karl Bühler's books. He was able to show, not only that the little child's real thought-phenomena follow special laws, quite unconnected with those of simple association, but he also proved that the child's other mental functions: perception, memory, imagination, drawing, etc., are all universally interwoven with the threads of thought-psychology, and it is these alone that give them their explanation. Bühler's writings are not yet able to show ultimate solutions of every point, but, even where they have to leave new problems unsolved, they are still an aid to the development of our science.

The "form-psychology" of the Berlin school [1] and the theory of complex qualities, put forward by the Leipzig school, have, in spite of much divergence, this in common: that they both combat the mosaic idea of psychic phenomena and show that every psychic form, in its coherent totality, is something quite different from the simple sum of its elements, and that, therefore, these psychic forms must be themselves understood in their structure and laws instead of being broken up into elementary component parts and thus explained away. This new point of view for the solution of development-problems was first used by Köhler in his animal-psychology; his pioneer researches into structure-functions and intelligent actions, as occurring in anthropomorphic apes, offered opportunities for extremely instructive comparison with the psychic phenomena of early childhood. Koffka then completed their direct application to child-psychology; the very centre of his study is the problem of fresh activity—or learning in its widest sense—that is, exactly the question which, as a branch of the theory of memory, had, at an earlier period, been the chief stronghold of the one-sided associative psychology. Volkelt has successfully applied the principle of complex qualities to the perceptions of

---

[1] Wertheimer, Köhler and others.

the little child. Still more closely allied to the "personality" theory are those writings that are known as "development"-psychology. The course of psychological development as such is considered as a uniform process of mental structural growth. The immediate result of this view is the necessity of showing the common conformity to law which is universally present in the early forms of psychic development, whether these are observed in child, savage, lower animal, in abnormal cases of human degeneration or in the more deeply hidden recesses of the soul of the normal adult. Thus we gradually gain an insight into the distinctive nature of primitive psychology, which presents such extraordinary difficulties to the complicated mind of those belonging to our modern-day civilization. Such a "development"-psychology, first put forward years ago by Felix Krueger, has lately been systematized for the first time by Heinz Werner. But then we are faced with the problem of giving structural pictures of definite stages of development. Either an attempt is made to represent such a stage in its typical growth, as Bernfeld on the one hand and Charlotte Bühler on the other have done as regards infancy, or a description is given of the individual character at some definite age; thus Elsa Köhler reproduces the psychic picture of a three-year-old girl, whilst Herr Katz and his wife give the characterization of their sons at the age of three and five years respectively.

The more recent, careful investigations of the Geneva psychologist Piaget into thought and speech in childhood also show a tendency to "development"-psychology.

Finally, attention must be called to the *"social"-psychological* point of view, which investigates the primitive connection of the child to its personal environment [Bühler, Grünbaum, Piaget and others].

In addition to the theoretical progress described, there is also in recent years that of method, particularly in the use of experiment, with which we shall deal in Chapter II.

With a certain regret we are forced to admit that the theoretical and experimental efforts of specialized psychological research in the last ten years, very remarkable as they certainly are, have been almost entirely directed to the understanding of the child's intellectual development. The psychological side of the child's life as regards emotion, impulse or will has, indeed, been almost entirely left to the mercy of other branches of science, which has subjected it to the one-sided treatment of psychoanalysis and of individual-psychology which we will discuss at once.

4. Off-Shoots

In addition to the main trend of work in child-psychology we find the development of two movements, dating from the beginning of the century, but only obtaining any considerable measure of application and credence in the last ten years.

Of these the Montessori movement is almost of the nature of specialized psychology, partly on account of its special reference to the experimental method of psychology, and partly by the very marked limitation of its point of view to development on the purely mental side. The significance of the Montessori Children's Homes—which are on a par with Froebel's efforts— as factors of social reform does not come within the scope of this book. The psychological views of Maria Montessori agree in one main point with modern child-study and the convictions expressed in this volume, for she emphasizes the principle of the child's free independence, which can be utilized quite otherwise than in the usual kindergarten methods of self-education and development. But against this advantage we have to set the fundamental bias of unyielding intellectuality. Exercise of the senses—and through the senses, exercise of the intellect; such is the main path taken by Mme Montessori in her general education of the little child. To distinguish, arrange without help, to name correctly colour, form, tone, material; to know and skilfully control their own physical movements; to feel by touch and then to draw outlines until the power of writing develops involuntarily; to count and calculate by little sticks— all this and much more is learnt by children of three to seven years of age, without compulsion, but with delight and astonishing speed. They learn by play—but all their games are learning-games, intellectually devised for the exercise of intellectual powers by way of the training of the sense and muscles. What becomes then of the child's real freedom if, in spite of the absence of command and prohibition, the unmistakable compulsion of the learning materials and the sober atmosphere of application to the performance in hand surround the child? What of all those activities which cannot be directly transmuted into training of observation and into intellectuality; that confabulation and imagining by means of speech or drawing, those games with dolls or personations, the looking at pictures and the singing games? Maria Montessori offers as her new contribution a splendid method—free from all force or mechanical drill—of training the child's elementary powers; but the psychological error of her teaching is that method in teaching is the all-important point in early childhood. She would be right if the little child's sole destiny was observation, or were he a being struggling for piecemeal knowledge; but he is created other and greater than this.[1]

Totally independent of all efforts hitherto described, and also with an entirely new assumption, the "psychoanalysis," originated by Freud, approaches the child's psychic life. Here, once more, medicine puts its hand to child-psychology, but now —otherwise than in Preyer's time—it is the emotional phenomena that form the chief centre of interest.

The aim of psychoanalysis is to illuminate those depths of impulse and desire that lie in the subconsciousness and use as symbols certain outer demonstrations and conscious phenomena to announce their existence. This fundamental thought contains a deep truth;[2] but its successful working-out is greatly diminished by the fact that this unconscious germ in the psychic nature is everywhere—even in the little child—looked upon as sexuality, and then finally, an interpretation, boundless in its freedom, is able to strike out a "real"—however unconscious—sexual note from every childish action and expression.

The interest of the psychoanalyst in the child's psychic life is by no means single-eyed. To begin with, the determining factor was the wish to understand the adult's psychic life; but, according to the theory of psychoanalysis, we find this greatly affected by the after-effects of infantile experiences. In order to investigate these sources of origin, psychoanalysis had, at last, to turn to the little child himself, and then, naturally, it was predisposed to see already in these first

[1] As regards the Montessori problem, cf. in addition to Mme Montessori's own writings, especially those of Muchow (IV) with her comprehensive bibliography, also Buchholz, Hessen, D. and R. Katz, as well as other passages in the present volume.
[2] Starting from an entirely different point, the personality theory has come to a somewhat similar view. Cf. *Die menschliche Persönlichkeit,* pp. 251 sqq.

phenomena nothing but hints and preparatory stages of maturer psychic formation (especially in erotic and sexual directions). This has doubtless led to the discovery of important —although hitherto unheeded—features of the child's psychic life, above all much additional light has been thrown on many psychopathic and neurotic conditions both in early and adult life. But the expert and unprejudiced observer of the healthy child's psychic life is struck again and again by the numerous misinterpretations, exaggerations and unreliable generalizations of psychoanalysis as applied to children. We are confronted here, once more, by the old defect in child-study in a new form, viz. the wish to see in the child nothing but the adult in miniature, and this error becomes more serious with decrease in the age of children subjected to psychoanalytic interpretation. The educational and therapeutic results are more especially dangerous for early childhood, since their tendency is to rob the child prematurely of his irreplaceable "innocence," and this fact needs particular emphasis since, at the present time at home and even more abroad, many enthusiastic followers of Freud are now recommending psychoanalysis of children as the general foundation of educational reforms.[1]

As early as 1904 Freud made known the main principles of his views regarding infantile sexuality; in 1909 he followed this up by the individual analysis of a five-year-old child suffering from fear-neurosis. Jung dealt with the conflicts of the child's psychic nature. Hug-Hellmuth endeavoured to give a summary of early childhood psychology from the point of view of pan-sexuality. Pfister, Stekel and others have, in their larger works, devoted special chapters to the psychic and sexual life in early childhood. Bernfeld has just published an exhaustive mono-graph concerning infancy. Most important and useful for child-psychology are, perhaps, the efforts of Alfred Adler's school, to a certain extent opposed to Freud's theories; this "individual" psychology in its methods of interpretation aims at discovering in the child's psychic life not one-sided sexual clues but those of general application and logical in character.[2] Albert Moll in 1909 published a general view of sexual life in childhood, independent, in its main features, of psychoanalysis and more restrained in its theories.

---

[1] See my *Protest-pamphlet*, 1913.   [2] Cf. *Heilen und Bilden*.

CHAPTER II

CHILD-PSYCHOLOGY METHODS

1. Methods of Observation

THAT what is simple is understood with greater ease than what is more complicated is a banal statement, and therefore, at first sight, it might seem as if no part of the whole of psychology could offer fewer difficulties to the investigator than early childhood, with its exceedingly simple and undeveloped psychic life. But this supposition is wrong and its consequences decidedly serious, for not a few are led astray into the mad idea that in child-psychology to heap up example on example is an easy matter, requiring no great training or critical caution. As a matter of fact, what is simple assumes a very different aspect in psychology from that which it has in other branches of science.

The understanding of psychic life comes directly to each human being, for himself alone. We only know what perceptions and sensations, will-power and feelings are directly through our own experience and self-observation.[1] The psychic life of another, on the other hand, we have to interpret by what that other shows outwardly, his expressional movements, utterances, actions and reactions, etc. The more the other,

---

[1] Hence self-observation forms the starting-point in general psychology. But it is another matter in child-psychology, for the child, especially the little child, has all his attention directed outwards, and is therefore entirely incapable of systematic self-consideration. Even if, now and again, he gives spontaneous expression to any utterance referring to his own inner life, yet it is never possible to construct a scientific method on such rare exceptions. But as soon as ever the child is induced to undertake self-observation of present or self-recollection of past thoughts, feelings, wishes, etc., he is at the mercy of the suggestions of his interrogator. This fact must be borne in mind in adjudging the credibility of many auto-pronouncements in early childhood obtained by psychoanalytic investigations. (Cf. with this last utterance my criticism of Freud's *Phobie-Studie*, 1913.)

The child seems somewhat more capable of observing himself as regards sensorial experiences. Thus G. Révész tells of a child (5 ; 6) who observed reflections of bright stimuli and other inner stimuli-effects in the retina and gave an exact description of them as they occurred. But such cases are, relatively speaking, akin to outer observation; also the child had a strong spontaneous interest in optical experiences; correct self-observation, when asked for, even of sensorial experiences would be obtained but seldom at this age.

The son of Katz (5 ; 4) noticed the contrast, and spontaneously drew the inference that negroes' teeth only *look* so particularly white because their skin is black.

C

whom we are observing, differs from ourselves, the greater
the difficulty in forming a correct interpretation, which, after
all, must have its origin in our own analogous experience.
And the fact that we adults, studying child-psychology,
already have a very complicated psychic life makes it difficult
for us to come to a right understanding of this primitive
psychic life, mainly because of its simplicity and consequent
dissimilarity from our own.

And we must own in self-resignation that the reason is,
in a certain sense, because childhood is for us paradise lost;
we grown-ups can never again come to a complete and absolute understanding of the special nature and construction of
the child-soul.

But even here the realization of ignorance is the condition of a surer even if a more limited knowledge. The
ignoring of the fixed gulf mentioned above continually resulted in the crassest misinterpretations of the child's outward
activity; this or that movement or utterance received psychic
explanations which in the case of older children or adults
might have been true enough. This is not only the case with
the undeniable—but very pardonable—mistake of every
young mother who acclaims the first intelligently spoken
word, the first appropriate movement, of her child as a
proof of infinite cleverness; but psychologists too, especially those of the earlier decades, continually dealt in such
exaggerations.

But there is also a tendency to err in the opposite direction,
and to look upon all differences between the psychic life of a
child and that of adults as defects in the former which one
either notices with a kindly smile or blames with pedagogic
superiority. The simple statement that a child does not know
this or that, that it does not understand, thinks or acts wrongly,
is, after all, not psychology. Our task is not to apply the
"normal measure" of our own psychic powers and nature to
the child and to make a note of the points where he falls short
of the standard, but rather to understand the different nature
of the child as being typically characteristic of his positive
divergent individuality. But we have by degrees learnt to
avoid these rocks of offence, and one of the most blessed results
of modern investigation in child-psychology is this very correction of such false deductions; mention need only be made

here of the important question of the apparent falsehoods of the little child.

He who would draw as near as may be to the tender, incomprehensible life of the child-soul without falling into such errors must observe some principles of procedure.

1. *In each observation made of a little child mark a clear distinction between the outward action, really observed, i.e. the action or expression seen, the utterance heard, etc., and the conclusions deduced from it.* Separate the record of each, and, whenever possible, justify to yourself and to others the reliability or probability of the conclusion advanced.

2. *The conclusion should be as much as possible in accordance with child-nature*; try to keep it as far as may be from the complicities of your own psychic life and give full weight to the simplicity of the child-soul,[1] it is of a more diffuse nature and the child's psychic experiences are much less sharply differentiated and more vague in their outlines.

3. No general psychological assertions, conclusions, explanations should be made which cannot be amply justified by actual observations.

Now, in what way and with the help of what persons are we to gather our materials for child-psychology?

The first place must, of course, be given to the direct observation of children by such persons as live with them in a constant relationship of confidence and familiarity. And because no one in these first six years is nearly so much with the child, sharing its smallest joys and sorrows, as the mother, she it is who seems destined, above all others, to do this service for child-psychology. It is true, scientific training is needed for such a task, and, moreover, but few mothers will ever find it possible to unite the objective turn of thought and interest required for purposes of investigation with the necessarily subjective mother-love and tenderness.

Other relatives follow in the second place. So far most material has come from them; thus Preyer, Stumpf, Dix and

[1] The little child translates its experience into expression much more directly than does the youth or adult. Those "symbolical" interpretations that read into the expression all kinds of disguises and displacements are therefore the least justified in the case of a little child, and it is just in such cases that the psychoanalytic method of interpretation is especially liable to error.

others as fathers, Ament as uncle, Miss Shinn as aunt, have kept observation-records of the children of their respective families. Up till now it is rare to find both parents carrying on an investigation of their children (Scupin, Stern, Katz).

We may expect valuable help from educationists who are concerned with the teaching of young children (governesses and tutors), and especially from those who have opportunity to observe the children outside their homes (the women-teachers in kindergartens and play-centres), also we may hope for similar help from doctors working in child clinics. So far the assistance derived from such sources has been very scanty, and the kindergarten literature, extensive as it is, has, up to the present time, been almost exclusively pedagogic and not really at home in child-knowledge.[1] But the assistance of such helpers will be all the more valuable, since they alone come into touch with the working-class child, about whose early psychic development we know, as yet, very little. The records of child-observation kept by relatives are, of course, only concerned with children of cultured circles.

There is now an excellent introduction to the psychological observation of kindergarten pupils. Judith Lichtenstein has published such an observation schedule with forty-nine questions, hints as to opportunities for observation and exhaustive model answers. The use of this introduction certainly requires not only interest and perseverance, but also a psychological point of view and training.

A keener interest on the part of psychologists of special branches will, of course, greatly improve the scientific nature of the investigations; yet a word of warning may not be out of place at this point. If the psychologist does not stand to the child in the position of a relative or a trusted teacher, but approaches him merely as a strange observer, that inner understanding which is so essential a condition of the study of young children may be entirely wanting. Without this atmosphere between the two, not only will the child behave differently than he would under normal conditions, but the investigator will find it impossible to understand rightly and appraise at its true value the real meaning and intention

[1] Mme Montessori has expressly requested the teachers in her schools to look upon themselves as, first and foremost, the observers of the children under their care. But I do not know whether this appeal has borne fruit already for scientific psychological child-study.

of the child's movements and utterances.[1] So that it would be very desirable that every psychologist, working with little children, should first take steps to be on intimate terms with them. And no less desirable is the co-operation of the psychologist with the children's ordinary educators (e.g. the teachers in kindergartens).

In this respect, the research tests both of individual children and of groups made by Hildegard Hetzer in the kindergartens of Vienna and by Martha Muchow in those of Hamburg, set an example that may be followed with advantage.

Child-psychology records can be made with two distinct aims in view. Either the observer undertakes them for his personal joy and instruction, to get a thorough knowledge of a child, near and dear to him, to have later on, for his own, a lasting remembrance of the child's tender, early years, above all, to clear his own vision for the ever-changing delicate stirrings, the infinite variety and the enormous speed of the development of a child's psychic life. Or he aims at contributing something to general child-psychological knowledge, wishes himself to work up the collected observations and to offer them, at any rate, as raw material for the cause of science. It is an error, pure and simple, to imagine that the capacity and wish to make observations of the first kind are, in themselves, sufficient to give such observations any scientific value. Observation for personal or autodidactic reasons is indeed desirable for everyone who approaches childhood with a warm heart and an open mind; YET ONLY THOSE SHOULD FEEL THEMSELVES CALLED TO SCIENTIFIC WORK— THOUGH THAT MAY BE BUT THE COLLECTION OF MATERIAL FOR THE SERVICE OF SCIENCE—WHO POSSESS THE NECESSARY PSYCHOLOGICAL TRAINING AND THE POWER TO STRUGGLE ON TO THE BY-NO-MEANS EASY TASK OF THE RECORD OF FACTS AND THE CONCLUSIONS THEREFROM. The value of investigation does not lie in the quantity of material gathered, but in its reliability and freedom from prejudice.

We will now give some hints as to the procedure to be followed in child-studies and their record.

Everything in the child is worthy of attention and needs

---

[1] The same also applies to a nerve-specialist; he is inclined to regard a child brought to him only from the point of view of his psychiatric or psycho-analytic interests.

observation, so that he alone who is able to keep his attention continually fixed upon the most varied activities of the child's mind gets a real insight into the overlapping and intermingling of all the awakening powers of the soul's life.

Any purposely defined limitation to one group of child-activities (e.g. his play, speech, memory, thought and love) undoubtedly makes the work much easier, and is therefore advisable where time or opportunity for research is limited, or when the observer is making his first essay in child-psychological investigation. But, in this case, there is always a risk of the result being one-sided and lacking in some important point, so that the mistake is made of looking upon the one part selected as if it were the whole of the child's psychic development.

Observations must be directed to the *spontaneous* no less than to the *reactive* behaviour of the child.

The term spontaneous applies to action that in its essential reality has its origin in and derives its character from the inner nature of the child; the play and chatter of a child left to itself, its quick change of interests and attention, its manner of intercourse with relatives, all come under spontaneous action which may be recorded by the observer.

On the other hand we test the reactive behaviour (or reaction) of the child when we notice how it acts under a clearly defined influence imposed from without (the so-called stimulus). In this way we determine the child's pleasure or pain, reaction to certain influences of taste, smell, colour and sound; we find out its reaction both in speech and intellect to pictures shown to it; we test its power of imitation by performing certain movements before it, its suggestibility by asking suggestive questions.

Both these methods of investigation are important and should supplement each other.

The superiority of spontaneous action is that it gives us a much clearer insight into the child's individuality than reactions do, for the child then acts under no compulsion, is entirely free from the compelling force of an instantaneous demand made upon it, and, therefore, often shows us surprising sides of its nature, which we should never have found by carefully thought-out experimental methods of investigation, sides indeed that are quite inaccessible to such kind of research.

To be sure, the natural spontaneous activities of the child are, as a rule, very complicated, and it is often impossible to determine in what degree different factors severally contribute to their origin and nature.

Here then an advantage of reactions comes to the front; their object is to provide answers to certain isolated questions, in which we are interested, and since we create these reactions by our experiments we have at the same time a certain power over the contributory conditions. We can so determine the pictures to be shown, the sense-stimuli to be used, that they may be most suitable to the investigation of the problem under discussion; we can graduate many factors to a mathematical degree of accuracy (e.g. the amount to be learnt as a test of the child's memory); we can measure the time required by the child for the mastery of the task; we can repeat the same experiment for purposes of comparison and thus obtain an exact record of the development which has taken place meantime in the point we are testing.

Yet we must emphatically state that for the study of any individual process of development experiment is far inferior to pure observation. For when we wish to follow the natural course of development in childhood we must avoid everything that is calculated to exercise an unnatural influence on development itself and thus to change its character. Hence the above-named experiments can only be recommended as occasional, and exceptional tests for the purpose of showing the psychic development in a certain specified point, without exerting any influence upon its later growth.

A few words concerning the technique of the keeping of records is here added for all those who have opportunity to make more or less continuous observation of one or several children; they are taken with but slight alterations from an introductory book published at an earlier date by my wife and myself.[1]

"The psychological reports should be supplemented by the principal facts of the child's constitution, heredity, environment, especially with reference to—

"Race, social position and age of the parents, brothers and

[1] C. and W. Stern: *Introduction to the Observation of Speech-Development in Children of Normal Mental Powers.*

sisters, surroundings in general, i.e. servants (dialect), relations and friends influencing the child, kindergarten.

"Home (large city, small town), country, factories, forest, sea, mountains, etc.

"Is the child often left to his own devices or constantly looked after? By whom? (Parents, relations, servants?)

"Change of impressions (travel, etc.).

"If the continuity of the observations has been broken by illness, travel or other circumstances, this must be expressly stated and taken into account in any deductions drawn from observations made after the break.

"It is best to keep the report purely chronological, with no attempt, at first, at grouping in respect of similar points of view, so that absolute freedom may be left for any after-treatment. At the same time every observation should have its distinctive word (as clue), and number of page entered in an alphabetical register, which, later on, will be the greatest help in making comparisons, finding places and arrangement.

"A separate book should be kept for each child.

"In the margin every observation should have its date and distinguishing word, and also the increase of age month by month, the best form being: ; 7 = at the age of 7 complete months, 2 ; 1 = at the age of 2 years 1 month, and so on.

"IT IS ABSOLUTELY ESSENTIAL TO KEEP THE CHILD TOTALLY UNCONSCIOUS OF THE OBSERVATION, first not to injure his character, and secondly to preserve intact the genuine simplicity of the child's self-revelations.

"It is essential to write down each observation as soon as possible after making it. If circumstances prevent immediate record, at any rate make a short note on a slip of paper. Any uncertain observations, reports by others of the child's doings or sayings and accounts, which cannot be written until some time after the observation, should be notified as such.

"A plain distinction should always be made between the definite objective fact (e.g. the use of a word on certain occasions) and the deduction drawn from it (that the child, for instance, already has some general idea). The description of accompanying circumstances should be as exact as possible, as only in this way can any light be thrown on the causal conditions of what has been observed.

"For the recording of the child's longer utterances, especially when the faculty of speech has reached a higher stage of development, the use of shorthand is advisable. This makes it difficult to keep older children (4 to 6 years) ignorant of what is being done—one observer must apparently be writing (in reality making shorthand notes) whilst the other keeps the child occupied with games, picture-books or talk. In such conversations a record must be made, not only of the child's sayings, but of the questions, answers, requests of the adult as well as of the actions of both, occurring in the course of the conversation."

. . . . .

2. Experimental Methods

The first research-experiments [1] in our field of observation were of a distinctly physiological character, to investigate the sensibility of young children (and its individual variation) to sense-stimuli of different kinds. The real methods of psychological experiment were slow to win a place in the study of early childhood. There they are of chief significance when it is not solely a question of the observation of some individual development but of some problem of comparative psychology. If a number of children are subjected under the same conditions to an experimental test, it becomes possible to determine certain psychological laws, for example, as regards the individual variation in children of appreciation of form, the simplest stages in the child's power of abstraction, their accuracy of memory, their early æsthetic feelings and their power of intelligent action, etc. By varied modification of test-conditions the child's psychic life may be subjected to a more subtle analysis, by extension of the experiment to different groups of children, psychological differences of sex, social position and age may be discovered. Indeed, comparison between children and animals as regards early forms of psychic life is made possible by experimental means, and then the method is of service in problems of *general* psychological development. Since Katz in his *Studies* 1913 demanded extensive use of experiment for purposes of child-knowledge a number of noteworthy studies have been made, and these will be mentioned in the detailed treatment of the

[1] We distinguish between research-, test-, and practice-experiments.

subject. A helpful review of the chief research experiments on young children has been given by K. Bühler, whilst Hans Volkelt gives a summary of the most recent results.

In spite, however, of many valuable results, it is not to be expected that the experimental method should ever be so important for the psychological study of early childhood as for school-age. That is due both to inner and outer reasons. The difficulty of mutual understanding and intimate relationship between the experimenter and the child upon whom he practises, the little child's quickly recurring weariness, his want of interest, the inexplicable diversion of his attention, and lastly the impossibility of extracting any statements from the child as to his feelings during the experiments, will all greatly limit the future use of this method during the earliest stage of childhood, at least for purposes of research.

The difficulty of really getting at the true psychic processes in early childhood by the experimental method resulted recently in the decision of investigators to renounce definitely the study of psychic experiences and to confine themselves to the determination of the objective attitude. In this the reactions of the child's organism to definite stimuli could be examined with great exactitude. This attitude- and reaction-investigation can only be designated as "psychology" in a wider sense of the word, but it can obtain useful material for psychology proper. It has been developed in America [behaviourism] and in Russia [reflexologie]; certain of Bühler's investigations have much in common with it.

Psychological examinations or tests are of use to gain knowledge of the individual child. The knowledge takes the form of a diagnosis when the mental state and power is determined at the moment of the examination, of a prognosis when it gives a picture of inborn capabilities and of the possible development to be expected.

Every such examination presupposes a standard; i.e. we must know the normal performances and capabilities of children of a certain category (such as those of a certain age) in order to be able to measure any individual child of the same category by reference to the normal.

Alfred Binet was the first to try to put this idea into practice. But his principles gained from experience were very insufficient for young children, and the credit belongs to

Alice Descoeudres (of the Jean Jacques Rousseau Institution, Geneva) of having drawn up a systematic examination (test) schedule for the ages 2 to 7; this aims at giving exact measurements for the general intelligence of children as well as for definite qualities. How far this aim has been achieved must be discussed later. But even here we must say emphatically that such short tests can only be looked upon, at most, as supplementary to, but never as a substitute for, thorough individual observation of children. Their chief sphere is to provide for children who are not under continuous observation a first appraisement of their powers in comparison with a normal standard.[1]

Dr. Maria Montessori utilized psychological experiment as we have hinted above for purposes of practice. Her teaching-games are, one and all, so arranged that a definite psychological power—such as differentiation of colour, form or tactual impressions—can be considerably increased by repeated occupation with the plaything, and she has succeeded along these experimental paths in perfecting certain accomplishments—such as writing or calculating—in children of certainly no more than average powers long before the usual school-age.

The "practice" experiment has a tendency to limit the significance of the "test" experiment. For the aim of the test is to examine the natural power, and hence to infer the degree of natural capabilities; the practice experiment, however, shows how greatly these capabilities can be increased by continuous practice.

The children of a Montessori Home, if examined by the usual tests for intelligence, would, thanks to their special sense-practice, appear to have a high degree of intelligence which they did not possess in reality.

3. Indirect Methods

There are other methods of investigation in child-psychology, but they are not nearly so important as direct observation. We might mention, first, adults' recollections of childhood. Every human being has such reminiscences, often painted,

---

[1] Huth in Munich and Winkler in Leipzig have lately brought out series of tests for the interval between early childhood and school-age (5–7 years). (Reproduced in Stern-Wiegmann's *Methodensammlung*, pp. 479 sqq.)

indeed, in very vivid colours, and it seemed natural to make use of them in our study. Reminiscences of childhood are found in numberless autobiographies, and the great majority of authors of such works are not content with the description only of outer circumstances, but also try to revive the psychic emotions of their youth.

The autobiographies of Augustine, Rousseau, Goethe, Gottfried Keller, of Helen Keller and others occur to one's memory.

And then it is possible by carefully worded questions to induce adults and even older children as well to revive reminiscences of childhood for special psychological purposes; e.g. the earliest occurrences they can remember, their interests at different periods of childhood, definite emotions, such as fear, tenderness, religious sense, etc.

But, attractive as such self-revelations may be, especially when made by those of outstanding personality, their scientific value can only be accepted with great reserve. Their extraordinary vivacity and often very circumstantial details are not, in themselves, any guarantee for the certainty and reliability of the memories described. There is always, whether conscious or not, the question of "truth and fiction";[1] the craving for artistic finish, and the writer's wish to look upon his life as much as possible as an unbroken and comprehensible inner development, show themselves in many inventions, deductions and additions; the author's sympathy with the soul-life of the child—a sympathy often very admirable —leads to descriptions which may possess subjective probability, but not, therefore, necessarily any objective value as reality.

Even less capable is the average human being of reviving to order the thoughts and aspirations of his childhood. The relation of the adult to his own early years is like that of modern times to antiquity, no longer natural but sentimental; supposition and invention, a more or less laboured "thinking back" and an unconscious "projection" in a backward direction of later emotional and imaginative experiences take the place of a real revival of past conditions.

---

[1] With keen insight, Goethe once remarked he had named the work he had produced with faithful care *Dichtung und Wahrheit* because he was deeply convinced that man in the present and much more in his recollections remodels the outside world according to his particular views.

Now all this is especially true of that early period which we are now considering with its usually very scanty store of reminiscences.

Yet in spite of all doubtful points we need not entirely refuse to make any use of this source of help in the psychology of childhood. What service it can render is seen in the book just published by Reichardt in which he has with indescribable industry made extracts from over four hundred autobiographies of important men and women to collect the earliest childhood memories of the various authors. Even if every passage quoted may be an uncontrollable mixture of truth and fiction, yet this collection gives an amazingly varied picture of the life of the child and one marked by strong intrinsic probability. The material thus collected may indeed on the one hand serve as an illustration of those features of the child's soul with which we are already familiar from other sources, but on the other, it also gives us fresh insight, for it contains so many spontaneous revelations of the inner life of the young soul which are never uttered by the child himself, and are therefore quite inaccessible to the direct method.[1]

A more sceptical attitude is advisable with regard to the abundant material offered in adults' childhood's recollections which has of late years been collected and used by the school of psychoanalysts. Their theory, already mentioned, of the after-effects of suppressed childhood-experiences led to an endeavour to find these unworked-off memories in their adult patients: i.e. the apparently dead and forgotten childhood-experiences were to be revived in the adult consciousness and thus brought to "abreaction".

What should be the attitude of scientific child-psychology to childhood-recollections obtained in this manner? As we have already stated, there are doubtless feelings in a child's psychic nature which cannot be ascertained by direct methods. The so-called repression which attempts to wipe out the occurrence of painful experiences or forbidden impulses by pushing them back into the unconscious, doubtless does occur in the period of early childhood (although not nearly so often as in later periods). Such repressed feelings might possibly

---

[1] Just lately in Leipzig Volkelt has collected more than 1,500 childhood-recollections, of which we have so far only a first preparatory report by Faulwasser.

so entirely lack all direct expression that they could not fail to elude all methods of observation of the child and only be revealed in some retarded manifestation. But whilst we have to do with spontaneous reminiscences in the autobiographies mentioned above, in psychoanalysis such spontaneity is entirely absent, and this considerably diminishes their objective value. When we consider with what suggestive means the psychoanalyst proposes to the patient certain interpretations of the fragmentary memories reviving in his mind, how he so impresses him beforehand with definite shades of feeling —especially of an erotic nature—that the patient can only see everything in such a light—then our suspicion is aroused and becomes more and more pronounced in proportion as these emotional experiences of early childhood and their sexual bias show greater and greater detail in the descriptions given of them in later, adult life.

It is strange how reminiscences of childhood more or less form a deviation from the laws of memory in general. As a rule memory fades with the lapse of time after the experience. For some decades of life this may be true of childhood's memories, and they grow constantly fainter, fewer in number and more uncertain; but at last, as old age approaches, the line takes an upward curve. Whilst we stand at life's zenith, the present and future fill far too large a part of our consciousness to permit any serious attention to the past; but the more marked the ebb of life, the more islands of memory appear above the waters of forgetfulness.

> I dream myself back in my childhood,
> And I shake my old grey head,
> How they follow me still, those pictures,
> Which I thought long since were dead!

One word more on the method of collecting data for the purposes of investigation.

This is no longer a question of exact observation of individual children, but of getting from very many children as copious material as possible from which to draw comparisons of a numerical nature, e.g. between the psychic condition at different ages or between the development of the two sexes or of different social classes, etc.

This collecting work, too, finds its chief field of enquiry

in school-age, although it has been, now and again, employed in early childhood. A beginning has been made in kindergartens and play-centres to make experiments: on the children's intelligence, susceptibility and so on. Sheets of questions have been sent out far and wide—especially in America —to collect from large numbers of parents, etc., material for psychological report concerning the effect of fear, kinds of play and other matters. Collections, too, have been made of drawings, bast-work, clay-modelling done during the first years of life.

Attempts have also been made to obtain an idea of the children of primitive peoples from ethnological material and reports of explorers.[1]

In conclusion we would point out that even the psychology of literature can be used for the solving of our problems. Charlotte Bühler (I) has been able to draw indirect inferences from a psychological analysis of the fairy-tale as to the child's imagination which can find complete satisfaction in such a story.

---

[1] Cf. the very interesting research work of Franke with Negro children.

CHAPTER III

PSYCHIC DEVELOPMENT[1]

WHAT does development mean and by what conditions is it determined? This question must be considered, even if very briefly, in all its more important ramifications, so that we may approach the understanding of the development of the child-soul from the right standpoint.[2]

1. The Principle of Convergence

Development takes place in an individual; but this individual is placed in a world of impressions and influences. In these two sentences lies the chief difficulty of our problem. Is development a process that, in its essential nature, has its real source in the individual himself? Or is development a result of that encircling world which rushes upon the child and makes him the plaything of incalculable influences, good and bad, helpful and harmful. Hard questions these, and doubly so because they arise not only from the desire for theoretical knowledge, but from the urgent practical needs of the treatment and education of children.

Answers diametrically opposed to each other have been given to these questions concerning the factors of development.

Some lean to "nativism", which maintains that all development, in its real essence, proceeds from the inborn nature of

---

[1] The important considerations treated in this division are to be found, almost in their entirety, though partly in another order and somewhat differently expressed, in my treatise published some time ago (1908). Meumann, in the second edition (1911) of *Introductory Lectures to Experimental Pedagogy*, gives utterance, amongst other subjects, to a number of similar thoughts on the same problem. The systematic foundation of the convergence theory has now been given in my book *Human Personality*.

[2] The following section is intentionally confined to the question of individual development—ontogenesis—with only passing reference to the fact that the psychic development of the race—phylogenesis—is also the subject of important scientific research, and remarkable parallels ("genetic parallels") have been found between these two lines of development, the individual and the racial. So that, of late, attempts have been made to utilize the facts of child-psychology in explanation of questions in psychic racial development—development of language, arts, etc. But the amount of space that a discussion of such questions would require makes it impossible here, in spite of their great intrinsic interest. I have on several occasions set forth my own point of view as regards the problem: *Persons and Things*, I. pp. 299, 324, 331; *The Human Personality*, p. 108; *The Language of Children*, chap. xvii. Cf. also Koffka, pp. 30 seq. and Heinz Werner (II).

the individual. Others, again, take their stand on an extreme "empiricism", which holds that man with his soul is, to begin with, but a *tabula rasa*, which afterwards contains only what is written upon it from without. And both points of view can support their position by weighty arguments. Nativism points out the development of talents and characteristics which have passed unnoticed and untrained by their surroundings, but which have surmounted all hindrances and made a way for themselves by some inner power that there was no gainsaying; it calls attention to the triumphant march of the theory of heredity, which applies also to qualities of the soul. Every child brings into the world those psychic qualities which have come down to him from his ancestors as his soul's inheritance. Empiricism, on the other hand, brings forward the amazing diversities of development which exist between children of different classes of society, of different educational advantages, and points to the immediately apparent results due to the influence, either of those concerned in their education or of playfellows, friends, brothers and sisters. And when nativism quotes the theory of heredity, empiricism answers with the no less successful theory of environment, which has opened our eyes to all influences—both apparent and hidden—of the outer world.

When two opposite standpoints can each bring forward weighty arguments in support of their position, the truth must lie in a union of both; psychic development is not simply the gradual appearance of inborn qualities nor a simple acceptance and response to outside influences, but the result of a "convergence" between inner qualities and outer conditions of development. This convergence is as potent for the broad outlines as for the minute details of development. It is never permissible to ask of any function or quality: "Does this come from within or without?" but rather: "How much of this comes from within, how much from without?" for both of these influences always share in its making, only varying in degree at different times. If inner development preponderates, we speak of it as "ripening" (*Reifung*); if outer acquirement is more marked, we call the process "empirical learning".[1]

The convergence theory, which will be our leading principle

---

[1] This distinction, first made in the present book with reference to the earliest progressive steps in infancy, has lately been applied by Koffka (pp. 28 sqq. and 114 sqq.) in a wider sense to all new achievements of children of every age.

in all after-considerations, is supported by a definite philosophical conviction of the essential nature of man. Here I briefly advance those arguments which seem to bear directly upon the problem before us.

Every living creature, and therefore the young, growing human being, is a "person" and not a "thing". A person, i.e. a whole, which indeed is not simple, but yet forms, always and everywhere, an undivided unity; not a "thing", i.e. not simply a chance collection of elements, not a mechanical linking together of processes. "IN-dividual" is no misnomer for what is indivisible indeed. The physical and psychic elements and processes to be found in him only owe their existence to the fact that they are component parts of the whole, and under the impelling life-force of an indivisible unity. The separate treatment meted out in later chapters to the several processes is only the result of methodical arrangement; in reality there are no special processes confined to the memory or mind, any more than there is a self-contained digestion or circulation; they neither exist nor develop independently of each other, but are only different manifestations and activities of the united corporate life of the individual.

ALL DIVISIONS INSIDE THE PERSONALITY ARE RELATIVE ONLY, MERE ABSTRACTIONS—which, however, are requisite for certain purposes of consideration and treatment—ALL DEVELOPMENT OF SINGLE FUNCTIONS IS UNFAILINGLY DEPENDENT ON THE DEVELOPMENT OF THE WHOLE.

Even the agelong division of man into a psychic and physical side is subject to this limitation. Man is not divided into a bodily individuality and a mental individuality, but, rather, his personality shows itself outwardly in a physical form, inwardly in a psychic, without thereby losing its unity, and hence there are in the personality many conditions which it would be quite arbitrary to ascribe entirely either to the physical or to the psychic side; they belong to both, are "psycho-physical neutral". What are speech, imitation, voluntary action? Is not the very essence of their being the fact that the united life-force of the personality produces activities whose component parts, some physical, some psychic, are blended in one indivisible whole? No less then is the DEVELOPMENT of speech or voluntary action a united psycho-physical development.

The fact of the unity of the personality as the compelling

force does not only hold good for elements and powers existing in man at the same period, but also for their "stratification" and succession in point of time.

The personality does not consist only of one dead level but has depth as well; in it we find "strata" lying above or intermingled with one another, hiding each other, in mutual opposition possibly or in complete harmony. Certain strata near the surface are in direct communication with their environment; others are so far down that they remain undiscovered not only by any outsider but by the individual himself, although they have their part too as hidden impulses in the building-up of the "personal" life. Occasionally manifestations that have their origin in the deeper strata break through the layers above, and give the impression of being strange phenomena which there had been no reason to expect; then too a change in the relative position of the strata may take place and cause a permanent turn in the direction of the life. But with regard to these strata, it must be continually remembered that the personality always is and remains an indivisible unity; it is not torn apart into several independent parts, but it is the living mutual relationship of the various strata, the way in which they are fitly joined together in the whole and their living interchange of power which makes the individual character of the personality.

Let us now finally consider the development of the personality as to time also from the point of view of its undivided unity. This development is no chance succession of events but the growth of one epoch from another as the result of a unity of effort. The aims of the personality consist of those arising from within and of those suggested from without. A human being strives to assert himself and to rise; but he also strives to attain goals outside himself: such goals he sees in other men, in societies of various kinds, or in abstract ideals. But in the end the unity of the personality triumphs by man's absorption of the aims suggested from without and his making them a part of the achievements for which his own personality is striving and thus an active mental centre of his world in miniature, the microcosm that he is.[1]

---

[1] I have dealt at length in my book, *Wertphilosophie*, with the phenomenon that lies at the root of all human aims, viz. "introspection"; at this point the reference given above must suffice.

With regard to the special problems of development in early childhood it is of primary importance to discuss in greater detail those aims connected simply and solely with the individual self. These show two main tendencies, self-preservation and self-development. The object of self-preservation is to maintain life, to hold fast what has been achieved; its action is as evident in the physical processes of change of tissue, respiration, etc., as in the psychic impulses of self-nourishment, self-defence. The aim of SELF-DEVELOPMENT is to raise the standard of existence; with each succeeding moment it leaves achievement behind to stretch forward to new aims, new values, to new tasks, new possibilities of attainment; it appears as physical growth and mental development.

But neither of these aims can alone fill the life of man. Self-preservation and nothing more paralyses the individual by the dreary monotony of actions which only provide for bare existence; self-development, by itself, would continually urge man on to fresh goals, but, in its onward course, would overlook the assurance of existence and the preservation of previous achievement.

So the marvellous teleological theory is manifest in the fact that self-preservation and self-development unite and blend in the process of growth. And especially in the years of early childhood is this union most apparent. The activities which first develop are exactly those which are of the most primary importance for self-preservation; and whilst self-development hastens on to ever-new triumphs in the growth of powers and the spiritual conquest of the material, the motive-power and capacity of self-preservation works away in the Subconscious with unerring surety of purpose.

But their mutual relation is even more intimate. Each single goal, aimed at by struggling self-development, is no sooner reached than it immediately exists solely to be replaced by others, and not only so, but it becomes a permanent acquirement of the personality. Thus it belongs, from that moment on, to its standing property, and becomes the object of its self-preservation. Hence, learning to talk or walk is self-development; the consequent power of speech and movement becomes the object of self-preservation on the level now reached. And the same is true of all achievements. For there is indeed nothing in development of only momentary value, everything keeps on working, even if only as a tool for other efforts, everything heaps up powers, makes reserves, opens roads, that determine future life. This principle of conservation is again true of the whole of man's nature; it appears in the most diverse forms: as memory, practice, habit, adaptation, sometimes on the psychic plane, sometimes on the physical, sometimes simultaneously on both. Lately it has been designated by the name of "Mneme" to distinguish it from the strictly psychic Memory.

Now those same activities which, through the action of "Mneme", become the permanent possession of man would very soon demand all his powers and make new developments totally impossible, if a new factor did not make its appearance. The Mneme has not only the power of conservation, but also of sparing or economizing; the oftener any action is performed, the less demand it makes upon energy and conscious effort, until at last it becomes quite mechanical, i.e. it is accomplished with the maximum of unconscious ease and the minimum expenditure of strength and conscious effort. Only thus is it possible that the larger portion of human strength and the real conscious activities should again be constantly available for the new tasks imposed upon man by his impulse of self-development. What is older, more familiar, more habitual sinks down into the mechanical, into the Unconscious, yet without losing its active effect on man's future life; and out of these ever-increasing substrata of the personality there constantly arises the impulsive urge to further progress, to new conquests for soul and body.

If man through his Mneme is the product of his own past, yet by his impulse to self-development he is urged forward towards a goal always ahead of his efforts, and is the master of his own future. Those inner conditions (dispositions) which through the principle of self-preservation have attained a certain toughness and durability we call "qualities", but those which only point to future unfolding, although plainly foreshadowed in the innermost being of the human personality, we name aptitudes.

Those endowments that a human being brings into the world are almost always only aptitudes that appear by degrees, ripen slowly, become fixed and develop into qualities. Very few powers of activity are, from the very beginning, so firm and unmistakable as to merit the name of qualities; if so, they are of the nature of those forms of self-preservation which each generation inherits from the one preceding. To this class belong, above all, the instincts which, too, are relatively least amenable to outside influences.

The child's aptitudes, however, also feel the influences of heredity, not, however, as conditions forced upon the child by its ancestors, but only as general tendencies whose specialization is left to individual action and to outer influences. The child therefore by cultivation of his aptitudes can develop himself far above his ancestors, whilst instincts fetter him to the primeval condition of humanity.

Since aptitudes are not finished products but simple potentialities, they require completion to achieve reality. This completion must take place from without, and here begins the relative correctness of the empiric point of view. A given seed can, as the result of its fore-ordained innate nature, only produce a plant of a certain kind. But with what speed, in what kindly growth and distinctive form its development takes place, depends in part only on the nature of the seed; its unmistakable determination is brought about only by sun and water, by soil and food, by competition with other plants, by the gardener's care, the restraint of the fence—in short, by outer influences. The application of the parable to the problem before us is self-evident. The child's aptitudes are not fixed predestinations of what will happen, but indications of the future, surrounded by a wide margin, leaving room for the influences of education and environment in the actual shaping of growth.

2. The Progress of Development

The progress of development in childhood is marked by two principles: (1) an increase of differentiation in function and (2) growth.

This structural change is the transition from a general diffuse confused condition into one of more pronounced demarcations, in which boundaries and divisions, differences and connections begin to be felt more distinctly. Each progress in structural growth is at one and the same time an increasing differentiation in function and a more pronounced centralization; that which at first was vague and confused becomes more distinct, but at the same time undefined want of form is succeeded by an orderly arrangement of the constituents of a whole which consists of a centre and subsidiary parts. The primary diffuse conditions are difficult to understand and still more difficult to describe because man's adult ideas and vocabulary are all borrowed from his own richly endowed and sharply defined mental equipment. And in such consideration, to understand the conditions in earliest childhood, we need to step outside our adult life, and this we find exceedingly difficult; the methods of most recent times are only just beginning to smooth the path.[1] The initial phases with which development begins cannot be at all adequately characterized by our familiar and plainly marked categories referring to sharply defined individual functions, for they still are inextricably intermingled. The part taken by different senses in perception is not yet differentiated, objective recognition is not clearly divided from sensational reaction, nor expression of feeling from a voluntary action. Speech utterance and gesture are still inseparably connected, and so on. Single definite functions and more plainly marked forms emerge but slowly from a chaotic initial condition and vague, fleeting images. But the advance in differentiation progresses by many deviating by-paths and is marked by most remarkable transitions in the child's idea of and attitude to life. This is true of periods far beyond that under our consideration, for in the sixth year the goal of differentiation as we know it still lies far ahead.

Martha Muchow (III) puts forward the view that in this respect the sharp distinction usually drawn between earliest childhood and school-age is destructive of actual continuity of development, since kindergarten and early school-age are very closely allied in their deficiency of distinct differentiation.

Moreover, these incompletely differentiated early images have also a positive side in comparison with adult-life. Just because the sharp clear distinctions and outlines are not yet existent, they are more intimately bound up with the personality. The child's whole being shares much more than does the adult's in all that he feels or does, just because the impulsive waves pass from the point of origin (e.g. the stimu-

[1] Compare particularly the theoretical treatment and practical examples in Werner's development-psychology. Attention is also drawn to Volkelt's, Muchow's and Piaget's writings.

lation of a sense-organ) with full force throughout the whole organism of the child.

These somewhat difficult facts will later on be illustrated by a large number of examples.

The second principle of development, that of growth, is more easily understood. The child's growth in psychic capability and psychic accomplishment corresponds to his continual increase in stature and weight. The manifold nature of the phenomena of his consciousness increases just as does his power to co-ordinate them. His power of receptivity is in the same ratio as his power of expression. The circle of his interests grows with the extension of his grasp of ideas of time and space, which rules his mind, and with the scope of his attention and of his will-power.

The impulse to psychic growth has its own inner rate, which can indeed be modified by the influences of education, but not entirely changed. A hot-house education, as is not very infrequently found in our times amongst the upper classes, may, as its immediate result, hasten and cause premature development; but it will not bring about any permanent growth in individual capacity nor anything but an increase of outer accomplishments at the cost of inner maturity and a risk to bodily health. And, later on, it will be the source of great disappointment when it becomes evident that the limit—imposed from within— of possible development can, in spite of all efforts, never be exceeded. All that happens is that the individual more quickly reaches the goal and the stopping-point fixed for him by his aptitudes.

On the other hand, neglect of education can considerably retard the rate of development, may indeed result in a stoppage of development at a point far below that possible to the individual's abilities. The same results may follow from an education which goes astray either from wrong theories or from carelessness, and so impedes or cuts short the possibility of development of aptitudes as yet dormant in the child. Thus the educator— and this is especially true even in early childhood—is faced with the difficulty of avoiding the threefold risk of too much, too little, too confined, in his attempt to promote healthy, normal growth in the tender plants of natural aptitude.

But even then the inborn differences between individual rates of development are very great. Quite apart from consideration of the specially gifted and mentally deficient—with neither of whom this book is concerned—the margin between normal children is still very considerable. Nothing is more erroneous than the expectation that normal children should reach the same stages of development at the same time (e.g. begin to talk) and keep up the same rate of progress. All standards set up in this respect are more or less arbitrary; they originate either in chance observations of single children, or are taken as the average of very varied individual conclusions. They form no ground whatever for the determination of what degree of variation from the average is beyond normal; this is a question for the physician alone.

This fact must be especially emphasized here, since in the following compulsorily fixed data as to the beginning and speed of development, we had to give some, at any rate, drawn from individual observations, so that they must be looked upon only as approximate points of comparison.

The rate of mental development is marked—also from an inner impulse—by its own particular rhythm. The dictum that nothing grows by leaps and bounds must not be misconstrued to mean that the growth of any psychic power is made at a constant rate of progress. It is rather the case that alternating phases of quick and slow progress are everywhere apparent. Sometimes the difference is so great that parents are, at first, so uneasy at what appears to be a complete stagnation of development that they are the more amazed at the overwhelming rate of the subsequent progress. This alternation of stagnation and expansion is specially marked in early childhood, as in learning to walk and talk, the development in understanding, play, emotion, etc.

In reality, the times of stagnation are no sign of real cessation, but they are being used for the storing up of strength and the inward assimilation of impressions; and, as a result, the inner creation of energy is so great that it is again transmuted into expansive action. The educator should beware—and more especially in early childhood—of speeding up the pace in such periods of stagnation; if he waits quietly he will always have the fresh surprise of finding the barrier has disappeared of its own accord, and that increased development, prepared in the slower stage, becomes again apparent. The alternation of quick and slow is found not only in the growth of some special activity (e.g. learning to talk), but also in development as a whole. There are periods when the child is altogether quieter, not so full of energy, less expansive, and shows slower mental progress; but others, again, where he is full of extensive energy in all direc- tions, and increases greatly in experiences and capabilities.

The degree of this variability in development differs very considerably from child to child. We find types differing in this respect, some with a comparatively constant rate of development and others with very marked alternations.

All who have to do with little children should bear in mind these possibilities of individual variation; it would be premature to prophesy, either favourably or adversely, the future of children from the observation of their development in their earliest years.

For so many mistakes may occur, some originating in the incalculable nature of all life's occurrences, but some too in our inadequate methods of recognition. In this latter point much is to be hoped for from the progress of research in child-psy- chology. Thus, in cases of specially gifted children, I think it highly probable that, in time, we shall learn to distinguish between precocious, over-hastened development which will hurry on to a premature end, and the early signs of real super- normality which will not reach its full stature until later on. I feel there is no doubt that both these cases can be distinguished by very early signs; if we succeed in recognizing and interpret- ing these signs at the right time we shall be spared many a dis- appointment in infant prodigies.

Presumably, too, the experimental testing of intelligence, when it has been brought to a greater degree of accuracy, will contribute to greater thoroughness and certainty in our prognostications. It has already been shown that in repeated tests of the same child the cases of great divergence from its usual standard of intelligence are not very often met with.

In conclusion attention must be drawn to the variation between the two sexes as regards the general rate of develop- ment.[1]

In the earliest years girls give proof of quicker development than boys; the well-known fact that they learn to talk sooner

---

[1] Of course, these statements only refer to the *average* degrees of intelligence of boys and girls of the same age; individual cases may show very marked divergence.

and more quickly is only a particularly noticeable side of a much more general application. The girl, however, does not keep up her early start through the whole of youth; indeed, there is manifold change during school-life. The girls make rapid progress during puberty, which occurs indeed earlier than with the boys; but instead the boy develops at a distinctly higher rate both before and after.

3. The Changes of Development

The simple increase of psychic powers as regards differentiation and amount does not, however, cover the whole character of development, for, looked at from the standpoint of quality, an *equally important* feature in it is its series of metamorphoses. If the baby of one year is compared with a six-year-old child, even from a purely physical point of view, the older child is not in any way a baby of larger growth, but something of different quality. Growth has not been proportional for all bodily elements, but rather a continual change of relationships. And this is true to a much higher degree in the corresponding psychic development. Although all the chief natural powers in their earliest stages are present in the new-born child, they do not all make equal growth with its increase in age, but, in far differing wise, follow one another through the essential stages of their development. So that, in development, there is a constant interruption of proportional progress to such a degree that, at any given time, a single innate power which, up till then, has filled a rôle in the whole development, so small as to be scarcely noticeable, may suddenly step to the forefront, and then, for some time, form the centre of the child's psychic activity, and in a short period accomplish an amazingly quick development; and when this onrush is over, a new branch of power and interest appears in like manner. The earlier powers of course continue to develop, not with such violence, but more quietly in the scope of the personality as a whole, and so, at every stage of his being, the child presents an entirely new picture as regards the quality of his development.

This succession of metamorphoses is not brought about by chance or outer influences, but is, in a high degree, the result of inner conditions. Consequently this psychic growth repeats itself anew in a definite succession of changes, no matter how dissimilar the conditions under which the children live. It is to be hoped that child-psychology will, in the future, be more and more successful in enunciating the laws for the mutual succession of the phases of psychic development, so that we may be as conversant with them as we are to-day with the stages of plant-growth from the seed to the fruit. An exact knowledge of the metamorphoses of development is not only valuable as theory, but of great importance for practical educational purposes; for ideal education should be "true to development", i.e. its rules and maxims should be in accord with the natural periods of the child's life.

So far as our present-day knowledge permits, an attempt has been made in this book to formulate certain laws as to the order of successive stages of development.

Hand in hand with ever-recurring general features of the qualitative facts of development are to be found important *individual differences*. These again are sometimes the result of education; if a certain branch—music, religion, sport— happens to be strongly emphasized in any home, the qualitative development of a child, growing up in that home, cannot fail to be greatly influenced thereby. But sometimes, too, the cause of the differences is to be sought within; an especially pronounced aptitude, an interest, developed unusually early, must, of necessity, impress the whole psychic growth of the child with an individual stamp. Thus, too, the breaking through of deeper strata—to which we have already made a brief reference—may be the cause of metamorphoses which could not have been foreseen.

Above all, the difference of sex is to be noticed here. We shall, at various points in the development, meet with differences typical of male and female. Their appearance in such early years is principally important as denying, in this case, the truth of the deduction from divergent educational and social conditions. For in earliest childhood the outward conditions of life for boys and girls differ only in insignificant details— and in spite of this we find this plain indication of male and female idiosyncrasy! In this case there can be no doubt that inborn differences are the cause of the special faculties of development which prepare in mind and practice for the future individuality of life's tasks.

In conclusion, in spite of the manifold nature of genetic

facts, we will try to name one feature, common to development as a whole.[1]

It is apparent then that, at the beginning of all development, there exists in every creature a condition in which we find an inseparable, indissoluble blending of the two activities that are both in contact with that which is outside (sensation and movement). The original source of this condition is the primitive unity of sensory-motor action, the interrelation of stimulus and movement, of impression and expression. The fact that, in the past, not enough stress has been laid upon these fundamental truths has led to quite erroneous ideas of the beginnings of psychic development.

The sensory-motor action passes from the outside (the effective stimulus) and immediately back to the outside again (the motor response). But all progress in development rests upon the fact that an ever-increasing interval slowly intervenes between these two actions, both occurring at the outer circumference. This fact gives rise to three distinct signs of increasing development. The sensory feelings develop in proportion as all of them are no longer transmuted into immediate and, so to speak, reflex movements, but are stored up as experiences; the motor activities develop in proportion as they no longer are nothing but the reflex response to sense-stimuli; and between these the inner activity, from the physical point of view, that of the brain, from the psychic, that of the consciousness, tends to become continually greater.

Now, development follows the same order in this central activity. At first we find development of such activities as are immediately connected with processes taking place at the circumference; and only later, development of those in which consciousness frees itself from its direct and intimate connection with the outside world and wins, for itself, an ever-increasing measure of independence. Now, many development tendencies, mentioned earlier as a general rule, prove their truth as formulæ of special parts. For the path of progress indicated above must lead from sight to memory-reproduction and to comprehension; from a preponderance of receptivity to spontaneous action (due to inner working, creative development); from simple voluntary action to choice and reason;

---

[1] That such development formulae must only be used with caution has been shown by me elsewhere: *Facts and Causes*, p. 18.

from the clinging to the immediate present to a sovereign power of also including and weighing the absent and the distant, the past and the future; from a subjective-emotional attitude as regards things to the calm objectivity of observation and thought; from unreasoning acceptance and imitation of tradition and suggestion to criticism and self-control.

These development tendencies, enumerated above—every one an exemplification of the general formula "development from the circumference to the centre"—do not, of course, all become apparent in the first six years of life, many not until much later. Yet we shall find the formula here touched upon of great use in the understanding of the first phases of development to which our attention is constantly turned.

K. Bühler has lately given a development formula, founded on comparisons between the development of human beings and of lower animals.[1] All phenomena of the intelligence can be referred to one of the three following stages: instinct, training for a special action, or intellect. Instinct represents the inheritance of capabilities ready to use, fixed, and not requiring to be learnt. Training for special action makes use of associative memory, and works on the foundation of instinctive tendencies, suppressing some things, developing others, and forming new combinations. In conclusion, intellect has the power to adapt itself to fresh situations, and makes discoveries by insight and deliberation; it gets for itself expedients, by-paths, tools to accomplish an action neither familiar by instinct nor learnt by association.

Now, it is one of the most important psychological discoveries of modern times that these three stages also apply to the lower animals, at any rate for the higher species. Intelligence is not only man's monopoly. Köhler's research work among chimpanzees has proved beyond doubt that these animals too, under certain circumstances, can act with insight.

If we now trace the development of the child, we find, at life's very beginning, instinct actions, after a few months actions learnt from experience (amongst these actions resulting from special training), and in the last months of the first year the first intellectual acts standing on the same footing as the chimpanzee's. Within the province of intellect the child very quickly passes over the mental boundary between lower animal and man.

[1] K. Bühler, *Abriss*, pp. 1 sqq.

The intelligent actions of the most highly developed lower animal are always confined to the immediate present, the evident single occurrence, the purely practical application. As soon as the child has become able to glance back and to look forward, to generalize, to ask, and not only to express his experiences, but to represent them (by name or drawing), he has finally left the animal stage behind.[1]

Finally, the question arises as to whether development goes through anything resembling "crises" in the period of early childhood. The only answer to that at present is an hypothesis put forward by Charlotte Bühler. She believes that in the very middle of this period, that is then about 3; 0, a change takes place of a violent and critical nature, resembling in a minor degree what takes place on a larger scale in the crisis of puberty. Manifestations of defiance, sudden increases in affection and other emotional disturbances are said to be the signs of this critical period. She even believes that a first suggestion of sexual development then takes place, "a brief flicker of emotion which ebbs away again later on and does not recur again before puberty "[2] The careful observations made by Elsa Köhler of a girl in the period between 2 ; 6 and 3 ; 6 might be interpreted in support of this hypothesis, but much more extensive material drawn from firmly established facts is required before we can venture to speak of this point as anything like a law in the development of early childhood.

The development-picture of "Annchen" sketched by Elsa Köhler is, however, of sufficient interest to justify a short description here. It shows the following phases: in the first observation-period (2 ; 5 to 2 ; 7) the child is still a creature of impulses of the passing moment, living in a pleasant, natural relationship to human beings and things in its environment; this period, however, is marked by a rapid development of thought. In a second observation-period (about 2 ; 9) during a summer holiday[3] the picture entirely changes. The child is in the midst of a crisis. Her relationship to her mother assumes the

---

[1] Köhler's chimpanzee research-work has been made the greatest use of in Bühler's and Koffka's works of child-psychology; we must be content with occasional reference to the parallels between lower animal and child.

[2] Cf. Bühler: *Das Seelenleben des Jugendlichen*, 2nd edition, p. 18.

[3] It is certainly difficult to say how far the outer condition of a change in environment is responsible for the change in the child's condition. E. Köhler herself speaks of a convergence of inner and outer influences.

character of a tormenting tenderness; the child will not let the mother out of her sight for a single moment, but "it seems as though Annchen wants her mother, not to take pleasure in her and to find peace from her, but to tease and provoke her and yet on occasions to carry out her wishes" (p. 128). In other respects too the child is over-excited, full of varying moods and fancies, and—it is evident that thought-development is at a standstill. In the third observation-period (3 ; 0–3 ; 6) the crisis is over. Her attitude to her environment is again more as it was in the first period, although with fresh characteristic features—"She knows and feels herself as an individual in the midst of the objective world . . . the emotional wave has subsided. The emotional feelings, still present of course and sometimes finding tumultuous expression, are now mainly founded on objective recognition, just as now the whole intellectual side comes once again into prominence. The pronounced emphasis of the ego almost assumes an "a-social" character; the child consciously separates herself from other human beings and takes up an attitude of opposition to them.

PART II

THE PERIOD BEFORE SPEECH[1]

CHAPTER IV

THE NEW-BORN CHILD

THE condition in which man finds himself at the beginning of his individual life has always been invested with quite special interest for the investigator. Is it not the starting-point for every consideration of human life, whether philosophic or psychological? A true understanding of this earliest of all stages seems therefore an indispensable condition for the comprehension of the whole development that follows thereafter.

It would, of course, be a mistake to imagine that the moment after birth is nothing but a mere point from which the development curve makes its start. For the child's life begins before this. It is evident in the later embryonic months as the so-called "quickenings", and it is very probable that the mute psychic stirrings which we think we perceive in the new-born child exist in their earliest beginnings before birth.

This conclusion is strengthened, moreover, by the fact that the state of development at birth is a very different one in different individuals—even if we except abnormal cases of premature birth—so that many children at once exhibit capabilities which do not develop in others for days or weeks; from which it is evident that certain facts of development belong to the pre-natal period, others to that after birth. Thus, entrance into the world does not mean a new beginning from exactly the same starting-point for every human being. But even so, the importance of the moment is fundamental enough, for it means the greatest and most sudden change made by man throughout the whole course of his life. He is moved from his narrow, dark, quiet, warm

---

[1] For these first epochs of child-life attention may be drawn now to the detailed exposition by S. Bernfeld of the *Psychology of the Infant*. Even those who cannot own to complete agreement with B.'s psychoanalytic standpoint may derive valuable help from the discussion—hitherto to be found nowhere set forth at such length—of the instinctive life, both from ethnological and sociological points of view.

prison into the wide world with its overwhelming variety of the most manifold stimuli; turns from a parasitic being into a real individual, still helpless and dependent to the highest degree, yet giving proof of separate existence to those who tend him.

Thus, the new-born child has already a past that cannot but exert an influence on his present life. Where and how this influence is chiefly felt has in recent times been more especially dealt with by psychoanalysts—particularly Freud and Bernfeld; we only call the reader's attention to these without being able to share such views without reservations.

The past history of the new-born infant consists of two stages: its embryonic period and the moment of birth.

In the lengthy embryonic period a number of different habits have been contracted which cannot be simply wiped away by the new situation, as if they had never existed, but which rather amidst all the fresh demands of individual life make efforts to persist and only grow weaker by degrees. The new-born child, unable to cope as yet with the never-ending stimuli of his new world, tends to take refuge again in his former condition of life, which was almost entirely free from stimuli or strain of any kind; at first indeed by far the greater portion of his existence consists of such a return. Thus the almost unbroken slumber of a new-born child is looked upon as a "regression" into pre-natal life; the attitude of the limbs of the sleeping infant corresponds to their embryonic position. One may assent to this view of the "regressive tendency" as far as the earliest stages of infancy are concerned, but find no justification for the much more extensive use to which psychoanalysis puts it in later periods of life. For since the old situation, corresponding to the embryonic form of life, has come to a final end, its after-effects must weaken with the progress of time until they are reduced to a minimum, perhaps even entirely disappear. Those "regressions" into embryonic life which are often assumed by psychoanalysts as an explanation of occurrences in the later stages of childhood, or even in adult life itself, are probably for the most part figments of the interpreters' imagination. The second phase of the child's previous history—of short duration indeed but so much the more catastrophic in its nature—is the act of birth itself. For this is indeed not only the boundary-line between two forms of existence, but an event that means an enormous shock to the child's organism. For hours the infant is exposed to the most severe pressure and dragging; demands of an entirely new character are made upon its organs, external and internal alike; lungs suddenly have to breathe, skin to endure marked changes of temperature, etc., etc. This effect of shock which undoubtedly occurs is known in psychology (Freud, Rank, Bernfeld) as the *"trauma"* of birth; and the important effects which in general are ascribed to traumatic conditions of childhood are also referred to the experience of birth. Thus according to Bernfeld the infant's cry when not a pure expression of hunger is such a revival of the birth-cry; in the same way, the infant's undefined fear-reactions to sharp and sudden stimuli are said to be repetitions of the birth-terror. Indeed, the "original fear" caused by birth is looked upon as the birth of fear in general, and said to exercise an ineradicable after-effect in the whole emotional sphere of man, as well as in later expressional movements.[1]

Here too, as in the previous hypothesis, no doubt it is in like manner true that such interpretations lose in probability with the increase of age in the child. In any case, there seems no point in transferring the expression "trauma" from the pathological to the normal as is done here.[2] By "trauma" we understand, in the word's general acceptation, a psychic "injury", i.e. then an abnormal interference with the course of the psychic life; but being born is the most normal of all happenings, and therefore by no means a "trauma"; we have indeed nothing to show how psychic life would proceed without this fundamental experience. Our question, however, takes on quite another aspect when applied to especially difficult and abnormal cases of delivery. A difficult complicated birth is, not only for the mother but for the child as well, a marked interference with the normal course of life; that, under certain circumstances, not only enduring physical but also psychic effects may be its result seems quite possible. But to establish the truth of such birth "traumata" we need comprehensive material of a statistical and observational nature as to the

[1] Cf. particularly Bernfeld, pp. 188 sqq.
[2] Bernfeld actually defines infancy as the time between the trauma of birth and the trauma of weaning.

psychic developments of individuals whose birth took place under abnormal conditions. But so far such material is entirely wanting.[1]

1. Movements

We will first consider the new-born child, purely from the point of view of his outward demeanour—without, for the present, discussing the question of the part played by his consciousness.

All-predominant for the new citizen of the world is the condition of sleep—probably a continuation of his only pre-natal state. His sleep is broken by comparatively short waking periods; yet even in the earliest days the natural alternation of sleep and waking begins, in so far at least that the inter-ruptions of sleep are fewer and shorter during the night than in the day. His waking state is marked by all kinds of movements, which, as closer analysis shows, are, even from the first day, very manifold both in number and purpose.

The presence can even then be detected of the two chief physiological kinds of movement existing in human beings, viz. those caused by a stimulus acting from outside: "re-active" movements or "reactions", and those which, apart from any apparent outside cause, arise from some inner urge: "spontaneous" or impulsive movements.

To begin with the second group, we notice that the child sometimes begins a movement when nothing in his sur-roundings has called it forth. Even the act of waking may belong to this class, as also crying or jerking his limbs. And since the child's general physical condition is continually changing, we cannot but conclude that some phase in this inner change is the origin of such movements; energy that must find an outlet[2] causes the waving of the tiny arms and legs; the gradual approach of hunger is expressed in screams, etc. But there is total absence of those spontaneous move-ments which do not originate in general physical conditions,

---

[1] The hypothesis of a relation between difficult birth and individual course of life is advanced by Rank.
[2] Bernfeld designates this group as "outlet movements" (*Abfuhrbewegungen*); they are stimuli-neutral, i.e. not due to the influence of any known stimulus.

but rather in special mental processes, or as the results of will-activity.

The impression given by these spontaneous acts of an absence of consciousness and definite aim is only apparent. Above all, screaming, the child's strongest demonstration of life, has the greatest value as a significant means of expression, for it is a sure sign to those around that the child is in a condition—hunger, dampness, pain—that demands relief. Nor should we underestimate the practical value of the fact that, in screaming, lungs and larynx are at once actively exercised, and that the waving arms and legs make full demands upon their muscular system.

And future developments are already foreshadowed when the movements of the little legs, as a rule, are not simultaneous but alternating—the right extending as the left is drawn up, and vice versa—the inborn aptitude for the power of walking to be acquired later on.

On the other hand, there are spontaneous movements in which no after-stage of development can imitate the new-born child. Certain muscular actions, for instance, which, later on, are only to be found in firm, indissoluble union with other movements—co-ordination—appear in the young child as isolated and independent movements. Thus many a new-born baby can move each eye independently of the other: one turns up, the other out, or one remains stationary whilst the other looks down. It is true these periods pass very quickly, sometimes even at the very moment of birth, so that such children only give evidence of co-ordinated eye-movements.

But even more numerous than the spontaneous movements are the reactions of the new-born child. These are seen in a series of the simplest sensory-motor combinations which lead from a stimulus on a sensitive part of the body to an immediate motor-response. The banging of a door, and the baby starts; a touch on the lip, and a sucking movement is set up; a bright light strikes the eye, and the pupil contracts.

All these reactions prove the immediate transmutation of sense-stimuli into movement; there is, as yet, no evidence of deferred reaction, no interval in which the sense-stimulation is further dealt with within the body, stored up, considered, joined to others, before at last the resulting movement follows.

But immediate reactions can be divided into two evident classes: *reflex* and *instinctive* reactions.

The *reflexes* are distinguished by the unmistakable associations of sense-stimulus and movement. With mechanical regularity a definite sense-stimulus produces a movement, and always the same movement; whenever a stronger light falls upon the retina, the pupil contracts to weaken the intensity of the ray; whenever the milk goes the wrong way into the windpipe, it sets up, as reflex, a cough or sickness to expel the foreign body. Our examples also show that these innate reflexes, in spite of their unmistakably mechanical nature, are at the same time of great utility to the entire organism.

But the so-called *instinctive movements* are far more remarkable in their purpose of utility; and, for that reason, scholars have always found them the greatest puzzle, whether in animals or in human beings, a puzzle of which, up to the present, no really satisfactory solution has been found. Perhaps there is none, and we are here face to face with one of those ultimate, inexplicable adaptations to purpose with which the whole life of the organism is permeated.[1]

Instinctive actions have this in common with reflexes, that they are the immediate result of sense-stimuli, that they are indispensable for the maintenance of individual life, that they are innate and unconscious. But instincts are no longer of a purely mechanical character, they are not necessarily determined in one direction only by the sense-stimulus, but they only act when some condition of life's process demands the fulfilment of the object which they serve.

These inner powers directed to a definite object which result in instinctive actions we call impulses (*Triebe*). Their characteristic feature is the elementary force with which a silent urge is transmuted into action, not however so unrestrained as outlet-movements, but directed to a goal—of course unknown to the child himself.

The best-known example of man's instinctive movements,

---

[1] With regard to the problem of instinct compare the more recent utterances of Koffka (pp. 64 sqq.) and the Summary of Karl Bühler, *Human Instincts*, in the Report of the Ninth Congress for experimental psychology in Munich (Jena, 1926). Both contest the theories of the American "behaviorismus", especially as expressed by Thorndike, who gives instinct a mechanical character, as nothing but a chain of reflexes.

and, at the same time, that which is most apparent in the new-born babe, is the action of sucking. For even on the first day this faculty reaches perfection. The nipple is put into the child's mouth, but a few moments pass in which unsuitable or not quite successful mouth-movements are made; then the lips close like wax round the nipple, and there begin with automatic regularity those alternating muscular movements by which the life-giving stream from the mother's breast is drawn into the mouth. That sucking is no simple reflex to the touch of the lips is shown a few minutes later. The child is tired or satisfied, and the still existent stimulus on the lips no longer calls forth the motor-response; he ceases to suck, his lips remain motionless, or he even makes an exactly opposite movement by expelling the nipple. It is just these complicated actions, adapted to varying circumstances, that make instinct so puzzling, for they it is that give to instinctive action such great similarity to the conscious voluntary movement of the more highly developed human being, and yet any participation, whatsoever, of thought, will, decision, or any form of consciousness, is out of the question.

It is often said that man has far fewer natural instincts than the lower animals; this is true only to a certain point. Certainly the new-born lower animal shows far more instinctive faculties than does man. Not only does it make correct movements when the source of nourishment is brought up to the mouth, but it tries to get its food with movements of its own head, often of the whole body; the mechanism of locomotion functions accurately from the first day; the instinct of flight and defence is shown at once in presence of dangers or enemies, of whose hostile character the young animals can have no experience (the animal crouches, rolls up, becomes motionless, seeks refuge with its mother or in a corner). But, then, since we know that innate faculties do not always necessarily appear in their perfection at birth, we ought not, as regards the question of instincts, to restrict our observations to the new-born babe; and, indeed, it is a fact that later on a series of instincts comes into evidence in man. They are only not so easily recognizable as in dumb creatures because they are joined with actions of a higher type, or lose their own identity as parts of these. But more of this in later chapters.

Yet even in the new-born child the sucking instinct is not the only one, as is so often affirmed. There is, it is true, but the barest indication of the very important instinct of defence, that, in its more finished action, already provides the new-born lower animal with a certain capability of self-protection; the human infant has only the afore-mentioned expressional movement of screaming by which he summons outside help. So much the more astonishing is it that the opposite of defence, the turning of the head as a sign of attraction, appears even in the new-born babe in a number of instinctive movements, doubly astonishing, because these movements of approach not only serve the purposes of purely animal self-preservation, but, to a certain extent, must be considered as the first preliminaries of the processes of attention and perception.

Up till now, isolated records have been made of these turning movements of the new-born child, but it has not been noted that they are only different expressions of a common instinct, the only expressions—except sucking—that appear in the first week of life. Thus some observers have noticed that a touch on the child's cheek with the finger or nipple results in a quick turning of the head to the object touching it, in such a way that it then comes into contact with the mouth.

As a result of our own observations we feel it is beyond doubt that the proximity of the mother's breast produces in the child these turning movements before any contact takes place; this "seeking" was noticed in our eldest daughter on the third day, in our son on the eighth (cf. the extract from diary appended below). If—as was probable—the sense of smell acted as instinct-prompter here, yet in other turning movements one of the higher senses, namely that of sight, already took part. Almost unanimously, the observers report that no later than from the first to the third day a strong light brought close to the infant caused the little head to turn towards it. And our notes concerning Eva run: "when the child was barely three days old, it was brought up to the lighted Christmas-tree, and turned its head to the candles as its nurse changed her position." Soon after we noticed the same thing with gaslight. But the turning can be even more specialized when a light is slowly moved from side to side close to the child's eyes; then indeed begins a "Keep your eyes on the light" sometimes even in the first week, which completely staggers the observer. Scupin's son showed this movement on the fourth day, ours on the fifth (cf. tests out of diaries given below), but other children not until later, as our own daughter and Dix's boy in their third week.[1]

2. Sensibility

The last considerations have already brought us to the further question of how far the individual sense-organs of a new-born child are capable of action. Natural observations can here be supplemented by little experiments, as was done by Kussmaul, Genzmer, Preyer, Miss Shinn, and others. We know that normally in the first days of life all senses function, i.e. they can serve as starting-points for motor reactions.

The reactions to the stimuli of touch upon the skin are the most numerous. Touch the lip, sucking follows; put a finger on the tiny palm, the little hand closes; tickle the sole of the foot, the leg is drawn up and the toes stretched apart. That temperature can act as stimulus we know from the state of well-being into which a child is put by a warm bath.[2] With regard to taste-sensibility, tests showed that anything very bitter, sour or salt placed on the tongue produced reactions of retching or sickness and comical grimaces of disgust, whilst sugar solutions were at once swallowed; the fact also that, at times, even during the earliest days, medicine or cow's-

[1] Observations of chimpanzees show that in these movements, following the direction of some object, we have to do with a form of instinct as elementary as it is widespread. As Köhler showed, "a wish that is concerned with a certain spatial direction but cannot be fulfilled for a considerable time at last produces action in that direction without much regard to practical value".

For instance, if a hungry chimpanzee, alone in his cage, saw others eating, he made all his movements, howling, arm-stretching, jumping, at last even quite senseless explosions of rage, fishing in the air with a straw, throwing pebbles through the wire, always in the direction of his more favoured companions. "In strong feeling that cannot be relieved the animal must do something in the direction of the object of its desire." The connection of this conduct with the attraction instincts of early childhood is obvious.

[2] This moreover is due not only to the actual sensations of warmth conveyed by the skin, but the whole of the little being is penetrated with the comfortable temperature when in his bath: then too the changes of position, the sensations of resistance and of movement of circulation and respiration, all have a share in creating an entirely different physical feeling. Hence Bernfeld is entirely wrong in his dictum (p. 31) as to the first bath: "that man has to thank the skin as a sense-organ for this first agreeable sensation, this first pleasure."

milk was refused points to a certain action of taste-stimuli. Yet we must look upon this as very slightly developed; only very pronounced and strongly concentrated differences produce markedly distinct results. We touched above upon smell reactions—turning of head to the mother's breast. Experiments also prove further that new-born children refused to close their lips on a nipple that had been rubbed with any strongly smelling substance.

Of the two higher senses, mention has already been made of that of sight. We must, of course, picture this first "seeing" of the new-born babe as of the most primitive possible nature; only pronounced differences in light produce the reactions mentioned. Colour, form, position, distance do not yet exist for the child, and any seeing of "objects" is out of the question.

Lastly, the sense of hearing is in the lowest state of development.[1] During the first days of infancy there is nothing of the nature of effective reaction, the stimulus arouses no movement, there are no varieties of response to varying stimuli, but only the one effect of shock; a sudden violent noise causes a sudden twitching, in milder cases confined to the face, in more extreme affecting the whole body and possibly accompanied by a scream.[2]

Sometimes noises will even cause twitching in sleep but without waking the child.

Thus the powers of the senses at birth may be classified as follows: THE SENSE OF TOUCH PRODUCES MANY VARIED REACTIONS, IN ACCORDANCE WITH THE POINT TOUCHED. TASTE, SMELL, SIGHT PRODUCE REACTIONS OF ATTRACTION, AND OCCASIONALLY OF AVERSION.

Temperature stimuli produce reactions of comfort or also of discomfort.

HEARING PRODUCES INVARIABLE SHOCK REACTIONS. This classification finds remarkable confirmation from quite another side, namely the anatomy of the brain. The Leipzig anatomist Flechsig has studied the development of the central nervous

[1] The statement often made that a baby at birth is totally deaf as the result of the stoppage of the ear by amniotic fluid is apparently not a fact. According to the more recent investigations of Hetzer, Tudor-Hard and B. Loewenfeld loud noises such as a rattle or clapping of the hands almost always produce reaction even on the first day of life.
[2] B. Loewenfeld explains this reaction as a primitive flight-reflex (*Fluchtreflex*).

system in the embryonic state and in the new-born child, and has found that the nerves leading from the sense-organs to the brain do not become vigorous (and therefore capable of functioning) simultaneously, but one after the other. Also, that at birth this stage of development has reached its highest point in those which connect the skin with the central organ (i.e., then, in the organ of the sense of touch), and its lowest point in the nerves of hearing; the other senses take a position between these two. Anatomical results are now of weight too for another question, which we will discuss in conclusion.

3. The Question of Consciousness

Has the new-born infant consciousness? And, if so, what is the stage reached by this consciousness?

According to the prevailing opinion, the brain is the real organ of consciousness; consciousness can only be present at birth so far as the brain is capable of functioning. A few decades since, general belief denied that this was the case. The nerves connecting the brain with the "subcortical" centres of sense activities and movements (lying in the spinal marrow and its upper continuations) were, it was thought, still so undeveloped that all sensory-motor activity at birth could only be carried on by the subcortical nerves, lying below the sensorium, and was therefore pure reflex action without a trace of consciousness. Since Flechsig's researches we know that the nerves, at the moment of birth, are in various stages of development, and reach perfection in the first weeks of life; it certainly remains true that the new-born child is mainly a creature of reflexes; but, even so, the first traces of consciousness may be present, and quickly develop into vigorous and varied psychic life.

We must, of course, exercise the greatest caution, if we desire to form an approximately true idea of the rudimentary consciousness existing at birth. Doubtless we shall have to reject all phenomena of consciousness of a really intellectual or voluntary nature; there is a total absence of inborn ideas or of any real perception, i.e. seeing and noticing outside objects and occurrences as such, nor is there conscious will or endeavour.

All that we are possibly justified in assuming is the presence of a dull, undefined foreshadowing of consciousness in which the sensorial and emotional elements are so inextricably intermingled that they might be designated either as "sense-emotional states" or "emotional-perceptive states". The presence of feelings of comfort or discomfort is evinced from the very first day by the bodily habit as a whole, by the expression of the face and by the active expression of screaming.

These sense-emotional states fall at once into two types. On the one hand they arise from inner conditions of the body (screams of hunger, comfort of satisfied appetite), then we are dealing with emotional-perceptive states. On the other hand they accompany reactions to outside stimuli (disgust at bitter tastes, attraction to light), and then they contain as a specific, component part, sense-perception. This division is important, for it forms the first foreshadowing of the later conscious distinction between the ego and the world without. The states of consciousness of the first class develop more and more into symptoms of the subjective idea of the individual personality, whilst those of the second grow into perceptions, and thus into symbols of the objective outside world.

At first, however, there is no ego-consciousness, no objective consciousness, but only the very first germs, entirely undifferentiated, of both.

A distinction must be made between the emotions along the lines of pleasure and displeasure. How are these distributed in the new-born child? This question receives the almost unanimous answer that displeasure greatly preponderates. For the infant's typical act of expression is a scream, i.e. the most pronounced sign of pain; with this he greets his entrance into the world, and with it accompanies every disturbance of his condition; whereas the corresponding signs of pleasure—laughing, crowing, indeed even the faintest smile—are entirely absent. In this circumstance Schopenhauer saw that even at life's threshold sorrow had the preponderance, a direct argument for his pessimism. Kant interpreted the infant's cry as a protest of man's spirit against his forced entrance into the fetters of the flesh.

A more exact observation of the child and a deeper consideration of the matter lead, however, to a much less drastic conclusion. First of all, the relation of any feeling to its expression cannot have the same significance in a new-born child as it has in after years.

Amongst adults, indeed, a scream is only known as the sign of feeling of pain so indescribably violent as to be no longer capable of any control; but it is the child's one and only expression of suffering, and may therefore be produced by pain of a comparatively undefined and moderate character. It is a mistake to represent pain as the infant's only emotion. The impression made by a child in a warm bath, or when lying in its perambulator dry and satisfied, is undoubtedly one of comfort, therefore of pleasure; it is certainly only noticeable for those who observe the child very narrowly, whilst strangers—and especially bachelors such as Schopenhauer and Kant—know the child only from the side of piercing screams. And that feelings of pleasure are so much less loudly expressed than feelings of pain is not necessarily any criterion of their respective depth, but no doubt has a teleological reason, viz. pain requires help, hence its signal of distress, whilst a state of well-being does not.

Possibly, too, Preyer's statement that "the first period of human life is amongst the least pleasant" may be correct. It is indeed no wonder if the complete change in manner of life which exposes the new-born child to all kinds of disturbances, hitherto unknown, should at first exercise an unfavourable influence on its general state; only by degrees can it adapt itself to the new conditions of temperature, food, etc., and so overcome the shock of organic equilibrium caused by birth. It is probable that all this may be dimly reflected in the consciousness.

In illustration of the above considerations I append a few observations made by myself of our little son during the first days of his life.

On the second day the boy showed signs of sound-reaction; we noticed several times that he began to scream when there was a loud noise near him (his sister shouting, heavy steps, scraping of chairs, etc.). Reactions were proved beyond doubt by a test of hand-clapping; they were shown by a twitching of the eyelids immediately after the noise. The test was first made close to him—at a distance of about three-quarters of a metre—any touch-reaction from the movement of the air by the hand-clapping being guarded against by a hanging towel. Then, too, tests at a greater distance were successful—from the door to the child's swaddling-table—about six metres.

Sucking: On the evening of the day of birth the child audibly sucked his thumb, and also in the following night. When he was twenty-four hours old and first put to his mother's breast, he quickly closed his lips on it and sucked away lustily, so that we several times noticed ten, six, thirteen consecutive sucking movements. Without any kind of hesitation, trial or learning, the sucking instinct functioned in absolute perfection.

Crying notes: "*a*" and "*a-a*" just as his sister's had been, only hoarser, and with a shriller timbre often ending in a squeak.

Eye-movements: Although both eyelids often open and shut independently of each other, strange to say, we have not been able, so far, to notice any unco-ordinated movements of the eyeballs themselves, rather indeed he always moved both in the same direction.

There was again proof of sound-reaction, this time in deep sleep, produced by hand-clapping at a distance of six metres and by one stroke of the dinner-bell at one and a half metres.

On the fourth day we thought we noticed that the hungry child when laid beside his mother grew restless and sucked his hand more violently. Further confirmation earnestly desired.

The following most striking observation is also mentioned with reserve: As early as the third and fourth days we thought we sometimes noticed that G. followed the movements of a watch swung close to his eyes. The experiment often had no results. But on the fifth day it had such continual consecutive success, that his parents thought it more and more probable that the child was looking at it! "He lay on his table while I swung the watch, changing the direction of his glance now a little to the right or the left, up or down. Often there was no result, but as a rule, after a few movements, the glance went in the same direction, sometimes even combined with a little turn of the head." Of course the watch had to be very close and the sideways movement kept within a very limited area.

Unco-ordinated eye-movements (squinting) were noticed once, but as a rule co-ordinated, always so when looking upwards.

Ninth day: "In the intervening days the following of the eyes could not be recorded with certainty. But to-day, after an unsuccessful trial, I again observed it as G. was lying on his table, face downwards. As a shining clattering bunch of keys was moved backwards and forwards beside him he not only turned his eyes in that direction, but followed this up by a little twisting of his head as well."

As he lies on his face, G. already shows the power of moving his head and lifting it from the mattress.

The association between the scent of his mother's breast and movements towards it is already apparent. To-day we made the experiment, an hour before his meal-time, of putting the child, lying awake on his pillow, against his mother's left side. The child, who had been busily sucking his little fist, turned to the right and began to "search". We laid him on his mother's right side, and it was not long before his head turned to the left. Once more we put him on the left side, and he lay for a long time quietly on his back, without sucking his fingers—a plain proof that he was not hungry. But as soon as he grew restless, he turned his head to the right, seeking his mother's breast again. In such tests the breast was about ten centimetres distant from the child's head, and also still covered by the nightdress.

CHAPTER V

THE DEVELOPMENT OF POWERS

1. The Infant's "Learning"

WHAT a number of accomplishments the child "learns" in his first year: to raise himself, to balance his head, to sit, creep, shuffle along, to stand, to walk; to drink from a bottle and eat solid food; to hold fast in its several modifications; to play with paper or a doll, a rattle or a spoon—games which involve the most varied activities, such as crumpling up the paper, tearing it to bits, moving backwards and forwards, lifting the arm, throwing away, etc.; baby talk in its constantly increasing variety; the repetition of words that have been heard and the imitation of actions seen; and to end with, a whole series of trained accomplishments and directly useful acquirements—a year's task, far exceeding what the very best school can teach in the same space of time later on.

The outward result of all these developments, viz. the transition from "not being able" to "being able", is all included in the comprehensive word "learning"; yet the inner process is by no means as simple as the name, rather the process of learning has an entirely different psychological aspect in proportion as it is chiefly concerned with innate aptitudes or outside acquirements or discovery.

(a) THE GROWTH OF THE INSTINCTS.

Since instincts are "inborn" aptitudes, we are only too much inclined to expect them to appear in full perfection at birth; or, if we grant that all instincts cannot function at the beginning of life, yet we think it only reasonable that, when they do appear, they should be in full working order and not have to pass through gradual stages of growth. This expectation may be justified in a certain degree—although certainly not entirely[1]—for other animals, but not for man. We have already seen that only two instincts are present at birth, one of which —sucking—functions perfectly at once. But the other—the instinct of attraction—only shows rudimentary powers of working: and the others are not yet in evidence. To bring

[1] Even birds have to "learn" the instinctive power of flying.

about the gradual development of a number of other instincts is now one of the chief tasks of the child's first year. How greatly this is the result of a process of inner development and not of outer acquirement is made abundantly clear by the fact that they appear in an almost unvarying order of sequence. Thus, the instinctive aptitudes of bodily movement appear somewhat in this order: in the first three months the normal child learns to lift and balance his head, in the next three to raise himself and sit up—at first with support, and then with none—in the following three to stand and crawl, to walk in the last three, taking his first independent steps about the end of the year.

Ch. Bühler and H. Hetzer have just fixed more exact periods of the instinctive aptitudes in an "inventory" of their different stages in earliest childhood; in accordance with this the *average* accomplishments are as follows:—

In the 2nd month: holding the head up even when lying face downwards;

,,   3rd   ,,   : holding up head and shoulders when lying face downwards;

,,   4th   ,,   : attempting to move sidewards when lying on the stomach;

,,   5th   ,,   : raising head and shoulders when lying on back; raising body and keeping it up from a prone position only supported on palms of the hands; turning from the back on to the side;

,,   6th   ,,   : sitting up with help; turning from a prone position on to the back; rolling over on to the side;

,,   8th   ,,   : lying face downwards only supported on one hand; sitting without help;

,,   9th   ,,   : rising to a sitting position without help; standing with help; kneeling;

,,   11th   ,,   : getting up with help into a standing position;

,,   12th   ,,   : standing unassisted; walking with help.

The instinctive aptitudes directed towards outside objects, the movements of head and eyes (attraction) foreshadowed at birth: staring, following, listening. In the next three, the child becomes, as Sigismund puts it, a little "grasper"; whilst in the last half-year imitation becomes the predominant feature of the child's development.

Every single one of these aptitudes appears at first in an imperfect and rudimentary stage, and advances by degrees to complete perfection. Hence, then, a thorough process of "learning" takes place. To grasp the fundamental difference between this "learning" and purely empiric acquirement, let us compare it with well-marked examples of the other kind of learning, e.g. the infant learning to grasp with the school-child's acquirement of writing; learning to walk with management of a bicycle; learning to talk with the mastery of Latin; then we see at once that the so-called "learning" of the little child is nothing more than the strengthening of inner powers by which the inborn possibilities are converted into realities, whilst learning to write, cycle or master a foreign language would never develop from within, but is entirely dependent on the empiric factors of example, direction and instruction.

Yet the infant's instinctive learning does not proceed with automatic, innate compulsion, but demands a kind of the most primitive effort of will on the child's part. Notice a child three months old, in whom the instinctive impulse to lift himself up is beginning to stir; how untiring his efforts to use the down quilt he has accidentally grasped or the edge of his perambulator as a help, and how he tries with mighty expenditure of energy to draw himself up, ever renewing his attempts until his strength gives out—those are doubtless simple efforts accompanied by great concentration of attention. The same thing can be noticed in ceaseless efforts to hold tight, and, a little later on, in his attempts to imitate, crawl, etc. It is therefore not improbable that the child's strength of will is, in this way, already achieving its first results. Of two children equally strong and healthy, and with instincts at the same stage of development, the one possessing the strongest will-power will more quickly bring them to perfection.

Neither is the growth of instincts quite independent of outside influences: to say the least, these certainly have something to do with the rate of development and the good quality or otherwise of the result. Thus, for example, poor nourishment may cause the child to be very late in getting sufficient strength to lift his head, draw himself up, creep or walk; too tight swaddling-bands may make it long before the little limbs get the agility necessary for certain movements. Occasionally, neglected children simply lack opportunity to begin and practise their instinctive powers; they have too few objects to learn to hold fast; they are not often enough put in the necessary position for the exercise of muscles required in sitting or for the contraction of the leg muscles indispensable for walking. On the other hand, good food and loving care promote and, under certain circumstances, hasten the development of instinctive faculties. Thus even at this age an education is, in a certain way, possible, although indeed a very limited one; still, care can be taken that the child has strength to carry out and opportunity to practise those faculties that, at every moment, struggle for development. But all direct forcing is unnatural, and may sometimes be a wrong to the child, e.g. the impatience of many mothers to see their child walk often results in crippling the little legs that were not yet strong enough to do so.

(b) EMPIRIC LEARNING.

The instinctive powers just discussed in their main features develop in much the same way in all normal children; they are, indeed, the common inheritance of the human race.[1] But in addition to these powers, the infant already learns a whole number of others which bear witness to his environment both as regards their nature and form. Of course, even here, a certain number of innate aptitudes must be presupposed to make this further learning a possibility; but the special transmutation of these aptitudes into actions, habits, accomplishments of a definite nature, is naturally the result of the special influence of the environment. And thus important divergence in children begins even then.

The empiric learning of certain motor-activities proceeds in a similar manner to that which we shall describe later in the acquirement of psychic experiences.

Certain groups of movements are lifted from the chaos of diffused and unregulated movements performed by the child spontaneously and aimlessly, and remain so permanently; sometimes the objective environment helps in this, thus the peculiar construction of some toy (e.g. a rattle) may bring about especial co-ordinated movements which the child would

---

[1] Naturally there are variations here, too, not only in the rate of development but also in its nature; thus there are children in whom creeping on all fours or bumping along in a sitting position forms a very marked period in their development of action before they begin to walk, whilst in others such a mode of intermediate progression is barely noticeable. Yet these differences are distinctly less in number than those development-powers which have just been discussed.

not have learnt with a plaything of another shape. Sometimes, too, the child himself makes the choice by preferring useful (i.e. leading to a desired result) co-ordinated movements and rejecting useless ones;[1] sometimes his elders intentionally induce certain movements on the child's part, for example the clapping together of the palms of the little hands or a wry face in answer to one they make themselves. This "lifting-up" of co-ordinated movements is further influenced by the familiar laws of memory and association.

There is just as keen a memory for movements as for sense-impressions. Every movement of the child's makes its repetition easier until it becomes purely automatic. And every sequence of movements which has been brought about by definite causes becomes, by frequent repetition, so closely knit that it requires but a slight impulse to bring about the whole orderly sequence which may result in very complicated actions. And, to conclude, associations can be formed between sense-impressions and simultaneous movements on the child's part even when these have no natural connection with the impressions, nor one comprehensible to the child, and are therefore empirical "sensory-motor associations".

The last kind of empiric learning is the most striking and therefore most familiar to the lay mind: it is the tricks (accomplishments) possessed by every child as the result of training.[2] These are certainly very generally greatly over-estimated, and interpreted as signs of the awakening "understanding". When a child answers "How tall are you?" by lifting up both arms, he neither understands the word "tall" nor realizes that he is to show his own height, but he has formed an association between the sound of these words heard so often and the raising of the arms at this sound; consequently, the sound alone is sufficient to set free the associated motor-impulse.

---

[1] Thorndike builds up a purely mechanical theory of learning on the difference between effective and non-effective movements, which theory is most justly disputed by Koffka.

[2] We limit then the expression training (*Dressur*) to such actions as are due to teaching by outside influence and in which a goal unknown to the child determines the sequence of movements. Bühler on the other hand gives the designation of training (*Dressur*) to all the second main period of development which lies between instinct and intellect, thus to everything that we call "empiric learning", and therefore logically also speaks of "self-training" (*Selbstdressur*), for instance in the example given above of the manipulation of the rattle. This extension of the use of the term "training" seems to me inexpedient as it might give rise to confusion.

The child's performance is indeed exactly on a par with the tricks of a trained horse, who goes through a certain movement at a familiar call from his master.

Amongst these artificial tricks, quite meaningless for the child, there are, it is true, some of undoubted utility. Thus personal cleanliness can be taught by the child learning to understand the association of certain positions and sounds, and this branch of "infant education" is often possible at six months of age.

(c) THE TRANSITION TO INTELLIGENT ACTION.

The instinctive and empiric actions considered so far have the one common feature of stereotyped efficiency. What has once been achieved has a fixed course and a limited path of progress, achieving at most by continuous practice gradual perfection, sure and automatic performance. But now new modes of action appear which break through this stereotyped efficiency, and that too in an intelligent manner. The child performs actions which are not strictly bound to inherited instincts or empiric learning, but which are specially adapted for special situations; the third stage—intelligent action—has been reached.

The opinion once so widely held that intelligence makes its first appearance with and through speech has been proved to be wrong; both child and animal psychology have simultaneously proved the existence of mental activity previous to speech. There is indeed a "practical intelligence" as well, and this is more elementary than that marked by speech; it is shown by the fact that fresh intelligent actions become possible by insight into the connection of means and end.

We find, of course, only very simple forms of such intelligent actions in the first year; indeed, in certain transitional phenomena it has to remain an open question as to whether we are dealing with an action, the result of highly specialized learning, or have already reached the fresh realm of intellect.

In this connection consider the three following examples:—

Hilde (; 7– ; 7½). At a period when the child took hold of everything that was brought near her, on one occasion she learnt another action in place of the useless seizing. After her bath she was often dressed in her little jacket by one arm after another being put into the open armhole. Once her mother, more in play than earnest, held out the sleeves to the child so that she could easily reach them. "The right arm moved forward, the hand approached the armhole, but strangely enough not to take hold but fully extended, so that it looked as though the child understood what it ought to do. In the course of the next two weeks the phenomenon was quite certain: the child with keenest attention tried to put its arm through the armhole."[1]

Hilde (; 8). "The child's bottle had been overfilled, and she had had enough before the bottle was empty. As the milk continued to flow into the mouth, the child slowly moved her right hand up to the bottle, took hold of the teat and drew it out of her mouth; then she gave a contented smile."

Gunther (; $11\frac{1}{2}$). "He has held the bottle unaided for the past four weeks, and for about a week regulated its position, so that he can, without any help, drink the last drop. When he has finished drinking he takes the bottle away from his mouth and plays with it."

The actions here described are not completely new to the child, for the little arm has often been put by the child's guardians through the armhole, the bottle teat removed from the satisfied lips and the position of the bottle altered to suit the milk still left. So that even here definite connections between movements and sensorial experiences may have been formed and fixed by repetition. Yet the difference between the passive acceptance of these connections and their active self-accomplishment, which suddenly begins, is so great, that we cannot exactly consider them as simply the effect of specialized training. That preparation by their elders has doubtless helped to facilitate the first flash of intelligence; we may, however, justly suppose that in these cases there is such a ray of mentality, a vague choice of the means for the sake of the end.

Nor are we restricted to supposition alone. Towards the end of the first year actions occur no longer in the accustomed grooves of practised performance, but presenting a new attitude, a finding of hitherto unknown expedients to achieve some particular aim. And here we have arrived at actions of undoubted, even if primitive, intelligence. The following

[1] The Scupins did not observe this same intentional effort until their child was twice the age (1 ; 3).

examples illustrate this in spite of the fact that the last is "an attempt with unsuitable means".

Scupin's son (; 10½). The child who finds creeping difficult tries in vain, when lying on the floor, to reach a distant object. His gesture asking to be picked up is disregarded by his mother. He then takes firm hold of her gown and tries to raise himself with its help. That he intends to use this new method to achieve his real object is plain from his further action, for he is barely on his feet before he trips along to the distant object and picks it up.

The same (1 ; 0½). He took a celluloid fish out with him for his airing. "To-day we noticed the child's restlessness; he moved back and forwards, at last turned right round and stared continuously over the back of his perambulator on to the pavement, then uttered impatient cries and looked at us with entreaty." A hundred steps back he had actually thrown away the fish unnoticed, and was now trying to find some means of calling our attention to his loss.

Gunther (1 ;). "When Gunther had entirely emptied his bottle, except a few milky dregs, he sometimes turned the bottle round and tried to put the other end in his mouth, as though he thought he could get what was left in that way."

Bühler, too, reports that his daughter at the age of eleven months in her play succeeded in all kinds of manipulations, in which certain "discoveries" formed a part.[1]

The problem of the very earliest phenomena of intelligence has now been brought into the domain of experiment by research work amongst animals. Köhler set before the apes he was observing tasks to excite their desires, by showing them bananas in a position they could not easily reach and leaving them entirely to their own resources, in the assumption that the apes would make use of the highest degree of mentality in any way possible to them. And, as a matter of fact, he was able to prove sensible acts which could not be explained as the result of instinct or empiric learning, but were evidently the work of intelligence.

Thus the bananas were laid by the experimenter well out of reach in front of the cage bars or hung from the cage roof. Köhler gives a very vivid description of the animals' behaviour. The first action is often to get some object which they try

[1] *Abriss*, p. 52.

to use as a stick to reach the bananas, but also unsuitable things such as wisps of straw or tendrils are seized for this purpose. This happens with such assurance that we are obliged to assume the co-operation of instincts of their wild life (possibly the use of boughs). But there is also other behaviour which develops new forms of activity never practised before: the chimpanzee is looking for a tool, and under certain circumstances makes it for himself, e.g. if there is nothing like a stick in the cage, but a box, then he breaks a piece off the lid and uses it to fish for the banana. If the banana lies so far away that the bamboo he has picked up will not reach it, he fetches another and tries to join the two. In this effort one chimpanzee (like Gunther) tries with unsuitable means, and endeavours to lengthen the cane simply by holding the other on to it. But the other chimpanzee succeeds in pushing the thin end of one into the wide hollow end of the other, and this invention is intelligently used again and again by him. The apes also make different inventions in their efforts to reach the bananas hanging up above their reach. One uses a long bamboo which he braces against the ground as a jumping-pole and swings himself up by its help to tear down the object of his desire. Another pushes a box exactly under the bananas to use it as a step-ladder. When one box is not enough, he even tries to put another on it, but he cannot manage to build up anything stable enough to be of any use.

These and other intelligent actions were not of course carried out with human definiteness of aim, facility and confidence; they were only occasional lights flashing, at moments of the strongest desire, out of the normal chaos of unplanned and unsuccessful movements. But that they are more than simple chance is proved by a number of reasons. First of all the animals' expression is unmistakable: to begin with, their senseless attempts in unceasing repetition, and consequent rage at their want of success; then, as intermediate stage, the expression of perplexity and puzzled endeavour, and suddenly the intentness of aim when once the solution is found, the dropping of ineffectual superfluous movements, the intelligent sequence of actions. (In the intermediate activity of breaking up the box lid, they do not forget the ultimate aim of "bananas".) As further proof of intelligence we have the fact that any solution of the difficulty, once found, is made use of repeatedly (without, then, the practice necessary in specialized training) and adopted by the other apes.

But no less important are the limitations of this ape—and therefore no doubt of all animal—intelligence. The intelligent, comprehending new act is not a daily performance of the creatures, but only appears as a rare height of achievement. It can only be produced by stimuli of strong affective tone, intimately connected with the elementary needs of life, especially the desire for food.[1] Such action entirely depends on sight, only dealing with a concrete existing situation, and even then only the simplest conditions can be grasped and mastered. If the optical image is but slightly complicated, or if several intermediate actions are necessary to reach the goal, the animal fails.[2]

These characteristic features of the highest stage of animal intelligence are of such importance to us because they correspond almost entirely wirh the first signs of activity in human intelligence, as shown before the development of speech. Every unprejudiced observer of children of about a year old will testify to this. It is no difficult matter to get experimental confirmation along the lines of Köhler's methods; unfortunately, the requests for this, so frequently expressed, have so far met with but very little response. As far as I know, all that bear on the first year of life are contained in a series of Bühler's experiments with his own daughter, the most instructive of which is here reproduced in his own words.[3]

A rusk tied on to the end of a string was placed before the child in such a way that it can reach only the string, not the rusk; and the object of the experiment was to see if the child would manage by itself to draw up the rusk by means of the string. "At first, in the ninth month, the child regularly stretched out her arm to the rusk without taking any notice of the string. If by chance it came into the grasping hand, it was dropped again or pushed perceptibly to one side. Only

---

[1] This is subversive of the belief that animals (horses, dogs) can by the exercise of intelligence perform actions so utterly foreign to the experience and nature of lower animals as calculating or spelling. These results are only due to training (*Dressur*), either intentional or unintentional.

[2] We must refrain from entering upon the intensive discussions which have arisen as to the true psychic foundation of "fresh acts" of the most primitive intellectual nature. Cf. especially Bühler, *Development*, pp. 270 sqq., and Koffka, pp. 136 sqq.

[3] *Abriss*, p. 52.

after two experiments did the connection seem to be understood, for several correct solutions of the problem followed in quick succession. I still think that this was so. But at the next attempt all was again forgotten, and it was not until the end of the tenth month that the situation was completely and permanently grasped and mastered by the child. After that time the string could be put in any position, e.g. on the left side whilst the rusk lay on the right, or vice versa, and the child always looked round for it, seized it and pulled up the rusk. But this only when it lay too far away to be directly reached. Several facts confute the idea here of specialized training: first, the attempts were only made once every other day, and care taken to prevent any accidental success, whilst in specialized training, both chance successes and continual repetitions are utilized; secondly, the characteristic transference of the action to other relations was entirely absent; and thirdly, our experience was the same as Köhler's: one glance is enough to distinguish in the child's look and bearing the difference between a clear, purposeful action and one mechanically learnt.''

We will now turn to two special groups of faculties that develop in the course of the first year and have special psychological interest—imitation and play.

2. Imitation[1]

Imitation is a movement the result of which is to copy or to attempt to copy some stimulus that has been observed. As we have mentioned before, after the first six months imitation becomes a strongly marked form of activity, but its very beginnings are to be found at a much earlier period. Its first appearances are self-imitations or "circular-reactions" (Baldwin). As everyone knows, the child endeavours at a very early age to repeat constantly some movements that were at first, accidental (of voice organs, hand, etc.). At first this is purely automatic, whilst the motor-impulse, once started, goes on without hindrance or interruption along identically the same lines. But now the motor-impulses are not the only constituents in the completed whole of this occurrence; there

[1] For the theory of imitation, cf. especially Koffka, pp. 230 sqq.

are also the effects which the consequent movements produce on the mental organs: the child hears the babbling
sound, sees the hand-movement, and his pleasure in the
action is united with pleasure in his perception of this action.
And by the repetition of the action a distinctive interval
is formed, *a, b, a, b,* i.e. there arises an inner association in a
definite series between the motor-impulses and the perception
of the resultant movement. But this sensory-motor connection
is two-sided: the sense-impression (e.g. the hearing of his own
utterance) does not only follow the movement of production
but increases the impulse to another production of the same
sound and the child imitates himself.

Now, it is certainly not at once possible to determine whether
the frequent repetitions in the child's babble or in the arm and
leg movements are purely automatic, or if they are self-
imitation caused by a sensory-motor connection. But the
question can be answered under certain circumstances by
means of experiments to find out if the child imitates the same
movements when they are shown to him from outside. For
instance, the same sounds can be made to the child as those
he has often used without prompting in his babbling to himself
—but not occurring, of course, just before our experiment—
and to our surprise recent observations show with absolute
certainty that the child is capable of this kind of imitation
even before the end of the first year. Since so early a date for
the beginning of imitation is opposed to current opinions, we
will support it by some examples.

Hilde (; 2½). "If *erre erre* is said to the child when she is in
a good temper, she often responds to the sound by repeating
the same syllables—spontaneously uttered without any difficulty—with evident effort often lasting for some seconds. It
could not be chance, since the experiment was often successful
when the child had neither before nor after uttered these
sounds of her own accord."

Gunther (; 3). "It often sounds like a primitive conversation
when we try with G. For they are simple sounds like those he
makes himself to which he responds (as e.g. *a* or *erre*), so that
his answer sometimes gives the impression of imitation."

Scupin's son (; 1½). "After *a brrr* had been said to him several
times, the child gave a shamefaced (!) smile, made one or two
preliminary lip-movements, strained himself with hands and

feet against the feather-bed, and with enormous exertion at last repeated *a brrr*."

Even if the child in these first imitations learns no new performance, yet he does learn to accomplish something without being prepared beforehand; hence the great exertion which the quotations are unanimous in reporting. So that here too a primitive voluntary action takes place, a preliminary to the very complex effort of will required for later imitation.

The path of self-imitation is not the only one by which the child reaches imitation of others; we still have to mention a particular kind of imitative faculty which cannot be anything but innate. The child has, namely, the power of imitating movements *noticed in others, but which it is impossible he can perceive in like manner in himself.*

Preyer's son (; 3) already imitated pursing up the lips, and Scupin's son (; 6½) always opened his mouth when he saw others drinking; our own son (; 9) imitated alternate opening and closing of the eyes. Now, what happens here? It is true that the child has often before made this movement of the mouth and eyes, he has, however, never seen them take place in his own body, but only knows it as a kinæsthetic[1] and tactile perception; now he experiences them in others as an optical impression, and is thereby prompted to corresponding movements himself. So that in the child's consciousness there is not a trace of likeness between what he has experienced himself and what he has perceived in others; the sight of the movement of my mouth cannot act as a stimulus for any learnt and practised sensory-motor association, and yet the movement is imitated.

This power, therefore, doubtless falls into the same category as the instinctive movements, considered in an earlier section; complicated actions with definite aims occur, and these do not find their origin in individual experiences and learning, but in inherited nervous processes (associations). The especial value of such an established truth is the fact that, up till now, imitation has been generally placed in opposition to inheritance. Imitation, it was commonly thought, was the result entirely of outside experiences, a passive moulding by pattern and

---

[1] Kinæsthetic is the term applied to those perceptions, directly possessed by man, of the movements of his limbs; they are caused by nerves of sensation issuing from within the joints and muscles.

example; now we see not only that the general tendency to and capacity for imitation must be an "inborn" aptitude, but that a number of elementary imitative acts must be provided for in the hereditary make-up (construction) of the central nervous system.[1]

The two factors we have been considering of self-imitation and instinctive imitation are the beginnings of that manifold imitative power which becomes so marked a feature after the first nine months. In addition to the almost reflex "infections" by something seen or heard, there are distinct efforts of the will accompanied by the deepest attention, hard, bodily exertion and fumbling first attempts.

The child is now able to imitate, not only those actions which, at an earlier stage, he has already performed spontaneously and independently, but also fresh co-ordinated movements, never practised before. Thus our daughter (; 9) copied the sound combination "pa-pa" which had never before occurred in her baby monologues; at the same age she could copy her mother so well in squeezing the india-rubber doll that she produced the familiar squeak. Major's son (; 8) imitated the somewhat difficult action of his mother as she held a page of the newspaper over her head like a cap. Scupin's son (; 11) energetically rubbed down a chair with paper as he had often seen the maid dust. The child of nine months sometimes tries to answer notes sung or whistled to it with similar notes—quite high squeaks for whistled notes. Rhythm, too, is imitated; thus our own boy (; 8) responded to a single *a* with *a* to a, doubled *a* with *a—a*. Progress is also shown further by mastery on the child's part of a whole series of imitative actions and the power of quickly interchanging them; from our daughter (; 9) we could get in quick succession imitations of the following sounds: cough, *rrrr*, *a*, high whistle, *dada*, and snapping of the fingers.

In these imitative actions we can now distinguish two more types which we will call DIRECT and INDIRECT imitations. By far the greater number of examples quoted above belong to the first class, in which the imitation follows without any pause the perception of the movement. The other type show a

[1] The elementary form of these imitative 'processes may perhaps best be compared with the many "infections" which we find in adults, e.g. "infected" yawning.

less striking but perhaps a more important result; there the perceptions are not transmuted into imitations at once, but only after a longer or shorter interval; the impressions must therefore have an after-effect in the form of tendencies or ideas which appear again at a suitable opportunity in corresponding movements.[1] This is, above all, true, of course, of impressions which are constantly repeated; the effects left by them accumulate until they become sufficiently strong to overflow into motor channels. In such cases, then, the utterance of definite sounds, the performance of certain actions, is only the conclusion of a long process of learning; but since this has gone on out of sight, the concluding moment often comes upon the observer as a total surprise; all at once the child can do something which apparently had never once come within his range of interests. "It flashes upon him."

This subterraneous path is really the chief road to learning. It is not by imitation of intentional examples that the child acquires the greatest number of powers, but by the constant acquirement of unintentional, unconscious impressions which, at last, in like fashion, are transmuted into action by the child. In this way the little child learns the intonation, dialect and vocabulary of those around him, no less than definite hand movements, games and a hundred other things, until he gradually becomes part of his environment, and permeated through and through with its outlook, manners and customs.

If we glance over what has been said about imitation and apply to it Bühler's three stages of instinct, specialized training and intellect, we are brought face to face with a noteworthy fact. As a rule, indeed, imitation is most closely referred to specialized training, and seems to be unintelligent action into which the individual can be coaxed or forced by the frequent presentation of any kind of sense-impressions. In reality, however, this imitation by mechanical learning is the least important, for, even in its primitive forms, imitation is distinctly more often a form of activity with inner, intelligent coherence. Therefore amongst the infinite number of impressions offering a possibility of imitation, a choice—unconscious indeed, but decided by adaptation to life—is made. The motives of this choice are, on the one hand, of an instinctive

[1] Whether these impressions continue in the form of conscious ideas until the imitative act follows cannot be determined in these early stages.

nature, determined by inherited biological needs (of these we spoke above); and, on the other, intellectual in character. There is imitation of movements which are not only a chance sequence of muscle contractions, but are grasped in their full intelligence, i.e. understood. We have every reason at the end of the first year—which in any case brings the first traces of intelligence—to assume the appearance of understanding imitation, and, as time passes, this takes precedence more and more of the other forms of instinctive imitation and of imitation resulting from specialized training. We shall be able to prove this chiefly in speech imitation.

We often apply the term "aping" to entirely unintelligent, mechanical imitation, as if apes gave preference to this special kind of activity. But Köhler's new research work forces us to an entire change of opinion. "The chimpanzee has untold difficulty in imitating anything without a full grasp of its meaning. Only when the action observed in man or fellow-ape is understood as intelligent in some way, does it awaken in him any impulse to imitate it." Köhler is speaking here only of the imitation of unaccustomed acts, and therefore does not consider instances of instinctive imitation. In any case, however, we can recognize even here the analogy between the child and the ape.

A third reason for the child's imitative actions is due—as Grünbaum[1] has lately pointed out with especial emphasis—to the *personal* factor. The child imitates where it is intimately bound up with another person, and imitates because the closeness of the connection is more keenly felt with the progress of his imitative action. As Grünbaum rightly says: "It is not the complex of perceptions which presents itself as an action which is imitated, but the person who performs this action." How fastidious the child sometimes is in his imitative acts will be shown later, particularly when these have to do with speech-imitation.

3. The First Beginnings of Play

Those actions which are directly aimed at the attainment of some object, such as trying to reach some person or thing, expressional movements demanding food, form only a quite

[1] Grünbaum has even—no doubt in too far-reaching a degree—made this factor into the ruling principle of all imitation in general.

inconsiderable part of the sum-total of the infant's activities. By far the majority of these have no direct aim outside themselves, but are self-sufficing; these are games.

Since the question as to the nature and conditions necessary for play will be very exhaustively treated later on,[1] we must content ourselves, at this point, with suggestions that have a direct bearing on the first beginnings of the child's play.

In these early stages the distinction we have just drawn between actions of play and those of utility exists only for the observer; there is no corresponding difference in the child's psychic nature. For it is seldom only that the child's serious actions for some definite purpose are determined by any realization of such purpose, whilst, on the other hand, the conscious intensity with which he pursues his play-interests is often in no degree less than the psychic action in absolutely essential movements, e.g. the taking of food.

Yet we must observe the distinction. We are faced with the curious fact that a young living creature, as a rule, performs such actions as appear aimless and therefore superfluous, and we ask ourselves how this can be reconciled with that concentration of purpose prevailing in all organic life. Why therefore does the infant play?

First of all, doubtless, as a result of living energy which craves for expenditure (expansion, expression), and cannot find scope enough in the serious business of life. And thus superabundant power changes into superfluous movement. These powers burst forth in kicking and stamping, in babbling, bubbling, snorting, in creeping and crawling, in throwing and banging all kinds of objects, in swinging a rattle and splashing water (Spencer's Discharge-theory).

As a consequence of this connection the extent and intensity of play must depend on the amount of superfluous strength, and, as a matter of fact, every diminution of strength is evident in a decrease of play. This is quite plain in all illness, for the child's store of energy is now required to fight the inner disturbance, and no superabundance is left over for play, the happy kicking, the well-pleased babble, joy in its toys, etc.; all these suddenly cease, and only return with recovery. As an example of the strength of these ups and downs:—

Hilde (; 6½). "Severe inflammation of the lungs with high

[1] Cf. Chap. XXI.

fever threw the child for four days into a condition of complete apathy and entire loss of appetite. As the fever diminished, her apathy disappeared, and when she took her food as before —in six days' time—a psychic change took place with unexpected suddenness. The child was overcome with excitement and delight; Hilde crowed, shouted and 'told tales' till it did one's heart good to hear her. It seemed as if after the illness her joy of life had grown more intensive and sought all possible means of expression."

But similar fluctuations in play-activity—which have not, as yet, received adequate attention—occur even without any accompanying illness; indeed, a certain rhythm between the increase and decrease of those primitive expenditure-movements seems to be a general and normal feature of early—perhaps also of later—childhood. We have particularly noticed this is the infant's babble, but it is also apparent in the play-movements of the limbs.

But although the theory of expenditure of energy gives some explanation of the origin of play, it throws no light upon its character. Is it then quite accidental and a matter of indifference as to the channels into which this energy should flow? Has the nature of play-activity no bearing on the child's life?

Karl Groos has given an answer to this question in his celebrated theory of play as TRAINING. Even if play seems to serve no special purpose, yet it fulfils a very important task as unconscious, autodidactic training for future useful activities. This statement lays bare the INSTINCTIVE foundations of play. The aptitudes for future powers stir into life long before the period of their real development, so that they may be trained in the freest possible way and on harmless materials for their useful work in the future.

Let us consider the chief stages of the development of play in infancy, with special reference to its value as preparatory training.[1]

The least complicated form is the child's simple play with its own limbs. Thus in the first three months the play of putting the hands in front of the eyes is of value as practice (cf.

[1] Cf. here also the "inventory" of Bühler and Hetzer, which contains an enumeration of play-activities observed in 69 children—with the dates of the appearance of the various forms of play.

G

Chapter VI, Section 3) in the perception of form and at the same time training in the power of holding. Apparently, aimless kicking exercises the leg muscles, and in its alternating rhythm hints at the specific movement of walking (cf. Chapter IV, Section 2).

Also, without the untiring play-babble of three-quarters of a year, the child would never gain that control over tongue, larynx, lips and lungs, without which future speech would be an impossibility.

Eva (; 4). "The gurgle has now grown into a loud delighted crow, and reaches notes as high as a young puppy's, and these notes seem to give her great pleasure, for she continually repeats them one after another—she plays on her larynx."

Scupin's son (; 10). "He produces all kinds of noise for pure enjoyment, smacks with his lips, bubbles, puffs, hisses (the first attempt at producing 's'), clucks, coughs, says *brr*, and chatters without ceasing."

As soon as the child can hold anything, that is then, after three months, the play with objects begins. It seems very monotonous to the onlooker, since, for the most part, it consists only in unwearied repetition of the same movement; newspaper is crumpled up in the tiny fist, then too—in later months—torn to pieces; the rattle is constantly moved to and fro; the spoon is banged on the table; the doll thrown out of the perambulator twenty, thirty times. And yet what a wealth of experiences the child gains in all this, and how deeply they are impressed upon the sensitive mind just by the purposeful impulse of continual repetition! Later on, everyone needs a thousand-sided capacity for dealing with things, to treat them rightly, to distinguish them, and to find himself a match for the tricks of the objective world; he begins his apprenticeship for this in his fourth month. With every blow that the child deals the table with his tin mug, he hammers into his little brain: "Noises can be made with things," and "I am the cause of noises." And when Scupin's son (; 10) kept on hammering with his spoon alternately on the table and on a tin tray he was learning: "Different objects give out different sounds." The child as he tears up paper gives himself a little lesson in physics and geometry; he notices that bodies resist division, that, when thrown into the air, they move downwards, that the most unlike forms arise from one another, that the greater becomes less by division, etc.

This must not be misunderstood. Of course the child himself has no idea of all these educational results which we have just deduced from his play. Such an absurdity as that the infant gets any ideas of causes or of cohesion is, of course, not meant. The immediate result is that the child becomes intimately acquainted with a large number of perceptions and of the relations between them, and that such store of experience in its ever-increasing familiarity forms a solid foundation on which to build later a real acquaintance with the world, an understanding of things and their interrelations. This preparatory work of all play is more or less done out of sight, in the twilight of total or semi-unconsciousness; any verbal formulation must more or less contort such intangible psychic happenings.

As the third group of infant play, we find in the second half-year, in addition to that already named, play with others; the child is no longer content with solitary play, but wants social games as well. If he were strictly limited to those relations with other human beings that are the real necessities of his life, how little it would be—fed, washed, garments changed—and that the end of it all! But play enlarges this sphere and strikes the first note of relations that only much later become realities; it is the first source of intercourse, of a real psychic relationship between the child and others. (Cf. also Chapter VII, 2c.)

Gunther (; $7\frac{1}{2}$). "For a week now Gunther answers a short exclamatory *a* with the same sound and does this several times consecutively. The reaction is especially quick if he is standing at the open door of an adjoining room, sees no one, and with this sound establishes a contact between himself and the unseen person."

The same thing exactly was recorded of our daughter (; $8\frac{1}{2}$): the child went on with this primitive conversation-game for seven or eight minutes without getting tired of it.

Concerning the attitude of the boy to his elder sister there is a record, shortly before the completion of his first year.

Gunther (; $11\frac{1}{2}$). "G. is very pleased when Hilde plays with him, gives him toys, pushes him about in his little chair, dances or hops about funnily before him, and so on. There seems some unseen tie between the two children; although neither of them can yet talk to the other, they yet understand one another through their childhood."

Competition for possession! What does a six-months-old child know about that? Or about parting and meeting again? and yet!

Gunther (; 7). "A game that gives him great pleasure is to hand over Hilde's doll and quickly drag it away again; every time this is followed by shouts of excitement and an attempt to seize it. So too Peep O! arouses his delight; whenever the playfellow's head comes out of its hiding-place, the little fellow shouts with joy."

It is very remarkable how this last-named game of Peep O! seems to be a typical game of children from 6 to 12 months old. In the most varied diaries of our own and of others, it is always mentioned again and again. Sometimes the playfellow hides behind a chair or a hanging of some sort, and the child watches attentively, greeting the other's reappearance with a triumphant "*da!*" to show his warm welcome; or he himself has a handkerchief thrown over him, and then pulls it off more or less cleverly, to make his reappearance beaming with happiness.[1] Apparently the remarkable attraction exercised by this game has its origin in the surprise of each discovery and in the contrast between being alone and in company.

[1] The game mentioned in Chapter VI, Section 2, belongs here too.

THE GAIN OF EXPERIENCES

1. Perception and Attention

THE question of the origin of human knowledge has at all times aroused the greatest interest both in psychology and in the consideration of the perceptive faculties, and often enough in these discussions the child is referred to in exemplification, since in him one has to deal directly with the beginning of first experiences.

Such reference is especially in favour with the exponents of empiricism who try to prove that all human perception, attention and knowledge are the result of sense-perceptions and their associations. According to this view the soul at birth is, to begin with, absolutely empty; the child has first to receive all material of experience from outside, to allow sense-impressions full play in his sense-organs, and to combine the originally isolated impressions with each other by association, thus creating complicated images, perceptions, ideas and thoughts.

The principal theses of this widespread teaching, which meets us in every possible gradation, are therefore—(1) the passivity of experiences coming from outside; (2) the atomic nature of the original consciousness, like the separate parts of a mosaic ("sensations"); (3) the building up of mental life by the mechanical union of these elements, originally separated. None of these theses explains the actual development of experience in the child, and their assertion was only possible as long as there was no access to actual observation of the child, for this shows quite another picture, and proves, in contradistinction to the first thesis, that perception is not a simple act of reception but comes into being through the convergence of outside impressions with inborn aptitudes of the child's own nature.

In opposition to the second, observation shows that the starting-point of psychic life is not a mosaic of isolated sensations, but a general condition of blended sensibility. Finally, in opposition to the third, it teaches us that experience is formed and differentiated not by mechanical juxtaposition of elements into complicated forms (association), but by raising certain component impressions out of the general undifferentiated state. It is only when such " forms of perception" have been achieved that "association" can begin to work.

Let us describe in somewhat greater detail these beginnings of human experience.

By "sensation" we understand the simplest element of all sense-experience. This idea is indispensable to psychology, but its significance must not be misunderstood. In reality it expresses an abstraction; if we could break up any perceptual image into its component parts and imagine this breaking-up continued until no further division was possible, we should call these imaginary final results "simple sensations." Accordingly these are only artificial products in thought, but not psychic realities. Such simple sensations—of a tone, colour, temperature, etc.—do not occur in actual consciousness; they are always only component parts in some united conscious images. And this lack of individual independence is greatest just in the earliest stage of childhood. For, as we have already seen, we must think of the earliest condition as one of entirely diffuse general sensibility, without as yet any isolated single experiences. In this first stage there are none of the "simple elements" of old psychology, nor of the "forms" (Gestalten) of the new. Just as, when we lie on the couch, dreaming with closed eyes, we do not notice the different impressions of the light that penetrates our eyelids, the distant noises from the street, the pressure of our clothes, the temperature of the room, but only their blended effect in the general condition of our sensation, so—only still much more vague and less keen—we must at first picture the sensibility of the little child. Therefore, before we examine how separate sensations become united, we must first ask how the child in any way manages to distinguish and isolate a single phenomenon out of the confusion of this general condition. Thus DISSOCIATION must precede association.

Now, this dissociation is only to be explained by "convergence."

On the one hand stimuli from without exercise their influence. The infant's sense-organs with very slight power of functioning in the earliest days grow daily more and more efficient, and bring about a certain *differentiation* in that confused general state of earliest sensibility. It is no longer indistinct and shapeless like a veil of mist, but rather contains spots distinguished by a certain quality (colour, noise, hardness), by certain boundary lines, by a sudden appearance and disappearance. Amongst these we should find such complex impressions as arise from the mother's face, voice and gentle touch, or from the shape and noise of the rattle. Yet the simple existence of such marked spots in the general sensorial condition does not yet mean any real perception; rather they do but form the one outside factor necessary in the convergence process of perception; they only represent the starting-points for that other factor, the individual activity of the child, which is partly of a physical, partly of a mental character. To consider first the physical character:

Some constituents of that general psychic condition, by their strength, pronounced character, special quality, are the cause of a physical movement which directs the sense-organ particularly to that element of sensation and so increases its strength, distinctness and continuance.

Picture a paralysed child, having a retina capable of functioning but incapable of moving the head or the muscles of the eyes: this child would certainly feel brightness of light and colours in his sense-perception as a whole, but he would never attain to separate optical pictures of objects and actions, because all those acquisitive movements of staring, following with the eyes, converging, etc., would be impossible. In the same way sensations of touch on the skin would never lead to the perception of objects touched, were these sensations not supplemented by the active movements of holding, scratching, stroking.

But these sensory-motor associations by which attraction and acquisition result from stimulus are by nature innate. Some of them function, as was shown in the last chapter, in the first days of life, others are developed so quickly in the following weeks that there can be no question of learning in a purely empiric sense. So that we are dealing with a quickly ripening instinct. But even the sensory-motor instinct of acquisition and attraction would not be sufficient alone to account for the fact of perception. For, since in the child other stimuli from without and within continually set up impulses to movements that cross the mechanism of the acquisitive movements, the birth of these would be constantly threatened, and, above all, their longer continuance would be impossible. This is borne out by the fact that in the first days of life, at any rate, evidence of any real attraction (turning) to stimuli seldom occurs, and this, always, only for a few moments.

But soon this condition changes as a central activity of the child's—ATTENTION—comes to the fore. The inborn faculty of concentrated attention is therefore the second necessary preliminary for growth in experiences.

A preliminary stage of attention consists to begin with in the fact that the child allows himself to be turned from his momentary occupation by a new attraction.

Sometimes no later than the third week, the child will stop a scream when he hears an even louder noise immediately follow or sees someone approach his cot. And now real active attention begins to work. The distracting stimulus not only stops the existing activity, but attracts the energy, thus released, to itself. Then follows that motor condition of the sense-organs which is especially favourable to the reception of the stimulus; a cessation of all other movements takes ·place, the organs not immediately concerned are often thrown into a state of peculiar expectancy, which doubtless is best adapted to prevent ineffectual action on their part; and lastly, this state of concentration is maintained by effort for some time in order to permit a quiet and intensive perception of the stimulus. Thus a purely instinctive turning to the stimulus of light becomes an attentive fixed look, and a start at a loud noise becomes equally attentive listening.

Hilde (*at the end of* 5 *weeks*). "Whistling and singing make an evident impression on the child; she immediately stops screaming and shows keen attention, i.e. her eyes are wide open, and both they and her whole body motionless."

Gunther (*third week*). "In the last few days there is absolutely certain evidence of the power of seeing. For instance, when anything—especially a human face — approaches the child, he assumes a look of fixed attention which is unmistakable. If the object looked at changes its position, his glance sometimes correspondingly changes in direction as well."

(*Three days later.*) "If the boy is having a good scream and someone comes suddenly up to him, the cry stops and he looks at the new-comer."

(*Fifth week.*) "His look becomes more and more wide-eyed and attentive; if anyone comes to his perambulator, he looks at him attentively; if he is lifted out or wheeled into another room, the change of impressions continues to keep his eyes fixed in almost expectant attention."

(*Seventh week.*) "If G. is lying on his swaddling-table he almost constantly turns his eyes to the light wall behind it; if he is turned round, he alters the direction of his glance correspondingly, so as to keep an eye on the wall."

Eva (*third week*). "She reacts to a sound, not only by starting but also by attentive notice, by cessation in screaming, especially to high whistling notes, jingling of keys and the chirping sound made by drawing in breath. Her 'attention' is shown by complete immovability and a fixed look. Faces, in full light, bending over her have the same effect."

At a somewhat later age—twelfth week—there is a record made by the Scupins of their son: "The mother was nursing the child on his cushion; he looked round attentively and gazed with the keenest interest at the fish swimming about in the aquarium. When a mudfish suddenly hurried round, he moved his arms quickly up and down and widely dilated his nostrils. After a time our bird began to sing, and the child at once turned his head towards it; he had recognized the direction of the sound quite accurately and never moved his eyes from the little warbler."

Of course, too much must not be expected from this concentrated attention in the first year. Especially is the child's persistence very small; however eagerly he has turned his attention to any impression, in the next few seconds there is evidence of weariness or turning to some new attraction. Even in a child of eleven months and a half, Idelberger found (p. 255), in a succession of little tests, that the length of time during which a given object was looked at with persistence never exceeded a few seconds; at the very most fifteen seconds, when the child looked attentively at a watch placed in his hand.

Thus motor movements and concentrated attention are the two closely connected means by which the young creature selects and retains separate elements from the original confused chaos of outer sensations, and immediately separates them from that general condition and reserves them as a special experience. Gradually they assume thus a character opposed to merely subjective experiences, they point outward to things—in short, they become perceptions. Only this process is a very gradual one: it is a long journey from the first stage, in which a sense-stimulus has an immediate effect through its subjective pleasantness or unpleasantness and produces reaction of attraction or aversion, to the moment when a person, a thing, an objective happening, is really experienced and "perceived". And it is not always possible to determine with certainty from the child's demeanour whether in any one special case it has already struggled through to the stage of genuine perception.

From B. Loewenfeld's experimental researches into the acoustic reactions in infancy, the following instances of psychological development may be given here. Whilst in the first month there occur only demonstrations of diffuse shock and reactions of displeasure, in the second month a first differentiation takes place, shown by negative reactions (i.e. with shock movements) to loud noises (rattle) and neutral reactions to sounds (whistling). In the third month the union between sight and hearing makes its first appearance, i.e. the eyes are fixed in the direction of the source of sound. This month is the distinctive "period of hearing"; also the duration of the response to hearing stimuli is particularly long. In the fourth month, the duration and number of reactions decrease, the shock reactions become less severe and take the form of expressional movements; the reaction of smiling appears for the first time. In the following months, response is only obtained by such auditory stimuli as make a special affective appeal.

Adalbert Stifter in his autobiography describes with subtle intuition this gradual transition from the diffuse condition of affective sense-experiences to the perception of an outer world separate from the individual ego. In this description we may leave it an open question as to how far we are dealing with real fragments of earliest recollections,[1] as Stifter himself believes, or how far with poetical reconstructions!

"Far back in the empty void of the past is something like

---

[1] For this passage I am indebted to Bernfeld's book (p. 261). The passage is the more remarkable since Stifter died as early as 1868, and therefore could not have been influenced by modern psychological theories. The italics are mine.

bliss and delight which penetrated my being with such mighty force as wellnigh to overwhelm me and which nothing in my after life resembled. The abiding memories it left behind were of brightness and confusion deep within me. This must have been very early, for it seems to me that the deep and wide-spreading darkness of a void enveloped the happening. Then something else followed that passed through my being like a soft and soothing influence and its abiding memory consisted of sounds. Then I swam in something swaying, swam to and fro. I felt moved then as though intoxicated, and then there was once more nothing. The following points grew ever more decided: the ringing of bells and a broad ray of bright light, a red twilight. Quite clear too was something that was continually repeated, a voice that spoke to me, eyes that looked at me and arms that softened all harshness of life. I screamed for these things. Painful unbearable experiences alternated with those that were sweet and soothing. I remember efforts that achieved nothing and the cessation of horror and overpowering misery. I remember brightness and colours before my eyes, tones in my ears and gracious influences pervading my being. I felt more and more distinctly the eyes that looked at me, the voice which spoke to me and the tones that assuaged all pain. I remember that I called all that '*Mam*'. Once I felt those arms carrying me. There were too dark points in me. Memory told me later that these had been forests which were outside me. Then came a sensation, like the first of my life, brightness and confusion, followed by nothing more. After this sensation follows a great gap once more. Conditions that existed must have been forgotten. In succession to the gap, *the external world rose before me*, where until now only sensations had been felt. Even Mam, eyes, voice, arms, had only been a sensation to me and forests too, as I have just said. 'Mam', which I at present call mother, *now took shape and form before me* and I distinguished her movements . . ."

If we consider more closely the result of this process we see it is not now the sum, so to speak, of its component simple sensations. The image standing out from the background of consciousness (mother, rattle, etc.) is rather, from the beginning, a whole, within which single tones, lines, colours, etc., only have significance as mutually dependent, necessary component parts of that whole. Such a defined whole new psychology calls a psychic "form", and the formation, and organisation of the parts its "structure".

Now, every such "form" has its own development. When it is first reached by sensation-movements and concentrated attention it is quite undefined and indistinct, but it works now and again as a fresh incitement to further physical and mental activity, and emerges from each such tactual and visual act in a more detailed and clearer form. The singling out of objects from their surroundings becomes more distinct, whilst in the inner structure one feature is more emphasized and others unessential pushed back—in fact, it is really individual activity in its general course that first creates the "form"—"formative" activity indeed.

We must in truth not only speak of "forms" as purely passive presentations of the consciousness, but as real apparitions, in which are included not only the sense-values of colour, sound, touch, but also the individual activity of the physical attitude and the duration of attention. The perceptual image "rattle" is for the child not only the interweaving of the shape seen and touched with the noise heard, but with these is included from the first his own rythmic movement of shaking and the act of attentive listening.[1]

We are now in a position to put the principle of association into its right place.

It is only when by means of dissociation separate perceptive forms have been obtained that these can be united. Such an act of union we call association, when one component part, appearing alone, is able to draw one or more others after it. This process can take place in two quite distinct forms as "intra" and "inter" association. The first is found within a single perception form; the component parts of the structure

---

[1] In the above presentation we have tried to refer the point of view of form-psychology back to the principles of personality. The "forms" are not of an ultimate nature, but proceed from the formative activity of the personal unity. It is, moreover, worthy of note that even the "form"-psychologists themselves feel it essential to pass on from those conscious totalities which they at first called forms and look for totalities of a higher order. In so doing they unintentionally approach the personality point of view. It is especially the consideration of early childhood that inevitably leads us to it. For instance, it makes Koffka not only place motor structures as a special group beside the sensorial and ideational (purely psychic) structures, but gives express recognition of sensory-motor structures, i.e. form-totalities in which psychic and physical are only mutually dependent parts. Such an attitude brings him quite near to the point of view put forward above, for such structures are only possible in the psycho-physical "person".

retain their connection with each other even when, at first, only fragments of the percept are reawakened by sense-stimuli. Thus the scent alone of the mother's breast may awaken associative sucking movements and signs of expectation in the child, because in the original perception-form of "the mother's breast" impressions of smell, sight, touch and taste united with sucking movements to form one indivisible whole. Inter-association, on the other hand, is found where two or more originally individual experiences come as a secondary process into union with each other and so form a new structure succession in time, spatial juxtaposition, causal relationship, etc. And again, in this case one part may cause associatively the following of another, as when the child has connected the objective percept tree and the (acoustic motor) word-form tree with the intelligently named object, and now at the sound "tree" looks at the actual thing.

This example shows at the same time that associations may exist not only between conscious ideas but between these and movements.[1]

The effect of association-connection extends beyond simple perception into the province of memory.

2. Memory Concepts

We must indeed assume that from the first moment when sense-impressions begin to act, the function of memory—understood in its widest sense—also becomes effective.

For instance, if any sense-perception occurs frequently, the sum of these successive impressions creates a general result possessing a certain durability. The first outward sign of these early acts of memory is the knowing—COGNITION—more exactly knowing again—RECOGNITION—on the part of the child, a capability which it is impossible to represent in a sufficiently primitive form.

Even in the second month of its age it can sometimes be noticed that the child does not remain indifferent to certain frequent impressions—especially its mother's face and voice —but greets them with a faint smile. After three months this

[1] The associative principle is therefore like that of form and structure psycho-physically neuter, thus forming an additional reason for the inference of personality.

cognition has advanced to DIFFERENTIATION, and the child's attitude is quite different to persons it knows and to strangers.

Gunther (; 3). "As I had just fed the child and was holding him on my arm—a position he liked very much as a rule—to show him to a visitor, G., who after a full meal had just been smiling at me, began to draw down the corners of his mouth sadly and to scream in piteous fashion, also more emphatically than he usually did."

Scupin's son (: 3½). "He smiles at familiar faces three metres distant. Strangers are known as such and considered with a serious look of astonishment; they cannot often get a laugh from the child, who is so gay as a rule. Generally he drops his head with only a bashful smile."

Eva (; 4½). "Yesterday I suddenly went up to her carriage with a lady; this stranger took the child by surprise as she bent over her, and Eva began to cry in utter fright. If father, mother, brother or sister bend over her she nearly always smiles."

Now, what happens in these cases? Certainly no recognition as such nor differentiation in the ordinary sense of the word. Probably a process somewhat of this kind takes place in the child's consciousness: "This face agrees with the one I just saw and have seen before, but that other I have never seen", for it can neither remember any impression previously made nor make any real comparison. In such a case the child is altogether incapable, as yet, of any conscious reference to the past. The only after-effect of earlier and repeated perceptions of its mother's face is to give a special shade of emotion to the fresh perception; the whole process of the present perception is made easier by that preliminary practice, the impression is added to already existent associations; memory finds her work run more smoothly, and can therefore, with the energy at her disposal, grasp and combine more details than in utterly new impressions, and so the act of perception can take on a suggestion of pleasure which we may name the quality of "familiarity" (Hoffding) or feeling of intimacy.

So we have—during the first three months at least—to deal exclusively with the united results of memory; the earlier perceptions do not leave behind them independent traces in the consciousness, but only subconsciously help in the formation of future perceptions. Yet this hidden working is also of the highest importance, for it makes the child acquainted and familiar with all the things and occurrences that exert a daily influence upon his sense-organs.[1] Each successive repetition deepens the impression, until at last the perceptions have penetrated deeply enough to leave behind an independent deposit in the consciousness as an actual trace of memory, i.e. an idea.

This EMANCIPATION OF MEMORY from perception proceeds, of course, only by degrees. Two transitional forms may be established: the primary memory-picture and the associative anticipation of perceptions.

A perception of some strength leaves behind, at its disappearance, a kind of after-shadow, the co-called primary "MEMORY-PICTURE", which fades away quickly, it is true, but may yet have a certain effect on the child's consciousness. Thus Miss Shinn reports of her niece:—

(; 3). "A brightly-dressed lady who had been joking with the child, through a change of place, suddenly disappeared from the child's sight. Then for some minutes she looked for the face that had impressed her and had suddenly disappeared." The impression, according to this report, must have continued in the less vivid form of an idea.

Some months later, the primary memory is so active that it can be used in the first simple play with the child. If an impression which interested the child has suddenly disappeared, he will immediately after be still so full of it, that he expects its reappearance; if this should happen, the child is delighted, and likes the game to be repeated.

Hilde (; 7). "For some days I have noticed in the child something that strikes me as a first game. When I am feeding her, she looks at me; I look another way, the child stops drinking, turns from her side on to her back and watches me with a roguish look, which, of course, I cannot notice, only my husband. If I now slowly turn to the child, a beaming smile of pleasure flashes over the little face, and she begins the teasing game again, takes a draught or two, stops, looks at me intently, and so on. Every time I turn round, a happy smile and utterance of gentle notes of delight follow."

[1] A more detailed treatment of the action of memory is to be found in Chapter XV.

But that not only impressions of the immediate past but those that lie farther back can be revived as elements of an idea is shown by the associated expectation and anticipation which also develop after the first three months. Such an association can be recognized in the child by movements of aversion or attraction in the direction of that part of the united impression which is not yet perceived, only expected.

Hilde (; 4½). "For a month now Hilde gets once a day broth given her with a spoon as she lies on her mother's lap. In the early weeks it was very difficult to induce her to keep her face up, for after each spoonful she turned it to one side, as she had been accustomed to do at her mother's breast. It was only by very gradual stages that she became used to the new way of feeding: now she holds her head straight, and often even parts her lips before the spoon touches them."[1]

"In her bath her face is washed with a sponge soaked in cold water. She always resists the cold by struggling with her head and body. For about a week I have noticed that these movements begin, and she jerks back her face, if the sponge comes near enough for her to expect to feel its touch."

In the course of the next few months there is a considerable increase in these feelings of expectation, both in number and variety; they already lead to real hopes, disappointments, fears, even if these only extend to the experiences of the next few seconds. The child notices that the down quilt is taken off his perambulator, and kicks with delight in the expectation of being lifted out; his pain is all the greater when he sees his mother coming up at once again with the quilt. Hilde (; 8½). ("During the period of weaning, the approach of the bottle or cup, instead of her mother's breast on which she had set her hopes, produces a most vehement protest, because the child already anticipates the coming unpleasantness of different food and of the inconvenient way of drinking.)"

It is characteristic of the whole early development of the

---

[1] Cf. the somewhat different interpretation which Koffka (p. 182) gives of the above observation. He does not think that it is a case of a real idea of expectation, but that in the whole process of being fed the spoon has assumed the position of a transitional phenomenon that points on to something further. It is, of course, impossible to fix with certainty the exact moment of this development at which actual "expectant-ideas" have made their appearance.

life of ideas that they do not appear so much as memories pointing to something in the past, but as expectations directed to the future—even though only to a future immediately at hand. We meet here for the first time a general law of development: REFERENCE TO THE FUTURE IS GRASPED BY THE CONSCIOUSNESS SOONER THAN THAT TO THE PAST. The reason lies in the utterly different bearing that the immediate future has on individual weal and woe. The past is a mere shadow, where nothing can be changed, and which can only be the region of a purposeless concept; but the future demands purposeful action, provision and care, aversion or desire, and is therefore the direct sphere of will-action. And the will dominates a mere concept.

Now, at what period memory reaches such a stage of freedom that it can, without any direct outer influence, raise spontaneous concepts in the consciousness cannot be accurately determined. For speech—the chief means by which man later on expresses his concepts—is still wanting, and other signs are not of an unequivocal nature. Has the child seven or nine months old, lying awake and alone in his perambulator, already any living concepts? Does his consciousness show him any inner pictures of those persons and things with which daily intercourse has made him familiar: pictures of his mother's face, voice, gentle hand, of his feeding-bottle, his rattle? Is his babble nothing but the expression of a condition of comfort unconnected with any objects or the accompaniment of some feeling of concrete consciousness, however vague it may be? We do not know, and probably never shall.

Towards the end of the first year, at any rate, the power to form a spontaneous and independent concept certainly exists, although this can only be established with the help of the speech now beginning. The following record shows particularly strong confirmation:—

Hilde (1 ; 0). "As I went this morning up to Hilde's bed, she signed with her little hands, 'Please, please', and said immediately after, 'dolly', although I had nothing in my hand. Here for the first time it was quite certain that the child was asking for something existing only in her own concept perhaps the rusk which the child always calls 'dolly' now or her plaything."

3. The Conquest of Space[1]

There is one side of human experience on which development, even in the first year of life, reaches a certain conclusion: the mastery of spatial perception. At the same time it is easier to follow progress from point to point on this side than on any other. And if we also grant that the psychic problem of the beginning of spatial perception, which has been the cause of so much discussion, can only be solved by child-psychology, we are justified in a special—even if short—treatment of the subject.

By the expression "conquest or mastery of space" we mean not only the consideration of the growth of spatial perception and ideas, but THE MASTERY OF THE SPACE-IDEA BOTH IN RECOGNITION AND ACTION. There is no division possible between these two, nowhere is sensory-motor association so sharply marked as in relation to space. The mental and physical grasp of space go hand in hand, and there can be no concept of it without a corresponding application in physical actions.

Consequently the isolated consideration of the space-phenomena of a single sense-organ would be an entirely artificial abstraction. Originally there is a total absence of special optical spatial-perception in the retina, of tactual by touch in the skin, of acoustic in the recognition of direction of sound, kinæsthetic in the performance and perception of bodily movements, or vestibular sensations for the regulation of balance; but, instead, the child's united spatial idea grows out of the elementary and uninterrupted intermingling of all these factors. That the psychology of space has so long been dominated by this misleading abstraction is only to be explained by the fact that earlier researches were entirely confined to adults.

The same cause has resulted in continual strife on the dark battlefield of nativism and empiricism. "Is spatial-perception natural or acquired?" This question, in any case, cannot be answered by the adult's perfect perception of and familiarity with space; but child-psychology shows that the question itself is wrongly formulated. There is no one act of perception

[1] In part, extracts from my earlier essay, *The Development of Spatial Perception in Early Childhood*, 1909. Fresh and important theoretical considerations as to spatial perception in early childhood are to be found in Bühler's *Development* (pp. 22 sqq. and pp. 57 sqq.), and also in Koffka's book (pp. 212 sqq.).

of or familiarity with space in which both natural and acquired faculties do not take part. The spatial-concept is so manifold in its categories—extent in line, surface, depth, form, size, direction, position, distance—that the power of its inward comprehension could not possibly be innate in its full perfection. Much must here first be "learnt". But, on the other hand, certain foundations—especially the general understanding of "extent"—are so evidenced by the senses, and so many sensory-motor associations act from the first or very soon with such accuracy, that it is impossible to deny to them a pre-existent faculty. Learning in the domain of space is therefore only partly purely empiric, but also partly a gradual ripening of instinctive aptitudes for which individual experiences only provide material for stimulus and practice.

Let us now follow this process of development in detail.

Space in its mathematical sense can, as we all know, be represented by a system of lines, which stretch from a point into the three dimensions. So too, psychologically, space as it exists in every man's spatial-perception, concept and familiarity, extends in three dimensions from a centre. But whilst in mathematical space the point can be fixed anywhere, in psychological space it has only one possible position, i.e. in the person of the perceptive individuality. For every man is the centre of his own space, understands from his own person the dimensions of front to back, right to left, from top to bottom. And whilst in mathematical space the point is a real one, in psychological space we cannot give such a point: the individual body as a whole—the head at least—is the starting-place. Thus one's own space stands opposed as a special concept-form to the outer space. All qualities and conditions of the outer space are in some way brought into relation with the individual space, and by this receive their psychological character.

But it must not be supposed that the little child first of all completely masters his own space, i.e. learns to know and use the position, movement, size and form of his own limbs, and then—and not before—sets about the conquest of outer space; rather both activities develop simultaneously and in constant interrelation.

The Individual Space.—The means by which the child gains the first experiences of the space conditions of his own body are, principally, the so-called movement-sensations, impressions which are caused by the sensory nerves in muscles and joints and brought into keen activity with every movement of the limbs. Even in a condition of repose there is a general consciousness of their position—"sense of position". As soon as stronger head-movements begin, especially when attempts are made to lift the head, and, later on, as the body is kept upright in sitting or standing, the vestibular activities begin to function, those three semicircular canals provided with nerves in the inner ear which help in a knowledge of the position of the head and thus by this means of the whole body. Very little is known about the development of these "own-space" perceptions in the child, but so much at least may be accounted certain, that from dull vague beginnings they come to maturity with the advance of motor capabilities—drawing up the body, sitting, standing, creeping, etc.

The sight-perception of his own limbs is not used for the space-concept of the body until quite late. When the child begins to look at his hands and feet, they are at first strange objects to him, just like anything else he sees; and these sight-impressions are only very gradually combined with kinæsthetic sensations and localized feelings, so that he becomes consciously aware that the limbs he sees belong to his own individual ego.

We are better informed as to the way in which the child gradually acquires knowledge of space outside his own body. Here we can distinguish between "original space", "near" and "distant" space. The principal organic contributors to this development are mouth, hand and eye, the senses of smell and hearing taking a secondary place in the understanding of direction.

The sequence named is on this account worthy of notice because it corresponds to the biological importance of the three spatial zones. What lies next to us in the spatial sense, is also near to us for self-preservation, the practical orientation, the interest in what is nearest. The young creature must first of all thoroughly understand his immediate surroundings and then an extension takes place in the sphere of space to which he has access.

The importance of the mouth in the first idea of space is of special note on account of its total disappearance in later stages of development. As the only part of the body which from the first day has a specialized activity (sucking), the mouth has opportunity to receive constant touch-impressions, which in this way will gain a relative distinctness and familiarity earlier than in any other organ. This "original space" is a kind of intermediate stage between "near" and "distant" space; for the unknown object must intrude a little into the sphere of "near" space to be touched. After a few weeks the mouth even develops the power of clasping (seizing) if the child's cheek is touched with the nipple; the open mouth tries to reach the cause of the stimulus, and the head is turned until the nipple is grasped by the lips. The mouth keeps this pre-eminence in the domain of touch for a long time, even when other organs have become active; see how the infant later stuffs everything he can get hold of into his mouth! Certainly, one of the chief reasons may be desire to eat it, but yet, at the same time, the mouth performs the intellectual task of explaining and confirming by its more familiar and exact touch-sensations the new and indistinct impressions of the other organs (hand and eye). Thus for a considerable time the mouth is the organ of control over space-experiences gained elsewhere.

But in the very first weeks the "near" space becomes accessible to the child, and for two or three months his mastery of space is practically confined to it. It consists, roughly speaking, of a hemisphere which with a radius of one-third metre extends in front of the head as centre; whatever lies beyond it remains for the present outside the child's sensory-motor control of space. The instincts of attraction already functioning in the first days of life (see Chapter III, Section 1) are at first almost exclusively confined to this "near" space. The turning of the head to the mother's breast—at a distance of a few centimetres—which is known by the sense of smell, shows this, as does also the following of glittering things with the eyes, which only occurs when the objects are brought close up to the eyes.

The chief organ of the "near" space is the hand.

To begin with, the hand is not yet an instrument, but a passive object of perception; its acquaintance is made by means of other organs, mouth and eye.

The constant sucking of the fingers—often lasting many

hours—must generate specialized touch-perceptions of this part of the body (the hands) in the organ of "original" space (the mouth); on the other hand, the child in his waking hours plays for a quarter of an hour at a time with his eyes fixed on his hand, turns it this way and that, spreads out the fingers, shuts and opens them, and in so doing gets the most varied sight-impressions. Since no other object, at this period, is so frequently in the child's optical "near" space, the first idea of optical form is certainly practised more on the hand than anywhere else.

But now the hand turns into an instrument itself, and this by two stages. At first only tactual-motor reactions take place, i.e. touch-impressions made on the hand set free motor impulses. Whatever is placed in the child's fingers or accidentally touches them is clasped, scratched, squeezed. In this way the form of objects within the "near" space is learnt in a twofold manner: by sight as forms of two dimensions, by tactual motor-action as bodies of three dimensions. By continuous repetition of these double impressions the child forms optical-tactual associations: he learns that things which appear round, cornered, narrow or broad feel at the same time spherical, angular, thin or thick, thus co-ordination between optic and tactual spatial form is doubtless acquired.

The second stage consists in the reaching out of the hand to an object which is not yet in contact with it. But even if the common impulse to grasp must be ascribed to an inborn aptitude, yet the direction of the grasp—that is, the association between the spot in visible space occupied by an object and the movement required to bring the hand to that place—must be explained in great measure by empiricism. Only when in innumerable cases the hand has happened to fall on the spot in the "near" space occupied by a visible object does the child get the length of directing the movement of his hand to visible objects; and some time again elapses before the fumbling, uncertain attempts develop into direct and certain movements of the hand towards the object seen. This surety of grasp is, as a rule, not attained until after the first three months.

It is noteworthy how, even in these later stages, the mouth still takes part in grasping. Often enough the child tries to reach some object visible in "near" space not with his hand, but directly with his open mouth, at the same time extending his head with great exertion.[1]

About the same time the idea of SOUND DIRECTION develops as well. If someone calls to the child several times from different sides, he always turns his head in a corresponding direction; and at the sound of a banging door, a dog's bark or of heavy footsteps, he turns to the source of the noise.

As soon as the child can hold things, opportunity occurs to make observations of his sense of distance. Our own observations are opposed to the frequently expressed view that the child at first sees all visible objects, far as well as near, lying by each other, and therefore without distinction tries to reach alike those in the distance and those close by. This stage, possibly true of children who have been operated on for congenital blindness, is not in our experience to be observed in normal children.[2] So long as the child's idea is confined to "near" space, it is indeed only close objects which arouse his attention and his impulses to movement. DISTANT OBJECTS ARE DURING THIS PERIOD NOT NOTICED AT ALL AS A RULE, since the powers of convergence and accommodation do not yet exist for them;[3] their diffuse impressions form the indefinite background for near things plainly seen and noticed, but they do not themselves become objects of perception or desire. At most, only exception can be made for things that give out light (a lamp, the moon), but even these do not act as so often affirmed. We ourselves have never noticed "the crying for the moon", and it is quite possible that other observers have not sufficiently distinguished between the *expressional* movement of desire which is set up by the attractive appearance of the shining light, quite independently of its evident unattainability, and the active movement of grasping, which includes in itself the supposition of the objects being within reach.

Learning to know things along the path of seizing and

[1] Dix has especially emphasized this seizing with the mouth, and, moreover, from the standpoint of his own observations, has associated himself entirely with my description of development given above.
[2] Our conclusions have meantime been confirmed by Dix (I, pp. 14 sqq.), and Scupin's drawings also seem to be in accord with them.
[3] Accommodation = adaptation of the greater or less curve of the lens to the distance, so that in every case a sharp image falls on the retina. Convergence of the pupils is the fixing of both optical axes on the object. The angle of convergence becomes more acute with increase in distance from the object viewed.

handling them implies a lengthy and intensive process of acquisition, which progresses from easy and simple tasks to ever-increasing difficulties.

Things that cannot be handled form a specially important stage on this path. They are, first, those things which are not near enough to be reached—of which we shall speak more below—and then those remarkable apparitions which, although near enough, present insuperable difficulties to the grasping little hand. With what delicate distinctions in the essential nature of space does not the child become acquainted by these ineffective efforts! They may be designated as *paradoxical spatial experiences.*

There he sees brightly shining, coloured spots; he tries to grasp them and comes to a flat surface, where the bright spots feel exactly the same as their surroundings. That is his first acquaintance with pictorial presentation. Or he tries to seize something, and before his hand can reach it he knocks against a smooth, invisible obstacle, thus getting familiar with transparency in the glass pane of door or window. Or he is given a flat object in which he sees a face, which, however, he cannot handle either from the front or back, and so meets with the mysteries of the mirror. And then the dancing motes that mark a clearly defined band in the sunlight but which cannot be caught, the stream of water trickling from the sponge in his bath and ever eluding his eager grasp; shadow, reflected light, the soap-bubble shattered at a touch—these phenomena, pointing, not so much to agreement as to disagreement between the impressions of sight and touch, are, after the first six months, all noticed by degrees, and in the form of a second group of experiences are added to the world of what is solid, firm and easily held.[1]

After the first three months "distant" space begins to open before the child's eyes. Convergence and accommodation for a distance of several metres begin, and soon there is continuous increase in the perception radius of the eye. The child sees and notices when he goes out, or from the window, vehicles and people passing by, recognizes his mother coming in at the

[1] These paradoxical spatial-experiences—but little investigated up till now—would seem to deserve a more exhaustive and, if possible, experimental investigation. The attitude to the mirror has been the only one dealt with in numerous observations by Preyer, Scupin and others.

door as well as the bottle in her hand, looks round enquiringly for new impressions to satisfy his love of looking. But even now there is no trace of that supposed indiscriminate grouping in the field of vision of far and near objects; rather there grows with the opening out of "distant" space the different perception of far and near; the immediate appearance of this perception is, besides, easily to be understood from a psychological point of view. During the period of "near" distance the child had only such object perceptions as were associated with marked signs of nearness, i.e. with the kinæsthetic sensations of strong convergence and accommodation and with great differences in the two retinas, and only sense-impressions possessing these characteristic accompaniments had been allied with grasping movements. Now "distant" space provides impressions with weak convergence and accommodation sensations, and with less divergence in the two images; the whole structure of the perception has been so changed that the grasping impulses miss their co-operating partner and thus do not work.

In this way, even in the first six months, the distinction between "near" (within reach) and "far" (beyond reach) comes into being as the earliest optical apprehension of depth.

In proof of the clear nature of this distinction we may quote an experiment practised on each of our children at about six months of age in the same way and with identical results. As the child was lying comfortably on his back in his perambulator a bright object (a watch) was brought slowly near him from above. The child stared at the approaching object and stretched his arms up, keeping them, however, wide open—a sign therefore of desire, not of reaching. As soon as the watch was within reach, the little hands rushed together on it and held fast. It was possible with each child to repeat the experiment time after time, and always with the same result.

In peculiar contrast to this accuracy in estimation of distance, we find a great inaccuracy in estimation of size.[1]

The apparent size of a thing as perceived by us depends on two opposed factors. From a purely optical point of view the size of the image in the retina changes with the distance of the object; the apple I hold out to the child makes four

---

[1] My former treatment of the apprehension of size has been somewhat modified as the result of Koffka's suggestions.

times as large a retina image at the distance of one metre as at that of two. If then the perception of size depended entirely on the extent of this image, we should continually have to change our idea of the size of everything, and we should never arrive at its "actual size". On the other hand, though our tactual-motor apprehension of size is "constant", the particular apple is at all times felt in one size only by the hand. Now, since from a practical biological point of view an object is only of vital importance if it appears as something of unchanging identity, this constant factor becomes the one determining component part of the idea of size, and we now "see" the object as well in its actual size in spite of variation in distance.[1] It is true this "seeing" is then not exactly the simple sensation of the image on the retina, but the united apprehension of an optical and tactual-motor totality-structure, in which the optical values are by no means isolated and independent. The size of the image is compensated by the impression of distance in the perception itself, and it is only when this impression is uncertain or non-existent that the simple extent of the retina image exercises an influence not to be found at other times on the impression of apparent size. Thus people at a distance so great as to be beyond our grasp (e.g. on a mountain peak) seem to us exceedingly diminutive.

Now since the child as long as he lacks the power of independent perambulation is not capable of a more accurate estimation of distance, this "constant" size perception does not act with certainty and occasionally grotesque mistakes occur.

Gunther (; 7). "His sister has a tiny doll's feeding-bottle, complete with teat, about one-fifteenth the size of a real baby's bottle. Now once when the boy was hungry the bottle was shown him in fun. He showed the greatest excitement and snatched at the bottle as if it were really the right one."

As the mastery of "near" distance was very incomplete so long as the child was only the passive object of sight and touch-impressions and could not hold things, so the conquest of "distant" space is exceedingly imperfect so long as the child has to wait passively until the distant impressions reach his eye. The development does not reach completion until the

---

[1] Thus we are usually quite unable to realize that a man twice as far off looks four times as small as the same individual at half the distance.

child *actively* masters the "distant" space and the difficulties to be found in it. This happens in several ways.

To begin with, "distant" space offers far more hindrances to sight than does near space. Objects lying behind one another form a mutual screen; some thing just before visible suddenly disappears behind another. After six months the child no longer accepts this disappearance with equanimity, but begins to look for the object; and at nine months he has got on so far as to overcome, by very practical efforts of his own, all hindrances to sight. At this time we find with especial frequency thar the child never grows tired of throwing things out of his perambulator, and as they disappear over the edge he raises himself up and bends over too, to find them again. (Scupin reports this even earlier, ; 4½.) We consider even more remarkable the following observation which we made of our daughter, and of our son too, at exactly the same age:—

Hilde (; 9). "When the child to-day was greeted by some-one standing at the end of her perambulator but hidden by the thick intervening down quilt, she took the annoying quilt in both hands and dragged it down a little, apparently to see who was calling. The experiment was again tried, and, after repeated calls, H. always responded to them in the same way, whether they sounded from right or left. She drew down the quilt always on the side of the direction of the sound, always finding the greatest difficulty with her left hand when the call came from the left side."

Then, too, the objects of distant space are beyond reach, and this hindrance is a special torment to the child. It is not enough for him to see, he wants to have what he sees; only what he can hold in his hands is really his; only thus does appearance become comprehensible reality. Just as the mouth in the first six months was the first organ of control for the hand and eye, so the hand now becomes the controlling organ for the eye, and remains so, even if in less pronounced guise, for all time to come.

"Distant" space is therefore only really mastered when changed into "near" space, and this is done by the child's own power of motion. After the first six months, with the exception of speech in its first preliminaries and efforts, nothing so occupies the child as his efforts to conquer distance. By crawling, creeping, and at last walking, he succeeds in bringing, one by one, distant objects into "near" space. Now, for the first time, a more accurate estimate of greater distances can be developed. The child finds out again and again how far he must creep or how many steps he must take to reach anything, and so the optical image produced by the object at a certain distance comes by degrees into ever closer union with just this consciousness of the exertion necessary to reach it. The perfection of size-estimate goes hand in hand with this as the optical perception of size is more and more closely associated with the corresponding distance. Consequently such misapprehensions in size as mentioned above no longer occur within the space which the child himself can traverse and measure by his own steps. The "constant size-perception" [see above] has now been acquired.[1]

So, towards the end of the first year, the spade-work in the mastery of actual space is mainly accomplished. The child can grasp the features of things as regards space—their position, distance, shape, size—and accommodate himself to them. He distinguishes far and near, great and small, round and angular, above and below, before and behind—in short, he has roughly a perception of space, which certainly is still capable of many misconceptions, and will need in years to come to be refined, made clearer and developed, but not enriched with any intrinsically new features.[2]

[1] H. Frank gave an experimental proof of this. He trained children (; 11 to 7 ; 0) to choose the larger of two hollow cubes standing side by side by placing chocolate for them to find under it. After the training, the two boxes were placed at different distances from the child so that the larger but farther off made a much smaller image on the retina than the cube which was actually less in size. In spite of this, however, the child almost always crawled or ran to the larger box, which therefore was recognized as the greater in spite of the paradoxical retina-image. This occurred even in the case of children only 11 months old.

[2] As there will be no further opportunity of referring to the accuracy of spatial perception in childhood, a remarkable discovery of Volkelt's is here added. At his suggestion, Dora Musold tested the power of three- to six-year-old children to distinguish differences in size with reference to objects of one, two, and three dimensions. The result (at first astonishing) is that measurement by the eye is more accurate for solid bodies (balls) than for flat surfaces (circles), and for these last than for visual objects of one dimension only. Volkert rightly interprets this result in accordance with "form" psychology as follows: The estimate of the size of an object is the more accurate in proportion not to its greater simplicity and paucity of detail from a geometrical point of view, but rather in proportion to its more involved form and nature and especially so, when not only optical but above all tactile-motor and emotional elements (as with the ball) enter into the form perception (p. 256).

CHAPTER VII

EMOTIONS OF THE FIRST YEAR

1. Pleasure, Pain and their Expression[1]

WE have already seen that we must grant to the first dull
conditions of consciousness at birth a certain shade of emotion,
and that, of the two opposing emotions, pain is more intensive
than pleasure, or at any rate has a much more emphatic outward expression. The marked development of emotional life
in the first year is shown first by an alteration in the normal
balance of emotions in favour of pleasure, secondly by continual increase in variety and delicacy of these emotions.

Schiller's designation of the "happy infant" is at least
applicable to the healthy, well-cared-for child. There are, it is
true, painful emotions of many kinds—of which we shall speak
later on—but these are no more than the shorter interludes
of a chronic state of well-being and delight.

If a six-month-old child cries and screams for an hour
a day—which is a fairly large estimate—the rest of his waking
time is filled with overflowing joy in life, eating and drinking
delicious food, pleasant baths, happy babble, eager play, the
delight of kicking, struggling limbs, observant surprise, joy
in the dear faces around him.

It is one of young parents' most beautiful experiences to
watch the earliest signs of pleasure in their child; at first only
somewhat brighter eyes, a gentle upward movement of the
corners of the mouth, then low, separate cooings of content-
ment, a pronounced smile, a really loud laugh, and at last a
joyous shout and delighted babble, a scale of active expressions
accomplished in the second and third months.

Now we meet in the infant who, so far, has scarcely passed
a purely animal stage a distinctively human feature; for animals
can neither smile nor laugh. There follow later other forms
of the expression of pleasure, especially the turning towards
the cause of pleasure, the snuggling-up to trusted friends, the
opening of the arms, the clinging to hair and beard of those
loved, and similar other movements.

[1] Cf. here Buchners' Monograph, illustrated with good expression-photo-
graphs, also Lewin's Supplement in this present book and pictures 8a, b, c on
Plate IX.

Also more variety is to be noticed in the expressions of pain. Crying—at first so monotonous—generally the sound *iau, iau* —in a few weeks develops such variation of tone that the mother knows whether it is caused by pain, hunger or discomfort; then, too, the distinctively human tears appear— in many children as early as the first month, in others very much later. Sometimes the cry increases to real paroxysms, when the child gets purple in the face, and his voice cracks or for a time quite gives way. On the other hand, less acute degrees of pain gradually find their utterance in the fall of the corners of the mouth and in an anxious fixed look in the eyes; it is often possible to observe clearly how these face-movements grow more marked until they suddenly pass into a regular scream. In addition, we find in the older infant whimpering or other more articulate noises that are the expression of hunger, pain, or keen desire; amongst these in the second half-year the sound-forms *ham-ham* and *nam-nam* are very conspicuous. Indeed, even babble, which, as a rule, is a sign of well-being, may assume under certain conditions an annoyed, scolding tone, a sure sign of displeasure (pain).

All these early movements of expression have an INSTINCTIVE character; there is in them—in distinction from those that follow later—nothing conventional or acquired. Compare in this respect, cuddling-up as an innate expression of tenderness with the kiss only acquired with difficulty, or the turning away the face as a sign of refusal, with the later shake of the head.

We find in Scupin's record a very vivid description of these varied expressional actions in the middle of the first year.

(; 5½). "Bubi was in his perambulator, and as we were busy reading he was left to his own devices, to amuse himself with his toy; but this evidently did not suit him, the toy was thrown aside, and the boy looked at us expectantly. Since we did not move, he began to argue the matter: '*Tae, agga, atta—ava, mamm ham.*' No result. Then he uttered short groans, drew up his body obstinately, threw himself suddenly forward, and, stiffening himself, fell back again directly, giving in these movements the impression of incredible wilfulness. As we did not yet respond, we suddenly heard a prolonged squeak on *ee*, and there sat our son with a purple face and clenched fists, casting furious looks at us with his half-closed eyes, whilst he made mighty efforts to continue his hoarse, never-ending 'EE' squeak! Then, when at last he was lifted out, quick as lightning his little face assumed an expression of contented gaiety and charming affection. The play of features was wonderfully varied, and expressed plainly and unmistakably the feelings mastering the child—anger, self-will, fear, defiance, disappointment.''

The instinctive character of the expressional movements calls our attention to still deeper connections between feelings of pleasure and displeasure (pain) on the one hand and the child's instinctive life on the other. Indeed, we may speak with justice of the child's instinct to acquire pleasure and to avoid pain. He not only passively accepts with pleasure agreeable stimuli but endeavours to get and keep them, and he not only shows aversion in his reaction to painful impressions but endeavours to avoid them as well. It is therefore impossible to draw a sharp distinction between the child's expressional movements and his intelligent actions; thus, turning to any person or thing is at once a sign of joy and an endeavour to intensify that feeling, and turning away is both an expression of displeasure (pain) and an effort to avoid it. The child shrinks back from unpleasant stimuli; he turns away and hides his little face from strangers; he pushes away things offered to him, throws himself backwards in fury or makes his back so stiff that there is no doing anything with him.

2. Gradation of Instincts ("Triebe") and Emotions

The general endeavour to obtain pleasure and to avoid pain, which we have just described, is not, however, sufficient in itself to give a full explanation of the development of instincts and of emotions in the infant. For in close and somewhat involved connection with it there exist clearly defined instincts ("Triebe"), i.e. innate impulses directed to quite definite aims—impulses which inner necessity and vague inevitability transmute into adequate movements. Their final development is of course again marked by great variation, owing to the influence of specific emotions; hence we have to deal with a complicated question that offers considerable difficulty in tabulation. It is clear that a general theory tried to find enunciation by means of many varied attempts at classification.[1]

Thus Bernfeld endeavours to refer the various manifestations in infancy back to two main impulses which he describes as follows: The "R-instincts" (classified as regression and rest instincts as well as those for self-preservation) are accountable for the endeavours to avoid disturbances, to secure self-preservation and the "regression" into the sheltered embryonic state. Whilst here the chief aim is above all the avoidance (passive or active) of pain, the sexual impulses are entirely directed to the positive attainment of pleasure. Following Freud's theories, every kind of pleasure stimulus is considered as a manifestation of sexual feeling, above all tactual pleasure, but in a wider sense the pleasure given by other sense-stimuli as well.

The application of this division leads to the following characterization of the three-month-old child: its principal efforts are acts of aversion, manifestations of greed—impulses, pleasure in sucking and in looking. The first two fall under the category of "R-instincts", the last two under the heading of sexual impulses. The developments of the next six months are classified under the desire of possession (*Bemächtigungsdrang*); it is manifested in the rising to an upright position, in creeping and above all in grasping. In this classification again the two main impulses make their appearance in a curiously involved fashion. The aim of by far the majority of possessive-acts is to get an object in order to put it in its mouth; the original greed impulse ("R-instinct") is here united with the joy of attainment which is induced by bodily contact of hands, mouth, indeed of the whole body, with the object desired (thus falls under "sexual impulse)".

Our own classification is other than this; it is arranged in accord with the chief aims to which instinctive impulses and emotions are directed in childhood.[2] At the same time the justice of this excessive extension of the sexual idea is contested.

---

[1] The grouping of such acts in childhood which formed the foundation of Ch. Bühler's and H. Hetzer's *Inventory* could not be made use of here as their book in its entirety had not reached me before these pages were in the printers' hands.

[2] Cf. also the similar classification in the treatment of games in infancy.

ORGANIC FEELINGS.

Lowest in the scale are those stirrings of instinct and emotion which refer to the vital functions of the organism as such. Hunger and satiety, the discomfort of being wet, pain, the comfort of the bath, are shades of feeling known even at birth; later on they still keep their fundamental significance. Motor discharge too of the stored-up inner energy, such as struggling with hands and feet, kicking, babbling, and, later, sitting up and violent backward jerks, etc., may be accompanied by a feeling of intense pleasure. And, above all, feelings connected with food, in whose primitive and unrestrained expression the infant often reminds us of lower animals; rage at any delay in satisfying his hunger, and the greedy quiver of desire at the sight of the feeding-bottle.

Our attention has been drawn by psychoanalysis to the great part played in the infant's life by certain stimulating feelings of organic pleasure. This is partly a question of general pleasurable conditions, caused by passive movements of the whole body (being wheeled about, rocked, nursed); we all know how quickly the child's restless cries can be changed into quiet comfort by these means. But it is also partly due to feelings in definite zones of the body whose pleasurable affective-tone incites the infant by his own movement to reproduce the stimulation time after time and to continue it as long as possible. As such zones we must give the first place to the mucous membrane of the lip and tongue and to the genital and anal zones.

The stimulation of the mouth zone is brought about by sucking movements. The act of sucking, at first serving as the means of taking food, is afterwards continued by the child as an end in itself—no matter whether the stimulus is a part of his own body (finger, toe) or some foreign body (a comforter). Sometimes this sucking is carried on with real fervour; there are children even in whom it degenerates into an almost unconquerable passion, continuing long after infancy.

As regards the genital and anal zones, it is noticed that infants often try to touch these parts of the body themselves, and also that the gentle stroking of those organs by other people seems to give a pleasurable sensation. Many mothers and nurses are said to use this easy but dangerous means of quieting tiresome children.

I

The psychoanalysts (Freud, Stekel, Hug-Hellmuth and Bernfeld) look upon these instances of organic pleasure and the child's actions connected with them as a proof of the existence of infantile sexuality, and speak of sucking ecstasy, "infantile-onanie", etc. They believe these inferences are justified by the two following reasons. First from the picture presented by the infant absorbed in his sucking; for they consider the expression of perfect satisfaction gives proof of pleasurable feelings comparable in character and strength with those of sexual lust. Moreover, in fully developed erotic and sexual life, features occur showing unmistakable likeness with those actions of early infancy. If we find amongst adults an ecstatic sucking—now with an undoubted sexual affective-tone—and other childish acts; if, further, in certain forms of sexual aberration one or other infantile mode of action can push its way into the very centre of the love demonstration, then we are justified, compelled indeed, to consider the corresponding phenomena in the infant itself as the first hints of eroticism and sexuality. We need not, however—so we are taught—confine the idea of eroticism solely to relationships with others or that of sexuality solely to certain functions of the actual sexual organs. Primitive infantile eroticism is auto-eroticism, i.e. entirely referring to his own person, and it has its special "erogenous" zones, amongst which the genital zone has at first far less significance than the oral zone.

In criticism of these inferences we will only refer shortly to a purely theoretical standpoint. The psychoanalytic theory takes its stand entirely on the ground of element-psychology when it argues that since the complicated phenomenon, always included under the name of sexuality, contains component parts similar to those occurring in infancy, therefore those infantile functions must be placed in the same category. But if we now approach from the point of view of form-psychology, then the phenomenon of sexuality, notwithstanding its extent and many-sidedness, represents a united totality within which the separated component parts first take on from the whole their sexual affective-tone. When such a unified form of psychic experience first arises, elements coming from childhood may well be included, may indeed play an emphatic part in it; and yet they are not the same as in childhood. The pleasure connected with sucking is psychically something entirely different when—as in the infant—it exists entirely alone as an independent sensory-motor form and when (as possibly in the adult's love kiss) it appears as a component part of erotic excitement or by transference is weighed with the emotions of other erotic states. AGREEMENT IN ELEMENTS NEVER JUSTIFIES US IN INFERRING IDENTITY IN UNITED TOTALI-TIES. We may therefore in great measure accept the actual statements of psychoanalysis concerning organic pleasure in infancy without necessarily agreeing with their sexualistic inferences.

Organic experiences of pain may be occasioned by definite momentary impulses from their environment, but again they may be connected with disturbances of longer duration arising from general conditions of life in infancy.

To begin with a few examples of the first class.

If stimulation of individual sense-organs occurs in too great intensity they are not accepted by the infant as perceptions but are viewed entirely as threatening harm to the organism, thus loud door banging, violent pressure, too hot milk produce pain and screaming. Even weaker impressions can have a similar result if they take the child unawares; thus, one of our children, lying half-asleep and all unsuspecting in its peram-bulator, was terribly frightened by the approach of its father's face.

Very curious is the effect of fright to be observed sometimes at quite an early age as the result of short interruptions of stable equilibrium.

Eva (; 1). "A strange start of fright was noticed several times: once as the child lay on the couch, and it yielded as her father leant upon it; then frequently in her bath Eva would in terror throw up both arms as though she was afraid of falling or sinking."

Since the child had never experienced the danger of falling or sinking, this was a case of an innate fear-reflex.

In the same way we see a similar reflex in strange idiosyn-crasies of some children towards certain sense-stimuli in which there is no assignable cause for the resultant fear.

We noticed on the seashore that one of our children (; 8) shuddered violently every time it touched the soft sand—just as many an adult does at the touch of a dry sponge or a slimy creature. Two of our children (; 2 and ; 7) showed a very strange fear-reaction to long-drawn-out notes, whether these were sounded by themselves or at the end of a tune to which they had listened with very great pleasure. Many observers ascribe the same effect to black as such; but we could not discover this at so early an age. It would be worth while to try to find out if such idiosyncrasies are found equally in all children, or if such manifestations vary individually, and whether heredity plays any part in them.

Amongst pain experiences of longer duration—apart from attacks of illness—two must be mentioned which belong to the normal life of every infant, viz. teething and weaning.

The cutting of the first teeth is almost always accompanied by a decrease in the infant's well-being, by fretfulness, restlessness and sometimes by a slight rise in temperature. At this period the child wants to bite on something hard, no doubt to overcome the local pressure and feeling of irritation. On the whole, however, the emotional upset, at any rate in healthy and well-cared-for children, is usually not very serious.

Apparently the first little teeth affect the parents more than the child himself. We find testimony to this not only in the mother's proved joy when she can make the ring or spoon rattle in the child's mouth, but in many strange popular customs everywhere, connected with teething in childhood. Bernfeld, in symbolical interpretation of these customs and of change in the child's behaviour, deduces the idea (pp. 199 sqq.) that teething betokens the beginning *asexualization* of the mouth zone (disappearance of the delighted sucking) and the conversion of this zone into one of attack and destruction (biting and chewing).

Just as teething is a physiological process, so weaning is due to social causes; the child is here the suffering object of a decision coming from outside and often enough determined by motives which have nothing at all to do with the development of the child himself. From the point of view of national psychology, it is exceedingly strange that the usual time of weaning is marked by extreme divergence.[1] There are civilized and uncivilized nations alike who, as a rule, wean their babies before the end of the first year, others where the mothers nurse their children up to two or three years of age, and lastly, others where the nine or ten-year-old children now and again drink

[1] Bernfeld, p. 217.

their mother's milk and gradually wean themselves without adult interference.

Weaning then is the first real encroachment upon the infant's sphere of life; his mother's breast, the source of his most pleasurable feelings, is taken away from him at a time when, if left to himself, he would be very far from ready to relinquish this pleasure. We can easily understand that this outside interference may have a very detrimental effect on the child. Very often the child at first refuses to take nourishment of a fresh kind, a sign that he is no longer governed only by a blind desire for food, but that the pleasurable condition of sucking at his mother's breast has become more important to him than the satisfaction of his hunger. Sometimes this refusal of food forms the introduction to a long period of difficulties in feeding the child, so that we may here indeed speak without hesitation of a "trauma" of weaning. Such shock-effects will be more marked in proportion to the sudden nature of the process; if other food is given by slow degrees in alternation with breast-feeding, which it gradually entirely supersedes, the process may take place without after ill effects.

For psychoanalysts weaning is under any and every condition a trauma. It betokens the "original disappointment" (*Urenttäuschung*) of man, the first real denial, and is used as the prototype of all refusals and deprivations.

FEELINGS WITH REGARD TO THINGS.

Even in the first months we find development of those feelings that are connected in some way with the objective world lying outside the child's own personality. The first objects to awake such feelings are those immediately affecting the child's senses or accessible to him. For the awaking sense-organs also crave their nourishment in stimuli, and every satisfaction of this craving—if not too violent—is a source of joy to the child. Everything gaily coloured, brightly shining or moving is considered with intense interest; sound-stimuli (human voices, piano-playing, the ticking of the clock, running water) or touch-stimuli, such as a warm bath or being stroked or breathed upon.

Again the psychoanalysts designate all feelings of pleasure that exhaust themselves in the sense delight resulting from stimuli as such and also the impulses directed to the creation of such pleasure-producing stimuli as "sexual". Here too in our opinion the idea is magnified and extended to such a degree as to rob it of all true significance.

But the child not only receives impulses from the objects around him; he is an active agent with regard to them; he seizes, moves works at and alters them. This activity is accompanied by feelings of accomplishment, of strength, of personal causality. And when these activities are themselves the cause of another delightful perception, of really loud noises, of visible movements or of fresh tactual experiences, then pleasure, as being both sensory and motor, has reached its highest point. Now we already meet with true play joy.

Gunther (; $11\frac{1}{2}$). "He makes a clatter with anything he can lay hands on—that is the finest game; the louder the better! Why do all children take such wonderful delight in noise they make themselves? I believe because their own efforts produce it and because causality is such a very early feeling. The child by beating an enamel tray on a wooden table creates something —something too that can be heard. And he notices that his blows are immediately followed by noise—cause and effect!— that produces one pleasant emotion and that he himself is the cause produces a second. Have we not here discovered the source of the meaning and joy of life for those no longer children? Creative work and to have a hand in the management of things!"

A further development in objective feelings is found in the fact that the emotions are not merely connected with the momentary perception as such, but with associated perceptual-forms which have often occurred previously, and through mnemonic processes have taken on a very firm and enduring character. (EMOTIONS OF FAMILIARITY.) Just as the child at last greets faces he has often seen with pleasant emotions of familiarity (see Chapter VI, Section 2), so in time, through the continual repetition of the perception-complex of sight, hearing and touch, certain objects become dear and familiar, and after six months the child already has "his own" toys— a little bell, a rattle, a ball or doll—that he knows so well as to resent a secret substitution of another plaything for any one of them.

Emotions of acquaintance (familiarity) are in the great majority of cases pleasurable, but we sometimes come across those that are not. Hence the recognition of things and persons which have previously produced unpleasant impressions may be associated with the emotion of fear. For example, our daughter (; 6) showed such fear of a piece of wadding which had been used to wipe her nose and also (; 9) of the doctor. This nervousness arising from experience must be most carefully distinguished from the inherited idiosyncrasies discussed above.

The emotions of acquaintance are not only associated with individual things and persons, but at last embrace the whole environment and all the happenings concerning the child and his immediate neighbourhood. The sum of these emotions forms the enduring conscious background of what is familiar and matter-of-course, from which henceforth everything new and strange will be distinguished by special mental reactions. But the child thereby again reaches a higher stage of emotional life; for as the emotions of familiarity belong to mnemonic action, the EMOTIONS OF NON-FAMILIARITY lead to intellectual processes.

If the familiar sequence of perceptions or the usual order of the association is suddenly interrupted at any one point by a strange impression, the emotional condition of SURPRISE results. In its pure form surprise is really a phenomenon of restraint (checking); a psychic check is imposed on the course of perception and on the emotion of familiarity, also a physical check on the capability of movement; thus a surprised human being always has a fixed expression. The second half-year gives proof already of such conditions of benumbed wonder; music has this effect very early, soon too the sight of persons and things, and, last of all, other sense-stimuli.

Preyer (; 5).[1] "When the child was in the railway carriage and I got in after a short absence, he stared at me for over a minute, open-mouthed (the lower jaw dropped) and with wide-opened, motionless eyes, his whole body immovable, a typical picture of surprise."

Scupin (; 6). "A pocket mirror was held up before him; with a laugh and shout of delight he looked at his reflection and snatched at it. Suddenly his look changed to one of enquiry, he leant over very much to one side and looked as if for something behind the mirror; unmistakable surprise was painted

[1] W. Preyer: *The Soul of a Child*, I. p. 108.

on the little face, surprise at the entire absence of the other parts of the body usually belonging to a face. Then the boy sat silent for some seconds, looking at us in helpless enquiry. Again he looked at his reflection, again bent down, far to one side, and looked for something behind the glass; it was evident the child was confronted by a mystery." (I. pp. 20–21.)

Hilde (; 11). "I have just for the first time given Hilde a cake to eat; she acted very funnily as she put the cake to her lips. Until then she had only (with the exception of liquid food) put into her mouth her fingers, india-rubber doll, or other toys of a like relatively hard nature. In surprise she took the cake out again, then nibbled it cautiously, and at last ate it up with enjoyment."

Surprise is accompanied by more than one emotion, so that we find joyful, frightened, and more or less indifferent surprise, although this last has a tendency to turn into pleasure at the novelty or into fear.

The surprise will, as a rule, be pleasurable when, after the first check has been overcome, the possibility is established of a continuous reaction to the new stimulus which now engages the child's undivided interest. What is perfectly new, totally unconnected with familiar impressions, when once entirely grasped by the child, generally causes pleasure, not fear. For this reason the child, in his first year, seldom shows fear of fire or of animals, not even those in a zoological garden, unless their cries and roars set up a purely sensory emotion of shock.

On the other hand, surprise has a strong element of pain when the impression is an admixture of the known and the unknown, so that the sense of familiarity can neither be pushed entirely to the background nor yet satisfied. This gives the child lost, uncanny feeling, which may produce the strongest sign of terror. THUS THERE EXISTS FOR THE LITTLE CHILD— and this is true for the next few years—NOT ONLY FEAR OF THE UNKNOWN BUT FEAR OF THE MYSTERIOUS.[1] This explains the frequent crying at the sight of strangers; they are in fact like his parent, and yet different; they speak too, but not with the familiar voice. The child behaves in much the same way when meeting again those he knows after a separation of some duration; if he does not recognize them at once, their appear-

[1] More detailed treatment of this fear in Chapter XXXV.

ance is strange, yet not so new as one he has never known; undefined feelings of familiarity are mixed with those of novelty, and the result is perplexity.

Scupin (; 5½). "He did not at first recognize his father's mother, who had been away for ten days. The boy uttered a note of fear when he saw her face and heard her voice, and sat motionless with wide-open eyes on her arm for a few minutes; then, and not till then, did he recognize her, and his little face assumed its usual expression of pleasure." (I 19.)

We notice a most remarkable example of this fear of the uncanny in our own son (1 ; 0) with regard to a doll, whose scalp his sister had half pulled off, so that its hair stood up rough and tangled and a great hole was visible in the head. Its pretty face was quite unspoilt. Now, his sister once brought this doll to her brother, who was in high good humour, but he then set up a pitiful cry and turned with evident disgust away from the doll to get her out of his sight. When he was happy once more, the doll was offered to him again with the same result.

(c) FEELINGS WITH REGARD TO PERSONS.

Feelings with regard to other persons stand out above organic feelings and those connected with things. They already exist also, at any rate in their first stages, in the first year of life. Sympathy with others is such an elementary action that, as is well known, we find it most strongly marked even in animals. In the human infant the first social feelings can be noticed towards adults as well as children.

The first infant smile appears in the second month when the child hears the human voice; no other sound can produce this effect.[1] And when we see how an infant of six or eight months greets his mother with extended arms and shouts of joy and how when sitting on her lap he snuggles up to her, it is impossible to consider this as egoistic joy, differing in no way from his delight in a bright gay toy; it is rather the first stirring of a personal emotional tie binding the child to another human being.[2] We find further that the child in the later months of

---

[1] This is proved by Hetzer and Tudor-Hart, who also see in it the very first sign of an emotion of a personal nature.
[2] Concerning the part played by purely sense-feelings in these first stirrings of tenderness of the child's, cf. Chap XXXVI. 2.

his first year is susceptible to a certain emotional infection; a kindly smiling face and gentle sounds from grown-up people are answered with smiles; unkind, cross looks and scolding words cause fear and an impression of pain. Of course, at first a real understanding of other's feelings does not exist, only rather an almost instinctive feeling, on a par with the instinctive imitation which we have already considered. But by degrees this develops into true sympathy—and do we not see how that has already been reached perhaps in the following case?

Scupin (; 11½). "When we (his parents) were fighting in fun, he suddenly uttered a wild scream. To try if it was the noise we made that had frightened him, we repeated the scene in silence; the child looked at his father with horror, then stretched his arms out longingly to his mother and snuggled affectionately up against her. It quite gave the impression that the boy believed his mother was being hurt, and his scream was only an expression of sympathetic fear."

Another symptom of the first awakening of sympathy is the "sharing" of which we saw the earliest sign in one of our children at the end of the first year.

Hilde (1 ; 0). "Yesterday I noticed, for the first time, that H. kept putting to my lips the rusk I had given her, without thinking of biting it herself. I pretended to bite off and eat a piece, and this pleased H."[1]

There are certainly other demonstrations which might be interpreted as quite the opposite of sympathy. Infants, in their play, love to take firm hold of the father's beard or mother's hair, to scratch their cheeks or seize their eyes, greeting with loud delight the cries of pain from those thus ill-used. But we have not therefore the slightest right to ascribe to the eight-month-old child delight in the pain he has caused or to speak of the "cruel" flash in his eyes and his "diabolic" greed (Scupin, I. 30/31). In reality, it is only a rough and untroubled expression of his seizing instinct; the child never suspects that his mischievous grasp gives pain.

Quite recently Charlotte Bühler (II) has arranged some very interesting research experiments into the relation of little children to one another. In an American crèche there were always infants in great numbers on whom to experiment.

---

[1] Further reports concerning the expressions of sympathy during the first year have been collected in W. Boeck's *Sympathy in Children*, p. 28.

Now in each play-pen two children were put opposite each other so that they could see and touch one another and their toys were laid between them. Each little couple was observed for about ten minutes and we have detailed reports of fifty-five pairs of children.

The interchange of courtesies between children up to the age of five months is confined to "sight contact" (*Schaukontakt*); they look at each other from time to time but for the most part show a mutual indifference. The beginning of the second half-year shows something very different. The child stretches out his hand to grasp not only the body of the other child but also his toys, even when they are in his companion's hand; the latter does not approve of this, defends his rights and tries to get back the object and quite militant movements may follow. Towards the end of the first year, however, actions occur which may be denoted "social" in the narrower sense of the word; toys are not only taken from each other but given to the playfellow, shown and exchanged.

Signs of order of precedence are already very plainly in evidence.[1] The one child seizes the predominant position, the other submits; the former carries out his activities without let or hindrance, the latter under definite restrictions. The dominating child turns to the other, struggles towards him, touches, grasps, takes away, gives, repulses, shows, sets an example, turns away when weary of it all, leads and organizes the whole situation. The subordinate child does not dare to take away anything, does not dare to refuse, loses his self-possession as the result of the other's activity and delight in attack, and falls a victim to the suggestion of affectual infection (screams when his companion does), etc.[2]

If both children are of the same social position, fresh signs of "rivalry" appear,—described in detail by Charles Bühler.

The order of precedence obtaining for the time being depends partly of course on special circumstances, especially on the children's difference in age. In 87 per cent. of all cases of despotism the dominating child was also the older. Rivalry was only possible when the age-difference was less than three months. But in addition to these factors of a more outward

[1] Exactly the same has been noticed amongst animals, e.g. in the poultry-yard (Schelderup-Ebbe and D. Katz).
[2] From Ch. Bühler's notes of a lecture to the International Psychologists' Congress in Groningen.

nature, the inner dispositions already play their part; for there are of course children who are inclined to "despotism" by temperament and will, just as there are others exactly the opposite.

We will conclude with a short extract showing the actual acts and deeds of a child towards the end of his first year.

Idelberger (p. 242), in observation of his son (; 11), noted down all the child's doings, utterances, and evidences of desire and emotion for the duration of a whole hour. We reproduce here only the chief contents of a quarter of an hour, but even from this we can draw three inferences:—

(1) The almost absolute predominance of the activities of will and emotions over the still very small intellectual functions.

(2) The surprising variety in kind and direction of the emotions—that one quarter of an hour shows us joy and sorrow, curiosity and surprise, anger and displeasure, desire and aversion.

(3) The impulsiveness and disconnected character of the psychic life, the incapability of any continuous concentration or of persistence in pursuit of any one interest.

"(6.10 p.m.) He utters a *chu-chu* of pleasure—seizes the inside of the sewing machine—picks up a matchbox from the floor—throws it down again—falls down himself—cries—pulls the hair of the dachshund lying on the floor—says '*wow-wow*'—asks to be picked up—looks surprised—lifts his first finger and says '*ugh-ugh*'—utters a *chu-chu* of delight—wants the little wooden milkcan—stretches up his arm to be lifted on to his mother's lap—wants to look in the bedroom after hearing a noise from that direction—stamps on the ground with one foot—looks at Frau S. and says '*bw-bw*' —bites his fingers—wants the matches—screams with anger—wants his toys—cries—points to a little bell and says '*ugh-ugh*' as a sign that he would like it— looks with surprise at a little rolling rattle—wants it—will not take the proffered piece of orange—pushes it away—wants to be lifted up from the ground—wants to walk—repeatedly refuses to eat the piece of orange—takes and tries it—makes a grimace at its sour taste—eats it—wants another piece." (6.25 p.m.)

PART III

DEVELOPMENT OF SPEECH[1]

DURING the first months of life, human activities scarcely rise above the level of a lower animal's; indeed, in many a point, e.g. in the development of instincts, the young animal is superior to the child. But human development quickly passes beyond that animal phase, and at the end of his first year the child achieves those two powers which have always been pointed out as the chief distinguishing marks between man and beast: the upright walk and speech. The upright walk, as we have seen, brings about a certain concluding stage of sense-mastery of surrounding space, but speech opens to the child the higher world of the mind. The power of language lends quite new variety to his relations with his fellow-men; speech becomes the instrument of enormous development in his power of perception, emotion and will; and to conclude, it is to speech alone that man owes the power of all real thought: generalization, comparison, judgment, decision, combination and comprehension.

Although this alone is sufficient justification for the peculiar interest shown in speech-development by all psychologists, yet another circumstance would increase still further interest in this subject: the ease and speed of learning to speak. What effort has, later on, to be expended at school in learning a second language, which is not really mastered even after many years of practice; whilst, on the other hand, the speech of his environment seems to flash upon the normal child of two or three years of age; without learning any vocabularies or studying grammar, he makes month after month the most astounding progress, and when he is four or five years old he can without effort make himself understood on every point that comes

---

[1] This division has very much in common with Clara and William Stern's book, *Children's Speech*. On account of its very detailed treatment of the problem of children's speech, I thought it permissible to content myself here with bare outlines of the chief features. For convenience, in a possible further study, the corresponding sections of the monograph are always given. We cannot here touch at all on the individual speech-histories of two of our children, which form the first main part of that work. The book, which made its first appearance in 1907, was republished in 1927 in a fourth entirely revised edition. Both in the text and bibliography reference is made to all previous literature on the subject.

within his range of interests, and give adequate expression to his abundant stores of perception and thought.

A third circumstance lends special attraction to the development of speech. "Children's speech" is not a lower grade of a perfected mastery of language, but has a particular form of its own, like a "dialect" which has its own laws of language and even its own special beauties. Certain features of the children's dialect are even common to different nationalities, thus pointing to elementary forms belonging to all speech such as are now barely recognizable in the conventional languages with which we are acquainted.

Thus the study of children's speech is of importance for the linguist when considering problems of speech-development in general.

CHAPTER VIII

PRELIMINARIES AND BEGINNINGS OF LEARNING TO TALK[1]

1. Preliminary Stages

THE beginning of speech is generally reckoned from that moment in which the child, for the first time, utters a sound with full consciousness of its meaning and for the purpose of communication. But this great moment has an earlier history, for speech grows out of impulses of the most primitive nature which begin to stir in the earliest months of life, only at first the sound-expressions are still embedded in the more diffuse activities of these impulses and only by degrees free themselves in independent acts.[2]

The first to make their appearance are discharge- and expression-movements. The setting-free of inner energies follows not only in kicking, struggling and gesticulation but also in a "struggling" of the speech organs and their utterances in the forms of crying and babbling are the most important preparatory exercises for speech. They provide practice, not only for articulations of the most diverse nature, but already build up associations between certain states of feeling and the sound-forms belonging to them, although the child may not yet be able to understand the sound as a symbol of the accompanying shade of emotion.[3] The child's impulse to this exercise of the voice organs is so strong that he does not even need the acoustic reaction; even the deaf-mute child babbles in quite a normal way, so that the child's infirmity may pass unnoticed for some time.

Speech has also another root of a social nature. The psychic contact with other human beings, which already begins in the first weeks of infancy and which the child tries to strengthen by primitive means, leads to an interchange of vocal utterances forming a preparation for later speech as well as for an understanding of what is said.[4]

[1] *Kindersprache*, Chaps. XI, XII.
[2] *Kindersprache*, pp. 121 sqq., and W. Stern, XII.
[3] Cf. the careful special examination of their child's babble by A. and G. Hoyer.
[4] This first understanding of speech has at first nothing to do with an intellectual grasp of the logical significance of words, in fact months pass before this stage is reached.

The impulse to imitation so strongly developed in the second half-year has, as its result, beside other perceptual impressions, many syllables and syllable-combinations that the child hears from other human beings; and even if the resulting "echo-babble" is, at first, incomprehensible, it yet enriches the learner's treasure with self-made sounds, sound-combinations, rhythm, etc., the raw material then for future speech.

The understanding of speech has a preliminary preparation in the early special trick-training [*Dressur*] mentioned earlier (Chap. V. 1). Even if certain word-combinations, e.g. "now do pat-a-cake, pat-a-cake", "where is the tic-tac", are for the child at first nothing but a vague sound included in a whole situation with which he has associated certain actions, yet the sound-factor may by degrees take on an independent character and be understood by itself from the sense of the action: a first vague understanding of the words has arrived.

The child therefore approaches speech along three paths:—

(1) The active expression of childish babble;
(2) Unintelligent imitations; and
(3) Understanding what is said to it.

As soon as these three actions, originally independent of each other, work together, real speech has begun. Examples of these three paths:—

Possibly the child has for months babbled *mamam*, and even objectively betrayed thereby to the hearer a certain condition of feeling—hunger maybe, or some longing—but the babble-sound becomes a babble-word, i.e. speech, when he subjectively connects some meaning with *mamam*—no matter whether the conventional one of mother or another of hunger maybe. Or again, he has in mechanical imitation repeated the word *dedda* (Bertha) when anyone said it to him, until, one day, as he repeats the word he looks towards the girl to whom the name belongs. Or, thirdly, for some time the child, without himself saying the word "tic-tac", has shown he understands it by turning to the big clock whenever he hears the word. When at last he says the word for the first time, he does so with complete intelligence.

2. Relative Times of the Beginnings of Speech

The time for these beginnings of speech is generally shortly after the end of the first year, yet individual variations are very marked. There are children of nine months who can already make intelligent use of one word or of several; yet there is no cause for anxiety when a child of eighteen months still uses nothing but signs. These are often so expressive that he needs nothing more to make himself understood. Observations so far seem to prove that girls as a rule begin to speak somewhat earlier than boys, and also keep ahead even in later development. Younger members of a family, too, learn to speak more easily and quickly than first-born children, because the latter only have adults to teach them, whilst the former can listen to the much more suitable childish speech of their brothers and sisters. Lastly, there is no doubt that speech development begins considerably later and proceeds more slowly in working-class children than in those of cultured circles; working people have not so much time or mental keenness to be constantly occupied with their children and talking to them.[1] The child's power of speech, however, after it has once begun, does not then increase at equal speed from day to day. Perhaps that general law of rhythm in growth is never seen so clearly as in the progress of speech. Periods of stagnation, sometimes a source of anxiety to parents, are suddenly replaced by periods of rapid progress, to be again followed in their turn by very slow development.

Very often this stagnation appears immediately after the first beginning of speech. The child has, at a comparatively early age, gained the intelligent use of one or several words; but then months pass without further success; indeed, sometimes what he has already acquired is lost again. Thus for six months Preyer's son had as his sole vocabulary *atta* (away) and *ta* (thank you), whilst for two and a half months our own son's only word was *da* (there).

3. The Nature of Children's Speech in its Earliest Stages

Let us try by an example to illustrate the state and peculiarities of the child's speech some months after those very earliest beginnings.

[1] Cf. Chapter XI of this book.

K

Her mother's notes give the following record of our third child, Eva, when she was 1 ; 0 to 1 ; 1:—[1]

First concerning the child's babble and imitation: "Eva is extremely lively and tells long tales in a double-Dutch which sounds like a foreign language—they are delivered so expressively and give the impression of a desire to tell something to a definite person. None of the other children have talked like this; apparently it is an imitation of the lively talk in our nursery."

"In these conversations of hers familiar names often occur, and we hear something like *hilda, elsa* (the nurse), and sounds she has often heard like *yes, yes, you, you*—said in playful admonition—are now constant features of her repertoire. The same may be said of words copied from us, not understood, of course, but sounding very comical: *'O where'* and *'dear me, dear me'*."

The report of her knowledge of speech goes on:—

"We are continually astounded, for we can scarcely keep up with its development, it is scarcely credible at this age: to-day the child grasps the sense of a word a little, to-morrow a little more, the next day entirely—no, rather, all at once, we notice that the child perfectly understands what we say."

The extent of her knowledge is shown by the appended note:—

"The child gives intelligent response to the following words and phrases, either by pointing out the thing named or by carrying out the request: *hoo* (bottle), *hap-pap* (eat), *by-bye* (sleep), *splash-splash* (bath), *tat-ta* (go for a walk), *ba-ba* (ugly), *give me, you, you* (admonition), *ahter* (father, applied to both parents), *gee-gee* (horse), *wow-wow* (dog), *dolly*."

To conclude, her own intelligent language up to (1 ; 1) includes the following:—

> *ahter* (; 9) for father and mother—the latter word she cannot copy properly in spite of much teaching.
> *dolly* for her doll and pictures of children.
> *wow-wow* for her toy dog, and occasionally for animals in pictures.

---

[1] The corresponding records of our two elder children are to be found in *Children's Speech*, pp. 18, 19, and on pp. 85, 86. The list of speech-beginnings of all the children in psychological records is there also on p. 159.

moo-moo for many animals in her picture-book and for the rocking-horse.

ba-ba (ugly) as correct response to "not suck fingers".

hap or *pap-pap* for her food.

peep O! in hiding game.

da when she offers a bit of her roll.

This report shows some qualities characteristic of the child's earliest speech.

From the numberless words which the child continually hears, his mind makes an unconscious selection by discarding most and only retaining a few. And this selection is twofold: the majority of rejected words are "beyond understanding", a small number of these have already been rejected as "beyond speech". The inferiority of what can be said compared with what can be understood is a peculiarity which continues even in adult years—for every one of us uses a much smaller vocabulary of words and phrases than he hears and understands in reading, lectures, etc.—but nowhere is the difference so striking as in the first months of speech. There are many children whose exceptional idleness in talking need cause no anxiety, since they give abundant proof of understanding what they hear. With such children the well-developed gesture-language (mimicry and gesticulation) takes the place of sound-language, non-existent as yet in them.[1]

Gesture has its value, too, in those speaking to children, as a help to the understanding of many words, for the meaning of some gestures is at once apparent to the child; when these are the constant accompaniments of certain words, at last the words alone are sufficient to convey the meaning. If at the words, "Well, come then", a child learns to get up and struggle along to his mother, it is because these words have always been accompanied by the highly suggestive gesture of outstretched arms.

The outward form of this early speech is very remarkable. It is not, in the least, a small selection from the adult speech constantly heard, but consists almost entirely of words not found there. What is the cause of this?

No doubt, to begin with, reasons of speech-technique make

P. Schäfer carried out special research work concerning the periods of actual understanding of speech.

the child's first words as like as possible to the sounds already practised in its babble; these nearly always consist of a simple play on vowels and consonants, the preponderating vowel sounds being LONG A (fāther) and SHORT A (dăy), and amongst the consonants (1) the labials (B P M), (2) the dentals (D T), whilst the gutturals (G and K) and the sibilants (S Z) the child finds very difficult or avoids altogether.

But these external reasons are second in importance to an inner motive which gives the child's dialect its own peculiar stamp, i.e. the tendency to use SUCH WORDS AS SHOW A NATURAL CONNECTION BETWEEN SOUND AND MEANING.

The great majority of adult words are "conventional" symbols; the sound "*dog*" is no more distinctive of the animal than "*chien*" or "*hund*", and only along the path of mechanical association can the child learn that word and object belong to each other. But the word *wow-wow* is quite different: it makes a direct appeal to a part of the perceptual-form of a dog, and that a striking part, viz. the sound it constantly utters; thus the word becomes a NATURAL SYMBOL of the thing.[1]

Such natural sound-symbols impress the child quite otherwise than do conventional words, for speech here is the outcome of long practised speech preliminaries; the child's strong imitative impulse, delighting in the repetition of sounds it hears, must, of itself, result at last in using such sounds as names. In this way child and environment meet in the use of word-pictures (onomatopœia) to build up one portion of early speech, and we see the origin of words like *moo-moo*, *wow-wow*, *ba-ba*, *miaou*, *puff-puff*, *tic-tac*, *pap-pap*, and many others.

A second group of natural symbols is formed from the sounds of active expressions. Even the cry of the first hour, "*iau, iau*", later on, crystallizes into the word *woe, woe*, which has left the nursery and passed into adult speech. The quite elementary note of aversion, *ă*, is used by many children as a real word, expressive of disgust, just as the caressing note of *ī* is used for a word of pleasure. The dentals are originally demonstrative in note, consequently the word *da* ("dere") is

---

[1] The association between sound and significance is therefore in the case of natural symbols "intra-association", but with conventional symbols "inter-association".

as natural a distinguishing gesture as pointing with the out-stretched hand or first finger.

The sound-form *mamamam* has a double value in expression. It is often used after the first six months as a note of desire or complaint: if the mother goes away or there is a little delay in bringing the bottle he sees all ready. The same sound accompanies the chewing of food, as can be noticed in older children. Thus it is not strange that this primitive sound for "hunger and love" becomes attached to the person whose business it is, above all others, to satisfy these needs.

It is easy to understand that these natural symbols are not confined within the boundaries assigned to national languages, hence children's speech of widely different nations and races has often points of astonishing similarity. For instance, a dog's name for children is not only *wau-wau* in German, but in Russian as well, *oua-oua* in French, *waf-waf* in Dutch, and *wan wan* in Japanese. And more than this: internationality is not confined to the nurseries, but from them penetrates into adult speech—just as many of the child's natural symbols are accepted by adults—and thus we find an explanation, amongst others, of the enormous universality of the sound complex *ma-ma* (*ama*, *mam*, or similar sounds) for the mother. For instance, this expression has been found in no less than one hundred African languages.[1]

It has been a frequent subject of discussion as to whether this early speech, with its preponderance of natural symbols, is the work of the child himself, or entirely the result of an environment which provides him with these words. Here again our idea of "convergence" must come to our aid. Early speech is the combined result of aptitudes and speech-impulses, inherent in the child's nature, and of stimulus offered for his imitation from without. It seldom occurs that a child quite independently raises a descriptive sound or a natural sound-expression to a real designation in speech, for he cannot, as a rule, reach such a stage because his environment deprives him of any opportunity, by offering him ready-made expressions (*wow-wow*, etc.). But that the child is not quite incapable of doing so is proved by some observations.

Ham—the sound of desire and snatching—is used by many

---

[1] A more detailed treatment of the connection between children's speech with the general science of speech in *Children's Speech*, Chaps. XIX and XX.

children of their own accord as a name for eating. Our own boy (1 ; 5) for some time designated all lights, lamps and such-like, with the sound *ffff*, which was nothing but an imitation of blowing them out. Hilde (1 ; 7) named a creaking little wooden mill—for lack of knowing any other name—with the picturesque title of *errr*.

Even in other cases the child takes an active part. People round him only, after all, offer him such words as they do because they know he will accept natural designations with much greater interest and keenness than he shows in conventional names. Often, too, adults pick up some sound that the child, so far, has not used for conversational purposes and make a real word of it. As an example:—

Eva (; 11). For a long time she has expressed a wish for food by smacking with her lips, a sound we imitated with *pap-pap* or *hap-pap*. If we ask her, "Do you want something to eat?" without showing her any food, she shows she understands by smacking her lips or saying *pap-pap*.

4. Psychic Activity in the First Stage of Early Speech

The analysis of the outer nature of speech is considerably less difficult than statements as to the psychic significance of these earliest utterances. For a long time the mistake has been made of transferring without much judgment points of view suitable for adult speech to this early stage. To arrive at a right understanding the enquirer must shake himself free from bondage of all systematized schedules and schemes. Although, considered from without, early speech consists of nouns and interjections, it has in reality as yet no parts of speech; although the expressions are used now for a narrower, now for a wider circle of objects, the child yet possesses no variety of conceptions. Early speech is innocent alike of grammar and logic, and the various categories of words and ideas which, in our eyes, seem to be a necessary element of every language are only in the most gradual way differentiated from the primitive embryonic form.

The child's first utterances are not words in the real sense of the word, but *whole sentences*; for the novice in speech does not talk to express concepts as such, but rather his own attitude to them. This is the only explanation of the fact that one and the same speech-unit can be used with such multitudinous meanings. It is not enough to translate the child's *mama* into adult speech by the one word "mother", but sentences must be used, as: *"Mother, come here"*, *"Mother, give me"*, *"Mother, set me on the chair"*, *"Mother, help me"*, etc.

The child cannot as yet express the manifold variety of his psychic feelings by a corresponding variety of utterances, and he therefore compresses everything he has to say into the one single sound-form, which corresponds to the culmination of his psychic feeling, and therefore stands in greatest readiness at the moment to cross the threshold of speech. Gestures, intonation and the situation as a whole all help to lend the necessary shade of meaning to the short utterance with its possibility of many meanings.

The capability of this "ONE-WORD SENTENCE" is so great that for a long time the child feels no need to extend the boundaries of his expression by the combination of several words. He therefore as a rule waits for six months or more at this stage; Preyer's son, indeed, waited no less than a whole year.

Psychologically, we may express this condition of things as follows: The first utterances have no purely intellectual character; they are not—as was generally accepted in the past—expressions for concepts, designations of things seen or remembered. Calm designation and statement are at first far from the child, emotion and will have to do their part before he can be induced to speak. Meumann indeed went so far in opposition to that idea of intellectual character as to classify all early speech-significance as purely subjective, and to deny it absolutely any touch of perceptivity. But this is not the case either; rather both characters—the intellectual and subjective—are unitedly comprehended in the one-word sentence, not to appear clearly distinguishable from each other till a future time. Certainly early speech is by no means purely self-expression, neither is it nothing but sounds of joy and sorrow, but it is a striving after something, a turning away from something, a joy about something. If this were not so, how could we understand, for example, that the delighted cry of *wow-wow* is only heard at the sight of dogs and similar objects in life or pictures, and not as the ordinary cry of joy on every occasion?

And lastly, the range of application for single words is by no means logically determined at first. There are, it is true, certain words only used for one single thing, as e.g. *mama* only for the mother, and others used for a number of similar objects (e.g. *dicky* for everything that flies, *dolly* for the most diverse toys). Yet the word "mama" does not signify an idea of one single thing nor the word "dicky" the idea of a whole class, in our sense of the word, for the child does not, to begin with, possess the fundamental requirements for the formation of any speech-idea, that is, the knowledge that every word has a continuous definite objective significance. For this, the child would have to be able to compare with each other the various applications of the word, whether to determine their identity (idea of one thing only), or whether by rejection of differences to arrive at what is common (idea of a whole class). But to make such comparison he must remember the former applications. And at first the child is not yet capable of such mental action as this. Former experiences take no part in a present utterance as "memories" or "objects of comparison", but only work in the background as founders of more or less firm associations and as the chief promoters of a feeling of familiarity bound up with word and perception, and the child offers a purely associative reaction to a present experience with one word only, because, at an earlier period, this or that point connected with the experience had appeared connected with the same word.

This undefined association explains why a word is connected now with one, now with another distinctive point in an occurrence, and therefore is used in gayest unconcern for the most widely differing objects. Hence the important part played in early speech by change and increase of significance of words, but always without a suspicion on the child's part of the "transference" or "generalization" of ideas. He lives entirely in the present, and uses a word that appears to him associated, often for reasons of a very vague similarity, quite untroubled by the fact that on another occasion he used this word for something else.

One of the earliest words used by our daughter Hilde was *dolly*, signifying the first time a real doll, but, very soon after, other toys such as her rag-dog and rabbit; on the other hand, however, not for another pet plaything, at this time a little silver bell. Apparently it only required a very superficial likeness (somewhat similar size, feel of material, a certain disposition of limbs) to bring out the same word. The little bell, which differed so entirely from the other playthings in sight, sound and touch, was, to begin with, unnamed.

It was a strange similarity that induced Hilde (1 ; 7) to call the toes of our boots *noses*. She was at this time fond of pulling our noses, and discovered the same possibility of pulling in the boot-toes too.

The little boy E. L., who was two years old before he began to speak, used (2 ; 3) *la la* at first for singing and music; then, after he had heard military music, for soldier as well; at last for all noises, however unmusical, such as knocking or being scolded. The interjection *ugh* was, at first, his expression when shuddering at the cold, then he said the same for heat, at last for everything uncanny—*ugh* for the dark, but also in daylight for an empty room; a mask was *ugh* to him, and so was a veil or spectacles!

The child's speech performances which we have described so far have still a certain likeness with what the lower animal can do. For it too possesses an undeniable—in many domestic animals a fairly extensive—power of intelligent reaction to certain human forms of speech and rudimentary expressions of its own which seem not far behind those of a one-year-old child. In both cases we find separate utterances for objects of affection or desire, utterances which are repeated in a purely associative way on corresponding occasions. The animal, too, has his special sounds for hunger, for delight at an approaching meal, for anxious alarm in danger, for pain, for joyful greeting of certain people. But the animal, no less than the child at the stage we are considering, has no speech-thought, forms no ideas, in his utterances pays no heed to comparisons and generalizations, and as yet never dreams that a sure and lasting designation belongs to everything.

This lowest stage of speech is never left behind by the animal, but very quickly by man. Further development then brings us at last to what is purely human.

CHAPTER IX

THE PSYCHIC FACTORS OF FURTHER SPEECH-DEVELOPMENT[1]

FURTHER speech-development, which after 1 ; 6 passes beyond the scanty beginnings already described, is, like them, only really to be understood if we look upon it as the product of the convergence between the speech-influences of his environment, continually pressing upon the child, and his own inner need of and aptitude for speech. The child, learning to talk, is no more a mere repetition machine than he is a sovereign creator of speech; but his speech-development is only effected by the combined action of imitation and spontaneity.

1. Imitative Speech; its Variety and Defects

Speech in its earliest stage, as we have seen, has scarcely any resemblance to language in its perfection; to transform the child's meagre double-Dutch into the well-ordered abundance of the mother-tongue is the aim of development in the next three years. The child can, of course, only become familiar with this mother-tongue, at first so strange to his ears, by continually hearing it, and only make it his own by repeating its sounds; thus imitation is, in truth, the factor which, above all others, makes it possible to learn to speak. This is so real a fact, that deaf children remain dumb as well; and if deaf-mutes later learn to speak by a very artificial method, in but slight accord with child-nature, it is by watching their teacher's movements in speech and by feeling with the hand, i.e. then, again by imitation.

Yet the process of imitation is not carried on by the normal child in such mechanical wise that every single word, every grammatical form, every turn of syntax is listened to, copied, and at last used independently in speech. Were this the case, the child, learning to speak, would indeed be not much more than a phonograph, that, as time goes on, gets more and more words on its cylinder to be reproduced at a fitting opportunity.

The very fact that imitation itself appears in its most varied

[1] *Children's Speech*, Chap. X.

forms (which we discussed in Chapter V) is sufficient contradiction of this. Sometimes imitation acts quite unconsciously
and unintentionally, sometimes as an energetic effort of will,
as when the child, with evident trouble, tries several times to
repeat a word, or when he asks the names of different things
or pictures and reproduces them again at once. The other
difference, too, between direct and indirect imitation is found
in learning to speak; with increasing age direct imitation,
which no sooner hears a word than it repeats it, "echolalie",
falls more and more into the background and leaves indirect
imitation to do most of the work. When this comes into action,
the sound-stimuli are constantly received without any immediate response in utterance—until at last the time comes
when the stored-up treasures of sound-impression have grown
strong enough to break forth in similar but independent
expressions. In this we find an explanation of those periodic
fluctuations of the rate of progress in speech-development;
those times of small increase of words in independent use do
not betoken real stagnation, but are really periods of inward
acquisition of word-concepts, which only in the fullness of time
cross the threshold of speech.

The most striking example of such an occurrence is to be
found in Carl Stumpf's son, whose speech-development showed
in every way very remarkable features.

For two years the boy stuck to the vocabulary he had
acquired at his very earliest efforts to speak, which mainly
consisted of natural symbols supplemented by a few contorted
words gathered from his environment. With these he formed
in royal fashion all possible word-compounds, long sentences,
and series of sentences, giving entirely the impression of a
foreign language. There was no evidence of any imitation of
the speech he heard around him continually; indeed, he directly
refused it by answering a request to say any given word, *horse*
for example, with his own babble word of *hoto*. In spite,
however, of this lack of response, the speech surrounding him
had its effect on the boy; he understood everything that was
said, and at last could no longer withstand the necessity of
translating the language he heard into the language of speech.
One day—he was now 3 ; 3—he, without any intermediate
stage, gave up his baby talk and began to speak intelligible
German and indeed at once fairly correctly—a sign that shows

how thorough had been the hidden preparation of those years of hearing only.[1]

In contradistinction to these long times of listening only, we often notice cases where a short change in the nature of surrounding speech—e.g. the companionship of a new maid or a journey to a district with a different dialect—shows its influence in the young child's surprisingly quick change of intonation and mode of expression.

On the whole, I think that the quick reaction to what has been heard with corresponding utterances is, in proportion, most frequently found in girls, whilst the longer storing up of impressions and only indirect imitation is more common in boys.

The fact that the child does not allow the technical difficulties in imitation of words and sentences to deter him from his attempts at speech, is the cause of more or less imperfect and faulty reproduction of what has been heard. That is why numberless mutilated forms are a natural feature of all early speech.[2]

Every word that has to be reproduced must be (1) heard, (2) noted, (3) pronounced, and (4) remembered. Hence we have four sources of error.

1. *Sensorial Mistakes.*—Since the child's perception is not yet sufficiently differentiated, fine shades of difference in sound are not noticed; only those that are broader and more striking.

2. *Apperceptive Mistakes.*—The child's weak and unstable memory causes a different attitude to the different parts of a word, whether he hears it or tries to pronounce it himself.

3. *Motor Mistakes.*—The power of articulation and the formation of the child's speech-organs are not yet sufficiently developed to enable him to reproduce correctly certain sounds or combinations of sounds.

4. *Mistakes of Reproduction.*—The capacity of the child's memory is not equal to the abundance of speech-impressions, so that slips of memory occur in the practical use of words previously heard.

Some of the most common sounds of children's speech must be referred to the combined effect of these sources of error, and may be classified somewhat as follows:—

[1] Cf. Stumpf and C. and W. Stern, *Children's Speech*, pp. 288 sq.
[2] *Children's Speech*, Chap. XVIII.

Vowels are more easy to grasp, pronounce and remember than consonants; hence they are less often mutilated.

Of the vowels, *a* (long and short, father, day) and *e* (long, degree) are the most easily said, hence least often wrongly reproduced.

Of the consonants, the guttural and palatal sounds and *sh* are more difficult to pronounce than the others, hence more often wrongly reproduced. The palatal sound *k* is often replaced by the dental *t*.

The more extensive the stimulus, the less intensive the attention turned to it, therefore extensive speech-forms (long sentences or long words) are more often mutilated than short ones are.

Since attention generally outruns pronunciation, and is principally directed to the more prominent parts of a word, the beginnings of words suffer most from mutilation, stressed syllables least. It is worthy of note that amongst the child's mutilations of words are to be found all those forms of word-change which comparative study of language has shown to exist in the general history of speech. So we meet in children's speech:—

1. The elision of single sounds (*o-o* = cocoa; *ittle* = little).
2. Or whole syllables (*mergence* = emergency).
3. Change of sound, substitution of dentals for palatals (*dood* = good; *toffee-tan* = coffee-can).
4. Assimilation, i.e. making one sound in a word like another (*gugar* = sugar; *goggie* = doggie; *bobbin* = dobbin).
5. Metathesis, i.e. transposition of sound (*waps* = wasp; *evnelope* = envelope).
6. Contamination, i.e. the combination of the elements of two words (*breakolate* = breakfast and chocolate).

To this must be added a feature perhaps peculiar to childhood—general assimilation; a sound has been so intensively noted that others, however different, are pronounced like it. Thus our son (2 ; 4) began the majority of his words with *h* or *k* (*hocking* = stocking; *hilk* = milk; *holl* = roll; *kather* = father; *kotty* = Lotty, etc.). Also, in regard to these errors, there seems to be some sex-difference: girls, who in general are more imitative than boys, pick up words they hear more correctly as a rule than boys. Yet of course there are exceptions amongst both girls and boys.

2. The Part Played by Spontaneity

The child's spontaneity, so far as it takes part in speech-development, is not in absolute opposition to imitation, but it penetrates even this and uses what imitation offers as material for further independent forms of speech.

The child's first attitude to the speech-stimuli offered to him is one of selection. In the flood of speech continually striking his ear, the child's imitation at first fixes on very little, then on more and more; and even if this selection is in no way under the direction of will and intention, yet it is "spontaneous" because the result of inner faculties and needs.

It is not the external circumstance that certain words are louder, more emphasized, less difficult to reproduce than others, but the internal reason, that the child's intellect has become capable of acquiring certain kinds of words, which is the reason why, at a certain period, a special number of verbs cross the threshold of speech, whilst, before and after this period, other classes of words are the chief additions to the vocabulary. Thus the selection apparent from time to time becomes a sign of the stage reached in mental growth. Now, it can be readily understood that, in spite of great individual differences in speech-development, CERTAIN REGULARITIES IN THE SEQUENCE OF SPEECH-CAPABILITIES are to be found in the child, for general laws of mental growth are at work here, and it is in consequence of these that every phase acquires the necessary supply of words and phrases. (Examples in the next chapter.) Since many of these laws act more or less independently of the kind of speech that influences the child or of any other conditions of environment, it is evident how strong must be the part played by inner faculty and its gradual growth in the development of the child's speech.

These regulations in development are especially striking when learning to speak takes place under quite abnormal conditions.

Thus the deaf and blind Helen Keller did not learn to speak until her seventh year, and then by means of the finger alphabet which was rapped on the palm of her hand. It is impossible to imagine a more unusual method, and yet the child went through exactly the same periods of speech as normal children do, only, by reason of her age, three times as quickly. I was able to show this by comparison in tabular form of Helen Keller's speech-development with that of our daughter.[1]

The principle of unconscious selection in imitation has, however, quite another field of activity. For the child's choice does not only extend to speech-material as such, but also to the persons whose speech is imitated. The child does not allow his speech to be influenced in the same way by everyone who talks to him, but remains remarkably indifferent, or even distinctly cold, to many people, whilst he at once shows a desire to imitate others and adopts from them vocabulary, intonation and distinctive dialect. In this the general rule holds good that imitation grows in intensity in proportion with the likeness of the copy to the copier. That is why, e.g., older brothers and sisters prove themselves much more efficient tutors than adults are; in the case of twins, however, the influence of older brothers and sisters has to yield to that mutually exercised by those of the same age on one another.[2]

As one example of the first case (influence of older brothers and sisters), we may point to the use of "I". First-born children speak of themselves for a long time by their name, and do not use "I" until very late, because the "I" of an adult cannot exercise any strong stimulus to imitation. Younger children, on the other hand, adopt the more effective, emphatic *"I, I"* from the lips of elder brothers and sisters at a remarkably early stage, and use it quite correctly.

The choice of the persons to be imitated is very striking where different languages are spoken by those with whom the child lives.[3] Then, not only is it generally the case that one language is evidently preferred to the other, but—and this is especially noteworthy psychologically—no real confusion arises between the two spheres of imitation; the persons with different languages form separate concept-centres for the child, and quite unconsciously he uses now one, now the other language as he needs them.

I have to thank Professor W. Volz for two examples of this. The scientific investigator had taken his wife and son (; 9) with him on a long exploration to Sumatra. There, as a result

[1] W. Stern, VI.   [2] A test of this in *Children's Speech*, p. 294.
[3] *Children's Speech*, pp. 297 sqq.

of continuous intercourse with Malay servants, the child learnt to speak nothing but Malay, totally ignoring his father's and mother's German speech. When they came home the boy was three years old, and from now on, with the exception of the Malay spoken by one servant who came with them, he heard nothing but German. A time of transition followed; the boy used both languages side by side, but without ever confusing them. His never-failing consciousness of which language he was speaking was a special characteristic of this period. But at 3 ; 3 a total change took place: Malay was totally discarded and, as may be added, shortly quite forgotten. It is true the boy's German was at first very faulty, and often had a touch of Malay in word-arrangement and construction; but the quick dropping of Malay was partly due to the fact that the boy noticed that coloured people, with all belonging to them, were considered inferior. Hence, though, to begin with, the simple nature of the native servants had made the boy prefer them as language-teachers, at a higher stage of development the lower estimation in which they were held caused the boy's endeavour to shake off their influence quickly.

JULES RONJAT, a Frenchman occupied with language research work, had a German wife. When their son was born they adopted the principle of *une personne une langue* and the father always spoke French, the mother German with the child. As a result, the boy learnt both languages simultaneously but almost quite independently of each other. He adopted each language as if it was his mother-tongue, took no longer over the process than a child with only one native tongue would do, and the acquisition of the two showed NO SPECIAL INCREASE OF MENTAL STRAIN. Each language was for him from the very first connected as a matter of course with one only of the two parents; e.g. if his father gave him (in French) a message for his mother, he would deliver it in German, without its being translated for him. Confusions between the two languages were rare exceptions.

Even if the principle of selection still goes on within the act of imitation, another function of spontaneity passes over these limits, as the child begins spontaneous working up of the material gained by imitation and in this way enlarges the sphere of his power of speech-expression. The general cause of all this working-up is a certain " language famine". For normally the wealth of experiences and the need of expression grows far more quickly than the supply of forms of words, resulting from imitation, so that the child makes a virtue of necessity and forms fresh language from what he has learnt, without, of course, having any idea of his arbitrary proceeding.

Neither does he supply his need by evolving sound-forms to which he now gives the meaning of a significant word. The occurrence of such "primitive creations" is indeed affirmed here and there, but careful examination very often shows that they were rather corrupted forms borrowed from adult speech.[1] Moreover, such speech-invention from nothing would psychologically be very improbable; the child always requires, so far as it is in any way possible, some relation betwéen sound and significance, and when the natural symbolism of imitative sounds and active expressions is no longer sufficient, then at least the words with whose sounds he is already familiar must be the tool wherewith he can make his own new forms of language.[2]

Thus these new language-forms are produced by analogy with what is already known. Some or other form-elements which have occurred in connection with one or more general perceptions, as representing a certain shade of significance, are used in designation of other perceptions, if the same kind of significance is also present in these. Examples of such sound-elements, transferable by analogy, we find in all signs of inflection, modifications, prefixes and affixes, which mark the plural, tenses or degrees of comparison. The child only needs to have learnt by imitation in a few verbs that past participles are formed by adding "ed" to carry out the principle on his own initiative in any number of other verbs. In the same way, derivatives which he has heard, such as rider from ride, hilly from hill, or other cómbinations of words, or syntactical connections and definite phrases, form the starting-point for an extensive activity by analogy. This means enormous saving of labour in speech, since it combines a minimum of learning with a maximum power of expression. The wealth of these analogous creations is certainly far greater than can be proved objectively, for they can only be recognized with

[1] *Children's Speech*, Chap. XXI, "Primitive Creations".
[2] Or at most we find occasional instances of the child, in obedience to a playful impulse, uttering a gibberish of strange sounds. But these sounds are seldom adopted in his language, and then only to disappear entirely.

absolute certainty when they introduce wrong or unusual forms of speech; when correct, it is impossible to decide whether the child has come upon them by imitation or by analogy. The tendency to analogy is often so strong that even the intensive influences of surrounding speech have hard work to overcome it. The child who uses the form "drinked" in analogy with other weak participles has heard the word "drunk" innumerable times and long understood it, but is not therefore to be deterred from using the wrong form. His own creation from an inner sense of usual speech is less trouble to him than the imitative learning of an irregular form. The actual learning of all possible forms comes along quite slowly in the train of his need of expression, and thus some approach to the correct speech he hears is only achieved with many hindrances and pauses.

Some other methods used by the child to help him in his need of language are appended here. Strange-sounding words, apparently quite unconnected with words he knows, are of course a hard task for the child's capacity of learning, and instinctively he protects himself against them by changing them until the sound has some connection with the meaning intelligible to him at any rate; thus "suburb" becomes *sollibub* (a less crowded place, possibly from analogy with solitude).

Such changes we call "child's etymology". Of course this changing process is generally quite unconscious, but, for that very reason, a sign of the part played by the child's innate nature in his speech-development; even where he intends simply to copy, he cannot suppress his need for inner mental assimilation of what he utters.[1]

In conclusion, the child's phraseology is the real arena of his independent activity; if he wants to express a thought-form for which he can find in the stock of phrases he has acquired no fitting expression, he comes to his own help, in his own way. Sometimes we hear strange laconic expressions in which, under pressure of haste and excitement, complicated series of thoughts are compressed into a few words, as for example, *Mama scolds in her eyes* (looks as if she wanted to scold. Scupin's son); *writing bed* (= the writing [of his father] should go to bed, i.e. stop. The Bergmanns' son (2; 5). Sometimes when the expressions wanted are not forthcoming, the

[1] *Children's Speech*, Chap. XXIV, "Child's Etymology".

child uses more or less original but always intelligible transcriptions; thus Gunther called the rail of a balcony which he had drawn: *something so that we don't fall down*; and Hilde found for matchboxes the almost poetical name of: *little boxes where the lights are hid.*

In these ways, then, the child's spontaneity in very different forms does its part in speech-development, and, under certain circumstances, may achieve results which lead children's speech on paths far from the usual forms of adult speech. Of course, there are all possible degrees in this spontaneous action: in some children, learning by imitation so preponderates that there is but little room left for spontaneous speech-development; in others, the influences of the speech around them fall far short of their own psychic needs of expression, and want of language sets spontaneity hard at work.

Since, as we have previously mentioned, imitation is, as a rule, more strongly developed in girls than in boys, spontaneity will be more conspicuous in the latter, and in fact such obstinacies and effervescing self-creations as we mentioned above in connection with Stumpf's son, or the clumsy originality which often marked our own son's speech, seems scarcely ever to occur in girls. Yet in many boys, too, speech-development shows no such peculiarities.[1]

[1] Examples of especially retarded speech-development followed by fitful periods of distinct changes are given in *Children's Speech*, Chap. XVI, Sec. 2.

CHAPTER X

THE CHIEF PERIODS OF FURTHER SPEECH-DEVELOPMENT

1. Leaving the First Stage Behind

THAT first period of unconscious speech for particular occasions which we described in Chapter VIII, as a rule, lasts for six months or a little more, without showing any very special progress within its own limits.

But then a decisive turn takes place once more in the development of speech with THE AWAKENING OF A FAINT CONSCIOUSNESS OF THE MEANING OF SPEECH AND THE WILL TO ACHIEVE IT.[1]

If, up till then, sound-forms have only been used here and there to express experiences, connected with them by some association of perception or emotion, now the discovery is made that there are in addition to those, other sound-forms of distinguishing (symbolic) value viz., a sign belonging to every object as a designation in speech concerning it, that is, that EVERY THING HAS A NAME.

This change has two evident symptoms:—

1. In the child's suddenly awakened enquiry as to names of things.
2. In the increase—often proceeding by leaps and bounds —of vocabulary, especially in important words.

Both changes may be active in varying degree, and do not necessarily occur at exactly the same time, since the words acquired by constant enquiry may lie hidden in the child's consciousness for a more or less lengthy time before they are used.

As Hilde was about 1 ; 6 we noticed a period when the question *"isn't that?"* or the demonstrative *that! that!* entirely usurped all her speech and thoughts in its demand for the names of all actual things and pictures of them, and at the same time her vocabulary increased rapidly. Gunther (1 ; 7) began his unwearied search for names with the question *that? that?* but, in his case, several months passed before he used what he

[1] *Children's Speech*, pp. 190 sqq.

had learnt in his ordinary speech. The record of Scupin's son (1 ; 10) reads: "His joy in naming things is great. To-day he stood in the middle of the room and said as he pointed to the several things: *lamp, the cupboard, the bassy* (basket)."

The occurrence just described must now doubtless be considered as a MENTAL act of the child's in the real sense of the word. The insight into the relation between sign and import which the child gains here is something fundamentally different from the simple dealing with perceptions and their associations. And the demand that some name must belong to every object, whatever its nature, we may consider as a real—perhaps the child's first—general thought.[2]

But of course the distinctive diffuse nature of the child's mentality must still be borne in mind. It is true that at this point words become "names" or symbols of things, but that does not mean that they immediately acquire nothing but a demonstrative and purely conventional relationship to the object designated [like any chance word or a chemical formula in adult speech]. On the contrary, the name has at once a much more original and primitive connection with the thing named; it becomes actually a quality of the object and also an expression of it as well. The thing itself gains from the fact that it can be

---

[1] Where speech-development takes place under non-normal circumstances, this moment of discovery sometimes makes its appearance with especial distinctness. For this reason the description is instructive which Miss Sullivan, Helen Keller's teacher, gave of the corresponding event. This child, deprived of both higher senses, grew up without speech to the age of seven years. At last Miss S. succeeded by touches on the palm of the hand in teaching her the finger alphabet; next, Helen acquired a few finger symbols by association with objects touched at the same time, but without having any idea of the symbolic meaning of the finger signs. At the beginning of the second month of instruction, the following occurrence took place (taken from Miss Sullivan's own report): "We went to the pump, where I let Helen hold the cup under the spout while I pumped. As the cold water poured out and filled the cup, I spelt 'water' on her empty hand. The word, immediately following the sensation of the cold water rushing over her hand, seemed to take her aback. She dropped the cup and stood rooted to the ground. Quite a new light passed over her features. She spelt the word water several times, then crouching down touched the ground and asked its name, and in the same way pointed to the pump and the grating, then turning round suddenly she asked my name. All the way home she was most excited, and inquired the name of everything she touched, so that in the course of a few hours she had embodied thirty new words in her vocabulary" (cf. W. Stern: VI).

[2] In *Children's Speech*, pp. 124 sqq., the general growth of speech in childhood is shown to develop from three roots, viz., the expressive, the social and the intentional. The first two become manifest in the earliest beginnings of speech —as we have already shown in this book, but intentional speech-activity (the designation of an ideal) is not possible until after this first general thought.

named, an increase in stability and permanence, and the name from its firm anchorage in the structure of the thing takes on some touch of its physiognomy; it sounds as the thing looks or moves or feels to the touch—a species of sound-painting which now appears side by side with the natural utterance. (See above.)

Frequent use is made of the instance of Stumpf's son (Stumpf, p. 25), who as a small child had invented the name of *marage* for a brick and gave his reason for this when 17 years old as follows: "The brick looked just the same as the word sounds." This peculiar double function of the name as being on the one hand a designation for the thing, on the other an expressive part of its very self, is found in all primitive vocal thought and involves that magic of speech which is quite evident in uncivilized peoples, children and in certain pathological psychic conditions, and indeed is never quite lost even amongst normal and educated human beings.[1]

About the same time (1 ; 6 to 1 ; 9), as regards syntax, the first period comes to an end; the sole dominance of the one-word sentence ceases, the child becomes capable of connecting several words to express one thought.[2] Here, too, understanding is generally in advance of power of expression.

Hilde (1 ; 4) could already obey the suggestion, " Touch your nose with your foot", and connected the two perceptions of nose and foot quite correctly; but not till 1 ; 5 did she utter her first sentence of more than one word: *there, see wow-wow*, and at 1 ; 7 the still more impressive one: *all, all milk!* (the milk is all gone).[3]

It is true these word collections were not all so fluently spoken as are our sentences; their characteristic rather was a jerky utterance (often interspersed by pauses) of the isolated words; in such case it is really more a question of a short chain of one-word sentences as: *Hilde—cocoa* (come Hilda, the cocoa is here), *ater—dolly* (father look, I have a dolly). It is only by degrees that such loose juxtapositions pass into the firm union of a really coherent sentence.

---

[1] Cf. particularly Heinz Werner, II, pp. 183 sqq. and elsewhere, also Koffka, p. 244.
[2] *Children's Speech*, pp. 199 sqq.
[3] Our own son was a remarkable exception. Although in other ways he learnt to speak with more difficulty than his sisters, at 1 ; 2 he connected his scanty words in sentences of more than one word: *moo hear?*—do you hear the cow lowing? *There is papa, see!*

2. The Second Period of Speech

Once the first period is over, rapid development generally begins; within a short time events follow so rapidly that we must confine ourselves to a consideration of the most important stages.

To show the quickness of the progress, we will first mention that girls at 2 years, boys at 2 ; 6 have a speaking vocabulary of about three hundred words[1]. In respect of constitution, this vocabulary is naturally of "paidocentric" tendency, i.e. it is grouped round the middle point of the child's interests, and the circumference of this circle gradually becomes wider and wider. In the first stages the exclusive material for the child's speech are words belonging to the most noticeable impressions of the immediate environment, such as parents, nurse, toys, animals, clothing and food, then sounds and movements as well as activities that attract the child's attention. Within this vocabulary the division into kinds of words now becomes clear; the interjectional kinds of expression, which in the first period were almost masters of the field, fall now more and more into the background, whilst expressions of objective import come to the fore in an easily marked sequence.

The necessity of learning names is confined at first to persons and things; so that at first (1 ; 3 to 1 ; 6) the vocabulary consists, with the exception of interjections, almost entirely of nouns. A few months later these are joined fairly suddenly by verbs in considerable numbers, whilst at the same time the store of substantives keeps on growing; it is not until a third stage that adjectives are added as well as the finer framework of language, prepositions, adverbs, numerals, etc.[2]

A later section deals with the significance of the three stages thus arising: " Substance", "Action", "Relation and Attribute Stage", for the child's thought-development;[3] we will now only consider these relations by means of a few statistics. The vocabulary of a normal girl shows roughly the following divisions—interjections not being considered: At 1 ; 3 substantives 100 per cent.; 1 ; 8 78 per cent. substantives, 22 per cent. verbs; 1 ; 11 63 per cent. substantives, 23 per cent. verbs, 24 per cent. other classes of words.

---

[1] *Children's Speech*, pp. 226–228.　　[2] Ibid., pp. 344 sqq.
[3] Chap. XXVII. 2.

But, after all, single words form only the raw material; the decisive step comes with the way in which they are used in the building up of speech. Here there are two outstanding points: the change of words by inflection, and their union by syntax.

3. The Third Period of Speech

For a year the words that the child uses are fixed forms only, at 2 ; o they begin to live, to bend, to move.[1] This, too, we have to look upon as the beginning of an important new period in speech-development, the third. The child of educated classes here already reaches a stage which has never been attained by many fully developed adult languages, for the study of language reveals many so-called uninflected languages that can only express all more delicate shades of meaning by the juxta-position of unchanging words. How much higher than these is a language which, by a slight modification, makes the same word express singular or plural, changes an action from the present to the past or future by adding a prefix and an affix, or expresses a quality in a greater or less degree by forms of comparison. Here the single word is no longer an isolated island, but the central sun whose rays represent the most delicate divergencies and relations of the main idea. The two-year-old child begins to acquire all this in the different forms of inflection (declension, conjugation, comparison) fairly simultaneously, so that, in reality, we are dealing with united psychic progress along the whole line.

It is true this fresh stage of development lasts some years; and four and five-year-old children often have a hard struggle with certain shades of inflection. As a whole, the regular, less inflected forms are more easily mastered than the more irregular and more strongly inflected, hence the frequent substitution of wrong forms of the first type for those of the last (*drinked* for drunk, *badder* for worse).

As to syntax, the end of the second year generally brings with it considerable development of sentences of more than one word.[2] Three, four, and more words are put together now to express one thought, not at first, of course, in the form of a fluent sentence, but as a jerky series of several short, little

---

[1] *Children's Speech*, p. 247, and Chap. XV.   [2] Ibid., pp. 202 sqq.

sentences. The same process, therefore, is repeated as in two-word sentences; the united structural form of a sentence only develops by degrees from elements but loosely knit together.

Thus Hilde (1 ; 10) expressed a wish that her mother should fetch pictures out of the back room as follows: *Mama—wanty pickies—room—wanty pickies—back—dada, mama fetch.*

The loose links of the original chain of words often produce an order of words in the sentence differing from the normal.[1] As the ideas bubble up into the little head, out rattle words, however wrong their order may be. Certainly the very strangeness of position often makes for impressiveness. Sometimes the word most emphasized by the child comes full-tilt at the very beginning; sometimes, on the other hand, the important word is used all alone as a special one-word sentence at the very end (this is specially the case for negation).

Gunther once at dinner pushed his high chair to a fresh place with the words: *A Gunther a father sit* (meaning probably, to-day Gunther wants to sit for once by father). When his mother asked: "Not by mother?" the answer came: *Yesterday a mumsey sitting a Gunter.*

Affix of negation: Idelberger's son (already 1 ; 6), *mama beat, no!*—mama must not beat. Stumpf's son (German boy): *ich haja kokadach mach olol kap—näh.* This very strange sentence in ordinary German runs: "Ich (hab) ein schones Schokoladen-haus; das macht Rudolf kaputt—nein?" I (have) a fine chocolate house; that Rudolf break—no!

But sometimes it is all confusion, and the mood of the moment decides now this position and, a second later, another; notice the negation in the following chain-sentence of our son's: *Gunther also a not make, Hilde also not a make—father also a make, no—no.*

With regard to meaning, the variety of sentences increases with astonishing speed. Although interjectional sentences containing an expression of will or emotion are still in the majority throughout childhood, yet statement-sentences continually tend to take a more important place, and they refer not only to the present (as giving an account of what is to be seen in a picture), but also to experiences and impressions which have lately taken place, and to end with, they are questions.[2] In addition to those questions, mentioned earlier, as to the

---

[1] *Children's Speech*, pp. 217 sqq.   [2] Ibid., pp. 212 sqq.

names of things (*isna that?* or something similar), we soon find questions as to the whereabouts of anything lost. Hilde (1 ; 9), *apple where?* Gunther (2 ; 8), *a, hat?* (*where is the hat?*); also questions to ascertain something (*may I eat these?*), and lastly, even questions of sympathy (*are you tired?*), said by Eva when she saw someone yawn. In these questions we often notice that the word of interrogation is discarded, or, to speak more exactly, has not yet crossed the threshold of speech. But the other words, the intonation and the situation, are sufficient to make the sense quite clear. Some other types of questions on a higher level intellectually are not developed before the fourth stage.

4. The Fourth Period of Speech

The beginning of this period is formed by the appearance of subordinate sentences.

Like inflection, hypotaxis (the subordination of one sentence to another) is a form of speech completely wanting in many languages that can only express the dependent relation of thoughts by placing sentences side by side (parataxis). The child of European civilization passes this stage in about two and a half years,[1] and thereby proves that he has grasped not only logical-thought relation but its word-representation in principal and subordinate sentences.

Thus Hilde (2 ; 2) could already express cause and result, but only in parataxis; *porridge lid not here, can't twirly, twirly* (spin). Not for another whole year was she able to show the same relation by a causal subordinate clause: *you rub your hands, because it is so cold.*

Just as in interrogatory sentences, the introductory particle may for a long time be omitted, so too in subordinate clauses conjunctions, relative pronouns, etc., that is, exactly the part of speech that determines (for the grammarian) the character of the subordinate sentence. Yet the clause in children's speech is unmistakable for the listener, even if the written form alone

---

[1] Many children even earlier. Thus our daughter Eva at 2 ; 0 uttered sentences such as: *look where glove is; daddy say if he can drink coffee.* Another girl of our acquaintance who had not begun to speak till very late (2 ; 0) then made such quick progress that at the age of 2 ; 7 she had got as far as subordinate sentences, e.g. Shop we buyed thing, was funny man (= in the shop where we bought something, there was a funny man).

leaves the reader in doubt. When Gunther (2 ; 6) uttered the sentence, *mother say, builded has Gunther*, his intonation explained that he meant to say: "I want to tell mother what Gunther has built", but not: "I want to tell mother Gunther has been building." For this reason the beginning of the period of subordinate clauses must not be fixed as only when the appropriate particles are really heard, for the stage of hidden knowledge of those words may often last for several months.

The following anthology of subordinate sentences which we recorded of Hilde (about 3 ; 0) shows how quickly hypotaxis grows when once it is grasped by the child:—

"*I will look in the kitchen and ask if she is coming here* (indirect question); *will whip the doll till it hurts her* (temporal clause); *that moves so to-day because it is broken* (causal clause); *you'll get no bread and butter if you're so naughty* (conditional clause); *you must take away the beds so that I can get out* (final clause); *dolly has disturbed me, so that I could not sleep* (consecutive clause)."

Nevertheless, many specially difficult constructions in subordination of clauses continue to be, for some considerable time yet, beyond the child's power; e.g. the hypothetical conditional clause with the conjunctive verbal forms—probably the most difficult of these clauses[1] —has only been mastered by our children at 4 ; 6.

Gunther (4 ; 8), of a friend who had undergone an operation: *If he were* (not) *cut at once, then he had died.*

With the mastery of such difficulties the period of children's speech, as such, may be considered as brought to an end.

The fourth period of speech-development is characterized by two other facts.

The child for the second time comes into an *age of questions*,[2] now, however, concerned with something higher—the time-question WHEN, the causal question WHY. But too high a value must not be set upon these questions. The earliest "when" and "why" questions are, for the main part, not the expression of unmixed desire for knowledge on the child's part, but are most intimately connected with his small ego and its practical needs; for this reason the first "why" meets the parents' ears

---

[1] TRANSLATOR'S NOTE.—Since, with very few exceptions, conjunctive verbal forms in English have given way to the use of auxiliaries, this statement loses much of its force when translated into English.
[2] *Children's Speech*, p. 214.

in the annoyed expression, *why not, then?* if some wish of the child's is forbidden or withheld. And *"when?"* the child asks to find out when the earnestly desired meal-time is to come at last.

Our son's (2 ; 11) first *when* was also extremely utilitarian. As he saw his elders biting the meat from fowl bones he asked: *"A shall we nibble? a are big, we can nibble* (the first *a* = when, the second = if we).

But besides such questions there are others from pure desire to know; not concerned with finding the justification of commands, but rather the reason of facts the child has observed.

At 2 ; 10 Gunther already asks: *"Tray so hot—why then?"* Hilde 3 ; 7 had so violent an attack of asking causal questions that sometimes she made a whole chain of them, each reason producing another enquiry as to *its* reason.

Thus about this time the following conversation—taken down literally in shorthand—took place as the child saw a whale in her picture-book:—

Child's Questions.	*Mother's Answers.*
What is he eating?	Fish.
Why does he eat fish?	Because he is hungry.
Why doesn't he eat rolls?	Because we don't give him any.
Why don't we give him any?	Because bakers only make rolls for people.
Why not for fishes?	Because they haven't enough flour.
Why then haven't they enough?	Because not enough corn is grown. You know, don't you, that flour is made out of corn?
Oh, I see.	

The little Anna, who forms the subject of Elsa Köhler's report, at the age of 3 ; 2 constantly asks *why*, but curiously enough only as regards other human beings. *Why will she be pleased?* (when hearing a fairy-tale repeated); *the wicked step-mother was dreadfully jealous, why?* "I never hear that questioning why in any other connection. Either she knows the reason, as is evident in her treatment of the matter, or she accepts the inexplicable with the silent attitude that is one of her characteristics."

Another characteristic of the fourth period, i.e. the making of new words, is not of such common occurrence as the peculiarity just mentioned; it is very marked in many children, but scarcely existent in others. It shows itself by an arbitrary enrichment of vocabulary in the form of derivatives and of compound words (of their own making). The child, as a rule, exercises his activity as speech-creator quite unconsciously; his creations take their place just as naturally as all the other words which he has heard from those around him. Sometimes the child evinces a wonderfully fine feeling for language; in other cases, though, we find grotesque and impossible turns of expression. In many children these new creations reach a fairly high number; in our two older children, up to the end of the fifth year, we noticed respectively forty and fifty new compound words, and twenty of their own derivatives. The majority have but a momentary span of life, but many are persisted in for some time.

The compound words[1] are the simpler forms, because in this case only the expressions for two distinctive features in the object spoken of are joined together. From our son's third year we may mention: *milkapple-jam*—an imaginary dish; *fire-box*—a fireproof casserole over a spirit stove; *children-rubbish-box*—a chest for toys, etc.; *holeplate*—saucer with perforated rim. From Hilde's fourth year: *child-soldier*— an officer, looking short in the distance; *hairflame*—stray curls.

Children show themselves very ingenious in the use of such aids to the expression of more delicate colour shades; amongst others, we notice *darkwhite, halfblue, greyred.* Compounds, too, are often formed in designation of occupations: *breadman* (baker), *beerboy* (the refreshment boy at railway stations), *lightman* (lamplighter). But the results of the other kind of word-formation, derivatives, are specially used for names of callings:[2] children who have often heard such designations as painter, carrier, etc., in like manner make *machiner, muffiner* (muffin-seller), *coaler* (coal-heaver).

Other groups of derivatives referring to objects: *the reading* (printed matter), *the smoke* (cigar, used by many children); for qualities: *raggy* (torn), *porridgey* (porridge-stained); for conditions: *splashiness* (result of splashing water), *funniness*, etc.

[1] *Children's Speech*, Chap. XXII.   [2] Ibid., Chap. XXIII.

5. Outline of Speech-Development in Childhood

From the fourth to the fifth year we may look upon the child's speech-development as mainly finished. Not that children's speech has, by then, already reached the stage of ordinary adult speech; it never does that at any period throughout childhood. Every one of the later development periods has rather its own special features; the eight-year-old does not speak like the eleven-year-old, nor like the fourteen-year-old, nor any of them like adults.[1] But, in any case, these later developments are incomparably less than those we have already discussed. The psychological law that every psychic function has its chief period of development is also true of speech, and this chief period is clearly marked between the first and fourth or fifth year of life.

We will now try to summarize the above considerations in a systematized plan; at the same time expressly stating that this must not be looked upon as a firm rule applicable to all, but only an attempt to give certain formulæ for the most generally prevalent tendencies in the development of early speech.

It will probably be found that each individual development will differ more or less from this outline, not only in details as to time, but even as regards stages reached within given periods; yet I think the outline has a certain value as a general guide.

‸ *Preliminary.*—First year. Babble. Imitation of sound-forms, first understanding of requests made to the child.

First Period.—About 1–1 ; 6. The child has mastered a few sounds used with special meanings, which must be considered sentences of one word. Speech-elements so far show no understanding of grammar or ideas (conceptions) and their significance, no differentiation as yet between the objective and what touches will and emotion. In sound they are still near to babble —the natural symbols; word-pictures and active sound-expressions are most prevalent.

‸ *Second Period.*—About 1 ; 6–2 ; 0. Awakening of the consciousness of the object of speech (that everything has a name) and the will to master it. The vocabulary suddenly shows great increase; questions appear as to the names of things. About the

[1] Berthold Otto has made well-known attempts to record such peculiarities in language at special ages, so that magazines intended for any age may be written in its particular style (which I, in passing, consider educationally wrong in principle).

same time the stage of " one-word sentences" is left behind; two, soon several, words are combined, first hesitatingly, then more and more fluently, in a complete sentence. Vocabulary contents are increased first by nouns, then by a large addition of verbs, and lastly by qualifying words and those expressing relation. Stages of substance, action, relation and distinction.

Third Period.—About 2–2 : 6. Complete mastery of uninflected speech. The child learns to express the finer shades of ideas by modifications of words, and about the same time different forms of inflection (conjugation, declension, comparison) begin to develop. Sentence-formation, although still in paratactic form (simple sentence), is very varied. Series of sentences—exclamations, descriptions (statements), questions —are formed. Questions refer to names of things, where, what information, etc.

Fourth Period.—About 2 ; 6 and on. The purely paratactic sentence-formation is left behind. The child learns to express varying order of thoughts (principal and subordinate) by hypotaxis, and there is rapid growth of the different kinds of subordinate clauses; although the finer differentiation of particles and the mastery of the harder verb-forms (e.g. the conjunctive or subjunctive) may yet require a considerable time to learn. The child's questions begin to extend to time and, above all, to the causal relations (*why*). Tendency to independent word-formation in compounds and derivatives.

6. Talk and Conversation in Childhood

Everything we have said so far has dealt exclusively with individual development in the use of speech. But this specialization is purely artificial; fresh problems arise when we consider the child's utterances as a whole from a more general point of view, i.e. in connection with its personal life and experience (talk, *Rede*) and in the natural communication with others (conversation, Gespräche). Two psychologists share the merit of having made thorough investigations in this difficult subject; viz., the French-Swiss scientist Piaget and two German parents, Herr and Frau Katz. The work of these investigators is mutually complementary, for Piaget studies children in the company of those of their own age, and Herr and Frau Katz observe them in their family life. It is shown that the talk and conversation of children assume an entirely different complexion, not only in its subject-matter, but in the whole structure and psychic form when the environment is thus changed.

Piaget has had records kept for a month at a time respectively of all the utterances made by several of the children in a Children's Home when in the society of other children and summarized this speech-activity in clever statistics.

He comes to the conclusion that the essential feature of the child's talk when with other children consists in the fact that it aims far less at communicating with or giving information to others (i.e. has a less social character) than does that of adults. It is rather to a great extent "egocentric", an automatic giving expression to the speaker's own emotions, ideas and thoughts, partly in the form of pure monologues and partly in pseudo-conversations, i.e. in the presence of other children, and undoubtedly incited by their presence, yet not with the idea of any interchange of thought with them by means of speech. Piaget counted all egocentric remarks and compared their numerical proportion to the grand total of all the recorded sentences. In this way he obtained "an egocentric coefficient", which is reproduced in the following table [1] :—

Child.	Age in Years.	Number of Recorded Utterances	Percentage of Egocentric Speeches.
I	3	1,500	56
II	3	1,000	56
III	4	1,500	60
IV	5	800	46
V	6	1,500	45
VIa	6	1,400	47
VIb	7	800	27
VII	7	600	50

Hence it is very evident that the egocentric character depends greatly on age. The three- and four-year-old child is more egocentric than social in his conversation, whilst in the case of the five- and six-year-old the egocentric coefficient is already somewhat below 50 per cent. and then in the seven-year-old shows an

[1] Piaget, II. p. 340. Child VI was tested twice (at the ages of 6 and 7).

abrupt decrease. In other words: It is not until early childhood is passed that the child's talk amongst other children assumes more of a social than an egocentric character. The picture is completed by a close analysis of the "social" utterances, which pass through several stages.[1]

It is only quite gradually that talking *beside* one another becomes talking *to* one another; at first indeed the individual child, quite on his own initiative (therefore with a pronounced egocentric character) speaks to the others and they listen, thus producing at last a real mutual understanding, since the talker now formulates the thoughts he had before from the social standpoint of a desire to be understood and with consideration of the thoughts of another. Piaget also considers that this highest form is not within reach of children before the age of about 8 years.

But how is it possible then that far younger children seem to understand each other so well in their common games? Piaget's answer runs as follows; because in early childhood speech is only one of the factors of expression. Gestures, mimicry, actions are the chief means of communication between children at play; the expressional movements are at once understood, actions imitated or continued, and spoken words act as tendrils rather than the main stems of supports to mutual understanding.

We have here a particularly striking example of the gradual nature of the increase in the individual working (*Ausgliederung*) of the different functions in childhood; vocal speech really does not exist at first for the little child at play as a separate fact, and only by degrees emerges as such from the undefined speech of the whole body, to become at a late period the one and only medium for the expression and communication of thought.

But Piaget's conclusions, exceedingly interesting as they are in themselves, must not be considered—which is sometimes done by the author—as general main rules of children's speech. The particularly tardy and slow development of the true social function of speech, for instance, is decided far more than Piaget assumes BY THE SPECIAL CIRCUMSTANCES UNDER WHICH IT IS

---

[1] Piaget, I, pp. 68 sqq. Cf. also Muchow's remarks, I, p. 349. The similarity of the above-mentioned stages with those of social games in childhood is at once self-evident. Chap. XXII. 2 of our book.

TESTED. In children's games with their playmates, there is comparatively little occasion for real exchange of thought, information, or interrogation, hence the expressive side of talking is here much more in evidence than the social. Also the specific nature of the Geneva Children's Home is not without its influence in this direction as well, for it—like the Montessori homes—consists of a number of children united by no very strong community interests, since all are busied with their different individual occupations. A further test by Martha Muchow (IV) in a Hamburg kindergarten gave quite another picture, for in this case the utterances of the five-year-olds only gave a good 30 per cent. of an egocentric character. But in that kindergarten the children were united in smaller groups more like families, an arrangement that tended to produce a more pronounced social attitude.

Now in actual family life the situation and, accordingly, the whole structural form of children's speech is entirely different. We see this very plainly from the collection of 150 conversations which the *Katz* parents carried on with their two sons (5 ; o and 3 ; 6). These conversations were never only the accompaniment of games but arose from the children's readiness to talk, from their desire to open their hearts and express their thoughts, from curiosity and wish for knowledge, from expressions of affection and also a wish to set up their own will in opposition to that of others, that is then, from entirely social motives. Soon the child takes an ACTIVE part by beginning the conversation himself, for instance in the form of questions by which he tries to find solutions of mental puzzles and doubts. D. and R. Katz reckon up a long series of typical questions (pp. 274 sqq.) illustrated by examples. Soon the child assumes a REACTIVE attitude, is responsive to instruction, tries, when requested, to remember his own small sins and good deeds, opposes a statement or direction of his parents', delivers a criticism on one of his younger brother's remarks, and demands exactly the same treatment for himself as is given to his elder brother. But all these mental attitudes are produced, as the author justly remarks, "by social psychological conditions; they arise in the social field from the interrelation of adult and child." We illustrate what has been said by an example from Katz; many other specimens of actual conversations are to be found in various parts of our book.

"The boys (T. 5 : 7. J. 3 ; 11) are talking one evening in bed to their mother about an incident that has occurred during the day.

"J.: *Elly (the nurse) ran away from me to-day. Have you ever seen such a girl? We will send Elly back.*

"T.: *In a parcel.*

"J.: *Yes, in a parcel; we'll make a hole in it.*

"T.: *A hole so big (shows the size with his hands).*

"Mother: What is the hole for?

"J.: *So that Elly will get air or else she might suffocate. Elly doesn't know that people must stay with children.*

"T.: *Once she was with us and went out; she said she was coming back directly, but she didn't come.*

"J.: *Then grandmother came, she didn't go out, she stopped with us.*"

7. Beginnings of Reading and Writing

Civilized man has not only the spoken language but the written as well. Reading and writing are the two forms of activity which enable him to use it. The speech-development of early childhood is, in general, limited to the spoken language, and this chapter treats of that alone. It is certainly no chance occurrence that in all civilized countries instruction in reading and writing begins immediately after early childhood has ended, that is then at 7 years of age; evidently the average child is not mentally ready before that time to understand speech in its written form and to produce it himself.

In special cases, however, this aptitude may develop earlier. The exception is due either to specialized instruction or to an unusual spontaneity of interest in written language.

(a) SPECIALIZED INSTRUCTION in writing and reading is given in the Montessori schools. As it is not the object of this book to deal with the instruction of young children, a short reference, touching on certain noteworthy psychological points, must here suffice.

Mme Montessori has shown undoubted skill in her methods of including the earliest instruction in writing amongst the play-activities of her schools. A beginning is made by the children tracing over geometrical figures with coloured chalks, then they are given little tablets on each of which a script letter cut out of sandpaper is stuck on to smooth cardboard; by tracing over the sandpaper model with the finger the writing movements are practised, at the same time accompanied by constant repetition of its name. Single wooden letters are then given to the child, who either by looking or feeling has to name them, find out any at request and, lastly, put them together into simple words. These exercises in the form of play, at first making no mental demands on the child produce in him at last a spontaneous desire to draw words on the blackboard—and the principle of writing has been mastered. Reading is practised in the same way in games. Cards of plainly written words are distributed and the child has to place them under their corresponding object, and is then allowed to play with this object, etc.

The results of these methods reported by Mme Montessori (p. 283) are astonishing. It is true there are always children who show no interest in these writing and reading games or soon turn away from them; they are allowed to do so if they wish. But as a general rule the children in these schools are supposed to begin writing at 4 years of age, and at 5 ; o they can read as well as a child usually does in its first school-year—which means an advance of two years. Even short orders written on cards can be read, understood and carried out by these little children.

Now ought we to conclude from these results that the child "in reality" is mentally fit at 4 years of age to learn to read and write and is only prevented by the procrastination of the ordinary instruction as a rule from taking advantage of his capabilities that are craving for occupation. I do not think so and consider that Martha Muchow's idea (IV) is very illuminating when she declares that it is the paucity of other games in the Montessori schools which makes the children take to this new occupation. In the Froebel kindergartens with their incomparably greater variety of occupations to exercise the child's powers of intuition and imagination, his interest and independence, as a general rule, scarcely any instances of liking for reading and writing exercises are to be observed.

(b) Our own opinion receives indirect confirmation by those occasional instances where reading and writing are learnt as the result of a real *spontaneous interest* in a young child without any didactic influences. For here the attainment of the facility generally follows quite other lines.

For instance in the case of especially keen and intelligent children it is often reported that their open eyes, eager to grasp everything, begin at last to notice writing especially when it is very striking. Names of streets, advertisements, notices of the electric tramways, headings in newspapers and announcements arouse the children's interest to such a degree that they ask their meaning, the names of the letters and of the separate words, etc. In this way at last a mental impression is made which is principally confined to printed capitals; the simple and distinctive forms of these letters make this preference intelligible. The same is true of numerals. These forms soon begin to make their appearance in the children's spontaneous drawings, often much deformed and above all in absolute defiance of their right position. It is true that real writing is only accomplished when the meaning of letters and their combinations is understood as sounds and words, i.e. when the child grasps that it can not only represent objects graphically but also express them by written speech. The discovery of the script symbolism, that "every sound has a script image", is like that earlier discovery—already mentioned—which unveiled for the child the symbolic significance of sound forms, i.e. that everything has a name.

This discovery is plainly revealed in the following example which was told me by a reliable witness. My informant's son (4 ; 3) had learnt the names of some large printed letters from advertisements and the names of streets. One day after a visit to the lavatory he came into his father's room and said: "I'll just write down for you what I've been doing", and drew on the paper a printed A—the sound he always uses in this connection.[1]

Of special interest is another case—unusual, it is true—in which a boy in his sixth year, the son of a university professor, makes use of the printed letters which he has learnt by his own

[1] We noticed a peculiar transition (border line) instance in Gunther (4 ; 10½). The boy, who had already acquired the simpler ideas of number but could not yet write figures, was listening as Hilde and her mother were doing arithmetic. Then he asked: *Can nought be drawn* (= written)?—*I expect it can't.* Mother: "Why not, then?" *Nought is nothing at all, isn't it?* Evidently then he still thought that it was only possible to write a name for things that could be graphically reproduced; he had not yet grasped the fact that every word—independently of its meaning—is capable of reproduction in writing.

unaided efforts to write with the utmost zeal (above all letters) and when doing so invents a peculiar but illuminating orthography (also self-taught). There was no possibility of help or correction from those about him, for the boy had no brothers or sisters older than himself.

His writings show the following peculiarities:—

1. He begins to write at the lower edge of the paper; the other lines are put in the same way above the first.

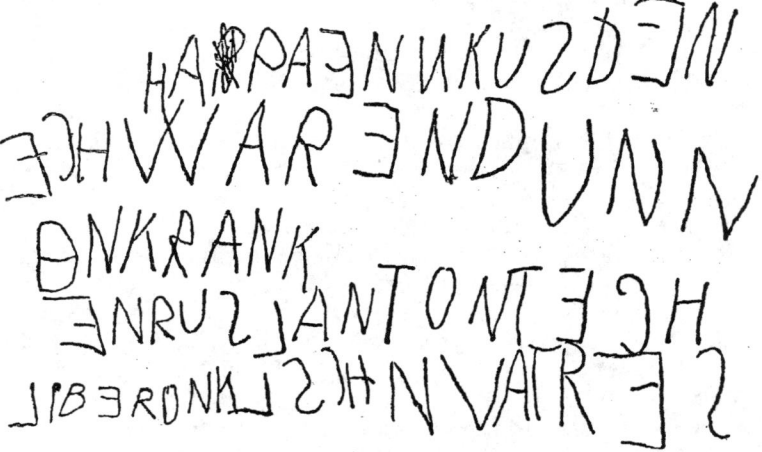

LIBER ONKL SCHN VATR ES EN RUSLANT
ONT ECH BN KRANK
ECH WAR EN DUNN HAP AENN HUSDEN

English translation = Dear Uncle Stern, Father is in Russia and I am ill
I was in Duhn, have a cough.

2. There are no divisions between the words.

3. The orthography is in part purely phonetic: SCHPIL = *Spiel*. Often the diffuse nature of sound-perception in early childhood is apparent, especially in the short vowels which seem to be most often confused; I, U, Ü, are identified with e, o, ö, throughout; ECH = *ich* (I), ONT = *und* (and), MOTA = *Mutter* (mother).

4. The letters are not used according to the sound they repre-

sent but for the sound of their respective names, familiar to him.

Thus the symbols R, H, N, B represent the combinations er, ha, en, be (pron. bay) as for example:—

VATR = Vat-er (father),
AENN = ein-en (a)
DUNN = Duhn name of a seaside resort
HP   = ha-b (have).

5. A number of letters are uniformly written in mirror (reflected) writing as e, s, c, l, many occasionally as n.

The following specimen, part of a letter to me (SCHN = Stern) gives examples of all the above-named characteristics; thus we must begin to read from the bottom left-hand corner. We have added an "interpretation" of the text in its proper sequence and with division of the words but without alteration of the lettering.

CHAPTER XI

TESTS AND MEASUREMENT OF POWER OF SPEECH

HITHERTO almost all research into children's speech has adopted the method of observation of children learning to talk, and only used experiment as an occasional expedient. But lately Alice Descoeudres in Geneva has made a noteworthy attempt to subject children of kindergarten age to an independent and systematic test as regards their power of language. And in so doing she had in view the same object as A. Binet in his test of general intelligence; first of all to find a normal standard of capability for each age (at intervals of six months), i.e. the power of satisfying the language tests shown by at least 75 per cent. of the children of the age under examination; then also an individual standard can be ascertained for every child tested by this method, i.e. the age can be given to which his power of language corresponds. For example, if a five-year-old child can only satisfy tests set normally for children of three and a half, then, in spite of his actual five years, he has in speech only reached three and a half years, and therefore is one and a half years behind.

After many preliminary examinations with extensive series of tests, A. Descoeudres at last settled upon a selection of nine especially characteristic groups of exercises. This series was "gauged" by means of 300 Geneva children aged from two and a half to seven years, i.e. it was ascertained for every six months what exercises were done correctly by 75 per cent. of the children.

The nine groups are in some ways similar to Binet's.

I. Children asked to name 20 opposites in objects and pictures shown to them. Each time two objects (or pictures) having opposite attributes are shown to them; e.g. a new and an old steel pen, a large and a small mushroom, a thick and a thin piece of cloth, and the examiner says to the child: "This mushroom is big, and that one is . . .?" The child has to find the opposite adjective himself.

II. To fill in missing words in ten very easy omissions.

III. Repetition of numbers said to them.

IV. To name six callings in answer to such questions as: "Who sells bread?" etc.

V. To name six materials: "What are keys made of?" "Tables?" "Shoes?" etc.

VI. Eight opposites from memory. "If your soup is not warm, then it is . . .?"

VII. To name ten colours.

VIII. To find twelve verbs. The child has to name actions performed either by the examiner alone—cough, sing, breathe deeply—or some in which the child has to imitate him: write, get up, jump.

IX. To give a list of twenty-five words of increasing difficulty (from house, ship, umbrella . . . to balustrade, hill, fog). It must be found out by the easiest possible questions whether the child knows the meaning of the words.

In fixing the normal standard, A. Descoeudres distinguishes between children of the working and upper classes. The social difference of power of language shown in this way is very instructive.

To solve all the exercises correctly would require 103 right answers. As a matter of fact, the different ages on an average gave the following number of correct replies:—

Ages	2½	3	3½	4	4½	5	5½	6	6½	7	7½
Educated classes	13	20	30	38	46	51	61	67	75	81	90
Working class	5	12	22	29	41	45	51	57	64	70	76
Collectively	8	19	26	34	44	48	56	62	70	76	83

The table shows that the number of correct answers increases with surprising regularity every six months, and that too in both classes of children. The average difference between the two classes at the same age is nine answers, roughly, then, 9 per cent. of the total answers. The average difference between the consecutive age stages in the same class is 7·4 answers, roughly 7 per cent. of the total answers. Hence the difference of the two classes corresponds on an average to a difference in age of eight months; or to put it in another way: the standard in language of a child of the working classes is approximately equal to that reached by a higher class child eight months younger. This calculation (which was not given by A. Descoeudres herself, but deduced by me from her figures) provides us for the first time with an exact finding of the degree of inferiority in language in the children of the proletariat.

Amongst the two-and-half-year-old children, the superiority of the educated class is fairly equally shown in all exercises, whilst for the ages three to four and half years it is principally the simpler tests, "callings," "materials," "colours" (these up to five years), and "omitted words" which show especially striking differences in the two classes; later on the results of these easier tests are more equal. On the other hand, amongst the six- and seven-year-old children the chief differences are in the more difficult tests; only a few of the working-class children can manage to satisfy the requirements of the test-group: "opposite attributes of the object" and list of words.

We cannot at present answer the very interesting question as to the origin of this social difference in the development of language. We do not know whether it must be entirely attributed to the unfavourable language influences in the working-class child's environment, or whether we ought to infer a naturally slower rate of development in children of the less educated classes. (Cf. W. Stern, "Intelligence," Chap. XI.)

The following example will show how A. Descoeudres calculates the individual age of any child as regards language:—

Boy Z. Age 5 ; 4. Position: Educated Class.

In every test the boy is compared with the normal standard of children of the same social class. In Test I (opposite attributes in objects) his results reached the level of children aged 5 ; 8; in Test IX (list of words) the level of children aged 6 ; 3, etc.

In Test	I reaches the standard of		5 ; 6
,,	II	,, ,,	3 ; 6
,,	III	,, ,,	6 ; 6
,,	IV	,, ,,	5 ; 6
,,	V	,, ,,	5 ; 6
,,	VI	,, ,,	5 ; 6
,,	VII	,, ,,	6 ; 0
,,	VIII	,, ,,	6 ; 0
,,	IX	,, ,,	6 ; 3

$$50 ; 3$$

$$\text{Average of all 9 tests} = \frac{50 ; 3}{9} = 5 ; 6$$

Thus his "language-age" of 5 ; 6 is two months in advance of his actual age.

It is very probable that this Descoeudres system of testing language is of definite practical use. First it enables us to ascertain a child's language-standard during kindergarten age and to devote special attention to any backwardness that may exist. Then, too, it gives confirmatory evidence as to fitness or unfitness in children about to go to school; for a certain capability of understanding and expressing himself in speech is an indispensable condition of success at school. Lastly, the method, in its author's firm opinion, is adapted for testing the language deficiency of abnormal older children; thus she found in a deficient Mongolian child of eleven years the language age of 4 ; 4.

But, on the other hand, we must not over-estimate its value, for, to begin with, it has the fundamental failing found in every measurement of psychic development; the great variety of qualitative phenomena is represented by a bald numerical statement which might give the impression that speech-development consisted entirely in differences of degree. Thus a number giving a child's language age, and obtained as the result of a half-hour's test, is never a real substitute for the full picture that is afforded by minute observation of the child; it only gives us a first preliminary idea of the approximate stage of development already attained.

Psychologically, the exercise system is not absolutely simple of interpretation, since power of language and the admixture with it of intelligence cannot be clearly distinguished. As a method it has the drawback of being one-sided, in that it is principally an inquiry into extent of vocabulary, whilst other no less important factors, such as phonetic, grammatical and syntactical development, are not tested.

It is therefore not advisable to adopt Alice Descoeudres' system of examination in its present form, but it may well be utilized as a suggestion and starting-point for similar systematic tests of speech-development in other places.[1]

The standard of speech-development reached in different social grades has very recently been tested by a careful inventory of 65 children of the Vienna *Kinderübernahmestelle* by

---

[1] Cf. with this my critical discussion of this method in Stern, IX . . ., some passages of which have been literally transcribed in the treatment above.

H. Hetzer and B. Reindorf. This showed that with regard to the very first, purely instinctive utterances, there were no differences between the social classes, but that these occur as soon as real speech begins. The children of the "uncared-for" classes when compared with those of the "cared-for" homes fell behind to the extent shown below.

Appearance of desire-words	6	months later
Appearance of naming words	3	,,
Use of different kinds of words	6	,,
Transition to inflected speech	4	,,
Transition to sentences of two or more words	4	,,
Extent of vocabulary	9 to 12	,,

PART IV

LOOKING AT PICTURES

CHAPTER XII

DETAILED CONSIDERATION OF LOOKING AT PICTURES

As we have already seen, the apprehension of the world perceptible by the senses makes very distinct growth even during the first year of life, but the period following brings with it great progress in sight-perception. A description of this progress in full detail would far exceed our present limits; we must content ourselves with such treatment as will show us some of the most essential features of the child's sight-perception.

For this purpose we select the child's relation to pictorial presentation. Looking at pictures plays indeed a very privileged part in early years. At the same time pictures offer the advantage, in case of need, of providing material for testing experimentally sight-perception; they can be shown in any order and in conjunction with definite questions and exercises; their presentation can be repeated at different ages or with different children for the purpose of comparison; or, lastly, simple representations can be drawn to order in the child's presence.

And also from a purely psychological point of view the picture occupies an interesting special rôle in the child's psychic development; it is almost, if not entirely, independent of sensory-motor activity.

To realize this fully we must remember that we found an almost despotic dominance of the combined sensory-motor action in the earliest development of perception, and that feature, which was so conspicuous in the very earliest period, is still dominant in the following years. It is this alone that gives the child of three to five years psychic possession of most perceptions, so that he is able to transform these perceptions into movement and independent action. The impression on the eye of events, on the ear of noises and speech, finds immediate expression in imitations of sound, mimicry, form; each new object is not only looked at, but seized, pulled to bits, subjected to all kinds of manipulation; and whatever arouses the child's attentive interest reappears at once in his play as a result of motor-activity.

Thus, then, purely sensorial "looking" as an independent psychological function is by no means so universally important in early childhood as is generally supposed; it is usually only of still indefinite power in the child's sight-perception as a whole. The quiet contemplation, which merely looks for looking's sake, is a condition of only very gradual growth.

Pictures, indeed, have the peculiarity of giving a direct idea of active life without setting in motion any active response. With real actual things the child can meddle and play, take hold of them, and change their shape; but those apparent things in pictures are only to be looked at, and can scarcely be treated otherwise than receptively. The great joy the child takes at the beginning of the second year in pictures is indeed a proof how, in addition to sensory-motor activity, the first beginnings of a higher form of activity—the contemplative—are showing signs of life; the immediate transmutation of sight-perception into movement is checked, and what has been seen can be subjected to mental consideration. Thus it is very significant that not only acquirement of speech and the upright position but looking at pictures should, at the beginning of the second year, appear as specifically human actions, fundamentally beyond the powers of the lower animals.

And yet the tendency to sensory-motor action still appears again from time to time in the child's consideration of pictures, more especially in the earliest stages. Not only does the child point at once to everything he sees before his eyes, and want to take up the picture in his own hand as well as to turn over the pages, but there is also a motor response to the contents of the picture. Above all, the turning of sight-perception into speech is entirely a matter of course to the child; silent looking is quite the exception. But also the picture sometimes, especially when it represents some vigorous action, impels the child to immediate imitation of the movement; occasionally, too, the purely pictorial nature of the picture is quite overlooked, and some handling attempted which would only be possible with actual things, and in this case is exceedingly comical. Some examples of this:—

IMITATIONS OF MOVEMENTS IN THE PICTURES.

These are at first no doubt of the nature of an unconscious reflex, as when Hilde (1 ; 7) sees in a picture a beggar holding up his arms, and stretches her own up as well; or when (1 ; 10) she sees the representation of birds' claws (in a book of drawing copies) and makes clawing movements with her own hands. But later the imitations are entirely conscious. Hilde (2 ; 10) sees a picture of kitchen utensils, and at sight of the carpet-beater she says: *What a great, big beater, it beats like this* (beats on the table); as she sees the grater: *getta does so* (rubbing on her frock). At 3 ; 0, when looking at Struwelpeter she imitates Hans-Head-in-Air by running a few steps with her head thrown up, and then bump and down she goes. The thumb-sucker is copied as well.

REALISTIC TREATMENT OF THINGS IN PICTURES.

Eva (2 ; 1) sees a large Madonna picture, thinks the naked babe ought to be dressed, and asks for a vest, which she earnestly begs should be put on the child. Miss Shinn's niece (2 ; 0) saw a picture that excited her sympathy: an eagle pouncing upon a chamois kid. Suddenly she put her little hand on the picture as if she wanted to form some defence between attacker and attacked; the same child (3 ; 0) saw, in a picture, a lamb caught in a thicket, and instinctively she tried to pull away the clinging thorny branch.

Nevertheless, on the whole, these motor-reactions become by degrees so much less apparent that, in the looking at pictures and in that alone, we can follow with comparative clearness the growth of sight-perception.

If we analyse this looking at pictures, we find it consists of three groups of factors, the sensory, reproductive and intellectual. It has its foundation in the optical impressions directly caused by the picture, but these are at once supplemented by the fragmentary memories of former impressions, and at the same time an intellectual process of treatment takes place on the shape of emphasis, neglect, combination and separation of the component parts, of classification of what is seen into certain categories, of interpretation and further development. But the separation of these factors only exists in theory and for psychological analysis;[1] for the child himself the picture-

[1] This must be borne in mind in order to appraise the following analyses at their true value.

experience is—in spite of the different nature of the constituent factors—a distinctly simple form of consciousness. For the young child has not yet reached the stage of being able to distinguish clearly between what he "actually" sees in the picture and what he fancies in it; the opposition between perception and imagination has not yet reached clear differentiation in the impression which to the child is an entirely simple whole.[1]

[1] E. Jaensch has recently voiced a similar opinion, viz. that the original cells of an idea of the outside world are pictures in which perception and imagination are inextricably mingled and from which only further development can differentiate on the one hand actual perceptions and on the other pure imaginations. Cf. also Chap. XVII, 2, of this book.

CHAPTER XIII

RECOGNITION OF PICTURES OF SINGLE OBJECTS

1. The Necessary Optical Conditions[1]

EVEN the child of nine months looks at an animal picture-book with keen interest or turns over an illustrated catalogue, and, with its scanty vocabulary, can already name many of the pictures correctly. This power of recognition is remarkable for this reason, that, looked at from an optical point of view, the pictures are in no way actual copies of the things represented. They are only flat, the objects mostly solid; the pictures either have no colours or those not corresponding with the object; they are motionless, and, as a rule, many times smaller than the things depicted. Yet the picture as a whole must make an impression which has an unmistakable likeness to that made by the object itself. Hence the question arises, on what features of the sense-impression does then this power of identification between picture and object depend?

(*a*) THE OUTLINE.

Observations tend more and more to prove that originally the recognition of pictures depends almost entirely or quite on the outline. And this is not always required in its entirety, recognition being called forth rather by a small portion of the outline, provided this includes the configuration that, in the child's opinion, is the characteristic distinguishing mark of the object. Strangely enough, these are by no means always the form-elements which would be considered as essential from a grown-up point of view. This attitude of the child can be supported by little experiments.

By the correlative method the child is shown numerous pictures of objects connected in some way (e.g. animals in an animal picture book). The child tries to name them, but, as a result of his weak differentiation in perception of his very scanty vocabulary, he has to make a few names suffice for the large number of pictures. Of course, in this case, every picture is correlated to that object with which it has the most similarity, according to the child's apperception.

[1] Supplemented by extracts from my treatise, *Development of Spatial Perception*, Part II.

We tried this method on Hilde (1 ; 7) with a natural history book. Some examples of correlation: a human skeleton and skull were called *Unkie* (uncle); the entire absence of surface-padding in contrast to her ordinary impressions of human beings, therefore, did not prevent her from a recognition for which she could have had absolutely no grounds but the outline as a whole.

Pussy was her name for the pictures, amongst others, of a bat and eagle-owl—in this case the decisive factors were the pointed, up-standing ears; *goos-goos* (goose) was applied, not only to the golden-crested wren, sparrow and ostrich, but also to the camel. Apparently, then, the rounded back, out-stretched neck, and the longish, somewhat pointed head formed the characteristic line for her apperception.

The *"formation"* method shows the minimum of outline required for recognition, as a sketch is made before the child's eyes, and stopped the moment the child gives the drawing a name. The drawings in Plate I were produced in this way in a test of our daughter (1 ; 10). It is astonishing how little is required before the lines take on a familiar shape for the child. The barely suggestive animal-heads, the few lines necessary for recognition of shoe, stocking, little frock, the "children" drawn in a frame, who needed neither complete limbs nor features for recognition, are striking examples of the truth of this statement.

The same attempt at the same age with our other children gave like results. Eva (1 ; 11) when the drawing had reached these three lines ⊓ at once exclaimed *chair*.

(b) FILLING IN OF SURFACE DETAILS.

This surface filling-in seems to take the second place as a means of recognition, far less important than outline, but early beginning to be helpful, and increasingly so as the child grows older. Thus, the circular outline of an isolated head-drawing is not recognized as a face until life is put into it by four lines representing eyes, nose and mouth. An article of clothing requires the addition of buttons for recognition. Similarly, quite early, a beard is considered the distinguishing mark of the male sex. Something similar is shown in Plate I, Fig. 16. When only the outline was drawn, it was named a house; but no sooner were the four key strokes added than it was recognized as a piano (*lala*).

But, in addition to the effects of these broader, more striking details, there are some cases where the delicate individual shading of the surfaces is the prime factor of recognition, such cases thus seeming to overstep the limits ordinarily assigned to children's capabilities. We speak here of the recognition of photographs, sometimes occurring at a remarkably early age.

Miss Shinn's niece (1 ; 1) recognized her father in a small photograph of a group of nine people. Our daughter Hilde (1 ; 3½) pointed out on a cabinet photograph she had never seen before her parents as *papa* (although her usual term for men in pictures was *uncle*). Both children, at the time, had only just a few weeks before reached the stage of recognizing pictures at all.

This early accomplishment can only be explained by the fact that here the recognition is of someone whom the child knows very intimately. The innumerable times the parents have been seen must impress the memory-concept with many more details than is possible with objects brought to the child's notice only occasionally or in varying degrees of similarity. Thus only is it possible that the distinctive features of the picture, especially the more delicate shading of the face in these cases, set free results of that more individual recognition which in normal cases lies quite below the surface of the child's attention or interest; for, as a fact, the normal condition in the second year is that pictures only act as rough images calling forth response from the few rough outlines of the child's *schematic concepts*.

This primitive satisfaction with the general impression has the remarkable result that many drawings, recognized at a very early age, later on are not. The child has grown harder to satisfy, more critical; e.g. just because Hilde's idea of a bottle had become more distinct with time, she could not recognize two and a half years later Plate I, Fig. 12, which at (1 ; 10) she had at once called *a bottle*.

(c) COLOUR.

The part that colour plays in the child's sight-perception and recognition is very peculiar and apparently contradictory.

That the child very soon recognizes colour in things is as

certain a fact as that colour awakens the keenest joy in him
This preference for all that is gay, gaudy, filled with colour continues indeed to later stages of childhood. The legend, occasionally heard, that children are, at first, colour-blind is to be
explained by the late appearance of the right names for colours
in children's speech. After the colour-names make their first
appearance in the third year, they are used in the strangest
confusion, until, as a rule in the course of the fourth year, the
child comes to their right application. So we are face to face
with an apparent contradiction: in spite of the strong emotional response to colours, they play no fundamental part in
the recognition and differentiation of things, nor in the child's
practical dealings with them, nor do they give him any familiarity with his surroundings. Whether a ball be green or red,
it serves the same purpose, and is exactly the same to the
sense of touch, which after all is the prime arbiter for conscious reality; the purely optical difference of colour has no
other effect but colour alone.[1] And it is just the same with a
blue or white cap, a red or yellow rose. If we only consider
how quite other is the part played by difference of form, we
shall understand that distinctions of colour, as being less
important in life, can only be of significance mentally at a
very much later stage. (At the same time, the comparative
detachment of colour from practical necessities of life no doubt
is the cause of its being an object specially adapted for the
beginnings of æsthetic development—but more of that later.)
The looking at pictures shows these points very clearly. In spite
of the joy that the child has in gay pictures, recognition in the
early years is not aided by colour, and in nowise disturbed
by wrong colours or entire lack of them. It looks as if the
importance of colour for the act of picture-recognition lay
quite below the surface of consciousness. Thus the black and
white pictures in catalogues and newspapers, photographs, etc.,
are just as well identified as those in the picture-book's gay
pages.

Hilde (1 ; 3) recognized her parents in a cabinet photograph and named a cock's black silhouette at once *cocky*.
(1 ; 6) Figures of animals which were cut out—a red dog, a
green cock, and a blue cat—and stuck on white cardboard

---

[1] Cf. with this the treatment in Chap. XXIX. 1 of experiments on abstraction
of forms and colours.

she named without any hesitation, nor did she in the least give us the impression of having noticed, for one moment, the impossible colours.

(d) SIZE.

Neither does the absolute size of the pictures—often in no sort of relation to the things themselves—seem to offer any real difficulty in recognition. Thus the tiny and only slightly suggestive drawings in Fig. 1, Plate I, Hilde at once called *children*. This independence of ABSOLUTE size is explained by the fact that even actual things vary in apparent size with distance from the eye, hence the child has learnt to identify images on the retina varying in size, if only form-conditions remain unchanged.

On the other hand, there is a surprising keenness of eye for RELATIVE sizes.

Hilde (1 ; 9) had wooden blocks painted with scenes from everyday life. She at once knew from their relative sizes whether the human figures were meant to represent adults, children or dolls. At 3 ; 6 when she could compare the pictures in her book with the animals in the Zoological Garden, it did not disturb her that the ostrich in the picture was only a few centimetres in height, but it did trouble her that his picture was no larger than the other birds standing near, and she said: *"Is that the ostrich bird? But isn't he bigger?"* And since, in her animal book, the armadillo was drawn about as large as the wild cat she could never get over the small size of the real armadillo in the Zoological Garden.

(e) POSITION OF PICTURES.

Whilst recognition of pictures continues in all later development to be independent of colour and size, there is one remarkable capability which the little child possesses in far higher degree than do older children or adults, viz. independence of the position of the picture. It has often been observed that it seems to make little difference to small children whether a picture is put before them right way up or upside down. If a mother shows a book to several brothers and sisters at once, it frequently happens that the children crowd round the table, so that some see the picture either sideways or wrong way up; but that seems scarcely to interfere either with their understanding or enjoyment of it.

Gunther ($1 ; 7\frac{1}{2}$). "He looks at pictures with great delight as he lies face downwards turning over the pages. It is all the same to him if the pictures are upside down—he calls a horse in that position *gee-gee* just as he does one the right way up."

Something similar occurs in a child of double the age.

Eva ($3 ; 5$). "The many cards of a picture lotto were put before her upside down, and she at once recognized the little pictures (she was of course very familiar with them from frequent games). If they were put into her hand, she turned every one the right way up before naming it. Then we showed her the cards also upside down belonging to the game, each of which contains eight pictures, and all of these too she named. When we asked: 'Are then the pictures right like that?' she answered without thinking: '*Yes.*' We again asked: 'Does a carriage then have its wheels at the top?'

"Eva: '*O where then, here is the top,*' pointing to the top of the carriage, which as the picture then lay was at the bottom. The relation of the different parts to one another was therefore as plain and natural to her when seen upside down as in the upright picture."

The older the child, the less of this indifference to the position of the picture; and in any case it varies very much with individuals, for there are children in whom it has not been observed at all.[1]

The recognition and production of pictures "upside down" is only made clear when we remember that, to begin with, the idea of form and the idea of position (i.e. of its relation to the spectator) are two distinct psychic functions, the second of which is only developed by a somewhat slow process of learning.

The importance of this fact as regards general psychology is by no means small, but cannot here be discussed in detail.[2]

(f) PERSPECTIVE.

The most complicated feature of pictures is perspective, by which the three dimensions of solid bodies are represented

[1] A feature—connected with this fact—of children's drawing will appear in our discussion of that subject.

[2] Cf. my essay, *Verlagerte Raumformer*. Re very interesting similar phenomena in the chimpanzee. Cf. Kohler, p. 128.

on the two dimensions of a surface. The correct representation of perspective is recognized as one of the latest achievements of the individual, as of the race; therefore it is to be expected that the perspective features—the shortening and diminishing in the distance, the acute instead of right angles, the foreshortening and hiding—offer special difficulties in the recognition of pictures. And that indeed is the case so far as the perspective composition of a larger pictorial representation (e.g. a landscape) is concerned. On the other hand, the child recognizes the perspective presentation of separate objects sooner than one would think.

Thus on Plate I, Figs. 13–16, which were in perspective, were recognized by Hilde (1 ; 10) and by our other children who saw them at two years of age.

The explanation of this must be found in the perception of real plastic objects (not their pictorial presentations). These, too, show in the retina-image perspective foreshortenings and angle alterations, and are recognized in spite of these; indeed, these alterations as such entirely escape notice. I see a plate as circular, even if I do not look at it perpendicularly from above; a table as right-angled, although its image on the retina, in accordance with the laws of perspective, must contain acute and obtuse angles. Only the highly differentiated perception of the artistically trained eye or a quite unusual position of the object, with regard to the eye, causes recognition of the altered form (an ellipse for the plate, a rhombus for the surface of the table).

But for simple perception under ordinary circumstances, it is a fact that, in spite of all perspective alterations in the retina-image, the object is seen in its "real" shape. And then the corresponding structural law of the perception can be transferred to the perspective pictorial representation as well, and the "real" shape be seen in the acute angles and foreshortening of a table.[1]

---

[1] This phenomenon is designated by Bühler as "Preponderance of Orthoscopic Forms", I. p. 157, by Koffka as the law of "Constancy of Form". We cannot dwell here upon the great theoretical significance, rightly emphasized by both; of one point only a short mention may be made. Koffka looks upon this constancy of form (independent of the retina-image) as a last Conformity with the law of visual perception, just as he did the constancy in size mentioned earlier, p. 95. But here, as there, we must remember that the purely optical form does not exist independently, but that rather structure ideas due to tactual-motor action are operative in the whole perception of a

This transference is doubtless made easier to children at our stage of civilization by the fact that the child is very early accustomed to the general perspective representation of modern pictorial art, for even the simplest picture-books have this feature now. Since all the objects drawn in this way are named to the child with the familiar expressions, he gets practice in identifying them in spite of this difference. We see here a case of premature development brought about by definite conditions of environment. Children of another stage of culture—say the Mahommedan—that knows, as a rule, only surface art, will doubtless come very much later to the recognition of perspective drawings.[1]

2. Comparative Tests as to the Recognition of Pictures

The child's power of recognition of pictorial presentations has often been tested by examination of considerable numbers; tests have been framed that make it possible to obtain an exact comparison of the powers of different ages, sexes and social grades. Some of these experiments extend beyond the sixth year; we are chiefly interested in the results for the younger ages.

The child's power can be tested experimentally in three directions: the recognition, distinction and classification of pictures. By recognition is understood the seeing in a picture not lines drawn at random, but an intelligible objective form; by distinction the pointing out in two pictures the differing elements; by classification the identification of a given picture

---

plastic object. Now these are always "real", the table surface as experienced by the sense of touch always offers to the perception angles of the same size, not with the varying degrees required by perspective. And this, so it appears to me, is what gives to the final perceptual form—and also to its optical factors—that quality of constancy of form. But if this has once been learnt, it can persist even when only the optical impression occurs, without therefore any help at the moment from tactual-motor action. Thus, then, a table which I cannot touch, and ultimately the perspective drawing of a table, is orthoscopically seen by me. In opposition to Koffka, then, I believe that purely optical constancy of form cannot exist without empiric help. Katz also gives a similar explanation founded on his experiments in copying solid objects and perspective drawings. (Cf. Chapter XXVI. 3).
[1] A sign of the difficulty in recognition which normally exists is to be seen in the attitude of primitive peoples to our modern pictures; they easily recognize outlines and surface details, whilst as a rule entirely misinterpreting perspective features.

with another in a series of similar pictures. The first two functions are tested by the Heilbronn Series, the third by the Geneva-Lotto method.

(a) THE HEILBRONN SERIES METHOD.

This method was originally designed by the psychic enquirer Heilbronner for psychiatric purposes; it was first used to test the normal little child by Van der Torren (Utrecht), and later in perfected form by Schober (Hamburg).

Simple outline pictures of any object, e.g. a church, are shown in successive stages of completion, viz., first, Plate II, Fig. *a*, then *b*, *c*, etc.; when a fresh picture comes, the preceding one is covered up, and at each picture the child is asked: "What is that?" thus testing at what stage of completion recognition follows. In addition with pictures 2, 3, etc., the question is put: "What has been changed?" and the child must then show or say what new lines have been added in comparison with the picture he has just seen. And thus capacity of discrimination is tested.

Van der Torren has with 17 series of pictures (a total of 103 separate pictures) tested 10 boys and 10 girls of several different ages. Frau and Herr Schober with 16 series, nearly all new (90 separate pictures), tested 6 boys and 6 girls at 5 different ages.[1]

The chief numerical results for the ages 4–8 years are tabulated below. They show what percentage was reached in recognition of the pictures shown and of correct answers as to the differences in two consecutive pictures.

Age in Years.	Van der Torren.				Schober.			
	Recognition of Picture.		Notice of Difference.		Recognition of Picture.		Notice of Difference.	
	Boys. %	Girls. %	Boys. %	Girls. %	Boys. %	Girls. %	Boys. %	Girls. %
4	37	20	89	—	52	37	36	35
5	33	24	89	91	56	55	49	57
6	47	33	95	92	69	61	72	60
7	53	37	96	93	70	62	82	76
8	55	35	97	95	78	76	88	82

[1] A selection of both series of pictures has been published for sale. To be obtained through Dr. Otto Bobertag, Zentralinstitut f. Erziehung u. Unterricht, Potsdamer Strasse 120, Berlin W.

The power of recognition now shows, as is to be expected, a considerable increase with age, with only two exceptions in Torren's tests, and none at all in Schober's. Thus with Schober the four-year-old boys had 52 per cent. of success, i.e. on an average they did not recognize the object represented until the first half of the series had been shown them; whilst the eight-year-old boys recognized the object after the first quarter of the series, that is, then, at a much less complete presentation (78 per cent. of success). A common feature of both tests (in T.'s very strongly marked) is the inferiority of the girls' performances.

On the other hand, there is a great difference in the two tests as to the absolute power of recognition shown at all ages and by both sexes. Still, it would be the greatest mistake to infer from this that German children are mentally superior to Dutch children. The reason is much more probably to be found in the fact that the pictures in the older test were less suitable; many series in it began with such utterly fragmentary suggestions that even adults were sometimes unable to guess what was meant.[1]

We note with surprise the disagreement between the two tests as to the children's power of distinction. T. found throughout such a high grade of success that age and sex differences almost disappeared. Even the four- and five-year-old children have in 90 per cent. of cases been able to show the additional lines in consecutive pictures. Schober, on the other hand, found the little children's power of distinction very small; it then markedly increased, but never reached that high degree shown by T.'s tests.

What is the cause of this? As long as we only had T.'s results, we might think that, as a general rule, the child finds it easier to recognize little differences in detail rather than the representation of the form as a whole.[2] But Schober now proves that this is not the case, but that the mutual relation of the powers shown must rather depend on the character of the pictures used in the tests. Indeed, we may conclude that exactly an opposite relation of the powers exists, especially in the earlier years. *Here the more recognition is directed to the*

---

[1] This failing is avoided by Schober, whose series always begin with the complete outline, which is then filled in by degrees.
[2] This was my own interpretation of the result in the first edition of this book.

grasp of the form as an intelligible whole, the less success is achieved in the observation of details in which two forms differ from each other.

For that reason in T.'s tests the four- and five-year-olds, just because they found the representations unintelligible for so long, paid more attention to the individual lines which were added in each picture. Only in later years do we find a different state of things; then recognition has become so easy that the attention can be turned as well to the separate elements of the picture.

Two further results remain to be mentioned. Van der Torren also counted the confabulations, i.e. the cases when, a picture not being really recognized, the name is given of some object which has no similarity or but a very vague suggestion with that represented. Such confabulations occurred more frequently with the girls (especially the younger ones) than with the boys, also with village rather than town children.

Frau and Herr Schober were able in their tests to differentiate between children of different social classes. The superiority of children of the more favoured classes over those of the proletariat on an average was as follows:—

	In Recognition of Pictures.	In Notice of Differences.
Boys	4 per cent.	14 per cent.
Girls	28 ,,	16 ,,

The great difference between boys and girls in "recognition" test is astonishing; perhaps the results of the working-class girls may have been especially affected by shyness. In any case, the social difference was most strongly marked amongst the younger children. Amongst the seven- and eight-year-old children the decreasing difficulty of the task, and probably too the influence of school, tended to make the results more equal.

(*b*) THE GENEVA-LOTTO METHOD.

The well-known principle of Picture-Lotto has been developed by Decroly, the Brussels mental specialist, and by the Jean Jacques Rousseau Institute in Geneva into certain educative games (*jeux éducatifs*) for abnormal and very young normal children. Alice Descoeudres then utilized these as tests of the powers of observation and distinction.[1]

The test of recognition and distinction is more difficult in lotto than in the picture groups described above. For the large lotto cards show a greater number of pictures, somewhat resembling one another, and a single small card has to be arranged on the same identical picture on the large card. The degree of difficulty is entirely determined by the points of detail in which the lotto pictures are alike or different.

Of the nine lottos used by A. Descoeudres in her tests, mention is here made of five; in every case, results are given at half-yearly intervals.

The Colour and Form Lotto and the Colour and Lamp Lotto may be treated comparatively. In both cases the lotto cards contain sixteen variously coloured pictures, the first all of different objects (red church, yellow basket, grey engine, etc.), the second all of lamps (which therefore can only be distinguished by colour). The standard of efficiency is the length of time required to cover the sixteen pictures with the little cards.

This time naturally grows less with increase in age, and that very markedly and without exception. In the first lotto the age of 2 ; 6 requires on an average nearly five minutes, 4 ; 6 one and a half minutes, 6 ; o one minute; in the lamp-lotto the same ages require seven, two and a half, one and a third minutes.

The greater difficulty of the lamp-lotto is psychologically very interesting. Apparently the test is easier, for no attention need be paid to the form (since it is always identical), the only consideration being the colour. But again we see that the separate recognition of elementary colour-impressions is more difficult than the recognition of objects in which distinctions of colour and shape are combined.

The other lottos are intended as tests adapted to different ages, so that the number of mistakes is noted, not the time taken. The large cards each contain eight pictures, the small cards are put singly on these and at once removed by the experimenter, so that each time the child has to select the right one from all the eight lotto pictures. It is noted at what age 75 per cent. of all the children accomplish the test with

[1] *Développement*, pp. 206 sqq.

not more than three mistakes, and again at what age with not more than one; the test is then considered as rightly graded for these ages.

EXAMPLES.

(a) Lotto, "Child and Ball". Every picture shows a child playing at ball, but each 'time the child's frock and the ball are coloured differently (e.g. child blue, ball yellow; child green, ball red, etc.). The child tested gets separate little pictures in corresponding colours, and has to put these on the right divisions of the card. Allowing not more than one mistake, it was seen that only 28 per cent. of the four-year-old children, but 73 per cent. at 4 ; 3, were successful, so that $4\frac{1}{2}$ years was the age fixed for this test.

(b) Lotto, "A laid table".[1] Again eight pictures of a laid table, and on each table four objects but of varying kinds, e.g. on table 1: plate, spoon, pot and cup; on table 2: plate, glass, pot, spoon, and so on. The arrangement of the little cards is now very difficult, because the child's attention has to be extended to four things, and not be led astray by great similarity. Result: allowing three mistakes, children of six, allowing only one mistake, children of seven, were equal to the test.

(c) Lotto, "Bodily position".[2] Eight pictures again, each representing a man with different positions of the arms and legs. Result: If three faults are allowed, suitable for five-year-old children, but if only one is allowed, almost beyond the power of children of eight years.

[1] Revised drawing to be obtained from the Psychol. Labor. Domst. 9. Hamburg.
[2] See the figure in Plate II; in the form there represented the lotto has been used in the Hamburg Psychological Laboratory.
[3] See Chap. XXVI. 1.

CHAPTER XIV

THE RECOGNITION OF GROUP-PICTURES
(COMPOSITIONS)

THE ever-growing part played by the mental powers in looking at pictures is shown by manifold signs. The power of perception grows, not as a result of the development of sense-organs and sense-impressions, but as a result of the increase in recognition, differentiation and vocabulary, in the synthetic power of attention and in thought.

As soon as the child reaches this stage he is no longer content with pictures representing one object only. He becomes interested in pictures showing a considerable number of things and actions and their relations to one another; for when offered such abundance his mind can make its own choice and associations. This intellectual growth is very plainly shown when the same picture is shown to a child at considerable intervals.

1. Tests of the Development of Mental Grasp of the Group-Picture

In our consideration of this development we give short-hand notes of conversations which we had with Hilde on different occasions, when looking at a certain coloured picture-book; reproductions—much reduced and uncoloured—of two of these pictures, "A peasant's room" and "A town room", are shown on Plates III and IV. Psychological explanations follow later.

I ; 8½. In every picture shown we pointed to the different objects with the question: "What is that?" In the peasant's room, she named correctly the boy (*child*), bed and cradle (*bed*), clock (*didda*), peasant (*uncle*), doll (*child*), *dish*, flower-pot (*sissy*), *hepsi* (= flower), peasant woman's shoes (*fiesse* = shoes). On the other hand, the peasant woman was not picked out, and consequently not named, no doubt because, on the flat picture, her body cut across the bed; however often we pointed to her the answer *bed* came.

THE TOWN ROOM.

Correctly named were the following: girl at piano (*child*), the piano (*lala*), music-book (*book*), dog (*wow-wow*), the man (*uncle*), newspaper (*read*), two little children (*child*), the woman (*auntie*), sewing-machine (*rrr*), hanging-lamp (*lamp*); this last recognition is remarkable here, for the lamp is much less clearly outlined against the mirror behind it than the peasant woman (unrecognized) is against the bed.

Six months later: Hilde (2 ; 2).

PEASANT'S ROOM.

Flowers.	Hilde points to the flower-pot.
Tic-tac, dere.	Clock, there.
Pitty flowers.	She means the crucifix with twigs.
Child goes by-bye.	Sleeps.
Lie bed.	Sleeps in bed; she again means child in cradle.
Window.	Points to picture hanging by window—an error older children (7 years) have also made.
Window too.	Points to the real window.
She too.	Points to doll.
Auntie got shoe.	The peasant woman's shoes.
Child.	Points to boy.
Uncle off.	=Undressed (the peasant has taken off his coat).
Chair up dere.	Means the empty chair.
(*Come elephant see*)	Takes her rag elephant standing on the table and rolls him over the picture to look too.
Ittie wow-wow.	Dog.
Ittie fwock.	(Little frock) points to the woman's apron.
Child has flowers.	Points to painted flowers on cradle.
	(Lengthy pause.)
Child on it.	Points to boy on the stool.
Go by-bye.	Means the doll.
Child not neep-nap.	The baby is not sucking its finger.
	(Pause.)

Father: "There are many more pretty things there."

Water.	Points to jug.
Ittie bed, da, bed.	Points to bed.

(The child is tired now and her unprompted remarks come to an end, though several more answers are forthcoming to questions: "What is there besides on the table?")

Child plays sand.	The boy's spoon reminded her of her own for sand.

(What is the child doing?)
Bite, bite, eat, eat.

What is he eating?
Soup.

We finished the test as the child was tired.

Four and a half months later $(2 ; 6\frac{1}{2})$:—

At another consideration of the same pictures only a few points were remembered, and these we particularly noticed, as they show how mixed the consideration of a picture now is with interpretations, fanciful conclusions and references.

PEASANT'S ROOM.

Dere, a child sleeps, has no cover, handies in.	She misses the coverlet and envisages the invisible hands under the coverlet.
Jam all gone, all eaten.	Evidently thinks the child's plate has nothing on it, and concludes it has been emptied.
When child run again, will get up.	I.e. when the child wakes, it will leave the cradle.
Where is child's apron?	She asked this after she had just noticed the woman's apron.
Is dere nother chair, uncle's?	She had noticed the boy's stool but not the man's, as he is sitting on it and thus hiding it.
Here is auntie's.	With a logical deduction points to the empty chair.

THE TOWN ROOM.

Here is lala, dere child plays lala	= Piano.

(After remarks between about something else.)

See? child plays lala, sunfink sung, a birdie flies in, sit down on my foot.	Playing has turned into singing, no doubt because she noticed the music-book; her father the day before had sung her a little song with accompaniment.
Where is bed for auntie to sleep?	A reference to the peasant's room. Because the woman there has a bed in that room she misses a corresponding one for the town woman.
Here is a lamp too.	She means the hanging-lamp.
Where is big lamp, stands?	Reference to the table-lamp on other picture.

Three months later:—

Hilde (2 ; 10) was showing her doll the picture-book and earnestly explaining the different pictures to her. Of the town room she said:—

See, that sings rallala.	She pretends to play the piano in imitation of the girl sitting at it.
Here someone sits in chair, not looking any more.	Grandfather. She means at the book which the grandfather is holding closed in his hand.

(Mother asks: What has he done then?)

Finished—shuts up.

(Mother says: At the back there is a . . .?)

Nanny—no a mummy sewing a vest.	(*Nurse.*)
She does so—like Mummy!	Moves her feet as if working a sewing-machine.

Then at a much later period we have one more short note about the town room.

"Hilde (4 ; 2) perfectly understands the relationships of the persons in the picture, counts the children, asks why the mother has three when we have only two, considers whether the stork brought the two boys together in his beak, wonders greatly whether the two children's building will be allowed to remain standing, if, maybe, it would fall down, where the box for their blocks is, etc., etc."

2. Psychological Observations

We will now add to these examples a few explanatory and supplementary remarks.

A picture containing a large number of details is far beyond a child's powers in its second year. By far the greater part escapes the attention, either because the object does not stand out clearly enough from the background [the peasant woman for Hilde (1 ; 8½)], or because the child's eye, at one glance, can only take in quite a small portion of the whole picture. Only a little is recognized and named, and nearly all this only in answer to questions. The spontaneous action of the child is evidently still very slight. Hilde (1 ; 8½) succeeded in naming in each picture nine or ten objects, and these only as nouns in simplest or allied form. The child then is still in the "substance" stage (cf. Chapter XXVII. 2).

The interest in one picture and the attention bestowed on it weary very quickly and the child asks for other pictures. From other observations we notice that at this period too the strangest mistakes in recognition and understanding arise; a doll is perhaps taken for a living being, a fortress with a tower for a railway engine, a white cloud for a high mountain.

Yet the stage of such a sparse total does not last long. Barely six months after that first trial, and quite spontaneously, double the number of things are named and adorned with many a detail. But most striking is the complete mastery of the simple recognition of things; now too the motionless representations are interpreted as phases of definite actions. In Hilde (2 ; 2) the first beginnings of this are evident, and she not only mentions actions actually taking place, but those that are finished (the peasant has taken off his coat) or nonexistent (the child is *not* sucking its finger).

After four months more (2 ; 6½) this "action stage" has grown to full, almost despotic perfection. The simple naming of objects has to give way entirely to the intensity with which life is put into the picture, and, as a matter of course, the child, in royal manner, steps beyond the confines of the picture's actual contents; he reads into it what happened before and what will or may happen afterwards with exactly the same certainty as what is happening at the moment.

The dramatic interpretation of pictures is by no means only the result of association which supplements the original optical sensations by the addition of memory-reproductions; the reality of what is happening is unmistakably clear. The child seems to seek some compensation for the enforced repression of his own motor-activity whilst looking at books by putting the more intensive movement into the picture.

When Eva (2 ; 2) looked at a new picture-book practically everything was translated into action: *the cat is here, there she lies down on the ground; here is the trees waving about; she is dirty, the woman is; she has shut up. The stars fly over on to the earth; here is Gunther, he lifts on to his lap—ah the basket. Lamp, there, look, see—he walks on high mountain, here is a man, he slip* (slides on ice). *Mummy cries on the step —the boys bathe—O the horses! goes ride ride.*

Exactly similar is the description given by Elsa Köhler (p. 90) of the monologues and duologues of the two-and-a-half-year-old Annchen when looking at her picture-book: *there is a cloud, do you see? there's the sun hiding . . . there the ducks are taking a bath . . . a nice little hare it is! sitting and playing, reading out loud—no it isn't reading! it's jumping. . . .* (What is that?) *A hare walking nicely. . . .* [A shrew mouse sitting on its hind legs is spoken of to the child as a "mousie".] *Yes, a mousie, it says please, please. Little angels, they will give the birdies somefink.*

What we miss above all in the performances considered so far is the power of synthesis. The attention is still fixed on one thing only at a time, and some detail or action is assigned to it; the indiscriminate juxtaposition of these separate objects of attention gives the child no feeling of discomfort, and a relationship between several component parts of the pictures is only made in those isolated cases when they are brought into special prominence, as some connection between different elements of the picture, e.g. when the child at the piano plays to another.

But the decisive step is soon made. Attention learns to grasp several details with one glance, and the logical necessity is felt of establishing some positive coherence between these separate parts; indeed, at last, the consideration of their mutual relation may become stronger than that of the individual details themselves. When this happens the child has reached the "relative" stage of sight-perception. Again to a certain extent his interest oversteps the actual content of the picture, and he discusses most eagerly, not only the connection of the objects represented amongst themselves, but also their relations to certain imaginary causes and effects or to former pictures, etc. The last test we gave in connection with the "town room" shows that Hilde, at the beginning of her fifth year, was already well in this stage.

The construction of relations is, at first, by no means carried out in accordance with the objective rules of logic. The child is not so much concerned with the discovery of connections, which the picture is intended to show, and which are fixed too by outward signs, as with the more or less unrestrained invention of such as seem in accordance with the particular bent and direction of the child's fantasy allied to them. In this the child's egomorphism is particularly evident as he reads into the picture the special conditions of his own life and his narrow environment.

Thus Hilde has at various times given a true egomorphic interpretation of a large picture of the Sistine Madonna and Child (half-figure) as follows:—

(1 ; 9) She said of it: *Hilde, mama.*

(3 ; 3) She remarked: *That is a mama and a Hilde, look, she takes hold of her, the little Hilde, because she's going out in her carriage* (referring to the way the Madonna holds the child as a preliminary to going out).

(4 ; 7) After a similar statement, it was explained to her that it was not a picture of herself and her mother, but a "Madonna", and immediately she broke in with another peculiarly child-like question: *Is that a friend of ours?* evidently thinking "Madonna" was the name of one of the lady-friends who visited her mother from time to time.

It is only by degrees that the child, in its interpretations, learns to pay more regard to signs given in the picture, and from them to draw a synthetic conclusion of the picture as a coherent whole. Success in this task naturally depends on the difficulty of the picture.

In passing, we may mention a stumbling-block in the way of synthetic understanding to be found in many widely circulated picture-books, such as Struwelpeter, and also in single picture-sheets, viz. the representation of a continuous story by several separate pictures in which—if possible on the same side—the same persons appear in different positions.

Thus Hilde (3 ; o), in the Struwelpeter poem "Paulinchen was at home alone", was confused by the many Paulinchens, and thought one was the mother who had forbidden playing with fire. Later on she learnt to identify correctly these repeated representations of the same persons.

The difficulty of the task determines not only the time of the right conception of the picture as a whole, but also the period at which the child reaches the several different stages mentioned above.

The pictures of the peasant's and of the town room are comparatively easy, because they only represent a continuous state (not movement). But it is a different matter with pictures serving as illustrations of some dramatic happening. As a rule, indeed, the tale connected with them is either read or told to the children; but if they are expected to find the dramatic meaning of the picture by themselves, a task is imposed that cannot be accomplished in early childhood.

For such pictures Binet in his graded system for intelligence tests has fixed a scale, similar to our stages in sight-perception, but later in respect of age. It is true the scale refers to working-class children, and children of the higher class are far in advance as regards this very question of capacity in the understanding of pictures—the natural result of their much more intensive acquaintance with pictures and of the more stimulating mental atmosphere of the home. Binet therefore expects at 3 years, enumeration of the isolated parts (our substance-stage); at 7 years, description of activities (our action-stage); at 12 years, explanation of the whole (our relative-stage). Bobertag has established the following grades for German children of the same class with other pictures of a similar kind; at 3 years, enumeration; at 6, description; at 9, explanation by the help of suggestive questions; at 12, independent explanation. The intellectual factors in the consideration of pictures are indeed the explanation of the great pleasure and unwearying interest the child finds in this occupation. The child does not look upon the picture primarily as offering the representations it contains, but as the stimulus that sets in movement the activity of his thought and invention. His consideration and under-standing of the picture is a game—if not an active bodily, yet a mental game—with what is represented. We find here the same unconcern as to whether the component parts are actually given or are only creatures of imagination, the same naïve application to his own personal experiences, the same activity of attention and fantasy as in other play of early childhood. No other toy has the power of his picture-book to give with each successive moment new and ever-changing stimuli for this mental-play activity, since it sets up connections with the whole of the visible world, and in this way enormously widens the child's narrow horizon.

Yet one must not forget that the use of the picture, looked at as merely the centre of the encircling creations of his own active thought and fantasy, has its dark side. This by-activity may very seriously affect the power of real observation, and indeed entirely overwhelm it. Then the child either gets no real gain in visual-perception from the picture, or what his eye really saw and his fantasy created are inextricably blended in his memory—and the most pronounced errors in relation are the result (cf. Chapter XVII, Section 3).

How little under certain circumstances a child really "sees" when looking at a picture is made clear by the following:—

The peasant's room picture had been shown to Scupin's son (4 : 7), and as he looked, he asked numberless questions connected with it, most of them concerning the family relationships (of which he himself gave an egomorphic explanation) of the different persons appearing in it. After he had looked at the picture for two minutes, it was taken away to give opportunity for a test of his power of description. But it was an utter failure, for the boy had not the slightest idea of what the picture really contained. The parents' report runs:—

"His mother now asked the boy to tell what he had seen in the picture. Quite taken aback, he looked at her: 'But I don't know.' Then he was asked how many men there were in it, how many children, whether he had not seen a table, what was on it; but, utterly at a loss, he looked at his mother and seized the book to see the picture once again."

Since real forgetfulness could not possibly have occurred so quickly, this complete ignorance can only be explained by the fact that the child, as a consequence of his lively imaginings founded on the picture, had never really arrived at actual observation.

3. Educational Hints

Our psychological considerations furnish us with some suggestions as to the educational use of pictures in early childhood. They should serve a double purpose apart from the awakening of æsthetic delight[1] on the one hand for the training of the power of observation, on the other for the incitement and guidance of the intellectual processes accompanying this observation.

The usual teaching of little children, whether at home or in the kindergarten, is inclined to lay relatively far too much stress on the second aim—as does also the ordinary school in the teaching of sight-perception. There, pictures are especi-

[1] See Chap. XXVI. 1.

ally used as starting-points of narrative and instruction, and doubtless valuable educational results may be achieved in this way amongst children of five and six years of age, provided that everything pedantic is scrupulously avoided. The fairy stories can be made much more intelligible by pictures; by means of geographical and historical pictures much can be told of other lands and peoples, and we can supplement animal pictures by many a tale of the life and habits of animals; also the picture can be shown again later, and the child himself be asked to repeat the information given in connection with it and other things as well.

But if the picture is always dealt with in this way, encouragement is given to the tendency the child already possesses to hurry too quickly away from the details of the picture itself and pass to the making of further concepts. For this reason education in real contemplation of the picture must not be omitted. The child should be encouraged first to say of his own accord what he actually sees in the picture and to put questions connected with it, which should be answered to the best of one's ability. When he can see nothing more, questions should be asked about the details omitted, the action of the people and animals in the picture, and the colour and shape of the various objects. Then he should be encouraged to find out himself other occurrences suggested by the picture, to test the fanciful interpretations—which he will always be ready enough to give—as to their possibility or probability, and to replace them by better ones. Naturally, in all this, the child must only be kept so long at a picture as he shows pleasure in and attention to it; in this the teacher's discretion must be the guide. But, as we have found out by personal experience, children take keen interest in these enforced lessons in sight-perception, nor is there any lack of educational success in the development of power of observation and consequent increase in accuracy of memory.[1]

If our own children in the reproductive tests to be discussed later (Chapter XVIII) acquitted themselves well, this, no doubt, was due to their having been accustomed from a very early age, not merely to nibble at a picture, but by affectionate observation to mark and inwardly digest its every detail.

[1] To dispense with picture-books then, as in the Montessori schools, means forgoing an exceedingly valuable aid to education and culture.

But the picture's educational value, as described above, may be diminished by one more factor, and that is the super-abundance of material to be looked at, which tends to deprive the child's consideration of mental effort and independent concentration. The present age is conspicuous for its failing in this respect, over-emphasizing, as it does, the value of numberless pictures flooding the home, kindergarten and school, not only in picture-books, but in a thousand other forms as well, as posters, advertisements, shop-windows and catalogues, decorations of room walls, magic-lantern slides, and cinematograph films. May not the easy possibility of getting every conceivable thing through the eye lead to mental idleness, and the excessive illustration of all fairy-tales and stories stultify imagination? Moderation therefore in this direction is earnestly to be recommended.

In passing, we would conclude by calling attention to the fact that education in observation and intellectual sight-perception should by no means be confined to the use of pictures. For a long time this was the mistake in sight per-ception (observation) classes in the schools, and, to some degree, is so still. But the education of little children should not imitate this mistake, nor use real life at second-hand, but rather take things and occurrences in their direct actuality, as the object of the observation it has to direct and develop. Of course, the grown-up person must then himself possess the gift of observation and joy in it, so that he may have in his hand that strongest of all educational influences—example. A simple coffee-bean that a mother puts before her child takes on quite another aspect when it is individually considered, described and discussed. The child brings up with every care a little beetle; what may he not learn to observe in it, if the grown-up helps him to look, meantime pleasantly telling all he knows about the tiny creature? As the child climbs some high hill he perhaps notices of his own accord that, in different places, the trees grow differently, that sometimes they stretch their branches in only one direction, etc. His grown-up friend shows the connection by explaining the influence here of wind and weather, and thereby incites the child to keep an open eye for other proofs of this.

PART V

MEMORY AND PRACTICE

To keep our feet on the right paths in the wide field of the nature and capabilities of memory we need a few preliminary definitions and general considerations.

By memory we understand the psychic power of reproducing the effects of earlier impressions. So that there are two stages in every act of memory: (1) the reception of the impression destined to produce the after-effect, (2) the appearance of this effect. The condition between these two stages, when the impression has passed but the effect has not yet had opportunity to show itself, we will call the "latent" period. This, therefore, is a state of present unconsciousness, but with powers of future consciousness. The time elapsing between the impression and the appearance of the effect, i.e. the "latent" period, is of great importance as giving a means of knowing over what length of time these psychic associations can extend.

The resuscitation of a former experience can happen in two principal forms. "Restricted" memory appears as an auxiliary factor of another present impression, gives to this a special feature (familiarity), makes possible its identification (cognition, recognition), smooths its present course (practice), but cannot yet take the form of an independent conscious presentation. The "free" memory-effect or reproduction, on the other hand, testifies its own existence as a phenomenon of consciousness and leads to memory-representation. These memory-representations must again be divided into two groups, which have quite different significance in the economy of the mental life. This classification depends upon whether there is still consciousness of the connection between the concept now appearing and its first origin or not. If this connection does not consciously exist, then these acts of memory are, so to speak, timeless images forming the inventory of the present psychic possessions—"knowledge" as we call it. If, however, the connection still consciously exists, then these memory-concepts are referred to a certain moment in the individual past in which they originated, and this stamp of time lends them historical value for their owners—these are "memories" or "reminiscences".

The negative sides of memory appear in the two facts of forgetting and repression.

Forgetting is in fact purely negative, it is due to the lessening sense of reality of an experience and to the filling of man's mind with continually new impressions. It is never possible to decide whether the act of forgetting is final or merely temporary; we are often enough surprised by the late revival of memories which had apparently lost their power and passed away for ever.

But in repression, on the contrary, the negative memory-result is produced by very positive causes, by the aversion, namely, felt by the consciousness to an experience. It is then pushed back into the Unconscious, and the self-deception awakened that it is wiped away. One might call repression the ostrich-like policy of the consciousness, a determination to know nothing of what gives it pain. Repression is often successful, becomes real forgetting, and thus a means of self-protection; sometimes, however, the repressed experience may create hidden disturbance and threaten the individual mental equilibrium.[1]

[1] Psychoanalysis has, more than all else, called our attention to these unfavourable after-effects of repression; their cure consists, in great part, of discovering the repression and by bringing the memory repressed into the Conscious to induce a final reaction. Cf. also Chap. XXXIII.

CHAPTER XV

RECOGNITION

In the first year, as we have seen, memory appears almost only in its "restricted" form (cf. Chapter VI). But a considerable change soon takes place, although the more primitive form continues to have an importance usually very much undervalued. For it is easy to overlook its effects, since they have no separate existence, but are only implicit in other psychic phenomena. Even the sense-perception of things is by no means the result only of the momentary sense-impulse. If the child names the animal in her picture-book, calls the doll "my" doll, understands a request made to her, or greets an aunt with affection, this can only happen if the present sense-stimulus calls to its aid the former occasions of a corresponding impression.

And all capabilities and actions are in like case. Speech depends every instant on earlier practice with the tools of speech and the acquisition of words. The manipulation of cup and spoon, the carrying out of little tasks, the care of the dolly, the practice of certain tests of skill—all these are but the product of experience gained in the preceding weeks, months, years, whilst the child itself had no idea of the "historic" necessity of his actions.

And lastly, the psychic inner life. When the child invents and tells his fantasy-tales, when he satisfies his first mental desires in comparisons, definitions, judgments and conclusions, when he connects his feelings of pleasure and pain or his efforts of will with definite objects and aims, he is working unconsciously but entirely with material provided by his former experience and now forming part of the new psychic forms.

The universality of this "restricted" effect makes it quite impossible to treat it in detail in every psychic branch in early childhood, we must therefore content ourselves with the selection of one group of activities with which this kind of memory stands in a special connection lending itself to more exact enquiry; such an activity is the development of recognition of people and places after a definite latent period.[1]

We met with a quite primitive recognition even in the first

---

[1] Considered by C. and W. Stern, II (Chaps. I and IV).

year of life, but it is strictly limited to some few people or things which the child has repeatedly seen, and it has only a very short latent period.

The extension of the possible latent period is then the most marked sign of further development. In the second year, familiar persons or objects are recognized even if they have not been seen for some weeks; in the third, after some months of separation; in the fourth, such recognition has been observed with absolute certainty after a whole year's absence. There are even individual cases where the times mentioned may be considerably exceeded, but, on the average, the latent periods we have given hold good for the respective ages. A few tests of this development follow:

Hilde (1 ; 0). After a visit to Berlin, she recognized her father, from whom she had been parted for a fortnight. At the first instant she seemed a little taken aback at sight of him, but was very soon as much at home as ever.

Hilde (2 ; 3). At the first moment recognized her grand-mother, whom she had not seen for three months, and was quite at ease with her. (3 ; 1) H. recognized her aunt, whom she had not seen for seven months. (4 ; 1) When she had been in the country the Whitsun before, H. had always seen in the garden a great shed and had sometimes been in it, e.g. to watch the mangling done. After a year's interval, when she came again the next Whitsun and went into the garden, she ran straight up to the shed, exclaiming: *"The clothes are mangled here,"* before she had had the chance of looking in to see the mangle.

The quick growth of the latent periods reveals to us important features in the structure of the child's psychic life. It is true that in these very early years the child is mainly a creature of the present, very seldom happening, of his own accord to go back in memory to the past, and it looks as though every former experience was forgotten as soon as it was felt. There are so many new things to claim the young brain's attention, that it is no wonder then if the effects of earlier impressions quickly have to fade away to give place to the new. And yet many of those experiences—to all appearance lost—have a much tighter hold than one would think; the weakness caused by the passage of time does not always mean their utter destruction, and the older the child grows, the greater this power of resistance, of which he is no utterly unconscious. The chance recurrence of the impressions alone inspires the sleeping memories with new life.

Development is also evident as regards the objects recognized. To begin with, there is only identification of those impressions connected, first of all, with individual persons and things (e.g. the feeding-bottle, toys), and these must have been frequently seen, but from the second year, the ordinary environment in respect of places and things, as well; for the child's range of vision and observation has by now become perceptibly wider.

When Hilde (1 ; 0), after a fortnight's absence, came back home, she showed no sign of knowing the house again. But it was quite a different matter at 1 ; 5½ when she had been away for six weeks.

"When H. came into the bedroom on her father's arm, she silently looked intently around; we could not help fancying that a light was dawning on her mind, and scarcely had she been set down on the cot she had not used for so long than she began to crow and shout in such unrestrained delight, that again we were forced to the conclusion that she remembered her dear bed, and hence the joyful uproar! When H. in another room first caught sight of the piano she stopped short, sang *lala* and beat on the closed front."

Another example shows how deeply this recognition may be tinged with emotion; under certain circumstances, even as early as the second year, it closely resembles homesickness.

Our son Gunther (1 ; 10) came back to Breslau after four months in Berlin, where he had never quite settled down. "The change in his whole demeanour was quite remarkable when he came into his old surroundings again. As soon as he entered the familiar rooms, he knew everything and was quite excited with joy; his first act was to pull open the drawer of his little table and take out a catalogue. He knew at once which was his and which Hilde's bed, and where to look for the little angels and the 'Ring-a-Ring-o'-Roses' picture—and this last had only been hung on the wall at most a fortnight before his journey. Six months later Gunther (2 ; 4), after nine weeks' absence, recognized his home as a matter of course."

From the child's third year the range of recognition includes the memory, not only of constantly repeated impressions, but of those that have only happened occasionally or even only once, a sign how much stronger and more permanent isolated experiences now are. Relations and acquaintances, people who were only a short time in the house, such as the dressmaker, are all correctly named even after fairly long intervals.

Impressions occurring but once, show at first, it is true, such after-effect only when they are associated with some deep emotion. This emotional emphasis then acts as substitute for the frequent repetition generally needed for a deep impression, and thus proves even in a two- or three-year-old child the truth of the old saying, "memory is interest".

As a rule it is the feeling of pain that gives to any experience so strong an effect in memory. Thus different observers notice that, at the beginning of the third year, children who had once only had to endure painful medical treatment, after several weeks' interval recognized the doctor and showed strong reaction in their aversion to his approach.

But an especially pleasurable incident has a similar effect as well. Thus Major reports of his son:—

His grandfather gave the boy (2 ; o) a toy, and spent the evening showing him how to play with it. Then, as it would easily break, the toy was put away. After a period of a fortnight, when the boy had his plaything again, he said *dahaw* (his word for "grandpa"). The child's psychic condition in the act of recognition itself, especially in the earliest stages of life, demands a few more remarks. In all those cases in which complete recognition does not immediately follow the renewed impression, we may notice a feeling of a strangely twofold character. The child indeed has that feeling which we express by "I feel as if I ought to remember", but yet he cannot quite place the impression either in the past—for of this the child knows next to nothing—or in the present, for other occurrences have taken place since, in which those other persons or things have no place. In this interval the earlier impressions have been "repressed" because they were incompatible with undivided attention to the new experiences; but now they are revived. Thus this incomprehensible revival of past with present impressions brings about a state of helplessness and fear which is reflected most plainly in look and behaviour. But now it is very noteworthy that this unpleasant intermediate state is very often ended by sensory-motor action. Either the new impression itself incites some definite motor response connected with it in the past, or the same result may be brought about by some outer influence; no matter which, as soon as the child has arrived at some accustomed activity, known from the past, the impressions belonging to it have lost their strangeness, and the intangible phantom of the past vanishes; whatever can be transmuted into action belongs indeed directly to the living present.

A few examples of this recognition by the help of motor reactions follow:—

Hilde ($1 ; 5\frac{1}{2}$). (After an absence from home of six weeks.) When her mother, soon after our arrival, laid the child on the swaddling-table, H. began, at once, as she had always done before her absence, to take hold of a little nursery picture on the wall to play with it. The familiarity of the whole situation acted as a stimulus for the almost reflex response of a grasping action not practised for six weeks.

Even more significant is the following observation on the morning after returning from a holiday. Hilde ($2 ; 0$) "after she was dressed she acted strangely. Before the holiday, day after day immediately she was dressed, she used to go to a cupboard where her toys were kept and beg for it to be opened. Then she would clear it out and carry the contents, one after another, to the window seat on the opposite side of the room. In Berlin nothing of the kind had ever occurred. Now, to begin with, she ran about the room aimlessly, quite at a loss what to do. At last her mother opened the cupboard, and then the joy of recognition began. No sooner was the first toy in her hand than the motor-response (namely the accustomed run to the window seat) appeared again, and the clearing-out began in the old way, after five weeks' interruption. With cries of delight every toy was greeted and named *map-map* (rabbit), *baba* (sheep), *rrr* (mill), etc., and when her mind, in this way, had recovered its wonted habits, her sense of familiarity with the house also returned at once; she was without effort as much at home in all the rooms as if she had never been away."

Here therefore is a lack of true recognition, the conscious identification of the present impression with an earlier one. This higher stage is reached by the child six months later.

Hilde ($2 ; 6$). On her return from a change lasting six weeks,

H. no longer simply accepted the old habits and places as a matter of course, but went consciously to work with the recognition of what had sunk so deeply into the past. "When we got out of the carriage before our house, she absolutely stamped with delight and said '*home, home*'. When we got in, she ran through the rooms with unhesitating delight and surprise, recognizing everything: '*pretty table, pretty window, Hilde's cupboard*', she kept on repeating."

Later years bring with them, it is true, gradual progress in the powers of recognition, but no intrinsically new features; on the other hand, they are the special period for the development of "free" memory, i.e. knowledge and reminiscences.

CHAPTER XVI
LEARNING AND PRACTICE

1. The Acquisition of Experiences

THE chief work of "restricted" memory was to enrich the child's renewed perceptions with the treasure of past learning, and thus to develop his observation, cognition, apprehension. But the older a child grows, the more he develops a mental life that is no longer directly bound by sense-perception; in thought, fantasy, play and production, in listening to tales, in hope and fear, etc., the child lives in spheres more or less distinct from the immediate present and the material it offers for perception, and he therefore requires for all those activities a memory-store, independent of the momentary sense-impressions.

We have already seen (cf. Chapter VI, Section 2) that even in the first year memory shows traces of this emancipation from perception, but it is not until later that the child has at his disposal A STORE OF FREE MEMORY PRESENTATIONS (knowledge which increases from year to year with amazing speed.

Now, how is all this knowledge gained, preserved and reproduced when required?

Knowledge is gained by "learning," so that here again we come up against this important idea.[1] And yet we immediately notice the strange fact that often the age after six years is generally spoken of as the time for learning, whilst that before is merely "play" time. This cannot, of course, mean that the child has learnt nothing in the first six years—on the contrary, in respect of amount, the knowledge then gained has nothing to fear from a comparison with school-years—but we must indeed allow that the manner of learning in these two periods is essentially different. Indeed, there is perhaps no feature so clearly distinguishing early from later childhood as the manner of learning. For the school-child, learning means a conscious systematic assimilation of given matter in the greatest possible perfection, and with the intention of using it again. Even if the impulse to this activity comes from without in the peremptory demand of the school, still its accomplishment is only

---

[1] Cf. Chapter V, Section 1, which treats of the "learning" of the earliest motor-powers.

possible because the child has already developed sufficiently
for such an act of will.

In the first six—or at any rate five—years there is not a sign
of all this. The intention to acquire anything as a lasting
possession is still very remote from the childish mind, intent
only on the present; and in the same way the child is incapable
of systematic consideration of any task, of its continual repetition, with attention fully concentrated on its assimilation,
or of any idea of its complete mastery.

At this age, learning, as an act of will, is at most only apparent
when it is a question of certain physical powers that seem
desirable at the moment (e.g. definite hand-movements in
playing ball, or some jumping or gymnastic feat), but not when
it is a question of permanent acquisition of knowledge. LEARN-
ING, THEN, NEVER APPEARS OTHERWISE THAN AS A BY-PRODUCT
OF OTHER PSYCHIC ACTIVITIES.

And yet the wonderful result! The interest with which the
child seizes on everything fresh, the intense observation he
brings to bear on things and events, pictures and sounds, the
unwearied desire for a fresh repetition of former impressions
(e.g. pictures and looking at books), the playhunger which
pounces on the thousand forms of life surrounding him, imitates
and changes them—such are the energies which, of themselves,
develop into the mental gain of knowledge. The child asks for
little songs, not to learn them, but to hear them, and to take
ever-new pleasure in the hearing; but, all the same, at last he
learns them. He listens to the confusion of surrounding speech,
tries to understand and imitate, not with any desire to make
progress in his power of conversation, but to stand in psychic
harmony with his environment; yet, in so doing, he learns by
play to talk. In his walk he stops at every shop-window and
expects all its glories to be pointed out and explained to him,
not that he may know them to-morrow, or in a year's time, but
now, at this moment; but he thus acquires lasting knowledge
of the appearance, significance, and use of things. The little
girl, in her play, imitates her mother's occupations, and so
learns what is the use of this or that, how this or that piece of
work should be done. In the child's consciousness there are but
momentary joys and present interests, but above and beyond
all intent, enduring future results are secured by an increased
store of knowledge.

It is true this learning by play is only possible because there are no tasks that *must* be mastered and no fixed time-limits within which they are to be accomplished. So that early childhood can in quite other wise adopt a principle that, later on in school-years, has, unfortunately, to retire io the background, the principle of UNCONSCIOUS CHOICE IN LEARNING. We met with it earlier in learning to speak, but it holds good, in like manner, for all early acquisition of knowledge. As a result of the economy of mental life, the child never understands nor is interested in more than a fraction of the innumerable impressions flooding upon him. The result of this selective apprehension is further reduced by Memory's refusal to retain more than a portion of material thus offered to her, and to transmute it into "knowledge". This is no misfortune, but an advantage, for the child's mind is then not drowned in the flood of acquirements offered to it, but floats upon them; he can, in his choice, obey the laws of his psychic nature, follow the straight paths of his interest, and satisfy the increasing demands of his development. This selective process then continues and whilst fresh impressions are constantly assimilated by him, the way is being paved for others whereby they, in their turn, may enter into the charmed circle of his knowledge; no matter though they pass unnoticed a hundred times, yet the frequent repetition forms a preparation for later understanding and acquirement. He finds intermediate steps without number: here only a name understood, there a hazy idea of the meaning of some word, elsewhere the comprehension even of a great association; thus slowly but surely these separate gay threads are woven into an ever-closer web of knowledge.

It is impossible to imagine a greater contrast than exists between this unconsciously selective learning and the principle that still holds sovereign sway to a large extent in school activity, viz., that every lesson should be exactly suited to the child's capacity. In accordance with this, knowledge is offered precisely in such shape and measure as the teacher thinks the child can understand and master in its entirety, and therefore may well be expected to do so. The Herbartian teaching of apperception and of formal stages is the best-known expression of this adaptation (suitability) theory.

This is not the place to discuss whether that other principle of learning in school-years is absolutely demanded by the exigencies of school-teaching, or whether more general recognition of the principle of selective learning might not be possible and desirable here as well. But in early childhood, where the levelling necessities of school do not yet obtain, the advantages of unconscious choice in learning must at any rate be preserved. It is perhaps not quite superfluous to emphasize this, for there are a few kindergarten methods[1] that seem, a little prematurely, to extend the systematic learning of "adapted" knowledge to this early age as well. I mean, in the kindergarten and nursery, teachers should not be too anxious to avoid a little "going above" their pupils' heads, provided it comes in the natural course of their teaching, but should leave the child a certain liberty in his selection and gradual acquirement of knowledge. It does not matter if a little poem is said without a perfect understanding of every part, nor is it a disaster when many things in nature and civilization work their will in somewhat wild confusion within the child's little head; it will all clear up in time. In short, it is no cause for regret that so much of what is shown or explained to the child seems to find no entrance or is so quickly lost again; in some way, unknown to us, it may prove a preliminary for future understanding, the germinating point of later processes of development.

Hilde (4 ; 9½). "Yesterday H. looked out of the window and we spoke about the dull weather. I said I thought all the snow must be melted since it was so warm, above zero" (centigrade).

H. *Does the snow melt when it is above zero?*

I. "Yes."

H., pointing to the thermometer hanging outside the window: *Did you look at that to find out, or do you know because the snow has melted?* Of course, she does not know what zero means, but each such talk brings her imperceptibly nearer to this knowledge. A further example: We have hung up a calendar in H.'s room; every day she tears off a little leaf and then reads to-day's date. What impression it makes on her—we do not know! But it would be quite a mistake to deprive children of such things which give them pleasure and preliminary practice as well, whilst certainly helping to make later concepts much easier to grasp.

This method of learning and teaching is, in the natural course of things, especially fruitful where there are younger brothers

[1] Cf. the next section on the Montessori method.

and sisters. For their natural desire to live in their brothers' and sisters' company brings them continually under influences, more especially intended for older children, whether in games, reading aloud, conversation or explanations. In the notes concerning our youngest daughter we find many remarks referring to this, and append two:—

Eva (4 ; 10). "As a result of being constantly with her elder brother and sister, her speech and manner are extraordinarily 'mature'. Her interests and knowledge extend to geography, theology, arithmetic, zoology, French, philately. She hears all they learn and do and is deeply interested in everything, whether beyond her understanding or not. Her father's journey fills her little head with phantoms of America. She speaks of New York, its bridges, its skyscrapers, of the Niagara Falls, and looks on the map as I explain to her elder brother and sister. Then she takes up a little toy globe and says, 'Now I will learn a little geography.' "

(5 ; 6). "The growth of younger members of a family when in the intimate companionship of older brothers and sisters controverts, as perhaps nothing else can. Otto's teaching of 'adaptation' to age. Not only our conversation at meals or out walking, but my reading to the children is practically all chosen in the interests of the older brother and sister. They would complain bitterly if I tried to put before them what they would have greatly liked at Eva's age. Little Eva, on the contrary, is quite content to listen, though, for the most part, everything is too deep for her."

2. Psychological Observations with Reference to the Montessori Exercises

The preceding consideration of the psychology of learning in early childhood now permits us to take a definite attitude with regard to the methods of the Montessori school.[1]

This is the more necessary since Mme Montessori thinks that her method is in strict accordance with scientific psychology. In my opinion this view is not correct. The very emphasis

---

[1] We may content ourselves here with short remarks, since an exhaustive and detailed discussion of this question has now been published (Martha Muchow, IV) which in its general tone exactly agrees with the standpoint adopted by ourselves. Cf. also Hessen's Essays, but then too the anti-criticism by Gerhards.

laid upon learning or "practice" in the Children's Home is unsuited to the character of this age-period. At this period, everything that the child handles or sees is the object of involuntary learning, and, for that very reason, is it less necessary to make this learning the conscious aim of the whole of education in early childhood. And if the unconscious choice of subject-matter to be learnt mentioned in an earlier section is to have its due weight, it is a mistake not only to prepare the child's occupations in such a way that in each something quite definite must be practised, but even to arrange these occupations in a systematic sequence.[1] That is premature transference of school methods to a period of a child's life which is not ready for the hard and fast system and the consciously fixed aims of school-life.

Mme Montessori, indeed, states that her method is opposed to that usual in schools, and emphasizes the fact that in her Homes the children carry out their occupations when and how they wish, being entirely free from compulsion to obey orders or follow any example; the teacher is to efface herself and make the child independent of her help as far as possible. Self-education by self-occupation is the new principle of her method. That is certainly true in great measure for the child's separate occupation for the time being, which is really left to the children's own choice. They are not forced in any way by commands or prohibitions. But, on the other hand, the child's freedom is the more limited by the whole organization of the possibilities of the occupations and by the restricted aims assigned to the separate exercises.

The Montessori system shows evident traces of its origin in therapeutic education. As a doctor, Mme Montessori tried to improve the methods of the French neurologist, Dr. Seguin, for the education of weakly children. In so doing she invented a series of very useful exercises for the training of the senses and bodily movements. When opportunity was offered her to start a home for the normal but younger children of a poor district in Rome, those methods were again employed there.

We have also to decide the further question as to whether the elementary instruction in schools might not derive helpful suggestions from the Montessori exercises. I think it by no

[1] Cf. the chapter "Graduated Provision of Material Exercises", Montessori, I. pp. 314 sqq.

means impossible that the main points of the Montessori method may by degrees be transferred from the kindergarten to the earliest school-years, which would be a decided benefit. For such occupations and exercises are undoubtedly much more suited to the psychic structure of the school-child than to that of the children still in the purely "play age", with whom alone we are now dealing.

There are in a genuine Montessori school only four kinds of occupations, which all either directly or indirectly aim at the furtherance of actions of practical utility and therefore are *not* games, viz.: (1) Exercises of the bodily senses and (2) of movements, (3) useful actions for practical purposes, and (4) the acquirement of elementary school-accomplishments (reading, writing, arithmetic)[1]. The exercises for the senses form the centre of the system; the specific Montessori material is designed first and foremost for them and these exercises are theoretically the very foundation of the system. For that reason, our present discussion may be confined to them as they clearly demonstrate the distinctive characteristics of the method in general.[2]

According to Mme Montessori, the chief mental function is the reception, recognition, differentiation, and naming of simple sense-impressions from the union and division, etc., of which all higher psychic activities (especially those of the intellect and of the so-called creative faculties) arise spontaneously. In earliest years therefore all the training required is in observation; if then a sure and firm foundation of clearly recognized and named impressions is secured, the development of those complex activities later on may be expected to take place automatically—so to speak. At the same time the consciousness

[1] For the reading and writing exercises cf. Chap. X, 7B, of the present work and for the practical utility exercises later chapters.
[2] When Gerhards, in his defence of the Montessori methods, points out that Mme Montessori also recognizes gymnastic exercises, modelling, building, free drawing, etc., Mme Montessori herself may be quoted as witness to the contrary, for in the new edition of her chief book (1926) she has omitted all the passages on which G. bases his defence, and with regard to spontaneous drawing explicitly states that it "is not included in my system. I avoid, indeed, those premature attempts which have the drawback of wearying failure" (quoted from Hessen, II). Therefore the utilitarian standpoint of success prevails without exception. That children in their play of spontaneous drawing find a means of self-expression, that it is a variety of the confabulation and tale-telling natural to them, and that it should be allowed them for these reasons, and not in any way with a view to some definite result for future writing, etc.—all this is neither recognized nor appreciated.

of reality will be so strengthened thereby that there will be no fear of any disturbances of the child's knowledge from the side of the evil imagination—which is, according to the Montessori theory, nothing but a remnant of imperfect stages of human development.

That this interpretation of development-psychology is wrong in its very foundations need not here be proved in detail; our book shows on every page how entirely different is the child's psychic development in reality. Important as may be, within this development, the gradual education of looking and observation, of classifying and comparison, etc., yet the detachment of sense-activities from the other psychic functions is exceedingly harmful.

But even within the sphere of sense-perceptions the Montessori method of detachment still continues. Every single sense-activity is sharply isolated and within this again a definite elementary characteristic is once more marked out. Thus there are exercises for touch, colour, sound, tone, smell, and so on; and indeed only such sense-stimuli are offered as are different in one respect and thus can be classified—"touch" plates of varying degrees of roughness, colour plates of different shades of brightness, dice of various sizes, etc.

The underlying psychology here is, therefore, purely the psychology of elements, which assumes that our perception consists of the sum-total of sensation-elements. But, in reality, the undivided form of a perception (e.g. of a tree or a movement-action) is something entirely different from the simple sum of the colour, form and sound-sensations contained in it, and therefore the natural path of training in observation is one which starts from natural unities and not from elements. The child learns observation much better in natural phenomena and objects, in things used in everyday life, and in pictures as well as in life's natural events, than in artificially detached and isolated colours and successions of sounds; and in the phenomena observed there follows a gradual detachment of the individual elements and their interrelations. Perhaps the child learns more slowly in this way; but what he learns has from the very first its place in the natural coherence of life. The child gets early enough in his school detached isolated learning, but, even there, more and more importance is attached to the principle that a beginning should be made from the whole as it naturally exists, not from the individual elements of which it is composed.

Of course the Montessori series of representations of forms, colours, etc., may now and again delight the child; he learns quite unconsciously so much in them, not only to distinguish and name the different members of the series but also the logical principles of arrangement, gradation, etc.[1]

And therefore the Montessori occupations may be welcomed as an undoubted enrichment of children's games if they are used as one group amongst several other toys and, above all, if they are used for purposes of play.

But it is just this use for spontaneous play which is banished from the orthodox Montessori method—and this brings us to the second serious psychological error: the one-sided nature of the respective occupations. It is true the child has unrestricted liberty in his choice of occupation-material and of the period he spends in the use of it, but he is restricted as to his method of dealing with it. The children's actions are adjudged entirely in accordance with the authority's point of view as right or wrong; and there is only one solution which is "right" in the adult's sense of the word (e.g. the arrangement of the gradations); all other activities are "wrong" and at best are only of value when the child from his very mistakes may learn what is "right".

Let us consider this in examples.

One of the best known of these consists of a board pierced with a row of circles graduated in size and the same number of cylindrical rods of different thickness; the child is to learn by himself how to put the rods into the corresponding openings, and thus to learn to distinguish different thickness and to grasp the meaning of a sequence. A description is then given of the child's independent action, of how he learns by his own mistakes, how he uses his sense of touch instead of his eyes, etc. But then we are told: "As soon as the child can place with

[1] The arrangement of "sense" series also presents psychological problems, problems which were attempted lately by Révész. When coloured tablets in the four main colours were put before 4- to 6-year-old children, 73 per cent. were able to find a principle of arrangement, and moreover—in about equal proportions—either the spectral succession according to similarity (red, yellow, green, blue) or the complementary order according to pairs of opposites (red/green, yellow/blue). In geometrical pairs of opposites the order of similarity preferred was as follows: triangle, trapeze, rhombus, square, pentagon, hexagon, octagon and circle.

apparent surety every rod in its proper place, he has outgrown these exercises, and *this material is of no more value to the child.*"[1] Here is a plain statement that these cylinders are only meant to serve the one purpose, designed by Mme Montessori; the fundamental fact that it is the little child's special gift to make everything out of everything is disregarded. What then if the child playing with this pierced board should hit upon the quite un-Montessorian idea to look upon the fattest rod as papa, the next as mama, the rest as the children, and so to play with them? Or to put the cylindrical rods under the board to roll it along like a train? In the whole book we never read a word of such independent actions, although these games are the first that are really free, that is, not prescribed by the teacher's intentions. I am convinced that the educative value of such entirely unrestrained activities is greater and above all more varied than when the child is limited to the performance of the different grades; for even thus the difference of thicker and thinner gradually dawns upon his mind, but with much else even more important as well. In their games with dolls and personations, children, all unconsciously, become familiar with human conditions and practised in certain voluntary mental attitudes, etc.

Here is another example of the practical working of a Montessori school (from M. Muchow IV). Two girls, sitting together at a small table on which they have emptied out the two little boxes of colour blocks, begin to build houses. "I shall build mine green," says the first; "And I a blue one," replies the second. They eagerly look out the colours they need and build the little houses with them. The teacher comes up to the table and without a word demolishes the buildings with a stroke of her hand, gives each child a block of brilliant colour as the first of a series and exhorts the children to finish the arrangement of graded colours. The children do so, but without any great pleasure; soon they give up the blocks from which at first they had hoped for so much creative joy.

Martha Muchow is quite right: in Mme Montessori's eyes the child is not an individual who should exercise the whole of his individuality—his needs, interests, imaginative joy, his attitude to men and things in play—but he is rather a psycho-physiological organism that should exercise his organs and capabilities exactly as prescribed in his occupations. And what is the result of this view? "The methods of the school destroy play."

3. Learning Poems by Heart

Learning by heart plays an important part amongst the different kinds of learning. It consists in the mastery of longer, ordered vocal sequences, which can be reeled off to the end after being once started.

Whilst the learning by heart of school-children and of adults has been the subject of much psychological research, the memorizing of little children, although it, too, has quite characteristic features, has so far received but the scantiest attention.

Children, from about their fourth year on, become capable of learning poetic text, and it affords them the greatest pleasure to rattle out the verses attached to the illustrations in their picture-books, to sing the necessary words to the dancing-games in the kindergarten, or to learn secretly and recite to their parents some little birthday or Christmas poem. Such poems, above all, give an opportunity of determining more exactly the extent of the child's memory capacity. We add a few tests at different ages:—

Eva (3 ; 0). "At Christmas the children had given to them a Caspar picture-book in which the 23 pictures—not connected with each other—were accompanied by little verses, each of about six lines. When the parents returned from a short stay away from home, to their surprise the children knew the book by heart. Eva said the 146 lines without a mistake, although, to be sure, as she turned over the pages, she generally had to cast a glance at the pictures on the next two pages to be able to go on. Besides this, at Christmas, she had said a poem of 12 lines to her father."

Hilde (3 ; 6). "The child knows several of Hey's fables by heart, to others she gives an independent ending; little verses she learns in play. A few poems that her parents made for her like 'Dolly's Washing' (20 lines) and 'Wherefore, Therefore' (12 lines) she was quite sure of, though there was not even one picture to help her memory."

Eva (5 ; 3). "The child had, for some weeks, been attending a private kindergarten of seven other pupils; at the term-end they had a spring festival in which every child had to say a little poem composed by the head-mistress. Eva mastered not only the verses assigned to her, but those of the seven others as well—altogether certainly far more than a hundred lines, and every evening, from her bedroom, there resounded the gay rhymes recited as far as possible with the intonation of each little actor."

Gunther (5 ; 6). "The 146 lines of the Caspar picture-book which the three-year-old Eva (see above) repeated with the help of her brother, he himself (2½ years older) could recite without seeing the pictures, and that too in correct sequence, although, as we have said, the pictures were quite unconnected."

Since, in the above passages, regard has been had to some only of the lines known by the children at the periods mentioned, it would be no exaggeration to credit a normal four- or five-year-old child with a repertoire, at any one time, of about 200 lines of verse. Of course there are great individual differences, due both to outer and inner causes. Working-class children, who have but little opportunity of hearing blank verse or poems, will not be able to remember nearly as many, whilst, on the other hand, training specially directed to this point can considerably increase the number of lines memorized. To quite another category belong those cases that sometimes occur of a naturally abnormal gift of memory which gives the child, even in early years, an astounding capacity for learning long poems.

But of greater psychological importance is the question as to how this learning of poems is accomplished. There again we find fundamental differences between it and the school-child's memorizing. The latter, almost without exception, sees the lines to be learnt on the printed page, and thus, in his learning, combines the sight-impression of the printed words with their sound and the feelings his own saying of them produces, learning, at one and the same time, by eye, ear and movement. But the infant, on the other hand, cannot read, and hence is limited to learning by ear and movement only. Now let us see clearly what that means. The little child not only loses all sight memories of the passage when read, of the poem's characteristic form with its short and long lines, its division into verses, etc., of the position of the different lines, but also he is quite unable, even if he wishes, to spend a little longer time on lines he finds more difficult, as the child who reads can.

Although, of course, in any case—quite apart from his inability to read—he is not at all capable of such independent treatment of the task, since he has as yet no conscious will to learn.

But now he finds compensation for the lacking visual help in something perhaps much more strongly marked in him than in an older child. That is, first of all, pure joy in the sound itself, quite apart from its meaning, the rhythmic formation of the lines, possibly the accompanying melody, the euphony of the rhymes, reduplications, refrains, the attractive peculiarity of strange-sounding or interjectional portions, such as "eia-pipeia," "kikeri-ki." All this is in an elementary way, emphatically pleasing to the child; and makes him demand frequent repetitions as well as being a great help to his involuntary learning of the poem. And so, in addition, is the child's sensory-motor nature. He knows no such thing as listening, pure and simple; all that is heard must at once be repeated by his own lips; he hears a little verse but once or twice, before he tries the next time to join in or to copy the recital—quite regardless of the fact that he has left out so and so many words or said them wrong, besides being always half a bar behind the original reciter. His half-knowledge becomes more and more perfect at last by his delight in singing and saying, as well as in the verbal accompaniment to his little dances and games; and the beautiful old children's rhymes, with many modern poems—not all so beautiful—become in this way the first literary possession of the future generation of our race.

And, although the little child cannot read the printed text, he finds optical aids to memory in the accompanying illustrations. We saw, indeed, how the four-year-old Eva only found the repetition of the Caspar poems possible when looking at the pictures, which, by association, prompted the words belonging to them. But her elder brother did not need to look at the pictures in his attempt, simply because he had in his mind's eye an extraordinary plastic idea of the whole picture-book with its pictures in right order; as he repeated them he gave the impression of mentally turning over the pages and knowing the position of the poems by the pictures.

The analysis of the learning process in early childhood shows further that sense and meaning are by no means so important then as in later years. With the school-child much emphasis is laid—and rightly—on his never learning what has no meaning for him; a text he does not understand is of no educational value to him, and yet, at the same time, demands infinitely more time and strength-expenditure than an equally long poem within his powers of comprehension. BUT EARLY CHILDHOOD IS PRE-EMINENTLY THE PERIOD OF SENSORY-MOTOR LEARNING BY HEART. If, as we saw, simple joy in the sound makes the child repeat it and ultimately memorize the poem without any conscious effort, this result is scarcely retarded by the fact that he scarcely ever really entirely understands the verses learnt— often, indeed, his understanding is of a very confused and fragmentary nature.[1] But it would even then be a purely pedantic mistake to force his understanding by long-winded explanations, or, again, to reject all poems not quite within his powers. And, indeed, it would be quite impossible at home or in the kindergarten to prevent the smaller children from learning—quite involuntarily and unconsciously—the poems meant for older pupils.

Eva (4 ; 2). "Klaus Broth's charming dialect poem of 'Lutt Matten, der Haas' was for a time extremely popular in our nursery. All three children knew it by heart and acted it, Eva with quite as much expression and assurance as the two older ones; but when I tested her understanding of it, I found most astounding gaps. This learning with others without understanding leads to comical mistakes. Thus, her elder sister had learnt, 'There sounds a cry like thunder-roll.' Little Eva stumbled through it one morning, and amongst other comicalities there came suddenly the words, 'Like clash of swords and rap of roses.' " A last peculiarity of early memorizing is the learning of poems as a whole. A school-child, who gets a poem of six four-lined verses to learn, almost always proceeds by reading the first verse several times till he thinks he knows it, does the same with the second, and not till all are learnt does he connect the verses together into the whole poem.

Experimental researches have lately shown that this "piece-meal learning," although quite universal, is a very wasteful

---

[1] The ordinary name for this of "mechanical memory" is not quite correct. For even unintelligible matter is not learnt by joining the separate elements (syllables) to one another by purely mechanical sound-association; this subject-matter consists rather of undivided sound-forms. In a single verse (e.g. Ring a Ring o' Roses) the features indicated above: rhythm, text, melody and expression-movement, are only existent from the very first as interdependent component parts, and as such a sensory-motor whole the verse is learnt and unites with others into the total shape of the little song.

proceeding. An amount that can in any way be mastered as one task will be learnt more quickly, as well as more thoroughly, if it is always attacked as a whole. Now, it is remarkable that this more economical way of learning is the only one practised in early childhood. This again is the result of the child's lack of will to learn; the repeated compulsory listening to any one part before going on to another would be quite against his nature, and, therefore, he asks for the whole picture-book with its twenty-three little poems to be read through again and again until he, too, can say them all.

"When the five-year-old Eva has to learn a Christmas poem for her father beginning:—

> Far in the forest stands a fir
> With needles sharp and keen;
> With these the dainty goldfinch sews
> Its coat of wondrous sheen—

with five more stanzas of the same length, it is enough if her mother for some days says over the whole poem twice when dressing the child; Eva repeats it and says it with her mother, and after a few days it is well known without the slightest trouble."

It surely might not be amiss to consider whether this natural "learning of the whole" might not with advantage be continued in the early years of school-life; but then, of course, the practice of giving a lesson one day to be learnt by the next or the day after would have to be discontinued, and a longer interval fixed during which the poem can be learnt without effort by frequent repetition of the whole.

CHAPTER XVII

REMEMBRANCE[1]

1. The Chief Forms of Remembrance in Early Childhood

WE have already had to emphasize in several places the very slight acquaintance between the little child and his past. It is true he owes all his knowledge and his capabilities to this past and its after-effects; but he is not yet able to look back to it. For as regards the past there is nothing more to desire, to expect, to hope for, only reminiscences to record, and children are not calm writers of chronicles, but creatures of will, emotion and action, all directed to the experiences of the immediate present or to an immediate future responsive to deeds. The experience which but just now occupied the child forthwith sinks of itself or—if it might cause disturbance or confusion in the present experience—is thrust into the Unconscious.

This condition only very gradually undergoes a change. Far back, the child already owns a great store of memories from his past, but he uses it only for present aims, as we saw in recognition and in the use of knowledge. But at last these stores of memories begin now and then to betray their origin, and the consciousness becomes dimly aware that they belong to an earlier period of the life, and they become memories (reminiscences).

In the mist which hides his own past from the child's consciousness, faint points of light appear here and there, indistinct and fleeting. With increasing years they grow plainer, more varied and frequent, later on to combine in somewhat greater numbers, as in the remembrance of some festivity, such as a summer holiday. But many years pass before these separate parts unite and form a whole, giving the child a connected picture—however simple and sketchy—of the portion of life's way which he has already left behind. This side of personal consciousness in which one's past appears as an historical sequence is not fully developed until after early childhood.

[1] With extracts from C. and W. Stern's *Monograph*, II.

Let us for a moment keep to our parable and consider the child's past as a path he has traversed and left behind in mist that is slowly lifting.[1] The nearest objects alone are visible in the mist, and thus his first flickering memories only extend to impressions but lately experienced; THE LATENT PERIODS ARE VERY BRIEF, and only gradually increase in length. And the mist, although it grows less dense, deprives the landscape of depth and perspective; the isolated points blend more or less indistinguishably in the same grey field. That is, the past has no distinct form for the child, and is not differentiated as to time, so that he can get no clear conception of greater or less intervals, of the relative times of events An indefinite "there was once" long takes the place of every time-distinction. This incapacity of localizing memories as to time, together with their want of connected union, mentioned above, is one of the most characteristic signs of early memory and, at the same time, a frequent source of errors.

Memories are phenomena of consciousness which are not necessarily—like other conscious acts—apparent to the onlooker. Therefore it is impossible for any observer of child-life to arrive at an absolutely certain judgment concerning the extent and inner working of childhood's memories. What we notice are always, indeed, only occasional indications, often the outcome of quite chance stimuli, or again performances that we have intentionally provoked by questions, etc.; what elementary memories beside these may be stirring in the child's subconsciousness we do not know. Sometimes only indirect signs show us how strong and enduring may be the after-effect in a child's mind of something which those around believed to be quite unnoticed or long since forgotten. Yet, in face of the child's wellnigh insatiable craving for expression, we must not attach too much importance to this elusive subconsciousness, as do the psychoanalysts for example. On the other hand, we must mention that sometimes we find in children gaps in memory that seem wellnigh incredible, especially as they are connected with impressions with a strong emotional emphasis. Here we get striking proof of how un-

[1] By this parable we show the analogy between the beginnings of remembrance and those—occurring a year earlier—of the first perceptual activity (cf. Chap. V). There, too, we showed that development does not start with single elements that afterwards combine, but with a diffuse chaotic state from which such elements are raised by selection.

systematic and unreliable a nature are the memories of childhood.

A remembrance can be brought to light in different ways, and we divide these into four main classes.

The simplest is its associative connection with a present sense-impression, either one of immediate contact or of a feeling of resemblance. We see the "contact" effect if the child sees again a place where he once was, and not only recognizes it, but also remembers some experience that took place there. The act of remembrance rests, on the other hand, on a feeling of resemblance when the child at the sight of a landscape is reminded of some district he has seen in the past when away from home. These two kinds of association, as Groos and others have rightly remarked, are not fundamentally different, for even in the recognition of "the same" place the impression is not identically the same as before, only similar.

But as all memory-functions are by degrees emancipated more and more from perception, so too are the acts of remembrance; they can take place without the impulse of any effective sense-impression at the moment. Associations also play a part in these, provided previous perception has led to that act of remembrance; but, besides this, there are also genuine "DETACHED" remembrances, i.e. those that suddenly and directly appear out of the depths of unknown consciousness.

These are explained by the "tendency to persist" (perseveration) inherent in perceptions (G. E. Müller). The effect of this tendency may, under favourable circumstances, cause a long-suppressed perception to break through the barrier imposed by other contents of the consciousness and to force its way into consciousness itself. The child-observer, of course, finds it difficult in any isolated case to decide whether any directly expressed remembrance is an effect of association or is "detached" in nature.

Both these varieties of remembrance, whether caused by sense-impression or the result of previous perception, have this in common that the remembrance arises without conscious co-operation either of the child or of anyone else. Differing in this point we find two further stages where there is DETER-MINATION of the remembrance by influences either from without or within.

If the child is required to give a reproduction—not

spontaneously arising—of a former experience, we call it a "PROMPTED" (suggested) remembrance. Prompting is chiefly done by questions which, in manifold variety, on every occasion are put to the child, now as a sign of affectionate interest: "Now, tell us what it was like there." "Let us hear all you have seen." "Did you meet so and so?"—now as a painful examination, when some smaller or greater fault has been committed. The first result of the questioning is to bring to the surface-consciousness a number of weaker or less prominent memory-concepts that would not, of themselves, have appeared there, and thus to increase considerably the supply of conscious memories (remembrances); on the other hand, it may tempt the child to state more than is justified by actual memory of the subject under discussion, and, for that reason, questioning is a prime factor in memory misrepresentations which we shall discuss later in detail.

Last of all, the child reaches that stage when by an effort of will he is able himself to determine his memories (remembrances, reminiscences). First of all, even the acceptance of the impression that is to be remembered is influenced by the will; we speak then of "MAKING A MENTAL NOTE" of a little errand, a number, etc. If, on the other hand, the will is set working to effect a certain remembrance, we speak of "TRYING TO REMEMBER". In early childhood only traces of these two will-activities can be found, a fact similar to one we noted when considering the acquisition of knowledge. THE PART TAKEN BY THE WILL IN THE MEMORY-FUNCTIONS, whether in regular learning, in especially noticing (making a mental note), or in the effort to remember, DOES NOT FULLY DEVELOP UNTIL SCHOOL-AGE.

2. The Development of Correct Remembrance

We have now reached the stage of illustrating the general features of the child's development in remembrance by examples from life. We shall at first confine ourselves to accurate remembrance. For errors of remembrance compare the following section.

The first signs of remembrance—although very fleeting— show themselves after completion of the first year. An impression has occurred and its primary effects have not quite disappeared, and a slight incitement is enough to bring remembrance to the surface. The following action is often told of one-year-old children: they had left their ball lying out of sight under a piece of furniture. A quarter or half an hour later they were asked: "Where is the ball?" and straightway shuffled or crept to where the ball was hidden to get it out.

But about the middle of the second year we find signs of remembrance after a somewhat longer latent period—the favourite time being twenty-four hours.

Impressions connected with definite hours return in the form of remembrance or expectation, as the case may be, at the same hour, called up by a corresponding situation (going to bed) or by a similar physical condition (fatigue, hunger).

Deville[1] reports of his daughetr (1 ; 6): "She has a succession of catalogued facts in her memory which she remembers every day at their special hour and at no other. She is barely awake before she demands her bath, from 9 to 10 a.m. she asks for her hat and talks of her walk, the basket to be taken and of the newspapers to be put in it. Breakfast is scarcely over before she asks for the coffee-pot to carry into the kitchen, and all this happens without anything being said or done to rouse her remembrance."

But even occurrences that only happen once may, for some exceptional reason, make such an impression on the child that they are sometimes remembered and reproduced days later, without anything having been done in the interval to refresh the memory.

Scupin's son (1 ; 7). The boy had once seen bacon fried and called an onion thrown into the pan a "ball". A fortnight later bacon was fried again, and Bubi at sight of the pan exclaimed: *Da, mama ball bah!* (I, p. 77). How quickly these latent periods may increase in length is shown by the following observation at the end of the second year.

Gunther (1 ; 11). He heard Hilde mention "board", and at once he pointed to our easel-board and said *wow-wow*. There was no dog to be seen on it, but two and a half months before their mother had drawn on that board large heads of a dog, horse, and cat, to Gunther's especial delight. To be quite sure that it was really a question of remembrance, his mother asked: "And what else did you see on the board?"

[1] Vol, 24, p. 29.

To which Gunther replied: *Gee-gee*. In the interval no picture at all had been drawn on the board to show the children, and also an absence from home had intervened.

Nevertheless, such remembrance is so rare, even in the third year, that it immediately arouses the observer's attention. As a rule, for the child at that age, it is still "out of sight, out of mind," and it seems remarkable sometimes how little he notices or feels the absence of persons or things that have formed part of his ordinary environment. It needs but little to revive his remembrance of them, but he never really misses them.

Eva (2 ; 2). Hilde and her mother had left home, and Eva at the window had watched them go in the cab. The first day she neither called for them nor mentioned their names; on the second, when someone happened to mention the word "mother", she said: *Away in the puff-puff*. If she was asked, "Where is mother?" she answered, *In the puff-puff*, or *Gone with the horse*, and with that dismissed the matter. On the third day there were oranges for the midday meal, and Eva exclaimed in delight: *Eva pleased, mother peel one*. When her father asked in astonishment: "Mother?" she stopped short, and after a momentary pause said: *Else* (the nurse). Her father asked: "Why is Else to do it?' Eva answered: *Gone with horse*, her laconic expression for: "Because mother has gone away." It was not till the fourth day that she said of her own accord: *Hilde gone with puff-puff*.

Scupin's observation of the same age is still more pronounced: "The boy had for some time had a live rabbit which he dearly loved. One day it was given away, and the boy did not notice its loss either on that day or afterwards. A month later, he left home for six weeks, and the new impressions completely effaced all remembrance of the rabbit. After the return home nine days passed before, at last, a chance sense-impression awoke the slumbering memory. He (2 ; 4½) saw the place in the kitchen where the rabbit had been kept and asked: *Dear, dear, where can Ninit in the kitchen be gone ?* The latent period was eighty-four days (I. p. 132).

By far the strongest acts of memory in these years are undoubtedly called into being by travel. All the fresh influences of nature, the railway, the different conditions of life, the strangers, leave deep impressions even in the two- or

three-year-old child, and on his return the striking contrast
of home conditions results not only in a mixture of impressions
but also in the travel experiences being distinctly marked off
from the present as a special perceptual-form. The child's play
and chatter for the first few weeks are entirely full of recollections of his journey, and even months later on he loves to
recall isolated experiences of that time.

Gunther (2 ; 3), after a holiday in the Riesengebirge. "His
principal remembrance was the cowshed, as he showed by the
herdboy's characteristic call *beda, beda*, and by crying out
hild cow (wild cow), his name for a cow with a particularly
loud voice. Every day he played, too, *puff-puff*, in recollection
of the railway. Three and a half weeks after our return we
also questioned him to test the presence of definite recollections. We asked him about our host's dog, about the village
children with whom ours had played, about the stable inmates,
and in his simple language he could answer us on every
point."

A very vague similarity in a picture called up in Eva
(3 ; 1) a most vivid holiday remembrance no less than four
months after the experience:—

"In her picture-book, as she came to a beautiful forest
scene, she grew excited and began after this fashion: *Now
once we were there : we sat on the seat and the sun glistened
through the trees. Then we ran round the hill and through the
seats.* Her recollection was of the forest church in the seaside
resort of Binz, which consisted of numbers of seats arranged
under the trees. We had seen a wonderful sunset there, as the
sun's fiery beams poured a flood of golden light through the
green branches. (There was no setting sun on the suggestive
picture.)"

As the examples show, the recollections at this early age
almost exclusively refer to the visible world of objects and
actions; the region of speech and logic to which the ear gives
access is, in comparison with this, of far less concern for the
action of memory. It is true the child has really great power
of memory for language—as is shown by its learning to talk
and its mastery of very many children's rhymes; but this is
knowledge gained by the combined effect of frequent repetitions, not recollections of a thought expressed but once. Such
recollections seem to make their first appearance about the

age of 3 ; 0, but even then only very seldom, and they are of much shorter duration than optical remembrances.

Scupin (3 ; 4). The boy had asked for his shells to play with, but his mother, who did not know where they were, made the excuse that before they left home she had given them to a little child, who had long since lost them. The boy was very distressed about this; ten days later, however, the boy found the shells, and, terribly upset, came to his mother: *"But, mother, you did say you had given them away, and the little child had lost the shells!"* (II, p. 38).

Eva (2 ; 11½). The child had had her photograph taken, and as it was to be a Christmas surprise for her father, they had to see that Eva did not tell him. So her mother impressed it on her with: "You mustn't tell father, mustn't tell until the tree is all lit up." When the child at different times after was reminded: "Mind, Eva, not to tell father," her quick answer came: *Of course not, only when the tree is all lit up*, and she obeyed the injunction too.

The example also shows that at 3 ; 0 the will can already be effective in specially noting anything. We noticed just the same in Hilde (3 ; 0), who was instructed one evening before she went to sleep to ring for the nurse next morning when she woke, and carried out the request correctly.

Another of Eva's recollections at that time referred to one of her thoughts to which she had given expression at an earlier date but now saw was wrong.

. Eva (3 ; 1). "At dinner one day, conversation showed that Eva thought 'ladies' were only women-strangers, so that her mother was no lady. One and three-quarter months later she said of some new clothes of her mother's: *Just like a lady's.* Her mother asked: 'Then am I not a lady?' Eva: *Yes, but once at dinner I said no, you are not a lady.*"

The fact that the young child has normally but little power of remembering speech heard only once, as regards the meaning, is also of educational significance. On the one hand the grown-ups rely unfairly on this weakness, e.g. they promise the child something for a future date only either to pacify him or to distract his attention. The child's forgetfulness generally, indeed, plays into their hands, but not always, and if the recollection unexpectedly comes to life, and the child notices that there is no intention of redeeming the promise, both his feeling of happy confidence and his natural sincerity are imperilled. On the other hand, grown-ups in their orders and prohibitions, especially given for the first time, do not sufficiently take into account the child's forgetfulness. Any definite order, e.g. "You are to keep out of the puddles", may be obeyed at first by a well-disposed child, only after a few minutes to be transgressed out of pure failure to remember.

After the third year, remembrance increases so rapidly, both in frequency and extent, that it is only worth while to mention cases distinguished by some special peculiarity.

A single memory-form may now include a large number of details, not in isolated detachment, but reproduced in their right relation. This is specially true in cases of place-remembrance. The topography of a landscape, the position of different rooms, the order of streets and turns in the road where a walk is often taken, are all remembered, and sometimes with quite amazing exactitude and distinctness.

Eva (3 ; 1). "A zither was casually mentioned in our conversation, and the word called forth in Eva the recollection of an incident that had occurred five and a half months sooner, and in great excitement she poured forth: '*Yes, I know a zither: in Krummhubel there was once a blind woman and a man: the man sang and the woman played a zither. They stood by the house Villa Marie and we stood by the tower, and you, mother, were up in the loggia listening.*' Every detail was right, and the incident had never been mentioned since."

Sometimes such place-remembrance is accompanied by a very expressive topographical demonstration; the child not only has a vivid picture of the whole scene, but mentally goes along the same roads, a motor-remembrance mingling with that of sight. The absolute size and length are treated with right royal indifference; the child reproduces on a smaller scale, just as we do in maps. Its whole interest is centred in the relative position, direction and change of direction, and these it accurately reproduces.

Hilde (4 ; 2). "After her return from a morning walk with her brother and the nurse she reported: '*Then we sat here with Marie*—pointing to a spot on the table—*and then played by this tree*—pointing to another spot—*and then we went so*— her finger marking the direction on the table—*and then round so and down here*'—showing the way all the time."

Children's memory for locality is shown, too, in their ability to act as guide along roads familiar to them.

Scupin's son (3 ; 4) undertook the guidance of the party in the Zoological Garden from cage to cage, and at 4 ; 4 the report goes on: "The boy knows the way to K.—about two miles—so well already that he goes right at every bend of the road, and then turns round to see if we are following" (II, 37).

With increasing mastery of space comes, too, corresponding mastery of time, and the latent periods grow longer and longer. In the fourth year it is no longer rare to find recollection of occurrences happening many months before with nothing to revive their memory in the interval; occasionally, even, we find reminiscence after a year's interval. It is indeed the recurring season that brings with it a return of events (the summer holiday, Christmas feast) that have not been thought of since, and so revives the recollection of the same event a year ago.

Thus Scupin's son (3 ; 3) on a summer holiday in the mountains recollected this and that experience of the previous year in the same place—that an aunt had lived in a certain room, and that a gentleman in a restaurant had threatened him in fun because he would not eat, etc. (II, 23); (3 ; 10) at a birthday party he not only recognized a lady whom he had only seen once, a year before, but at once asked if she would play the same game with him again as she had done then (II, 80).[1]

In the fifth year it is actually possible to say that the child has recollections of his youth! Any chance incident may suffice to call from the depths of unconsciousness an event experienced more than half his life before and never since renewed. We noted down two observations of this astonishing capacity in our son, and since then Scupin and Frau T. Ehrlich

[1] That such remembrances are possible at a much earlier age is evident from a written communication for which I am indebted to Dr. Sperber (Vienna). Herr and Frau Sperber went with their little daughter (2 ; 1) in the summer of 1924 to the same holiday resort as the year before, but to a different house. The child led her mother to the last year's flat, ran straight into the empty rooms where it had lived: *there Detta lives*; showed when asked where the bed stood, where the milk was kept, and such things. Also another remembrance came to light. The mother pointed out the hairdresser's little house, asking, "What did we do there, then?" The child, it is true, did not remember the haircutting, but had not forgotten once sitting with her mother on the seat in front of the house and playing with a little dog: *Detta plays with bow-wow, sat on bench.* The latent period lasted 10 months.

have recorded similar confirmation. These examples are as follows:—

Gunther (4 ; 6 and 4 ; 11½). "Our present nurse put on a blue and white striped blouse, and at once Gunther cried: *You look like Marie, Marie wore a blouse like that.* His little sister had on for the first time a frock of black and white check, when Gunther remarked: *Eva, you are Marie.* His mother: 'How do you mean?' Gunther: *Well, Marie she had a dress like that, only not the blue and black* (pointing to the trimming). As a matter of fact, a former nurse wore in the summer, when she left us, a blouse almost identical in colour and cut with the other maid's; moreover, at the same time she used to wear a black and white check dress."

Both facts had never been mentioned in the intervals of respectively two and a quarter and two and three-quarter years.

Scupin's son (4 ; 2). "To-day he suddenly recollected a gollywog that was given him in his first year, but thrown away, worn out, as soon as his second year. Now, Bubi had got, later on, another gollywog, and we thought it was this one he referred to, but he said with decision: *'No, I want a gollywog like the one before ; he had yellow tassels, and the other hadn't.'* That was right too. The first year's gollywog had yellow metal tassels, a decoration wanting in the other, so his is a reminiscence dating from nearly three years back."

Lore Ehrlich (4 ; 11). "Lore said lately she remembered the visit of a relative who came to see us nearly three years ago. I thought such a long memory impossible, and tested it with questions; but she knew quite correctly: *The lady was in mourning and we sat in the blue room.*"

What now are the original factors that give to certain experiences that unexpected persistence which fixes them in memory for a considerable time? This question can be answered on general lines, but in individual cases the child's fragmentary remembrances are, often enough, distinctly puzzling.

To begin with, it is certain that many impressions (especially optical) of a purely sensorial nature have unusual after-effects. They keep their form and colour quite otherwise than in adults, almost indeed with the force of an hallucination; even a long interval during which they were not recalled to consciousness does not deprive them of this sense-distinctness. Thus, indeed, it is characteristic of all our last examples that,

in every case, colours and brightness have been remembered
from an age when the children knew no colour-names, and
therefore remembered not their designations but the colours
themselves. These psychic contents are presumably allied to
the so-called "vision pictures" which were lately investigated
by E. Jaensch (Marburg) and his school, although amongst
older children.[1] Jaensch gives this name to those effects of
optical impressions which are not of so weak a character as
the reproductions of memory, but, in appearance and functional
laws, resemble perceptions. He designates the disposition to
such distinct mental pictures as "eidetic faculty", and looks
upon it as a phenomenon of development appearing especially
in the first stages of puberty and dying away afterwards. It
would be well worth while to investigate the occurrence and
nature of such pictures in young children as well.

But we must now enquire further why certain experiences
keep this character of distinctness which is lost by most others.
In such cases, our minds turn to the special affective-tone
which also played its part in other memory phenomena. An
experience strongly tinged with emotion makes a far deeper
impression and keeps more persistent form and colour than
one that is indifferent. It is true the emotions that deepen the
impression are not always so apparent to the spectator as
in our son in the example above; there, evidently, the keen
feelings of attachment felt by the two-year-old boy for the
nurse contributed to the certainty of the after-remembrance.

In less transparent cases, the psychoanalysts have in readiness the expedient of accepting as the real reason of the
remembrance an erotic or even infantile-sexual impulse; this
is rendered possible by the familiar symbolic interpretations
which see in far-off contents of consciousness covering pretexts
for sexual emotions whose accuracy can be tested by no
scientific standard.

For example, if we read the chapter "Remembrance" in
Hug-Hellmuth's book, we might imagine that the little child
had scarcely any but sexual reasons for remembrance.

We quote here a striking instance of the way in which
one of our own observations receives an entirely arbitrary
interpretation.[2]

[1] Compare the summarized treatment by Jaensch and Kroh.
[2] *Monograph*, II., p. 56.

We reported: "Gunther (2 ; 4). The picture of a serpent with double rings called forth the words *bille* (= brille = [spectacles]) and *Ella*. Explanation: Their mother a month before in Schreiberhau had made and given the children cardboard spectacles to play at 'Doctor'; and a playfellow, Ella, had also brought such spectacles once for herself. The serpent's double rings reminded the boy of the spectacles, and these of the game with Ella."

Hug-Hellmuth now remarks on this: "The pronounced sexual note of the favourite Doctor game and the eroticism of young children's friendships are a sufficient explanation of the occurrence of this vivid remembrance."

The little child's emotional life is, after all, in reality much more varied and beyond our comprehension than these stereotyped sexual interpretations will allow. Let us rather concede that we are not always in a position to determine, at any given time, the nature of the feeling-tone that bestows upon an impression an unexpected revival later on.

Similar consideration is also true for the reverse side of memory, namely for chance lapse of remembrance. That is, there are impressions which at the time of occurrence were accompanied by the strongest feeling-tone, and, for a shorter or longer period, took entire possession of the child's soul; and, later on, seemed absolutely wiped out, as though they had never existed. Here it is true psychoanalysis will certainly be right with the weighty explanatory principle of the power of repression; the painful impression must be banished, and the banishment is successful.[1] Other cases, however, are only due to simple fading away and forgetting. Thus it seems to me that only the first of the two following instances of amnesia (loss of remembrance) is a case of possible repression.

Gunther (3 ; 1) saw the breaking-in of horses at a circus; at the very first he was terrified, had to be taken out, was afraid for his sister, who had stayed inside, wanted to go back again, and only after much hesitation and terror and anxiety did his delighted interest win the victory, and for many days after his favourite game was "circus". Barely two years later we chanced to speak of it again. We tried by questions and suggestions to revive his recollection of an experience so charged with emotion, but entirely in vain!

[1] On the subject of "Repression", cf. Chap. XXXIII.

Scupin's son acted in much the same way with regard to the rabbit he had owned for nine months from the age of 2 ; 2, loved very much, and mentioned afterwards from time to time.

When (4 ; 8½) he saw a photograph of himself with the rabbit he asked in surprise: *"I never saw such a rabbit as that, why is one like that taken with me?"* We reminded him of different details, but he looked at us in astonishment, shook his head, and assured us he knew nothing about it (II, 141).

3. Later Recollections of Early Childhood

If even during childhood's years memories are so scanty and quickly become even scantier by forgetfulness and repression, it might be thought that in the later periods of human life there would be no traces at all left of any recollections connected with the earliest years of earthly existence. But that is not the case, however, as we learn from the collection of autobiographical childhood's remembrances which we owe to Reichardt. Even though we have to subtract large portions of these narratives as having a possible origin in subsequent interpretations and poetical embellishments, yet there still remains sufficient material which evidently bears the genuine stamp of truth.

Here it is only possible to note some general results from Reichardt's investigations. First of all we notice that such recollections may under certain circumstances go back as far as the second year. We should think this impossible if the date was not fixed by some objective characteristic, as in the case reported by Carus—the psychologist from the beginning of the eighteenth century who has lately come into fresh repute once more.[1]

"I should myself scarcely believe that a reminiscence from such early childhood could be retained, but I cannot doubt it because my mother's second son was born not quite two years after me and because my memory plainly shows me this boy, who so soon after left this world again. I know that I saw an elderly woman in a gold-embroidered cap—the midwife—dressing a little baby."

[1] From Reichardt, p. 16. The *portion*, too, of Stifter's autobiography quoted in Chap. VI of this present book may be referred to again.

Carus designates this picture as being "of a daguerreotype nature, very firmly imprinted" and also the examples of others from this earliest period are similarly characterized as something like flashlight photographs which stand out as isolated pictures in the complete darkness and void of that early time.

In addition there are examples of experiences in which for some reason or other the purely sense impression has been of such an especially intensive character as to leave behind an enduring picture. Amongst these—as regards the part played by the various senses—the sense of sight is especially noticeable. But recollections of definite experiences of bodily sensations, of a sense of situation and movement, also play a certain part; acoustic memoriés (musical impressions, noises) are rare, whilst memories of smell and taste never have an independent character but only act as the incentive of other reminiscences.

Amongst the early memories due to the sensorial persistence of the impression, there are to be noted those in which the part played by the senses may be much less pronounced; in such cases emphasis is laid by careful observers on their incomprehensibly vague and indistinct character ("Pale pencil notes from the diary of one long gone" they are called by the astronomer-workman Bürgel). If these pictures, in spite of their faint outlines, possess such astonishing persistence as to enable them to return again after tens of years, we must once more attribute this persistence to their emotional emphasis. Reichardt's material provides very ample opportunity to confirm this assumption. All those childish emotions which we shall discuss in detail later on here appear as a fixative of memory; we hear of feelings of tenderness, of hatred, of experiences in which self-confidence was strengthened or shaken, of terrifying or eerie impressions, of feasts and deaths. Here too the selection is mystifying. For the child has indeed had experiences much more charged with emotion; how was it then that it was just some of these mental excitements with their attendant circumstances that took firm root in the psychic nature whilst innumerable others finally disappeared entirely?

Of course too there are examples of sense emphasis combined with a strong emotional factor, an illustration of which is given us by Bertha von Suttner in a record from her third year.[1]

She was to go to a picnic with her mother and relates as follows: "I was dressed in a white cashmere frock made up with narrow red borders—a beautiful thing, cut low at the neck—I can still see the pattern of the stitchery, I could even draw it. How astonished everyone would be when they saw it! I felt beautiful, positively beautiful in it." But clouds began to cover the sky, the order was given for the child's frock to be changed. She resisted with all her might and main. The next picture shows me the brilliantly dressed, beautiful and energetic creature lying face downwards on a big table, the red embroidered frock lifted and the mother's hand inflicting a shower of blows on the body below—"To-day I cannot tell why this occurrence made so deep an impression in my soul; was it due to my injured pride in the charming frock or the insult inflicted on my feeling of self-respect by the disciplinary measures adopted? Possibly to both."

Amongst affective experiences, remembered in later life, occur such as are not capable of expression during childhood itself, either because they had been at once banished into the Unconscious or remained hidden from the outside world in the inner recesses of the soul, or lastly because the child still lacked words to tell of the emotional impulse.

Hebbel in his diaries tells how when he was sent to the infant school at the age of four he straightway lost his heart to a little girl. He paints his feeling with poetic licence and then continues: "But no one must guess what my feelings were, Emilie least of all. I took the greatest pains to avoid her not to betray my secret."[2]

Here is another example by J. W. Grosse.[3] "I had once abstracted a small silver sixpence—yet this coin lay on my conscience for endless years. I believe I would have confessed this sin of a four-year-old child at my preparation for confirmation if such a course had been customary. No one either then or later ever knew of it."

The strong emotional tincture of those recollections makes it permissible here to draw certain educational conclusions. In these reminiscences of early childhood there is evidence of the persistent effects that may be caused by mistaken

[1] Reichardt, pp. 69 and 78.   [2] Id., p. 57.   [3] Id., p. 313.

measures of education. Our attention is called to this fact by
Faulwasser, who quotes a number of examples from the—as
yet—unpublished Leipzig material in the Volkelt collection.
The terrorizing with wicked men, animals or ghosts, unjust
punishments, broken promises and other educational sins may
make so deep an impression that the sufferers under such
methods after many decades still remember them with marked
feelings of pain. Amongst the 1,500 childhood's recollections
in this collection 100, roughly speaking, are of the variety
just mentioned.

Another division which we must make within these adult
reminiscences of their early childhood is that between memories
that always persisted and those that only recurred after a long
"latent period". We are told of many individual impressions
—especially those of an optical nature—that they were never
quite lost and reappeared on many occasions. But then there
are others that awake from their deathlike trance after an
interval lasting tens of years—to the excessive and often
terror-stricken surprise of their owners. Sometimes these arise
of their own accord quite without any special cause, especially
in old age, but often they are produced along the lines of
association by some apparently remote impression.

Gabrielle Reuter relates[1] that the night-light used to make
a great impression upon her as a small child and especially
the oil. Whilst the water remained clear, in time there collected
in the oil a multitude of tiny things—dead flies, moth wings,
match-heads, cotton-ends, that shone in the thick golden mass
as if imprisoned in yellow amber. All that had been long since
forgotten until once, almost fifty years later, the writer was
sailing on an Alpine lake, "through whose blue water we
could see such strange shining things on its bed, in reality
nothing more than moss and algæ. Then suddenly the 'won-
drous joy' again revived which had once upon a time been
born in her as she gazed into the night-light oil."

Lastly we find in many reminiscences the quality of MAG-
NIFIED REMEMBRANCE, especially whenever the adult returns
to the scenes of his childhood and compares the actual impression with his conception. Almost always then, it happens that
his memory of dwellings and distances differs greatly in size
from reality. What does that betoken? That there is no stan-

[1] Reichardt, p. 267.

dard size in his former pictures, but their measurements are in accord with the size and powers of those who possess them, as compared with the environment at the time the original impression was made. The child retains, as it were, the significant note, the relative measurement, and therefore distances that required distinct effort to traverse in early childhood are remembered as large; a square, a garden, seems gigantic because in those days its boundaries seemed almost to correspond with those of the known world. This significant note sometimes persists to a certain degree in spite of the fresh corrective-perception, as is shown by the following remark made by de la Motte Fouqué concerning his paternal home:[1] ". . . of the first pictures of external environment offered to the mind of the child and still existing in the aged man's consciousness and that too in exceedingly large dimensions, reduced as they may often be to smaller scale when the reality is seen in later life, they yet retain in the depths of one's mind their quality of strange enlargement."

4. Errors in Recollection

After this digression into adult reminiscences of childhood we will now return to the memory of the child himself.

The work of memory is rendered less efficient not only by forgetting but also by error; and this last is the more to be feared because it does not betray itself at once, but speaks with the assurance and certainty of a positive fact. The "psychology of expression", studied so much in the last few years, has considerably increased our knowledge of the amount and kind of errors in remembrance; yet these researches have been almost entirely limited to school-children and adults, with but occasional notice of early childhood. Yet even then we can prove certain fundamental features.[2] These are verified, on one hand, by errors in recollection noticed in the little child's natural life, on the other by simple experiments with pictures.

We only speak of an "error" in recollection when with SUBJECTIVE SINCERITY a statement OBJECTIVELY FALSE is made concerning a past experience. None of those false state-

[1] Reichardt, p. 276.
[2] Further details in *Monograph* II, by C. and W. Stern, Chaps. III, VII, VIII.

R

ments where the misstatement is consciously made, either in
joke or earnest, belong to this section; we shall not deal
with them, until we come to the later sections on play and
falsehood.

Now, how can it come to pass that human remembrance
sometimes not only gradually fades away but also becomes
absolutely misleading?

Here, to begin with, we are helped by the distinction we
have drawn between "memory" and "remembrance". In our
memory we have numberless presentations, arising from earlier
impressions; but a remembrance is only such a presentation
as refers to a definite time, that is, then, having a time-index.
Now, if any memory-presentation—however correct and vivid
it may be in itself—gets a wrong time-index, the remembrance
is in error. The individual thinks then that an occurrence in
reality belonging to a period x, happened in period y, and
brings fragments from the periods x and z into a description
which, according to his idea, belongs to y. So we find the
paradox that someone may have a very rich, tenacious and
clear memory, and yet be liable to many errors in remembrance, in so far as he is wanting in keen and cautious differentiation of time. Now, in early childhood, as we have seen,
there is already no lack of memory-presentations, but time-
consciousness, at any rate for periods fairly far back, is but
very poorly developed, and the worst errors would take place
then if the child, in spite of this, should try to provide his
memory contents with a definite time-index.

But fortunately this is not usual in the child's presentations,
at any rate, when these are spontaneous, because he lacks the
desire as well as the power to fix a definite time. The four-
year-old child has indeed an indefinite impression of "long
ago", and the broad distinction between "earlier" and "later",
but it is impossible for him to refer back an event to "the day
before yesterday" or "last week", to say nothing of a definite
month. Sometimes he can indeed say with some probability
of accuracy: "Such and such a thing was to-day", or, "That
wasn't to-day", but scarcely use "yesterday" as a more exact
limit for remembrances in the less immediate past. So far as
he is capable of making any time-distinction between his
remembrances, he does so generally by the help of respective
differences of place; an expression such as "that was Schrei-

berhau" is in his eyes not only information as to place, but an indefinite time-indication as well.

And it is just this indefinite fixation of time which gives him a certain protection from erroneous remembrance. But the defence ceases to be effective when the child is forced to give a definite time-remembrance, as he then, without a second thought, assigns any memory-presentation that happens to appear to the time suggested to him. And, indeed, questions referring to the child's remembrance do, as a rule, demand a more or less special determination of time. The child is asked, not if he ever happened to meet his playfellow X. in his walk, but if he met him to-day; not, if he has ever brushed his teeth, but if he did it that same morning, and so on. The inevitable result of such harmless questions as provocation in early childhood is to call forth a whole host of entirely innocent errors in reminiscence; the child says "yes" because the question really revives the memory-presentation of his playfellow or tooth-brushing, and the specialized idea of to-day has not yet been grasped by him.

A very general pronouncement of the psychology of self-expression states that far fewer errors in remembrance are to be found in spontaneous accounts than in answers to questions; we understand now why this appears especially true as regards early childhood. Every educator ought clearly to realize that questions referring to remembrance may have a twofold result: (1) the positive result of bringing to light correct and important details which would not have been mentioned without the question; (2) the negative result of obtaining random answers which, to a great extent, may be wrong.

This injurious result becomes so much the worse as questioning passes on to regular cross-examination. For the greater the force exercised on the child by questions, the more pronounced the tendency to wake from its dark, confused slumber any memory-presentation whatsoever, and then—since the questioner seems to wish it—to refer it to the matter under discussion. Yet the child acts in all good faith, as does too his cross-questioner, who has no idea that his inquisition alone is the real cause of the misstatement.

It is especially serious when the question is so framed as to suggest a definite memory-presentation; e.g. "Didn't you see your little brother break the cup?" In the case of such suggestive questions the child finds it much easier to say "yes" than "no", and the younger the child, the greater the "suggestibility". This is plainly proved by the experiments described below.

But let us go back to erroneous remembrances, not directly caused by questions from without, but to be explained by some cause from within. And first we may name transitional remembrance; if a certain attitude has been frequently produced in the child by definite questions, it may afterwards happen that in recurrent conditions he gives corresponding information apparently on his own initiative.

Gunther (2 ; 4). "To-day Gunther came back from a walk with a tale—unprompted but incorrect. *Met Nanny and Polly.* These were two little friends that they had often met, but not for the two preceding weeks. The apparent spontaneity of this statement, I think, was really the result of my usual question to the little company on their return: 'Have you met anyone?' Gunther in response to the suggestion in the question had several times given a wrong answer, and now he anticipates my enquiry by his information."

A special case of incorrect time-determination is to be found when some former object has been removed for a considerable time without the child specially noticing it; the existence of this object is then transferred as a matter of course to the present, even if its last real appearance took place a month before.

Hilde (6 ; 0). "We have a bust of Goethe which in a former house used to stand in a turret room behind the piano. In the house we have lived in for ten months now, there is a similar turret room, but Goethe's bust is not there, but in another room between two windows. One day as we were talking about books Hilde asked if the books had been written by the man who stood on a stand behind the piano. In answer to our astonished question she repeated her opinion: *Yes, behind the piano in the next room.* She thought, therefore, that an arrangement which had been changed nine months before still existed, and persisted so obstinately in her assertion that only the evidence of her own eyes would convince her otherwise."

Another fruitful source of error is the transmutation of imagination into reality, a change that is more frequent in earlier years than at any other time. The sharp demarcation between objective and subjective—of real and apparent—is, after all, of very gradual growth, and—as we shall see in our discussion of plays, falsehoods, etc.—passes through all possible degrees of transition. There we shall also discuss play with reminiscences and statements.

But quite apart from any play-motive, the child often gives proof of flagrant change from imaginary to real, especially when the presentation is associated with a strong feeling of self-interest, of expectation, or even with a decidedly logical probability. Then, in the reminiscence, hearsay becomes personal seeing, a lively hope fulfilment, or a supposition certainty. We append examples from each of our three children:—

Hilde (3 ; 10). "In February, when we were going a walk in the Park, I talked to Hilde a good deal about the swans on the lake there, and we both wondered if we should see them. But no swans were out, as the water was covered with a thin coating of ice. We talked some time as to whether they were in the water under the little swan-house, and what it might look like inside there. As we went home we talked of other things, and I asked Hilde: 'What will you tell Father?'

"She promptly answered: *That we saw the swans.*

"I: 'What did we see?'

"Hilde: *Lots of swans.*

"I: 'Did we really see swans, Hilde?'

"Hilde (thoughtfully): *No, they were inside the little house.*"

Eva (4 ; 10). "I went with the children to a dairy with the expressed intention of buying milk-cheese, which they all liked. But there was none to be had, and instead I bought some pickled cucumbers. Half an hour later Eva told her father: *To-day with mother we bought some milk-cheese.* Gunther contradicted this, and Eva corrected herself with: *Oh no, pickled cucumbers.* To her father's astonished question as to whether these were much the same thing she explained: *No, but we wanted to buy some milk-cheese.*"

Gunther (4 ; 6). At dinner the following conversation took place: "Where is Eva's soup cover? has she thrown it away again?" Gunther: *Yes, she has thrown it away.* Mother (emphatically): "Have you seen her do it?" Gunther: *Not seen her to do it, but I see it is not there, so I know.* Thus a supposition has become certainty in the boy's statement. If we had not seriously questioned him further, he would have persisted in his positive statement, but then the boy of four and a half was self-critical enough to grant that it was not a real observation, and sufficiently logical to be able to justify his conclusion. But the expression "so I know" shows, after all, how little distinction a child's simple mind makes between "think" and "know".

The issue will not always be so happy as in these three cases, in which the error could be immediately corrected. In cases where other witnesses are not forthcoming, or there is no careful test of the statement, only too often the objective error in the subjective presentation may become so firmly rooted that neither the child nor anyone else can distinguish it from reality. A few more considerations about errors in remembrance in early childhood will be most conveniently dealt with in our treatment of experiments in descriptive observation (aussage) in Chapter XVIII. But before then we must discuss conclusions of directly practical importance as regards the capacity of the child to give evidence as a witness in a court of law.

5. The Young Child as Witness

All statements before a court of law should reproduce remembrances of an earlier experience; the investigation of errors in memory-concepts is therefore of direct importance in adjudging the credibility of witnesses' pronouncements. And as children are more liable than adults to such errors, the problem in their case is of special moment and can only be solved by the closest co-operation between lawyer and psychologist of childhood and youth.[1]

Now certainly in the vast majority of cases it is children of school age or older who are summoned as witnesses in a court of law, but occasionally younger children's testimony is required, either because they themselves are said to be the objects of criminal action—maltreatment, or criminal assault —or because they are either ear- or eye-witnesses of some other crime.

I quote therefore from my book some thoughts and facts referring to early childhood.

[1] Cf. my summarized statement XI.

First of all three examples from actual life. In the first case an innocent man was condemned because the court had too much faith in the child's statement; in the second case a psychologic specialist was able to prove in time the unreliability of the young witness's testimony; in the third case a verdict of "not guilty" was given as the result of the credible witness of a young child.

1. An actor was accused of an indecent assault upon a six-year-old child. The child had, a few months before, been the victim of a similar assault, which of course reduced the unprejudiced character of her testimony. When first shown the actor by the police, the child declared he was not the guilty man; it was not until later, under her parents' influence, that she named him as her assailant. The court believed the child and the man was condemned to three years' imprisonment. In another trial the verdict was confirmed by another court, and it was only in the court of appeal that the child's statement found less credence; it turned out that she had only been induced by her father's threats to withdraw her former denial of the man's identity; moreover her statements now contained so many contradictions and discre_ _cies as to the place of assault and the appearance of the assailant that a verdict of "not guilty" had to be given. The man meantime had suffered two years' imprisonment.

2. Max Doring, the Leipzig educational psychologist and a specialist in children's statements (aussagen) writes the following: "I have once dealt with a case where two children below school age pointed out different men as the guilty parties, although the circumstances of the case made it exceedingly probable that only one was concerned in the case. So a number of persons other than those suspected were brought before the children. Their statements were not only mutually different but changed so often that the investigation ended in no decision. As a matter of fact descriptive statements offer more difficulties than any others. And in such cases of confronting the witnesses with the suspected persons an expert will of course also closely observe the children in order to form a judgment as to the degree of certainty in the child's designation of the culprit."

3. The wife of a foreman had committed suicide after a dispute with her husband. At first the man was suspected of

having murdered his wife (by hanging her in the storeroom) and was arrested. But a verdict in his favour was largely due to the announcement of his little daughter (3 ; 6) who had been with her mother immediately before she went into the storeroom. The child on the next day told what had happened to an aunt and also to the judge: "On Sunday morning mother quarrelled with father and hit him too, then father went into the sitting-room and mother stopped in the kitchen." Her mother had kissed her in the kitchen for being a good girl, then put on her stockings, gave her a little cap and bade her tell her father that mother had gone into the storeroom to put on some clothes. The child had heard her mother lock herself in. Then father had burst open the door, brought out her mother, laid her on the bed and poured water on her face. Then lots of people had come." This statement in no way gave the impression of having been learnt. It is certain that several things have crept into this report which the child could not have said in exactly that way (e.g. no child of that age could have definitely fixed a time-period like "Sunday morning"). Yet the statement is particularly rich in details which it would not occur to the examining justice to suggest to the child (mother's words, stockings, little cap, etc.). Consequently it gives the impression of being a true recollection in the main and no doubt is worthy of the credence it found with the court.

The first case shows how a man's life can be ruined by the statement of a little child because those who had to judge the truth of this statement were not sufficiently conversant with child psychology. Those who have made acquaintance in the preceding chapter with the manifold sources and striking examples of errors in child-description are no longer surprised that a six-year-old child in all good faith answers the judge's questions by reporting things that never happened or accusing people who had no hand in the matter, but from an average lawyer—and police officers particularly—we can no more expect any real knowledge of a child's nature (*psyche*) than we can expect methods suited to childhood as a whole in the treatment and interrogation of the little witness. As indeed the whole terrifying formality of a legal proceeding is peculiarly adapted to put the child into an uncomfortable position and thus prejudice even more the spontaneity of its statements.

On this account the demand has sometimes been made that the witness of children under seven years of age should not be accepted for legal purposes. But under certain circumstances that might only prove an incitement to crime if the offenders knew that their victims were not allowed to tell their tale.

Our third example also shows that in certain cases—though they may be rare—the positive contents of a child's statement may be of the greatest importance.

A solution of the difficulty might be found in the proposal made in my book, mentioned above, which runs as follows:

"Children not yet fit to attend school—i.e. then normal children to the end of their sixth year and sub-normal backward children relatively longer—shall not be summoned as witnesses but only questioned before the case is tried and then by a lawyer, versed in child psychology, who should call to his aid someone professionally trained in the education and psychology of young children. A report shall be made of this examination, giving questions and answers, a description of the child's behaviour and an opinion of those conducting the examination as to his credibility. Those who took any part in the questioning shall moreover be summoned as witnesses at the actual legal proceedings." The most important condition in this is the co-operation of an expert in child-psychology (cf. Example 2), who should be summoned as soon as possible before unavoidable suggestions of the most pregnant nature—whether from the side of the police, parents or others—have exercised their influence on the child.

CHAPTER XVIII

EXPERIMENTS IN DESCRIPTIVE OBSERVATION (AUSSAGE)[1]

EXPERIMENTS in "aussage" on little children have so far been made entirely by means of pictures. The test can be carried out principally as follows:—

1. The child is asked to describe a picture seen only once either—

(a) Immediately after looking at the picture ("primary aussage"),

(b) Again, some time later ("secondary aussage").

2. A "continuous impression" is used as the test for description, i.e. a picture which has been a considerable time before the child's eyes, e.g. hanging on the wall; this continuous impression may be either—

(a) One that has existed up to the moment of the description, e.g. a picture hanging in the next room;

(b) One that in the past has existed for a long time, but has been non-existent for some time before the description, e.g. a picture removed from the wall some months before.

The "aussage" can be given in the form of a description (connected narrative) or of a cross-examination (answers to separate questions, a series of which have been drawn up as the result of systematic trials); as a rule both methods are combined. It is valuable, both from a psychological and educational point of view, after the test is over to put the picture before the child once more and let him find out what mistakes he has made (self-correction).

1. Tests with Pictures Seen Only Once

As an example how such aussage-tests may be carried out at a very early age, we append the result obtained from Eva (2 ; 11). A picture she had not seen before, "The Breakfast" (cf. Plate III), was laid before her for two minutes, and she was

---

[1] *Aussage* = statement or description, as the result of observation.

asked to say all she could see on it; then the picture was taken away and an account and examination followed.

During the Two-Minute Observation of the Picture.

A. Observation and Description.	B. Examination.	
	Question.	*Answer.*
Gunther eats bread—and here is Tony (the cook)—flower. What is that? (Mother answers: A satchel.) *For the boy—that is a cupboard there and that a room* (pointing to the door). *Where do you go into? And that is the kitchen. What is Gunther eating I wonder? Bread.*	Is the woman standing or sitting?	*Standing—Gunther sits.*
	Has she got an apron on?	*Tied round her.*
	What colour is it?	*Green.*
	What has she got in her hand?	*I don't know without being told.*
	Can you see a table?	*Yes.*
	What is lying on the table?	*Bread.*
	What else?	*Nothing else.*
	Isn't there butter as well?	*No.*
	Has she got a knife in her hand?	*No.*

After Taking away the Picture.

A. Description.	B. Examination.	
	Question.	*Answer.*
(Mother: Now try and tell me all you have seen.)	How is Gunther dressed?	*Suit, stocking.*
Gunther, Tony, Flower in room.	What is he doing?	*Eating.*
	How does he hold it?	*In his hand.*
(What else?) Door.	Is there a door in the room?	*Yes.*
(What more?) Tony.	Open or shut?	*Open.*
Gunther.	Can you see what is outside?	*No.*
	Can you see a box?	*No.*
	Can you see a flower-pot?	*No—yes.*
	Where was it?	*On the cupboard.*
	Can you see a satchel?	*Yes.*
	Where?	*Down on the ground.*
	What does it look like?	*Like the table.*
	Can you see a jug?	*No.*

Secondary Aussage, three days later; the picture not seen in the interval.

A. Description.	B. Examination.
(Mother: Do you remember my showing you a picture here on the table? What could you see on it?)	1. Was the mother standing or sitting?
	1. *Standing. Gunther was sitting.*
	2. What is the woman doing?
	2. *She was cooking soup and the satchel was there too.*

A. Description (contd.).	B. Examination (contd.).	
Gunther, Tony, Mother, Door.	3. Had she an apron? What colour?	3. Yes. Green.
(And what else?) Else (the nurse), Tony.	4. What was she holding?	4. A spoon for the soup.
(You saw Tony and Mother?)	5. Had she a knife in her hand?	5. No.
Yes, and Else too.	6. Had she got bread in her hand?	6. Yes.
(Do you remember any-thing else?)	7. Can you see a table?	7. Yes.
Door.	8. What lies on the table?	8. Bread.
(Anything else?)	9. What else was on table?	9. Nothing else at all, but the bread was on the table.
Hans—nothing else there at all.	10. But you said Tony was making soup.	10. But it was bread.
	11. No soup then?	11. Only bread.
	12. How was Gunther dressed?	12. Suit and stockings.
	13. Wasn't he bare-footed?	13. No, shoes and stock-ings.
	14. What is he doing?	14. Eating bread.
	15. How does he hold it?	15. In his hand.
	16. Is the door shut or open?	16. Open.
	17. Can you see what is outside?	17. Yes, nothing but little pots.
	18. Do you not see a window?	18. No.
	19. Do you see a flower-pot?	19. Yes, there is a flower-pot.
	20. What is standing on the ground?	20. A school satchel.
	21. Do you see a jug?	21. No.

Explanatory.

The number of statements given in the "primary aussage" was 35—5 wrong; in the secondary, 37—8 wrong; if the extreme youth be taken into account, the sum-total remembrance was therefore quite excellent. It must be owned by far the greater number of statements were extracted by questions; in the unaided accounts we only find four and five respectively, hence spontaneous remembrance in the three-year-old child is still very small. The effect of the interval between the primary and secondary aussage is not shown by an increase of forgetfulness (for the number of right statements at worst remains the same), but it is in an increase of error. The mistakes made are caused in great part by confusion with impressions arising from other pictures, e.g. this is the cause of the indecision shown in the secondary aussage, when Eva first makes a wrong statement about making soup, but then rightly substitutes bread-cutting. The colour-mistakes are of no importance, since at that time the child was not yet sure of colour-names. In addition, some things really there (jug and knife) were not allowed. On the other hand, exactly the opposite error, the invention of objects not to be seen, does not once occur in the primary aussage and but seldom in the secondary, a proof of the child's good power of observation and her extreme freedom from suggestibility. For in the examination strongly suggestive questions were purposely introduced, e.g. "Isn't the boy barefooted?" "Isn't there butter as well?" But Eva's sure remembrance and great independence of mind prevented their having any effect on her, although they very often have on children of that age or even older.

In such an "aussage"-test, then, in spite of its shortness, we get an insight into the different aspects of childish individuality.

We applied the same test to her brother, two and a half years older, and since want of space forbids our giving the full result, we will only mention a few points showing the decided progress in aussage proficiency between 2 ; 11 and 5 ; 5.

Now, with Gunther we were able to secure such SILENT consideration of the picture as is usual in aussage-tests, which was not yet possible with Eva. The number of statements is about twice as large, 67 compared with Eva's 37, but most striking was the great development of spontaneity, for whilst Eva in her unaided report only gave 4 to 5 statements, Gunther gave 20. Moreover, whilst Eva in her report only gave a bare enumeration of nouns, Gunther, on the other hand, rose to description of the actions represented, and even some reference to relative positions. The persistence, too, of the memory-presentations has increased, for although the secondary aussage did not take place for a week (in Eva's case three days), it was in no way inferior to the primary, either in quality or quantity.

The relative number of Gunther's mistakes exceeded Eva's; $13\frac{1}{2}$ statements (20 per cent.) were wrong in the primary test, 12 (18 per cent.) in the secondary. Of these mistakes far the greater number were made in the answers to questions, so that with him, as with Eva, we find proof of an important point in aussage-psychology mentioned earlier (see Chapter XVII). The errors were partly due to the fact that Gunther tried to give a great deal of information about the colours depicted (five wrong colours followed seven correctly given), and that he often succumbed to suggestive questions, e.g. he adopted the suggestion of a window and of a lid to the jug.

The greater maturity of five and a half years is shown, too, in the power of self-correction. When after the secondary aussage the picture was again put before him, he could, either quite unaided, or with very little help, find out his mistakes: *The pot is not like what I said, it is green*—(his answer had given it as white-blue); *it has no lid*, etc.

This self-correction is not only of psychological significance, but is doubtless of educational value as well, for to find faults oneself makes a much deeper impression than to have them pointed out by others; thus the request for self-criticism after the examination is a help in getting more correct observation and reproduction.

Scupins have also proved that even children of four and a half are capable of this self-correction. About that time they made with the picture of the peasant's room (Plate III) a test similar to the one described above, and when after the secondary aussage the picture was put before the child again, he at once said: *About the kitten I said wrong—white and yellow colour I said, and it's black and white instead. And the lamp I said wrong, it's not hanging*, etc.

Lately in England a small number of three- and four-year-old kindergarten children have been tested by Winch in exactly the same way, with the same picture. Unfortunately, statistics have only been given of the right statements and not of the errors.

In the primary aussage, the spontaneous descriptions gave 8·3, the answers to questions 13·2 right statements; in the secondary (after a week) the figures are: description 9, answers 15·8.

As with us, it was found here, and indeed without the exception of a single child, that the lapse of a few days in no way diminished but rather increased the number of correct memory presentations. Evidently the first aussage suffered from the novelty of the task; but it formed an experience which was all to the good in the second aussage.

Winch tried too to get the children to correct their own mistakes, but without any success; evidently then this power does not exist before the fifth year—which we also found in our test.

The effect of suggestive questioning, touched upon several times already, had once been made the subject of a special enquiry held by Lipman and Wendriner amongst the pupils— six boys and six girls aged from four to six years—of a private kindergarten. The children had to look carefully for one minute at the coloured picture of the peasant's room, Plate III, and were then required to answer suggestive questions, all framed differently, about nine objects in it. By a particular turn of question it was possible for every object to test the effect of three different grades of suggestion. A few examples will make this clear.

The question as to the colour of the woman's apron (blue) was put (a) to four children in the non-suggestive form: "What colour is the woman's apron?" (b) to the four other children in the form of an expectant suggestion: "Isn't the woman's apron red?" (c) to the remaining four children in the misleading form of either, or (both wrong): "Is the apron red or green?" The result was: Question (a) produced three right, one wrong answer: Question (b) four wrong answers, i.e., assent to red; Question (c) two wrong and two undecided (*I don't know*). Thus no right answers at all were given to the suggestive questions.

The attempt by questioning to get a jacket fastened on to the peasant sitting at the table had a somewhat different result. Although the questions (a) and (b) were fairly suggestive: (a) "Has the man got his jacket on?" (b) "Has the man got on a torn jacket?" the wrong "yes" did not once come in reply, but instead five correct and three undecided answers. But it was an entirely different matter with the children who were tormented with a false hypothesis: "Is the man's jacket torn?" By this form of question the questioner seemed to assume the man's jacket as self-evident, and only to wish information about its condition, and that matter-of-course assumption misled the children; not one of the four gave the only right answer that the man had no jacket at all.

A third series of questions touched on the object in the man's hand. The non-suggestive form (a) "What has the man got in his hand?" led to three right answers (a spoon) and one indefinite. The suggestive question (b) "Hasn't he got a knife

and fork in his hand?" produced two noes but two wrong
affirmatives as well. The false hypothesis, question (c): "What
is the man cutting with the knife in his hand?" was answered
wrong three times and indefinitely once.

Limited in extent as these tests are, yet they are sufficient
to prove how carefully the form of questions must be watched
in testing little children. The less suggestive the question, the
greater the likelihood of a correct answer.

2. Aussage after a Continuous Impression

Six months after the experiment on our children mentioned
above (Section 1) we made a second; Gunther was now 6 ; o
Eva 3 ; 6½ old. This time a picture was chosen which the
children had seen not once but endless times, namely a nursery
frieze "The Goosegirl," which for years had hung in their nursery
in a position where they could see it easily. One would think
that this continual repetition of the impression must create
recollection of extraordinary extent and intensity, but a test
showed that this supposition is by no means self-evident. The
children were examined in another room without any preparation, i.e. they had not been allowed one more look at the picture
beforehand. We give the result below—in the case of wrong
statements the right answer is added thus (   ) (cf. Plate II).

Gunther 6 ; o.

A. DESCRIPTION.

The woman that was walking had a white (black) apron and a red
skirt, I think. Green trees with apples falling down and many geese.
The woman had a kind of rake (shepherd's crook), something like a
long pole.

B. QUESTIONS AND ANSWERS.

(Colour of apples?) *Yellow.*
(Have the trees long stems?) *No.*
(What then?) *There is scarcely anything to see of them.*
(Can you see all the trees entirely?) *No; here (pointing to the right)
    where the picture finishes there is a quarter tree, and here (left) another
    quarter.*
(Are there more geese before or after the goosegirl)? *After.*
(Colour of their beaks?) *Yellow.*
(Bodies?) *White, end of tail a little black in a good many.*
(Feet?) *I think, yellow.*

(What do we see on the meadow?) *Flowers, grass.*
(Can we recognize the flowers?) *No, they are round with point.*
(What does the goosegirl look like?) *White cap, white [black] apron and, I think, a red skirt.*
(Do we see her full face or sideways?) *Sideways.*
(Do the trees stand close together or with spaces between?) *Quite close.*
(Is the woman barefoot or has she got shoes on?) *Slippers. I think.*
(To which side is she turning?) *To this.*
(How many trees altogether?) *Four, five or six.*
(About how many apples on each tree?) *About ten.*
(How many geese?) *Eight.*
Self-correction *after looking* at picture.
The apron is black.
The trees stand close together.
She hasn't a rake.
There are six geese.

Eva (3 ; 6½).

(Do you know what sort of picture hangs by the nursery-door?) *Little geese.*
(What can you see in it?)

A. Description.

A woman—and geese walking on it—the woman is feeding the geese (wrong).

B. Questions and Answers.

(Are there trees in it?) *No, but on the road* (wrong).
(Are there any apples?) *Yes, yellow apples.*
(Do the geese all run behind the woman?) *No.*
(Do some run in front of her?) *Yes.*
(What do their beaks look like?) *Red.*
(And the body?) *White.*
(Feet?) *Red.*
(What do we see in the meadow?) *It isn't a meadow* (wrong).
(What does the woman look like?) *White cap.*
(Skirt?) *Blue.* (Red.)
(Apron?) *White.* (Black.)
(What has she got in her hand?) *Food for the geese.* (Shepherd's crook.)
(Do we see her full face or sideways?) *Full face* (sideways).
(Shoes or barefoot?) *Shoes.*
(How does the woman stand?) *Like me* (faces me).

Evidently the task was harder for Eva than in the earlier experiment, for out of seventeen statements, seven (40 per cent.) were wrong. Although the picture had hung constantly before her eyes, the child had never looked at it with conscious attention, and she now tried to supplement her hazy recollections with guesswork and memories of other pictures. So it is clear that EVEN FREQUENT REPETITION OF THE IMPRESSION, IF THERE IS BUT SLIGHT ATTENTION, PRODUCES LESS EFFECT IN ACCURATE MEMORY THAN THE IMPRESSION OBSERVED ONLY ONCE WITH CONCENTRATED ATTENTION.[1]

This is confirmed by the different result of the one on Gunther. He gave thirty-four answers with only four (12 per cent.) mistakes; this superiority was not only due to his greater age, but principally to the boy's stronger visual capacity.[2] He is accustomed to study optical impressions with great attention and to study them in detail, so that the task did not find him so unprepared as his sister. Also of the many colour statements (nine) made by him only one was wrong. After the test he took the picture of his own accord and compared it with his aussage, thus giving us the self-correction recorded above when he found out almost all his mistakes, without any help from us.

Such little aussage-tests as those described are to be recommended for occasional use in the nursery and kindergarten. They, like the consideration of pictures described in Chapter XIV, serve to train the power of observation and recollection, also to strengthen resistance to suggestion and to induce a certain caution and self-criticism. Of course such tests (which must be regarded by the child only as a short game) need not be confined to pictures; we can get experimental aussage practice with regard to any real circumstances and occurrences, e.g. a walk taken shortly before, the position of the furniture in a neighbouring room. Certainly for educational purposes the best objects for aussage are those that can be shown to the child again for practice in self-correction. (Pictures and interiors.)

[1] This is a quite universal conclusion in aussage-psychology both as regards school-children and adults.
[2] This special visual gift enabled the six-year-old boy to get better results in this test than even his elder sister who (7 ; 8) had also the same examination. She gave thirty-one statements, with 6·19 per cent. mistakes.

PART VI

FANTASY AND PLAY

WHERE shall we begin and where end? The material available is nowhere so overwhelming as in the consideration of fantasy and play. For the period of life with which we have to deal is indeed the "age of play", and imaginative perception has here reached a stage of development far in advance of any other perceptual activity or mental function.

The estimation in which this central activity of early child-hood is held has been, and still is, very varied. On the one hand, childish fantasy on account of its apparent nonsense, lack of method and judgment, is considered of very slight value; on the other, the child's power of building, in royal fashion, a world of his own in fairy-tale and play is held in high esteem as a wonderful, almost creative power. We must try to find the happy mean between these extreme views.

We will first discuss in general the characteristics of imagina-tion in early childhood, and then treat separately the most important manifestations of its activity.

CHAPTER XIX

CHARACTERISTICS OF FANTASY IN EARLY CHILDHOOD

1. General Considerations

CONCRETE and spontaneous perception is a feature common to all fantasy. The fantasy-percept is always concrete, containing one single definite image, being thus akin to apperception and remembrance, and distinct from thought, with its abstractions. The concrete imagery of the fantasy-percept is not, however, the direct production or reproduction of outer impressions, but the result of inner working; in fantasy-pictures man frees himself from direct connection with the outer world. The percept is experienced and enjoyed as his own creation. By this subjective feature of spontaneity, fantasy-perception is raised above the other two forms of concrete perception, apperception and remembrance, one connected with present objects, the other with those past.

Yet this difference between spontaneous fantasy and the receptive activities (apperception and remembrance) is not of the nature of an absolute opposition, in fact there are many points common to both.

Fantasy is never capable of creating from nothing; its elements must rather be founded on actual experiences. Its creative nature consists in the use of these elements, in the power to dissociate them from their former setting, and to form from them new combinations, ever changing and ever more extensive, so that the fantasy-percept, in all its varieties, is a presentation of something "that never was on land and sea". The power of this dissociation of elements and their different reassociation which we call the "play" of imagination varies greatly with the individual.

Moreover, the obvious nature of the fantasy-percept depends upon the vigour of the apperception and the memory. Only that man who has very keen and distinct sense-perceptions of colours, forms, tones, etc., and can reproduce these impressions with the same clearness, is able to endow his fantasy-percept with a touch of the same life-like reality. The varying grades of this quality we designate by speaking of a more or less "vivid" imagination.[1]

Sense-perception not only provides imagination with its raw material, but often enough incites it to action as well. Some one outer impression, as a word, a picture, a movement, sets in motion the perceptions already waiting in readiness, and these speedily weave the impression into their web, or in their ramifications wander far from their starting-point. Nevertheless, the sense-perception had to play the part of fantasy-stimulus, and we shall see how important this is, above all for childhood's stage of development. The readiness to allow such stimuli to set imagination to work might be called "quickness" of imagination.

If, then, imagination is influenced by the receptive functions of apperception and memory, a reverse process is no less true; those psychic activities, brought into play in the perception and reproduction of objective facts, are not without their subjective moment of imagination. In proof of this we need only refer to what has already been said. For we found that the child's apperception and remembrance were continually crossed by fleeting ideas (perceptions), which on the one hand gave life and richness to concept and statement, but on the other diminished and endangered their objective value. THIS MUTUAL, INTIMATE INTERMINGLING OF REALITY AND IMAGINATION is a fundamental fact, the full significance of which has only been recognized in the last ten years, and yet it is the source of the most important psychological knowledge of equal significance in the highest form of imagination as evinced in art, and in the simplest in primitive man and in the little child. If imagination was, as used to be believed, an independent "psychic power", sharply differentiated from the other powers of apperception and remembrance, then of course each process could be at once ascribed to its own specific psychic pigeonhole; the imaginative percept would be experienced as a subjective appearance, apperception and remembrance as signs of objective fact. How little this is the case will be shown in the following section.

[1] Whether strong fantasy-percepts are connected with the "eidetic faculty" mentioned earlier (Chapter XVII, 2) cannot be stated without further investigation.

2. The Child's Untrammelled Imagination

The child's individual fantasy-percept is at first indistinct and insignificant. This is a result, not only of the general laws of perceptual development, but also of certain symptoms in the working of imagination itself. For instance, the little child shows striking unconcern as to the character of the outer object with which the fantasy-percept is associated. Any chance shape of a torn morsel of paper is greeted as "shoe", although in our eyes the likeness is very remote. A circle with four little lines in it, that the child has drawn, stands without any scruples for "a face", perhaps even his little brother's. The hobby-horse on which the child rides and the real animal have practically not a point in common; the one fact, that the child can put the hobby-horse between his legs, is enough to give reality to the imaginary concept.

This disregard of detail is considered a favourable point of early imagination, and rightly so, for it shows how quick and how strong is the inner urge to perceptual ideas even at that time. But, on the other hand, we must not forget that the whole process is furthered by the comparatively sketchy nature of the percept. If the little child had a sharply defined colour- or form-percept of shoes, then the sight of a torn scrap of paper would not so easily reproduce the shoe-image; the differing features would at once effect a psychic impediment. And the hobby-horse as steed does not upset the little boy, only because all other features, particularly that of the special form of a horse, have, in his percept, to yield entirely to the chief point of being able to ride upon the animal.

The indefinite character of the isolated percept, however, in no way detracts from the capability of the child's fantasy. For his imagination, unlike that of the creative artist, does not wish to form a permanent inner picture as correct and complete in detail as possible, but rather, in quick movement, to hurry from percept to percept, from action to action; so that those hazy memories and echoes are just fitted to make any chance objects the halting-places for the different stages of this motor-action. And thus, too, we understand how one and the same object can serve in quick succession as the stimulus of the most varied perceptual images.

Hilde (2 ; 2½). "Hilde holds in her hand a flat square little piece of wood with which she plays as with a ball. Suddenly she lays it on her head, shows it me: *Lovely hat!* Then after a little while again: *It is a thaler.* (2 ; 5.) The child was sitting at table with an aunt and began to play with her apron. First she rolled it into a ball and pretended to throw it, then she twisted it, like a bandage, round her finger and said: *sore finger*; then she gathered up the bottom hem and held it out (as if to catch a ball) saying: *plate."* The child has reached a higher stage of development when it is conscious of the discrepancy between the fantasy-stimulus and the associated percept, but is unmoved by it. At this stage, the object perceived sinks to a mere symbol, to the simple stimulus required for association or incentive by the keen inner perceptual process. The child putting three chairs behind one another to play at trains knows quite well that a train looks very different, but he overlooks the differences in order to make use of the one feature he considers essential, the arrangement of carriages behind one another, as the tangible foundation for his play-fantasy. Thus we here meet with something the same thing as in the development of language-thought: a conscious symbol takes the place of a mechanical association and immediately raises the process on to a higher level.

Hilde (2 ; 7) symbolized the trains as follows: once by four chestnuts one behind the other, then a row of building-blocks, then again a metre measure that she dragged behind her.

Gunther (3 ; 11) once even used his hands for trains. He pointed suddenly to his thumbs: *These are the engines and those* (stretching out the eight fingers) *are all of them carriages: and here* (pointing to the air) *is the railroad and the lines.*

In many of these extremely strange representations, we grown-ups can scarcely believe that the child overlooks crass dissimilarity to connect his comparison to some solitary, insignificant feature.

Gunther (3 ; 2) untied the apron of his mother sitting in her chair and dragged, as he made clumsy efforts to move backwards, at one of the strings, saying: *Mummy, will you be a net? I pull you out.* He had recently seen how fishermen move backwards in their strenuous efforts to drag a full heavy net to shore. The possibility of dragging and imitation of the backward movement were enough by themselves to identify his mother, in the game, with the full fishing-net.

In Hilde (5 ; 10) we again noticed the following remarkable personification: "She was playing with a coffee-mill; the lid consisted of the usual two half-circles joined by middle hinges so that they can be opened to meet or shut away from each other. That was quite enough to suggest human movement to the child. She made both lids meet: now they are kissing. She parted them: now they are going a walk. She pretended a shower of rain: then they both return; one side was turned out and down: he was going another walk; but the other means to wait till the fog has gone."

This unconcern reaches its highest point when imagination dispenses entirely with a tangible starting-point and brings into being something very like hallucinations.[1] When the child begins its "confabulations", or when, lying in its cot in the evening darkness before sleep comes, it holds forth in a monologue blending, in wild confusion, relatives and toys, the day's events and wishes for the future, then all imagination-stimuli have disappeared, and we see the play of the inner perceptual power in its purest form. But one step on from this brings us to dream-fantasy, and it is characteristic of the child that very often the dividing lines between real experience, waking-fantasy and dreams entirely disappear.

This feature of hallucination becomes specially marked in play-fantasy. Here, indeed, the child touches and handles airy nothings, e.g. in his game with an imaginary ball, which he can carry on with the same engrossing zeal as when he has the real plaything in his hands. But yet in this, we always find present one real and apparently essential condition, and that is, the child's own movement in the game; this cannot be supplanted by a simple movement-percept in the imagination. Hence the motor elements of the percept have to play a different part from that of the visual, auditory or tactual elements. The thing that can be seen, heard or touched can be replaced by an imagination-percept, but not so individual movement. It is, however, very easy to see the reason of this difference in the part played by imagination. We are not always able to secure the actual presence of objects, man has to content himself with the subjective substitute of his fantasy-percept, but

---

[1] The following examples show that Bühler is not right in considering an outer stimulus through sense-impressions as a necessary condition for the working of imagination in childhood.

movements we can always go through once more, so that we do not need to provide for them a corresponding substitute in imagination. The following instances of hallucination-play give distinct confirmation of what has just been said.

Gunther (2 ; 6½). "His little sister has just been washed and is scarcely out of the bath before G. climbs on to his little chair and looks into the empty bath, with the words: *do, as if baby was there,* and admires the non-existent baby in the bath."

Hilde (3 ; 5). "H. is playing at marketing, i.e. we send her with imaginary money to buy imaginary things; she runs to the shop in an empty corner and brings away make-believe butter, chocolate, etc."

Gunther (5 ; 10). "A very favourite game with the children is hop-scotch. A plan is drawn on the ground with numbered divisions; a little stone has to be thrown into a certain division and fetched out again by hopping all the time, without the foot touching one of the boundary lines. G. sometimes plays this game in the room without any kind of apparatus. He pretends to draw the plan on the bare boards, pretends to throw the pebble, exults as if he had got the 100 division (apparently the plan stands out distinctly before his mental vision), hops along cautiously to avoid boundaries that are not there, etc."

Hilde (5 : 10). H. was keeping shop. Her mother, who had bought something from her, said she would send for it the next day. To get that "next day" quickly, H. symbolized the intervening night by going into her "shop" and, as she stood there, snoring several times loudly with great good will. Then she said contentedly: *Now it is to-morrow.* Thus for her "night" she needed no bed, no darkness, not even to lie down—the expression-movement of snoring was accounted a quite sufficient foundation for the fantasy-percept of "night".

This unconcern as regards objective perception distinguishes the fantasy of early childhood from the really æsthetic imagination of the artist and art-lover; for it is an essential part of æstheticism that the imagination-percept should find an adequate objective presentation, and since the little child entirely lacks the feeling for this agreement of inner idea and outer form, the essential principle of art is still quite foreign to his nature.[1]

A certain relationship between childish and artistic imagina-

[1] Cf. chapter on "Enjoyment and Creative Activity".

tion is not to be found in the matter of form, but in the power of illusion, of rising superior to the constraint and compelling force of reality. But such efforts of imagination are, as we have seen, in early years only possible by unconcern as to outward presentation; if this, therefore, is unduly restrained, an undesirable crippling of imagination takes place.

Yet how little regard does our toy education pay to that feature of untrammelled imagination! With dolls and dolls' houses, toy animals and soldiers, no trouble or expense is spared, until everything that the child's imagination can picture is presented objectively as well. In this realistic treatment, what becomes of the child's power of making everything out of anything? Do we really believe that the rolled-up rag bundle or the stiff wooden form awakes less joy and imagination in an unspoilt child than the most expensive and elaborate doll with a life-like head, eyes that shut, and clothed with all the dainty refinements of the latest fashion—and consequently leaves but little opportunity for imagination to give any additional touches? In such cases we often see that the doll only wins a place into its owner's affections when it has lost its first beauty, and can now without any qualms be transferred to any situation that may please the child's imagination.

A self-evident consequence of this fantasy unconcern is that there is no more ideal plaything than shapeless material on which the child can practise his power as he pleases and put into it everything his imagination pictures. There is paper that can be torn, folded, crumpled up, stuck together, scribbled on; sand that can be dug, shaped, kneaded, scattered; water, clay, snow—what inexhaustible treasures for the joys of childhood's imagination! It is, indeed, no mere chance that children of all ages are nowhere happier, more persistent in play, and therefore better behaved, than at the seaside, where, week after week, they enjoy to the full the endless possibilities of play offered by sand and water.

Much greater use ought to be made, too, in the child's daily environment of such shapeless material. A big sand-heap ought to be found in every public square, in every garden, above all in every kindergarten. That there is no place in the Montessori theories for this means of play and education—which nothing else can replace—is one of the failings of its methods. Similar opportunities should be offered at home as well; a great lump of clay should always be handy for the child to model and play with to his heart's content. Mothers, who indignantly repudiate such suggestions from consideration for the children's clothes or their fine furniture, have no idea how much joy and imagination they suppress in this way. And in the same way we should let the children splash about and sail their boats, etc., in the bath or some big pan.

3. Illusion and Consciousness of Illusion

We know to-day that the distinction between subjective and objective experiences has not existed from the beginning in human consciousness, but is the final aim of long psychic development. Between complete confusion of apparent and real and a keen critical sense of their differentiation, there are endless intermediate states, many of them very difficult to understand. We, sober critical grown-ups, in all our perceptions have almost always to decide whether they affect or are affected by the practical conditions of life—when they are of an objective nature—or whether they are solely the products of conceptual pleasure in and for itself—when they are non-real fantasy-images. Since we are used to this distinction, we can at first scarcely picture conditions in which it is either entirely absent or only dimly apprehended, and have even more difficulty in fully sympathizing with such a state. Yet it is only thus that we obtain the key to the most important characteristics of the child's psychic life.

The child is much more a creature of the moment than we are, and the result of this concentration on the present is that it is free from the adult's desire to bring its perceptions into connection with the past and the future, and thus to test their reality. "Real" for this early stage of life is simply what is keenly felt, and it remains real as long as feeling is absorbed in the experience. The child is engrossed in an imaginary concept, and whilst it lasts its content is no less real for him than, at other times perhaps, his food, a memory image, or a push that hurts him is an objective reality. It is in the nature of every perception to bring with it a suggestion of its own truth, a prompting to believe in it. And the strength of this belief depends far less on objective tests than on the subjective intensity of consciousness. When we see the child's absolute absorption as he listens to a fairy-tale or tells an imaginary tale of his own, how earnestly he carries on his games, and his despair at any interruption, then we recognize that the illusion of reality is here complete indeed, or very nearly so.[1] We shall see examples later on.

And yet the child begins fairly early to feel dimly that other stern idea of reality possessed by us adults. He notices that many of his conscious experiences cannot be ended or changed in accordance with his fancy, but that they force themselves upon him and make their consequences felt; in short, he begins to realize his dependence on things outside himself and to endeavour to adapt himself to them. And, in so doing, he comes into contact with a reality harder and more powerful than that he knew before, so that, henceforth, that undifferentiated state of simple, trusting acceptance of every vivid percept is no longer sole master of the field, and the distinction between objective and subjective begins to struggle into consciousness. But even this is a slow process, and passes through the strangest intermediate states. Sometimes there is abrupt alternation between absorption in the illusion and superiority to it, sometimes the child intentionally turns away from everything that might destroy the illusion. Then, again, there are psychic conditions when the child is conscious of this discord, and hovers between the opposite poles of taking reality seriously and playing with his percepts. The æsthete Conrad Lange affirms that such "conscious self-deception" is quite general as the characteristic feature of artistic enjoyment— a dictum which is too pointed to be entirely true. But as regards the child, and particularly the little child, this condition is undoubtedly significant. That arbitrary power of alternation confers a sense of sovereignty and at the same time a feeling of very pronounced pleasure.

If the self-deception is conscious, we speak of a conscious illusion. A few examples will show the various phases and intermediate forms of illusion in childhood.

---

[1] Karl Bühler (I, pp. 208 sqq.) maintains a somewhat different view. In his opinion these fantasy-games are almost always only make-believe; however intent the child may be on his play, he is always conscious of the essential unreality of the game. Bühler is right in the main as far as the more advanced forms of imaginative play are concerned, but he does not do full justice to the fact that, in early stages there is but imperfect power of differentiation between the real and the apparent, and remarkable forms of confusion between them.

To begin with, an example that shows how early undoubted conscious illusion is to be found with an admixture of playful make-believe.

Hilde (2 ; 2). "It is not always possible to decide where the child's consciousness of the self-deception in her game begins or ends. When Hilde puts her dolly and toy animals to bed, feeds them, washes them—in short, treats them as she herself is treated, she may be conscious or unconscious of self-deception. The child expects no answer when she directly addresses her doll or stuffed dog, etc. But conscious playful self-deception is certainly shown in another stage now reached by Hilde. This morning she missed her little chair; first she asks: *Where is my little chair, then?* Then she consoles herself with: *Look for little chair on the floor*, and, sure enough, down she stoops on to the carpet, looks about as if finding a pin, and at last says decidedly: *No, it isn't there*. So comical the whole proceeding was!"

But yet, six months later, the child's actions seem to point to a certain degree of illusion still.

"Hilde has got fresh coverings for her dolls' beds, and now an intensive game; all day long, the dolls have to go to bed; get up and again to bed. She tends her children with touching care, and in tones of motherly affection rocks them to sleep, asks them if they have slept well, and expects us to do the same when she comes in the morning with their perambulator into our bedroom. This is the expression of actual warm feeling, free from fancy or make-believe. And this is certainly no case of pure and simple fiction, but a remarkable mixture of real belief, half-belief, playful acquiescence and intentional make-believe. Just as we think: 'that is all conscious pretence'; in the next moment it is evident that the child is entirely under the sway of illusion and really believes what she says about the doll."

"When Hilde is 4 ; 7 this play-illusion still moves her to actual tears. One evening—the bedroom has already been darkened—she suddenly calls out quite anxiously to know if one or other of the dolls has been tucked up in the thick blanket; she is evidently afraid that, if not, her doll will catch cold in the raw November weather. And when we try to induce her to be quiet, her tears flow; anxiety for her little sister's health could scarcely be more genuine than this care of her dolls. Would this be possible if she had a conscious mental picture of the fact that the treasured doll was only a piece of leather stuffed with chaff?"

And sometimes her treatment of her little sister leaves us in doubt whether she really wants to have personal relations with her, or if she is treating her as a doll. Thus, she (4 ; 7) goes to the six-month-old baby in her carriage, and says: *I want to show Eva my work*; then she dangles the stocking at which she was "working" before the little one's eyes and talks affectionately: *Yes, yes, I'm four years old now, and go to the nursery-school. I learn to darn now.* Now, it is remarkable that this make-believe did not sound the least like a joke. Sometimes she has no idea of her little sister's powers (lately she doubted if she could hear), at others she speaks to her, evidently more or less confident that she is not preaching to deaf ears.

We find this alternation of confidence and doubt shown by the child, not only in its self-illusions, but in its attitude to those offered to it from without, viz. in fairy-tales, Santa Claus, and the various fantasy-games.

Our eldest daughter, ten years later, still remembered her strangely mingled feelings when one of her elders chased her in fun round the table, yapping like some animal. There was always a touch of real fear in her knowledge that it was only pretence, and, strangely enough, this consciousness of mixed feelings persisted when similar jokes were played upon the same child at a much later age.

The following episode recounted by Herr and Frau Katz shows similar feelings. Children's ages: J, 3 ; 7, T. 5 ; 3. One afternoon when playing their mother said: 'Now I'm going to growl like a bear." She does so and J. cries and screams. Mother: Why do you cry? J.: *I thought you had changed yourself by magic.* T. comes into the room and the mother growls again. J. runs away and hides. T. (nervously) *I was a little frightened too.*

In conclusion an example in which the illusion-concept is not only plainly evident but is also aptly expressed, namely as knowledge of an imaginary not-knowing.

Hildegard Hetzer reports, p. 37, of Christine (4 ; 2): She brings her doll something to eat, *There's a roll for you* (a fragment of pasteboard). *Well no, it's not a real roll. But I don't know either.*

The child finds a great source of pleasure in fantasy's power of illusion. For the more man learns to grasp the hard fact of reality, the more conscious he is of its compelling, constructing power. The little child, meeting hindrances on every side, so dependent on grown-ups in its real activity, may well have some more or less indefinable sense of this oppressive power, and seeks freedom from it by flight into the world of imagination where he himself is lord and master—aye, in very truth, moulder and creator. Moreover, the stronger the illusion by means of which he loses himself in a life of his own creation, the stronger his feeling of liberation and the greater his pleasure.

And the child's real environment is narrow indeed. The rooms of his own home, the members of his own family, the servants, the daily walk, and his toys—these alone are his world. The rest of the wide world only casts its reflection from afar over the child's existence. But as he receives this reflection by the light of his own imagination and play, he widens the sphere of his life. In this way, he not only charms into his play-kingdom all objects of the outer world, horse and carriage, railroad and ships, etc., but—and this is far more important—human beings as well, by transferring himself into their shoes. The exchange of the individual personality with that of another, in spite of the great demands it makes upon the power of illusion, may sometimes happen with a quite surprising intensity.

We see from the above that the part illusion plays in one and the same fantasy-image can vary greatly. One human being may have a rich, lively and sensitive imagination without confusing its images with reality, another with comparatively poorer imagination may possess a higher degree of illusion. The power of illusion, therefore, is a special quality of the imagination.

In the child, illusion depends chiefly on age; it steadily decreases with years, whilst other qualities of the imagination, such as extent or quickness, simultaneously increase. But besides this, even in early childhood, there are great individual differences; many children very early acquire a sharp distinction between reality and appearance, others remain an exceedingly long time in that confused state where experience and make-believe blend in chaotic intermingling. Among these, doubtless, there are cases within pathological limits, and therefore requiring special educational—and curative—consideration and influence. But, on the other hand, we must not forget that a certain degree of illusion assuredly belongs to the normal character in early childhood; it is therefore an entire mistake to condemn, root and branch, or to combat in education (Montessori) the consequent confusions between seeming and reality, whether in play, fantasy-tales, reminiscences, etc., or to be inclined to look upon them at once as pathological symptoms.

4. The Symbolism of Imagination in Childhood

The relation of fantasy to reality appears in a new light as soon as the ideas of fantasy are considered in a symbolical sense. Then what is fantasy only is neither entirely divorced from reality nor identical with it, but is the symbol of a reality of another kind.

Such a theory of symbols is developed by psychoanalysis. In accordance with its point of view, a fantasy is not experienced and enjoyed for its own sake, but is rather a disguise under which secret desires find expression and seek an outlet. The child lives—such is the assumption—always and everywhere for himself and for nothing else, even when his fantasy-forms appear to have an entirely different object. And, indeed, fantastic disguises allow the appearance of those sides of his ego to which direct expression is denied—either because the child is as yet entirely unconscious of them or because they dare not show themselves in their true form, and are therefore pushed down into the Unconscious.

A sharp distinction should be made between the principle at the root of this symbol-theory and its application. The principle is certainly justified, and it cannot fail to be recognized when the psychic life is considered from the point of view of personality. In the unity of the individuality there is no sharp dividing line between the life of imagination and of impulse; all separate psychic phenomena gain meaning and import only when understood as offshoots of essential features of the personality; thus we are justified in an enquiry also as to the personal significance of fantasy-forms. Such an enquiry shows often enough that the true conscious content cannot be simply inferred from what is apparent, but that it needs interpretation; and this interpretation may lead to deeply hidden motives, which, all unconsciously to the child, may yet exercise a strong influence upon him.

To refer to comparatively simple examples, it is certain that in many play fantasy-forms, instincts of power or contest or cruelty or protective care find a disguised expression all unconsciously to the child; later on in discussing the theory of play we must refer to this again. This symbolic reference to the ego in the fantasy-form is very plain in the following case reported by M. L. in the periodical "Parents and Child" (*Eltern und Kind*) [Vol. 7, No. 5, p. 82, year 1925].

Two boys (6 and 4 years old) "have quite spontaneously invented fantasy-forms of the dear good beautiful child and of the naughty tiresome fellow, both of which they look upon as a kind of friend and example outside themselves and yet again in some fashion identify with themselves. Each boy has his mysterious Hans who counsels and does all that is bad and naughty, is the universal breaker, a dirty fellow who falls about, howls etc., and on the other hand as a model of virtue, 'Schleifle', who is always good, pleasant and clean. *My Schleifle said at once I shouldn't do it but of course Hans——.*" The parents used these childish personifications of good and evil as a means of education. In the Katz children's conversation, a witch plays an important part as the personification of everything hateful and loathsome. Even though this figure may be the result of some outside presentation, yet their parents believe that it satisfies some deep need of the young soul to have at its disposal a personal representative of the negative side of their estimation—perhaps as the opposite to the image of their mother, who appears to them the personification of every virtue.

The case presents several noteworthy features from a psychological point of view. Since the fantasy-forms are distinctly on a parallel with the ideas of "folk" thought (demon and angel, fairy and witch, etc.), but yet seem to be a spontaneous growth of the young soul, the personification of the two root qualities in morality may be considered as a general characteristic of primitive psychology. But then again we recognize certain unconscious motives which have had something to do with the creation of these fantasy-forms; a shelving of the child's own disagreeable impulses on to another in order to absolve himself from personal responsibility. It was, of course, not his doing; it was Hans who happened to be stronger than good Schleifle (who is evidently more closely identified with the child's own inner self—with the desire-ego).

To a certain degree the symbolism of "above" and "below" (and of similar fantasy-forms) is obvious. This symbolism is interpreted by the "individual"-psychologist, Alfred Adler— in my opinion somewhat one-sidedly—as follows: "Children's preference for the idea of being above, for what is literally large and high, for big numbers, supernatural powers, etc., is an unconscious attempt to compensate by a kind of illusion of self-glorification for their own feeling of weakness and inferiority."

But there are numberless other cases in which the symbolism is less apparent—no wonder then that the child's fantasy-utterances become the happy hunting-ground of all kinds of arbitrary interpretation. FOR AFTER ALL EVERYTHING CAN BE SYMBOLICALLY INTERPRETED IN EVERY CONCEIVABLE WAY and a preconceived opinion or a foregone hypothesis may easily determine the methods of interpretation, and may even push to one side an unforced explanation in favour of one that is far-fetched.

We see abundant instances of this in the different schools of psychoanalysis and especially in Freud's. The theory that the child's unconscious impulses are chiefly of an erotic-sexual nature leads to interpretations that make every fantasy-form into a sexual symbol.

The jealousy- and desire of death-complex plays a great part in the psychoanalytic interpretations. The boy has an unconscious sexual complex for his mother,[1] sees in every other member of the family a rival whom he looks upon with jealousy and desires to get rid of—all of this, of course, is deep in the Unconscious. He is chiefly jealous of his father,[2] of his younger brothers and sisters. And if little children, in all innocence, use the word "death" or something similar in any fantasy-utterance, psychoanalysis sees in it the result of that motive-complex, as is shown in two examples from Hug-Hellmuth.

"When little Scupin says of his own accord: 'But I will put my papa in a pot and keep on pouring hot water over his face

---

[1] The so-called incest-complex.
[2] Œdipus-complex. In a well-known Greek myth, Œdipus kills his father and marries his mother.

until he is nice and soft' and then eat him up, the origin of such fantasy is not only to be looked for in the fairy-tale *Hansel and Gretel* with the greedy witch, but is to be found in the unconscious intention of seizing an opportunity to get rid of his father, his most formidable rival as regards his mother, and the fairy-tale is nothing more than a pretence to hide the evil wish in sheep's clothing."[1]

In a long imaginary conversation of our daughter's[2] (2 ; 10), when, amongst other things, she shows and explains to her doll a picture of different people and a child in a cradle, the following sentence is selected:—

"Aunt and Uncle and a Gunther and he is dead," and Hug-Hellmuth now asserts that such mention of her six-months-old brother justifies the Freud assumption of an unconscious desire for his death. But now, if it is known that, at this period, Hilde used the designation Gunther for all little children, and also the expression "to be dead" was quite common with her for all lying down, and if, too, the child's general attitude to her brother at this time is known, the interpretation put upon her words is seen to be entirely without foundation.[3]

In these instances it is, at any rate, the child's relatives that he directly mentions. But the psychoanalysts are convinced that the same hidden emotions find their abreaction in fantasy-forms apparently totally unconnected with them.

Thus Pfeifer interprets a boy's (4–6) repeated game of "pig-sticking." He used to stab old blocks of wood with a saddler's awl (the father was a saddler), kneeling on them and squealing like a pig that is being killed. As his mother over-indulged this boy, but his father was strict, Pfeifer thinks he is justified in assuming that the pig-killing was only the unconscious symbolic expression of his wish for vengeance on his father.

And psychoanalysis allows itself an increasing licence in its interpretations, crediting the child with an extraordinarily keen interest in the sexual act, and all connected with it, especially, too, in the sexual organs—an interest whose origin

---

[1] Hug-Hellmuth, p. 77. From Scupin, II, p. 81.
[2] Hug-Hellmuth, p. 95. From Stern, *Kindersprache*, p. 62.
[3] Herr and Frau Katz in the "Conversations" point out that the child has become acquainted with such expressions as "to kill", "to be dead" through the medium of fairy-tales, and then often makes use of them himself. But he understands and uses those words in the simple meaning of not being present, of the disappearance of the person in question from the existing state of affairs, without any idea of the deeper tragedy of death.

they ascribe to observation of his own body and those of his relatives and playmates, as well as to the hearing of certain scenes (of course not quite intelligible to him) in his parents' bedroom, and lastly to what he learns at the birth of a younger brother or sister. This sexual interest, entirely undisclosed by the child, now finds expression—so psychoanalysis maintains—in disguises of a hundred different kinds. All longer objects used in play, mentioned in confabulation, seen in dreams, are, according to its views, symbols of the male organ; just as circles, holes, openings in which anything can be pushed are of the female. In every action of a striking nature (e.g. the cracking of a whip), in the knotted-handkerchief game, it sees a symbolic expression of sadistic impulses; in all throwing or letting fall, a symbol of the action of birth, etc.

Following on Freud's lines, Pfeifer works out the following interpretation: A five-year-old boy is never weary of playing one particular game with an india-rubber doll. He sticks his mother's penknife into the squeaking hole in the doll's body, then by pulling its feet apart lets the knife fall out again.[1] The unconscious meaning of this game is that the doll represents the mother, and that the whole performance is nothing but the desired, imagined, and—in this symbolic substitution —accomplished union with the mother, that is, then, incest, with its consequent natural result.

And this one example can give no adequate picture of the overwhelming number of the most varied interpretations which give the impression sometimes of being very wide of the mark.

They lose sight of all limits, recognize no boundary line, and the real object of these considerations ceases then to be the child at all, and becomes the unbridled chain of association, originating in the interpreter's own particular psychic-sexual constitution. When at last Pfeifer psychoanalyses the game "Fox in his Den" (knotted handkerchief corners), he is no longer making a psychological study of any real children, but deducing from the symbolic interpretations of the fox, his limp, the den, and the knotted handkerchief the hypothetical repressed sexual instincts of the child at play. And he supports his contention by numerous analogies from myths, religious rites and popular customs, quite overlooking the fundamental difference between such actions and child's play. For the

[1] Pfeifer, p. 243.

former are productions of adults in the life of whose personality it is recognized that sexuality plays an important part; so that, in this case, there is objective justification for enquiry as to how far the forms of fantasy may or must be interpreted as symbolic expressions of these instincts. In the child, on the other hand, there exist only outward similarities with those forms of fantasy; and from these alone, conclusions are drawn as to the existence and nature—in any case very problematic— of the instincts prompting them. There would be much more probability in an inverted method of conclusion, viz. that even in those games which have gradually fallen from original popular adult customs into the children's sphere, they will indeed keep the outer forms, but invest them with quite another meaning (or even simply enjoy them as they find them), because their life of impulse is entirely different from that of the adult.

The extremely difficult task of the right interpretation of children's forms of fantasy will therefore only be successfully accomplished, when it takes the child himself as its starting-point, and assumes as foundational motives and feelings only those which can be proved by other auxiliary methods as well as those of symbolic interpretation.

5. The Connecting Links of Imagination

We have now finally to find out how the detached fantasy-percepts are united into a connected chain of imagination. That such chains are formed at a very early age is beyond doubt; when children confabulate, draw or play they are but very rarely occupied with a single or even with only a few fantasy-percepts, but with a more continuous sequence, which may sometimes extend, without a break, over a fairly consider-able period.

An obstacle to this connected chain is at once apparent, i.e. THE WANT OF A CONTROLLING AND CONNECTING SYNTHETIC POWER. A condition, only known to adults in dreams and pathological cases, is the normal state in the earliest phase of the child's imagination; the percept-union of a and b, b and c, c and d, etc., is formed by mere association without any connec-tion being present or formed other than that between the two adjoining links. When the child reaches d, a is already forgotten.

By this predominance of the association-principle the chain

of imagination in early childhood forms an interesting contrast to the other mental processes. For these, as modern psychology of thought has shown us, are certainly not to be attributed to association alone, one perception does not bring another in its train, and so on *ad infinitum*, but a goal fixed, from the first, for the whole process determines its direction, decides the appearance of certain percepts and thoughts and the rejection of others. This conscious aim as a "determining impulse"[1] (dominant interest) is effective during the whole process, and guarantees a synthesis of the elements in an intelligent connection for the attainment of the definite end. The Self is therefore not simply passive under the flow of his perceptual process, but confronts it as an active agent, and, in later years, his determining impulses control not only the course of his thought and will, but also of his imagination, especially in all artistic activity.

In the imagination of early childhood, on the other hand, a determining impulse, if any such should ever appear, is so short-lived that it only extends over a small number of the percepts, and is so weak that any element happening to arise in the perceptual process—a similarity in sound, some relation of space and time—can, by association, turn all further progress into quite another direction. Any chance object, meeting the child's eye in his confabulation, provides an immediate reason for a total change in the perceptual process; a line the boy has scribbled to draw a definite object reminds him of something else, and, in a twinkling, this second end becomes the determining impulse of his further drawing, until a fresh change of intention comes to pass.

This VOLATILE CHARACTER is one of the most prominent features of the child's imagination, and, at the same time, one that results in a great difference between childish and artistic imagination.

"Gunther (3 ; 2) sitting by my side on the sofa asks me where exactly I wish to go in the train, whistles, hisses, and for a couple of minutes really plays at trains. A few moments later, he is sitting on the end of the sofa as on his horse, and now he is either a wild horseman or a cab-driver. He jumps down, pushes two chairs together, gets in, and now he is rocking on a steamer, in a sailing-vessel or a motor-boat. He sees the

[1] The expression originated with N. Ach.

funnel, the smoke, whistles, lands; after a little time, the chairs pushed together are a room 'in which he lives,' and Hilde comes to visit him, or they are a stable where a number of circus horses are housed. The blind-cord, too, is extremely useful in forming all possible places; he fastens it from the window to the bed, and behind this imaginary partition he then entrenches himself. After a while he is very busy 'sewing', i.e. he runs serviette ties through the seat of the cane-bottomed chair.''

Once when the boy was four years old, we managed to listen to him when he was drawing all sorts of things on his drawing-slate. The different stages of the drawings and the words accompanying them could be noted without his knowledge, so that we have an absolutely true reproduction of the leaps and bounds of his perceptual process.[1]

At first he wanted as requested to begin a camel. He drew Fig. *a*, presumably the head projecting from the body. But the camel was already forgotten—the protuberance on the side reminded him of a butterfly's wing. He said: *Shall I draw a*

[1] Taken from C. and W. Stern, III.

butterfly? rubbed out the top and bottom portions of the perpendicular line and drew a second wing (*b*). Then followed: *another butterfly* (*c*). *Now I'll draw everything that can fly, butter-flies, bird* (*d*), *and then comes a gnat. Now a gnat! Gnats have something that sting,* and he put two dots on the slate (*e*). The perpendicular stroke between was also part of the gnat, yet as soon as it was drawn, he cried in delight: *O a face in the moon. Shall I draw a face in the sun?* and he drew Fig. *f*. Then he went back to his starting-point. *Now I'll make the gnat!* Again he dotted two points and drew an irregular oval round them (*g*). *That is a gnat.* Then the idea struck him to copy a bird-picture hanging in the room. He began with the beak (*h*). But immediately his idea entirely changed; he saw in the two strokes the beginning of a star, and asked: *Shall I make a star?* which he then did (*i*).

In apparently strange opposition to this capricious chopping and changing of ideas we find another feature also commonly found in early childhood, i.e. perseveration. There are chains of imagination which consist of the most monotonous repetition of the same links; and grown-ups who marvel at the child's capricious ideas and want of perseverance look on in equal amazement at the patience and self-content which is continually pleased with the same unvarying play-movement and demands the same little verse or song again and again.

Thus Preyer once reports that his son (1 ; 1) opened and shut the hinged lid of a can not less than seventy-nine consecutive times.

Scupin's son (2 ; 11) spent a full hour and a quarter in uninterrupted stirring together with a porridge-stick of meal, water and salt. He kept on pouring from one pot to another and back again, finding the monotonous employment so enjoyable that he protested with tears when he had to give up the porridge-stick.

But, in spite of all appearances to the contrary, caprice and perseveration have this one point in common, that neither has any synthetic power: even in the monotonous repetition, the separate elements are only associated as distinct forms without any connected idea in which all are included. How near these two forms of a chain of imagination may be to each other is shown in the following report of Hilde's confabulation:—

Hilde (3 ; 9). "It is remarkable in her fantasy-tales how on one hand the child jumps from one point to another without any connection, and how, on the other, she brings in a thought that may have especially pleased her several times in almost literal repetition with the excuse: *Then I did that again,* or *Then that was like this again."*

As the child grows older, then it is true the imagination grows out of this condition of simple association by contiguity of identical or derived ideas, and the forces of dominant interests and synthetic powers make themselves felt. On the one hand, the aim becomes a task to be undertaken. The child fixes, even if only dimly, a programme of what it will draw, play or confabulate. And on the other, this dominant interest is really for some time sustained and followed, so that now we get connected chains of imagination.

This growing power, however, does not depend on particular capability of imagination, but on more far-reaching conditions; for the strength and endurance of the dominant interest is, when all is said and done, a quality of the will which is seen alike in outer will-activity and in those inner activities of thought and imagination. When, therefore, imagination for too long shows a lack of strong dominant interest and keeps to the stage of caprice or monotonous perseveration, it is due to some weakness which calls for energetic measures to develop will-power.

In addition to the dominant interest, there is another condition which gradually produces increased coherence in early imagination, and that is continuity of concept. Certain conscious ideas may become predominant for some time under the most diverse conditions. The best-known example of this is the idea of the doll as a definite individuality. As soon as the doll has received its name and relationship to its owner (daughter, son, etc.), the child, in all her dealings with the doll, acts in accordance with this relation, and keeps up the idea in its games from day to day. Again, this acting of a special rôle can, by such ideas, become permanent, as we once saw happen in Gunther in very characteristic fashion.

At the age of 2 ; 9 the boy began at times to call himself *hig hister* (big sister), and his real big sister *Mietze*. This illusion took root, and after ten days his mother wrote: "He calls himself nothing but *hig hister*, Hilde is Mietze, I am *hand mummy* (grandmother), and his father *hand daddy* (grandfather).

He corrects us very frequently when we call him by his right name, and tells strangers he is called *hig hister*. The game continued unbroken for another week, and that the change of characters was indeed deeply ingrained was shown by the fact that he kept it up, not only in merry play, but also under quite real circumstances of pain and excitement. Thus he remembered, when night had already come to the nursery, that the balls had been lost in the walk, and crying in the dark he called out: *To-morrow hand mummy must go with hig hister to look for the balls.*"

The excess of such continuous games is under circumstances not without its dangers, for the predominance of the ruling idea may bring with it an undesirable limitation of the child's interests and definite loss of susceptibility to the varied stimuli which would otherwise appeal to him; also, as a result of the constant repetition, the illusory idea may become more and more life-like, so that the child becomes absolutely absorbed in the fantasy-concept, and loses all sense of its perspective to reality. Fortunately, in normal children, there are other qualities—caprice, quick change of interest, absorption in the present—which effectively counteract the undue influence of such fancies, so that their continuance, either in play or imagination, after some time generally comes to a natural end. Yet there are children that need careful watching in this respect; in these cases, an attractive, new impression, a fresh toy, a change of environment will provide the necessary diversion and change of ideas. There are instances, too, of more obstinate phantasms which show mental weakness and require special medical treatment.

CHAPTER XX

DREAM-FANTASY

IF it is difficult to give a detailed description of one's own dreams, the difficulty becomes wellnigh insuperable in examination of other people's dreams, and especially of those who, like little children, are almost or entirely incapable of self-analysis. For it is significant of the dream that whilst it lasts, it generally gives no outward sign either of its existence or character, and that its after-remembrance is amazingly short-lived; and since, as we have seen, the power of remembrance is much less in the child than in an adult, we can easily understand why his dream-reminiscences are few indeed.

We have therefore to resort to somewhat exceptional observations: on one hand of the chance expression-movements during sleep (screaming, crying, sleep-walking), on the other, of those isolated dream-remembrances which the child tells of his own accord. Even these spontaneous statements must be used with caution, since it is easy for confusion of dreams with waking ideas or even downright confabulations to occur in them; yet the trained observer will soon be able to judge of the genuine character of the accounts. These are especially credible when they occur in connection with the first-named symptoms (e.g. a bad dream with scream, consequent awakening and immediate expression of the terrifying dream). On the other hand, *prompted* dream-remembrances are quite worthless. If the child is asked in the morning: "Well, what beautiful dreams did you have last night?" his suggestibility, combined with his poor power of recollection, provides the most favourable soil imaginable for the growth of the crassest misstatements.

Dreaming, very possibly, BEGINS as far back as the child's first year, for even the sleeping infant shows at times reactions such as screams, sudden sucking movements, etc., which lead us to infer a dream-concept, no matter of how indefinite a character. Only suppositions are possible with regard to the FREQUENCY of childhood's dreams. It is thought, no doubt with justice, that dreams are an accompaniment of the lighter degrees of sleep only, whilst deep sleep is a condition of complete unconsciousness. Now, in early childhood normal sleep is very sound indeed; when children are once asleep, they are not awakened even by the loudest noises or by a shake, etc., indeed, sometimes they do not show any reaction even by the slightest quiver; dreams, therefore, are improbable in these periods of sleep. Most likely only the lighter sleep periods, just after falling asleep, or shortly before awakening, also the restless sleep of sickness, are accompanied by vivid dream-fantasies. This is supported by the fact that children, as soon as they show motor-symptoms of dreaming—are comparatively easy to wake, and therefore cannot have been any longer in quite a deep sleep.

Let us begin with some of those BAD DREAMS which afford the most direct insight into the child's dream-life.[1] The cause of the sudden state of fear cannot as a rule be discovered; the probable reason is most likely momentary indigestion, an overfull bladder, disturbed circulation, or something similar. But the dream-concepts, evidenced with this affective-tone of terror, have generally some connection with the day's experiences.

Gunther (2 ; 9) often had such bad dreams. Once he cried and woke up, calling out that someone had pulled down his building bricks, another time that a bear came in and bit his hand. The second time we turned up the light, encouraged the boy till he was sure there was no bear and that his hand was not hurt. Perhaps he was haunted this time by memories of Red Riding-Hood and the biting wolf. In the same way the Scupins' son (3 ; 0) was disturbed in his dreams by a fictitious spider, often used by those around him as a deterrent. He screamed suddenly in the night and asked to get into his mother's bed because a spider wanted to bite him. Even when he was really awake, he still thought the spider was in his bed, and cowered nervously away in one corner. It was only with difficulty that they could succeed in persuading him to lie down.

That such nervous fantasies are especially violent in feverish attacks is a matter of common knowledge. But, quite apart from health, even outer circumstances likely to disturb sleep may affect the child's dream-fantasy by producing terror; of this we have a very plain instance in Hilde.

Hilde (4 ; 9). There was great unrest in the house during

[1] Cf. with this the chapter on "Fear".

the night when her little sister was born. As Hilde was taken in her bed to a distant room she woke up and did not sleep soundly again for some hours. Confused noises, strange voices, etc., reached her ear. Several times she started up in terror and called for her father. *Such ugly children and women keep coming, so black, and then they go away from one another again; so ugly! And when I shut my eyes, I still see them.* We turned up the light, and that calmed her a little, but it was not until her father could at last stay with her that she fell asleep, Evidently this was a kind of half-dream, a middle stage between sleep and waking. The fantasy-images were intensive enough to terrify her, but her consciousness far enough awake to recognize at once the unreality of the apparitions.

A bad dream which in consequence of the strength of its hallucinations continued, even after waking, to show its effects in a belief of reality is told by Herr and Frau Katz (II, p. 247). The boy T. (5 ; 0) came early in the morning to his father's bed and felt both his hands to find the wound made as he had dreamt by a bite from a horse. The care shown in his examination and the boy's concern, according to the parents, made the psychoanalytic statement incontrovertible that the desire to enquire into his father's injury had made its appearance in his dream.

Bad dreams have, as we see, a strong tendency to expression-movements, but there are motor results in dreams that are free from any trace of fear. To this class belong many cases of sleep-walking, one of which we experienced with Gunther.

Gunther (3 ; 8). "In the middle of the night Hilde called out that G. had come into her bed. We lit up, and sure enough the boy had found his way, for some distance, in the pitch dark to his sister's bed, and explained the reason of this excursion by saying: *Well, Hilde said I was to get the crumbs out of her bed.* Probably the boy had not only been asleep when he dreamt these words, but also when he accomplished his journey."

We will pass on to those dreams of which we occasionally know something from the subsequent accounts of the dreamers: children scarcely seem capable of such narrative below their fifth year of age.

Hilde (4 ; 9½). "Some weeks after the birth of her little

sister Eva, the child one morning, as she was dressing, related the following dream: *To-day I dreamed about everybody. How Eva says eh-eh, and how darling she is, and how Gunther screams and wants to take everything away from me, and how mother is still ill, and that I love mother and I love father and go a walk with Miss W.* (the attendant). So there is no high-flown fantasy to be found in this dream, but simply the repetition of her everyday doings and interests."

The following report of Gunther's (5 ; 0) sounds more imaginative, but his mother, who heard it, was doubtful if it was a case of a real dream or a confabulation: *I have dreamt something so nice ; a whole lot of little boys came and they had on soldiers' tunics, and then there were ferns, and they were nothing but little fir-trees for them.*

The first dream that Herr and Frau Katz's son T. ever related was at the age of 5 ; 3 and ran as follows: "Daddy, last night I dreamt I went across the street with Elly and when we had got round the corner, there was the moon fallen down and rolled across the road. It wasn't the whole moon but the half moon."

In one case the Scupins could very plainly observe the transition of a real dream-account into a confabulation; at the same time this example is interesting from the wealth of detail in the dream-account.

Bubi (5 ; 5) one morning described his dream of a thief that had wakened him in the night, "very seriously and as though searching his memory: *I was alone with Clara and you were away—then I went down the steps, and down in the garden stood a watchman—then I came rolling down and he said: Don't roll! Then I stood up quick and went up again—but before that was, the lamp in the parlour was lit, but now it was quite dark—only in the gentleman's room all the lamps were alight that Papa has—and through the door I saw how the thieves stealed—then I went into the kitchen to Clara and the thieves kept on stealing.* In the account of his dream, the whole style of the recital, it seemed extremely probable that this was a case of a genuine real dream. The child's behaviour was quite different when we asked what further had happened with the thieves. With no more deliberation, no more pauses, Bubi chattered on in gay invention: *And then I went into the street and fetched the watchman; he locked all the doors, and then the thieves were shut in, and then they have been shut up in prison, and there the mice run, and now the tale's done.*

"This second part of his recital was quite evidently an invention tacked on to the dream."

As is well known, the psychology of dreams takes an important place in psychoanalysis. In Freud's opinion, dreams are deeply rooted in the life of impulse, and in them wishes that dare not come into the open in real life find an abreaction, since they appear no longer as mere desires but as their actual fulfilment. Certainly this happens but very seldom in a direct way, for, as a rule, even in dreams, the repressed desires only appear in symbolic form, and then the familiar symbol-interpretation must once more come to the fore. This general theory is also applied to children's dreams, and we get from Freud, Stekel, Hug-Hellmuth and others numerous interpretations of dreams of children aged two to six years, in which we find almost always the well-known sexual symbolism.

Criticism of these attempts must make a threefold distinction:—

(1) The theory of "wish-fulfilment". That this applies to a large number of dreams is undoubtedly true.

Freud[1] himself relates an unmistakable example of this in a boy aged five and a half. When staying amongst the Alps he had often seen in the distance the roof-stone with the Simony hut and heard a great deal about mountain-climbing. On one excursion he asked of every rock he saw: "Is that the roof-stone?" and at last he was much disappointed when the excursion ended without reaching the point he was longing for. But next morning he said with great delight: *Last night I dreamt we were at the Simony hut.*

Here then the dream-distortion only consists in the fact that a mere wish is transformed into real experience, a metamorphosis which we often find in the young child's waking confabulations.

But according to psychoanalytic teaching, cases of such direct evidence of wishes form the exceptions only. Psychoanalysts therefore lay the chief emphasis on—

(2) The interpretation of the dream-content.

Here we have a repetition of all that we found above in the symbolic interpretation of the child's fantasy in waking hours

[1] I, p. 133.

or in play. There is no dream-presentation which under the clever arts of interpretation may not become the symbol of some object of sexual desire; and there is no criterion enabling us to discover amongst this infinite number of possible interpretations those that are really correct. Here again we are standing beyond truth and falsehood in the region of unfettered fantasy, viz. the interpreter.

Thus Hug-Hellmuth,[1] in an analysis of her little nephew's dream, interprets the railway appearing in it as a genital symbol, since it meanders along (and since the boy, in his games, always guides the train with his hand, and thus by transference performs an act of onanie!). In the same dream cigarettes appeared, "just men they were," and "at the top of each there was a lot of tobacco hanging out and that was their hair". These interpretations given by the child himself did not satisfy the psychoanalyst. In the hairs there was an upward movement; the hanging out signifies again the genital organ.

According to Stekel, a dream of any excretion has the same symbolic interpretation; thus, if anyone dreams that he has a cold or is bleeding from a cut, the interpretation is always sexual excretions. In addition to sexuality, Stekel affirms that it is innate criminal instincts that find expression in children's dreams, for the repressed wishes for others' death, lust of cruelty, etc., are then brought to fulfilment.

(3) The determination of dream-content.

Here, psychoanalysis is entirely wanting in the critical caution, so especially necessary in dealing with children. We noticed, above, that spontaneous recitals of dreams seldom appear before the fifth year, and that even then the child has difficulty in distinguishing between the real account of his dream and waking confabulation. The psychoanalysts, however, accept and make use of the dreams of two-year-old children. Their material is deprived of all value by the fact that, not content with the child's spontaneous statement, they only make of it the starting-point for an inquisitorial cross-examination by which they hope to extract from the child a still further dream-content, and, if possible, the interpretation of the dream-symbols. It in no way astonishes us that it is always possible by this method to obtain from

[1] III, p. 470.

the child himself the interpretation presupposed by the analyst.

As an example of this, we may take the tale of the dream of a five-year-old child which has gained notoriety by Freud's Analysis of Phobia[1] [V]. The dream ran: "In the night there was a big and a tiny giraffe in the room, and the big one screamed because I took away the little one. Then it stopped screaming and I sat down on the little one." The dream had so frightened the boy that he took refuge in his parents' bed.

The boy's father, a follower of Freud's, saw in the two giraffes the two parents with their respective sexual organs. To determine this he now used a method about which he says himself:—

"On Sunday I am going with Hans to L. At the door I part from my wife with a joking: 'Good-bye, big giraffe.' Hans asks: 'Why giraffe?' I replied: 'Mummy is the big giraffe,' when Hans says: 'Yes, isn't she, and Hanna (his younger sister) is the little giraffe.' In the railway carriage I EXPLAIN TO HIM the giraffe-fantasy, and in reply he says: 'Yes, that is right.' " And in another place the father reports: "As a matter of fact my wife CROSS-QUESTIONED HIM ALL MORNING until he told her the giraffe tale." Thus the tale of the dream-content as well as the acquiescence in its interpretation has only taken place under suggestive influences so strong as to be irresistible.

[1] For a criticism of the psychoanalysis made on this child cf. W. Stern, V, p. 91.

CHAPTER XXI

THE FACTORS OF PLAY-ACTIVITY

1. The Instinctive Principles of Play

THE chief field for the expression of the child's imagination is play, and so, in earlier chapters, we had in many ways to touch on the subject. But play demands quite other methods of treatment, if we wish to give it its full weight as the very centre of the psychic life in early childhood; not only the consciousness present in play (with which we have so far been principally concerned) but the play itself, its significance for individual development as a whole, its origin in deep instinct and in the wide influences of environment—all these deserve separate treatment.

Here we traverse paths already well trodden. Since Rousseau in *Emile* impressed the play-attitude to the world and life with the stamp of an educational ideal, and since Schiller[1] glorified the play-instinct as a special human gift—"man is only man indeed when he plays"—the subject has never been forgotten or neglected, until, at last, in the second half of the nineteenth century, it led to a succession of more or less exhaustive play-theories promulgated by Spencer, Lazarus, Stanley Hall, Carr, and, above all, by Groos. In recent times, too, psychoanalysis has also added its quota. All who wish to investigate the play problem more closely must be referred to the fundamental work of Groos; his theory of play is not only the most carefully thought-out, but, at the same time, the most satisfying, and in the detailed considerations we are now giving we have to thank his writings for many weighty suggestions.

To understand the problem before us, it will be best to start with an apparent paradox.

What is play? VOLUNTARY, SELF-SUFFICIENT ACTIVITY. This indeed must be its definition, if we wish to characterize the CONSCIOUS CONDITION existing in play. Play is self-sufficient, i.e. quite content in and with play *per se*, not directed to the achievement of any end outside itself, in opposition to work that is never anything but the means to some other aim.

---

[1] In his *Letters Concerning Man's Æsthetic Education.*

Only that being can play whose consciousness is not quite subjugated under the yoke of necessity, under the stress of the struggle for existence. The aim of play is reached and fulfilled in the player's consciousness when the game is finished. As soon as any other aim is consciously connected with the play, as money gained in cards and roulette, or the "record" in competitions, the activity loses its character of play, pure and simple.

But if play has no aims outside itself, it is also free from all outside compulsion; play is neither demanded nor imposed, but bubbles up spontaneously from the individual's deepest craving for action, and its nature, form and duration are determined by the player himself. Compulsory games cease to be play. Even the rules of the game, which represent a certain compulsion, in no way contradict this, for the recognition of these rules, in the submission to their dictates, is a voluntary act on the part of every player.

But now it becomes evident that the definition just given of the state of consciousness in play cannot apply to play itself. For it speaks of self-sufficiency, and yet there are inherent in the child's play aims which reach far beyond the moment of the immediate act of play, which indeed make play of basic service in the universal tasks of life. The definition speaks of spontaneity and freedom, and yet play originates in a deep compulsion of human nature that almost brings it into line with the compulsory functions of instinct.

The solution of the paradox lies in the fact that, in the first case, we consider play as a phenomenon of consciousness, but, in the second, as a personal function independent of its conscious representation. It is now recognized that the true motives and associations of human life by no means always rise to the surface consciousness; we must rather look for them in that teleological unity of the human personality which functions in great measure apart from the Conscious. All human activity—hence play as well—has its personal significance, and is, in its own place, an essential factor in the accomplishment of the whole development of the personality. Viewed from this standpoint, play activity is indeed closely related to those elementary principles of life which we call instinct and impulse. Play shares with them that inner urge to whose irresistible force the child has to yield without doubt or question.

In support of this a note in the diary concerning Hilde:—

Hilde (4 ; 2). "Just as the poet, in the stage of inspiration, says of himself: 'A poem burns in me,' so Hilde might justly say of herself, 'play burns in me.' Play is like some higher power holding the child fast in its bonds. Sometimes when I try to fetch H. from a game to some other occupation, very welcome as a rule (e.g. watering the flowers), she answers: *No, I must play now*, and that sounds like no capricious refusal, but as if the child had to submit to an irresistible impulse."

Nevertheless, no useful purpose seems to be served by giving a special place to the play-instinct or "play-impulse" (Schiller) in contradistinction to the other instincts. Play is rather a particular form of activity of all instincts. When the child is playing, all unsuspecting, he brings his life and action at the moment into line with that whole chain of instinctive activities which stretches from his ancestors across his childish present away to his own adult life. Thus the personal significance of play falls into a significance of the past, present and future.

(*a*) The significance of the past consists in the inherited principles of play especially emphasized by Stanley Hall's theory, in accordance with which play is a kind of atavism, i.e. the revival of original instincts of earlier primitive races (possibly, indeed, of lower animal ancestors). Every man—so Hall teaches, taking his stand on Haeckel's fundamental law of biogenesis—receives from his ancestors the inheritance of their psychic development, and must therefore pass through the lower stages of psychic development before he can reach the stage existing at his own time. Thus in the chasing, fighting, destroying, climbing, throwing and other children's games we see the effects of old, so to speak outgrown, motive forces. They no longer possess their former power of determining the real adult life; but in the child's life they reappear once more to work themselves off in the harmless form of play-activity. According to this theory, the positive personal significance of play is to be found in this discharge and abreaction of atavistic instincts, a significance we may indeed concede, but one which does not play the important part ascribed to it by Hall.

He lays especial stress on the essential agreements between the attitude of mind and action in young children and human beings of early civilization, but there are also formal agreements that have not, necessarily, anything to do with atavism. All psychic development, whether in the individual child or in humanity as a whole, follows certain laws of sequence, in accordance with which primitive and more roughly hewn life-forms precede the more complicated and finely differentiated. Hence the little child's games may show in their simplicity a certain kinship with the actions of primitive races, although the content of the game may be entirely borrowed from his modern environment.

(b) THE INFLUENCE OF THE PRESENT in play is to be seen in the fact that the trend of the aims dominating the child's life at the time comes into evidence in it. Certain associations are then clearly recognizable: the wish for knowledge, movement, adornment, appearance and imitation are the direct causes of definite forms of play. Other associations are of a more hidden nature; to these belong those expressions in play which psychoanalysis in some cases proves, in others only asserts. In the main they may be divided into two groups, impulses of mastery and erotic impulses; the former (as especially emphasized by Adler) are the child's protective instincts against his feeling of weakness; they provide for the child, in his play, the satisfaction of a fictitious feeling of power and superiority. The erotic impulses (to which the Freud school give a foremost place) are regarded as most intensive although entirely repressed personal features, which rule even the little child, and can only find an outlet along the symbolic paths of play. We have already in another place spoken of these theories.

But now the influence on play of these impulse-forms—in so far as such an influence exists—does not consist so much in their nature at the time as in their prophetic hint as to future development. This is especially emphasized by Adler, who is inclined to think that demeanour in childhood is the surest indication of the lines that will be followed in after-life. Freud's school, on the contrary, are chiefly concerned in proving how great is the sexual part in the child's present life; thus they maintain that instincts find in play a means of discharge rather than of preparation.

This is, for instance, distinctly stated in Pfeifer's psycho-analytic theory of play; in his opinion it is this working off of infantile erotic impulses that makes real play of play;

otherwise it would only be an "unpleasant piece of work". But, in reality, the child is by no means that pronounced little sexual horror which it here appears; those tendencies are present, at the very most, in quite a vague, indistinct and undeveloped form, and thus their significance in children's play exists in a much wider connection, which we must now consider somewhat more in detail.

(c) The significance of play is developed chiefly by Groos in his theory of preparatory training which we endeavour to connect with our personality point of view. In his play the child anticipates his future in the present, for PLAY IS THE INSTINCTIVE SELF-DEVELOPMENT OF BUDDING CAPABILITIES, THE UNCONSCIOUS PRELIMINARY PRACTICE OF FUTURE FUNC-TIONS.

Every new-born creature, whether man or beast, brings with it a number of ready-made powers into the world, whilst others only develop more or less slowly in the course of the individual life.

The lower animal is, as we have seen, at first more favour-ably placed than man, as it possesses a much greater store of these inherited capabilities; in his early years man is not yet able to do much that, later, he must achieve. It is true this human disadvantage is only apparent; his manifold and complicated tasks in life cannot be accomplished by fixed inborn mechanical powers, for the reason that, with ever-changing aim, they must progress with the progressing con-ditions of life around him. An inevitable consequence of this progressive principle of human mentality is therefore the gradual disappearance of the conservative principle of finished, inherited powers; certainly man has first to learn very much, but, in compensation, he is also able to learn much that his forefathers could not, whilst the lower animal can only travel along the well-worn tracks of the inherited powers of his kind.

That period of life which is destined slowly to mature powers existing, as yet, only in their preliminary stages, to practise them and bring them into correspondence with the conditions of their environment, is called childhood and youth. It lasts in man relatively much longer than in any other animal, embraces, indeed, no less than one-third of the average human life.

In this preparatory process play takes on a special significance; hence the child plays more intensively and for longer than the young animal. Play, then, represents the most intimate interaction of those inner capacities which must be practised and of those surrounding impressions which must be met and conquered. Let us first consider the part played by the inner conditions, then that of those without.

The different human capabilities and powers become "due", i.e. necessary to life, at very different times. But now it is evident that the awakening of the inner dispositions, leading to these powers, by no means corresponds with this demand of necessity, but takes place much earlier. This premature appearance seems to be a general law; no psychic function is exempt from it. Active tendencies suddenly appear as an instinctive matter-of-course—tendencies not in the least appropriate for the existing stage of life, but often betraying by their elemental force the end to which man was unconsciously striving. These are play-activities. In the infant's restless limbs and babbling tongue we see already, in play, instincts of speech and movement not due till a full year later; the boy's sham fight and the girl's love of dolls are the first signs of the adult instincts for strife and fostering care not "due" till tens of years later. EVERY PLAY-IMPULSE IS THE DAWN OF AN INSTINCTIVE REALITY.

We might think that the premature appearance of certain activities would not only be of no advantage but might even be harmful. Yet premature activity means at the same time preliminary practice, and this practice exists, without exception, for all functions that may be valuable in life, whether psychic or physical, social or individual. Bodily strength and technical skill, management and handling of things, patience and perseverance, deliberation and decision, wonderment, interpretation, working with others for the general good—all this and much more is practised in play.

The power of play in such self-teaching is possible from the fact that the practice takes place in harmless material; play is indeed to life as manœuvres to warfare. Failures and losses which, in real life, would cause the greatest harm are experienced and endured in the game without any actual damage, with advantage, indeed, as a kind of self-control is exercised to rise above them. Insight thus gained is much more useful than teaching from others. "Knowledge by suffering entereth", even when it is only play-suffering. The boy playing with his bricks will try ten times in vain to lay a cross-beam on two pillars, just because the pillars are too far apart or of different heights; at last, by trying and trying, he finds the right pillars and position, and has also gained some insight into statics and skill in handling which, later on in practical life, will prove very useful.

Also, from a mental and moral point of view, we find this premature play of the instincts. In play the child faces the task of drawing up plans, forming resolves, exercising presence of mind and of disposing his forces (for instance, in sham fights) at a period when he is, in real life, entirely dependent and unable to make any plans. In his game, the child soon learns to submit to its rules, i.e. voluntarily to recognize and obey the obligation of an abstract law. How much later it is before he arrives at regulating his actual life, not in accordance with direct personal authority, but from a compelling sense of duty! Thus the child's play-life is psychologically several stages ahead of his actual development. But, of course, this is only possible because these premature play-activities are devoid of consequences and of responsibility. The play-instinct is concerned, not with the result as in actual reality, but with the action as such, and the value of the practice provided by this action forms the personal significance of play as regards the future.

2. The Influence of Environment on Play

We have intentionally given pride of place to this instinctive, and therefore inner, factor of play because it is often under-estimated or entirely disregarded in opposition to the outer factor, the influence of surroundings on play. The effects of these influences must be apparent to the most superficial observer. The child's sense-impressions, the objects at his disposal, the forms of life in his environment, the companions with whom he associates—all these exercise the strongest influence on his play. The psychic function that causes such influence is imitation, according to Spencer's theory the only factor determining the kind and nature of the play. His philosophical teaching is, namely, that if the natural energy of any individual is not entirely used in life's stern tasks, it must find some other outlet (e.g. in play), no matter in what way. But the most convenient way of providing an aim for this superfluous energy consists in doing what others are seen to do, and thus imitation is the only determining factor of all play-activity.

This theory is wrong in such a one-sided view, yet, at the same time, it must be granted that imitation exercises an enormous influence on play, as a consequence of the child's natural motor-reactions. What he sees and hears is not only perceived and noticed, but transmitted, either directly or indirectly, into personal action. The child directly imitates when he is induced by the sight of soldiers marching past to play at soldiers himself, or when he sees another child playing in the sand and at once wishes to do the same. And the imitation is indirect when the example is not present at the moment of play, but has been more or less frequently perceived before. These indirect imitations are very frequent even in the two-year-old child, as the following test shows:—

Hilde (2 ; 0). "If we notice H. at play we can often see how intelligently she imitates adult occupations. For example, the day before yesterday she put her right hand into one of her little boots and rubbed it with a rag, saying meanwhile *dirty*. Lately she had a little flat-iron given to her; I wanted to put it away for a time, as I thought she would not understand how to use it in any way. But I was entirely wrong. She called out energetically *iron, iron,* and, to our astonishment, she began, standing at a little chair, to move her iron cleverly back and forwards over the material, even once, between the movements, placing the iron on its stand. Also she will often 'fold the clothes' if she has a serviette or something similar given to her for the purpose."

It is reported of the same child at the age of 3 ; 7 that she treats her doll, in every detail, as her mother did her little brother, that she washes her doll's clothes, scrubs the doll's house, etc., all in imitation of her elder's activity.

As a result of imitation we find in the child's play reflections of the child's native place, its father's calling, the recurring incidents of the season and any remarkable happenings. The mountain child plays at poaching and smuggling, the child of the seashore at steamers and fishing. In any place where a Zeppelin or aeroplane has been seen for the first time, this sensation will doubtless be transferred for weeks to the sphere of the children's play. The boys' sham fights at one time were called Russians and Japanese, at another French and Germans, and thus the world's history casts its shadows over the region of the children's play.[1]

In early childhood it is not so much these historical events, but rather the experiences resulting from the district in which the child is living, that are most eagerly imitated. When our children's holidays had been spent at the sea, their play was greatly influenced by it for weeks afterwards; they played at steamers and sailing-boats, at swimming, and fishing, whilst in the years of mountain holidays, minding cattle and other country occupations often left their impress on the games.

In this chapter on influences of the environment toys must also find a mention. The child of poor parents, who really has no objects on which he can exercise his play-instincts in handling, building and busying himself, is certainly adversely affected in his play; but, on the other hand, the superabundance of toys found in the case of many children of the upper classes tends to render the child superficial and restless, at last even blasé, and thus makes play of very doubtful value.

Still more important is the influence of the playfellows. Undesirable as it is that games should be played to order, yet it is impossible for the child to do without encouragement, help and, above all, hearty sympathy. In children that are left a great deal to themselves we often find, therefore, a crippling of the play-instincts; it requires a large amount of spontaneity not to suffer greatly from such neglect. But even when some older person is greatly in sympathy with the child, he is not in himself a sufficient playfellow. The want does not make itself so much felt in the very earliest years, but, from four to six years of age, the child feels strongly attracted to other children; the infectious influence of delight in play, the mutual stimulation, the community of interests and of mental growth are indispensable factors in the development of play, especially play of a social character. That is why younger brothers and sisters, who belong from the very beginning to a childish play-society, have totally different

[1] Especially characteristic of this point are the Soviet children's games in Russia.

play-development from that shown by first-born or only children; it is here that the kindergarten gives some of its most important help. Here, too, we see the force of that law of imitation already mentioned (cf. Chapter IX, Section 2), viz. that the more the imitator feels himself like his model, the more intensive is the imitation.

The imitative factor of play has the further significance of introducing the child to the great process of civilization. In play the child obtains his first knowledge and mastery of the forms of life and the achievements of culture, of the manners and customs characteristic of his nation, his local environment, his social group and of his family, which in all probability will form the foundations of his own adult life. Long before the school consciously begins to give to the young generation the mental riches of their age, they have begun on their own account in their imitative play to provide for historical continuity.

3. Convergence of Inner and Outer Conditions Influencing Play

In spite of the great importance which we must assign to imitation, it would be a great mistake to ascribe, as Spencer does, all play to its action. For that is proved erroneous, first of all, by the fact that there are very many games— especially in earliest childhood—which are quite independent of imitation. Groos rightly calls attention to the elemental significance of "experimental" games. When the child happily beats with his spoon, now on the table, now on the plate, delighting in the difference of sound, or when he destroys some toy to find out the secret of its inside, he is not imitating in any way.

But even more convincing is the fact that the child, even in imitation, is not so passively absorbed in his models that his games are entirely decided by them. Rather we are here brought face to face with a typical example of the convergence of innate and acquired powers; the outer factor of environment is directly responsible for the possible play-material and models, the things to be imitated, but it is the inner factor of the play-instinct that alone determines when and how imitation is to take place. For the unconscious choice made of the models, as well as the way in which they are grasped and worked up, entirely depends ON NATURAL DISPOSITIONS, ON THE INNER INFLUENCES OF DEVELOPMENT AND OF DIFFEREN-TIATION.

The child may live in the same surroundings year after year, may always receive the same impressions; yet with every changing year he copies different models, in accordance with his existing stage of growth and the development of his interests. And this is brought about by development-laws of such force that the same play-instincts appear at the same period of growth in children of the most divergent lands and times, in spite of all differences in conditions of environment. Thus games with dice, dolls and sham-fights rise superior to time and place, to social rank, different nationality, degree of civilization. The specific material used for the expression of movement, nursing or fighting instincts may vary with surroundings, but the general forms of the play remain unchanged.

But, on the other hand, the greatest diversities are shown in the games of children in the same environment but of different individuality, thus again affording proof of the part played by the inborn impulses. The difference of psychic gifts between man and man seems indeed to appear nowhere so early as in the child's play, and that because this is an anticipation of the future individual development.

Whilst the actual life of the first years is almost completely under the levelling influence of universal childhood, the special individuality of the growing character, the future nature of the intelligence, etc., already show themselves in play. One child plays with energy and perseverance, another with indifferent fickleness; the one in group-games throws himself into the leadership, rules and commands his playmates as a matter of course; the other allows himself to be led by others, shows but little initiative and joins in the game as one of a crowd. Imitation, in one case, is slavish, an exact replica of the model; in another, more tinged with personality, an independent development and transformation of the things imitated. Are not all these essential features of the future adult prematurely budding forth? We might feel strongly tempted to foretell children's later character and mental development from carefully observing them in their games, and even if we cannot be quite sure of escaping considerable error, yet, at any rate, there is no other province of the child's existence where we find such clear indications of the future as in the games of childhood.[1]

In this point the kindergarten might have a psychological task which, up till now, has been entirely unrecognized. It might trace characteristics of its pupils with special reference to their bearing in play; from these, later on, the home, school, and even the discussion as to calling in life, might gain hints for the better understanding, treatment and advising of the child. It is true that this requires—what to-day is very rarely found—thorough training in psychological observation and interpretation.

In this connection, attention might again be drawn to Judith Lichtenstein's introduction to observation.

No psychic differentiation is so marked as that of sex. The assertion that the psychic differences between the sexes is the direct result of outward environment receives no more striking refutation than in the play of early childhood; for if even in three- and four-year-old children we find quite elemental differences in interest and manner of playing, this can only result from a difference of instinct, deeply rooted in man's very being.

This sex distinction not only exists in the play-temperament (a boy's, as a rule, being wilder than a girl's), but also in the subject-matter of the games. The girl sees the fire-brigade driving, the soldiers marching past, etc., just as much as the boy does; the boy, like the girl, sees his mother busied about the house, and looking after his little brother, so that both are influenced by exactly the same models for imitation; and yet the girls rarely think of playing at soldiers or fire-brigades, and the boys just as seldom dream in their games of imitating cleaning and scrubbing or the care of a little child. Perhaps it may be objected that the boy plays at fire-brigades, etc., because he sees men engaged in this work. But even this limitation itself of imitation to models of the child's own sex requires an explanation; for apart from the game, the consciousness of sex is still so small that the child

---

[1] Even psychopathic features of a later age may be foretold in certain peculiarities of childish play. Pfister describes such a case in which the child's play seems to him "an early symptom of unhealthy development".

is equally susceptible to the influence of either men or women. There is no other alternative: in that choice of interest we find the distinct natural trend of both sexes—the dominant interest in the girls' play is "the home," in the boys', "public life".

A second objection is sometimes put forward: that even these differences are the result of training. The boy is prevented from playing with dolls or turned from it by ridicule; girls are forbidden playing at soldiers and similar games for the reason that "little girls do not play at that". Such a reason may sometimes partly explain the difference, but what were the reasons, to begin with, that certain games were considered characteristic of boys, others of girls? On one hand, because, in the majority of cases observed, boys gave their chief preference to one form of play and girls to another; on the other hand, the games were valued in their relation to the future serious activities of the two sexes. In this way, therefore, popular opinion already presupposes the instinctive and anticipatory significance of play.

Besides, it is by no means correct that children are deprived of the opportunity of playing games peculiar to the other sex; but even when it is offered, they make another use of it, more in accordance with their own nature.

Even little boys get dolls and play with them, but it is quite exceptional to find in them the tender anxious care with which the girl surrounds her dolls; the boy makes his doll hop and march, play tricks, ride as passenger in his cart or on his rag animals, gives it medical treatment, and— soon tosses it aside.

The boy F. L. (3 ; 0) had a doll given to him. He looked at her and especially admired the way in which she could shut and open her eyes, praised her shoes and pretty scarf, and ran round to different members of the family to show with delight his new possession. Then he set her down beside him and said: *Look now, how I can build.* That was her dismissal for that day. On the next, one of her arms was torn off. After that he took no further interest in her.

On the other hand, a girl gets a box of bricks, but does not use it nearly so often as a boy; she does indeed build a room with furniture and a little garden of no very striking construction, but with more care expended on decorative details;

whilst the boy builds houses, and castles, towns and railways. The following instance given by the Scupins shows this sex distinction in spite of identically the same outward conditions for play.

Holidays by the sea. Bubi (4 ; 3) is playing with a little girl-friend of about his own age in the sand. "Their favourites were buildings with an arched roof. Bubi's and Lottchen's buildings were very much alike, although based on different ideas. Lottchen, for instance, had concerned herself chiefly with the building of an oven; by means of a mussel-shell she put little pebbles representing bread and cakes into the oven; Bubi, on the other hand, builds bridges, tunnels and dams." His little playmate has passed bridges and tunnels just as often as the boy, but she never thinks of including them in her sphere of play.

Of course, these and other differences, to be discussed later, between boys' and girls' play are only to be looked upon as a general rule for the average child. It is only a question of preponderance, not of the utter exclusion of one or other kind of play. It will therefore not be difficult to quote isolated instances of an opposite nature. There were times when our own boy was so infected by his elder sister's play with her dolls that he too adopted the girl's way of playing. But such actions were only temporary, and soon showed, by their constraint, that they did not originate in the spontaneous impulse of the child's soul, but were adopted from outside. It is true they may sometimes be of an inner nature, for there are innumerable degrees between typical boy- and girl-hood; thus there are many girls who show a distinctly boyish touch in their games, and *vice versa*. In such cases we must again remind ourselves of the prophetic nature of play: a boy whose inner instinct leads him often to play with dolls like a girl has doubtless a certain prospect of showing, as a man, a touch of tenderness, almost womanly—perhaps even womanish —in character.

CHAPTER XXII

CHIEF VARIETIES OF PLAY IN EARLY CHILDHOOD

WE will conclude the discussion of play with a survey of the principal typical forms of play; this can be short, since numerous details were mentioned in earlier chapters, and others will be considered later on in the section "Enjoyment and Creative Activity".

In the present chapter we will especially fix our attention on, first, the growth of development, and, second, the sex distinctions. The question whether the child plays by himself or with others forms the main division. Both forms begin very early, but solitary games develop more quickly than group-games, and for that reason greatly preponderate in the earliest periods.

1. Solitary (Individual) Games

The development of play passes through the same stages as the mastery of the spatial-concept; starting with the individual self, it extends its activity in concentric circles of an ever-increasing radius.

The first games of all are limited to the child's own body; in our treatment of infancy we have already discussed the babble-games of the organs of speech, the movement-games of hands and legs (cf. Chapter V, 3).

But, even later on, these bodily games maintain their important office; an unquenchable thirst for action causes the child in its earliest years to spend the greater portion of its waking life in performing play-movements, which, in spite of their apparent aimlessness, are most valuable for the practice of skill, strength and perseverance—in short, for progressive mastery of the body; thus the young child's life is filled with struggling and walking, hopping and jumping; climbing and balancing, swinging and dancing, bawling and shouting—and even swimming and skating—can be managed very happily by many a five-year-old. Sometimes the purely play-motive is joined by a feature of something like sport, and the child tries to surpass his own or others' performances: to jump a little higher or farther, to stand still longer on one leg, or to utter louder shouts, etc.

The second class of non-social games aims at the mastery of things. Now the child wants other toys than his own limbs, he wants to seize and conquer something outside himself (cf. Chapter V, Section 3). The distinction between actual toys and other things comes but gradually into being, and, to begin with, the child plays with everything that falls into his hands.

Hilde (2 ; 7). "The child looks upon everything from the play point of view, in every case tests its possibility as a plaything, and afterwards more or less promptly uses it as such. Thus she plays with a torn paper as if it was a doll, with a ball of wool like a rag animal, and with the carpet-beater as with her ball. Many of these things serve only as momentary objects of play, and are straightway discarded and forgotten; to others the child returns again and again, they are continually used for games, and therefore become 'playthings' in the narrower sense of the word."

The simplest playthings are objects left unchanged in their original form and only used as auxiliary to the aforementioned body-games: as when the child thumps on the table with a lump of wood to satisfy his craving for movement and his hunger for noise-stimulus. But of more importance as practice in the mastery of things are those games in which the objects themselves or their mutual relations are altered by the child himself. This happens in the two forms of destruction and construction which show a distinct sequence of development; for, as in all historical developments, so too in the child's psychic history, tearing down always precedes building up.

Hilde (1 ; 6). "Until now Hilde's play has chiefly consisted of destruction (tearing to bits, throwing away, etc.); as yet she shows no constructive sense at all. Building bricks, for example, are dashed in all directions, but not yet put upon one another, either in couples or more."

Six weeks later it is reported for the first time that she tries to arrange wood blocks properly in their respective boxes. After another six weeks she tries to fit a number of hollow wooden dice of successive sizes into one another. Here we catch sight, no doubt, of the first beginnings of constructive action.

DESTRUCTIVE GAMES.

The child's love of destruction is well known. A piece of paper that comes into his hands only leaves them in fragments, toys are bent and broken, the insides of dolls ransacked, things, arranged in proper order, are ruthlessly thrown into confusion, and even the beautiful tower his mother has built out of his bricks, to the child's great joy, is overthrown with even greater delight. We must not put too low or too high a value on this desire for destruction. It would be quite a mistake to see in it the expression of natural spite and malice, for the child has, as yet, not the faintest idea that he is destroying anything of value. But that other explanation of the child's craving for knowledge and investigation is only occasionally correct, at any rate in early years. The matter is much simpler. The child, in handling things and practising his strength on them, meets with opposition, and is spurred on by this to so much the greater exertion, and delights in the final victory without heeding any other results. The consciousness of being the cause, which has so strong an affective-tone of pleasure, can never be exhibited in a more elemental form than in destruction. All upbuilding takes time, can only reach its goal by single stages, but the impulsive "I will now knock down the tower" brings about a violent and immediate result.

In this destructive activity the child will learn much even without any desire for research. First, the physics of resistance, the inertia, stability and weight of objects, then their inner constitution, which often appears as a consequence of the child's action, although quite unintentional. When the child is four or five years old, a real desire of knowledge may then lead to a more systematic dissection of things.

Of course, CONSTRUCTIVE PLAY which combines elements in new associations has reached a much higher stage. For it already presupposes a fairly developed power of psychic synthesis as well as a dominant interest which, for some time at least, must be fixed on the destined goal. To these necessary conditions, however, there is now added as the really decisive motive a certain creative desire to produce results, not only in imagination, but in actual reality. The joy of being the cause which finds only blind expression in destruction is now refined, on one hand, to the joy of mental strife as it fights with the self-imposed task, on the other to the joy of creative power when it succeeds in impressing objects with a new shape.

These instincts of dominance, strife and creative power are qualities belonging in greater measure to the man than to the woman; in accord with this fact the constructive games at a very early age show an unmistakable SEX DISTINCTION. The smaller productivity in the psychic life of the female is now generally recognized by impartial judges; yet we are astonished to find this difference emphasized as early as the second year. About this time boys, indeed, already begin to show signs of an active desire for the independent fitting together of things of some sort or another—in the third and fourth years they are filled by a rage for building which is not nearly so strongly marked in girls. Not only building-bricks of wood and stone, but all sorts of other things: rods, cotton-reels, logs and boxes, all serve as materials for the boys' imaginative buildings.

Gunther (1 ; 2) already tried to put his wooden dice one on the other, and could manage to do it with two, whilst the third still came rattling down. (1 ; 6) His towers now have reached six blocks.

(1 ; 7.) "When he has made anything new he laughs aloud with delight. To-day he put another little doll on a toy rocking-horse that already had a rider; huge delight followed. At dinner he plays with the things on the table, e.g. he puts one napkin-ring on another and a knife-stand through both, etc., etc."

(2 ; 4.) "He gets great pleasure from building, especially with unusual materials. He likes to put reels of cotton on or beside one another, playing, of course, at *puff-puff*; he makes a lamp of napkin-rings placed on one another, etc. Lately he took a piece of wood shaped like a mushroom used in darning stockings, put it down stalk uppermost, round which he arranged four or five little cotton-reels."

(2 ; 8½.) "With his blocks he builds, with much skill and caution, very high shaky towers, which he thus adjures: *No, no, don't fall down, no! no!* At dinner he made a railway of remarkable symmetry from two knife-rests, two teaspoons and two porridge-sticks." See figure on p. 324.

From the fourth to the sixth year there is great development in constructive games in girls as well, although boys

still keep in advance; in many other constructions as well
as building, e.g. the formation of patterns with little sticks or
coloured slabs (mosaic work), threading and sewing on beads,

and the putting together of cut-
out pictures; modelling in clay
and drawing[1] also belong to the
same class.

It is interesting to determine
the part played by imitation in these games. In many there
are patterns to be copied; often, too, someone else will
copy these for the child to see or begin the work for
him, in which case there is direct imitation. In other
cases, the imitation is only indirect and accompanied by
more spontaneous action: the child builds a house, not
like his copy, but from his recollection of some actual
house that he may have seen. And lastly, there are constructive activities free from all trace of imitation, such as
imaginary buildings and the invention of new patterns with
the gay mosaic slabs.

The part played by imitation in constructive games is
evidently greater in the case of girls than with boys. For
many boys totally disregard the copies supplied with the
building-bricks and similar games, and when they do use
them, copy them much less faithfully than girls do. On the
whole they prefer indirect imitation, which leaves them greater
scope for independent action; at first, indeed, they must alter
the house, the bridge, the railway which they have seen in
actual life into the form, size, etc., necessitated by the play-
materials to hand and their own power of using them. At
last we find purely imaginative constructions and inventions
almost entirely confined to boys.[2]

On the other hand, girls, as a rule, welcome a model or
copy as a guide and limit for their production, and are perfectly contented in aiming at a close copy of such a model.
Compare the two following descriptions of the same game at
the same age:—

[1] For drawing cf. Chapter XXVI.
[2] Doctor Czerny, in *The Physician as Educator*, p. 46, puts forward an entirely unpsychological view of the importance of a copy for the young child.
He considers only building to a copy of any educational value, and adds: "If
we give the bricks to the child to do what he likes with them, he only learns
how to pass the time with profitless play."

Eva (4 ; 10½). "For a month she has played happily with a mosaic game. Every day—sometimes for hours—she puts the gay, variously shaped pieces together, generally like the copy, but often in 'invented' stars. She is always equally delighted with her success, shows us her work and the sheet of copies, asking us to guess which star she has made."

Gunther (4 ; 11½). "The 'star' game, i.e. one of bright cardboard pieces in different shapes, continually gives him the same pleasure. If we want to fix his attention, we only have

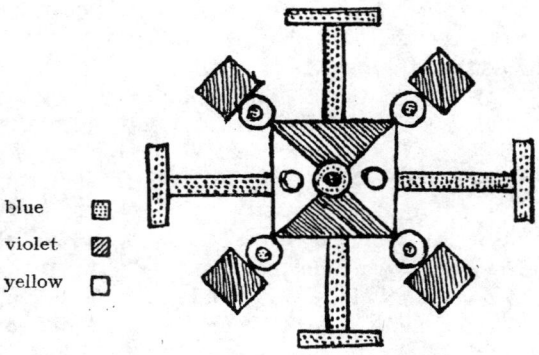

blue
violet
yellow

to give him the box of coloured figures. He never uses the copies, not that they are dull in any way, for they represent the most amusing things, beside patterns of the most diverse kinds: houses, ships, trains, etc. G. makes the most manifold pictures always out of his own head; he is always inventing fresh stars and figures; often he designs 'real' people, and a little while ago a train with engine and trucks that was quite a success; here no doubt he had been unconsciously helped by the copy he had so often seen. I often noticed him at his work and saw how he used to set out the figures symmetrically with both hands, starting from the middle and working up and down, right and left. A special feature, indeed, of his patterns is their symmetry. Lately we succeeded (without his seeing us) in taking away a star and fixing it exactly as he had made it (see figure above). It is remarkable that he has arrived quite spontaneously without any teaching at such symmetrical form. We parents have very seldom indeed set out a pattern."

The Scupins' boy was a particularly zealous builder. He began at the age of two and a half, and soon perfected himself in the erection of ingenious and very complicated buildings without troubling about patterns or copies. This was such good practice that (4 ; 7), at his first attempt to work from a copy, he put up a difficult church without a mistake— a refutation of Czerny's statement as to the uselessness of independent building.

We have a copy of one of this boy's buildings at the beginning of his sixth year, which shows of what complicated work he had already become capable (Plate V). His parents give the following explanation:—

Scupin (5 ; 1). (II, p. 161) "The child feels building an absolute mental necessity—a labour of love undertaken of his own free will. He is barely dressed in the morning before he betakes himself to building, generally with all five boxes of bricks. He often builds for two or three hours together, sighing from time to time: *But what hard work it is!* If, however, from fear of overtiring himself, we call him off or propose some other occupation, he gets beside himself and tells us he must finish his building, for *I build because I am so glad when I have a nice building.* As he works, the boy will listen to no suggestions; even our proposals to build something in such and such a way are completely ignored; indeed, he screams at the top of his voice if we only venture to touch one of his blocks. So that we leave him an entirely free hand. We succeeded in securing a picture of one building of his. In the foreground is the courtyard, on the right the roofed-in cellar, adjoining it, the washhouse with a tower. The archway represents the entrance to the house, the space as far as the steps, the hall; the staircase, which was carried out with special, loving care, leads to the first storey. Under that we find the carriage-drive. Since there were not quite enough bricks to complete the first storey, the boy pressed his slate into service and used it as the floor of the first storey."

Another class of individual games is acting a certain part. Here the interest is not chiefly directed to objects and their changes, but to the personal self and its alteration. Then immediately all the surroundings are made to fit this metamorphosis; the child who feels himself a sea-captain makes the chairs and tables into his ship. If two boys are playing at horses, the cord round the horse serves not only for reins but for the carriage as well in which passengers are driven.

These personating games with their strange metamorphoses of the individual ego have always been the object of special interest to all concerned with theories on play. Most of the play theories we have already discussed have had as their aim the explanation of this form of game, and tend to show that the tendency to play such games and the special choice of rôle are due to one and the same principle. But closer consideration shows this, in every case, to be an insufficient explanation.

For instance, in accordance with Stanley Hall's atavism theory, the boy climbing trees, bird's-nesting, shooting with catapult, bow and arrow is once more enacting in his own person the early stage of the primitive hunter; and in his soldier and robber games we see the revival of men of a bygone age of development. This explanation does not go far, for, besides such parts as these, the child, with great relish, plays too those that belong only to the development of his own time, not to an earlier one, e.g. airman, motor-driver, postman, etc. In these cases the choice is most certainly determined, not by inheritance, but by imitation.

After all that has been already said, it follows, as a matter of course, that Freud's psychoanalytic theory sees in the choice of rôles nothing but the child's repressed erotic desires. Hence in the case of the boy, all rôles in play are direct or symbolic "father" rôles. For instance, the jealousy the boy feels for his father as a rival in his mother's affection is said to induce, consciously or unconsciously, an imaginative personation of his father—a fictitious supplanting of his rival as it were. This assumption may be true of an occasional suggestive prompting of the choice of personation, but there is absolutely no foundation for it as a universal rule.

The decisive motive in the choice of personation seems to lie in the general tendency of the child to enlarge the narrow boundaries of his ego. But this tendency appears in different forms.

To begin with, every personation of another—quite irrespective of the special nature of the rôle assumed—tends to widen the child's horizon and extent of feeling. The very personation resulting from imitation brings with it a change in the child's attitude to his environment. The child, playing at postman, shopkeeper or mother, not only imitates the outward movements and actions, but gives proof of an inward adaptation—in however simple a form—to the manner of thought and feeling of that other person, and thus the child's ego grows in kinds of experience and understanding which would not have been gained by simple observation of others. This primitive self-identification with persons of the most varied kind knows no social distinctions; it is to be regretted that such power of sympathetic understanding greatly diminishes with increasing years.

But now the special choice and performance of the rôle personated is also of use in the tendency of the ego to expand. If play, as a whole, is the forerunner of future development, then the personating game is, in detail, the forerunner of the abundant performance and power which it is hoped the future will bring. The child wishes to prove to himself or others—or to beguile them into believing—that he can do something worth doing, tries to show his superiority by giving or ruling, and to taste the joy of seeing others—whether men or things —either offering him service or requiring his help.

Often enough the choice is influenced by a kind of unconscious protest, as Alfred Adler has perceived, rightly enough, although giving it too general an application. The child's painful sense of weakness and dependence tries to seek relief and escape by feigned power and grandeur, and therefore he plays emperor and princess, magician and fairy. The boy whipping up his hobby-horse, the girl ruling her doll or baby brother with a rod of iron, are both unconsciously seeking to avenge themselves for all the restrictions and limitations they so constantly have to endure in actual life. The fiction is but an inward protest against the real sense of inferiority.

Hilde (6 ; 0). "Hilde and her little brother are playing at mother and child. The house is tidied up, the child put to bed, and Mother Hilde is walking about, scolding; the child's every movement is looked upon as forbidden and punished with a slap. Punishment is, at all times, a favourite pastime in children's games. Every human being has a touch of the tyrant in him, and the poor child, always compelled to obey in ordinary life, tries in play at least to taste for once the joys of ruling."[1]

Now, whether this motive of "Power" or "Performance" is of a more negative character in the endeavour to repress the consciousness of weakness, or more positive in the anticipation of future stages of actual superiority, in either case it can help us greatly in the understanding of the choice of many rôles.

Thus the boy in various ways puts himself forward as ruler, leader or fighter; as commanding officer, ship's captain, engine-driver or guard; rider on his hobby-horse, driver of his little handcart, or architect and builder with his blocks. Even there, where he has consented to a subordinate part, he makes a marked protest at any rate by unruly defiance, and shows that he will not put up with anything. Thus the boy who wears the reins as horse feels it all-important to jib and rear, so that the driver knows that it is the horse, not he himself, who is playing the chief part.

Similar games are played by girls, but they never form the central point of their interest. Also girls show a remarkable monotony in contrast to the multitude of rôles assumed by boys. All other rôles have to take a very inferior place in comparison with one—that of mother—since all other budding instincts are secondary to the one of giving, tending, nursing. Even little girls of three or four years often show, in the treatment of their doll, such affection in look and voice, devotion and care, aptitude for the minor details of nursing, that a veritable halo of motherhood seems to surround them. That is no longer simply chance imitation, but a foreshadowing of future destiny. And the child, too, pours out her nursing instincts upon the whole of her little play-world, for, in the earliest years, not only her dolls but her toy animals, indeed all kinds of things, such as spoons and rattles, are fed, washed and put to bed. And, later on, the doll, even when not immediately present, is the object of much care and attention. Its clothes are washed, the doll's house put in order, some adornment or other—(e.g. a row of beads)—made for the doll; if the child gets a pretty present, the doll must see it, etc.

From all this we get the remarkable result that playing with a doll no longer continues a solitary (individual) game.

[1] This extract from my notebook was written in 1906, consequently before the promulgation of Adler's theory.

Even when she has no living companionship in her play, the child does not feel alone, for she is playing with or for another creature that has life and personality, though they may be but illusory. The real "individual" game in which the child, in solitary independence, meets the world of things and tries to conquer it, only exists in lesser degree for girls, whilst it forms a great part of the boy's life, either in constructive play or in many personating games. Many of the girl's individual games, on the other hand, are already group-games in disguise.

Hildegard Hetzer has carried out some interesting experiments as to personating games at different ages on twenty Vienna boys and girls (3 ; 1–6 ; 3). She took each child by turn and proposed it should play either "father" or "mother" and do everything that its father and mother did through the whole day—a doll was provided as child. For half an hour a full record was kept in each case of all words, actions, instances of help or the opposite and so on. The girls almost without exception and 75 per cent. of the boys chose the rôle of mother —a sign at any rate of how far from universal application is the Freudian thesis that the boy continually pictures himself in the rôle of his father. (Of course, in this instance, the choice may have been due in some degree to the fact that little children see far more of their mother's daily doings than they do of their father's.)

Some children refused to play, either from a spirit of self-will, poverty of ideas of their own, or incapacity to carry on the game without help from playfellows. One six-year-old of too realistic a turn of mind felt he was already beyond make-believe and laughed at the others who "are so stupid as to take the wooden chair for a bed". The remaining children were all, without exception, independently of age too, capable of carrying out the representation and with the simplest apparatus gave the personation of themselves, the doll, and of other objects and actions. The consciousness that it was only a pretence-reality seemed evident in all.

The differences in age show themselves chiefly in the manner of the presentation. The number of activities carried out in the half-hour is not only dependent upon increase in age, and for this reason, that the younger children indicate the different individual activities by but one movement or by only very few (with scarcely any speech accompaniment) and quickly pass on to another, whilst the older children give a more detailed treatment to every single action (e.g. the "washing" of the "child" or the marketing). In the case of the oldest, the speed is again quickened by their use of verbal presentation as a help or sometimes even as a substitute for actual movements. The lack of consecutive fantasy, the capricious character of their play, does not show any appreciable change from 3 ; 0 to 6 ; 0.

Very recently noteworthy observations and numerical results as regards children's group-games have been made in kindergartens.

In a Vienna kindergarten, Sonia Vislitzky for several months observed a company of 36 children (3 ; 0–6 ; 0). The grouping of these young children is still very unstable in its character and a group seldom remains unbroken for longer than an hour. The DEVELOPMENT of the social sense is shown in the following points: (1) Amongst the three- and four-year-olds there is always in existence a number of ASOCIAL children (those who prefer to go alone), but in the five- and six-year-old groups they have disappeared; (2) up to five years of age, the quite small groups (not exceeding three members) predominate, and it is not until about the age of six that the groups of four–seven members form 50 per cent. of the sum-total. The motive for the formation of a group is in 89 per cent. of the cases some toy or game which brings the children together, and only very seldom is it direct need of personal contact. Newcomers are at first ignored or even avoided; it is only after some days that a chance circumstance may lead to a breaking of the ice. Generally, in group-games, the rule is one and all alike, but sometimes there are upper and lower positions as one child assumes the function of leader, now for the duration of a single game and now again for a longer period; the latter it is true not before we reach the six-year-old groups.

2. Group-Games

The child's first playmates are not its equals but the adults that nurse it, and the child, even in its first year, responds to their jokes, songs and hiding-games. But the older the child grows, the greater its desire for childish playmates and the more its capacity of joining with other children in common games. In these group (social) games several stages of development can be plainly perceived.[1]

The most elementary expedient to give meaning to social intercourse is imitation, which in primitive play takes the special shape of psychic infection. Some child, A, accomplishes some action or other, claps his hands, runs shouting through the room, perhaps quite heedless of the fact that others are there, perhaps, however, urged on by the presence of spectators and possible playmates. Child B, infected by this, instinctively imitates what he sees or hears, joins A, and thereby incites him to fresh effort; thus the play-enthusiasm is increased by the common action of the playfellow to an intensity seldom found in individual play. In the first three or four years the group-game scarcely progresses beyond these earliest forms, having more the character of playing *beside* rather than *with* one another.

Hilde (4 ; 3), Gunther (2 ; 0). "It is extremely interesting to watch the children playing together. Until now, their chief game consists of rushing together through the room to the accompaniment of ear-piercing screams, reminding us strongly of savages' primitive dances and games. Yesterday we stayed, for a quarter of an hour, dumb witnesses of such a representation of dancing, howling dervishes. At first, both children turned ceaselessly round and round in the smallest circle so persistently that in one short pause Hilde exclaimed: *The whole room turns round with me*—(but none the less she begun her circling again immediately)—and Gunther, several times, came down with a crash, but was quickly on his feet again, twirling round once more. And, all the time, both mouths emitted a loud monotonous *la, la*; each seemed to incite the other to continue. After a short time this first game developed into one of puff-puff; each demanded a little bell, and they rushed one behind the other through the whole length of the room from one end to the other, shaking the bells to and fro, making a terrible noise, half-singing, half-hissing, and their faces beaming with delight."

If a considerable number of children are together, this

[1] Similar stages of development in the nature of children's games are given by Piaget, I, p. 68.

mutual incitement may increase to a regular "mob-infection";
the children then show on a small scale something similar to
what social psychology knows on a larger scale as "mob"-
fanaticism, enthusiasm and suggestion.

In the example given above, the same action is carried on
without any regulation by children beside each other; if this
is reduced to a definite order we get dancing and singing and
kindred games. For the greatest delight to the child even in
Ring a Ring o' Roses, is that so many at the same time sing
the same words and perform the same actions, but the very
fact that every word and step is prescribed prevents even in
this game, as a rule, the strong effects of psychic infection
that existed in the first case. An additional delight lies in the
representative action which is included in many games of this
nature—especially those played in the Froebel kindergarten;
they are regularized personation games.

We find in the games of primitive peoples something analogous even to this quieter form of group-games. As a result of
the many voices, the rhythmical impression made by text,
melody, steps and gestures is increased and thus the physical
movements become disciplined and at the same time a simple
æsthetic pleasure is produced. This kind of game is the first
"common work of art" that binds music, poetry and dance
inseparably into an æsthetic whole. Girls have a greater liking
for the common æsthetic rhythm of such games and keep such
a liking longer than boys.

On a higher intellectual plane we have the development of
those games in which those who take part have DIFFERENT
things to do, and for the first time we can really speak of
playing *with* one another, when each player undertakes a
special activity in the game. The child is faced with a twofold
difficulty: on the one hand he must not yield to the impulse
to comfortable imitation, but on the other he cannot follow
any chance play-impulse that may come to him, but must
recognize and maintain, as a dominant interest, his own special
office within the common aim of the game. That is so difficult
that, as a rule, a three-year-old child requires continual
prompting and help to take part in such a game, and an
independent capacity for this form of play does not seem to
develop until the fifth year.

Political economy shows us how gradual is the development

of a work-society where all do the same tasks into one with division of labour, and the same gradual growth is seen here from the group-game, where all have similar activity, to one with "division of play".

The first example that we noticed corresponds to the age conditions given above. Hilde (5 ; 1), Gunther (2 ; 10): "The children now often play at 'Doctor.' Hilde is the doctor, Gunther is ill, and has to submit to the strangest packing up of head and legs, etc."

Games of this kind are almost exclusively "personating" games, and are very similar to games with dolls, where a division of parts also takes place between the child-mother and the doll-child. Moreover, "Mother and Child" is, far and away, the most popular of these games of different personations in all nurseries, at least in those with several children. With our children this game was a direct development of playing at dolls, and lasted for years, with the addition of continual variations.

A note from the time when Hilde was 8 ; 2, Gunther 5 ; 1, Eva 3 ; 5, runs: "With our children, there is, so to speak, a fundamental game, or rather a fundamental idea, from which the most manifold games are developed. It is called 'playing at dolls,' and has originated in the way the children occupy themselves with their dolls. The children and the dolls represent different members of the family, parents, servants, relations and doctor. By degrees the dolls are quite dropped out, and only the children keep on the game amongst themselves, but the name continues, for the idea is the same. Such a game often lasts for several hours—lately H. and G. played all Sunday in this way, passing in imagination several days, having meals, going to school, to bed, etc., etc."

In these common personating games, one child, as a rule, takes the leading part, either to incite the others and to divide the parts or to make the continuation of the game possible. Generally the older and more mature child will take the reins, but it is partly a matter of temperament, so that sometimes a little scrap of a thing will rule his older playmates as a matter of course.

Hilde (4 ; 4½) made friends in the summer holiday with a number of village children, some of her own age and some considerably older. The friendship was entirely unclouded, no doubt chiefly because the little peasants agreed, without a protest, to Hilde's wishes and proposals.

When the common personating game is carried on more systematically, if possible in accordance with a prearranged programme, it develops into regular acting, and the leading child becomes stage-manager. Although the actual development of this kind of game belongs to later years, yet early beginnings are already to be found in the period with which we are concerned. For instance, our own daughter recorded her first success as stage-manager at the age of five and a half years.

Hilde (5 ; 5), Gunther (3 ; 2). "For some time Hilde likes to play certain fairy-tales with Gunther, such as Red Riding-Hood or Hansel and Gretel. G. is Red Riding-Hood, H. the wolf, and, when required, they change into any other characters needed, grandmother, huntsman, etc. Hilde prompts G. the whole time as to what he is to say: *Now you must say: Good-morning, dear grandmother, how strange you look! What big eyes you have!* all of which G. faithfully repeats.

"They play Hansel and Gretel too. Three chairs are pushed together to make the witch's house, and Gunther, the witch, has to creep under them. Hilde represents Hansel and Gretel both in herself. Hansel has to stretch out his finger somewhere, then Gretel is to creep into the hearth; she says to the witch: *Show me how*; and when Witch Gunther does so, Gretel gives her a push forward and the witch is burnt in a moment. Whilst G. is still kept at repeating the prompted words, Hilde is very drastic in her acting. She snores loud and deep as the wolf, emphasizes the plumping into the well, pushes the witch furiously into the fire, and delights in the successful joke."

The first stage of group-games showed simply play in one another's company, the second real play with each other; a last stage shows development into play against each other, as in war games and sham fights. But the real development of these last seems to lie almost entirely beyond the age which we are considering.

Olga Doroshenko has made very interesting investigations into the group-games of young children in Kiev. For it is shown that the sociological conditions in the Soviet Republic —entirely different as they are from those in Western Europe,

exercise an exceedingly marked influence on the nature of the
games spontaneously chosen by the children. Frau Doroshenko
made her observations in two kindergartens; the first (I) contained children of trades-union artisans and officials, the
other (II) on the outskirts of the town was made up of children
of unskilled workers, the very poor and the unemployed.
Whilst the circles in (I) are quite at home in the new ideas
and conditions of life [the family replaced by communal life
in public], the parents of the children in (II) take no interest
in politics and have also preserved more remnants of the old
family life, religious observances, etc. A comparison of the
children's group-games offers the following picture—we must
of course bear in mind that the Ukranian kindergartens keep
the children until their eighth year.

Games of the "old style of life" (family, mother and child,
neighbours, kitchen, etc.) in (I) only reach a total of 6 per
cent., but in (II) up to 49 per cent. Also in (II) the constructive
games (imitation of manual occupations which they have seen)
are very frequent, amounting to 36 per cent. compared with
only 14 per cent. in (I). On the other hand there is a total
absence in (II) of the following games, which we find forming
the play-activity of (I) : civic communal life (elections, meetings,
etc.) 24 per cent., means of intercommunication 10 per cent.,
revolutionary phases of life and games (revolution, Lenin's
funeral, etc.) 23 per cent., boy-scouts (pathfinders) 10 per cent.

Another difference consists in the fact that the group-games
in (I) are of a more lasting character and include a larger
number of children. Whilst in (II) a play-group only as an
exception contains more than five children and never more
than eight, in (I) it is quite common for ten–fifteen children
to join in a game, sometimes even as many as thirty [a fact
easily understood in such large group-games as a revolution
or public funeral]. Both schools, however, have one point in
common—testimony to the never dying spirit of childhood,
independent as always of its environment—viz. that the
voluntary formation of the little children into groups is almost
exclusively for play-purposes only and that the submission
of the majority to one leading spirit is nearly always observable.

PART VII

ENJOYMENT AND CREATIVE ACTIVITY

CHAPTER XXIII

PRELIMINARY STAGES OF ÆSTHETIC FEELING

A RELATIONSHIP between æsthetic imagination and that of the child has often been noticed, but as a rule wrongly interpreted, for, æsthetic enthusiasm having been in inverse ratio to real insight as regards child-psychology, the child has been credited with artistic capacity and efforts which in this form were either entirely non-existent or only to be met with in cases of exceptional endowment. Real æsthetic feeling and creation presupposes a mental development which, as a rule, does not exist before puberty; in earlier years we only find their preliminary stages and foreshadowings. Therefore, when discussing "art in childhood", "genius of early years", etc., we must not only notice the relationship to æsthetic feeling, but keep our eyes keenly fixed on the marks of differentiation as well. The younger the child is, the more decided must be the insistence on this point.

Man shows æsthetic feeling in three distinct forms, viz. receptive, imitative and creative; and all three forms are found in the child at a very early age. He is very sensitive to everything giving pleasure to the senses: to bright colours, pictures, figures, to singing and piano-playing, to little verses of pronounced rhythm, poems and fairy-tales. From this purely receptive attitude the child quickly passes to imitation; he says and sings the song with or after the singer, tells the little tales again, revives them in dramatic form, and reproduces optical figures in accordance with the copies. Lastly, we meet with individual creative effort in the imaginative drawing, clay-modelling, confabulation, improvisation of melodies, and in the continual invention of new games.

An additional characteristic is to be found in the play-nature of æsthetic feeling upon which Schiller has laid such emphasis. The satisfaction given by imaginative creation as such, the power of illusion to carry above and beyond the narrow bounds of reality, and to create an imaginary world amidst hard everyday fact, these bring artist and art-lover into close relationship with the child.

But at this very point we are brought face to face with fundamental differences, and these, curiously enough, even more marked in æsthetic enjoyment than in creative effort.

In its absolutely pure form, æsthetic enjoyment is disinterested pleasure in the form of things as they are perceived by the senses. Now, the little child—as we have just shown—experiences lively pleasure in his sense-perceptions. But he is very lacking in disinterested feeling and concentration on the formal side of the sensation. Concentration, free from desire or action, on the æsthetic pleasure is only rarely possible to the child, and then is but very transitory; as a rule he desires what pleases him. In his earliest years he stretches out his hand for everything bright; when he goes for a walk, at 4 or 5 years of age, and sees the splendours of the shop-windows, he does not only say: *that is nice*, but also *I want that*. If he hears music or singing it is more natural for him to join in, as best he may, than to listen in quiet enjoyment. But even where he does adopt a receptive attitude (for example, when looking at a picture-book, listening to stories, seeing an acted fairy-tale), it is not the æsthetic form but the matter portrayed or related that holds his attention and secures a response of pleasure or the reverse.

When Scupin's son $(4 ; 7\frac{1}{2})$ was present at a performance of a fairy-tale, he was quite carried away by the plot. The greater the action on the stage the more unrestrained his delight. "The boy's sense of justice was greatly outraged when the wicked king of the dwarfs rewarded Snow White and Rose Red for releasing him from the unpleasant position of having his beard nipped in a tree by dragging them off to his cave. In the greatest excitement, Bubi continually beat the air as if chastising the wicked king as he cried aloud: *Oh, the ugly old man—horrid !*" (II, p. 129). Of course, that is anything but æsthetic feeling.

This clinging to what is represented is, moreover, by no means confined to early childhood; we might indeed say that even in adults, especially when uneducated, a true and unmixed æsthetic attitude is comparatively rare. Complete detachment from the content, from a basis of any kind, from sympathy and antipathy, i.e. then from all non-æsthetic factors, is, as a matter of fact, scarcely possible to simple human nature; and we ought not from the point of view of a theoretical prejudice to despise the attitude in which æsthetic appreciation is intermingled with that of the subject treated. Although the little child practically never displays unmixed æsthetic feeling, yet it exists within him, and, with more mature growth and appropriate, careful guidance, his pleasure in pictures, dances, songs and stories will increasingly develop into the capacity of enjoying the purely æsthetic qualities which are offered in these forms. We must, however, be careful not to allow a false æsthetic feeling to drag even the little child away from his interest in the subject-matter and thrust upon him purely æsthetic enjoyment and judgment.

But even if we cannot expect continuous states of æsthetic feeling in early childhood yet we do find occasional æsthetic response of shorter duration. Individual capacity plays an important part in this. There are children who, at an exceptionally early age, evince silent delight at musical sounds, others again who possess a keen feeling for harmony of colour and of light and shade. Later on we shall find examples of this.

The other difference between æsthetic feeling in the child and the artist is still more universal, being found not only in enjoyment but also in creative effort. It is essential in all æsthetic work that the inner imaginative concept should find in the outer world an adequate representation by means of which its value may be presented in a tangible form. It is this union alone of valuable content and effective æsthetic form that constitutes a real work of art. But for this the child, especially when young, lacks the necessary power. For his imagination is entirely dominated by the feature of "unrestraint" (Chap. XIX. 2), and however much this feature may enable the child to give the most manifold expression to his play-activity, in spite of its poverty of presentation, it yet undoubtedly cuts off all childish performances from the realm of "art". The same may be said of the want of synthetic power in the child which causes his continuous feats of imagination to vibrate between monotony and erratic unconnected flights. Artistic creative work, on the other hand, is always ruled by dominant interests; even the wildest imagination—as in the case of E. Th. Hoffmann—is yet restrained by the unity of the desire for æsthetic form; and it is just this which the child lacks.

Even though in this way we assign to the creative efforts of early childhood a place far removed from real art, we are by no means of the opinion that they are of no significance.

The sense-expression which the child accepts or shows is as yet by no means an isolated part of his whole individuality but deeply rooted in the personality; it is received and formed as a part of a whole, is not yet separated from emotional or motor-impulses, or conscious contents of other senses. But it is this diffuse nature of the child's impressions and creations that lends them marked significance as a means of expression so that both drawing and confabulation may serve as symptoms demonstrating certain psychic features—whether temporary or permanent—of the young child; in the same way as play, so the product of the creative instinct may have great significance for diagnosis and prognostication. But only those who pay homage to untrammelled impressionism will see in this form of self-expression any æsthetic value. And, on the other hand, we can now understand why the impressionist form of art is often so similar to the creative forms of early childhood.

To sum up then: In the young child's enjoyment and creation of forms perceptible by the senses we can as a rule see only the preliminaries to—in exceptional cases the earliest potentialities of—æsthetic feeling; the activities and objects of this feeling belong to the sphere of play, not to that of art, and are therefore to be classified amongst the psychological and biological conformity to law which we have set forth in earlier chapters with regard to play-fantasy. This done, we have laid the foundation for the consideration of different forms of this feeling.

CHAPTER XXIV

FAIRY-TALE IMAGINATION AND PLEASURE IN CONFABULATION

WE will begin with the oral side of this subject, for as soon as the child has sufficient mastery of language to understand without difficulty more simple connected narrative and can express himself, he begins to evince great pleasure in hearing and telling connected imaginative tales.

1. The Child and the Fairy-tale

Every normal child from about the age of four years has a great desire to hear stories; many of these are invented on the spur of the moment by the mother or kindergarten teacher, but more are drawn from already existing sources, viz. from the storehouse of the familiar fairy-tales. The child's first acquaintance with literature is at once marked by the deepest interest. The fervour with which children listen to tales and keep on asking for them again, their unwearied attention to a never-varying repertoire of stories, the severity indeed with which they control the verbal accuracy of the narrative and reprove every variation, are points that always awake wonder in adults, and indeed observations such as the following disclose one of the most striking differences between an adult's and a child's evidence of interest.

D. and R. Katz report (p. 81) the case of a boy (3 ; 6) who listened to the tale of the Frog-king fifty times in the course of a few days without showing any sign of weariness in his attitude of listener. "The child seemed to experience the same keen interest in all the turns and astonishing solutions of the narrative as if he had no previous knowledge of them."

So far there has been but little direct study of the young child's attitude to the literature thus offered to him; but Herr Bühler and his wife have come to very interesting conclusions by means of an indirect method, i.e. not by analysing the child, but the literature which is shown by experience to arouse the greatest interest in children at this early age, namely fairy-tales, and hence deducing from this standpoint certain characteristics of the imagination in early childhood.[1] We

[1] Karl Bühler devotes some sections of his *Mental Development* to this subject, and Charlotte Bühler a special book.

must refer the student to these more exhaustive studies, and confine ourselves here to a few notes in passing founded to some extent on Bühler's opinions.

K. and C. Bühler distinguish in early childhood three separate periods of literary interest, which, having regard to the characteristic material peculiar to each, they name (1) the Struwelpeter, (2) the Fairy-tale, (3) the Robinson period. The middle period reaches its height between the approximate ages of four to eight years. Thus we see that the supernatural fairy-tale lies between two phases of more realistic interests. For Struwelpeter has still to do with the quite ordinary important everyday happenings of the child's earliest stages—eating, washing, finger-sucking, etc.; whilst in the Robinson period, preference is shown for adventures, exciting episodes and heroic deeds which might be experienced in real life. The unreality of the fairy-tale period is evidently connected with that condition we have already described, hovering between totally unconscious illusion and conscious illusion, which is so characteristic of early childhood. Whether this "Once upon a time" refers to fact or pure fancy is quite beyond the sphere of childish enquiry; the child gives himself up to the delight of the tale without any wish to confirm or question the probability of any point.

It is true that this indecisive state of mind is not achieved at once. The earliest fairy-tales still cling very closely to real life. Red Riding-Hood, Hansel and Gretel are themselves children, and their experiences are distinctly those of children. Later on, of course, the introduction of kings, princesses, giants and fairies, as well as the continual occurrence of miracles, transformations, etc., opens a new and strange world to the child. K. and C. Bühler, however, aptly show that these creatures of the imagination are, for the most part, only big children, and behave in an exceedingly childish way.

No doubt it is this very intermingling in fairy-tales of the strange and the familiar that is calculated to gain such favour in the child's eyes. And to explain the attraction found in what is strange and unfamiliar we must again refer to the idea mentioned in connection with personating games. The royal or supernatural personages in the fairy-tales are indeed nothing but the disguised embodiments of the child's own wishes. His desire and imagination lift him out of his own weakness and poverty into this strength, might and majesty; so that these are no strange romantic forms, but embodiments of the child himself—no wonder then that they betray childish features.

In the following example there is clear evidence of the feeling of personal relation to the hero of the tale that had been told; the effect on the child is totally uninfluenced by the fact that it is not a fairy-tale but a Bible narrative.

Gunther (3 ; 11). When G. saw in an illustrated Bible the picture of Samson and the lion, he was anxious to hear the tale, which so charmed him that he is continually asking now: *tell about strong Samson*. He says he is as strong as Samson, and if he should ever meet a lion, then he would kill him too.

Gunther (4 ; 7½). "Gunther's favourite hero still continues to be Samson; lately when the name was mentioned, he said: *O yes, Samson, that I am so fond of!*"

Other features of the fairy-tale correspond also to the primitive nature of the child's ideas and feelings; e.g. the simplicity of the plot, the want of every more refined human characteristic, an evident, boldly outlined moral tone in which the reward of virtue and the punishment of vice immediately follows the good or evil deed. The formal construction of the fairy-tale also fits in with those characteristics of the imagination in early childhood with which we are already acquainted, especially in the small demand it makes upon the power of synthesis. It offers no logical coherence that has to be grasped with one glance, but only one event joined to another, one picture following another; moreover, no demand is made for complexity even in the consideration of single characters, so that we never find in fairy-tales such complex figures as nixies (half-men, half-fish), etc.

In short, the fairy-tale has but one universal method of art, namely a continual increase in gradation; as occasion arises it requires the child to translate well-known ideas into other dimensions; thus the dwarfs and giants, the fairies and witches are nothing but quantitative embodiments of familiar qualities. In the same way the continued action is by gradation brought together into a very simple unity; the hero has to accomplish tasks ever increasing in difficulty, or the splendour increases from silver by way of gold to precious stones, from the lowly hut by way of a house to a palace.

Up to the present we know very little about the psychic *effect* of the fairy-tale. Rationalistic educationists are sometimes found who condemn the fairy-tale because it displays to children a world of deception and marvels, suppresses the sense of reality and love of truth besides cultivating vague imaginations. Anyone holding this view as a general rule has no sense of the important part played—and rightly so—by imagination in these early stages. Individual cases may occur now and again that a child with over-developed leanings to imagination may cling too long to fairy-tales and find difficulty in finding the path to a world of reality.

Another question deserving of more serious investigation is whether the very simple and fixed moral standards set up by the fairy-tale with its opposing factors of good and evil exert an entirely favourable influence on the child's moral education. So long as these standards are applied to purely imaginary characters (e.g. fairies and witches) they are harmless enough, for the child, later on, finds out that there are no such beings. It is a different matter when an actual human being is marked by such a standard. An example has been brought to my notice by a work produced in my institute. It is a matter of common knowledge that in fairy-tale the STEPMOTHER often enough plays the part of witch as well. In Grimm's collection there are twelve stepmother fairy-tales, amongst them the well-known stories of Hansel and Gretel, Snow White and Cinderella; all twelve stepmothers are bad, most of them even intent on disposing of their stepchild. A more recent psychological investigation by Hanna Kühn has now shown that the fairy-tale thesis of "all stepmothers are bad has found wide acceptance in popular opinion and that this view meets EVERY stepmother in the form of a compact mass of suspicion, aspersion and instigation—this too even in cases where the stepmother may be taking up her difficult task with the very best of intentions. We wonder if the fairy-tale is not a contributory factor in this state of things.[1]

---

[1] Further doubts of certain psychic effects of fairy-tales are mentioned by D. and R. Katz, I, pp. 79 sq.

2. Confabulation

Children of lively temperament are not content with simply hearing pretty tales ; they wish to create them themselves, and therefore begin to confabulate. Probably often enough they are first incited to this by the fairy-tales and stories they have heard, but also, quite apart from this, there exists in the child at one period an irresistible craving to express in speech the ideas that come surging into his mind; and these confabulations show us in paradigmatic distinctness all the qualities of the connected links of early imagination. The confabulations of early childhood can be divided into several groups: first the *non-egotistic*, i.e. having nothing to do with the personality of the narrator—e.g. self-invented fairy-tales, stories of animals and dolls—and secondly, the *egocentric*, that relate fancies concerned with the child's own past or future.[1]

We give three examples of the first group, one for each of our children, which we managed to take down in shorthand, unnoticed.

Eva (3 ; 4½). The child had often heard the tale of Little Red Riding-Hood, and one day she told it to us, but purposely changed it, and thoroughly enjoyed our astonishment. As characteristic of childish caprice we may mention that after a short time only the names of wolf and Red Riding-Hood remain to remind us of the fairy-tale, and, in the end, even these remnants disappear, and the whole tale is concerned with other things.

"There was once a little girl called Red Riding-Hood and she had a red cap. And the grandmother, she was ill. And the wolf—well, now where is the wolf going? He went to the ,grandmother and then the grandmother was afraid. Then she dressed herself quick and went quick to Else. And the father of the grandmother—and the grandmother when she was well, then she went into the forest too with Red Riding-Hood and the wolf went into the garden with them too. And then they runned

---

[1] Psychoanalysts maintain that ALL products of the child's imagination are indeed egocentric, the only distinction being whether the reference to the personal desires is quite apparent or appears in symbolic form. But a perusal of the following examples compels the admission that there is such a thing as pure joy in confabulation. The interpretation would be strained indeed that would find in all these merely expressions of hidden personal desires, and those too of an erotic nature.

away fast. And the wolf has runned too and then they runned to the water tower and then the wolf said: 'I can run as quick.' And the daddy was afraid too of the wolf. And Red Riding-Hood has cried too and the wolf bit her finger and made it bleed. And Red Riding-Hood's kitty cried. And the wolf went to kitty but then kitty screamed: he runned quick in the wood and kitty didn't cry any more. (A little pause, and her mother asks: Is it finished? However, Eva does not succumb to the suggestion, but answers): *No, not yet. The water-tower too could run to Berlin. Now it's done. Kitty of the little Thea comes up. Kitty that has to be carried.* (Her mother asks: Who is Kitty?) *A little girl. Once we saw at the building-master's (mason's) house a kitty but a real one, an animal kitty. Thea's, that was a girl kitty."*

The confabulations which Hilde at 3 ; 0 produced were much wilder. For some weeks the child was possessed by a veritable confabulation mania (which afterwards died away completely). Especially in the morning she gave us the benefit of unending tales; she did not require us to follow them in detail, to answer or to ask questions, only someone must be present to give her the feeling of a sympathetic hearing. Want of space allows us to give only a short extract here. The tale had, it is true, no dominant interest, but yet at least a conceptual-motif, the fowl-yard, and so everything that went through the child's head was referred to fowls. In other respects, certainly, everything is chaos, any chance associative connections—a glance happening to fall on anything in the room, contact with something else— determine the continuation. She often begins sentences without knowing the end. It seems as though the flow of words must not be interrupted at any price, and, to avoid any gaps any sort of padding must be used, which in its turn becomes the starting-point for other associations. The whole body seems to join with the speech-organs in a craving for movement. H. hops and tears about, throws herself on the sofa, jumps up again directly, and eats an egg quite without her usual interest, only impatient to be able to continue her tale. A few fragments and explanations now follow.

And then they shut the fowls' door, and the fowls lie down alone, shut their eyes and go fast asleep. But look, I saw they didn't ate grass to-day but they ate hay. (Her Mother says: "But hay is the cut, dried grass.") *But see, it was on it, and the fowls bit it off.*

But now listen: there came a great chair (she had just run against a chair), *and then the fowls sat down on it.* (Her mother says: "Dear me!") *Well, now then they got one of those birthday books. . . .*

Look at the fowls' stove—the chickens burnt themselves on it. Then they fetch out of the kitchen wood and coals and a little box where lights are hidden (description instead of the unknown word matchbox). *Then the cock strikes a light. Now what are the cock father and mother going to do to-day?* (She evidently did not know yet what she should do with them.) *They go to dinner to-day and eat soup. . . .*

And there is a washstand and all the fowls have washed themselves clean, and laid the little fowl-brother on the swaddling-table and dried him again.

Then came too such a pretty new book, so many pictures. There were so many witches in it, so black they were. But they had no long noses, they had made their noses small again; then they washed themselves clean. Look at a fowl-witch.

Gunther (5 ; 6). A much higher degree of development in confabulation is shown by the tales which our son used to tell to his mother in the evening when lying comfortably in bed. We give as an example a fire brigade tale. It was during a summer holiday in Binz, and the day before he had watched with great interest a practice of the firemen in a tower. The beginning, which could not be taken down at the time, ran somewhat as follows. The fire brigade men climbed on a tower—and now the literal continuation follows:—

"And then they fell on a rose-tree with no thorns on it and yet they pricked themselves. Then they gathered roses and went home to his wife. There the fire brigade stood and the fire brigade (man) made a wreath for his wife out of pale and dark roses, he took it to his wife and she was asleep. Then the firemen put it on gently not to wake her. Then they took away the big ladder and climbed up without: then the man said: 'That is easy in other houses, then you must practise in another way, when a house is burning you can't do so, then you will want to fetch a ladder and you will lose your way.' The fire brigade have said and have not lost their way. Then they were tired

*and undressed and went to bed and slept. Then robbers came
and quietly put a lamp on the ceiling and lit it and then made
it all dark again and not stolen anything."*

We still notice here the supremacy of caprice in imagination; the history consists of four or five phases which are
held together only by the initial motif of "fire brigade",
or even, as at the end, are connected with what goes before
by a simple "then". But within the limits of each phase,
at least, the effect of the dominant interest is already plainly
evident, as in the motif of the wreath of roses and the putting
out the burning chimney.

Further, the boy already shows also the conscious intention
of giving his story the stamp of a fairy-tale. To effect this
he uses the amazingly simple means of the paradoxical contradiction. The fire brigade men fall on a rose-bush without
thorns and—yet get pricked! Robbers specially light a
lamp—and yet steal nothing at all! In this way the child
tries to introduce into his own tale the same touch of the
unexpected and wonderful that he has felt in the fairy-tales
told to him.[1]

The "egocentric" confabulations in which the child makes
his own individuality play a part have somewhat different
characteristics. For instance, the tale loses its want of time
definition, and is referred to the child's life-time in the past,
present or future.

To begin with the last, the fantastic description of future
joys is peculiar to every child. How many tales begin:
When I am big, or *When I'm a mother*! But the real period
of castles in the air is at a later age than that we are
considering. The little child still lives too much in the present,
he does indeed picture to himself this or that detail which
he intends to carry out when he is big, but there is no question
as yet of a more comprehensive and connected confabulation
of his picture.

As far as we have observed, the first of such chains of
imagination appear in the fifth and sixth years; but they
still refer to a near future. Coming festivals act as special
incentives, so that in the weeks before Christmas the child
not only feels eager joy, but also indeed, in imagination,

---

[1] A further example of such "confabulations" by young children is to be
found in Groos (5th ed., p. 152).

anticipation of the delicacies expected—hence too sometimes certain disappointments when the feast really comes.

When Gunther was 4 ; 9 old, his sister had her birthday treat, and from then on his little head was haunted by thoughts of his own. "Almost every day he repeated—with a few variations—the programme he had drawn up—a programme whose prevailing feature was of a culinary nature, but which also contained a few more ideal pleasures. Once it began: *Please for my birthday, cocoa you know and cracknels even for breakfast. For dinner I should like white soup, red cabbage and—well, carrots. On my birthday I'll get wallflowers and forget-me-nots on the table and chicken, etc."*

A fantasy of the future produced by his sister when she was a year older (5 ; 9) was on a higher plane. Her mother was to give her some work so that she could earn money. This she would give to the owner of the house so that he could build on a really big room to our flat and that should be her doll's house. She had thought out too how the furniture was to stand and pictures to be hung in this new room.

In these fantasies of the future the illusion is presumably complete, the child is convinced, at any rate for the moment, that everything can and will be just as his fancy pictures; he has, as yet, very little idea of the difference between possible and impossible, probable and improbable. Consequently Hilde was seriously disappointed when her mother had to tell her that there were considerable difficulties in the realization of her plan of a room built by her own earnings.

If the confabulations refer to the child's present, then we have to do with play indeed which has already been discussed.

On the other hand, the fantasy-tales dealing with the past need a little more discussion. In their outer form they resemble accounts of actual experiences, and since they are really founded on unreality, the observer may easily mistake them either for slips of memory or for untruths. As a matter of fact, they are neither one nor the other, but a special form of wrong aussage. (*"Fantasy errors in aussage."*[1])

The distinguishing feature is the playful character of the aussage with all the qualities of play, especially that conscious illusion present either in suggestive or clearly marked form.

[1] A more detailed treatment of this in Chap. IX, *Monograph* II, by C. and W. Stern, from which much has been literally transcribed.

The child does his best, even if without much success, to fill the gaps in his reminiscences and reconstruct his real experiences; in the case of untruth, reality is intentionally misrepresented in the hope thereby to obtain some benefit or avoid something unpleasant. In either case the action is performed in serious earnest. The fantasy-aussage, on the contrary, is a game, like any other, only that the child fills his illusory rôle in the game not in the present but in the past. There is no fundamental difference between the fact that the child, pretending to be "shopping", runs about the room, stops at a door as at a shop, asks for butter and eggs, says "thank you very much", etc., and, with the omission of the movement, transfers such imaginary actions to the past and says now: *I have bought that.*

So far as any conclusion is justified by observations up till now, this fantasy aussage-game is at its height especially in the fourth year.

"Eva (3 ;) was in the kitchen with her mother, who was going to tell her a tale. But Eva anticipated her by the following: *Shall I tell you something about a little baby? The little baby pricked a hole in itself, pricked a hole with an umbrella, it did. When she put it up she pricked a hole directly in her head. Then I went out quick and fetched some sticking-plaster. Daddy gave me a great bit of sticking-plaster and I tore it up* (adding by way of explanation: *you see I am called mother*) *and licked it and then stuck it on her head: and when it came off, then I stuck on another. But then the baby cried.*"

This confabulation is remarkable for its logical coherence and utter absence of fantasy's usual leaps and bounds.

. The report on Hilde at the same age (3 ; 5) runs:—

"H. has long enjoyed telling, as her own experiences, tales often originating in something she has heard but greatly changed and brightly adorned by her imagination. Of course, we never think of interfering in any way in these creations of hers."

"Thus she told her mother when out for a walk in Schreiberhau the following: *I went with my doll up to the new mountain hut, there were cats up there, a big cat and kittens, the big cat was black and the little cats were white, etc.*"

By the addition "with my doll", Hilde consciously marks the illusory character of her tale, not only in this special case but in many others as well. Sometimes she even pushes her little sins on to her doll, as when she was admonished not to pull off leaves in the garden: *Dolly has pulled off leaves, she'll get slapped.* She never attributed guilt to real persons—a sure sign that these statements were made in fun.

In these instances the child stands completely above the illusion. But in these aussage-games there is just, as in other games, that desire to be entirely absorbed, at any rate for a time, by the illusion, to keep the appearance of truth. This may result in such a contradiction of correction as may have every semblance of a real untruth without being one.

Eva (3 ; 5). "We were talking of Hilde's work-box, and Eva said in fun: *I've got a work-box too, a present from Granny.* Hilde and Gunther were much astonished, and I explained: 'O, Eva is only joking.' But Eva answered: *No, I really have had one given me by Granny.* Whereupon her brother said indignantly: *That's just a lie, Eva.* Out of regard for the older brother and sister, who already scrupulously distinguished between truth and untruth, I could not let the fantasy-aussage rest there, so I asked Eva to fetch the work-box. Then she was very cross and fought with her tears, but it was not till long after that she made up her mind to answer our repeated questions as to whether she really had got a work-box with *no*." Many people possibly would classify this action as a lie; but the simple written record is not enough to justify a judgment of an occurrence that needs, for its interpretation, personal, visual knowledge of the whole situation and its development and observation of all the accompanying incidents (expression, mimicry, etc.).

In those early years when the real and apparent are constantly confused by the child, it is of no importance when it transfers this game with reality into its own past as well. In later years, of course, the child must be required to distinguish when he may allow his imagination to play with his narratives and when he must reproduce reality only.

CHAPTER XXV

THE CHILD AND MUSIC

THE relation of the young child to music has so far received but scanty attention as far as conscientious child-study is concerned; with the exception of two very thorough experimental investigations there only exist a few stray observations.

We will begin by some quotations from our own notes.

Gunther—as is proved later on—seems to possess more than average musical talent, far outstripping his sisters. This difference is noticeable in the very earliest years.

Gunther (1 ; 10). "G. much enjoys singing; he often twitters away to himself, generally the tune he knows: 'Hop—hop. How the pony does gallop.' Indeed, he sings practically everything that interests him to this tune, e.g. he picks up a lotto-card, representing a horse, and sings: gée-gée-gee-géegeegée-geegée! The song is always rhythmically quite correct, so too is the understanding of higher or lower, even though it does not yet always keep in the same key. 'Bunny in his Hole' is also sung—of course without words—half-way through in absolutely correct rhythm and fairly right in other respects. We really think the boy has a turn for music."

Gunther (1 ; 11). "Gunther sings a great deal and with evident enjoyment; his repertoire is certainly not very extensive but what he does sing has plainly marked rhythm and is fairly in tune. His chief melody is the song 'Hop—hop. How the pony does gallop,' which he sings in two variations:—

Of course, intervals and key are not quite correctly maintained; yet sometimes the first consecutive thirds of the first variation are perfectly true; in the descending scale the intervals as a rule are somewhat too large. He has very seldom heard the tune from us, scarcely at all lately, but he is continually singing it, especially in bed when we are still playing with him. The text varies considerably; now being *gee, puff, bow-wow,* and again, *Mama, Papa, Lilde.* Once when we sang the first half of it to him as *mama mamama,* he roguishly finished with *papa papapa.* To-day when he was singing in his bed, unobserved, as he thought, by us, we heard him first sing the tune to *mama,* then give the order '*all together*' and repeat it to *papa.*

"The following observations is more full of interest. Many weeks ago—possibly three months—we have heard him constantly singing a tune which must be one of his own invention, since it has no resemblance to any of the tunes sung to him. Lately, after a long pause—we heard it again as he sang it time after time to *ha ha.*

The *g* was sometimes a little too deep, and the last note hovered between *e flat* and *d.*"

Gunther (2 ; 9). "G. seems to be musical. He likes singing, and is quite happy when his father plays the piano. Then he sits quite quiet in the next room or stands close by his father, looking at his hands and then moving his own little fingers gently along the wood in front of the keys, whilst he gives but scant attention to the words of any of the songs. If he is ever allowed to play, he gently taps about on the keys in great contrast to Hilde, who 'makes music' with two fingers or even her whole hand."

Gunther (4 ; 6). "He is now very fond of whistling—in imitation of his father and, strangely enough, he whistles more correctly than he sings; he makes us guess what song he is whistling—just as his father does with the children."

Gunther (5 ; 6). "To-day when their father was having a little concert with the children, Gunther sang a few nursery rhymes and folk-songs quite correctly. So then he was allowed to try if he could pick out a tune with one finger. Consumed by ambition, he tried this note and that, now and again wiping his eyes, bright with unwanted moisture—tears are always very near when he is fired with ambition—and with his father's help at last he gently strummed: 'From the wood, hear the cuckoo's call.' In his excitement and delight he called out to us that he could play the piano, and eagerly hastened to give us a proof of his power."

Hilde (3 ; 8). "We notice in Hilde a great desire to sing just now. She sings continuously for a long time, and the text of her songs is a conglomeration of all kinds of words from the songs familiar to her with unintelligible sounds, which she produces with great ease. Her song is by no means tuneful—indeed, from an ethnological standpoint it has only reached a very low degree of culture—but it is vigorous and full of vitality." (A few days later:) "Amongst many inharmonious notes there sometimes appears here and there a fragment of real melody, as, for instance, almost without a mistake the beginning of 'Ring a Ring o' Roses'. In every case the rhythm is very nearly accurate. If her father sings her something, she cannot yet join in on the same notes, but rather sings quite unconcerned the same words in the same rhythm to tunes of her own composition."

We will now try to point out briefly some of the principles underlying the child's relation to music as this develops in its three chief forms of receptivity, imitation and creation of melody.

In a certain sense, music is the first of all the arts accessible to the child, for even before it can speak, it listens eagerly to song and piano; and even the simple monotonous tunes that the mother sings to the child have a strangely soothing effect, for the restless child grows quiet and at last falls asleep. For this singing, in its unchanging repetition, apparently exercises a direct, physiological influence similar to that of rhythmical rocking, with which indeed the song is often connected.

In subsequent years, then, real pleasure in hearing music makes its appearance, although as a general rule it is true this cannot yet be looked upon as æsthetic sensibility. We do indeed meet with silent, absorbed listening, but it seldom lasts for any considerable time; when it is a pronounced feature, the presence of more than average musical gifts may be assumed. But most little children at once translate the music they hear into bodily movement; the unity of sensory-motor action is still a matter-of-course for them. This motor sympathy extends not only to the tone-productive organs—as the child joins in the song—but to the whole body. Children beat time with heads, arms and legs, march with the soldiers' bands, jump and dance to the songs they hear, and join in accompanying the singing with acting-games. The fact that music, to begin with, sets in motion in the child involuntary sensory-motor action is the reason why, at this early period, rhythm makes a special impression on children. For it, unlike melody, is not confined entirely to the region of sound, but can be grasped and copied by all sensory and motor organs.

Baldwin and Stecher carried out an experimental investigation (p. 141) of the rhythmical capacity of kindergarten children. The children had by means of two pieces of wood to beat time to a march played on a phonograph. The rhythm thus beaten was electrically recorded and could be compared with the actual rhythm of the piece of music. The result was shown in all degrees of rhythmical capacity from entire irregularity without any recognizable connection with the music up to really exact and persistent agreement with the emphasized beats of the march. A remarkable point was that SUCCESS, DID NOT DEPEND UPON AGE; some of the best performances were those of the youngest scholars (3 years). Investigations amongst school-children produced similar results. Rhythmical capacity evidently depends so greatly upon inborn differences of the gift that in comparison with it advance in age is of no perceptible value.

Belaiew-Exemplarski has obtained some interesting results from 6-year-old Russian children as to the effect produced by pieces of music. Different pieces were played to the children who were to guess what each was. The children's pronouncements were very varied; the features that had most influence upon the children's decision being rhythm and time—this was quite evident in the verdicts of "dance", "march" or "lullaby", but very often the rhythmical impression was connected with directly concrete optical impressions which were looked upon in a very naïve fashion as part of the contents of the piece of music, e.g. *'The music was as if they were burying Lenin'*, or *'The cows are being driven to pasture'*. In so far as the musical factor takes part, it becomes descriptive in tone:—*it is as if ponies were running.—The fire-engine comes driving up* and so on.

The feeling for harmony seems entirely wanting in early childhood. At any rate the experiments made by Rupp and Belaiew-Exemplarsky on 6- and 7-year-old children show that they listen to piano melodies with equal pleasure whether they are played with their right accompaniment or with one entirely out of harmony, unendurable indeed for adult ears, e.g. a melody in D major with an F sharp major accompaniment! Only children of quite unusual musical gifts proved an exception to this rule. Thus the musical development in the individual progresses by the same stages as it apparently does in the human race as a whole in the following order; rhythm, melody, harmony.

The power of recognizing tunes also comes under the heading of receptivity. Children of four and five years of age are often able to name quite a number of songs when they hear them either played or sung.

At this age they already have the power of recognizing a song from the rapping out of its rhythm without the tune.[1]

The second phase is reproduction, i.e. joining in and copying a song they hear. Here, indeed, the average child displays in full that æsthetic unconcern of his. If he is singing with others he is totally indifferent as to whether he sings in the same key or in quite another; if by himself, his intervals are anything but correct, often indeed he is quite content to mark the tone-gradations of the melody by a chance raising or lowering of his voice. And again, it is the rhythm that is proportionately the best in reproduction. If at a very early age children sing their little songs fairly correctly, we may look upon this too as a sign of special talent—principally, it is true, in the matter of a musical memory.

Other kinds of reproduction may also occur, e.g. whistling, —almost exclusively confined to boys; occasionally, too, first instrumental attempts.

Worthy of note is the case made known to us from a trust-worthy source of a two-year-old boy who could sing a number of little songs fairly correctly with *la, la* even before he could speak. The child used his songs then as a means of expression and communication instead of ordinary speech, pointing out a flying bird with the tune, "A Little Bird Comes Flying",

[1] Silverstolpe has proved this in his own children.

and calling attention to trees with the tune, "O Pine-tree deep in the Forest".

Since we have a distinct type of musical literature intended for early childhood in children's songs and singing-games, it would seem possible to carry out an enquiry on the same lines as Ch. Bühler's with regard to fairy-tales, i.e. to find the early musical constructions that appeal most strongly to the child's mentality. On this point I have heard of an earlier hypothesis put forward by König that there is a kind of "foundational melody" which runs somewhat as follows:—

Its characteristics are: first ascending, then descending tone-gradations, a compass not exceeding a fourth, the absence of semitones, and the third occurring as a third minor.

It is true that the simplest little songs, such as "Jump, Horseman, Jump", "Ring a Ring o' Roses", and many cradle-songs show this construction,[1] and the observation concerning Hilde, quoted above, gives evidence that this form, more than any other, is most readily noticed and remembered by the child.

Yet it would be a mistake to see in this motif the germ of all human forms of tune. It may indeed be the simplest and most attractive to children of all the motifs that our European musical system can offer them, but still more primitive than this music which is heard and reproduced by children are those forms which they invent without help, that singing for themselves which is simply the outcome of their innate energy, and therefore direct and independent evidence of their inner life. The observation of Hilde already given shows plainly enough that their earliest singing has a predominance of tunes which need some adaptation to accord with our melodic and harmonic systems.

These real primitive melodies of the child's are by no means lacking in interest; and even if they do not correspond with the points of view of our own cultured musical feeling, that should no more deter us from a psychological study of them

[1] Silverstolpe reports a Swedish melody of similar construction which is apparently made by children.

than a similar non-correspondence does with regard to the child's early efforts at drawing.

We therefore owe a debt of gratitude to H. Werner for his attempt to reproduce accurately and to analyse these first musical creations of early childhood. He used the phonograph and induced children between the ages of two and three-quarters and five years to sing something into the fine "automatic chocolate-machine" that rewarded them by the production of a piece of chocolate, and greatly reduced the children's self-consciousness by this apparent game. The phonogram was then carefully examined as to pitch, rhythm, etc., and transcribed into staff-notation. In this way sixty-five different specimens were obtained.

According to Werner, the foundational form of childish tune is the minor-third motive, and this in descending order. A preliminary stage of this is the child's scream, which proceeds "glissando" from a higher to a lower note. As soon as this gliding is superseded by two distinct notes, we get the beginning of "melody". The earliest interval is descending, because the main energy of the melodic discharge is displayed to begin with, and a deeper note is automatically produced with the diminished power of expiration. But since such a simple motif does not occur only once but in continual repetition—in common with all other childish forms of expression—the transition from the final note of the first movement to the beginning note of its repetition shows an ascending tone-gradation; by the synthesis of several simple movements we get at last the descending-ascending movement:—

etc. The smaller intervals (tones, semitones) are due at first to two causes: (1) the tendency to fill up the gap between the two notes of the minor third; (2) the decrease of initial energy as singing goes on, which gradually reduces the intervals and produces modulations and tone-gradations which—in contrast to the original interval—are not true and plainly marked. So that the quarter-tones now appearing are no sign of an especially advanced development—as in our most modern music—but a quite unintentional result of intonation in total disregard of correct intervals.

The factors which Werner names as determining the form of the child's spontaneous melodies must, I think, be supplemented by one more—the swaying movements which accompany them. We must indeed never forget that this primitive singing is not only a matter of ear and voice organs, but that the whole body has a share in it. But these accompanying movements are always marked by a successive alternation: the lifting and dropping of a limb, the change from the right to the left foot, bending the head first to one side then to the other, rocking the body to and fro, etc. THIS SWAYING NOW IS EXPRESSED IN THE TUNE BY THE CHANGE FROM HIGH TO LOW. Thus the child will probably scarcely ever produce the monotonous repetition of the minor-third motif without accompanying it by a swaying movement of some part of the body. At a somewhat higher stage of development not the single tones, but the ascending and descending tone-gradations are associated with the bodily movements; to this stage belongs König's foundational melody, which—as we mentioned before—possesses an elementary rocking character, with its notes first ascending and then descending.

Werner, on the strength of his investigations, tries to fix five grades of development in the young child's invention of melody. Plate VII contains a specimen for each grade from his phonographic records. The stages are characterized by Werner as follows[1]:—

First Type.—Descending two-toned minor-third motif with derivatives, produced by contraction of the compass—continual repetition. (Up to three years of age.)

Second Type.—Descending or ascending-descending three or four-toned motif of a compass up to a minor third; rising and falling last note of motif; a similar low-note ending; compass of a major third; greatest intervals minor thirds; diminishing compass and constant repetition. (Age up to about three and a half years.)

Third Type.—Ascending-descending, many-toned motif with repeated cadences; contraction of the cadence-compass; broken cadences; ascending first note of repetition of motif;

[1] "Ambitus" = compass of the whole melody. "The same low-note ending." The melody ends with the continued repetition of the lowest note.

descending last note, same low-note ending; compass up to a diminished fifth; tone-gradation from a minor third to a semitone. (Age up to four years.)

Fourth Type.—Ascending-descending, many-toned motif with ascending repetition; repetition of part of cadence; first tone of repeated motif either ascending or descending; ending on middle tone; compass of a diminished fifth and smallest intervals down to a quarter-tone. (Age up to four and a half years.)

Fifth Type.—Double-phrased many-toned motif with harmonious broken intervals; smallest intervals, quarter-tone-gradations; ascending-descending first note of repeated motif; greatest compass a diminished fifth. (Age up to five years.)

In these undoubtedly interesting compilations we must not forget the limitations which must have been imposed on them by the experimental method of producing the melodies. The children did not sing spontaneously but to order; thus their whole psychic "habitus" (habit, attitude) is entirely different from that when they sing entirely to please themselves. Yet it is worthy of remark that Gunther's first spontaneous melody taken down by us (reproduced at the beginning of this chapter) has the descendiug tendency in common with Werner's plan, but not the minor-third motif nor the small general compass of the melody.

But how near that theme must lie to child-nature is shown by the astonishing fact, that almost exactly the same tone-gradations have been noted down in the case of an English child (2 ; 4) as the first melody which it sang spontaneously.[1] Here too, therefore, there is possible the occurrence of something like a foundational melody.

The notes made by the English musician, W. Platt, on the first spontaneous song melodies of his two sons up to their fourth year can only be mentioned briefly here. The themes already show in great measure a close resemblance to

[1] Platt, p. 5.

ordinary music; it is uncertain whether that is the result of exceptional musical gifts in the children, the constant hearing of music in the house, or from the nature of the record in the regular note and bar system. It is interesting that the two boys at the respective ages of four and three years without help discovered the principle of the canon. They sang, for instance:[1]

[1] Platt, p. 16.

CHAPTER XXVI

THE VISIBLE WORLD

THE infinite range of optical impressions has already often claimed our attention; here it will only be treated in so far as these impressions prove a means of enjoyment, expression and graphic representation.

1. Æsthetic Feeling for Optical Impression

In this feeling we find two varieties. as we did in music; the general-personal feeling and that which is specifically optical in its nature.

To begin with, the child sees not only with the eye but with its whole being. The eye only forms the gate of entrance for a general feeling of strongly marked content. What this means will first be illustrated by a few examples; later, when dealing with drawing, it will be possible to give a further explanation.

I have been surprised to observe the following facts in my grandson: The boy (2 ; 1) in a house that was strange to him had been given a doll and made it smell the plants standing in the winter garden, each time saying *ha-psi*. The syllable *ha* was spoken on a middle note of the voice, then, after a pause, *psi* delivered in an incredibly high chirp. A similar sound had often been made to him no doubt when smelling flowers. But now something else followed. After he had made the doll smell a number of little flowers standing in a low box, he came to a fairly large india-rubber-tree standing on a higher table far above the others. The height of the *hapsi* at once changed; instead of the shrill chirp the syllables were uttered in a rather low muffled tone. Thus we see that the high chirp belonged as a matter of course to the little flowers and the tall appearance of the india-rubber-tree at once created a change in the whole situation, a general feeling of size which produced, as a direct result, a corresponding change in the vocal expression.

Gunther (3 ; 2½). A meaningless pencil scribble which he had produced (see figure) was at once named *a scolding hand:* later, when he was again asked what the hand had looked like, he characterized it with the words *it always said no, so!* The vague resemblance of the strokes to a hand with a forefinger raised in warning was sufficient to rouse in him the emotion of a whole situation (Mother's indignation and prohibition). It is not in any way that the lines reminded him of such happenings, no, he saw them directly expressed in the strokes; they themselves "scolded" (which expression is again quite robbed of its specific acoustic character and only means the underlying emotional nuance[1]).

When Gunther at 5 ; 6 was much occupied with counting, the figures, whether printed or in his own writing, took the form of most active individuals. *The 5 looks rushing along and the 6 as if it was walking slowly.* (The 5 was somewhat smaller and more slanting than the 6.) Scupin's son at the same age expressed himself similarly, when he had written figures in a wrong position: *the number has come bang on its head—it is turning a somersault;*—a 7 in reflected writing *only wants to say good morning to the other.* (Scupin, II, p. 189.)

Much less primitive than these personal optics is the æsthetic feeling for specific optical impressions; in this an understanding of an individual impression must already have occurred which is only possible to the average infant on rare occasions and then only in a fragmentary form. A more frequent occurrence testifies to special optic and æsthetic gifts.

We will begin with examples of pleasure in colours and colour harmonies.

Perception—and also sensibility—of harmonious blending developed very early in little Lore E.[2] Even at the age of 3 ; 6 the following observation was noted by her mother: *Mother, you are too bright for me.* ("Why?") *Because you have a blue blouse and a lavender skirt.*—(4 ; 4.) *Who has made the dish so beautiful just like a picture? How nice it looks— apples and vine leaves you see, yellow below and green above.*— (4 ; 9.) *Just look how lovely the clouds look, sky blue, white and pink.*

We noticed the first similar remark in H. at the age of 4 ; 8½. She put a leaf into a little silver bowl and said: *Green and silver—but don't they go well together!*—H. (5 ; 11½) was

---

[1] Cf. with this the analogous use of the word "scold" by Scupin's son—mentioned previously.
[2] Toni Ehrlich, p. 510.

watching a fly: *How nice it looks when it flies.* (Mother: "How does it look then?") *So gold and shimmery.*

Gunther (5 ; 11½). "He grasps all colour harmonies and in all honesty, admires beauties that others never see. This power is natural to him; he is brought up in the same surroundings as his sisters, but they are not so sensitive to these impressions. Yesterday evening we called the children out of their playroom, which was still fairly light, to come and have some music in the drawing-room. The lowered blinds threw this into complete darkness, only relieved by the golden-red light of the lamp by the side of the piano. The sisters had come in and noticed nothing; G. came a little later, stopped short at the door and said with admiration: *O how beautiful it looks, so dark and then the lamp.*"—"He was watching me get breakfast ready. As I put dark red strawberries on the yellow cream of the sour milk, he called my attention to the effect: *How beautiful, isn't it, the red and the yellow!* Yesterday, on the same occasion, he begged me to make a star of strawberries on the milk. Even here he looks at things not with desire, but æsthetic enjoyment."[1]

The little child seems at first to find more æsthetic pleasure in natural phenomena than in works of art, perhaps because material interest and selfish wishes must take a secondary place when confronted with nature. The charms of a landscape, the songs of birds, clouds, and stars—all these we do not covet, but only rejoice in their splendour. Love of nature seems to awake from the beginning of the fifth year.

Lore E. always used the word "holy" for such impressions as filled her with devout joy. (4 ; 3.) *Just look, how holy the moon looks.* ("How do you mean, 'holy'?") *Because it looks so yellow and beautiful and like evening.*—(4 ; 1.) *Mother, I want to whisper something to you. Yesterday, I had such a holy feeling it was so lovely and sunny. I was singing in the arbour and the sound of the bells came in and then I looked out of the window.*

Of our own children, Gunther showed the keenest and most spontaneous delight in nature.

"Full moon in the mountains. The children had been taken out of bed again to look at the moon above the mountains, and G. (4 ; 1½) said in a tone of rapture: *O that is lovely, lovely: I say, how lovely that is!*" (4 ; 1½.) "G. studies nature; he has a

[1] For G.'s especial interest in colours, cf. also Chapter XVIII, 1.

genuine enthusiasm, a really innate joy in its beauty. A few days ago, he chanced to look out of the window and said: *O Mummy, how beautiful the trees in the garden look when the sun shines on them!* After the sun had set, he remarked: *The sky was golden before, now it is red."*

(4 ; 10.) "When out for a walk, he admires every natural object; every little blade of grass, tiny flower or bird's feather he brings to us, delighted with the beauty of his treasure."

(4 ; 10½.) "We planted in our flower-boxes on the loggia some carnations which are not yet in flower. A little while ago G., when he saw them, clapped his hands, jumped high into the air, exclaiming: *O how glad I shall be when the carnations flower!"*—(4 ; 11.) "Now the great event has come to pass— we found a bud opened and called the children to the loggia. Then G. came walking up with his eyes shut, and passed through our bedroom, in this fashion, so as to let the full beauty burst upon him when he reached the loggia and stood close in front of the flower."

(5 ; 11.) "He has always delighted in a forest, and is especially happy when the trees stand so close together that there is the real forest twilight below their branches."

2. Creative (Spontaneous) Drawing[1]

Handling a pencil is indeed a fruitful source of pleasure for every child, and as in this branch it is comparatively easy to collect and study the productions, this form of childish activity has been the object of particularly searching enquiry. Special attention has been paid—quite rightly—to "free" drawing, i.e. drawing produced by the child's spontaneous creative desire, and therefore offering an unequivocal picture of his inner feeling.[2]

[1] The other creative branch of MODELLING has been accorded but scant attention in comparison with that aroused by the child's spontaneous drawing, although children at home and in the kindergarten are very fond of modelling in clay or plasticine. Up to the present no scientific investigation of this branch has appeared, but several publications by Frau Bergemann-Konitzer may be expected in Jena very shortly.
[2] A great deal has already been written about this "free" drawing. Ruttmann gives a short compendium. Kerschensteiner's monumental book, *The Development of the Gift of Drawing*, treats almost exclusively of the schoolchild's drawing powers. The summary: *The Child's Free Drawing and Modelling* (published by Grosser and Stern) contains essays dealing with all ages, including early childhood. K. Bühler has lately given an exhaustive psychological

We can best understand the real nature of the earliest attempt at drawing by a negative proposition. It is not *arte dei bambini* as Ricci calls it, not children's art, but children's play. For at first it is not only wanting in all æsthetic aim, but even in any tendency to imitate copies put before them.

In its beginnings drawing is simply an outlet for motor energy, the hand, armed with a pencil, moves over the sheet of paper, and the visible results of these movements incite to repetition and variation. This is the stage of meaningless scribble within which there is development from the straight awkward movements of the entire arm to the finer spiral and encircling movements in which the wrist now takes part.[1]

Scribbling is to drawing much what babbling is to speech, and just as the latter proves a preliminary to intelligent speech, so the former is valuable preparation for intelligent drawing. For the child soon begins to put some additional meaning into his own strokes that were quite meaningless to begin with, and to call them "a man" or "a house"; at last, too, the moment comes where the aims from the very first stroke of his pencil at the presentation of some definite object, and then actual drawing begins.

It is possible to follow these stages very plainly in our monograph on the early development in drawing of our son (C. and W. Stern III).

Hildegard Hetzer's investigations amongst three to six-year-old children gave the following information as to the transition from scribbling to representation (pp. 72 and 99). Three-year-old children are almost without exception still in the scribbling stage; at least only ten per cent. supplement

---

analysis of "free" drawing in childhood (*Mental Development*, Chap. V). B. also deals with higher stages of development, with the connection between speech and drawing, and lastly with the parallels between children's drawings and the symbol-art of primitive man—subjects which we must leave untouched. Corrado Ricci's little book which first called attention to the problem is devoted specially to early years, as is also Sully's Chap. X. The work of C. and W. Stern, *A Boy's Development in Drawing*, contains the most exhaustive treatment of the early stages in drawing of individual children (with numerous illustrations). Dix, the Scupins and Hartlaub give further tests and tales of development in individual children. In more recent times there have appeared the experimental tests of Hildegard Hetzer and the individual histories of the development of drawing in children by W. Krötzsch and Helga Eng. The latter gives in her excellent monograph—which is provided with numerous illustrations—both a survey of the development and psychology of drawing in childhood and reference to the whole literature on the subject up to 1927.

[1] This development has been proved by Krötzch by careful observation.

their productions with names. Amongst the four-year-olds, a third of them have named their presentations whilst drawing them and another third did the same before beginning. Amongst the five-year-olds eighty per cent. have reached this highest stage in intentional presentation, the girls before the boys and children of higher social grade show distinct advance when compared with those of humble position, viz. one hundred per cent. against sixty per cent. Amongst the six-year-olds drawing is already exclusively real presentation.

Here we must distinguish between the method and the aim of the presentation.

Krötzsch has again given us some very far-seeing explanations as to the method of production, showing that the determining factor of the final form is not mainly the visible drawing aimed at, but the rhythm of the movement in drawing. According to Krötzsch, the finished picture as it appears in collections of thousands of children's drawings is of psychological value, only if we are in a position to reconstruct the causal activity to which it owes its origin. It is therefore best to try and catch this activity "in flagranti", by observing not the finished drawing but the child as he produces it. Krötzsch therefore especially sees in drawing a particular form of expression-movement. He points out how the desire for rhythmical movement, up and down this way and that, the spiral and angular, is represented graphically; how strength of will, more or less pronounced, conscious aim, etc., finds an outlet in drawing. The primitive craving for the repetition of definite movements leads either to the production of repeated series of similar motifs or—if the same movement is carried out in opposite directions—to symmetrical forms.[1] Thus a tendency is given to ornamental effects, which it is true do not reach a more independent development before the end of the sixth year. On the other hand, the practice in drawing has, as its result, that the rhythmical movements belonging to any special drawing take on a fixed character, both in their constructive stage and result, so that the finished production becomes fixed into a mechanical picture incapable of further change.[2]

[1] With regard to symmetry, cf. Chapter XXII of this book.
[2] Krötzsch calls the production of such an automatic drawing a "schema". Cf. with this the next footnote.

As soon as we look upon drawing as an expression-movement, its products become an important aid in diagnosis, disclosing under certain circumstances deep-seated qualities of the child's psychic dynamics: weariness, want of concentration, inner steadiness or its opposite, energy or lack of will-power, etc. In this sense Krötzsch considers children's spontaneous drawings—especially when access can be had to a number of productions by the same child—as affording evidences of character; the child has his drawing "handwriting" long before his real handwriting has become sufficiently formed to have any graphical significance. Here we find a new, possibly very fruitful, means of interpreting character in childhood, not however before its application has been systematized.

Krötzsch gives an example to explain his meaning. He came across a six-year-old girl's drawings of men, all of which had great similarity with the early outline sketch (schema) of the "fine fellow" (cf. specimens a few pages further on in this section), and showed no further development in the course of a whole year. This arrest in development induced K. to make a graphical analysis of this child, who was totally unknown to him; he came then to conclusions which were acknowledged by the child's teacher to be of far-reaching accuracy. These conclusions, it must be noted, are not drawn from the finished result, but, as opportunity offered, from the action in drawing itself: all the sheets, from first to last, show an exceedingly confused, aimless formation and arrangement. The child makes ten or twenty attempts before it accomplishes a figure, often scribbling over the paper with wild spiral lines, hundreds of dots or short meaningless strokes. The different parts seldom show any intentional meaning, and this when present is never carried on consistently. As a rule the strokes are bold and decided, without many breaks, and showing no abnormalities as strokes. "When I saw these productions, they gave me the idea of a confused, erratic, unrestrained imagination, of a weak-willed and yet, in many respects, a determined child, wanting in self-control. There was scarcely ever any sign that the child had a feeling of any standard, or any limitation of what was allowed. She is continually showing degeneracy in some point or other, is of a restless, excitable, nervous temperament. This activity—or rather restlessness—may be partly of a physical, partly of a psychic nature."

We have secondly to consider the aim of childish drawing: what does the child wish to represent in his sketches?

Here again we meet with one of those phenomena which from the adult point of view seem paradoxical. Children in their drawings never think of trying to represent visual reality, indeed their strokes are nothing but the marking down of the ideas and thoughts that come scurrying through their heads. The very scantiest indication is enough, if only it offers the child a reminder sufficient to awake the imagination in the direction he means. Yes, "means"! for the child draws what he means, thinks, knows—not what he sees.

The fundamental significance of this simple fact has only lately been recognized. It throws a dazzling searchlight on the insufficiency of older theories concerning the beginnings of human apprehension and experience. The belief that contemplation, pure and simple, forms the beginning of all apprehension, and that, from it, abstract knowledge and judgment slowly develop, can no longer be maintained. The proofs to the contrary already given in the beginning of the first perceptions and in the treatment of looking at pictures are supplemented by the argument gained from the study of children's drawing. It is found that, to begin with, the pictorial representation is only looked upon as the symbol of something meant, something thought of, and that it is only after much effort that the power develops of keeping the pictorial representation of things as they appear to the senses free from all "intentional" features, i.e. those that correspond to the drawer's knowledge and ideas (cf. Chapter XXVII, Section 1).

Since Kerschensteiner put forward his theories we are accustomed to designate this first period of intelligent drawing as the "schema" (outline suggestive sketch) stage. In this connection a "schema" is an optical picture in which a mental idea is represented by "natural" optical symbols.[1] We call

---

[1] This definition thus pays regard to the object represented. We feel we must retain it, in spite of Krötzsch's attempt to limit the designation "schema" to that special kind of representation which consists of a drawing that has become mechanical. He says: "So long as a child is still looking for shapes and making attempts to represent them, we cannot speak of a 'schema' in spite of the primitive representation of form. . . . A 'schema' means fixation. Fixation is shown only in the automatic application of the same rhythmical movements." According to this definition, therefore, the first representations of any object could never come under the heading of "schema", because they could not possibly be produced by automatic, rhythmical movements, resulting

these symbols "natural" because their meaning does not first require to be learnt (as in the case of letters or mathematical signs), but directly occur to the child, and are used by him as a matter of course. Thus a long stroke is a natural symbol for an arm or leg, a small circle for an eye or head. The stroke in a "schema" must therefore have some likeness, however distant, with the object represented; but in the way this likeness is treated we again see that "unconcern" of the childish imagination with which we are already acquainted. It never occurs to the child to look at the object he means to draw before he begins or continuously during his sketch. The drawing from copies or models is, therefore, not for the child, as for the art-student, a necessary preparation for free creation, but seems perfectly unnatural to him; it is only when the child has drawn from memory for years that he occasionally begins to venture on the task of copying or drawing from life. In the early stages, however, he cheerfully confabulates with his pencil, noting down line by line what he knows of the object he means to draw, or, to speak more correctly, the features occurring to his mind that seem to him the most interesting and which he happens to remember. For remembering is of course more fragmentary than knowledge, and therefore these first designs are often grotesquely incomplete. Thus a four-year-old child knows that men have ears; but he does not remember to materialize this knowledge in his actual drawing, and never notices in the finished sketch the lack of these parts of the body. The stage of the "schema" extends, as a rule, far beyond early childhood. Kerschensteiner found that, even in the first years of school-life, nearly all spontaneous drawing was of a "schematic" character. It is only in later childhood that we find then the higher stages of development, when efforts are made to reproduce what is apparent to the child's power of vision, and, at first, even these efforts only extend to flat objects; still later—and only within the reach of very few—does the power develop of reproducing in drawing solid objects and things seen in perspective.

In addition to the "unconcern" of the childish imagination in early years, we have shown its lack of synthetic power,

from practice. But it is these very first representations, e.g. of a house or animal, that have a special pronounced "schema" character in the ordinary acceptation of the word.

which is also betrayed in the first drawings. Even the simple
task of maintaining the dominant interest until the intended
drawing is finished proves to be beyond the child's power,
thus we see that lack of steady purpose which changes the
subject in the middle of the drawing (of which we have already
given a specimen in Chapter XIX, 5). Even if the original
intention is carried out, the child does not, to begin with,
succeed in representing the various parts of an object in right
mutual relation or proportion. In fact, there are cases even
in which parts of the face were shaded in outside the head,
and others where the legs were made shorter than the head.
The size in which any portion of the picture is given depends
primarily much more upon its importance in the child's eyes
than upon any laws of proportion.

With increasing years comes the growth of synthetic capacity
and we find increase in the power to grasp the different parts
as constituents of the whole,
and to observe more accu-
rately their relation to one
another. At last, as early as
the fifth and sixth year,
the increasing constructive
power in drawing, as earlier
in building, enables the child
to produce larger "composi-
tions"; at this age our boy
drew landscapes, houses with
gardens and people, sea-

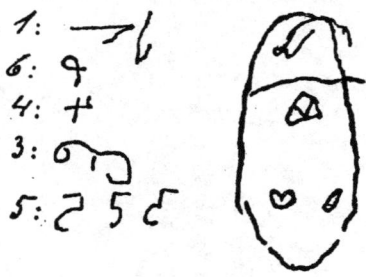

Misplacements.

pieces on which appeared sailing and steam ships, fishermen
and divers, all executed with the simplest means, often only in
the roughest of sketches, but yet with a certain sense of
arrangement and space division.

The child's unconcern as to whether his drawings correspond
with the objects drawn is also shown in the remarkable
"misplacements" which occur fairly often in the very early
stages. Above and below, vertical and horizontal, right and
left, are interchanged without the child either noticing or
being disturbed by it. We give as examples some drawings of
numerals which Hilde (4 ; 9) made on her slate, partly from
copies, partly from memory. We find here all possible misplacements; the tilting over at an angle of 90°, the position

upside down, the reflected image. Still more remarkable is the face that Eva (3 ; 0) drew. She began with the oblong, then placed close to herself the two eyes, over these the nose, and, above, the stroke across for the mouth. Other examples (of letters) will be found in the reproduction of a sample of writing at the end of Chapter X. This misplacement is on a parallel with the recognition of pictures upside down (Chapter XIV, 2). For the psychological significance of this phenomenon the reader is referred to my treatise on *Misplaced Positions*.

We turn to a short consideration of the typical beginnings of two chief subjects of the child's drawing. The child's favourite subject is that which every artist undertakes as his last and most difficult, i.e. man. But how differently the child attacks this problem. He draws at once—and no artist can imitate him in this—the idea of Man—man in himself, not any individual in a definite position, mood or clothing. Such a drawing is therefore a remarkable intermediate stage between individual representation and abstract idea. But what does the child consider as essential to man? Figure *a* (drawn by Scupin's son (2 ; 11)), representing about the simplest plan of the human representation, shows it: head, legs, arms, and an upright position. Not only feet, hands, hair and clothes are wanting, but the very fact that there is a body between head and legs is disregarded. It seems almost incredible to us that even the child when he has produced such a "fine fellow" does not notice what is missing when it is so poor a representation or likeness. This "fine fellow" type is, moreover, not confined only to the earliest years. Figure *b* is one of the many examples found amongst six-year-old children in Primary Schools, no doubt, of course, only amongst those who in early childhood have had no opportunity of drawing.

a   *b*
"Schema" of Human Beings.

Next to human beings, the favourite subject is a mammal of some sort. The child considers them quite sufficiently characterized (cf. Figs. *c* and *d*) by the horizontal position of the body, position of the head before, not over the trunk, several legs, not by any means necessarily four, as we see in these samples. In the earliest form, therefore, we find not only no distinction between different mammals,[1] but no difference in the form of the head between the lower animal and man. Who would guess that the monster with the human face (*d*), the production of a six-year-old boy, is meant to represent a pig?

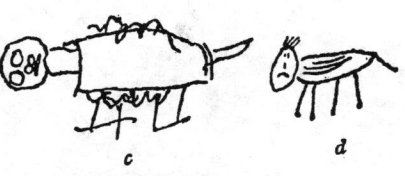

"Schema" of Mammals

In sample *c* (by Scupin's son (4 ; 11)) the child feels that the hair strokes and the large nostrils are quite satisfactory evidence that it represents a dog. Who knows whether such animal forms produecd in the first age of civilization by bygone generations with their artistic incapacity have not contributed to the origin of certain myths (Sphinx, harpies, etc.)?

As long as drawing remains in the "schematic" stage, it has great similarity with expression by means of speech,[2] for, like this, it aims—only with different means—at reproducing thoughts and opinions; like this, too, it is a frank expression of inner experience totally untroubled by considerations of attractiveness or accuracy. But whilst vocal speech maintains, in the case of every normal human being, throughout life the rôle it achieved in early childhood, drawing loses its general human significance from the moment of transition from the "schematic" stage to that of conformity to vision. Whilst all children—no matter how gifted or talented—enjoy "schematic" drawing, really cultured drawing has always been and will always remain the possession of a select few; of only that type of men with a definite interest who feel the craving to translate their inner vision into a corresponding representation and men of definite talent who can successfully carry out the self-imposed task of reproducing in similar form the object perceived by their outer or inner vision. For this reason graphic

[1] I met with the following instance in a nine-year-old girl. She produced, in response to my request to draw an animal, a figure similar to specimen *d*. When she was asked what kind of animal it was, she grew confused and said hesitatingly: "Well—just an animal." So she had accomplished the feat of drawing the general abstract idea of a mammal!

[2] K. Bühler has given very instructive observations concerning similarities and dissimilarities between expression by drawing and by speech.

art can in later years only be a general human accomplishment in so far as it maintains a close connection with the symbolic character of speech, as a form of "writing". Even the modern methods of teaching drawing and the inclusion of graphic forms of expression in the various subjects taught in kindergarten and school will be powerless to bring about any fundamental change; yet we shall be glad to see as a result of these efforts that the child can find a more intensive and fuller power of expression within the scope of his "schema" form of activity, and if talent rising above the average is recognized and developed.

If now we transfer these points of view to the earliest years of childhood, we can understand why pleasure in drawing is more universal in the first years of life than at any other later period. Then the child still scribbles away gaily, he has no sense of inadequacy to his task, no struggle with difficulties, for he is making no attempt to produce a representation with any apparent correspondence to what he sees. But, even at this early age, there is preparation for that parting of the ways which we mentioned above; from amongst the average children who draw their clumsy "schemata" from pure play- amusement, others begin to be differentiated by performances that stand out above the level of a simple "schema"; indications of a likeness to what is seen become recognizable, occasionally indeed in a certain range of subjects rise to an astonishing degree of similarity.[1] (Cf. with this Plate VI.)

How such rudimentary forms can develop gradually through more complete and correct designs into the beginnings of artistic representation is illustrated by the specimens of drawing of a man which we have from our son (Plate VI). The boy had an extraordinary love of drawing, and also an aptitude a little beyond his years. The series extends over two and a quarter years, from 3 ; 3 to 5 ; 6.[2]

Fig. 1 (3 ; 2½) is still on the border line of scribbling, but is raised to a higher stage by the intention he expressed beforehand of drawing his sister. The curves, twisting into one another, give an undefined representation of head and trunk;

---

[1] Only the highest degree of optical reproduction, that including three dimensions, as in model or perspective drawing, seems a closed door for even the most gifted of young children.

[2] More details over this boy's early development in drawing in C. and W. Stern, III.

some were drawn during the production as eye, nose, mouth; arms and legs are recognizable.

After nine months' pause in drawing, his interest awoke again, and now more distinct sketches were made. Fig. 2 shows nothing wrongly localized except the comb-like fingers placed along the whole length of the arm; the swellings on the legs represent the knees. In the actual drawing he had, as yet, no specific intention, but afterwards he would utter a kind of humorous criticism of his work, saying: *He is an old man, has no hairs but one. The old man is waggly too.*

Six weeks later, he drew another portrait that shows further progress in the trunk and arm-formation and the additional feet. Fig. 3. Very peculiar are the four appendages to the head; in answer to our astonished question as to the four ears, we got the explanation: *Why of course those are meant for the cheeks* (pointing to the one pair of handles). He had thought of the cheeks, so they had to be specially marked out somewhere.

The portrait in Fig. 4 at the age of 4 ; 8½ shows considerable progress, in spite of its imperfection. The drawing is meant to represent the side-view of a man looked at from behind so that only the back of the head and one eye is seen. When G. had just finished the drawing and we, misunderstanding his intention, said: "O poor man, with no mouth and no nose", G. took up a position with his back almost turned to us, and asked: *Can you see his mouth when he walks like this? but you can see his eye, can't you?*

And with this he leaves behind the period of the primitive sketch. G. has recognized that drawings have not to reproduce what is objectively present, but that which can be seen from a definite point of view.

In his sixth year the boy's power of drawing takes a considerable step forward towards pictorial representation; at 5 ; 6 he drew in his sketch-book a girl (Fig. 5) showing a somewhat primitive body and quite wrongly placed arms, but all the more surprising in the characteristic head. The face is not drawn in the usual circle, but the hair is included in the shape of the head (certainly a little too long), and hangs down over the forehead; on the top it is tied with ribbon. The ears are at the right height and properly shaped.

To end with, Fig. 6 represents a combination of the art of drawing and cutting out. Santa Claus was first drawn on white paper, then cut out roughly, and at last stuck on a dark background. G. knew the distinguishing features of Santa Claus, not only from pictures, but also from his own experience, as he had played the part three months before at a little Christmas celebration with a long beard, pointed cap, net of apples in front, and on his back a sack of toys. The bent position of the top of the body is the result of good observation. All the drawings just described were from memory, in accordance with the natural tendency of early childhood. But in his sixth year G. sometimes ventured on other tasks. He began to draw from a book of simple copies, and at 5 ; 6½ he made an attempt to draw a blue crayon portrait of his little sister sitting facing him.

The result (Plate VI, Fig. 7) is—mercifully—not a speaking likeness, but yet shows the boy's keen observation. He quite left the usual lines followed in his face representations and tried to do justice to what he really saw and noticed. Thus he reproduced the more delicate modelling of the face in the folds and lines which appear below the eye, along the bridge of the nose, between mouth and nose, in the corners of the chin and in the lobe of the ear. The curve of the cheek was somewhat strongly produced by circular lines running into one another. In the eye, too, he gave many details not noticed as a rule (the socket, eyeball, pupils, eyelashes, eyebrows).

As an example of supernormal performances we give in the second part of Plate VI two drawings by a four-year-old boy. This child, an architect's son, who showed for many years a zeal for drawing that amounted almost to monomania, with a pronounced preference for all imaginative drawing; bright dresses, fire and hell, sea-pieces (although he had never been by the sea), processions in alternating confusion fill the pages of his bulky sketch-books. The stage of the simple schema was passed almost immediately.[1] As the last example shows, in the province of drawing, natural aptitude may be so great as to obliterate all difference in age; by far the majority of adults are far behind the four-year-old R. B. in their artistic powers. But though natural talent is the chief cause of this difference in accomplishment, yet we must not overlook the other contributory factors. The child's keen interest may sometimes induce a practice of certain motifs which will lead,

[1] More details concerning this boy in Kik, pp. 94 sqq.

even at a very early age, to relatively important success on special lines, without the existence necessarily of any considerable artistic gift. For the young child with any liking for drawing nearly always concentrates—at any rate for definite periods—on a single subject or on a very narrow field, and thus gradually achieves familar types sometimes marked by characteristic features of the object represented. Thus there are little horse-specialists, some that only draw human figures, others who consider engines the only things worth drawing.[1,2] Finally, the influence of favourable opportunity must not be underestimated. A child with paper, pencil, coloured crayons, and if possible a nice big blackboard and unrestricted chalk, who is not made shy by ridicule, criticism and continual correction, will often take up and enjoy his graphic play. But his elders must accustom themselves not to look at the productions from an æsthetic point of view, but rather to rejoice that the child's perceptual life finds in them new and unrestrained expression.

Imitative Drawing

Whilst for an adult copying seems to be much easier than "free" drawing, the case is exactly the opposite in childhood, particularly in early childhood. It is a negative quality that first strikes the observer, viz. an amazing incapacity for reproducing a copy—no matter how simple—with any degree of accuracy, even in those children who are able in imaginative drawing to produce quite recognizable schemata. The task is alien to the child's nature; of his own accord a child, even if very keen on drawing otherwise, will scarcely ever attempt it. We are therefore forced to the almost exclusive use of experimental tests.

Van Gennep, at his five-year-old daughter's request, made outline drawings for her of simple objects and printed letters;

[1] This last class includes Dix's son. Cf. *The Grades of Locomotive Drawings*, Dix, II, pp. 73–82.

[2] We find something similar in human development. The prehistoric man who by his magic adorned the walls of his cave with those startlingly realistic figures of buffaloes or reindeer evidently had the same specialist's practice for the object of his life's interest. Yet we are not justified in drawing the conclusion (Verworn) from such performances that realistic art appeared earlier in the human race than representation of a more symbolic nature.

the child attempted to copy them, but in such a form that onlookers would not as a rule discover which of her attempts belonged to any given copy. It was noteworthy that drawings having some meaning for the child, e.g. a tree, doll, pencil, etc., were more like the copies than printed letters, which, although so much simpler, both from the point of view of optics and technique, are for the child nothing but an unintelligible combination of lines.

The like result, with regard to letters, was obtained by Huth's experiment on thirty-seven kindergarten pupils. Huth started from the query as to whether instruction in writing could begin —as so many people wish—before the age of six, and tested whether children averaging four and a half years of age were capable of copying the simplest of all script forms, viz. the small German *c* ($\mathcal{N}$). In the first test the finished copy was shown to them, in the second it was formed before their eyes, in the third they had to say whether their drawing was like the copy or not. The result is astonishing in the variety of types produced, amongst which those that were correct or nearly so were decidedly in the minority.

In the first test not half the children had even noticed that three strokes were required; angles pointing in all directions were offered as well as curves, and a variety of zig-zag lines instead of the simple up-down-up $\mathcal{N}$. But even the three-line drawings show all possible variations, misplacements, separation, and bending of the single strokes. The second test yielded somewhat better results, no doubt because the children could see and imitate the sequence of movements from left to right, but here, too, the number of meaningless performances was large enough. In the third test fewer than half the children were able to notice whether their imitation was right or wrong.

Huth concludes from his results that the power of kindergarten pupils to copy meaningless combinations of lines is greatly over-estimated, and that it would, educationally, be absurd to burden children of less than school-age with writing characters.[1]

But now it is not enough to stop at the statement of this

---

[1] It is another matter, of course, when children from spontaneous interest begin to copy letters and numbers which they see on posters, etc., or to imitate the writing exercises of older brothers and sisters.

incapacity; we must endeavour to find a psychological explanation of the child's attitude to copying.

Here we must distinguish two contributory causes. If the child is to copy an object with which he is already acquainted, or at any rate knows some of its definite qualities, this knowledge of his (just as we find in "free" drawings) must make an unfailing appearance in his efforts at copying, indeed it will not even allow the purely optical impression of the copy to come first.

We find an example of this in tests made by Katz (II) who gave copies to the children, consisting of geometrical figures—plane and solid; especially instructive are the results with forms of three dimensions, such as dice, table (a square surface on four supports), etc.

The results we can know indeed from children's unprompted imaginative drawings, but they are still more remarkable when face to face with the objects themselves: the child does not reproduce what he sees, but what he knows of the object to be copied. Perspective is entirely ignored; dice and table-top are always shown with right angles, and all lines in their actual relative length, not foreshortened. This point of view still persists, too, even if they are given a copy drawn in perspective of the same objects: in any attempt at copying, the knowledge of the actual shape again comes to the front and surfaces all become rectangular. The following figures *a* and *c* are the "table"-drawings of a six-year-old girl, *a* from the solid model, *c* the imitation of the perspective copy *b*.

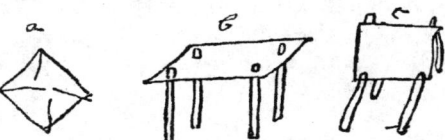

In other unfamiliar copies in which the child has to let himself be guided by the impressions they make upon him, the phenomena of the primitive *general* character of the impression appear (cf. Chapter III, 2). Indeed it is possible—as Volkelt, Werner (II) and Muchow (III) show—to test this peculiarity of his psychic perception—which is so important a factor in our understanding of the child—in copying tests with experimental distinctness.

The child does not look upon the copy as a purely optical impression with fixed lines, angles, points, etc., but as a vague whole of which motor instincts, tactile ideas, emotional feelings form a part and often are the chief factors in determining the character of the drawing. Then all that remains of the optical perceptual form is only something indefinite in accord with the general feeling; e.g. in a square only the circumstance that it is an enclosing line; it will then be called "something round" and drawn as a circle with beginning and end coinciding. If here the diffuse perception leads to a weakening of the inner formation of the figure, so the exact reverse may take place in sharp-cornered figures, and these sharp points take on an independent significance of something pricking or piercing; thus in the copy they are made into independent outstanding strokes or directly translated into motor-action— i.e. dotted down hastily on the paper.

A particularly striking instance of the optical impression being translated into a motor-expression of strength is given by Muchow (III, p. 47).

A boy (4 ; 6) was given a copy to draw of two larger black circles with a smaller black dot between them. First he drew with a light movement the dot; then he set down his pencil close to it on the paper and pressed with all his might to produce the big dot (i.e. one of the large circles), until the point broke and he sat perplexed before the hole he had made in the paper. "The 'big dots' had probably impressed him as something produced by great exertion, something important, hard; he therefore thinks that he too must produce them by great pressure." The purely optical feature that they show a larger extent of surface had not yet been differentiated in the diffuse general impression.[1]

---

[1] Cf. the entirely similar action of Gunther in his "free" drawing of a gnat; the gnat's sting was illustrated by two "stung" dots on the slate (Chapter XIX, 5).

PART VIII

THOUGHT AND INTELLIGENCE

THIS part of our book is devoted to a subject that in each of the preceding chapters has played a more or less considerable part. But in those we were only concerned to find the degree and kind of influence exercised by the intellect in the functions of speech, memory, apperception and imagination, whilst now we propose to deal solely with this motive power itself, i.e. with the child's thought, and above all with its evident and fundamental distinction from the other psychic activities, especially those of the perceptual life.

Such consideration of the psychological problems of thought *per se* is still of fairly recent date. From Herbart on, psychology has been in the habit of looking upon thought-processes as complicated perceptual movements, and of identifying power of thought with the power of forming perceptions. It was not until the beginning of the twentieth century that a change took place, and then it is true that with regard to this point modern psychology followed two fairly distinctive paths. One turned to thought as the substance and activity of consciousness: Psychology of Thought. The other concerned itself with the human tendency to thought in action—with enquiry into intelligence. Both points of view have only extended to early childhood within the last ten years.[1]

---

[1] A third problem, which is of especial interest for childhood, can only be mentioned here in passing, viz. the system of thought in which man lives. What is the nature of the child's view of life, i.e. what is the child's mental attitude to the world as a whole, in so far as it is accessible to him, to what is perceived and thought, feared and hoped? Up to the present there are few attempts to give descriptions of the picture of the world as seen by the child or to understand it from the conditions of early psychic development. Herr and Frau Katz have recently made such an attempt for their two sons. Cf. also Piaget's writings and Werner's supplement to the present book concerning "magic" thought in childhood.

CHAPTER XXVII

FORMATION OF IDEAS AND JUDGMENT

1. Psychology of Thought

WE have already mentioned in Chapter I, Section 2, that the thought-psychology which originated in the Wurzburger School has recently been applied by Karl Bühler to questions arising in child-psychology.[1] Bühler's researches and the subsequent expositions in this book are mutually complementary. Bühler lays especial emphasis on the premises of general psychology which aim at the explanation of primitive thought; he examines theoretically the facts of the certainty of remembrance, of the grasp of facts and their bearing to each other, of the conditions of the processes of judgment, formation of ideas and the drawing of conclusions, in order subsequently to prepare a systematic psychology of thought in childhood. But to make this possible we require something else, viz. an insight into the manifold nature and special structure of those thought-phenomena that actually occur in childhood. Our book aims at contributing to such a collection of the phenomena of child-thought; at the same time the interpretation of our observations leads to psychological theories which correspond with Bühler's in many respects.

First of all, a few statements for general guidance. Psychological theory must distinguish thought from conception in two ways: in difference of content and difference of process.

As regards contents we must distinguish "thoughts" from "conceptions". By this is not meant that a thought here, a conception there, possesses independent and isolated psychic life; both rather are only factors in the united mental condition, but as factors they have quite different qualifications. We understand by "conceptions" the concrete contents of consciousness, produced by perceptions, their after-workings, intermingling and combination. But thought deals not only with concrete contents, but refers to objects which lie outside its experience. The child has had the most varying apperceptions of its doll, optical and tactual, in sizes altering with distance, in different lights, from different sides; these apperceptions

---

[1] *Geistige Entwicklung*, Chap. VIII.

continue in many more or less distinct perceptions; but it is not these apperceptions or inner perceptual ideas that the child names when he speaks of his doll, but the actual thing outside, which cannot become a concrete experience, but yet is known as the common and unchanging point to which many experiences are referred. This is the mental part in the psychic condition. The direction of the consciousness on something we name "intention" (Husserl). In so far as the thought has objective significance, i.e. is appropriate to the object to which it is directed, it is called "idea".

In the above example the intention extends to a single object and brings us to the individual idea. But we are also able to think of generalizations ("man", "animal"), and also of relations between things ("aim", "place", "causality", "number"). And just as surely as all these thoughts need concrete perceptions as their starting-point and working material, so surely are they themselves abstract, indistinct—yet essentially unmistakable—content of consciousness. The same is true of judgment: it only comes into being, if I add to my perception, or unification of perceptions, the positive or negative intention, the conviction of the existence or non-existence, of the coherence or unity of what is thought of.

The second distinctive mark of thought consists, as mentioned before, in the resultant form of its activity. Here associative psychology utterly fails in its attempts at explanation. Thought does not consist in the reception of impressions, the perceptual ideas resulting from these impressions, the mingling and combinations of such ideas, and—in consequence of associations so formed—the reappearance of these impressions when occasion requires. Such construction had indeed been proved insufficient in every department of psychic life, as it overlooked the never-failing personal interference of the ego-activity, intent on reaching some goal. But in thought this sentient activity—and therefore superior to simple associative impulse—appears with especially marked distinctness. The thought-process has a characteristic time at which all component factors are subordinated to the final aim, the "task" to be fulfilled. Then and then only does it become thought when the ego out of the abundance of available contents of consciousness and of associative connections chooses those which are "intentionally" valuable, and when, not only is use made of combinations already existing, but conscious conceptual ideas never before combined are for the first time put into synthetic union. For it is the distinctive mark of a real thought-process that its result is new as regards the individual's existing thoughts and conceptions; all thought is a passing beyond perceptual data. As soon as the conscious activity is only repetition of former conscious processes, it is not thought, but only perceptual reproduction, hence it happens that psychic processes may assume the logical form of acts of thought in their expression without being such psychologically. In this fact we have a great, though generally not sufficiently recognized, difficulty in psychological analysis. The intentional thought as a conscious element and the dominance of this conscious activity by active striving for new "intentions"—these are the two psychological foundations of all thought.

First traces of such thought-processes have been seen in the period prior to speech (Chapter V, Section 1). But they are still only germs then, and even the early attempts at speech scarcely contain any intellectual factors.

The transition from the first to the second period of speech, of which we treated in Chapter X, is the earliest date we can give as a turning-point. For if we say of that period: now there comes an awakening of a consciousness of the significance of speech and the will to conquer it, then we have the fulfilment of the two conditions of real thought as formulated above. Our consideration of the development of thought in the child will have then to begin at this point.[1]

2. The Development of Ideational Activity

(a) Perception as a Factor of Ideational Activity.

Ideas are something different from percepts, but they are closely connected with them, and develop on perceptional foundations, and it is the special task of child-psychology to follow gradual process of growth and to find out the positive part played by concrete perception as starting-point for abstract thought-activity.

[1] The close connection of thought with speech was the reason why our book, *Children's Speech*, contains so many considerations on the psychology of thought. We must refer to them those readers who desire more than the brief treatment of the next few pages.

Separate percepts and memory-presentations of objects (cf. the example of the doll in Section 1 of this chapter) are in consequence of their individual concrete nature connected with definite separate situations, and therefore not adapted for use as starting-points for the general and unvarying knowledge concerning the object. But now we have in schematic conceptions become acquainted with contents of consciousness that are literally concepts, that is, resembling a definite sense-impression, but yet no longer so detailed and individualized as in single memory-presentations.

They are, as it were, sense-abstractions, generalizations, still partaking of the nature of sense-impressions, indications of the most striking features, and therefore fitting representations, not only of the subjective experience of the individual impulse, but of the real object. This alone explains the significance that the "schema" has in the most diverse provinces of the child's psychic life. Since it belongs to a world of sense-experience, psychic power is able to form it at an early stage of development; since it is so scanty and empty, it is a suitable starting-point for the generalization of thought.[1] What, therefore, is a failing from the point of view of sense-experience is an advantage from that of development of ideation. We have met with such "schemata" in dealing with visual and sound-perception; in the one, as the schematic drawings representing "man" or "animal", in the other as the sound-pictures, that abstract from the entire perception-complex of an animal or of an object the simplified percept of its sound-expression (bow-wow, tic-tac). Development from this stage of schematic percepts proceeds in two directions: one leads to the conscious, most accurate presentation of the sense-image free from what exists in idea, but not in sight—we followed its path in drawing, where we saw the gradual development of a representation true to appearance from the early "schema". The other development, which concerns us here, endeavours more and more to neglect what is seen in order to give greater weight to its more purely logical character of an idea. The schema (image) still has a certain, even if vague, similarity with the impression which it constantly recalls, but gradually the need for this similarity between what is meant and its image disappears,

[1] Bühler too emphasizes this intermediary significance of the schema (I, p. 268).

and all that is required is a mere trace of likeness to mark the reference, i.e. the intention, to the object; the schema becomes nothing but the symbol.

This is the path from the graphic image by way of picture-writing to the ordinary script, and in the province of hearing and speech from natural symbols (sound-pictures and expressional-movements) to the chance, conventional names of things.

We understand now too why no real ideational thought is possible without speech. Verbal presentations are less burdened with chance details of any particular time of apperception than are actual percepts; they are, it is true, still concrete conscious images, but only through their sound; and whilst this unvarying sound is connected with various similar actual percepts, it is freed from the ballast of separate detail of a temporary nature, and can become an intelligible means of conveying the invisible, constant object-thought. For this reason we feel justified in looking upon the child's discovery that everything has "a name" as his first real effort in thought. And the activity of thought, too, becomes apparent at this period, for the child is no longer content with the knowledge of speech coming to him without effort, by chance as it were, but endeavours to make progress by his own enquiry as to names. With every newly-acquired word he gets the opportunity of now identifying something that before had only been given him as a momentary, perceptual experience as a lasting object, so that this questioning as to names is not a mechanical snapping-up of words, but a striving after the mental conquest of the objective world. Forty years ago Lindner very aptly compared this mental process with the progress that walking brings to the child in his mastery of the world of space. In one, as in the other, the child is no longer satisfied with what is brought up to him, but carries himself and his endeavour to meet the things he desires to conquer.

(b) The Increase in Objective Power.

Yet another condition is connected with the development of ideational power, and one whose nature can be shown most clearly in the development of speech. In all early speech, as we have already seen (Chapter VIII, 4). perceptual activity is most closely connected with emotional and will elements. The first words gave expression to the subjective reaction still inseparable from objective stimuli. This subjective tone in experience must have been already suppressed before the formation of ideas of things (of which we have just been speaking) can become possible, and, by degrees, the progress in objective power extends over an ever wider field. We can trace in the use of single words, as in the conquest of certain parts of speech and inflections, the steps forward from a state of personal desire to one of real statement and the consequent uninterrupted progress in ideational power.

We will illustrate the change to objective significance by some single words which had, to begin with, a purely interjectional, hence emotional, character.

Hilde by degrees gets to use the petition *please* as the actual name of a roll, even when not asking for it. The exclamation *look*, often connected with the gesture of an outstretched first finger, comes at last to be used as the name for hands in that position (nothing but *looks*, said our daughter when she saw the picture of many such hands in an advertisement). We find a similar objective use of the exclamation of regret *a pity!* and of disgust *bah bah!* in these instances: *the* (broken) *doll looks such a pity* (Hilde); *Händel looks bah bah* (Scupin's son, 2 ; 2).

The designations of qualities show something similar. The first appear without exception as words for a temporary condition of the child requiring relief (*tired*, *wet*), or for the way it is inwardly affected by persons or things. If he say *Mummy good*, he means Mother is good to me; *milk hot* is the exclamation of pain, meaning that the child has burnt his mouth. The child, at first, only succeeds in the abstraction of special features, when these make themselves especially felt as disturbing (less often pleasurable) factors of his emotional attention; not until some monthe later is he able to name those features which are noticed without special co-operation of emotional activity and recognized now as appertaining to the object. When the child is in a position to say *a big doll, a clean tablecloth*, he has mastered the ideal character of qualities.

We will now mention, to begin with, two ideas of relation showing a similar course of development: "No" and "I".

The child's first "noes" always have the subjective significance of refusal, meaning, "No, I won't have that", "No, that is not to be"; whilst its significance as a statement, a negation of the objective, "No, that is not so", is not yet existent. An eighteen-month-old child can certainly scream *no, no* very energetically when a toy is taken from him, but if his hand is touched and he is asked: "Is this your little eye?" he cannot yet say *no*, although when asked he can quite correctly show his hand and eyes. In the case of our own children the first no as a statement appeared two or three months after the early use of the word with its affective and will tone.

Gunther (2 ; 10) had adopted as a general expression of negation and contradiction the expression *it is dear* or *it is too dear*. The original of this is quite clear: his parents had sometimes refused his wishes for a toy or dainty that he saw in the shop-window with the reason: "No, that is too dear." The boy had not understood the actual meaning of "dear", only the negative attitude; and in this affective significance he also considered *it dear* when he was to be fetched from play to bed or disturbed in some occupation or other, etc.

The intervening time between the first and second significance of "I" is often even longer. The reflective words I, me, mine, as expressions of strong self-will, were heard from our two eldest children as early as the age of 2 ; 0. *I look for ball—me too*, when others received anything; but its use as statement did not follow until after 2 ; 6: *I am small.*

Another sign of the gradual growth of objective power in thought is shown in the child's attitude to time-divisions: past, present, future. To begin with, the child knows only a direct sense (with a pronounced affective-tone) of the present, and a desire or aversion directed to the very immediate future, but the past which can only be grasped by the loss of the subjective will-impulse, i.e. by a process of objective statement, does not appear in the child's consciousness until a much later period. We already discovered this in our discussion of the first percepts (Chapter VI, end of Section 2), and of remembrance in childhood (Chapter XVII, 1), and it occurs again when time-divisions have to be mastered in speech. The subjective time-relations of the present and future are first mastered in speech; the Infinitive form of the verb expresses the immediate present, and still more frequently that which is directly hoped for or dreaded. Past time, on the other hand, does not find expression (by participles) for another six months. And the same sequence is seen in adverbs of time; the expressions of the present and future, such as *at once, then, now, to-morrow, soon*, have long since been adopted when words referring to the past, as *just then, yesterday, before,* creep in with laggard step.[1] This question has been closely investigated by Piaget, of which we already quoted an instance (Chapter X, 6). Cf. also Chapter XXVIII, 1.[2]

Closely connected with the increase in objectivity is the progressive "socialization" of thought. Thought-contents can by means of words only be expressed and understood in the society of others if they are freed from their purely egocentric form and converted into a super-individualistic shape. Adult thought is in this sense entirely subordinated to the principle of social objectivity; in the child however the process of adapting thought-activity into sympathy with others' thoughts is one of very slow growth.

(c) THE CATEGORIES.

Another advance in thought which also seems to be founded upon a far-reaching law of development consists in the successive mastery of the different ideal categories. We have already met with some expressions of this law in earlier chapters, we will here only review the most essential points in order to throw light on the manifold working of the principle. To begin with, thought stands in the "SUBSTANCE STAGE"; out of the chaos of unnoticed experience there emerges at first substantial form, independently existing persons and things as the separate material of thought. Then follows an ACTION STAGE; the existing activities of persons and things are emphasized in thought and attract special interest to themselves. Not until the third stage does the child develop the power to separate from things their inherent qualities and the varying relations existing between them, in the STAGE OF RELATIONS AND ATTRIBUTES. Of course, as the new stages appear, the powers of the earlier ones show steady increase in extent and variety.

In order not to mark these stages too sharply and above all not to consider them too much in the sense of category thought in the adult, we must keep clearly in mind that the principle

---

[1] Limited space unfortunately forbids a more detailed consideration of the very interesting problem of the comprehension of time in childhood. The reader is referred to the careful study on this subject which Decroly and Degand have published, founded on continuous observations of one child.

[2] Piaget formulates the opposition between adult and child thought in the following somewhat pointed antithesis (I, p. 56): *L'adulte pense socialement même lorsqu'il est solitaire, et l'enfant en dessous de 7 ans pense et parle de manière égocentrique même lorsqu'il est en société.*

of gradual differentiation is applicable to them also. (See Chapter III, 1, 2.)

The beginning is to be found before a categorical differentiation, i.e. then in a pre-categorical phase. As long, for instance, as the child's speech is still in the interjection and one-word sentence stage, feeling and conception, objective and action appreciation are so undifferentiated in the consciousness that there can not yet be any question of the presentation of a category.[1]

The successive differentiation of the individual categories then begins, but still in the child-like diffuse manner. The keen ideational distinction between object and activity made by adult—and particularly by scientific—thought represents a mental performance which is only possible at the end of a long process of development. To place a child's mental performance in a category does not therefore mean that this category stands out independently and by itself in the experience, but that it is especially accented, and becomes the central point of its structure.

Now, these stages are not to be regarded as mental states which the child as a whole passes through in succession, so that at one period he is a "substance-thinker", at another an "action-thinker"; they are rather transition-phases through which the different kinds of intellectual activity severally pass. Difficult processes which in any case do not begin until later will therefore still be firmly fixed in the substance stage, whilst others have reached the action stage long before.

These successive stages are found first in the development of the vocabulary, which adopts one after another substantives, verbs, and the other parts of speech (cf. Chapter X, 2). A little later, the same process takes place in the development of the child's power of spontaneous remembrance. The earliest recollections mentioned by Hilde (1 ; 6) referred exclusively to objects, principally persons. At 1 ; 9 she began to remember occurrences, especially actions of her own; at last, people and actions were definitely localized in the memory, and with this the easiest kind of relation, that referring to locality, was acquired. Memories of distinctive features, such as the appear-

---

[1] I have always accepted such a pre-state of category development (cf. Chapter VIII, 4 and Chapter X). The statement of Bühler and Koffka, that the substance stage is not the very first, accordingly does not mean any ground of opposition to the development principle which I have enunciated above.

ance of certain persons, etc., did not come into evidence before the age of 2 ; 9. At a later period of childhood we more especially think of the child's attitude in the consideration of pictures; we have already proved the course of development here by examples. As the task increases in difficulty—for instance, when the picture has to be described not at the time of seeing it, but afterwards from memory—each separate stage does not appear until very much later, yet the same sequence is maintained. Thus in the aussage-tests with the picture of the peasant's room it was found that the reports of the seven-year-old children in the elementary schools were almost entirely in the substance stage, those of the ten-year-olds in the action, and of the fourteen-year-olds in the relation stage, whilst the spontaneous mention of qualities developed still later.[1]

Another interesting proof of the working of the law is the change of stage in a child of definite age, as soon as the task is made more difficult. The report in Chapter XVIII, 1 of an aussage of Eva's plainly shows this. Whilst looking at it, there was often evidence of the action stage (*Gunther is eating bread: where are they going in then?*) ; but as soon as she had to describe the same picture from memory she confined herself entirely to the substance stage, and gave an unbroken enumeration of one thing after another.

We must still consider two more special aspects of development, one taking place within the period of substance-thought, the other in relation-thought.

(d) INDIVIDUAL, PLURAL AND COLLECTIVE IDEATION.

The logical opposition between individual and collective ideation is, as we have seen (Chapter VIII, 4), not yet present in the first period of speech, but it must be developed as soon as thought refers percepts to objects. As a result of the strong subjective admixture of feeling-tone still existing, the first isolated objects to which thought refers are those to which the child stands in a special personal relationship, and thus they it is that first develop the mental idea of "individuality". The name is now the expression of a conscious identification. *Dolly* is always the same doll, the child's dearest plaything, *Mummy* always the same person, who satisfies his desires.

[1] W. Stern, I, p. 120 sqq. Cf. the critical remarks on this in Bühler's *Intellectual Development,*

And, starting with these objects so familiar to his mind, the power of conscious recognition and of identification arising therefrom will, in the end, extend to the many other objects of his environment.

"Collective ideation" needs, on the other hand, a much longer time for its development. It is quite true that the child from the very beginning has used certain words for many similar individuals, e.g. *dicky* for every flying thing, but it is still a long journey from such a name that is connected in a purely associative manner with any chance-recurring feature to the consciousness that the word and what it expresses includes all members of that group. And on this journey we meet with a peculiar intermediate form which we have called "plural ideation".[1]

The child now already knows that "a horse" is not an individuality existing only once, but that he can meet with it in many instances, but his statements always refer only to this or that particular horse which happens to be the object of his apperception, recollection or expectation. He places each new specimen, whose likeness he recognizes, among the many others that he has already perceived, but he does not yet place them all under a general (collective) idea.

A characteristic example of this gradual distinction between individual (singular) and plural ideation follows: "Instead of the word *papa* which Hilde at first had applied without distinction to her father and all other men, at the age of 1 ; 7, a second appellation came into use, the child reserving *papa* for her father alone, and calling all other men, whether in real life or picture, *uncle*."

We noticed that Gunther, at the same age, discovered the likeness between all members of the same class of objects. "Pointing to a door he asked *that?* We said 'a door', and, as if to assure himself that the same name would always be forthcoming, he ran to a second and third door in the room, repeating his question. He did the same with the seven chairs in the room."

So that the child was trying here to form a plural idea, even before the corresponding word existed in his vocabulary.

The chief help in the formation of the plural idea is evidently then the arrangement in series and this principle, at certain

[1] *Children's Speech*, p. 179 sqq.

periods, plays quite an important part in the child's spontaneous thought as an excellent preparation for the development of the logical power of abstraction.

Eva (3 ; 8). "Everything now is arranged by her in series, she counts up what each one does, all the things that are alike in the house, etc. Thus, as four of us, all provided with something to read, were sitting on the garden seat, *Gunther has something, you have something, father has something, I have something. And Hilde* (who she knew was reading somewhere else) *has something too.*"

Counting is closely related with these logical performances.[1] For real counting (not of course the unintelligent gabbling over of numbers) begins with the conscious adding together of similar objects. If the two-year-old child has in front of him several apples or building-blocks, he indicates the successive repetition of the same impressions by the repetition of the same words, e.g. *one, one, one,* or *one more, one more,* or some similar expression. It has never been observed that dissimilar things have been added to one another in that way; it is therefore indeed a formation of the plural idea. By slow degrees, then, with small numbers, successive numerals take the place of the same words, thus giving, as it were, to each object its special place in the succession. But the child still clings fast to individual things; only after much effort does it see that the last-named number is also the general summarized term for all the objects enumerated. The "sum" or cardinal number representing a collective idea, therefore, develops later than the ordinals, which are plural ideas. (Of course, the fact that names of ordinal numbers always appear much later than the cardinals need not be considered in this connection.)

Hilde (3 ; 7). "If we stretch out five fingers to her and ask: 'How many fingers is that?' she says, *I will count,* and does so correctly from 1 to 5. But, then, if we ask her immediately after the last number: 'well, then, how many fingers?' she begins again from the very beginning to count once more, and so on for several times. The last finger is certainly the fifth, but the collective group of fingers is not yet expressed for her by the number five."

---

[1] Cf. with this what is said in this book over experimental tests of power of counting (Chap. XXIX, 2) and Bühler's explanation, *Intellectual Development,* I, p. 92 sqq.

If the summary of given units in a total idea offers great difficulties to the child's thought, these are considerably increased in the attempt to think of a common object in such a way that it includes not only those objects actually perceived, but also all others of the same kind. But this production of real generalization in ideas is only possible by a regular inductive conclusion, and therefore cannot be discussed before our next chapter.

(*e*) RELATIONAL IDEAS.

In the idea of numbers just mentioned there is to be observed another peculiarity as regards the child's relational thought. We get real relational thought only when the relation is recognized as no longer dependent on the concrete objects between which it exists; some relation or other of place, number or causality may exist in an identical way between any objects. But the child's idea is really only relational when he begins to understand it; never, it is true, immediately in this independence and general applicability, but, at first, as limited to a more or less narrow circle of applications, and these confined to such objects as are specially associated with the child's personal interests and needs.

For example, one would think that a child having once recognized the significance of "two" would be able to apply this numerical relation whenever two things of the same kind entered his field of vision. But no such thing: "two" is at first looked upon as a quality inherent in certain, especially interesting objects, but not recognized in others. Relational ideas assume their abstract quality but slowly and with great difficulty.

Thus Major and Lindner both agree in reporting that, towards the end of the third year, their children could, it is true, distinguish with unfailing accuracy between one and two apples, but on the other hand were incapable of recognizing as "two" eyes, ears or hands. And even of a boy aged 4 ; 3 we get the following report: When his grandfather asked: "How many fingers have I got?" he answered: *I don't know. I can only count my own fingers.*[1]

[1] Recently Beckmann thinks he has reason—founded on his own experimental observations—to refute the statement that the child's abstraction of number does not exist apart from the objects counted. He found, namely, that children who had acquired by experimental practice any definite mastery

We are told that savage people's ideas of number are also confined to certain things. And we catch sight of the last trace of this wanting power of abstraction in the fact that we use number-expressions such as "a dozen" and "a score" only in reference to certain things.

Naturally, the child finds it most difficult to grasp relations which, with the same objective, change with the change in the speaker's point of view.

Such "standpoint relations" are personal degrees of relationship (the same person as the child's mother is aunt to another child), the pronouns (the same person who says "I" is "you" for the child), and points of time (some occurrence is on one day "to-morrow", on the next "to-day", and on the day after "yesterday"). We can now understand why the child finds it so much easier to speak of himself with his name rather than with *"I"*. For the name always signifies his own identity, whether uttered by himself or by any other; but the various "I's" which the child hears always refer to another person, and it requires considerable power of abstraction to recognize that the very essence of the "I" idea consists in its reference back to the speaker in utter disregard of who this may be.

And lastly, time expressions! What confusion reigns for a long time in the child's little head before he grasps that the ever-moving present turns to-day into yesterday and to-morrow into to-day!

In her fourth year Hilde was continually asking: *Is to-day to-morrow? Is now to-day?* in order to dissipate the chaos. (3 ; 5). She said of a coming journey home: *If we go home, then it will be to-day.* And still at 4 ; 3 she confuses even to-morrow and yesterday: *We will pack to-day and start yesterday.* But soon

of number with blocks or something similar (e.g. the difference between 2 and 3), and knew it with certainty, could also show the same knowledge with any other objects whatsoever brought to their notice. From this result we may indeed conclude that in experimental practice mastery of number is not confined to special objects. But in the cases mentioned in the text, the choice of certain objects did not depend on the practice-experiment, but on an entirely spontaneous practical interest. The question whether he is going to have one or two apples is one of great affective interest for the child, so that in this case his attention is called to the total quite differently than when he has to consider blocks or marbles. Abstraction of number in practical life develops no doubt in closest union with efforts of will and mental feelings, whilst the experimental test of mastery of number deals with objects all of equal indifference to the child. At this stage, then, the experiment, on account of its artificial exclusion of spontaneous interest, is not an adequate expression of the child's usual attitude.

after she has got her time-relations quite clear. (5 ; 1.) She dictates to her mother the following message for her absent father: *To-day we are cooking nice things*, and adds as explanation of the "to-day": *To-day—do you know because it is to-day father will know at once it was yesterday* (that is, when he receives the letter on the next day). And (5 ; 6) she enjoyed explaining to herself difficult time-relations. When she hears we are starting the day after the day after to-morrow she says: *The day after the day after to-morrow is, to-morrow, the day after to-morrow.*

(f) PSYCHIC IDEATION.

We must consider it one of the highest stages in the child's ideation when he succeeds in realizing psychic conditions in thought. For even if, at first, in direct experience, we find a predominance of the subjective emotion and will, yet conscious-intentional thought is at first exclusively directed to the world of outer objects, and it is long before the child can look objectively upon his own psychic activities.

The child, of course, only attains by degrees to the logical mastery of the subjective. Thought, up till the present confined to physical objects, is inclined, at first, to seek an explanation of psychic phenomena by connection with something material, and thus, to begin with, it is the physical expression-movements that are simply identified with the corresponding psychic action.

Thus our children have long used *to love* as having the same significance as to "to show love" (stroke, caress, kiss). Other examples are:—

Eva (3 ; 1½) had once for fun kissed a chair.
Father: "But the chair will laugh now."
Eva (laughing herself): *Why, it can't laugh.*
Father: "Why not then?"
Eva: *Well it hasn't any teeth.*

In exactly the same way, the little boy Katz at about the same age (D. and R. Katz, II, p. 261) said: *the fish are not glad, they haven't any voice of course.*

But, even much later than this, the child is very apt to identify the inner psychic activity with its outer accompaniment. Thus we had the following conversation with Hilda (4 ; 9). Father: "What is thinking really?" *Don't know.* "Well, what

what do we think with?" *Animals think with their mouths.* "And people?" *With their tongues.* "What does a man do then when he thinks?" *He speaks.* It is the same thing with personal qualities; goodness she connects with smiling, as is shown by the following criticism of a stranger: *She is certainly very good; she smiled so at me.*

But then it slowly begins to dawn on the child that a psychic act and its equivalent are not one and the same thing; the psychic by degrees ceases to be material.

Rasmussen's daughter (4 ; 11) said (II, p. 196): *First I think about something and then I say it—first I think and then I speak.* Mother: "Did anyone tell you to do it like that?" *No, but I cannot do it at all any other way.*

Hilda (6 ; 0), in answer to someone's remark that new-born babies could not hear, said: *Yes, they can, they can't understand what is said, but they can hear it all right*—thus a clear-cut distinction between physiological perception and psychological apperception.

The conscious recognition of the subjective can, however, be developed from another side. The objective is what refers to all, the subjective what, on the contrary, belongs to me alone. This view of the subjective as "individual only", and therefore not applicable to others, was discernible in the four-year-old Hilde, and that, too, with regard to taste.

(3 ; 11.) *Oh, that is horrid coffee, it tastes nasty* (in explanation): *to Hilde it tastes nasty.*—And when later on her father thought the soup rather salt, Hilde (4 ; 2) said: *No, it isn't salt.* Father: Yes. Hilde: *Not to me.*

3. Chief Kinds of Judgment in Childhood

Any perception or perceptual association only becomes a judgment when the self assumes a positive or negative attitude to it, i.e. recognizes or rejects it as actual fact. The vocal expression of judgment follows in a statement (proposition); but not all statements are indicative of actual acts of judgment. As a rule they only contain reproductions of judgments, uttered by others, or that have been formed before by the speaker, and the mental conservation of energy as a rule tends in these cases to prevent any fresh judgment being formed as a result of one's own mental decision. Thus man gets through his ordinary life with a very scanty supply of genuine acts of judgment, and the same is true, in even greater measure, of the child, whose thought-combinations depend—as a result of imitation—so greatly on environment, and as greatly on former acts of thought—as a result of habit. A forceful impetus is given to judgment when the more convenient expedients of thought-association fail, that is, when the child is confronted by a new situation with which he is unable to cope either by adoption from without or by habit from within. Such a case must at first be shown by a change in the feeling-tone (as we saw even in the infant as feeling of strangeness) (cf. Chapter VII, Section 2); the child is taken aback, either because the new will not fit in with the usual course of perceptual activity, or because, to say the least, he still has a feeling of uncertainty as to whether the old familiar trains of thought will meet the case.[1] This state of mind awakens all the intellectual activity of judgment, and with it that further mental activity of understanding, concluding, enquiry, etc. "Wonder is the beginning of philosophical impulse" (Plato).

As regards quality, the child's earliest judgments are all of a positive nature; they state a condition of things that attracts the child's attention. The comparatively late appearance of negative judgments is all the more noteworthy, since negation, in the form of an expression of will, makes itself felt at an exceptionally early age. But it is, of course, one thing to ward off an unpleasant treatment and quite another to assert the non-existence of a fact. Cf. what was said about the use of "no" (Chapter XXVII, 2).

Negative judgments usually appear in two successive stages.

First in a shape that is not unlike the affective negation, i.e. as an antithesis either in thought or speech. The denial is here, therefore, a reaction to the positive opposite, whether this has occurred as an actual fact or simply as an assertion. Thus the child's positive consciousness of having or knowing something leads to a denial of the other's having the like possession or power.

Badon pas à Zazan, non, à bébé (le ballon n'appartient pas à Suzanne, non, à bébé), a little French girl of only 1 ; 9 ex-

---

[1] K. Groos sees in this two separate sources of critical power; but this sharp distinction seems to me somewhat artificial. Cf. on this point of "psychic surprise" as a criterion of real judgments Bühler, I, p. 297.

claimed. Our own son (2 ; 9) said: *G. has made a sandpie quick. H. has not made one quick.*

But, above all, other people's statements which the child considers wrong call forth antithetical answers:—

G. (2 ; 9) answered a joking "you old boy" with: *Me not old boy me new boy.* On a higher stage we find the second form of negative judgments which, as one would expect, does not begin to develop until antithesis is fully developed. This second form is the sense of loss. Here negation does not appear as reaction, but independently and spontaneously. The disturbance, experienced in the usual course of association by the want of one member of it, is directly translated into an independent intellectual act, and a statement is made as to the want of the missing part. The richer the conscious activity, the more percepts of all kinds brought into consciousness by any impression, so much the more frequently is the opportunity presented to the child of noticing the non-agreement of the fresh impression with these recollections, i.e. of missing something.

Our children showed proofs of missing something at 2 ; 0, and especially when looking at pictures.

Eva (2 ; 1), when looking at a picture of leafless trees, remarked: *No fir-trees, no* (i.e. there are no fir-trees): when at another picture, which no doubt revived a memory of one representing animals: *The dromedary is not there.* In the same way Hilde (2 ; 2), looking at the picture of a child in a cradle, said: *The child not nup, nup* (does not suck its finger).

The sense of something wanting is much more conscious in Scupin's three-year-old son, who examined a carriage of his toy train on all sides, and then cried: *Where is the door then? but, Mummy, how can the people get into the train?* In the same way he noticed the absence of a plate on the engine, of smoke from the chimney, etc.

That the statement of non-existence is of higher mentality than the statement of existence is besides true for all the child's after-life (even for adults as well). Thus Binet, in his graded system of intelligence-tests, requires even the three-year-old child to recognize and name the objects to be seen in a picture, but does not expect children until they reach the age of seven to notice in an imperfect figure what parts are wanting (arms, eye, nose, etc.).

The statement of defects—criticism—is closely allied with

the statement of non-existence. It is true the child only too often experiences in his own person outside criticism and correction of his actions and claims; he has learnt to distinguish between right and wrong by the approval or disapproval of those around him, and now he hastens to pay back like with like.

Gunther (2 ; 5½). When his father called a picture in his book "fine", the boy, who no doubt did not fully understand its details, contradicted with: *ugly*, but at the next picture emphatically stated: *Now that is nice!* (3 ; 11). The young critic would not allow his little sister to call one of her own scribbles "a flower-pot": *It is not like a flower-pot to me.* And, finally, we must here mention the Scupin boy's lordly behaviour in continual fault-finding of the gardener, busy with the flower-garden. *But, man, you really mustn't scatter the earth about so: that is quite naughty—don't hold it like that, it's the wrong way— there, now, you have poured it over—you oughtn't to, Mummy will scold you.* All this is in great measure an echo of scolding and exhortations heard by the child, yet the main fact remains that he notices faults (or what he considers to be such), and this impression produces the speeches reported above.

Thus the child sees the mote in his brother's eye; what about the beam in his own? Self-criticism is much harder than criticism of others, for that aloofness from the object indispensable in criticism is very difficult to achieve with regard to one's self. Hence, instances of self-criticism in children are apparently very rare.

But we see it beginning in the self-correction Hilde (2 ; 3) uttered of her own speech. She is looking for a pencil: *Isn't a write-write been put here, Hilde's,—*HASN'T *a write-write been put here?* Soon after she asks for letter-paper to write on: *Lettel too—* LETTER *it is called.* With regard to self-correction in aussage, cf. Chapter XVIII, 1.

Interesting sidelights are thrown on the genesis of moral self-criticism by the Scupins' observations. When the boy (2 ; 3) did anything forbidden, it often happened that he admonished himself just in the same way as he had so often heard his mother correct him "If the naughty boy climbed, the good one warned him: *Now you, you, will fall directly! little lad, don't knock yourself!* Or if he disobeyed orders: *Stop that, you naughty boy! Mummy will whip you directly.*" I, p. 115. Here, then, direct imitation of warnings constantly heard is more evident than in criticism of others. But even if at first these warnings are uttered from pure association with similar actions, yet gradually the child becomes conscious that he himself, at one time, represents the actor, at another the critic; and whilst uniting in his own person two people hitherto separated, without however quite confusing the points of view, real self-criticism begins to grow out of the imitation of others' criticism, and that warning at last develops into "the voice of conscience". Cf. also example Chapter XIX, 4.

At a somewhat later age self-criticism may become of much more serious value. Gunther, from his fourth year, took very great and frequent pleasure in drawing. But, whilst other children for a long time are perfectly contented with the most faulty of scribbling, Gunther began as early as his sixth year to be a severe critic of his own productions and to destroy them, until he was satisfied with their fulfilment of his intention.

Thus he once attempted to draw on his slate from memory a kitchen-knife that he had just seen; at first the handle was too narrow to please him, then too broad; he rubbed out his attempts six or seven times until a faultless knife was achieved. In this, however, we no longer see an occasional flash of self-criticism, but CONTINUOUS, WATCHFUL JUDGMENT of individual action.

The following example of self-criticism is noteworthy because in it the child expresses the relative nature of a judgment of his own hitherto considered quite final.

The elder son (5 ; 6) of Herr Katz was exceedingly fond of Robinson Crusoe and once when his mother said: Robinson Crusoe is a nice book, I will read it to you, he answered: *Once I used to say Berni* (by Scharrelmann) *was the nicest book. Now I say Robinson Crusoe is the nicest and later on I shall say too another book is the nicest.*

Another side of early power of judgment has to do with what logic calls the "modality" (mode of proceeding) of the judgments.

The difference between the assertory and apodictic method of judgment[1] is probably non-existent in early childhood. What appeals to the child as fact, he at once accepts as if it must be

---

[1] Assertory = judgments asserting facts, e.g. it rains to-day. Apodictic = judgments asserting necessities (axioms), e.g. the part is less than the whole.

so, and he does not yet recognize any other necessary condition (for instance, the logical) as connected with fact; such recognition requires complicated deductive processes impossible until a much later period.

On the other hand, the development from the dogmatic stage to the problematic, and hence to the purely fictitious, takes place at a very early age. It is remarkable how the sense of validity already varies in assurance.

At first every act of judgment is accompanied by absolute conviction of its correctness; thus thought in the individual, as in the race, begins with dogmatism. But doubts soon begin to rise, and about 3 ; 0 we can already find in the child's questions and statements expressions of the problematic stage: *perhaps, probably, I suppose.* And still more: about the same time the conscious comparison between the subjective supposition and the objective reality takes place, and is vocally expressed in the right use of *I think, fancy, believe.*

Gunther (2 ; 9). "When the soup is brought in he supposes: *Snow soup:* but when it is served out he notices his mistake, and says—cautiously now: *Rice soup I think.*"

Eva (2 ; 8). "The child after her morning nap often does not get to the dinner-table until we have finished one or two courses; lately she came a little earlier, as we were still at our soup, and expressed aloud her astonishment: *Why, you are eating soup: I thought you were eating potatoes and vegetables.*"
Frau H. Neugebauer (II) reports much the same of her son, who, at the age of 2 ; 7, often used such terms of speech as: *I thought you weren't here: I thought you were in the kitchen.*

If in such supposals the assurance of validity still leans to the positive side, it no longer does so in "fiction"; something is thought of as actual fact, although there is a conscious sense of its non-actuality. The significance of such fictitious judgments in the child's life, especially in play, has been fully discussed in the section on Consciousness of Illusion (Chapter XIX, 3).

CHAPTER XXVIII

FURTHER STAGES OF THOUGHT

Enquiry and Deduction

1. GENERAL CONSIDERATIONS.

IF the origin of individual judgment is to be found in a mental condition of startled "surprise", the same process may be repeated in the power of judgment now gained. The child does not remain satisfied with the isolated fact that he states, or with the use he makes of it; astonishment awakes in him anew and tries to take effect in a further act of judgment.

This need for further thought is the starting-point for important thought-structures in the child. They all have one point in common, viz. that he finds himself faced with problems. Side by side with what is known and familiar there suddenly appears an X, demanding transformation from the unknown to the known. And this X, his mental task, becomes the motive power of the thought-process. That which must now first be discovered decides the separate steps. The child enquires, reflects, thinks over the matter, seeks for new light. Now we can understand children's well-known persistent questioning, understand, too, the fact—which will be illustrated directly by examples—that causal thought and conclusions more generally proceed by questions than by statements.

Before we discuss the mental processes in early childhood from the standpoint of our own material we will briefly call attention to the very interesting and important researches carried on recently by Piaget in this subject. His books I and II, it is true, follow the child far on into school-age but contain weighty conclusions too concerning the early mental processes of the young child.

Piaget lays chief stress on proving the essentially different nature of thought in the child and in the adult. In the child's thought we find present at the same time two apparently incompatible principles, viz. "syncretism" and "juxtaposition". Syncretism is the blending of all the contributory factors of a thought into a diffused whole, in which egocentric desire and imagination are certainly the determining partners, although the whole is accepted in all simplicity and without criticism.

Juxtaposition is the unconnected and unaffected following of and nearness of thoughts to each other instead of their hierarchical arrangement in a logical connection.

Piaget now tries to show the process of PROGRESSIVE OBJECTIVITY of thought in general, just as we endeavoured to carry out the same aim with regard to individual ideas in the preceding section. And here, too, he introduces—as a very noteworthy fresh point of view—the SOCIAL motive in his explanation. As long as the child's thought is egocentric, there is no necessity for the process of a really logical nature, viz. the VERIFICATION (reason and justification) of his thoughts. But this need arises as soon as the child wishes to arrive at an understanding with his companions as to their particular world. Then his thoughts must take on a shape which can also be understood and recognized by the others; the demand of his fellow human beings for an objective world that all may share opposes the purely subjective individual world. Then he has to occupy himself with the reasons, proofs, justifications of his thoughts, has to bring them into connection with other circumstances. *"La preuve est née de la discussion."* But in the working-out of this fruitful thought Piaget goes too far if he dates the beginning of that objectivity process no sooner than after the period of early childhood, i.e. not before the seventh or eighth year. As we have already mentioned, this is possibly due to the fact that Piaget gets his material from children's conversations amongst themselves. But it is the distinguishing feature of children's thought that its natural development takes place in the intercourse with their mental superiors, with people who can give help in their mental difficulties and an answer—no matter how simple—to their questions. But this development leads—as the examples in the following pages will show—much earlier to children's thought of really logical structure than Piaget would lead us to expect.

In other directions too Piaget is inclined to ascribe too long a duration of the simple forms of thought in childhood. Our examples of clauses which from three years on express the logical division of thought into main and subordinate positions show that simple juxtaposition of thoughts may be ended as early as the middle of early childhood by the comprehension of their interdependent relations (see Chapter X, 4 of this book). The following sections select for consideration from among the manifold facts of progress in mental activity, causal thought, drawing of conclusions in childhood and mental games.

2. Causal Thought

As a preliminary stage to causal thought we have become acquainted with a number of phenomena taking place entirely in the region of perceptual activity. On the one hand, the child had associated the sensation of individual movement with the sight or hearing of actions so produced, and thus formed firm connections between his personal activity and its effects (cf. Chapter VI, 1). On the other hand, he had so closely linked together two or more outer impressions, frequently following on one another, that a fresh appearance of the first impression was sufficient to awake expectation of the second (cf. Chapter VI, 2). According to Hume's well-known theory of causality, this is all that is required to produce a causal ideation. But even the child shows how insufficient is that derivation from psychological association alone. For it would not explain how the child arrives at asking why, as regards facts lacking that natural associative completion. And this "why" question does not aim at getting any presentation that can be connected with the momentary perception, but is directed to the intentional object, which is thought of with the perception. The child who asks: *The tray is so hot; why then?* (Gunther, 2 ; 10) does not want to know why his fingers feel the sensation of heat, just then, but how the quality of heat belonging to the tray fits in with other objective facts.

In other words: Causal consciousness is not a phenomenon of perceptual-activity, but an element of intentional thought. It is true, acquired perceptions are indispensable to stimulate it and to provide it with raw material for its operation. Yet causal thought is as little the result of a frequently repeated succession of perceptions as objective thought is the result of the simultaneous union of perceptions, but it is an independent product of man's growing capacity of thought.[1]

The "why" question is only one amongst the manifold symptoms of the awaking causal consciousness; other questions

[1] The psychological genesis of causal thought has indeed nothing to do directly with its theoretical value; nevertheless, it is noteworthy that even child-study decides to discard the purely empiric origin of causal consciousness, to accept an *a priori* element (the growing power of thought).

too (e.g. who made that), attempts to find a reason unaided, understanding of the reason given by others, the mention of a consequence following from a former perception—all these show what efforts the child is making to think beyond the simple individual thought and to master causal relations. That something unique and in its way new is taking place in the child's psychic life is corroborated by the suddenness with which these different symptoms of causal thought all make their appearance almost simultaneously.

We made especially characteristic observations of this in the case of Eva; the importance of the subject justifies, I think, the illustration of the strong and varied nature of causal consciousness by a considerable number of examples. (The various stages were reached by this child at an unusually early age; the same thought-development in other children does not show itself, as a rule, until a few months later—after three years of age.)

We had our first proof, to our surprise, as early as 2 ; 3. The child, who up till then had drunk her milk from a bottle, was to be accustomed to a cup, but had so strenuously resisted all attempts to teach her, that the idea had been given up for the time. Soon after, the child happened one evening to break the bottle. The next morning the nursemaid brought her milk in a cup again, with the explanation: "You broke the bottle yesterday, so now you must drink out of a cup." And she actually did drink. That the explanation had been really understood was shown shortly after, when her mother praised her for drinking from the cup. Then the child said: *Eva broke the bottle, Eva drink from cup.*

A whole number of further examples occur in one month (2 ; 5). She saw a man in the garden watering with the hose: *Why does he sprinkle?*

(2 ; 5.) She was told not to take hold of the sugar-basin: *Why, my hands are not dirty!*

(2 ; 5.) She was told: Don't sit on the sand, it is too cold. Eva: *Has it been raining?*

(2 ; 5.) When she came in from the garden her father said: "Your hands are icy-cold." Eva: *My hands are not icy-cold, why, I had a little coat on.* Thus she emphasized that she was not cold because she was more warmly dressed than usual.

(2 ; 5.) E. had seen a captive balloon floating over the houses

but had not noticed that it was fastened by a line. After some days the following conversation took place. Eva: *Is the air balloon still there?* Mother: "No." *Have people taken it down?* "Yes." *But there wasn't any string to it.*

(2 ; 5.) We were talking of going a walk when a chance look into the garden made her say: *But the trees can't go with us.* To the question: "Why not?" she answered at first: *Because they don't want,* but on being asked again: *Because the tree is so firm in.* A few days before she had seen how little trees were planted, and so had got an ocular presentation of their being "firm in". Six months later (2 ; 11) the report runs: The "why" question is now finding its culmination. In numberless things that attract her attention, she enquires as to the cause: *Mummy, you have got a ring on, why then? The man in the picture has such a big tummy, why then?* That this was in no way a stereotyped unintelligent figure of speech is shown, even more plainly, by other examples. She notices that her parents do not take their coffee in the ordinary room: *Why don't you have coffee to-day in the study?* Indeed, she is already beginning to connect causal questions with occurrences, not actually taking place at the moment, but only occupying her memory. In this way one question referred to a rain-cape, used indiscriminately by both parents: *Father, why did you then, this morning, put on mother's cape?* When her father once happened to be present when she was going to bed and played with her, she remembered that this did not often happen, as her father was generally busy at that time, and, quite unprompted, put the surprising question: *Why must you then be always working?* [1]

From these examples it is clear how far from accurate Hume's theory is as regards the real genesis of causal consciousness. For the first incitements to its awakening do not in the least consist in the expectation of accustomed associations, but in fresh situations, for which no expectations or feelings of familiarity have yet been formed. Indeed, it might perhaps even be said the movement of perceptual activity along wonted paths does indeed result in an instinctive expectant attitude to the recurring causal connections with the objective facts, but would probably never, by itself, lead to a causal consciousness. This needs for its awakening the shock which an unaccustomed arrangement produces in the child; now instead of the habitual

[1] For further examples of the "why" question, see Chapter X, 4 of this book.

course of associated percepts, thought is set working, and demands a causal origin for what has attracted the attention.[1] For the first time in his life, Scupin's son had noticed that his fingers had a rosy light when he held them up against the sunshine, and immediately he formed a causal synthesis between this impression and the sun visible at the same time—that is, then, between two impressions never before associated—*"the sun makes my fingers blood-red"*.

The fact that wonder at what is unusual is the signal for the awakening of the need for causal thought explains a psychological phenomenon in childhood, especially emphasized by psychoanalysis, viz. the interest taken in the question of birth. Undoubtedly the child is keenly interested in finding an answer to this problem; this is indirectly proved by the invention of the stork and other fables to satisfy their thirst for knowledge, and directly by the varied questions propounded by the child. But there is absolutely no reason to look upon this problem as the pivot round which revolves the whole of the child's early view of life. Psychoanalysts believe that the question as to the origin of children plays consciously and unconsciously a part in the child's psychic inner life, such as adults never suspect; and this part is again connected with the sexual relations attaching to the problem of birth; that the child unconsciously creates for himself marvellous systems of "infantile sexual theories" which are secretly set up in opposition to the adult's stork and other fables apparently accepted in all good faith by the children.

The unprejudiced observation of healthy children gives no support to this assertion. So far, indeed, it is correct that the question of causality is principally aroused by experiences of a most pronounced affective-tone. And such an experience—in the sense of the breaking-through of the already existing—is the sudden appearance of another little human being. This brings home to the child that his own life, up till now accepted as a matter of course, also once had a beginning. So this interest, too, joins all the other causal questions called forth by striking and unusual occurrences, and so belongs amongst the manifold expressions of childish curiosity. Psychoanalysis is, indeed, on that account, inclined to look upon these other apparently harmless questions as masked sexual questions hidden under

[1] Bühler, too, emphasizes this point in his exhaustive analysis of causal thought in children.

symbols; we would rather, contrariwise, conclude that all those questions as to the origin of beautiful Christmas presents, whether those from the tree or those of little babies, have their source in A COMMON FEELING OF WONDER; this feeling may indeed have many modifications, but really sexual factors are—at least in the age with which we are concerned—scarcely ever to be met with. Also at this period it is a fact that children are very quickly put off with any answer and completely satisfied with it. Their desire to know the cause of anything unusual is indeed keen, but has as yet no depth nor persistence; they are, in reality, in far higher degree creatures of the moment than psychoanalysis supposes. In this point we again meet with the erroneous projection of the adult's psychic attitudes into the child.

And does not the same law—that causal thought develops, not from the familiar but from the new—hold good for all human mental growth? The mythological causal explanation is always connected with experiences out of the ordinary course of events, with elementary natural phenomena and particular dispensations of providence. The sequence of events in their daily repetition is accepted as a matter of course, and is immediately shown in the automatic attitude of expectancy and in an adjustment of action in accordance with it. It is not until very much later that thought becomes ripe for the knowledge that causal problems lie hidden in these everyday events. Every single branch of science, too, follows the same course, developing its need of enquiry on the striking abnormal phenomena of its special province, and only by slow degrees addressing itself to the riddles offered by the normal.

The causality at first accessible to human thought is therefore the individual causality of a special happening, not the general causal law that the same effects always arise from the same causes. (For the application of this principle, cf. the discussion later of conclusions by transduction, Chapter XXVIII, Section 3.)

The primitive causal consciousness is moreover to a great degree anthropomorphic; the cause is looked upon as "intention", the occurrence as a purposeful action, as a "making"— even in cases not concerned with human life.

Piaget (I, 212 sqq.) made a note of all the spontaneous questions asked by a boy (6 ; 0—7 ; 0) during a period of ten months. Of the 1,125 questions 360 were "why" questions; of these 183 referred to human motivation, ninety, it is true were concerned with non-human things but under the influence of the personifying point of view were considered as intentional making. Only thirteen questions evidenced the need of mechanical causal statement by positional contact.

Piaget, who evidently only recognizes the last method of causal connection as causality, therefore designates the child's thought as "pre-causal". This designation seems misleading to me; the child quite evidently feels the need of grasping what is given as "worked" (effected) by something or other, and in this rather than in the special method of the coherence of the process of "working" lies the actual germ of causal consciousness.

Another generality of the causal law, namely that it is true of everything that exists, is apparent to the child comparatively early, and indeed in a train of thought most evidently not acquired from outside influences, but as a necessary consequence of his thought-development. The child is here confronted with the well-known antinomy that, on the one hand, for any cause discovered, another more remote cause must be demanded, and on the other, that thought, in spite of this, demands satisfaction in some final cause. We may well see a first trace of this mental difficulty in the following conversation between Hilde (4 ; 2) and her mother.

Hilde: *Who was with me then when my mother was little?* Mother: "Then, Hilde hadn't come yet; when I was little I was with my mother, Hilde's grandmother." *Who was with grandmother when she was little?* "Your great-grandmother." *And who was with all mothers?* The child was, it is true, content with the answer: "Each one was always with her own mother."

The problem grows plainer when the child has heard of God as the cause of all things. That, to begin with, completely satisfies his enquiry as to the causes of all separate things and occurrences. But as regards God Himself? "Who made God? seems to be a question", says Sully,[1] "to which all young minds in their thirst for knowledge come at a certain stage of childish thought." I am inclined to doubt whether this is really so generally true as this statement maintains. But that occasionally a child stumbles upon this question by itself may be shown

[1] 3rd edition, p. 110.

by two examples both occurring in children of the same age. Gunther (5 ; 4): "A few days before the child had been told the Creation story. Without any further questions as to details, his little brain must have found many a problem to solve, and one evening, as he was being washed, he suddenly burst out with: *How remarkable it is that the good God can create Himself!*"

The thought of *causa sui*—of that formula with which the greatest metaphysicians have tried to cut the knot of the above antinomy—has here been found unaided by a little boy of five and a half.

Herr and Frau Katz report (II, p. 124) the following conversation with their son (5 ; 5). Theodore: *Was God born?* Mother: "I will tell you when you are bigger." T.: *But God made men so he must then have been born himself.* M.: "God was not born and God never dies. . . ." T.: *If God does not die, then no men ever die.* This last step in the boy's thought, a pronounced transduction conclusion, leads us on to the next section.

3. The Child's Power of Drawing Conclusions

Some of the functions of causal thought discussed above already took shape as conclusions, but we must give separate treatment to this highest operation of thought. The theory of the conclusion is recognized as the fundamental fact of ordinary logic; but the difference between the logical and psychological point of view is nowhere seen so distinctly as here.

All conclusion is a progress from given judgments to fresh ones. We can therefore from a psychological point of view only speak of the actual drawing of conclusions when we think of what is given as well as what is found in the form of judgments. Hence many psychic processes which, according to their logical effect, might be classed as conclusions cannot psychologically be regarded as such; and it is misleading to use such names for them as "unconscious conclusions" (Helmholtz). We can certainly represent the child's (0 ; 6) shrinking at the approach of a cold sponge (before it touches her) as a conclusion somewhat in this way: the ocular impression of the sponge had often been directly followed by the unpleasant impression of cold and wet; now the ocular impression of the sponge reappears; therefore there is again expectation of cold and wet. In reality, however, not a single one of these better judgments is present, but only an associative completion which has nothing at all to do with thought (Chapter VI, 2).

It is more difficult to decide whether we may talk of "conclusions" in all those cases in which only the final step of the process, that is the so-called conclusion, is expressed, as a judgment without any mention of premises, but, in early development, such cases are, however, the rule. When Hilde (2 ; 6) sees her supper prepared by her mother, and not, as usual, by the nurse Bertha, and asks: *Bertha away?* such an utterance can arise in one of two ways: either the sight of the supper-preparation from association called forth the idea of the maid, and this perception gave rise to the negative judgment of a sense of loss as the only act of thought; or, again, she might think, "usually Bertha gets supper", but not express her thought, and this latent judgment leads in correct conclusion to the expression of the supposal that the maid must be absent. Karl Groos thinks that only the first explanation is correct, that the apparent conclusion is only a simple judgment, and, at very most, those premises are realized afterwards, only if the child is led by a question (e.g. why, then, should Bertha be away?) to justify its supposal.[1]

No doubt Groos will be right in many cases, but there is no reason at all to exclude the other possibility. The non-expression of a judgment does not necessarily imply that it has not existed in thought. It is much more in accordance with child-nature not to mention parts of an act of thought, which, in themselves, have no significance, and only to translate into speech the conclusions of the process. We may conclude that the conclusion passes over the threshold of thought as well as of speech. The premises have much less conscious power; whether in consequence of this they remain behind the threshold of speech only, or even of thought as well, cannot be determined in the cases mentioned.

Karl Groos is, no doubt, led to his opinion by a belief that the child's conclusions only appear in this shortened form of a judgment-conclusion. This is certainly the first stage, but at an early age we also meet with the expression of several judgment-conclusions in which the different links of a chain of thought are plainly discernible. Thus Hilde (also 2 ; 6) once said:

[1] I, pp. 234 sqq.

Cannot say "morning", have such greasy hands. That meant: my hands are so greasy, therefore I cannot give you them in good-morning greeting. And after 3 ; o we often find expression of long trains of reasoning, arising quite spontaneously from the child's own desire for thought, not, in any way, as only the result of adults' suggestive questions.

With regard to the form of these conclusions, the psychogenetic consideration is the reverse of that of formal logic. For that form which, in logic, is the main type of the conclusion, namely the syllogism, takes quite a secondary place in the development of the child's conclusion. The inductive conclusion takes a second place in logic, but it is much more important in early thought. But the real genesis of the child's conclusion has to do with those forms that as analogy and similar conclusions play a very unimportant part in logic. These we designate as transduction-conclusions. Since the child's early judgments are directed almost exclusively to single facts or ideas, there is, at first, no possibility either of their derivation from general judgments (deduction) or of a leading-up to general judgments (induction), but always rather only a leading-over from a single judgment to another approximate single judgment, that is, then, a mental process which we can best designate as transduction. These transduction-conclusions of the child can be subdivided into conclusions of Exact Similarity, of Difference and of Likeness (analogy).

In the first case a conclusion is drawn that the same result will arise from the same causes, e.g. if a relative brought the child something on his last visit, he will easily expect another present on his next. In the following example, too, an earlier experience leads to a judgment under like circumstances. Hilde (3 ; 2). Along the balcony railing a string had been fixed for some reason or other. The child, on seeing it, asked: *What hangs here then? Is it put up for the washing?* Such and similar psychic processes take place daily in great number from the third year on, but their real intellectual value is very slight, often practically nil. For, as a matter of fact, the conclusion may arise as a purely associative process, owing to the similarity of the suppositions. Conscious conservation of energy declines mental exertion when mechanical, perceptual process will produce the same result. We therefore find the same truth in conclusions as in causal thought; real mental work only begins when the associative process is broken off by new experiences, or at any rate obstructed.

The conclusions from difference are therefore acts of much more pronounced intelligence. If the existing situation differs in character from the usual one, the child may be impelled to draw similarly different conclusions from it, or to make different hypotheses about it. That in so doing he states the conclusion as a cautious question instead of in the form of a positive assertion makes no essential difference in its psychological mental nature.

Hilde (3 ; 0). "Her father was lying on the balcony on a lounge-chair, and the child was sitting with her back turned to him on his lap. An umbrella, to keep off the sun, had been put up over both, and its handle (invisible to H.) had been fastened to the balcony railing, so that it did not require holding. As her father took her hands in both of his, she at once exclaimed: *Is the umbrella alone?* Since her father had two hands free, Hilde concluded that the umbrella could not be held in the hand as usual."

Scupin's son (3 ; 6). The boy, standing on a bridge, noticed, for the first time, that the river-water was moving and asked where it flowed to. When his mother told him that all water ran into a great basin, the sea, he replied: *Well, but when all the water has run out, then the ships will not be able to float any more.* (II, p. 133.)

A year later, the same boy had some talk with his father about a skull lying on the writing-table. He had often seen the skull before, but not until he was 4 ; 8 did he enquire as to its origin. When he learnt that it came from a dead man, he said at once: *Why didn't the poor man turn into an angel, see, here is his head?* Since, therefore, he supposed that the whole human being after death went to heaven, he concluded from the head left on earth that he could not have turned into an angel. (II, p. 133.)

The following example shows conclusion from difference in a higher stage of development. Gunther (4 ; 10). At dinner we were giving him little counting-tests in play, and he counted the cheeks of those sitting at table correctly as ten. The next question: "How many eyes have we got all together?" he answered from analogy and correctly again as ten. To the further question: "How many heads?" he said at first ten again, but immediately corrected himself: *O no, I'll just count*—and he counted five. When he was now asked: How is it we have ten cheeks and only five heads, his answer ran: *Because cheeks are always two and heads always one.* This difference in each individual had led him, after a short confusion, to the insight that the total must be different as well.

Sometimes conclusions from difference take on the form of a reversed conclusion. If *a* is referred back to *b*, then *not-a* must be referred back to *not-b*, and vice versa.

Thus our Eva (2 ; 10½) made a positive conclusion from negative propositions:—

Her mother, not being well, was in bed, and Eva asked her father: *Why are you not in bed?* Father: "Because I am not ill. Eva said to her mother: *Why are you lying in bed?* Mother: "Well, now, why do you think?" Eva: *Because you are ill.*

Hilde (3 ; 8) drew an even more spontaneous conclusion. "Her father at dinner would only take a little vegetable, and gave as reason in answer to Hilde's enquiry that he had eaten too much breakfast. Hilde: *Then you are only a little hungry, and so you only eat a little.* Then she noticed that her mother had more vegetables on her plate, and drew a conclusion at once as to her smaller breakfast: *Then have you eaten only a little bread and butter.*"

Conclusions from analogy are a combination of the two previous kinds, since certain agreements are noticed in some difference, and hence further correspondences are inferred.

Eva (3 ; 7). "When her mother said she was going to lie in the hammock, Eva said thoughtfully: *Then it will certainly burst. When Else sat in it, it burst too, and you are just as big as Else.*"

Scupin's son (5 ; 1) asked: *Is there gas in the cloud to make it fly?* He knew in any case that it was gas in air balloons that made them fly. (II, 167.)

The chief field of application for analogy-conclusions is offered to the child in the comparison of himself with other people, and vice versa.

Thus Scupin's son (4 ; 8) concluded from his own body that there must be a skeleton belonging to the skull already mentioned. *But where is the bone then that is inside the stomach? And* (instead of "for") *there are bones in my legs and arms as well.* Gunther's conclusion at 4 ; 6 takes the opposite direction, passing from others to himself. One evening, when washing, he noticed his breasts, and asked with hesitation: *Can men give milk to little children as well?* And when he was told "no", the intelligent causal question followed: *But then why do men have breasts?* But such childish comparisons of himself with others are, above all, called forth by the observation that people at different ages can and do act differently; as soon as that is noticed the relation between great and small, and the expectation of being big himself, and all the changes that this will bring forth, begin to occupy the child's mind very greatly. But the conclusion from analogy lies at the root of all variations of this inexhaustible theme.

Scupin's son (3 ; 3), after considering his father's beard for some time: *And my beard is still inside my skin.*

Hilde (3 ; 5) is constantly uttering such speeches as: *When I'm big, I'll learn to knit. When I'm big, I can open the door by myself,* etc. Gunther (4 ; 7), as he looked at a sacred picture, asked: *When I have got to be as good as Jesus, shall I get such a pretty shine round my head?*

On the other hand, a child of barely three may already feel itself big compared with a brother of six months only. Her father asked Hilde: "Ought Gunther to eat cake?" Answer: *Not a bit.* Father: "But isn't he hungry?" Answer: *When he is big, then he can eat.*

Hilde (3 ; 2). "Her father is laughing at her little brother's eager greed when he is being fed. Then he had to submit to Hilde's precocious exhortation: *Before, when you were little, you always did just the same.*"

Rasmussen reports the following intelligent remark of his daughter Ruth (age not notified; about six years). Her younger sister had done something in a wrong way, so Ruth said; *No, Sonia, if I'd been you I wouldn't have done that . . . but if I'd really been you, I would have done it of course.* (II, p. 186.)

We cannot draw any sharply dividing lines between the transduction conclusions discussed above, consisting only of single judgments, and those conclusions in which generalized judgments are pronounced—induction and deduction conclusions. For it is quite possible that in transduction the two single judgments are not the only thoughts, but that a generalized judgment co-operates as intermediary without finding vocal expression. For example: the boy who infers from his father's beard that he himself will get a beard at some later time may perhaps have had the intermediate thought: all men have beards; in this case his inference from his father's beard to a beard common to every man was inductive, but that from the common beard to his own, at a future time, was deductive. And since psychic conservation of energy, even at that early age, results in the non-expression of intermediate steps, many inferences, apparently due to analogy or consideration of difference, may be in reality, especially at a somewhat later age, such disguised inductive-deductive conclusions.

Yet this must not, in any way, be looked upon as a general rule. The direct leap from a concrete single judgment to another of a similar nature is, without doubt, the earlier form, and by exact observation we are also able to trace how very gradual is the development of the power of abstraction (i.e. the formation of generalized judgments).[1]

We have already spoken of "plural" ideas (Chapter XXVII, 2) which dwell on the similarity of many objects without proceeding to grouping of them together into a collective (group) idea. This grouping together is only possible in a generalized judgment obtained by the way of induction; and now it is evident that, at a certain stage of his development, the child is not yet capable of such a generalization even when it is suggested to him.

Hilde (3 ; 6). "When looking at an animal picture-book, she began to ask if a certain bird laid eggs. Her mother replied: 'Yes, all birds lay eggs.' But this general affirmation had as yet no meaning for her, for she pointed to every other bird with the same question: *Does this one lay eggs, this one too?* Her— mother always repeated: 'Yes, all birds lay eggs,' but without any result."

Yet as early as 3 ; 8 the signs of abstraction appeared. "As some one in fun tried to persuade her that the meat on the table was not a joint, she said: *I call it a joint, Mummy does too, we all call it that.* Soon after she noticed a brown horse with a white spot on his forehead, and asked: *Do all horses have a white spot?*"

Even a little earlier we noticed an exactly similar question in Gunther (3 ; 5), who, when he saw a cupboard with glass doors, asked: *Are there always glasses like that in all cupboards?*

[1] Cf. with this subject the "abstraction" tests made by Eliasberg, discussed in Chapter XXIX, 1c.

It is true these generalizations have only very little logical value; their question-form alone shows that they are not yet actual inductive inferences, but only a vague supposition, produced, moreover, by an entirely isolated momentary perception. Real induction, in the sense of forming into one general statement all that is common in a sequence of observations, and of enquiry as to its application for all further cases, seems normally not to occur before the end of the fifth year. We now give several instances which again represent various stages of induction. Induction appears in the first case in response to an outer impulse.

In the counting-game mentioned above, Gunther (4 ; 10) was asked how many fingers he had. He counted them: *ten.* "How many has mother?" He again counted ten. "How many have Hilde, Eva, the nursemaid?" Each time he said ten without counting, drawing his conclusion from analogy. When he had thus found the number of fingers in many people, his mother looked at him enquiringly: "Well, then?" And from his slow deliberation came the answer: *Then . . . everybody has ten fingers.*

The other case of Hilde is especially instructive, because, in the child's attitude to a definite problem—that water apparently takes on the colour of the vessel containing it, we have observations of two different phases of development: in one she stops short at analogy, in the other she steps forward without help to induction.

Hilde (3 ; 5½) got water to drink in a blue glass whilst we had white ones. Then she said: *When the glass is blue, then the water is blue.* We pointed to our glasses: "And what is the water?" *There the glass is white, and there the water is white.* It would be difficult to find an inference from analogy more aptly expressed.

One and a half years later Hilde (4 ; 10) for the first time had water handed to her in a nickel cup. We others again had ordinary glasses. This time the child remarked: *Whatever water is put in, anything that is silver or yellow, that's how the water always looks. And yet it is always white really. How does that come so then?* She proves therefore, that although water is always white (i.e. without colour), yet it always looks like the vessel in which it is put—an induction quite correctly drawn.

D. and R. Katz (II, p. 117) report the following conclusion by their son 5 ; 4.

Frau Katz told the mother's help that it was ten o'clock and the young lady replied that her watch was only half past nine. The mother replied: "My husband's watch and mine are both ten o'clock, I think that is right." Theodore: *Yes Mummy, Auntie O's watch is wrong.* Mother: "Why do you think so?" T.: *Yes, because two watches are ten and one watch half-past nine.* Thus drawing the conclusion from the majority of watches that they gave the right time.

The following example, in conclusion, shows a very advanced stage of generalization.

Gunther (5 ; 5). Hilde having complained that she was kept waiting for some delicacy G. was already enjoying, her father reminded her of the proverb: "Who laughs last, laughs best." Shortly after, G. ate first the more tasty yolk of his poached egg and then the white. When he was reproached with this he said: *That might be turned into a proverb too: The worst is eaten first, and then the best.*

We are here dealing with a double generalization: the understanding of the general sense of what is meant by a proverb; and the concrete experience with the egg is enlarged to a general statement.

The child makes a less frequent use of purely deductive inferences. This may be due less to their logical difficulty than to the natural mental needs; for when the child makes a special statement he but seldom needs to mention the generalized suppositions from which it may be derived. Indeed, the child is not as a rule conscious of that generalized suppoal until he is induced by questions to justify his special assertions or convictions.

Eva (3 ; 1). The mother's dress with a train was on view, and her father asks Eva in fun: "Is that your dress?" E. (laughing): *Children cannot wear a giant dress like that.* Father: "Is the dress for me?" E. (laughing again): *Uncles* (her general name for all men) *don't wear dresses.* Father: "Am I an uncle then?" E.: *You are a father, you know, so of course you are an uncle.* It is noteworthy that, in the first and second answers, the conclusion itself—as being self-evident—is not expressed; only the major premise is said each time: "children cannot wear giant dresses" In the last answer the major premise (all fathers are men) is unexpressed, but that it existed in thought is evident from the faultless execution of the subsumption.

Scupin (4 ; 1). The boy had been given some acorns that he

wanted to plant and turn into trees. Then he remembered a re-mark of his mother's that "gnats always come out of trees". So he continued: *Well, I suppose there are gnats inside the acorns ? Trees always come out of acorns, and then the gnats must be inside them too.* The "must" in the last sentence shows that the boy already had a sense of the necessity of deductive inference.

An instance, to end with, of an unusual form of conclusion whose analysis may be left to the reader's intelligence. The child expresses but one single judgment, but this presupposes on account of the unusual, particular negative idea of the subject a fairly involved power of thought. "Hilde (5 ; 2) knew that her grandmother had a bracelet-watch, but had never yet seen anybody else with one. Now, one day, she heard her father say to her mother: 'You must have a bracelet-watch too.' Then H. asked: *Do many people, not grandmothers, have one?"*

4. Exercises in Thought

From about their fifth year intelligent children readily respond to mental exercises requiring a little thought. The alteration between keen effort and solution is often accompanied by real pleasurable excitement; if the child so long as he has not found the answer feels the superiority of the better-informed adult, so much the greater his satisfaction when he manages to solve the problem; his own small ego now feels raised to the same level as his questioner. Children also like to enjoy the superior position of being themselves the propounder of problems; they set tests and riddles with an extraordinary feeling of clever superiority. Lastly, there is a third possibility: the child sets himself problems and makes eager efforts to solve them. This is undoubtedly a higher form of mental activity than the other two, for it requires originality to discover mental tasks as well as the mental effort needed for their successful accomplishment. Within the age-limits with which we are concerned, this form of mental activity is only to be found in children of special talent and of unusually keen mental interests.

The height of development reached in all mental problems depends, moreover, very greatly on outside influences, i.e. it is largely influenced by the frequency with which these mental games are played in the nursery and kindergarten.

The whole subject of these recreative mental problems has so far received little attention in child-psychology, and we too must content ourselves with giving a little material for consideration.

We will begin with an example of mental problems set by adults and solved by children.

Eva (5 ; 0), Gunther (7 ; 5). "At dinner to-day we tested Eva with addition of things of different denominations. 'What is one tablecloth and one dinner napkin?' Eva only answers: *Two*. When we ask: 'Two what?' she cannot answer. Evidently she does not understand the meaning of the question. Gunther interposes with: *Two cloths.*

"Then we again ask Eva: 'An eye and an ear?' Now she answers correctly: *Two parts of the face.* (Gunther: *Two parts of the body*.) 'An apple and a pear?' Eva: *Two fruits.* (Gunther: *Two different fruits*.) 'A glass and a cup?' Eva: *Two pieces of tableware*. Then Gunther says with admiration: *Ah, I hadn't thought of anything yet.* 'A brooch and a clock?' Eva: *Two bright things*. (Gunther: *Two useful things*.) Gunther always waited for Eva to speak first. The actual intelligence shown consisted less in the different right answers than in the speed with which Eva —after her first failure and Gunther's help—had grasped what was wanted."

Frau and Herr Katz report of their son 5 ; 5 when in a railway carriage travelling with his father: Father (in fun) "Has the railway carriage got eyes?" Theodore: *Yes, the cushions.* F.: "And its mouth?" T.: *The line under them.* F.: pointing to the luggage rack, "And that?" T.: *That's the brain.* F.: "And the arms?" T.: *The doors.* F.: "And the legs?" T.: *The wheels.* F.: "The father?" T.: *The engine.* F.: "The mother?" T.: *The tender.* F.: "What does the train eat?" T.: *People that he spits out again.* (After some deliberation.) *The other trains are his brothers.*

Question and answer followed each other at lightning speed and Theodore really enjoyed this intellectual game.

The following example shows questions put not only by adults but by the child as well:—

Scupin (5 ; 7½). "To-day when we saw in the distance a boat drawn up on the shore, he asked: *Now, Lotty, why do you think the boat looks so small now and is so big when we get close to it?* He was pleased she did not know and that he could give a very circumstantial explanation of the smallness of everything seen from a distance. In order to make the boy think, we often answered his questions, even when quite intelligent, with others; thus when Bubi wanted to know why most of the tree-trunks along the bank of the Oder looked so black on the one side and greener on the other, we told him to think over again himself why that should be. The boy considered, and then said: *Perhaps because the snow comes from the one side and not from the other.*"

Next comes a record of exercises that the child sets himself, and this one of arithmetical problems for which Gunther in his sixth year showed a quite spontaneous interest.

Gunther (5 ; 7½). "Gunther shows remarkable pleasure in reckoning; we help him very little in his attempts, and he—following the self-help method—sets himself tasks of his own invention. Amongst these a series-form is very typical; he goes from one to another by a kind of analogy, e.g. *1 and 1 is 2; 2 and 2 is 4; 4 and 4 is 8; 8 and 8 is* 16, etc. Yesterday he said suddenly: 9 *and* 8 *is* 17. His mother: 'How did you count that?' Somewhat embarrassed, he answered: *Well,* 9 *and* 9 *is* 18, *isn't it?so* 9 *and* 8 *is* 17."

(5 ; 8½). "He has an irrepressible liking for calculation; he is always assuring us how nice it is to calculate.   He is beginning to divide, e.g. the half of 60 is 30; makes discoveries such as: *2 and 2 is 4 and twice 2 is 4, but it is not like that with 3 and 3 and 3 times 3*—and wonders why not. Everything suggests a problem to him. Eva happens to have on her napkin-ring the figure 9, Gunther 3. Eva says in fun: *O, I'm* 9 *years old now,* to which Gunther answers: *O, I'm only 3 years old, so Eva is* 6 *years older than me* —Or he calculates how old Eva will be when he is such and such an age."

We will end with some examples of riddles, where the children not only guessed but invented some for themselves.

Many children's riddles show a primitive logical form and a sharp contrast in the problem (e.g. "What ring is not round?" or, "It has a throat and yet cannot speak, what is that?"). The answer (herring, bottle) then changes the antithesis into synthesis. We have already in various places shown the liking shown by children for the obviously logical form of antithesis (Chapter XXVII, Section 3); in riddles this pleasure is increased by the final solution in some surprising association.

Children's self-invented riddles are very remarkable, mostly having no solution. The child thinks his own mental connections between the problem and its solution self-evident, having no idea that his hearer cannot possibly follow the tortuous paths of his mental leaps and bounds.[1]

Gunther (4 ; 4½—6). When out for walks we often set the children riddles in the form of antitheses, such as: It can strike, but has no arms (clock). These spurred the children on to think out riddles of their own, and we took down the following of Gunther's: *It is large, but is not a town.* (Heaven.)—*It is fine but is not gold.* (His aunt's wedding, at which he had been present.) —*It is a mountain, but yet not solid ground.* We guessed gingerbread mountain, and such-like, when he said: *O, nonsense, it is on human beings.* He meant "a nose".—*It is large, and yet to be eaten.* (Gingerbread house.)

Gunther (4 ; 9) is setting Hilde riddles, amongst which we heard the following, whose solution shows a strange mental jump: *It is a house, but you can only walk on the roof.* Neither Hilde nor any of his grown-up audience could guess it, and at last he gave the startling solution: *Well, doves can only walk on the roof, can't they!*

Gunther (5 ; 1). His mother was talking to him about the little song, "A mannikin stands in the forest", which ends with the familiar riddle: "Now who may this mannikin be?" (Mushroom.) On this occasion he was asked what a riddle really was. After some deliberation he gave the following explanation: *When someone says something and someone has to think a long time before he finds it out.* By the first "someone" he means the propounder, by the second the guesser.

---

[1] This is not the case in a riddle which the little boy Katz, aged 5, propounded to his mother: T. *Mummy, what is larger than an elephant, but it is not an animal nor a man?* Mother: A church tower. T. *Yes.*

CHAPTER XXIX

EXPERIMENTAL TESTS OF MENTAL POWER

THOUGHT in childhood has often been subject to investigation by means of tests. Some of these have already been discussed by us, for mental processes formed great part of speech-facility (Chapter XI, Section 1), the tests of comprehension of pictures Chapter XIV, Section 2), and aussage-experiments (Chapter XVIII).

This chapter deals with three further groups of tests; the two first concerned with mental activity of a special nature, the last with determination of general intelligence.

1. Enquiry into "Abstractions" of Shapes and Colours in Childhood

The so-called abstraction experiments owe their origin to Külpe's Wurzburg school, who carried out initial tests first on adults, then on school-children, and lastly on children of younger age. In these experiments the term "abstraction" has a definite significance, meaning that mental activity which can distinguish the points of similarity in several impressions to the exclusion of points of non-agreement. The aim of the children's tests is to determine when the abstract relation of LIKENESS is mentally grasped and in what form this idea of LIKENESS develops.

(a) FORM AND COLOUR COMPARISONS.

The method consists of putting before the children two collections of objects to be considered which are alike in colour or form, never in both, and of these those alike are always to be chosen. But these very experiments—first tried by Katz (I)—show the special difficulties that occur in the testing of young children. A slight alteration in the order of the test or in the way of speaking to the child may produce the greatest discrepancies between the results of individual investigators. Katz, working with geometrical figures, found as follows.

Varying figures of different colours ("subordinate figures") were put before the children, e.g. three red triangles and three green circles. Then a figure was shown to them which resembled one before them in colour and another in form, e.g. a red circle ("principal figure"). The experimenter now asked the child to give him one of the subordinate figures "that looks exactly like" the principal figure shown to him. Thus the children were forced, in spite of only partial likeness, to notice one of the points of agreement, and then to choose a subordinate figure either of the same form or of the same colour as the principal figure. If a child's principle of selection remained unaltered throughout a considerable number of tests, this was a proof that it did not choose indiscriminately any chance figure, but had noticed and taken into consideration the likeness of some point. The test had a positive result from the age of 2 ; 9. Up to the age of 4 ; 8 similarity in colour was without exception the determining factor of selection, in spite of pronounced difference of form; from 4 ; 10 there were some children who gave up figures similar in form but differing in colour.

Recently Volkelt had the same results in similar but more exact tests. Indeed, he found even greater preference given to similarity in colour; and if by a change in the tests he tried by degrees to induce the children to consider likeness in form, the persistency with which they clung to their adherence to colour similarity was astonishing. On the other hand, Countess Kuenburg in the use of several methods got quite different results.

The object of one was to test the understanding of likeness in its preliminary stages in a child less than two years of age. It liked playing with cardboard boxes and fitting on their lids. Boxes of different shapes and colours with their lids were mixed up and given to the child, whilst a watch was kept as to whether he would find the right lid to every box. After a number of trials a certain progress could be proved. At first the child took any one quite mechanically without thought, so that of course many mistakes occurred; later he now and again looked for the right lid and rejected one that did not fit, so that during his play there were signs of an occasional consciousness of the necessity of similarity. In opposition to Katz's conclusion, it was evident that he paid least attention to colour, for often box and lid were fitted together because they were alike in shape although of different colours.

Another series is designed for children between 2 ; 5 and 3 ; 11.

Small meaningless figures were cut out of white cardboard and two collections of such figures were given to the child; in each collection one figure matched one in the other, but the remaining figures all differed. The duplicate was taken from one collection and the child asked to give one like it. In the great majority of cases the attempt was successfully made, and as a rule quickly and without waiting to think. Then the test was complicated by colour, the two form duplicates being different in colour, whilst one of them was similar in this respect with a figure of different shape. But even then two-thirds of the children handed the figure of like shape, thus ignoring variation in colour. So that this series also shows that abstraction of shape precedes that of colour.

An attempt to explain these diversities brings us to an important psychological fact.

The preference of colour likeness found by Katz and Volkelt seems at first paradoxical. The normal attitude in ordinary life is doubtless that already described by us in Chapter XIII, 1, viz., that the young child pays little heed to colour in his recognition of things but on the contrary identifies a characteristic form, no matter how different its colour.[1]

If then the experiments with geometrical figures give a different result, it is probably because the conditions of choice are so little in harmony with those of ordinary life. In the latter, forms have always a meaning, they signify something, but in the experiments meaningless figures were offered them. The sense of any form is an inseparable part of its conception as a whole, so that the picture of a pony, even if coloured green, is always called a horse. But if the child is faced with an entirely unknown choice, to observe form either by itself or colour alone, then certainly colours call more loudly for attention. Volkelt will doubtless be right in saying that the children when they consider the simple mental impression and are quite at a loss as to its import see in representations of the same colour portions of a coloured whole and therefore point out these two parts of the combined whole as belonging together. There is no attempt

[1] Other investigators of child-psychology are also convinced of the preference for form in the child's natural recognition and comparison. Bühler (I, p. 82) and Kuenburg (p. 276) suppose therefore that in many cases the children did not really understand what was wanted. Révész has lately proved by experiment that monkeys, too, in similar tests give preference to form-similarity.

at all at comparison and abstraction first. And now we understand the differing result of Countess Kuenburg's box test; in this case, when the proper lid was to be found, likeness of form was once again of importance, for only a lid of the same shape not of the same colour would fit the box—and straightway preference is given again to form.

Colour and form are therefore reasons for choice of quite varying nature. Colours are noticed, compared and assorted to one another chiefly on account of their appeal to the senses—forms (shapes) by reason of their intellectual significance.

Since the above attempt at explanations was written, some further series of experiments have been made public and these we will briefly notice.

In entire agreement with our explanation we find the result of the "mass" test which Hans Tobie made on 700 Munich kindergarten children by means of everyday figures (animals, dishes, etc.), but otherwise in strict conformity with the test used by Katz. Tobie now found that even in the sole use of geometrical figures (triangle, square, circle, star), the colour was not given undivided preference but only a little more than twice as often as the form. But in the comparison of figures of significant objects the situation was reversed, the cases of form preference being to those of colour-choice in the ratio of 2 : 1. At every age there were children in whom form-preference entirely suppressed that of colour.

Tobie's very interesting psychological development results are here reproduced from his summary (p. 85).

1. In the early years up to about the fourth year, there is a phase of psychic development in which the observation of component factors is determined by the insistency of the appeal of those factors. (Zone of susceptibility.)

2. From the beginning of the fourth year to 4 ; 10 there exists a phase of development in which the child from essentially constitutional reasons spontaneously chooses colour, which is superseded by form only in response to very suggestive conditions. (Zone of colour preference.)

3. At 4 ; 10 a tendency arises to the displacement of colour preference for that of form. (Initial displacement zone (4 ; 8—5 ; 1).)

4. Once the threshold of this zone is crossed a phase begins in which, as a general rule, form is chiefly noted, and with continued intellectual development, comes the capacity for abstraction in both directions. (Zone of observation of form and the consciousness of identity.)

5. This capacity depends in individual cases on the special personal gifts and may make its appearance earlier.

6. At later age periods (from about four years on) the transition from colour to form is easier than from form to colour and may already be brought about by slight influences and lead to identification, whilst the reverse process only takes place under special conditions. At lower ages the change is effected without difficulty in both directions; the child's attitude here depends mainly on surrounding conditions.

7. The preference of colour is not an essential primary condition in the child but in a psychogenetic sense of a more primitive nature than that of form.

(*b*) COMPARISONS OF FORM.

Another test has been made by Countess Kuenburg—which now deals only with comparison of form, again, it is true, of artificial, i.e. meaningless forms.[1]

Two groups of meaningless figures, each containing one duplicate with the other and all others dissimilar, were put before each child. After looking for a short time at a "selection strip", i.e. a longer series of shapes put in front of them, the children had first to find those that were duplicates in the two groups (Principal Test), and then to find those that corresponded with the shapes that varied in the original groups (Subordinate Test). The experiment makes much more demand on mental power than those preceding: the task must be understood before they begin to look, which is only possible when there exists a conscious general idea of "likeness" apart from any special object of consideration. Further, the task once understood must continue as the dominant interest during the consideration of the groups of figures and that following of the "selection-strip"; and, lastly, the real "abstraction", i.e. the

[1] The method was taken from the tests by Koch and Habrich on school-children.

choice of like elements from the total combinations of the figures inspected, must be made.

These manifold mental demands of the task were only fulfilled by the children by degrees and with great difficulties. The diagram shows an example of a two-group test with its selection strip; attempts were also made with groups of three and of

four. With the groups of two, 851 trials resulted in 132 (fifteen per cent.) successful accomplishments of the principal test, i.e. "in 132 cases the same figures were selected from amongst the unlike figures". With groups of three, there were ten per cent. correct solutions, and with groups of four, seven per cent.

The following notes refer only to the two groups:—

The increase of success with age is especially noticeable from 4 ; o to 5 ; o; here the percentage rises from an average of seven to twenty-five; and the percentage of complete failures falls from twenty-nine to twelve. Individual capability is shown amongst other things in two children aged five and a half, who had more than fifty per cent. of success. The subordinate tests (finding out dissimilar figures in the selection strip shown later), proved more difficult; correct solutions were not given till a somewhat higher age, and very seldom equalled in number the solutions of the principal test. The abstraction aiming at the selection of like figures from the groups does not leave enough energy available to grasp dissimilarities.

(c) ABSTRACTIONS WITH CHOICE OF METHOD:

The very interesting experiments which Eliasberg tried on children and adults are of a somewhat different nature from the abstraction tests described above. The exercise given to those tested consisted only in the nature of the objects put before them, the understanding of the task and its method of solution being left to them. They were offered sheets of cardboard in two colours (e.g. five blue and five yellow), all mixed. together. Cigarettes were stuck under the sheets of one colour but it was impossible to see from the surface of the spread-out cards whether they contained cigarettes or not. (+ sheets, — sheets.) The test-controller showed the child some specimen sheets from the heap. Even at this stage it was possible to determine WHEN the child understood the rule and consequently looked for cigarettes under a definite colour (blue) and no longer tested—but even directly pushed aside—the sheets of another colour (yellow). But in the following tests there was a continuous change of colours, e.g. five + red and five — yellow sheets or even five + yellow and five — blue, hence an exact reversal of the first test, and so on. This brought about a disappointment of any firm rule of the union of a certain colour and cigarette which might have been formed by the foregoing test, so that for a new arrangement a new conscious rule had to be formed. Gradually a more general expectation of rule may arise from this, and at the next test the child was eager to see which colour would now be connected with the cigarette. Thus the rule then of the relation between cigarette and colour was no longer connected with any special colour.

A series of very thorough reports shows us now whether and how, at what speed and with what signs, a series of children mastered the different tests. We can follow all stages—often in the same child—in the course of the test series—from blind seizing of all cards passing through a diffused uncertain sampling to the systematic choice of those cards where the first trials justified expectation of cigarettes and the no less systematic neglect of cards of a different colour. It is generally possible to recognize from its method of working without any need of words when the consciousness of a rule has taken place. But sometimes utterances come that throw a flash of light on the insight gained; of this we give the two following examples:

Hannah 2 ; 10 (the author's daughter). In the first test, + yellow and — blue cards were put before her. The child looks through them all, puts back the blue ones but picks out the yellow.

In the second and third test the same cards were laid out; in the second only one blue was tested, in the third not a single blue was touched but only the yellow ones selected: *I will take the same again.*

After a few tests with other colours, at the seventh a reversed test was put out: four blue (+), five yellow (—). She takes up a yellow: *that won't do.* A second: *nor that.* A third: *no, none of them do. Will those do then?* (tries a blue one). *Yes, they will do.* Then she picked out all the blue cards.

That a child not yet three years old should pronounce the complete generalization from a series of individual observations (*no, none of them will do*), must be classified as very early. Cf. also Chapter XXVIII, 3 of this book.

Trudie ($4\frac{1}{2}$). After she had learnt in several tests that only the yellow sheets had cigarettes (in the end she paid no more heed to the blue cards) a reversed test was made. As soon as she had found the cigarette on a blue card she only picked up those of that colour, saying: *If they are under the blue, there won't be any under the yellow*. Thus a logical and clearly formulated insight into the connection of the cigarettes with one colour (which however need not always be the same).

Eliasberg arranges his three- to five-year-old examinees into three groups:—

1. Those with good mental and speech development: Positive classification begins even in the first test. The non-connection between a minus colour and cigarette is grasped comparatively quickly; the independence of definite component parts is soon mastered: thus the child frees himself from the control of what is apparently given and this is particularly evident in a reversed test.
2. Children of good mental but backward speech development. The positive connection is soon grasped but a reversed test offers difficulties.
3. Children of poor mental development and backward in speech. Great observational weakness, so that it is only after a series of tests that the positive connection between colour and cigarette is grasped; persistent feeling of the mutual permanent dependence of one colour and cigarette.

2. The Development of the Sense of Number and Calculation

The young child has an acquaintance with simple numbers long before he begins to get elementary teaching in arithmetic. But it needs closer examination to find out the psychological significance of this "acquaintance". For it is not as though his use of numerals in early speech signified his possession of a sense of number, or even of the general idea of number-counting or of sequence; children in their races repeat the one, two, they hear without any suspicion of these being numbers, just as, somewhat later, they rattle off 1, 2, 3 . . .[1] in counting-out games. So that a careful analysis of the child's attitude to number must be made in order to understand his actual development in its comprehension.[2]

In recent times several practical experiments on a fairly large scale have shown us that there are varying kinds of grasp of numbers and also very varying rates of development. The Belgian investigators, Decroly and Degand, thought out a number of ingenious exercises specially adapted for practice. Alice Descoeudres extended and improved these exercises, making them into real tests, which have been tried on numbers of Geneva children. Quite lately Beckmann carried out careful examinations of several hundred German children as regarded their number-capability, whilst Filbig tested about one hundred kindergarten children.

In some of Descoeudres' tests we find the happy thought of dispensing entirely with the use of numerals and only requiring number-imitation from the children; the examiner in irregular sequence puts out of a number of buttons or counters, now one, then two or three before the child, each time telling it to put the same number. The problem becomes more difficult when it has to be carried out in something different—as when three fingers are shown and an equal number of buttons asked for. With such silent tests a child unable to talk, with no knowledge of numerals, may occasionally show that he sees in what is shown to him not only an indefinite quantity but has a correct idea of counting.

Other methods, utilized by A. Descoeudres, Filbig, and most carefully by Beckmann, make use of numerals either by requiring the child to understand them or to use them himself. Beckmann distinguishes in the child the following chief number capabilities:—

(1) Number-building. (A number of dice lie in front of the child. Test: "Give me three dice.")

(2) Number-distinction. (A group of two and a group of three are successively pointed out with: "Is this

---

[1] Alice Descoeudres found that most children of 3½ could say the numbers up to 6, but could not make use of this knowledge for actual counting of objects before 4½ years.

[2] Cf. also observations on number-power in Chapter XXVII, 2, d.

two or that?" Or there is only a group of three on the table: "Is that two or three?")

(3) Number-finding. (A chart is shown with different groups of dots: "Show me wherever there are four dots".)

(4) Number-naming. (On the same chart the various collections of dots must be pointed out by their correct numeral.)

Beckmann examined almost 500 little children of different social grades with nothing but numbers from two to five.[1] It was found that number-building was the easiest, but number-naming the most difficult and latest in development. The number two by itself was correctly built up and distinguished even by two year-old children, who, however, were not yet able either to find or name it. The number five appears rightly used about the age of 3 ; 6, but then only in building and distinction. It is only the five- and six-year-old children who often succeed in correctly finding and naming the five group on the dot-charts.

By a summary of the children's performances the three above-named investigators were able to find a simple expression for the general progress in the child's attitude to number; they determine, for instance, at what average age the idea of the numbers 2, 3, 4 is mastered. Since the tests employed and the methods of striking the average were different in all three cases the degree of agreement is the more remarkable—and it is evidently a question of a general law of development (see tables below). Whether the slight superiority of the Geneva children is due to race or to difference of method cannot be determined.

Average mastery of numbers by children

of the ages here given	2	3	4
Beckmann's results	3 ; 6–4 ; 0	4–4 ; 6	5–5 ; 6
Filbig's results	3 ; 9	4 ; 2	5 ; 6
Descoeudres' results	3 ; 0	4 ; 0	5 ; 0

To the above law may be added another law of development—deduced from Beckmann's results—with reference to the general rate of development in mastery of number. If the results as regards all numbers tested are collected and the five-year-old

[1] One, to begin with, is considered by children as an article, not as a numeral. Children when asked to give one dice respond correctly, but show doubt or even entire failure when the request is made with a different intonation and emphasis on the "one".

results are looked upon as 100 per cent., then the mastery of number develops to this maximum at the following speed:—

At the age of 2 ; 6–3 ; 6 the progress is 23 % ⎫
　　　,,　　,,　　3 ; 6–4 ; 6　　,,　　　　,,　　43 % ⎬ of the total increase.
　　　,,　　,,　　4 ; 6–5 ; 6　　,,　　　　,,　　23 % ⎭

Thus arithmetical development makes its greatest progress about the age of four, i.e. at the time when the child masters the distinction between 1 and 2. As soon as the 3 idea is conquered, the way is apparently clear for the higher numbers as well.

The real understanding of any definite number may come to pass in two entirely different ways psychologically: by the direct grasp, at sight, of the total (as we adults see the six on a dice), or by successively adding units with the help of a sequence of numbers, that is by counting. As Beckmann discovered, the children were capable of a wonderfully sure self-observation regarding this difference. If they were asked after rightly naming a number of dots how they had got the result, they answered either: "Why, that anyone can see straightaway," or, "I counted that". Of course, counting is only done where the direct grasp at sight cannot be managed. In this again the progress of development can be gauged. The majority of four-year-old children have to count at the number 3 before they get the correct result, but six-year-old children can as a rule grasp a total of 4 or 5 at first sight without having to count.[1]

The power of direct grasp of a number depends of course greatly upon the senses involved. A. Descoeudres experimented with acoustic stimuli by a series of taps that the child had to copy. It seems that the correct result only occurs if the child unites the raps he hears into a rhythmical form without having to count first. It was shown that the task was more difficult than with objects that were seen. Not before the age of four did the children correctly reproduce the bar of 2, or before the age of five the bar of 3. This test, moreover, showed remarkable differences of innate capacity, so that sometimes younger children did better than the older ones. Evidently this is a sign that mastery of number pure and simple is in this case

---

[1] Alice Descoeudres got the same results with six-year-olds, but her four-year-olds were, for the most part, able to grasp 3 without counting (Chapter XXI). Filbig tested under much more difficult conditions, for he only let the children look for one second at the objects arranged in rows or groups. It was only the six-year-old children who were able after such a short look to recognize correctly groups of even 3–4.

crossed by quite another factor, namely that of a sense of rhythm.[1]

Beckmann also carried out ingenious tests as to children's early powers of addition (up to a total of 6), using dice that showed the different numbers of dots. The test was, amongst others: "Put (to a dice with 2 dots) another to make 3." Or (the child himself throwing 2 dice): "How many dots have you thrown?" Here again there were cases in which the children at once "saw" the sum, others where they counted it up, passing from one dice to another. In the older years a third type also appeared—each group was grasped by itself and their sum was given by means of a formula already learnt: "Of course, anyone knows that 2 and 2 make 4."

These addition results are also first possible about the age of four,[2] which is thus again shown to be the critical age for the first sense of number. Throughout, those exercises were the easiest where one of the numbers added was only unity, and those the most difficult where the sum-total reached 6. It is very remarkable that some of the children could so far see no connection between a purely verbal addition sum and the adding together of visible objects. Children who could combine 2 and 3 dots and give the correct sum of 5, answered the same sum, when purely verbal, with: "I haven't learnt that yet." They never thought of the possibility—even if a formula had not been learnt—of finding out the answer by a mental picture of 2 and 3 dots or other things. At this period, then, the real understanding of number is entirely dependent on sight.

There are of course exceptions to the periods given above for the development of the power of counting and reckoning. Gifted children with a strong spontaneous interest in numbers often of their own accord at an early age get as far as setting themselves arithmetical problems—and solving them too— which are far beyond the stages given above. We gave instances of this in Chapter XXVIII, 4. And also didactic methods of a special kind may lead to earlier achievements, as is shown by the Montessori methods.

Mme Montessori describes a long list of additions and multiplications up to 20, even division and multiplication by 2, adding: "All this is not difficult for five-year-old children."

[1] Cf. with this Chapter XXV.   [2] Filbig obtained the same result.

Now, the method invented by Mme Montessori to familiarize young children easily and pleasantly with numbers is certainly most ingenious and successful. The principal exercises are done on wooden rods of graded lengths with coloured insets of centimetre units. The shortest rod measures 1 centimetre, the longest 10. By a step-like arrangement the sequence of rods can be used as a very clear calculating contrivance. Systematic use of this and similar play exercises seems now actually to result in a considerably earlier familiarity with numbers. But that, after all, this is really only a matter of artificial drill seems to me proved by the presentation given above of the general laws of development as regards children's sense of number. For at this age, which is not yet ready for systematic instruction, the natural rate of development ought to be the foundation of any pedagogic interference. Mme Montessori prematurely turns her pupils into school-children to be trained first of all in useful obedience to teaching. That she exercises in this no direct compulsion upon the child, rather indeed makes its work as enjoyable as possible, is no justification from an educational point of view. We cannot pronounce a final judgment on such teaching of small children until the two following questions have been answered: (1) Do children that have gained such pre-cocious facility in counting and calculation retain their superi-ority, or are they soon on the same level as the other children? (2) Does not this one-sided occupation of the children with didactic tasks keep them back from other possible occupations more suited to their age? It seems to me that what ought *not* to be taught in the Montessori schools is a far more important problem both from a psychological and educational point of view than what is undeniably actually accomplished in them. (See also Chapter XVI, 2.)

3. Intelligence Tests at Kindergarten Age

By intelligence modern psychology understands that general capacity by which a human being can successfully meet fresh demands of life through the help of mental effort. It is signi-ficant of intelligence that it is not confined mental effort of any definite kind (e.g. the power of synthesis, calculation, criticism), but that it signifies the general mental level of mankind. The designations of different degrees of intelligence refer to this general mental level: clever (=highly intelligent), of normal intelligence, stupid, mentally deficient, of weak intellect.

Even since Alfred Binet's pioneer attempts, psychology has endeavoured to develop test-methods by which the degree of a child's general intelligence can be exactly determined in a short time. Although this method was at first chiefly designed for use in the determination of abnormally low degrees of intelligence, improvement in investigation has made possible a more exact determination of supernormal intelligence and a finer gradation of grades of intelligence within the compass of normality. There exists to-day a most comprehensive literature and numberless more or less trustworthy test-methods,[1] destined certainly for the most part for use in school-age and later youth. Not until quite recently—and that in other countries—has greater interest been taken in testing the intelligence of children of kindergarten age.

The "step-method" introduced by Binet consists of a series of varying tests for every year which normally can be solved by 75 per cent. of the children of that age. Thus the intelligence-age (I.A.) of every child tested can be determined; e.g. a child that answers all the five-year-old tests and perhaps three out of the six tests meant for six-year-old children has an I.A. of $5\frac{1}{2}$. We can now compare these figures with the actual (literal) age of the same child. For this comparison I suggest the term now universally adopted of Intelligence Quotient (I.Q.), expressing, as it does, the relation of the intelligence-age to actual age:—

$$I.Q. = \frac{I.A.}{L.A.}$$

For example, if the child mentioned above is already six years old, whilst as regards intelligence he has only reached the level of 5 ; 6, his I.Q. is $\frac{5 \; ; \; 6}{6} = 0 \cdot 93$. The I.Q. 1 designates an entirely average intelligence; if the figure is larger than 1, the child's intelligence is in advance of his age.

There is no longer any point in preserving the original form of Binet's "step-method". Numerous re-examinations have

[1] Summaries and bibliography in the following books: W. Stern, VIII, and Stern and Wiegmann.

revealed many defects, and it was just for the younger ages that the tests were not gauged accurately enough.[1]

The system has been most thoroughly revised in the last few years by the American psychologist Terman; his series of tests has been tried on thousands of children of all ages, and may be considered to-day as the most generally useful step-method. In addition to this, the investigation we have so often mentioned by Alice Descoeudres has led to a frequent proposal of a fresh "step-test" for the ages of 2½–8. Neither of these test-series is suitable in its present form for use in Germany, but both furnish very valuable hints for making in the future a German normal series.

Terman's series[2] gives the following tests for ages 3—7. [Notice resemblance to Binet's well-known series.]

For three years:

1. To point out parts of the body. ("Show me your nose," etc.)
2. To name familiar objects—clock, dish, etc. ("What is that?")
3. To look at a picture and, unprompted, to name at least three things in it.
4. To give sex. ("Are you a boy or a girl?")
5. To give name. ("What is your name?")
6. To repeat (in imitation) six or seven syllables.

Four years:

1. To compare lines of different length. ("Which is longer?")
2. To distinguish difference in shape. (A circle is shown and the same shape is to be chosen out of a number of different figures.)
3. To count four coins.
4. To copy a square.
5. Intelligence query, first grade. ("What must you do if you are tired [hungry, cold]?")
6. To repeat four figures (in imitation).

---

[1] By gauging a test we understand the determination of the age-period characterized by a definite solution of the test.
[2] Terman, I.

Five years:
1. To compare two weights (3 and 15 grammes). ("Which is heavier?")
2. To name colours. (Four papers—red, yellow, green, blue.)
3. An æsthetic test. (Three pairs of faces, in each one ugly, one pretty. "Which is the prettier?")
4. To define six everyday objects. ("What is a chair, horse, doll, etc.?")
5. "Game of patience": To make a rectangle like one shown out of two triangles.
6. To carry out three requests. ("Put this dish on that table." "Shut the door." "Bring me those boxes.")

Six years:
1. To know right from left. ("Show your right hand, left ear, etc.")
2. To find omissions in pictures. (A face without a nose is shown, the full figure with no arms, etc.)
3. To count thirteen coins.
4. Intelligence query, second grade. ("What must be done if it is raining and you have to go to school?" etc.)
5. To give names of current coinage.
6. To repeat (in imitation) sentences of sixteen to eighteen syllables.

Seven years:
1. To give number of fingers. ("How many, first on one, then on the other, and then together?")
2. To look at a picture and describe the action depicted.
3. To repeat five numbers.
4. To tie (in imitation) a simple knot.
5. To distinguish from memory. (Difference between a fly and a butterfly; a stone and an egg; wood and glass.)
6. To copy a rhombus.

A fine medley of tests, as is evident; side by side with real mental questions, tests of observation, skill in manipulation, comparison, and even a certain amount of general knowledge. Such mosaic-work can never quite satisfy a theoretical psychologist but the system is intended first and foremost to serve the practical purpose of a diagnosis of the general level of intelligence, and for this it seems quite well adapted.

Terman gives an account of tests set by Miss Cuneo on 112 kindergarten children between the ages of 3 ; 6–7 ; 0. The I.Q. of these children varies between 0·61 and 1·52, i.e. between pronounced weak mentality and unusual super-normality (a four-year-old boy with the intelligence of the six-year-olds). Three children stood on the borderline between normality and mental inferiority. The distribution of intelligence amongst the 112 children was normal (cf. the diagram); most cases crowded together round the average I.Q. As super- or sub-

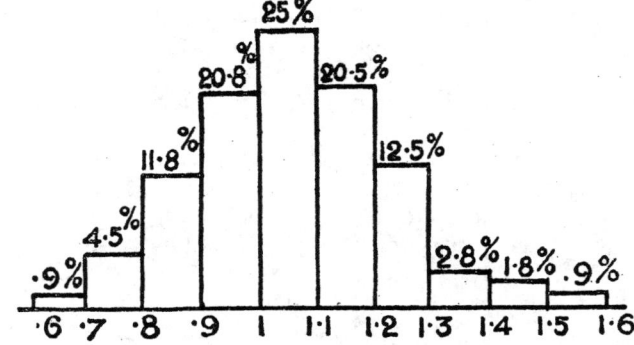

Distribution of I.Q. amongst 112 Kindergarten children.
Each column gives the percentage of children reaching the I.Q. notified at its foot.

normality was approached the numbers decreased at much the same rate.

The question as to whether such a test at so early an age has any prophetic value as regards future mental development is answered by Terman on the whole affirmatively. Of course, the test must be carried out with the greatest care and delicate psychological insight, so that the results of the various tasks should not be influenced in any way by shyness or chance occurrences. Also later examinations of the same children—after a longer or shorter interval—have shown the infrequency of considerable change in their I.Q. This is true, too, for the extreme cases on either side. The four children who in the kindergarten had an I.Q. above 1·3 (i.e. possessed a more than four-thirds average intelligence), two years later again showed an I.Q. of over $1 \cdot 3$, and were above the usual average at school. And, on the other hand, Terman is convinced that a child showing at five or six years of age only two-thirds average intelligence (I.Q. $= 0 \cdot 61$) will never develop beyond the intelligence-standard of the nine- or ten-year-old. If this is so it would be possible to find out pronounced cases of weak mentality even in the kindergarten, and there would be no need to wait until the eighth year before sending them to schools for defective children.

Terman considers such intelligence-tests especially needed in the kindergarten. For whilst later on at school mental capacity becomes more or less apparent in the school tasks, the occupations in the kindergarten are in his opinion less adapted to show the degree of a child's intelligence; consequently kindergarten teachers often make mistakes, especially as they ascribe to difference in intelligence a good deal which ought really to be attributed to their pupils' varying ages. Consequently there was no great correlation between the results given by intelligence-tests and the kindergarten teachers' estimate of individual intelligence in the children.

There was very little difference as regarded sex in these intelligence-tests. The boys' average I.Q. was $1 \cdot 03$, that of the girls $1 \cdot 08$. This coincides with the well-known ordinary experience that girls are especially in advance of boys at a very early age.

The comparison of kindergarten pupils with children beginning school showed a noteworthy result (see diagram on next page).

If the frequency of cases of intelligence-age is represented by lines, these in great measure coincide, although the maxima occur at different places: the kindergarten children reach the maximum frequency at $4\frac{1}{2}$ years of age, the school beginners at $6\frac{1}{2}$. But the whole time lying between these two limits shows fairly marked frequency in both sets of children. Terman concludes from this that a large percentage of school-beginners are not very different as regards their intelligence from the children below school-age, and that there is therefore no justification for a sharp distinction at the sixth year of age and for the sudden imposition on the children of totally new kinds of mental requirements. So that the results of intelligence-tests support that reform which aims at making the first year's school curriculum a gradual transition from kindergarten to school methods.

Alice Descoeudres has by systematic research amongst children aged two to seven endeavoured to provide a new series of graded tests of speech-capacity (Chapter XI), of power of counting and calculation (Chapter XXIX, Section 2), the lotto-method of determining power of observation (Chapter XIII, Section 2, *b*).

Some of the number-tests, as well as the lotto-method, are so-called "silent" tests; it is one of the merits of this Geneva investigator that she attaches great value to the development of such tests without speech. In the case of children who have

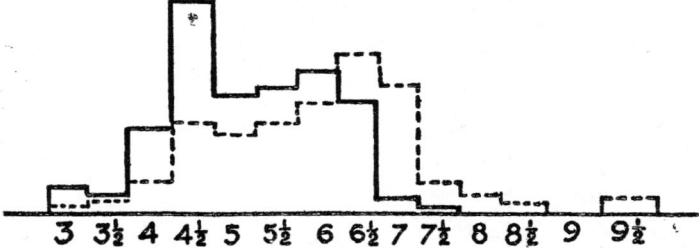

Distribution of Intelligence-Age in Kindergarten Children and School-Beginners.

not yet acquired a ready use of language it is very easy for some speech difficulty to obscure intelligence that really exists, so that, especially with young children, test-methods should be used which permit the display of any existing mental power independently of its expression in speech.[1]

A. Descoeudres, therefore, in addition to tests already named, made use of one for skill in manipulation—threading twenty beads (she took as standard the time occupied)—and of some silent judgment-tests, which required the arrangement or correct grouping of pictures.

Twenty-four different little pictures, divided into groups of four of the same nature, were put in confusion before the child and he was asked to sort them out into their different groups. The varying groups were successfully selected at different ages

[1] This is the proper place for those simple test-methods for determining animal or infant intelligence (Chapter V, 1, *c*). In Binet's and Terman's series there is a great preponderance of tests requiring speech.

as follows: first, the flower picture (at $4\frac{1}{2}$), next mammals and birds (at 5), last, articles of food ($5\frac{1}{2}$).

This test is worthy of methodical development with better pictures.

To end with, A. Descoeudres is now trying to form a new "step-series" from all her separate graded test-methods; this contains six tests for every half-year, partly spoken, partly silent.

This attempt is very valuable as a beginning; for a series of new test-methods has certainly more connection with the natural course of development in the child's intelligence than Binet's and Terman's series of somewhat haphazard tests. But her collection must be in no way considered as a final system; for the grading of the individual tests is founded on far too few results to give any assurance of certainty, and besides no attempt has ever been made—even by A. Descoeudres herself—to find out whether the total series was of any practical use in determining the intelligence-age and quotient. For this reason we cannot here give a copy of the proposed series.

In America too there has lately been a change to more frequent or even exclusive use of tests that are independent of speech.

Thus two series have been made in Detroit. One ("The Detroit kindergarten test")[1] asks the children to "react" to pictures by pointing with the finger, e.g.: A picture contains the moon, a cup, a sledge: "Show me the thing that is up in the sky." Or, Picture No. 1 contains a bicycle and a mail-cart for children. Picture No. 2 shows a dog, a child's perambulator and some apples. Test: "Show me (on picture 2) the thing most like these two (on picture 1), etc." The test is used to find which children are to be moved into a transition class from the kindergarten and which should be kept longer where they are.

In the other Detroit series[2] the power of accomplishing certain practical actions is to be tested and in this we find the following tests: To pack 16 dice into a box out of which they have just been emptied; to fit into each other four hollow dice of different sizes; to build a copy of the tester's pyramid made of 3 dice; to join 2 pieces of stuff by means of one button and button-hole; to do the same with 2, 4 buttons, etc. The frequency of the correct solutions is determined for all ages—in half yearly stages—from $1\frac{1}{2}$ to $5\frac{1}{2}$ years.

[1] C. Baker and Kaufmann.   [2] Cf. Stutsman.

Lately too in America use has been made of a GROUP TEST (the simultaneous testing of a large number).[1] Those to be tested get a little book containing nothing but pictures. The tests to be performed are to find out pictures of certain objects, and point out special parts of a picture which are to be shown as belonging to persons or things mentioned in a tale that is read aloud. The reaction of the children consists in simple pencil lines to mark the parts of the picture in question.

The results are said to correspond well with intelligence tests by other methods. But I am inclined to think that such a mechanical method of testing which prohibits all consideration of individual peculiarities of the different children must be open to more objection in early childhood than at a later age.[2]

The most extensive experimental examination of young children has recently been carried on by Baldwin and Stecher. In Iowa there is a special "Pre-school Laboratory" in which the physical, mental and social development of the child is to be scientifically observed and promoted in accordance with educational principles. The laboratory is conducted like a kindergarten, but at the same time experimental tests of the most diverse nature are made on the children. The two investigators now report the measurements taken of the 100 children, which comprise those of height and weight, sense-perception, agility in movement, power of combination and distinction, grasp of number, time, rhythm, etc. It is here as impossible to enumerate the individual methods of the exceptionally comprehensive series of tests as it is to give the numerical result of the progress in development; in every test it is shown how the numbers achieved by the two-year-olds change up to the children of six.

Thus only a few results which Baldwin and Stecher have obtained with the Terman method mentioned above will be given as complementary to our former considerations. As the majority of the children in the Experimental Kindergarten come from cultured homes it is intelligible why the average I.Q. was somewhat higher than Terman's, viz. 1·15. The lowest and highest were 0·79 and 1·56. A number of the children were tested not only at entrance but frequently afterwards; in many there was shown a certain increase of the I.Q., which however the

[1] Cf. Pintner and Cunningham.
[2] For school-children and adults it is sometimes only possible to test large numbers by written group-tests. These, however, only constitute a last resource *faute de mieux*.

authors attribute not so much to a real change in intelligence
as to the fact that the children become more and more accustomed to experimental tests. (Possibly too the children by
degrees get used to the special tests of the Terman series.) The
difference between the sexes was found, as by Terman, to be
small, but for the girls on an average the I.Q. was $1 \cdot 17$, for the
boys $1 \cdot 13$.

We must here mention the comparative tests made by A.
Huth with a series of experimental methods on Munich kindergarten children in their sixth year. These researches, carried
on as early as 1913 but not published until now, had for their
object to find out the sex-difference. In speech-expression, etc.,
tested by imitating the utterance of sentences, the girls showed
greater exactitude and better use of imagination in making up
for defects in remembrance; the boys had the advantage only
in such sentences as referred to their own experiences. Graphic
expression was analysed by drawings and tests of painting and
cutting out of very different objects. The boys' work was
more to the point, plainer, more adapted to the subject, careful
in placing, richer in presentations of actions and means of
communication; the girls' work was more imaginative, cleaner,
with more appreciation of colour and a preference for conditions
and personal affairs. A test of *reproduction* lastly determined
(by drawing, description and answering questions) the number
and contents of the conceptions that still remained from an
expedition made the day before. The result showed the girls'
power of reproduction to be far greater than the boys' and again
the different direction of their interests was clearly brought out.

On the whole girls of five to six years are mentally superior
in most respects to boys of the same age; but boys at this
period are making more pronounced progress in development.
Moreover the boys almost everywhere show far greater differences between themselves; their performances were much more
varied than were those of the girls, and also the work of
individual boys gave evidence of more mental fluctuation.

Huth concludes his report with the following characterization
as a summary which in my opinion certainly seems to over-
emphasize the sex-differences:

"The boy under school age is at a period of quick but erratic
development: but his perceptions are still, so to speak, coarse-
grained, rough-hewn, undifferentiated. In observation and work

he is reliable as to facts but falls short in form; his power of verbal expression is still very clumsy. His interest is centred on the life of action, distance and the means that carry men to that distance. The main trend of his nature is to reason—he is above all 'rational'.

"The girl under school-age develops more slowly but more steadily; she is in every respect more mature than the boy; the emotional psychic life already seems more finely tuned and differentiated in many ways. The girl astonishes us by the startling technique of her work and by many individual observations but her rich imagination lessens their exactitude and reality. Everything personal attracts her interest. The quintessence of her nature is entirely 'irrational' and intuitive."

PART IX

IMPULSE—EMOTION—WILL—THE VARIOUS FORMS
AND DIRECTIONS OF ENDEAVOUR

CHAPTER XXX

THE PERSONAL PSYCHOLOGY OF EFFORT[1]

1. Consciousness and Aim of Effort[2]

WE will begin with the problem of consciousness, mentioned above.

The consciousness of effort undoubtedly confronts psychology of a descriptive and dissecting nature with a number of important and interesting questions. For the facts of inward compulsion and independent action, of determination by aim, of desire, choice, decision, etc., require careful investigation; the question as to the part played in this consciousness of effort by pleasure, *dis*pleasure, feelings of activity and expectation, anticipation of success, thought of the task, and the further question whether, over and above all this, there does not exist an act of will as the real content of consciousness, have been, and still are, the subject of much discussion.

And yet these questions do not touch the central problem of effort. For we cannot stop at consciousness as our final goal and content ourselves with determining its content; we are compelled instead to ask ourselves what is THE SIGNIFICANCE OF CONSCIOUSNESS IN THE TOTAL LIFE OF THE PERSONALITY, and in what relation conscious effort stands to actual effective endeavour and action.

This relation between experience (consciousness) and life (effort towards an end) exists in various forms, one of which is reflection, i.e. man tries to reflect his own self and the world

---

[1] This chapter is in a sense somewhat of an intrusion, as it is not, properly speaking, child-psychology. The author, however, felt compelled to touch briefly on those foundational philosophic-psychological views and to explain the ideas which seemed to him indispensable for the understanding of his further treatment of child-psychology. Unfortunately, this has had to be done in very cursory fashion; those readers who wish for further explanations and proofs of this difficult discussion are referred to my book, *Human Personality*, as well as to a publication to be brought out in 1929 on "Personalistic Psychology".

[2] For Introductory Observations see p. 572.

in his consciousness. His feelings of pleasure and displeasure reflect his inward attitude to that which is either advantageous or harmful to his ego; in his conscious will-impulses he is conscious of aims to which his line of life is actually directed. Thus, sometimes more veiled, sometimes clearer, an image of the direction of his aims is projected upon the consciousness of man struggling onwards.

But this reflection is not perfect. The real self is not all comprised in the self-consciousness; the abundance and involved development of man's struggling powers are but partially realized in his emotional, perceptive, craving consciousness. What consciousness offers is but a SELECTION of life-determining tendencies; indeed, even more, it is partly but a REMODELLING of these tendencies.

To consider first the selection. Consciousness only appears where reasons of personal teleology require it, and this is only in cases of conflict. As long as human life flows on smoothly in innate assurance of aim or along accustomed paths, so long as "convergence," i.e. the mutual relations of environment and inner dispositions, proceeds without friction, life functions normally without intermission and needs no inner reflection. It is only when inner or outer disagreements arise that the friction strikes the spark of consciousness. All consciousness—even when pleasurable—bears testimony to restraint and strain, opposition and conquest. Thus conscious reflection has not to do with the whole of life's content and meaning, but only with its CONFLICTING SIDES.

But even these are not always adequately represented. THE MIRROR OF THE STRIFE BECOMES AT THE SAME TIME A WEAPON IN THE CONFLICT, and thus the reflection turns into a false (delusive) representation. The fighting problems of consciousness determine how far it will identify itself with the inner reality of the ego, and how far it must avoid this or even veil it. This does not imply any intentional deception on the part of the consciousness, but rather indeed quite involuntary modifications of conscious representations, issuing from the unconscious striving after aims of the individual. There are certain impulses and tendencies which are not consciously known in their true form, or, if they once were, cannot remain in the Conscious without affecting detrimentally the unchanging nature of elementary life-aims, and to secure unconsciousness of them other conscious ideas replace them. The negative side of this procedure, namely the pushing away of some conscious content which, as such, might disturb the personal equilibrium, is known as "repression".

We have now reached the point where the individualistic theory maintained by us most nearly approaches the psycho-analytic standpoint. Both schools consider it desirable to enquire into the SIGNIFICANCE of consciousness and to attempt the INTERPRETATION of its content, and both hold that to limit their consideration of simple consciousness as such would result in merely surface psychology. The ripples and waves of this surface derive indeed their significance from their con-nection with the depths below. But psychoanalysis looks upon these depths as the simple opposite of consciousness, "the Unconscious", that, like some independent psychic phantom, has his seat somewhere in man, using some complicated machinery to outwit the Conscious wherever he can. The individualistic theory, on the other hand, sees those depths filled with the ego in whose undivided and indivisible life-unity are hidden the first stirrings of consciousness no less than the first strivings of endeavour which, without the help of consciousness, are directed towards their goals.

The two schools are also at variance in the fact that "the Unconscious" of the psychoanalysts in reality has but the one aim of sexuality, whilst the "person" of the individualists consists of a unity of many aims and consequent directions of effort.

The multiplicity of aims is the natural result of the "person's" position in the world. Every human being is the centre of HIS world. There is first his own more narrow self to be main-tained, protected, developed, then the objects of his environ-ment, the facts of nature and civilization to be perceived, grasped, used and furthered, or conquered, then the other persons around him, intercourse with whom is a practical necessity for each individual, then his relation to those superior bodies, membership of which influences the life and activity of every individual, and lastly the abstract ideas of value (ideals)—these all constitute those aims to which all human effort is directed. And of these, no one is the primary aim with all others derivative from it, rather are they interrelated, belonging to each other from the first; and however great their differentiation, yet they always shine forth together again in the unity of "the person", who is the embodiment of all these strivings. This united gleam is the final miracle of all personal existence, the personalistic school designates it as "introception". The service of the narrower Self, the striving and working for aims not identical with the ego, for things and persons near me, for communities and values above me, are not, when all is said, contradictory, but they endeavour to unite in forming a higher Self; the striving after a goal above the ego is what alone lends to the ego itself its special worth and true meaning.

This, then, is the fundamental endeavour of every individual, so to achieve valuable aims that they become part of that self which is guarded and served by the subjective efforts of self-protection and self-development. But this fundamental endeavour is never perfect, never occurs in unmixed purity; separate aims of some sort or other push forward in their exclusiveness, opposition, complication and entanglement, yet in this confusion of many (often inharmonious) tones the bass note of "introception" makes itself heard in its endeavour to preserve the unity of the personal line of life.

2. Fundamental Ideas

The following divisions will be of help in the understanding of the fundamental ideas present in our consideration of human effort. The first group (a) refers to permanent characteristics (dispositions), the second (b) to separate phenomena of effort appearing not constantly but at special times.

(a) The entire sum of personal effort (entelechy) breaks up into a number of branch efforts, each directed to a separate form and variety of aim. They may be defined as dispositions in certain directions or tendencies.[1] When these tendencies are innate in the individual, and only roused into action, but neither created nor determined by outer influences, they are called "instincts" (impulses); but when their special nature

---

[1] Cf. *The Human Personality*, p. 83 seq. There tendencies and potentialities are contrasted, the former containing a direction to special aims, the latter offering the means of their attainment. This last group also comprises "capacities", the most important of which we have already considered, viz. the gift of observation, memory, intelligence.

and aim is only possible as the result of convergence with experience, they come under the heading of "inclination" (bent of mind) and "interest". As soon as the various tendencies in the course of continual battling with the outer world have been built up into a united and permanent whole, so that each isolated tendency or its expression only appears as a component factor of this united whole, "character" has been formed and the individual shows his personality.

All these considerations so far treat of the tendencies in their psychological neutral direction to aim; an instinct (impulse), an interest, or inclination sets the individual in motion as a living whole, and is often evidenced no less —possibly even more—in physical action than in psychic experience.

Whenever, on the other hand, the psychic factor becomes the chief point of interest, we get the ideas of emotion (feeling) and will. Feeling is namely that tendency which gives a conscious reflection of constantly enduring inner nature; will the tendency which presents images to the consciousness of objective aims to be realized.

(b) The remaining considerations treat of separate acts of effort occurring at special periods. We will again begin with the psychophysical neutral ideas.

In every effort man takes up some attitude to the world. This ATTITUDE is always alternative, moving between negative and positive poles. This polarity is the general fundamental form, which may appear in many gradations, as pleasure—displeasure, desire—repulsion, consent—refusal, love—hate, pursuit—flight, attack—retreat, etc. Nevertheless, the two poles are not separated with no possibility of reconciliation; there are pains and sufferings that are not avoided but embraced, hatred which is hidden or repressed love, selfishness which strangely enough finds pleasure in suppression of self.

These inner dialectics of effort[1] warn us to avoid attempting too great a simplification of the personal life by formulated classifications.

In accordance with their origin, the acts of effort show themselves as reactive or spontaneous, reactive when an outer object provides the stimulus for the individual positive feeling

[1] Psychoanalysis speaks of "ambivalence".

(pleasure, desire) or for the negative feeling (displeasure, aversion). On the other hand, the action is spontaneous when, arising from the inner self, it seeks its own object. In reaction man is tied to the effect of outer conditions beyond his own control; in spontaneous action his subjective attitude is free, i.e. not indeed without a cause, but determined by the immanent aim-effort of his own personality.

Such direct opposition between reaction and spontaneity it is true never exists in reality, for every subjective attitude assumed by man is dependent on outer no less than on inner conditions.

The reaction is so much less mixed the more the attitude is determined by the MOMENTARY CONNECTION of actual conditions; spontaneity, on the other hand, is freer the more the inner nature, reaching out beyond the immediate moment, impresses a distinctive mark upon the subjective attitude.

The reactive efforts we must further subdivide.

Every reaction is set working by a stimulus. There exists normally between stimulus and reaction a connection of aim, since the reaction signifies that subjective relation—psychic or physical—to the stimulus which lies in the direction of the personal life-aims in the individual. But it is not therefore essential that there should be any similarity between the two factors of the connected aim. A needle-prick and its reaction in a feeling of pain have no similarity, nor has the sight of a cake and its reaction in the desire to take it. Most reactions belong to this heterogeneous form, especially in adults. But besides these there is a group of homogeneous reactions, less extensive certainly, but of the greatest significance, especially in childhood. In these the tendency is to REPRODUCE THE STIMULUS IN A SIMILAR WAY.

Now, the homogeneous reaction may extend to the physical as well as to the psychic side of the subjective relation. The first case is well enough known to us in the form of IMITATION of bodily movements, whose significance we have seen in speech, play and elsewhere. On the other hand, the second case has only now and then been touched upon, and must receive more detailed treatment in Chapter XXXII; this is SUGGESTION, which in reality is nothing else than imitation, but an imitation of psychic attitude. Whoever assumes a certain subjective attitude, not because he develops within himself such an attitude to any object, but because some other of strong personality takes up such an attitude before him (or even only appears to take it up), is influenced by suggestion.

To end with, we come to the purely PSYCHOLOGICAL considerations of efforts.

Two action groups correspond to the above-mentioned tendencies of emotion and will. We call an isolated, temporary act of the emotional sphere a "stirring", and in this the effort, as such (apart from its translation into action), appears as an inner reflection in the consciousness. Thus there are stirrings of emotion, moods, stirrings of desire, and of interest. An isolated temporary act of the will-tendency we call a desire; here the representation to the consciousness is the pressing urge to REALIZATION.

This representation indeed can be one of very varying intensity. A desire which consciously only ends in a dull wish for its realization—i.e. does not anticipate action as its result —we might name an "urge". But if the object of the effort is the central point of anticipation in the conscious process, we are dealing with an act of will, and the consciousness of aim becomes the conscious motive. This act of will is "simple" when a single motive determines from the first both the aim and course of effort; it is "complex" when several motives cross in the consciousness. In this case special inner attitudes —choice and decision—intrude between the conscious motives and their accomplishment.

It must, however, not be imagined that the factors and phases of acts of will are all present in the consciousness, rather is it the case that only fragments of this involved inter- and contra-working are consciously known. It is here we often find a personal effort resisting its conscious realization, and thus the contributory causes which man exercising his will thinks he knows may sometimes be other than the impulses which in reality have determined his action.

CHAPTER XXXI

EFFORT IN THE YOUNG CHILD

1. General Characteristics

In dealing with the subject of effort it is much less possible than in any other to look upon the child solely as a miniature adult. The whole personal structure is different, and hence the separate forms of aim, of impulse, the stirrings of emotion and acts of will are of quite other significance. It is true indeed that the infant is from the very beginning a "person", i.e. a life-unity where all parts are blended together to form the whole; but there is still lacking that stability of form which we call "personality", that mutual inter-toning and permanent mutual accommodation of all aims and efforts that make of them one clear individual image. In this, as in all other functioning parts, we find at the beginning a lack of distinctness as well as ambiguity, instability. Aims and efforts mingle in confusion. For instance, if in the adult we can treat emotional feelings and desires in clearly distinguishable psychological categories, it is not possible to do so in the same way with the child; his desires gush forth directly from strong, impulsive, elementary feelings; emotions pass easily into desires and action-impulses.

This diffused confusion of manifold affective feelings and desires is plainly shown in a description which Elsa Köhler gives (pp. 154 seq.) of a fright intentionally given to a little girl. Anna (2 ; 8), rather clumsy physically, goes for a walk with some grown-ups and children in the forest. In a narrow cutting she is allowed to walk on the raised path, which was wide and not high, whilst her aunt walking on the level ground below it holds her hand, but suddenly leaves go and encourages her to follow the example of the other children and go by herself. Anna stops, gives a little groan, stretches out her hand, and hesitates. But her aunt, instead of taking her hand, goes on. One of the older girls steps up the slope and offers her hand only to be refused with screams and angry gestures. "What now rages through the little soul is certainly no longer only fear; perhaps it is a sudden access of anger with me, for putting her in such a position?" And even more; Anna's mother is on a few paces ahead, leading a stranger child by the hand, apparently not troubling about Anna and leaving her farther and farther behind; so do her aunt and the older girl whose help she had scorned. "Now the child stands alone in its fear, anger and, no doubt, its jealousy, forsaken in body and spirit alike. . . . It seems to me she must experience some such feelings as would be mine, if my friends left me on a rock in the middle of the sea, although they could have helped me. Then a strange thing happened. The child who, up till now, had been so timorous in her mortal fear summons up all her strength and shows utmost daring—and right judgment. She sits down on the ground and, bit by bit, slides down the incline of less than a yard high, screaming meantime and deathly pale. . . . A. has undoubtedly had a little shock but has gained an experience of the greatest value."

The lack of clearness and of differentiation is closely connected with the strongly marked "preliminary" nature of its efforts. Even in the discussion of play we discovered that what intensifies, later on, into pronounced forms of instinct and separate interests is present in the child as a germ only.

And just as in an embryo the various organs only appear in vague misty indications, so—to pursue the metaphor on to the field of psychology—in the young child efforts lack that definite aim and decision of purpose which belongs to them later. It is therefore not without some hesitation that we employ here the same names as have a clearly marked significance when applied to the adult; names such as egoism and kindness, deceit and candour, love and jealousy carry with them such an emphasis of adult-psychology that they place the young child in an entirely wrong light. And the danger of a distorted image increases with the distance of time at which impulses—for whose early beginnings we look in the child—actually arrive at maturity. Especially is this the case with the region of erotic-sexual ideas.

If we wish to escape the danger of this wrong application of names, we must not now turn our attention at once to the different kinds of effort, but first deal in a general manner with the formal structure of efforts in early childhood, having in view the twofold aim: (1) To point out the strongly marked points of difference between the nature of effort in childhood and in later periods of life; (2) to describe the gradual approach of psychic life in children to that of higher grades. We shall therefore have to lay so much more stress on development from the purely psychological points of views in proportion as they have suffered neglect at other hands.

An important part is played here by the relation between consciousness and unconsciousness.

The variance between these two spheres of life in the individual—on which psychoanalysis lays special stress—is itself a phenomenon of but slow development. In infant life, consciousness only exists in the undefined rudimentary forms already described, which do no more than rise from the hidden depths of unconscious life to sink back immediately into them again. By degrees life, in the increase of its complicated and conflicting demands, requires foresight, consciousness of aim, power of choice; and the increasing maturity of the individual brings with it the requisite possibility of greater intensity and clarity in the part played by consciousness. This progressive development will be considered in a special section of the present chapter.

But now, to begin with, consciousness still has its roots firmly fixed in the Unconscious. The child's acts of will are not so much hostile interplay between the earliest feelings of impulse and instinct as their refinement, regulation and development; the child is only able to aim consciously at those ends which already exist as pronounced tendencies in the Unconscious.

If, then, it is wished to form in the young child attitudes not in accordance with the carrying out of unregulated impulses, it is not to be expected that this counteraction can be effected by an appeal exclusively or even especially directed to the childish consciousness. At no period of life is simple instruction and explanation so barren of results as in early childhood. Then a special effort must rather be made to anchor the new attitudes and suggestions desired in the Unconscious itself, i.e. to supplement the inborn germs of impulse and instinct by a system of acquired reflexes, or, better still, to see that they merge into this system. This system is habit.

A principle of development comes to our help in this, a principle too that is very marked in early childhood: the tendency for action to become mechanical (Chapter III, 1). This principle proceeds along the opposite "regressive" path

to that followed by the development tendency already discussed—from consciousness to unconsciousness. Newly imposed
forms of action must at first of course arouse consciousness,
at the very least produce feelings of unfamiliarity and perplexity, then again awaken processes of perception, thought
and will, especially if their accomplishment is confronted with
outer difficulties or inner opposition. But repetition quickly
diminishes this expenditure of consciousness, and soon the
effort required has become entirely unconscious. This regressive
form of development begins in the weaning of the infant and
its training in cleanliness; later on the actions of eating,
speaking, care of the person are regulated in the same way
by habit, as are also behaviour to others, growth in cleanliness,
in order with regard to toys, etc. As a result we get those
everyday virtues (and in some cases vices) which speedily
become the child's second nature and overpower his first
nature, i.e. the first undisciplined beginnings of impulse and
instinct.

Thus, by means of "regressive" development through habit,
the path from the Conscious to the Unconscious is both easy
and gradual. But there is quite another kind of transition,
a forcing into the Unconscious which at the same time leads
to a sharp division between the individual conscious and
unconscious life. This forcing into the Unconscious is called
REPRESSION. If we are right in our theory that a sharp differentiation of the two spheres (Conscious and Unconscious) is
attained by slow development only, then repression in which
both show a very distinct individual existence can only be
present in early childhood in an exceedingly rudimentary
form. The opposition derived from this reasoning to the child-
psychology promulgated by Freud and his school demands
special consideration (cf. Chapter XXXIII).

Whilst the principle of repressions credits the child's psychic
nature with a very great measure of inward independence,
the principle of suggestion lays emphasis on the child's pronounced dependence on the mental aims prevalent in his
environment. Since sensitiveness to suggestion—i.e. want of
inner independence—decreases with age, it is especially marked
in early childhood. But this, too, will be treated in a special
chapter (XXXII).

2. Dynamics of Effort in the Child

The economics of individual strength never find more direct expression than in efforts. The young child shows characteristic pictures in the intensity, persistency and distribution of the energies displayed in emotion and will.

The energy of the momentary emotion and desire is often far greater in the child than in the adult. The reason for this lies in its incapacity to stem the flood of excitements pouring upon it and in its complete subjection to the one impulse before other crossing, enervating, retarding impulses can make themselves felt. Displeasing sense-stimuli show special results of this kind; we need only think of the violent screams when the child has knocked himself or of the rage when some delicacy is denied him; yet the delight and darting upon a new toy may show equal excess and unrestraint.

But now the duration in no way corresponds to this impelling force; the child gets over a grief that has just shaken him to his very depths with surprising quickness; any distraction can bring about with almost lightning speed a metamorphosis of tears to smiles. Probably there is some connection between the slight endurance of emotional disturbances and the slight effect of dominant interests which we found in the child's imagination and thought-activity. The psychic power of dominance for considerable periods is indeed a quality which in every functional region only gradually develops from small beginnings; later on we shall have to notice the same in real acts of will.

The child's want of inner stability is also seen when we consider the diffusiveness of subjective relations. There is as yet no firmly welded habit to determine what stimuli in general shall move the child to strong excitation of will and emotion, rather at first, indeed, all is in a state of chaos. An impression which to-day excites greatly may fade to-morrow; what was passionately desired yesterday is refused to-day. There are experiences in our opinion calculated to upset completely the childish mind—and they are passed by indifferently as everyday trifles. Yet other occurrences, in reality of but slight import, exercise on the child a quite unexpected effect of jubilation, fright or rage. Of course, this strange attitude in the child rests partly on intellectual causes—on an imperfect understanding of the occurrence or a wrong interpretation of it. But this does not explain everything. Evidently, then, emotional development partly follows its own laws, which do not always coincide with those of intellectual growth.

Children's individual differences with regard to the dynamics of effort are very strongly marked. And as it is not so much a question of its content as of formal differences, they are not as a rule greatly altered by the experiences of life; hence they are of decided prophetic significance.[1] That trait of character here makes its appearance which was designated by Kerschensteiner as "excitability". The differentiation extends not only to intensity as a whole, but may even touch the different side of some experience as pleasure or displeasure. Of this we find a striking example in a comparison of two of our children.

Of the children, Gunther has the strongest excitability of temperament. His enthusiasm for all beauty that met his eyes, especially for the delights of Nature, was not only of the greatest intensity but of rare permanence for his early years. (Examples in Chapter XXVI, 1.) But he is even more susceptible to displeasing stimuli. For example, every visit to his relatives in Berlin meant for him an emotional upset of absolute pain. The strange faces and conditions, the unaccustomed bed, the want of his toys, all this quite upset his equilibrium; he often cried, made scenes before going to bed, was more disposed than usual to be disobedient. This excitability, too, showed itself on isolated occasions. Defiance and self-will, but then, too, repentance and tenderness, seemed in him to come from greater depths than in the other children.

In one case his violent reaction to a shock led to long continued results. "In the summer holiday the children had been left alone and locked in by an unconscientious nurse. Gunther (2 ; 4) had unexpectedly awakened, called to the maid, and became greatly excited when she did not come. His parents heard his cries, but could not get to him at once as he was locked in, so his father had to break a pane of glass and climb in through the window. Everything happened in the dark. This occurrence upset the boy completely for a long time. Even the bare thought of going to bed, whether in the day or

---

[1] The value as a prophetic symptom which we before indicated in the manner of play (Chapter XXI) and of drawing (Chapter XXVI, 2) is especially pronounced in the dynamics of efforts.

at night, made him afraid; once in bed, he had the most violent fits of crying, which only ceased if his mother stayed with him till he fell asleep. Our one attempt at severity only made matters worse; and he did not get over it until his bed was permanently moved beside his mother's."

His sister, Hilde, two and a half years older, had gone through the whole experience as G. had done, but showed no fear at the time, nor any after-effect. This was due, no doubt, not only to her greater age but to her less excitable temperament.

But now, how does the following behaviour agree with this strong excitability? Again it was in the summer holidays. Gunther (4 ; 2) is standing on the edge of a small pond, bends too far over the edge, and falls in without a word. He was completely under water, and no help came till brought by the call of a stranger who had seen the fall from a distance. Meantime he had made efforts himself to struggle out of the still water. As he was carried home dripping by his father he showed not a sign of fear or excitement, only saying in a whimper: *Herr K.* (the owner of the pond) *ought to put up a railing.* A little scolding, a little tea, and a little warm bed soon sent him into a sweet sleep, from which he got up well and lively for fresh tricks. The experience had simply slipped out of his mind—one of those paradoxical reactions mentioned above.

Eva belonged to quite another type. In early years her excitability in response to painful stimuli was strikingly small. Not that it was a case of general emotional insensibility, for she was exceedingly receptive of the joys of the brighter side of life. "Her temperament is sunny, she laughs and shouts on the slightest occasion", the report runs of her at 2 ; 5, and we find similar remarks continually recurring later on. When we went to relatives in Berlin she, unlike Gunther, felt at home immediately. (At 3 ; 8.) "Her bright amiable temperament makes her everybody's darling, the whole house yields to her charm. The child scarcely cried once in the four weeks in Berlin."

This butterfly gaiety accepted, too, everything easily that might have occasioned great pain to other children, e.g. frequent visits to the dentist's. (4 ; 2½.) "In the most joyous expectancy she paid the visit she found so interesting, seated herself in the chair, beamed at us all, opened her little mouth to its full extent, let the instrument be put in as if it were a bit of chocolate, and had several teeth stopped without an eyelid quivering." If her parents took a walk or visited a museum with her elder brother and sister, she was indeed dejected for a moment, sometimes even to tears, but she only needed an explanation that she was still too young or a proposal of some nice game to be completely reconciled to her fate again. Gunther under the same circumstances was always very unhappy.

Pleasant as this gaiety was in such circumstances as those mentioned, at other times it might easily impress others as a want of sympathy. One summer holiday the children once saw a caterpillar in which an ichneumon had laid eggs, and now the grubs were creeping in their hundreds out of the living caterpillar. The sight was horrible to us grown-ups and to the ten-year-old Hilde. Gunther, too, thought it dreadful, but in his case his thirst for knowledge got the upper hand, and he examined what was happening with a magnifying-glass. Eva (5 ; 8) alone remained unmoved; she looked at it as the others did, and indeed repeated their verdict of *it is horrible*; but she by no means gave the impression of being the least affected by it. (Further instances in Chapter XXXVI, 4.)

The two sons of Herr and Frau Katz show very interesting variations in the dynamics of effort and these are put forward in psychological comparison by their parents. Since both boys grew up in the same environment and educational influences, it is without doubt a case of different dispositions in temperament and character. (D. and R. Katz, *Conversations*, pp. 211 sqq.)

The older boy is the more delicate, gentle, thoughtful and sensitive, the younger rougher, bolder, more thoughtless and less complex. If they feel aggrieved, the elder brother withdraws into himself, but the younger takes up the attack, etc. The former loves animals dearly, it is true, but at a distance; the latter goes up to them, takes hold of them and is not to be frightened away, as, for instance, when a white mouse bit his finger he no sooner had it bandaged than he went for her again.

Now it is remarkable that these characteristics show themselves as general personal structures and are, therefore, not confined to the purely dynamic force of effort. They show themselves too in the physical side as well; the older boy is slightly built, the younger inclined to be stout and sturdy; and in this connection there is a great difference in their tastes as to diet. The former prefers vegetarian food whilst the younger takes meat dishes with outspoken preference.[1]

On the other side, the differences extend to the relation between the individual ego and other human beings.

" Of the two brothers J. is the greater egoist, probably he is not more careful of his own interests than the average child at his age, but of T. it must be said that he excels his contemporaries in self-sacrifice and ready self-denial. It is very difficult to induce J. to give away any of the delicacies that fall to his share, whilst it is correspondingly easy to persuade T. T. has a larger portion of psychological power of sympathy, enquires after the fate of others, is troubled by their sorrow and does not like to hear of other people's misfortunes, whilst J. is not greatly affected by them." (D. and R. Katz, II, p. 220.)

3. The Development of Spontaneity in Will

Even in the new-born infant we have noticed spontaneous movements as well as reactions, although the latter class show a pronounced predominance. And also later on in the first year it was found that most actions followed the paths of sense-impressions with the corresponding motor activity, that is the direct transmutation of a sense-impression into the reaction of movement, and we could only find traces of the emancipation of the child's actions from outer impulses. In the succeeding years, certain psychic developments presented a similar picture; memory and imagination, at first closely connected with existing sense-impressions, freed themselves but slowly from this connection and reached spontaneity.

We must now trace a corresponding development in the child's subjective relation and shall prove that with increased spontaneity there is also an increase in the part played by consciousness; at first he clings almost entirely to the present

[1] D. and R. Katz rightly call attention to the fact that the connection between taste in diet and the constitution of body and character has up till now been practically unexplored, but that the small child offers the best opportunity for such investigation, because such firm taste-appetites have not yet been formed in him as in an adult.

and its chance stimuli, his sensations of pleasure and displeasure, of attraction and aversion, his first uttered judgments
come and disappear with the changing impressions offered by
the world without. Then the first traces of spontaneity begin
to appear; here and there his attitude is connected with inner
experiences, with memories of previous or expectations of
future impressions; processes of deliberation and choice creep
in between the sense-impression and the ultimate reaction,
a dominant interest, ever growing stronger, may maintain a
certain fixity of aim in spite of many diversions tending to
effect other reactions; at last the power is felt of motive-groups
which may oppose firmer inner attitudes to the outer momentary incitement and may already be looked upon as the initial
stages of real character, i.e. sense of honour and duty.

One of the earliest signs of awaking spontaneity in will is
to be seen in the fact that the child of fifteen months will set
himself little tasks which he tries to accomplish. The kind of
task is certainly still entirely dependent on the object which
may chance to be at his disposal.

Gunther (1 ; 3½). "Sometimes G. lays his roll, after he has
taken a bite, up on the big dinner-table by which he is standing to fetch it off the table again; the little fellow is still so
small that he cannot catch a glimpse of the roll he has put
up, and can only reach it with difficulty, but as a rule he
manages to get hold of it again. He acts in the same way with
a dinner-napkin ring: throws it away, runs or creeps after it,
only to throw it away once more when he has laboriously
fetched it out from under the table or behind the chairs. In
this way he makes demands upon himself."

In the course of the second year the child becomes capable
of expressing wishes which cannot in any way be connected
with a perceptible cause, but only with the inward revival
of some former perception.

Gunther (1; 5½). "We often used to play with the boy by
stopping at one end of the room and rolling a ball to the
child sitting at the other end. To-day G. suddenly plumped
down very comically at one end of the room with the imperative exclamation: *Ball !*"

Hilde (1 ; 9½). "A pencil is now often demanded with the
word *ite ite* without her having seen paper or pencil."

Hilde (2 ; 7) has been, for days now, filled with a continuous wish to possess a doll's perambulator. This wish was not only expressed when she saw other children with such perambulators, but often enough quite spontaneously since her imagination was continually dwelling on this idea.

Even those attitudes which result in reactions may in character and performance be more or less influenced by inner spontaneous factors.

This is principally shown in the gradual development of the power of "choice".

At first the child has chiefly to deal with simple reactions, i.e. with those in which a definite stimulus produces a definite attitude; some request is made to the child—he carries it out; a piece of chocolate is handed to him—he takes it, etc. Even when the stimulus leaves open several possibilities of reaction the child at first finds it more convenient to seize indiscriminately any of these contingencies without the intervention of an intellectual decision, a "choice".

We notice the simplest applications of choice at the age of 1 ; 8.

"Hilde (1 ; 8) was accustomed in the morning to empty her playthings out of the cupboard, and bit by bit to lay them on the window-seat; other objects, too, in the room, such as her father's things on his cupboard, travelled to the same hoarding-place. Then one day her father said: 'Bring me back everything you have taken from me.' Hilde at once found collar, tie and pocket-knife and brought them. There only remained a pair of gloves folded one in the other lying half-hidden between toys, so that the child might easily overlook it. At the exhortation: 'You must bring back something more,' she cast a searching, lingering look over the number of things, once hesitatingly took hold of a little doll's hat, but at once put it down again and looked and looked. At last H. caught sight of the gloves, seized them immediately with full assurance and real joy to restore them to their proper place."

Hilde (2 ; 4). "She was to have a cake, and the maid handed the full cake-dish for her to choose. H. took a long time deciding without touching one, *Which is it?* At last she made up her mind—*I'll have this here*, and took one."

Not long after, the child becomes capable of choosing between possibilities, each of which is accompanied by a strong feeling-tone, so that the ultimate attitude of the will only develops from several preceding emotional attitudes. The child in such cases goes through a regular contest of motives.

Such inner conflicts of the little child's may seem to the adult no more than a storm in a teacup, all the more so because as a rule he has only a smile for the value of the conflicting motives. But the psychic enquirer views them differently. Here, indeed, is the opportunity to see the surprising variety of the child's emotional life and what mutual connections opposition, incitement and suppression, the emotional elements, may produce, to lead at last to a decisive attitude or to a sequence of such relations. There are motives set free as pure reaction by a sense-stimulus; these may be confronted by motives of a spontaneous nature originating in a sense of honour, sympathy, duty or curiosity.

An example in another connection was given in Gunther's (3 ; 2) changeable behaviour on his visit to a circus. Here we had a motley collection of motives; fear for himself, anxiety for his sister, a desire to be brave, confidence (in his protector), curiosity and a wish to see, within a few minutes followed each other and raged in wild confusion through the child's mind. We would refer the reader to the instance of little Anna, lately reported on another page.

The contest of emotion and will called forth by way of experiment in Scupin's son was of a different character. It was a battle between egoism and self-denial on his mother's behalf; as a further shade of feeling, something like uneasiness of conscience appeared after his decision.

Scupin (3 ; 8). "To-day his father in play gave his mother a little slap, when Bubi stood up before him ready to fight: *You, not to beat my mother, or else I beat you!* His father declared quite seriously that one or other he must beat, and Bubi could choose either to be beaten himself or to have his mother beaten. Bubi looked quite at his wit's end, evidently fighting with himself, turned crimson, and at last answered: *No not me, beat Mummy only very little*, laying particular emphasis on the *very little*. Whilst the answer showing undisguised childish egoism but yet a good heart as well quite pleased us, Bubi did not seem quite satisfied with himself,

GG

indeed looked up to his mother in a somewhat depressed and anxious way, and did not recover his cheerfulness again until she gave him a friendly nod. (II, 65.)

Which motive wins the final victory in such inner conflict and decides the attitude depends on a thousand circumstances, which vary not only from child to child and from year to year, but also from case to case. That the reaction to the momentary stimulus—a passing fit of greed, a defiant ebullition, a feeling of fear—very often conquers other less outward forms of feeling, is only to be expected from the primitive stage of the child's development; in this he plainly resembles uncivilized man, who in like manner is first and foremost a creature of the moment and of impulse. But yet, however, we must not think too lightly of the child. In the character development even of children from the fourth to the sixth year those motive groups, which are not bound up with the sense-stimulus of the moment, but permanently anchored in the child's nature, become so strong that they sometimes appear in opposition to fairly energetic momentary impressions; that is then a victory of spontaneity over simple reaction. Certainly these motive-groups are not spontaneous in the sense that the child has produced them directly by himself; teaching and example must be presupposed in order that ambition, sense of honour, and of duty, consideration, etc., may develop in a certain way. And yet teaching and example alone could never produce these kinds of attitude if the fruitful germ of such qualities were not already inherent in the child's nature; indeed, often enough their appearance, their sudden development, the specific form of their distinctive feature, is so surprisingly little influenced by conditions of the outer environment that we think we have directly solved the secret of "inborn faculties".

The different provinces of subjective relation will each occupy our attention later on; here we will only add a few examples of conflicting motives ending in a victory of higher reasons over the momentary impulse. In these cases the question is generally one of self-mastery (self-control), whose appearance in little children surprises as much as it delights us.[1]

[1] Further examples, some from somewhat more advanced ages, are to be found in *Aus einer Kinderstube*, by T. Meyer and C. Stern, Chaps. II and IX.

Self-mastery is shown either in the acceptance of something disagreeable or in the refusal of something agreeable.[1]

Striking instances of the first case occur in our children from the fourth year. Hilde and Eva both had a strong aversion to the skin on the surface of hot milk or cocoa, yet at the age of three, by appealing to their sense of honour, by explaining how wholesome this detested skin was, by the example of their elders in partaking of the skin with apparent enjoyment, and lastly, by their mother's emphatic but quietly expressed wish, without any penalty or threat, we succeeded in inducing the children to swallow the skin of their own free will. This aversion, however, still continued undiminished, so that Eva (5 ; 9) could once more in the same matter test her self-mastery, which had now attained a high grade of spontaneity; for she did so without anyone asking or influencing her in any way—only because her brother and sister had done it the day before. So that she actually came to tell her mother with sudden pride: *I have just taken the cream (skin) out of the cocoa and eaten it. I couldn't yesterday evening because I didn't have any : that's why I've just done it.*

Akin with this is the attitude to certain medical measures, for taking physic and submitting to cold wet compresses are proceedings that give children a painful shock, to begin with at any rate.

In the case of Gunther (3 ; 8) it was necessary to renew such a compress every hour. "Sometimes he refused with screams; but I always induced him by appealing to his self-respect, without using any force, to yield to it. Once I said when he was little he had been so good about having the compresses, next time I persuaded him by whispering that Hilde in the room expected him to scream at the compress, so he must be quite quiet, so that she would not notice and be astonished to find it all done—and he kept as quiet as a mouse whilst it was done. The third time I coaxed him with the prospect of the doctor's praise."

The other kind of self-mastery—refusal of pleasure—is not quite so difficult as submission to pain, thus we get instances of it at an even earlier age.

Scupin's son (2 ; 9). "The beginning of self-control is evident

---

[1] A third form, the restraint of a personal state of emotion (defiance, rage), will be considered later.

in the boy's talk to himself when eating a buttered roll: *Bubi don't lick down the butter from the roll—big children don't do that, only quite little children do : that is very ugly, you know*; and looked at us for approval." (I, 75.)

We find similar voluntary self-denial on a far higher stage in Hilde (4 ; 3). "For some naughtiness at dinner her cherries had been taken away from her until the next day. In the afternoon her mother, who had long since forgotten the incident, said to the children: 'Now, you'll get a chocolate cigar for your walk.' But H. at once saw the contradiction in this to the punishment imposed upon her, and was not silenced by the prospect of the sweet, but at once with some strength of character drew the logical conclusion, *But I shan't get one, Mummy, you see I was naughty—only Gunther.* And she did not make the slightest attempt to persuade me, having once said it, to give her a chocolate cigar as well." In connection with the time conditions of the child's attitude we meet with the same law of development as in our discussion of imagination and thought; the dominant interest, i.e. the power to decide the course of psychic activity for a time by some mental aim, or by a task, is included in general continued growth. The stronger the dominant interest in the region of desire, the more possibility of more complicated and extensive will activities, the more consistency in the child's life, and the greater the power of resistance to interruptions and distractions from the fixed aim.

When the child at eighteen months begins to take little messages from its mother to the maid, it requires not only to remember the words but also the fact of its errand all the way to the kitchen. Even this little distance offers so many distractions, and the child's imagination may meantime have followed so many side issues, that we must not wonder if the determining thought, "I have to take a message", has meantime lost its power.

But it is not only fresh and outer impressions that may destroy the dominant interest; hindrances in the performance of a given object may arise from within as well.

For it is only in very easy tasks that the will is able to be fixed upon their fulfilment. If more difficult demands are made, it must first fix and attain intermediate aims, i.e. SEVERAL DOMINANT INTERESTS OF A LOWER ORDER MUST BE

PRESSED INTO SERVICE, without, however, losing sight of the chief interest. Almost all serious forms of activity are in adult life composed of such mingled, diverse, superior and subordinate means and aims, whilst in childhood such systematic arrangement is but weak.

Again and again we may notice in the child the most striking disparity in intention and execution, and this, indeed, not because the intention was lacking in earnestness, but because the first aims used to the last thread all the energy available in the dominant interest. The child comes to a stop at some intermediate aim, turns it into the main object, and connects with it others quite different not belonging to it at first; in short, his action is a striking instance of the principle of the "heterogeneous character of aims" as propounded by Wundt. In addition to the difficulty of the task, its duration may prove a stumbling-block for the dominant interest. To begin with, a motive with a strong feeling-tone may bring about some action; the boy zealously undertakes to put up a great building with his bricks, the girl falls in joyfully with her mother's request to arrange her scattered toys tidily. But the performance takes time, the pleasure feeling of the first impulse diminishes, weariness sets in, new pleasure motives arise, and against these powers the dominant interest of the task, even if it still happens to be consciously present, cannot permanently prevail—and the child drops the work he has begun.

We gave abundant instances of this weakness and caprice in the dominant interest when dealing with play, confabulation and drawing, so that no fresh examples are required of exactly corresponding cases in the emotional and desire attitudes.

But it is well worth while to offer examples of the exceptions to this rule. For that unsystematic action and the want of motive-persistency decreases year by year, and the gradual strengthening of the dominant interest in the child forms one of the most important helps in the formation of will and character.

First of all we show by an example how the chief dominant interest may survive many intermediate tasks in a task offering difficulties to the child.

Hilde (2 ; 9). "H. was told to carry a footstool on which she had been sitting back to its place under a work-table in front of a chair close by. H. carried it up to the table and then asked some of us to move away the chair standing in front. We suggested she should do it herself, which she did. Then she picked up the stool again, but now the chair was pushed so close to the couch that she doubted at first if she could get through. To manage this better she first put the stool on the chair, squeezed through and lifted down the stool to put it under the table. Her next business was to put away four cushions she had used; they belonged in four different rooms, but without any hesitation she sorted them out correctly."

Further instances will show that the child can at times show a fair amount of perseverance in carrying out a task once undertaken. We have already mentioned how indefatigably a child will persist for one or several consecutive hours in some games, but here it is the lasting pleasure in the occupation itself which automatically secures its continuance.

It is on a much higher stage when the DOMINANT INTEREST itself provides the child with a sufficient reason for carrying out a task once begun to its completion, even when the feelings of pleasure, present at first, disappear or are dispersed or crossed by those of an opposite nature. In this case we already meet with the awakening of a sense of duty.[1] It does not matter what the special nature of the duty is nor whether the task is one chosen by the child or imposed upon him from without: it is enough that THE AIM OF THE TASK IS FELT AS A COMMAND NOT TO PROVE FAITHLESS; the whole act from the inception of the dominant interest to its accomplishment in its unity and necessary coherence is understood and appraised at its full value. We are here doubtless brought face to face with those natural moral faculties mentioned above which can indeed be awakened, strengthened and guided by education, but not created.

Hilde (3 ; 8). "If any work is required of her, she remains mindful of it for a considerable period and carries it out. A few days ago I left the child, telling her to gather up in a basket the innumerable paper snippings she had scattered in her play, and that I expected when I came home to find everything tidy. When I returned in an hour's time she ran

---

[1] This word, of course, here is only used as an analogue, a germ-form, so to speak, of what in the adult is understood by a sense of duty.

at once to tell me she had gathered up everything. On similar occasions if I come in to her as she is working to see what she is doing, full of her task, she calls out to me: *Do stop outside a bit—I've not finished yet."*

The following instance shows the triumph of this sense of duty over inclination:—

Scupin (3 ; 5). "Just lately Bubi has developed great zeal in putting away the toys he has used during the day; he refuses to have his supper until he has put all his toys in their places. To-day we offered him a piece of apple, as a rule a great tit-bit of his; his face gave signs of a short struggle between his desire for the apple and his sense of duty, but soon the latter conquered and Bubi quietly said: *No, afterwards : first I must tidy up all the muddles."* (II, 42.)

Of course, we must not make too many demands on this self-control. If the temptation, calculated to lead the child away from his intention, continues for a considerable time, the more primitive motives get the upper hand again. It is no less droll than interesting from a psychological point of view to watch how virtue at first triumphant grows gradually weary in well-doing, and how the little ascetic of four or five years of age once more becomes a real impulsive child.

Gunther (4 ; 7). "At dinner we had stewed plums, a very favourite dish of his. In spite of this he declares he was going to keep his for his supper—a heroic resolve! I looked at him encouragingly once or twice to tell him to eat them up, but he stood firm. Then he played with his spoon, threw it down, and begged to have it picked up again. His father said: 'What is the use, he is not going to eat!' We gave him the spoon 'to play with', as he said. His father remarked that it was getting darker, evening would be there directly—then he almost cried and persisted he would wait until real evening. Then we left him in peace. Suddenly he said: *Or I'll eat it at afternoon coffee.* We suggested: 'Listen, our afternoon coffee is served (we grown-ups were having a cup of coffee), so you can eat them at our afternoon meal.' G. *No, I mean proper afternoon coffee when we have ours.* Then the maid began to clear away, and I said: 'Save G.'s plums for this afternoon.' Then he suddenly seized the spoon as if some sudden light had come to him and made the great concession: *Well, yes, then I'll just eat them at your afternoon coffee,* and fell to with

great good will! Hilde laughed heartily, for she had already
said: *Now we shall see when Gunther's evening is.*"

Scupin (4 ; 8). "A couple of marzipan sausages had been
given to Bubi. He at once broke off one little sausage and
put it back in the bag, saying it was for Lotty. But not long
after, when he had eaten his own sausage, he opened the bag
again and began to play with Lotty's marzipan. We purposely
let him alone to see if, uninfluenced, he could remain true to
his first resolve. Suddenly Bubi broke the sausage in two and
said: *O dear, now it's broken in two! I'll eat the little bit and
Lotty will get the big one.* So he did, and put the bigger piece
back in the bag for Lotty. Then he began to play at trains
with chairs and footstools. As he looked through his toys to
find passengers for his train, he suddenly caught sight of the
bag. He laid it beside him on the edge of the chair with the
decision: *Lotty's sausage can come with me.* But unfortunately
it did not stop there; Bubi opened the bag again, fetched out
the sausage and broke off another little bit: *Mummy, can I
eat just a tiny scrap more?* His mother pretended not to hear,
and Bubi, glad not to hear 'No', quickly ate it up. When
Lotty at last came in the afternoon there was only a morsel
of marzipan about as big as a nut left in the bag, but Bubi
held it out to his visitor in triumph: *Here, Lotty, take it, I
saved it on purpose for you.*" (II, pp. 135 seq.)

But here two years bring with them greater moral strength.

Gunther (5 ; 11½). "Yesterday he showed me four cherries
which he meant to save till the next morning. And he really
did accomplish the feat, although the cherries lay on the end
of his bed as a constant temptation."

4. Freedom and Independence in Early Childhood

As the last section has shown, the development of independent
will makes certain progress in early childhood, yet it covers
but a small portion of the path to the goal of the inner independence and personal responsibility of the individual, and it
is not until this goal is reached that man is really free. Hence
it is requisite that education should aim at promoting the
scholars' freedom, and it should be her ideal gradually to
withdraw her authority in proportion as the inner self-deter-
mination of the developing child becomes able to take the

place of outside influence. But this withdrawal of educational powers can only take place by very gradual stages, just as the child's psychic nature only takes very short steps in its approach to the goal of independence. In other words: Freedom is the goal but not the one and only principle of education.[1]

We recognize the aim of this consideration. In modern pedagogics we often meet with an idea of freedom of quite another nature; its chief exponent for early childhood is Mme Montessori. Freedom in this sense means left to one's own nature and withdrawn as far as possible from outside influences, especially those of persons in authority. Education should confine itself (a) to being in readiness to create for the children the environment in which natural tendencies to development can come into activity with opportunity for their practice, and (b) to guard against influences which are found unsuitable for the child's nature, for example, according to Mme Montessori: dolls, fairy-tales, etc.

The enthusiastic "Montessori mother" D. C. Fisher writes these very words (p. 64): "The corner-stone of the Montessori system, on which rests firmly every smallest item of educational material, every technical detail, is the full recognition of the fact that NO HUMAN BEING CAN BE EDUCATED BY ANY OTHER WHATEVER. Each must educate himself or it will not be done."

Now we might oppose to this point of view an apparently paradoxical thesis. "The child is to be left to his own nature." Well and good! But the little child's own nature consists to a great extent in an essential lack of liberty; dependence on others and their support, stimulation, guidance and control are essential features of this stage of development, moreover they are positive features by which he is led slowly along the path to independence of will and mind. If we neglect these needs of childhood from a wrong conception of freedom, another power—perhaps of less educational value—takes control instead, as we found when considering earlier in this book (Chapter XVI) the "atmosphere of the Montessori school".

The reader must not misinterpret these sentences. How greatly I favour the free development of the child's powers is shown throughout this book, but especially in the consideration of

[1] Cf. similar trains of thought by Muchow (IV). On the other side, Gerhards (p. 38 sqq.).

play in childhood; here where the child lives in his own world, all outside authority should be confined to providing opportunity and encouragement, example and guidance, but should never extend to command or compulsion. Here I think much more uncontrolled freedom is requisite than is recognized by Mme Montessori.

There is too a second activity where the little child's emancipation from adult help is to a greater degree both possible and desirable, viz. the everyday performances of dressing and undressing, personal cleanliness, eating, orderly arrangement of toys, etc. It is in the education of this independence that we find one of the chief merits of the Montessori system. The example of their schoolfellows and the daily practice have as a result that these children alone and without help wash their hands at the end of a meal, put on their coats for themselves, clear away the toys they have used, and that some whose duty it is lay the table for the whole company, etc. Many acts in which the child has to wait for the adult (and also therefore the adult for the child) are here considerably reduced in number.

But this independence is acquired by habits, not by decisions or in other words by the daily routine, not by continual fresh ideas for forming and educating the child's character.

That this distinction is not made, is perhaps the chief failing in the Montessori psychology and educational methods. Where habit is a preparatory step to or even the acquirement of fixed standards of behaviour, then the educator may to a great extent efface himself, but where a demand is made for continual striving up to higher stages of mind and will, the educator must to a far greater extent be in evidence. Concerning the insufficiency of the Montessori freedom in mental education enough has been said already in Chapter XVI of this book. As regards the education of the will, our description of development (Section 3 of this chapter) has shown how essential is the convergence between the inner unregulated impulses and the first germs of a regulated will on the one hand and the outer adult influences on the other. Later chapters will bring fresh material concerning suggestion, punishment, and want of truth. Is then a mature adult, with a sense of his duty to the child, to have less right to act as a factor in its development than a collection of varying gramophone records?

It is true that for a long time there has been too much restraint and compulsion exercised in the training of the will in early childhood, and this practice still continues in certain circles; the modern freedom in education is the natural and to a great extent beneficent reaction to this. But now this benefit should not fall into disrepute by a deficiency in the matter of real education.[1]

[1] It is very remarkable that the keenest upholders of the "freedom" movement in the school should at this very moment begin to see that they have gone too far in the removal of definite educational measures and in the proclamation of the uncontrolled rule of the child's own nature. This change of opinion finds emphatic expression in the excellent paper in which E. Zeidler, a leader in the movement of the Hamburg *Gemeinschaftschulen*, describes "The Discovery of the Boundary Line", *Die Entdeckung der Grenze.*

SUGGESTION

SUGGESTION is the awakening of like mental attitude by means of inner imitation. Thus in every suggestion we find two agents involved—the transferer and the imitator; therefore an active and passive side appear in the occurrence. The activity in making a suggestion is called "suggestivity", the passive reception "suggestibility". For instance, the mother's attitude is strongly suggestive and the child's attitude to her one of suggestibility. These few words in explanation of the main ideas.

The people surrounding the child continually assume attitudes in the form of judgments, feelings and resolves, which they make known either in word or deed. These attitudes now act upon the child as stimuli. As long as the stimulus has only the effect of making the child grasp and understand those psychic processes, there is no question of suggestion. My attitude only acts as suggestion upon the child when it produces in him, by way of imitation, the same attitude—but without the child knowing anything of its character of pure imitation; he thinks he has made an effort himself—then his judgment is nothing but an appropriation of mine, his feeling an imitation of my feeling and his desire a copy of mine.

The imitation by which a suggestion is adopted presupposes a higher mental development than purely physical imitations. All that is required for these is that the child should see others' movements and be able to carry them out. But suggestion requires the child to penetrate another's outward signs of words, expressional movements or deeds, to reach the inner judgment, feeling and will lying behind them. It is only physical imitation when the child begins to scream as soon as he hears other children screaming; on the other hand it is suggestion when at sight of tears he understands the sadness they express and then becomes sad himself (Emotional suggestion). It is only imitation when the child, seeing me clap my hands, claps his too; but it is suggestion when in a sham fight the enthusiasm and courage inspiring the leader infect his play-fellows, and his determination to make an attack is adopted by all (Will-suggestion).

Even from these examples we can see that the transition between simple physical imitation and psychic adoption is a very easy step; even we grown-ups often enough do not know whether the furious applause in the theatre carries us off our feet too, because the MOVEMENT of clapping awakens our imitation, or because the spectators' ENTHUSIASM, thereby expressed, by suggestion kindles ours as well. Frequently, too, imitation, only physical to begin with, forms a little entrance-gate through which suggestion manages to creep. All this concerns the child greatly, because in him physical imitation plays such an ever-present part, and because, at the same time, his physical expression and inner psychic activity are much less sharply differentiated than in the adult.

As in imitation, so in suggestion, the child exercises his power of choice with regard to the PERSON to whose influence he submits. Without exception mothers exercise the strongest suggestive influences; what they consider beautiful or ugly, right or wrong, appears so to the child as well. Their belief becomes the child's dogma: what the mother earnestly desires she is able with pedagogic instinct so to impress on the child's will, that he never dreams but that it is his own wish. But, in addition to hers, there are other suggestive forces: father, relatives, early teachers, servants. We are often utterly unable to explain why some particular person has won a specially strong power of suggestion with a child, whilst others, in spite of the most honest endeavour and real educational gifts, can find no entrance at all. Here, no doubt, is a case of those last personal mysteries which, up till now, are quite beyond the reach of psychology. Also, we must not forget playfellows and, above all, older brothers and sisters, for they it was indeed who awakened imitation in such intensive wise, especially in play; it is they, too, who play the part of chief suggestors for the kind of will, judgment and feeling specially belonging to the age of childhood. Most of the suggestive influences exercised by these persons are unintentional. The comparison with imitation again forces itself upon our notice. The child imitates, not only what is purposely put before him, but all kinds of things, often, with strange persistency, just what is least desirable (grimaces, mistakes in dialect, etc.). And, in the same way, owing to his strong susceptibility, he reaches out to all possible attitudes and assumes them as his own; here he picks up some judgment uttered in his elders' conversation and produces it—real *enfant terrible* that he is—on the most unsuitable occasions as his own; there he allows himself to be infected by a senseless ghost-superstition or fear of thunder from the servants; and, again, he adopts from elder brothers and sisters interest in games or collections which are quite unsuited to his age, and therefore show no sign of the usual spontaneity of children's play, etc. Thus amongst the suggestion-phenomena of childhood we find what is desirable and undesirable from an educational point of view, as well as what is valuable and harmful from a moral standard surging together in wild confusion.

But suggestions differ from physical imitation in one very important point: the attitude assumed by the child has never indeed been actually perceived by him in another—for it is essentially an inner act—but only inferred. It is therefore not at all necessary that the other should really hold such an attitude; as soon as the child merely presupposes it in him, its suggestive effect is possible. Thus then simulated and acted attitudes may equal real ones in power of suggestion. Anyone telling horrible tales to a child in very expressive tones, without himself feeling a trace of fear, may yet thereby suggest to the child the strongest feeling of terror. Moreover, the child may read in some outward act of the other a hidden attitude which perhaps has only appeared unconsciously. In this connection we have the extensive field of suggestive questions. If I ask: "Hadn't the man a stick?" the child already attributes to me the opinion that he did indeed have a stick, and this attitude, imputed to me, may have the well-known suggestion-result of a wrong answer.

The following little collection of examples of successful suggestions may begin with the dispersal by suggestion of negative attitudes (pains, disinclinations, etc.). We have mentioned children's aversion to cold compresses. (Chapter XXXI, 3.) But it is by no means always necessary to awaken the child's self-control, as is there described, by an appeal to his self-respect; when the child is still younger, by means of suggestion he can even be persuaded that the compress is something pleasant and worth striving for.

Scupin's son (2 ; 3½) joyfully accepted a compress which forced his head into an uncomfortable position, because he had been told "Bubi has been a good boy and is getting a compress now in reward. He lay there motionless, murmuring happily *a tompress*" (I, 124). The cod-liver oil, so detested as a rule, assumed the rôle of "the nice juice" given as a reward after a successful meal in the little girl observed by Elsa Köhler. "The same boy (4 ; 4) came running up to us with every sign of horror to tell us that an ugly worm was creeping up the window. It was a wood-louse, which his father picked up carefully, saying: 'What a pretty little creature it is!' " The child's look of disgust disappeared at once; he came up, full of curiosity, took hold of the animal with a smile, and followed with interest its every movement. The path of suggestive example is a very sure one to conquer the fear in children of the handling of certain creatures (frogs, cockchafers, etc.).

Cure by suggestion plays a special rôle in every nursery in the healing of children's many minor aches and pains from falls, knocks, scratches and pinches. In ours it was "blowing" on the tender spot that worked wonders, year after year.

Hilde (2 ; 0). "I achieve the finest cures with my 'blowing it well'." Begun in joke, this blowing has now become serious earnest for Hilde.

"I used to blow when she had given herself a little knock, and now H. has got so used to it that with every little pain she runs to me or her father crying: *iaow, iaow, blow! feet iaow!* or whatever other ill afflicted her. I do not even need to blow quite close, but after a very few puffs in the direction of feet or stomach, I get in answer to my question if it is better a pleased '*yes*'."

The same method is still in full swing with Hilde (3 ; 5), and already successful with Gunther (1 ; 6), "the poor little fellow is forever knocking himself, but his screams are nearly always silenced if I blow a little".

We are here at the source of all cure by suggestion, which only requires faith in the healing power of the means employed, no matter what its specific nature. Even the adult cannot look down with contempt on these little healing miracles of the nursery; for what part does not faith, awakened by suggestion, play in his life, whether by means of a certain method of cure, a renowned name or a wonder-working sacred place! It is but a step from a cure by blowing to a cure by prayer.

The dispersion of unpleasant feelings by suggestion is unfortunately counterbalanced by their suggestive invocation, thus all the examples above can be confronted by their opposite. A child who has scarcely hurt himself by a fall or a knock can, by his mother's too-ready sympathy and anxious cosseting, be made to fancy a much more serious pain, with the result of louder and longer screams; if such instances often occur, the child learns by suggestion a permanent self-pity. But this kind of suggestion rages most cruelly with reference to fear and allied emotions. We find an opposite effect to that in the wood-louse incident in the numerous cases where their elders do not hide, even before the children, their senseless fear of touching certain animals, such as frogs and cockchafers.

And then, above all, the ineradicable attempts to make the child afraid, the threat of the black man, the tales of ghosts lying behind the stove, the exclamation: "Ah, now the police-man is coming to fetch you", and all the thousand other variations of this senseless educational method! The child does not notice that the speaker has no belief himself in all these evil things; by nature he has a certain disposition to timidity, and thus falls a helpless victim to such suggestions of fear. It is not speaking too strongly to say that no other outer influence can so embitter a child's early years as threats like these. Even severe punishments, after all, cause only passing pain, but suggested feelings of fear bring permanent suffering to the child; every time he is alone, in the dark, or in unusual surroundings, may be a real torture to him.

Therefore it is parents' most urgent duty to restrain com-pletely themselves from such fear-suggestions and strictly to forbid them to servants, who are, as a rule, very prone to their use.

We have been successful ourselves in this respect, so that I am glad to say we have no examples of our own of this kind of suggestion. The Scupins, too, made the same endeavour, not, however, with perfect success. Shortly before their child was two years old, he had been persuaded by a servant that a ghost —the Bubu—was sitting behind the stove, and at 1 ; 11 the parents' report reads: "Unfortunately the child has again been told about 'the Bubu'. Whenever he hears a strange noise now, he stares in horror and asks: *Bubu?* Often when we have thought the boy long since asleep he was sitting up in his little cot, and when we came in, pointed to the stove, saying: *Stove Bubu is toming! No, no, not toming!* Probably the nursemaids have told him that the Bubu will come out of the stove and punish naughty children." (I, pp. 95 sqq.)

Now comes another instance of the good educational result of suggestion; in this case not in effecting an attitude of feeling and emotion but one of the will. The old saying: an ounce of practice is worth a pound of precept is, at root, nothing but an application of the principle of suggestion to action.

Scupin (5 ; 2). "A bag of sweets was brought out on a picnic, and his father gave a sweet to a little ragged girl at the roadside, much to the surprise of Bubi, who more than once looked thoughtfully at the last two pralines in his hand. When he saw a village boy coming in the distance, he snatched his hand out of his father's and saying: *I will give him one too*, pressed a sweet into the stranger's hand; afterwards he smiled a little nervously, as if he was half-ashamed of his action. A simple request to give the child something would certainly have had no result." (II, 171.)

AUTO-SUGGESTION.

In all the suggestions, considered so far, the active and passive factors were supplied by two different individuals; but there are also cases where the giver and receiver of a suggestion are found in one and the same person.

In this "auto-suggestion",[1] the individual transfers an attitude of his own from one period of time or from one psychic activity to another. For instance, a child is afraid of the dark; this phase of feeling now influences his critical attitude in such a way that the spontaneous foundations of judgments, viz. calm observation and deliberation, cannot make themselves felt, fear turns into the expectation of some evil sight, this into the assurance that an uncanny something is sitting in a corner and—the auto-suggestion is complete. Another variety of auto-suggestion is shown by the following:—

Hilde (4 ; 11½), Gunther (2 ; 8½). The two children often play together at "The Lion or the Dog is Coming", or some such game. One of them then creeps on all fours across the room and the other runs away in apparent fear. The lion or dog does not make any terrifying noise or even show his teeth or claws—

---

[1] This, too, has its parallel in the province of purely physical imitation. Cf Self-imitation (Chapter V, 2).

they are the tamest of animals—but, none the less the child pursued often begins to cry in such terror and so hastily takes refuge with his mother that we feel quite convinced that the fear is real, not simulated; in this case auto-suggestion adds a spice of actual terror. (Cf. the similar notice about Hilde, Chapter XIX.)

CONTRA-SUGGESTION.

The phenomenon of the so-called "contra-suggestion" seems to differ even more from real suggestion, but in reality these two forms are most closely connected. Here an attitude is chosen which is the exact opposite of the one observed; instead, therefore, of submission we find express opposition dictated by the child's violent desire of independence. But its further progress shows anything but this, for the attitude does not originate in the child's own inner nature, but is directly produced by the example he sees, exactly as in direct suggestion; the one very scanty contribution made by the child's own initiative is that he gives to his attitude the appearance of an exact opposite. The adoption of a contra-suggestion, then, is nothing but wolf's clothing which the lamb puts on, the pretence of strength meant to hide the consciousness of weakness.

A characteristic of this disguised weakness is the fact that if the suggestor's attitude is changed (by apparent agreement with the child's opposition), in a second the child reverses his attitude, either because it was never meant seriously, or because the fighting attitude must be plainly maintained at any cost. There is an excellent Munich picture-series which illustrates the state of affairs better than any theoretical explanations. A peasant is taking a young pig to be killed. The pig is obstinate and refuses to go in at the slaughter-house door. As long as the peasant tries to drag him forward, it pulls back with equal strength, and there seems no end to the battle. Then the peasant turns right round with the pig and drags it away from the door with all his might. And the pig, persisting in the contra-suggestion, drags himself in, to the peasant's hidden and malicious delight. The tale holds good psychologically, not only for young pigs but for human beings too, and is of educational value. For often a child who obstinately refuses to do or take something required can quickly be brought to it by apparently forbidding him or withholding the thing refused.

The phenomena appropriate here seem to become more strongly developed in the fifth year.[1]

Gunther (4 ; 7). If we think anything nice and he does too, as a rule he will, in spite of this, say, to begin with: *I don't think it's a bit nice*, or *I don't like it at all*. It is only when we begin apparently to draw the logical conclusion and take the food away that he confesses: *It is nice after all*.

Scupin (4 ; 11). If he has once decided not to eat a certain dish, we have proved it perfectly useless in any way to press the new food upon him; if he refuses the dish, he gets something else, and when the same food again appears at table it is not at first offered to him but some other food instead. As a rule, then, he asks of himself if he may taste the other for once—if we only grant this request with some hesitation and every appearance of consideration, we are certain of victory. Bubi is then firmly convinced that it is something especially good and eats the food, but lately despised, with marked relish. (II, 152.)

The quality of suggestibility depends greatly upon age. Since susceptibility to suggestion requires a certain mental growth, it cannot possibly exist in the earliest stages of life (in which there is already physical imitation).

But as soon as the necessary inner conditions, above all understanding for the attitude of others, have developed—i.e. about the middle of the second year—we find suggestion-phenomena, and in a short time suggestibility becomes very strong. The child's great dependence on those around him, his unbounded confidence in them, his uncritical attitude, the convenience of assuming a ready-made attitude, one which the child could not create himself or only with the greatest effort, all this makes suggestibility one of childhood's most outstanding qualities. But the growth of spontaneity with increasing years (already treated in our last chapter) has to make itself felt in opposition to suggestion, for the more spontaneity in the attitude, the stronger the independence and critical power, and the less the child's need to adopt others'

---

[1] That there are indications of the contra-suggestible attitude at a very much earlier age seems indicated by the following observation of Alfred Adler's (*Healing and Forming*, p. 96): "I saw a boy of thirteen months who had barely learnt to stand and walk. If he was put in his chair he stood up; if we said to him, 'Sit down', he remained standing with a roguish look. His six-year-old sister on one such occasion called out to him, 'Keep on standing', and down sat the boy."

attitudes or his satisfaction with them. Thus decline in suggestibility is one of the surest laws of the child's development.

Apart from age, there is much individual variation in suggestibility. We need not think this can be simply referred to intelligence, in the sense that the less intelligent child is always the more susceptible to suggestion. For suggestibility is partly a MATTER OF TEMPERAMENT. If a child, with a very active temperament, likes to take up a definite relation to all kinds of things, if his ambition urges him to do and to believe what others do and believe, if his blissful confidence has not, as yet, been too much weakened by criticism and opposition, he may be very susceptible to suggestion, without detriment to his intelligence.

The large number of examples of suggestion put forward by the Scupins point to the fact that this boy was fairly susceptible to suggestion. On the other hand we could notice distinct resistance to suggestions in our youngest daughter at a very early period. Beside the instances of this already given in the aussage-experiments (Chapter XVIII), the following example may throw light on this special quality in the child:—

Eva (2 ; 11). "When she was trying on new boots, which she declared did not hurt her, we could not succeed, however suggestive our questions: 'But don't you think the shoe pinches just a tiny bit here?' in inducing her to own to any pressure. We were playing lotto with her; she could already manage to put the marked counters on the cards with corresponding figures or those that looked similar; if we tried by suggestion to induce her to put a counter on a figure she did not think right, she always refused our request."

What then must we think of the educational significance of suggestion in early childhood?

Its most striking effects are indeed without question those of an undesirable nature; for instance, suggestion of false statements, of fear, etc. Too great suggestibility is also of doubtful value in the general development of character, for it signifies dependence, want of critical faculty, credulity— in short, lack of personality. But yet we must not forget its counterbalancing advantages. We have already mentioned that the use of suggestion for dispersal of pain, fear, aversion, etc., is a useful, often indeed, an indispensable educational expedient.

But suggestion is even more important when we wish to excite unobtrusively and without force or to fix valuable permanent interests in the child's attitude and to suppress those of harmful tendencies. It is, especially in early childhood, really impossible to leave to the child the self-creation of his judgments, shades of feeling or decisions of will; and thus in all questions of importance, whether touching on religious, ethical, æsthetic, national or theoretical feelings and convictions, suggestion will hold its rightful place in early training.

Of course the teacher must clearly remember that suggestion, as a means of education, must be less and less used as the child's age increases. For growing spontaneity makes it possible—as demanded by the ideals of training—for the child gradually to reach a stage when he can found his own feelings, desires, judgments and values on attitudes of his own inner creation.

CHAPTER XXXIII

REPRESSION

One of the outstanding merits of psychoanalysts (and of Freud especially) will be that they proved the fact of repression and recognized its significance; but the special manner in which the idea of repression is referred to early childhood has no scientific justification.

According to the theory of psychoanalysis there exists, even in the little child, below a deceitful surface consciousness and apart from the outward expression of the innocent life of the moment, a many-sided, permanent mechanism of repressed desires and aims—of such a nature that all the most apparent phenomena of the child's action and consciousness are of far less significance than this hidden inner psychic life, in which alone the real man is to be found. We have already mentioned it in several places where we had to deal with the hypothetical symbolic interpretations of repression-complexes in play, dreams or imagination. But we must now discuss the existence of repressed desires themselves and their alleged significance in the individual life-structure.

It is affirmed that in early childhood's unknown psychic depths lie hidden all erotic and sexual desires and their de-generate offshoots (Freud); that every child, all unsuspecting, carries about in himself an elementary criminal nature (Stekel); that lust of power and a hostile attitude to the world under different disguises fills their unconscious being (Adler)—and so on.

Further, psychoanalysis devotes itself to the results which are supposed to follow from these repressions. I will arrange these results in three groups:—

1. Passing (momentary) results.
2. Primary after-results.
3. Secondary or later after-results.

The first occurs when a desire—aroused by outer or inner causes—in consequence of opposition in the consciousness, remains from its earliest stage in the unconscious, and only gets indirect expression in symbolic forms of feeling and action, but at the same time finds an abreaction in such expression. It thus forms a temporary, quickly passing event. To this class belong, for example, many manifestations of self-will, pose, shame, of which we shall have to speak later.

A primary after-result occurs when a repressed emotion remains obstinately fixed in the Unconscious, and from its unassailable point of vantage makes disturbing inroads upon other provinces of the personal life—even into the field of consciousness, although here under disguises as constantly changing as they are difficult to penetrate. But these incursions do not always lead to direct discharge, the "abreaction" may possibly not take place until assisted after a fairly long interval by natural means of discharge, sometimes even not at all. Hence neurotic weakness of varying nature, especially abnormal fear conditions (phobia), may be produced by such persistent, firmly fixed emotional states; also many forms of behaviour not quite normal, naughtiness, bad habits, peculiarities in play and behaviour, strange predilections and idiosyncrasies, are said to have their real origin in this hidden "repression-system".

Lastly, too, the repression may be so complete that for a long time its object does not attain to any consciousness whatever or to any outward sign. And it is only by late after-results, occurring perhaps years or tens of years subsequently, that proof is given that, in spite of appearances, no real forgetfulness takes place. For in later childhood, puberty, or even as late as adult-life, there may appear neurotic phenomena, sexual degeneracy,[1] etc., explained by psychoanalysis as emotions experienced in earliest childhood, repressed then, and never again consciously realized in the interval; relief is brought about by bringing into the Conscious and thus removing the fatal complexes of childhood. Freud, in this connection, speaks of "infantile amnesia" as a fact of great positive importance. That general inability of human beings to remember their earliest years does not arise simply from the fading and ultimate disappearance of the earliest memories, but is man's self-defence against the disturbance of equanimity which might result from the continuance in consciousness of early erotic-sexual emotions. In later years the child neither will nor dare remember that he has already gone through such a first stage of strong

[1] Cf. for instance, Stekel's comprehensive book on Psycho-sexuality in Infancy (*Psychosexuellen Infantilismus*).

impulse-life, and thus the whole period is repressed into the Unconscious.

Such are the chief features of the psychoanalytic repression-theory in so far as it refers to early childhood. Criticism must be limited to proving exhaustively that in such teaching psycho-analysis has for the most part ignored the standpoint of develop-ment-psychology.

Just as consciousness, to begin with, struggles slowly out of indistinct uniformity into greater clearness, inner differentiation of content, and persistency of working, the same course is followed as regards content and function of the sphere of the individual Unconscious, and as regards the mutual relation of the two spheres (Conscious and Unconscious).

It is quite possible that much may be already anticipated in the Unconscious for which the Conscious is not yet ready (cf. the anticipatory nature of unconscious play-tendencies, already discussed), yet nevertheless there is correlation between the lines of development in the two spheres, and it is absurd in face of the low stage of development of the child's conscious life to credit him with an Unconscious so perfect, full and differ-entiated as really to be capable of no further development, for the little unconscious human being two or three years of age is, according to this view, equipped with all those impulses, emotions, wishes, desires for knowledge, vices (possibly virtues too) which we find in the full development of mature human nature.[1]

That the same holds good for the mutual relation of the Conscious and Unconscious has been mentioned already; the opposition between the two is to be found at the end, not at the beginning of development. Both—Conscious as well as Un-conscious—are in the young child still entirely subordinate to the fundamental sensory-motor attitude; their life of the moment is mainly filled with sensation and response. The inner life must first have gained a certain fullness and stability from constant contact with outside impressions, and the subsequent motor-reactions directed outwards before it can achieve any independence as an "inner life". The repression theory, on the other hand, considers it quite the rule that in the Unconscious of this infantile psychic life there should be development of

[1] Cf. with this what has already been said concerning the diffuse and in-definite form of desire and effort in earliest childhood (Chapter XXXI).

permanent conditions which persist obstinately apart from outside influences, apart, too, from their motor-response, and not
only apart from but in opposition to these.

Such a purely inner persistence of psychic experiences is now
in reality the chief characteristic of puberty, and may possibly
extend to a certain degree into the preceding years of later
childhood, but is entirely foreign to the personal image of the
young child.[1]

Repression and the division it brings between the Conscious
and Unconscious is therefore a phenomenon of development; it
does not begin, as Freud thinks, in the young child with special
force and that silent persistence ("infantile amnesia") which
often does not give any sign of life until its late-effect in adult
life, but as a rule has but minute and transitory beginnings.
As age increases it assumes more pronounced and less fleeting
forms. This, at any rate, is true of the normal child, and as we
are confining our consideration to him our later examples can
only bear witness to rudimentary and fleeting forms of repression.[2]

The picture sketched by psychoanalysis of aims and desires
of childhood takes, therefore, the shape of an unjustifiable
reversed projection upon the earlier and earliest life-phases of
the complicated structure of the adult individuality. And it is
possible to recognize the real source of this reversed projection
as being in the CHILDISH MEMORIES OF NEUROTICS. For we
must continually emphasize the fact that psychoanalysis has
not derived its peculiar and decided conception from the child
itself, but that it rather has sought in the child for what it
expected to find there on the ground of its experiences with the
adult. We must here, therefore, once again consider the authen-
ticity of those later childhood memories which we shortly
mentioned in our introductory remarks (Chapter II, Section 3).

The need and capacity to transfer oneself back into childhood

---

[1] There are at this age, it is true, persistent effects which we discussed earlier
as habits; but they are only made possible by continuous and ever-renewed
repetition of outside interference and by constantly anchoring them in
psychophysical action, and they do not possess the independent inner life of
the so-called "repressions".

[2] In children of psychopathic tendency, or in otherwise normal children
showing temporary psychopathic conditions (e.g. phobias), repression may
play a more considerable part at a relatively early age. But even here I think
an excessive use is made of the psychoanalysts' idea—which again is only
possible as a result of their symbolic interpretation already mentioned.

is not only characteristic of old age, but of every human state with conditions resembling in any way those of childhood. Helplessness and need of assistance, therefore, in certain respects transform every sick person into a child; and the same is true in a special sense of that psychic malady which we call neurosis. Feelings of weakness, of inferiority, of incapacity to cope with the demands of the world and the responsibilities of life, need of support, the desire to take refuge in simplicity from the complicated refinement of existence; and then again as make-weights for these desires: wilfulness, defiance, the eagerness to make his power felt, to tyrannize over others—all these things fill the neurotic mind. Such tendencies must make childhood seem to him a paradise lost of which he would gladly preserve some trace at least. Thus he luxuriates sometimes with full consciousness in memories of childhood, and sometimes his infantile presentations and traces of memory play a part in his Unconscious and can be brought into consciousness by the methods of psychoanalysis. But now these reminiscences are so deeply embedded in the adult's present experience and attitude that to separate them entirely therefrom is utterly impossible, and especially so with regard to the emotion with which, as a result of the intermingling, they are now tinged. For these revivals of diffused childish feelings are now interpenetrated with the concrete feelings and desires peculiar to adult life as such, and projected all unintentionally into the past. For instance, if a neurotic suffering from sexual perversion is reminded of childish mental attitudes—e.g. of his pleasure in striking others —he then ascribes to that childish pleasure the sexual factors that he now connects with it; and if these memories of his are accepted as a fact, there is apparent proof of the "sadism" of early childhood and its repression for tens of years.

It is evident that an adult can renew childish conditions in himself, more particularly by certain formal emotional peculiarities. It is these that Adler has especially emphasized and designated by the names of a feeling of inferiority and male protest, but even then it is very questionable how far a real revival takes place, and whether it is not rather a case of a vague similarity. But now, the more aims are determined by their CONTENTS, the less possibility is there of unerring remembrance. It is no longer possible to distil out of a present emotion of jealousy or erotic cruelty the same feeling in childhood; it is rather a case of projecting something foreign to childhood into the child's indefinite emotions. And by this transference, the concrete incident of childhood is itself changed and so altered in its objective contents as to make any distinction impossible between truth and fiction.

We find these thoughts uttered in no dubious tones in the following quotation: "That scene . . . will not be a memory of L.'s, but a fancy which he formed later and transferred to his childhood. Man's childhood memories often have no other origin than this; they are not as a rule, like conscious memories of mature age, determined and repeated by the experience, but are not reproduced until a later period when childhood is passed, and *at this reproduction are changed, falsified, pressed into the service of later tendencies, so that not infrequently they cannot be clearly distinguished from simple fancies.*"[1]

These utterances are the more remarkable since they are made by none other than Freud himself.[2] But they stand isolated and unheeded as a foreign body in the literature of psychoanalysis.

Had they achieved their logical result, psychoanalysis would have lost its chief *point d'appui* in its dealings with the child's psychic life.

[1] The italics are mine.—W. S.
[2] A childhood's memory of Leonardo da Vinci's. Freud endeavours to escape the very clear negative inferences from this statement by treating the so-called memory of childhood in spite of the fact that it is only an adult's fancy of his childhood as an unconscious symbolic interpretation of the infant's actual desires. Leonardo's report runs: "When I was still lying in my cradle, a vulture came down to me, opened my mouth with his tail and struck my lips several times with it."

CHAPTER XXXIV

THE EGO IN CHILDHOOD

THE usual method pursued by older schools of child-psychology in treating the problem of the ego was to enquire for the earliest conscious perception of the ego and to take as sign of this the first appearance of the right use of words referring to self (I, me, etc.). This was erroneous in many respects. To begin with, the language-mastery of "I", "mine", etc., depends in greater measure on the development of fluency in speech and on surrounding influences than on the ego-consciousness. Secondly, the search for the ego-perception is much too intellectual; for it is just in the early stages of development that the ego-consciousness is not, first and foremost, knowledge of the Self, but a desire-filled, emotional experience of the Self. But—thirdly—even the ego-feelings are on their side only significant as proving the defeat of the entirely personal aims which regard only the individual Self. This unconscious aim must be our starting-point, for it alone can throw full light on the conscious phenomena of the realization of the ego.

1. Self-Affirmation and Self-Assertion

The most direct and uninterrupted manifestation of the ego-aim is self-affirmation. The child demonstrates, deports and realizes himself as a living entity, a one complete centre of power. He does not only aim at attaining a pleasure here, avoiding a pain there, but he wishes to affirm himself, his existence, his importance—and to increase it—in his desire of pleasure and to protect all three in his efforts to ward off pain.[1]

It is often said that the little child is an absolute "egoist", that he recognizes nothing but himself, and only follows those impulses which are of service for his own self-preservation and development. We can later on discuss the question as to what justification there is for this appellation and the moral criticism it implies. But here, at any rate, we must grant

---

[1] All theories that give the attainment of pleasure as the real aim of the child's action confuse the accompanying consciousness with the real nature and import of the action. Even psychoanalysis, which as a rule lays such strong emphasis on the importance of the Unconscious, in this point remains faithful to "conscious" psychology.

that desires concerned with the individual self appear at first in much greater variety and intensity than those connected with objects outside the ego. That is also quite natural, for the child's life-circle, of which his ego is the very centre, extends at first only by slow degrees; at first he has to get a sure and firm footing before he is capable of entering into living relations with his environment and the strange aims it presents to him. Hence the desires and impulses that first develop are above all of an egoistic nature. They aim at the maintenance of the self: hence the wish for food, the longing for healthy activity of the limbs, the impulse to aversion and attraction, the need of protection, help and tendance. Also they aim at further self-development: hence, above all, the play-instinct, the desire to know, the wish to learn and imitate, and at last the longing for importance and power.

As long as self-affirmation can express itself unhindered it is reflected in the consciousness as self-enjoyment. This is the child's ingenuous pleasurable absorption in his own being, feeling, power, his delight in himself. In this the sense and mental factors are most intimately connected and inter-mingled. When the two-year-old child dances about delightedly in nature's garb, admires himself in the mirror, then lying on his back kicks his legs in the air, pats himself all over, and with greatest enjoyment sucks his fingers, etc., etc., then this superabundant life is filled with curiosity, astonishment, with the joy of sight, touch and movement, and with the desire to continue as long as possible all this pleasure in his own indi-vidual self. But is it fitting to look upon such feeling—on account of its component factor of purely sense enjoyment—as an emotion of a sexual nature? Not only in the infant,[1] but even in later years of early childhood there is as a rule no justification for such a judgment. The so-called "Narcissmus" (passion of love for oneself) may occur much later as a direct preliminary to or as a substitute for the hetero-erotic emotion, and is then undoubtedly of a sexual nature. But here it is indeed true for the young child, that if two people do the same thing, it is not the same thing. The very use even of terms applied to mature human beings, such as "auto-eroticism", "Narcissmus", "self-love", distorts from the very first the

[1] Cf. Chapter VII.

representation of the childish mental condition which is supposed to be adequately described by these words.

We would not deny that isolated cases of pleasurable autoeroticism may occur even in the first six years. Especially is it said that onanistic manipulations may sometimes become bad habits. Many doctors say, indeed, that these are only movements caused by irritation—resulting from eczema or worms—in the region of the sexual organs; other observers, notably the psychoanalysts, are convinced that these hand-movements are of a pleasurable sexual character. If this last interpretation is correct, it can scarcely hold good for normal and healthy young children, although it may be possible that psychic disturbances and mental defects may tend to produce this effect. The fact that psychoanalysts as doctors are for the most part acquainted with neurotic children would predispose them to draw a general conclusion from what they observed in them.

The primitive self-affirming ego finds itself in a world with which his conscious relationship has yet to be acquired. It is at first an objective world, a chaos of things, happenings, states which act on the ego as restraining or developing influences, threaten and frighten as well as delight and exhilarate. Above all, it is a world of persons, a system of other egos meeting his own ego as will-centres demanding individual recognition. So the child is confronted with two possibilities only: to increase his self-affirmation into self-assertion, or to amalgamate his own ego in the company of other egos.

Here we will only discuss the child's first effort, one with a presupposition of a negative nature, namely the hostile character of the world.

The world of strange persons and things has a direct effect upon the child in a limitation of his feeling of self-importance, which consciously exhibits itself in disturbance of his self-enjoyment and in a feeling of personal weakness and inferiority. The child in every direction meets with limitations and obstacles to his desires; prohibitions, commands, compulsion all oppress him from without; helplessness, bodily incapacity, want of understanding from within prevent his doing what he would, his comprehension of what he longs to know, his facing of the world on equal terms. One of the most direct results of this feeling of weakness is the sense of fear and the—especially characteristic of childhood—disposition to nervousness which we will discuss in a later chapter.

Especially striking is the individual nature of this ego-weakness and feeling of inferiority in different children, and in this direction we owe many valuable suggestions to the "individual-psychology" of Alfred Adler and his fellow-workers. Adler has developed the theory that IT IS THESE VERY POINTS OF SPECIAL WEAKNESS THAT MAY BECOME THE STARTING-POINTS FOR THE FORMATION OF THE PERSONALITY. He is even inclined to find in this an all-sufficing explanation, and wishes to show that each individual has a fundamental weakness which determines the direction of his life-line. The acceptance of the exaggerations of the principle is not necessary to enable us to recognize its importance in spite of them.

These points of least resistance are of the most varied nature: physical failings, such as a speech-impediment, a limp, incontinence, etc.; or psychic, such as shyness, readiness to cry, aversion to certain animals or foods, etc.—any of these may press upon the child as constant sources of detriment and embarrassment, as limitations of feelings of conscious worth, and hence starting-points for self-derogation.

In other cases, again, the feeling of distance from adults, of still being small and stupid, may prove such disturbing elements. Amongst these we find the one especially emphasized by Adler, viz. uncertainty as to the child's own sex-character; childish curiosity is soon directed to the differences between boys and girls, father and mother, and the incapacity to solve the problem leads to fears of individual inferiority.

Typical limitations of self-estimation finally arise from the "position" of the individual child within the circle of brothers and sisters. Here competition threatens the full achievement of self-affirmation in very different ways. The child who has hitherto been the only one is very prone to see in the appearance of a younger member of the family a decrease in his claim—so far undisputed—to his parents' affection; in succeeding years the older child is required to yield to the younger, to let him have his toys, to look after him, and to restrain his own liking for power as far as the younger is concerned. Again, the younger member continually feels that he has neither strength nor permission to do as much as the elder, and that the latter utilizes his own physical and mental superiority to tyrannize over him.

The fact of belonging to one special class of society is also a frequent source of a feeling of inferiority, as is especially emphasized by Rühle with regard to proletarian children. The circumstance that these children are bound by birth and environment to a portion of human society which is marked by physical and social inferiority has its effect—so Rühle maintains—at a very early age on the young creature in the sense of a collective feeling of inferiority, for which it then finds compensation in appropriate collective counter-measures. It is certainly doubtful if these attitudes of resentment in proletarian children are noticeable at the early age with which we are dealing.

Now, what is the child's attitude to these derogations—temporary or chronic—of his self-affirmation? Like every living creature he responds with defensive action, and practises self-assertion. An entirely passive submission to the hostile power would be a contradiction of the idea of personality, which actively endeavours to preserve its individuality as a whole. Thus the child, although still so helpless, may set in motion reserves of strength to counteract more or less efficiently the disturbing attack, sometimes indeed in his defence he may display astonishing strength of will and persistence.

But self-affirmation does not always follow such a smooth path that an effort of will really gets rid of the disturbing factor. There are, indeed, as we have already mentioned, chronic derogations of the ego which cannot be mastered; how does the child deal with them? In this case, again, we find evidence of the inner teleological structure of the human personality: the points of weakness themselves maintain the function of the strong.

Here we are confronted with the second part of Adler's theory, to which he has given the not very appropriate name of "manly protest." The appearance of any manifestation of strength is according to this theory the attempt to over-weigh a weakness. Just because the child has a feeling of derogation, and in the very point where he experiences such a feeling, he endeavours to give proof of strength and to deaden the sense of inferiority in the enjoyment of the consciousness of power. Because he feels too weak for defence, he prevents its necessity by aggression; he avenges himself for his continual compulsory obedience by endeavouring to tyrannize. These are tendencies of self-protection and security functioning in an entirely natural manner, not simply in any way feigned desires.[1]

The means adopted by the child to assert himself in this way are very varied, both in nature and value: from the still more or less meaningless defiance up to the fancying of himself in rôles of emphatic power, from an occasional pretence (pose) of strength to the habit of ruling those around him with despotic power, by means of his weaknesses, ailments and nervous fears, ranging from a momentary expedient to systematic deceit. We have met with some instances already (Chapter XXII), others will be found in the following pages.

It is difficult to give the exact boundaries of this paradoxical emphasis of strength, for its manifestations at first sight are very like the expressions of primitive will-power. But, in any case, it would be an error to look upon every childish demonstration of obstinacy, or desire for recognition, as a disguised over-compensation for feelings of inferiority; there are also cases of defensive response of the nature of literal strength. Taken as a whole, these paradoxical efforts cannot hide their real character of weakness from a keen eye, for they lack the genuine nature and depth of real strength-manifestations. It therefore appears improbable also that they should, in the manner Adler ascribes to them, normally determine the direction of the development of the personality. Undoubtedly such forms of defence play an important part in neurotic characters, whether children or adults—also in people with pronounced weaknesses. In healthy children that paradoxical form of effort need only be taken into account as at the very most a side issue within the total representation of the personality.[2]

The more recent development of the theory of "individual psychology" has led then to the following psychological and at the same time educational results. The childish feelings of inferiority, possibly originating first of all in real shortcomings in the child himself, become fixed, perhaps even immovably so,

[1] Cf. Section 4 of this chapter as to "pore".
[2] Erismann, too, in his monograph on defiance distinguishes between the two forms of defiance, one from excessive self-will and the other from a lack in power of resistance.

by the inexpedient treatment of those around him. Too high demands which cannot be fulfilled, reproaches and punishments, perhaps too mistaken over-indulgence, produce in the child deep discouragement, which in its turn defeats any incitements to a directly personal achievement. If the child is continually told how weak, stupid, bad-mannered, etc., he is, he is the more ready to accept this suggestion as the condition thus stigmatized is a refuge from the higher demands of his world: "I am just as you make me out, and so you must take me." Something like this is the unconscious motive power for the way in which the child now organizes his life. There is only one method of counteracting this vicious circle of education and that is "ENCOURAGEMENT". The child must regain confidence in his indwelling powers and possibilities, he must get courage for himself—and many shortcomings, indeed not only these but the unsatisfactory habits of concealment and self-protection as well which the child has adopted, will disappear of themselves.

Undoubtedly, this is the enunciation of a very valuable educational maxim worthy of extensive use in the case of children with some psychic defect; i.e. the victims of chastisement or over-indulgence, those of weaker mentality, psychopathic children, cripples, etc. In many cases apparently those children who are difficult or impossible to educate, the awakening of their own strength and courage to achieve may work wonders. And we must put it to the credit side of "individual" psychologists if by their one-sided emphasis of the "courage" principle they wish to inspire teachers, and especially teachers of pathological cases, with courage for educational optimism. But as psychologists we cannot allow certain exaggerations of the new principle to pass uncontradicted. The "individual" psychologists are inclined ultimately to ascribe almost all individual differences in children to their differing degrees of courage in facing life and action, that is then, as differences which can be eradicated by right educational encouragement. Certainly any child who always has to hear how stupid it is will thereby be even more handicapped in the development of his individual capabilities than he was destined to be by his inborn deficiencies, but for that reason to say that original differences in capacity are quite insignificant in comparison with this courage-factor implies an enormous undervaluing of an incontestable psychological fact (in which perhaps the political ideal of the equality of all men may possibly be one of the contributory factors). Moreover, is not then the capability of courage also an innate quality which may vary greatly in different individuals?[1]

We will now consider some of the chief ways in which the child makes the assertion of himself the end of his endeavours.

2. Wilfulness in Childhood

The earliest form of self-assertion is wilfulness. It gives hints of its existence even in the child's first year; from his second, it develops quickly and plays a more or less considerable part in the life of all healthy and fairly strong-willed children.

Scupin ($1 ; 1\frac{1}{2}$). "The boy feels an irresistible impulse to act in defiance of our commands. For instance, if he wants to put something forbidden in his mouth, he first looks round shyly at us. If we then forbid him with: You, you! No, no! he repeats with a roguish laugh: *No, no!* hesitates a moment —and with sudden resolve puts the thing in his mouth in spite of us. To-day his father slapped his hand every time he tried to put the comb in his mouth; the slaps grew harder and harder and the child more and more furious and wilful; sometimes, certainly, he was a little overawed by his father's stern look and hesitated with the comb half-way to his mouth, but defiance gained the victory, until, at last, we took the comb away from him." (I, 58.)

Defiance may take on such an affective tone of violence that it can even overpower such a strong elementary impulse as desire for food.

Eva ($2 ; 5$). Even this sunny-natured child had now and again fits of defiance. "One day E. at dinner gave the command: *Father, pick up the spoon.* We asked: 'What else should Eva say?' She understood perfectly she should say 'please,' but she only made a wry face and wouldn't say it. We let one dish after another pass by her, without result, although she cried bitterly each time her full plate was sent out untouched—but she remained obstinate."

It is, at first, perhaps matter for astonishment that self-

[1] Cf. with the above Gina Kau's and other contributions in the *Handbook of Individual-Psychology*.

will (wilfulness) should be so prevalent at the very time when there is so little sense of the individual self, i.e. of real independence of thought, will or action, and that it should decrease with the increase of maturity and independence. But the very nature of self-will consists in the fact that it is not rooted in the individual volition to attain some valuable aim, but entirely in a continued wish for its own way. The childish ego identifies itself with the chance desire of the moment, and would feel its relinquishment as a derogation of the self. And thus that purposeless self-affirmation comes into being.

Von Hattingberg, who has devoted an interesting psychoanalytic study to the psychology of self-will in the child, distinguishes three kinds, in accordance with their root-motive.

ACTIVE SELF-WILL—we might call it obstinacy—is intent on the attainment of some object, on which the child has set his mind, under all circumstances, even when the impossibility of such attainment is evident, or any reason takes all point from the object. We should thus classify the behaviour of the little boy who sets his mind on getting an apple down from the tree. And although his climbing feats are doomed to failure, and even though he is offered an apple he can easily reach, he persists in his resolve simply to avoid the confession of failure to himself or to others and the conscious sense of self-derogation.

REACTIVE SELF-WILL is shown in opposition to the imposition of another's will. The child, at first, may be induced by some motive to do something forbidden, to demand something refused or to neglect some command. But, as his defiant feeling continues, it loses all sense of purpose, and the fact alone of the order or prohibition becomes its motive; the superior power of the other is felt as an attack upon the self, and "defiance" is born. Meantime the immediate cause for it may be quite trifling, the defiant child is not rebelling against the one chance request of his guardian's, but against his general power of ordering, and he wishes to make him feel the strength defying him. This explains why defiance depends so greatly on the person exercising authority. It may be specially roused by persons with whom the child stands on a footing of love and devotion, for here the danger of losing himself calls for the more energetic reaction of the wish for recognition. And if such attempts on the child's part have often been successful—e.g. with his mother—then he will only be too glad to make use of this means of power.

Von Hattingberg adduces instructive observations on this point made by him in his child-clinic (p. 21). The very child who screams himself black in the face when his mother is there, and resists in the greatest horror with hands and feet every examination, who will heed no kindly persuasion even when supplemented by a chocolate-box, and who fears no threat—that very same child may stop with magic suddenness if, after emphatic warning of what would happen, his mother is really sent out of the room and he is told she will not be allowed back until he is good. The result of this experiment is often amazing, especially with two- or three-year-old children whom no one would credit with so much understanding and command of their feelings. It is surprising how quietly and fearlessly children of this kind will then submit to examination. In many cases, it is true, the reappearance of the mother is the signal for fresh outbursts of emotion.

Erismann in his study of defiance, mentioned above, calls attention to the occasional connection of this phenomenon with contra-suggestion. Perhaps the child had never even thought of a certain action, but the harshness of the prohibition first suggests its possibility and suggests its performance as a subsequent protest against the intentional measure of restraint. He also calls attention to another mistake in education. Often enough the adult reacts to a burst of defiance not with any educational measures but with defiance on his own part too. He is not concerned with the attainment of any definite objective aim, but only to carry out his own will in the contest with the child's opposition. In the struggle there is a mutual increase of defiance, and if at last the adult "breaks down the child's opposition" he has so far conquered but not educated him.

The third form of self-will—PASSIVE SELF-WILL—consists of an almost purely negative attitude. The child does nothing, is absolutely silent, refuses to make the simplest movements, and shows a peculiar state of immovability. In so far as a real act of will is here directed to the doing nothing, the case is not fundamentally different from the one just mentioned; but von Hattingberg is convinced that this is not simple stubbornness, but a paralysis of the will, which may be referred back to deeper obstacles that can only be explained by psycho-analysis. Passive self-will is thus very closely connected with manifestations of shame and nervousness, of which we shall speak later on.

In self-will, the ego shows its most elementary attempt to assert itself. If persisted in at higher stages of development, it betrays a constitutional weakness of the ego. For opposition only for the sake of opposition, refusal to listen to reasonable appeals in order to enjoy one's own obstinacy, bears witness to a very small measure of self-confidence in the ego and to the low order of its aims. The really "self-willed character," therefore, is—as Adler and von Hattingberg justly maintain—not a strong but a weak type. Here, indeed, self-will is, above all, the screen which weakness puts up in self-defence.

3. Sense of Honour and Ambition

A finer form of self-consciousness which makes an early appearance is the sense of honour. Even a nine-months-old child shows traces of it now and again, and that in circumstances when one would least expect it. As we know, the use of corporal punishment for little children is often defended on the ground that other penalties, especially those touching their honour, are not understood, so that bodily pain is the only effectual reminder. But there is proof that children who have not previously been hardened by blows feel their psychic, i.e. their humiliating significance, quite apart from the physical pain. With our children, who were as a rule not struck, we made observations for which there could be no other explanation.

Hilde (1 ; 3). "H. tried to slap me in fun; then her father gave her a tiny playful slap on her cheek, and I a gentle tap on her little hand. She evidently took this in earnest, for she burst into an extraordinarily violent fit of crying, threw herself back in anger, and could only be pacified with difficulty. The little taps had certainly not hurt her, so that they can only have had a psychic effect. But where could the child have learnt that blows were a humiliation? We noticed just the same with Gunther (1 ; 3½)."

As years increase, the child becomes more and more sensitive to any measure of punishment, however slight, that touches his sense of honour. For example, exclusion from the society of others (sent into the corner or another room) may be felt as a deep humiliation; how to use such feeling in making punishment a means of education will be discussed in Chapter XXXVII.

The child's increasing sensitiveness to humiliation is closely connected with the fact that he begins to realize more and more clearly his own weakness and inefficiency. A child who can as yet do so little feels it more important not to be reminded of his weakness and to find recognition of what he really can do—indeed, if possible, to make himself and others believe that his powers are greater than is supposed. Fear of slight, a wish for respect and genuine ambition, are the different expressions of this endeavour. Thus even a two- to three-year-old child can show an angry response when laughed at, made fun of, and not taken seriously, because in all this he finds contempt of his individuality; he also feels hurt by reproof. On the other hand, he feels a craving not only for sympathy but for applause for his little accomplishments from those around him. No child really flourishes without the sunshine of this praise, with the encouragement it gives to ever-renewed effort.

Hilde (1 ; 9) already called out proudly to us: *See, see!* when she pushed along her little chair or held the cup in her own hand. The same pride was written on Gunther's face when (5 ; 6½) he told us of his first success as a teacher: *I have taught Eva how to put on gloves.*

In his artless way the child also tried, by sounding his own trumpet, to present his small person in a right light.

Thus Gunther (2 ; 6), when he had, on his own initiative, dragged a chair up to the dining-table for his sister, said: *that is Hilde's chair, sweet boy!* (4 ; 3½.) "G. feels himself a mighty man; he boasts of his heroic deeds, how he has pulled over his grandmother or his father and what trees he has climbed."

Sometimes even moral self-praise is to be heard. Hilde (5 ; 3) was sticking pictures in a book to give to a little girl she did not know very well. And as she did it, she said: *It is really good of me to do this : when people give me anything, that is good of them, isn't it ? And when I give something that is good of me. But this is even better of me, isn't it ? because people know me and I'm giving something to strangers that I didn't know before.*

It is impossible to be vexed at such self-praise on the child's part, but it should be kept within moderate limits and the child protected from that idle self-contentment which is the enemy of further effort. Fortunately, this danger is counteracted by a strong opposing element forming another side of self-consciousness, viz. ambition.

We call it ambition when a desire to emphasize his own individuality urges on a human being to maximum effort. It is strongly developed at an early age in the child. Since at so many points he has to rely upon grown-up help, he is all the more consumed with desire to be able to do without that help, whenever he possibly can. *Do it by myself, walk by myself, build by myself,* is his cry at every turn.

Ambition is most closely connected with that wish for respect which we mentioned above. A child, even when alone, will, it is true, from pure joy of achievement, strive to reach a certain stage of efficiency, but the incitement is far greater if he knows that he has a sympathetic public or a rival. Under certain circumstances the higher feeling of ambition is strong enough to overcome feelings of bodily pain.

Scupin (3 ; 3). The boy was climbing on to a projecting stone in a wall and jumping from it on to the ground, a distance of nearly a yard. Each time he fell and grazed his hands, once even bit his tongue, but he climbed up again at once and jumped down thirty-two times in succession. "But before every jump he uttered a long drawn-out squeak, to attract our attention as we sat in the meadow at some little distance. Bubi was so proud of his heroic deed that he could not do without an audience, who, he felt, would be able to appreciate his courage; our praise spurred him on to continuous effort, and he paid no heed to his grazes." (II, 27.)

This ambition assumes strange guises sometimes when others carry out what the child either could or would do. The childish desire "to do it myself" will go so far as to undo what has already been done, simply that he may accomplish the whole action himself.

Gunther (3 ; 1½) is playing on the sands. "If he will not come home and the nurse picks him up, he struggles and screams a request to '*walk by myself*'. He wriggles down from her arms and goes right back to the starting-point to act independently without yielding to force. If I say to him, 'Bring the bucket for Eva', and someone else, quicker or more obliging, brings it, he takes it back in deepest dudgeon to its original place to carry it all the way himself."

Scupin (3 ; 6½). "He considers he holds a mortgage in perpetuity on whatever actions he has once been allowed to perform. If, by any oversight, his prior right is not respected, there is great unhappiness, and it has even come to pass that his drawers and stockings have had to be put on once more to allow him to come into his own again and exercise his right to take these garments off by himself." (II, 56.)

4. Pretence and Shame

The dependence of self-realization on an audience leads to two more distinctive attitudes of outward behaviour. By pretence (pose), in its broadest sense, we mean that change of behaviour which is the outcome of an expectation of a response from others. It is only in the rarest cases that we find any conscious deceit, often rather the consciousness of a spectator produces quite automatic expression-movements or other behaviour which the original expression by itself would not have produced in that form of intensity. Between this quite involuntary and unconscious change of behaviour and intention there is a gradual process of half-conscious, half-unconscious actions. It is the same intermediate state between apparent and real which we all know in the child at its play and the actor on the stage. The child may, indeed, half think he feels differently when the consciousness of being observed is added to his former experience; he is acting a part, not only for others but for himself as well. Some characteristic instances of this pretence are seen in Scupin's son:—

(2 ; 4½.) "If we are angry with him, he often cries quietly to himself, a sniffing and sobbing comes from his corner; but if he thinks he is noticed he at once pulls a much more piteous face—indeed, we have often noticed him looking happily enough round the room, until he felt our eyes upon him, when at once he broke into sobs again." (I, 132.)

Very much later we find a very similar pretence, this time of physical pain, and it is noteworthy here that the injury connected with the pain is turned into a source of pleasure and used to emphasize the individual worth—a phenomenon that, when chronic, is in the eyes of the psychoanalysts a prominent feature of hysteria. We reproduce the first of two instances given by Scupin.

(5 ; 7½.) "A little girl of his acquaintance had given him a slight scratch. Bubi talked more than was necessary about this incident, repeated and repeated how naughty Lotty was, refused to have the plaster washed off for days, pretended it hurt him dreadfully, winced and whimpered if anyone touched the place. He evidently enjoyed the rôle of martyr and was anxious to play it as long as possible." (II, 20.)

Of quite a different nature is the pretence of courage very frequently found in children. Whenever the child is confronted with an uncomfortable or terrifying situation, the presence of spectators induces the child not indeed to conquer its fear, but to suppress its outward expression and to try to prove, at any rate in face and bearing, the more and less genuine wish to be brave.

Scupin (5 ; 4). During a stay in the country the boy, when with the village children, felt a certain shyness, which, however, he would not show. "To-day, when two of them about his own age came into the room, he went without a word away into a corner. At last he put both hands into his overall pockets and walked up and down whistling. That was meant to look very brave, but was, in reality, only the expression of extreme embarrassment. Bubi evidently felt shy with the two bare-legged little girls, but tried to hide his confusion behind as indifferent a manner as he could muster." (II, p. 179.)

A sense of shame forms a contrast to pretence (pose) in so far as it causes the individual to shrink from an audience. In every ego we find, together with a desire for self-surrender and a corresponding response, the opposite craving as well to belong to oneself alone, and to keep certain sides of life as entirely personal, not to be exposed to other people.

The question as to the natural and inner causes of this bashfulness is difficult to answer in our days when certain outward forms of this bashfulness at any rate are impressed upon the child by his upbringing. The expression, half-playful, half in earnest: "be ashamed of yourself", is very frequently to be heard in nurseries; also the child early learns that certain things may only be done in strictest privacy. Even the innocent joy in the use of limbs, when entirely unfettered by any garments at all, is damped at much too early an age by word and deed of unwise "educators".

Nevertheless, with minute observation it is possible to determine the natural, inborn component parts of this bashful feeling, and they are apparently of three kinds: (1) The tendency varies—quite apart from educational influences—to an extraordinary degree in different individuals. (2) The first stages of development have nothing to do, either directly or indirectly, with the sexual side of human nature, as affirmed by the Freud school of psychoanalysts, but can be referred to quite other sources. (3) Bashfulness (sense of shame) is shown in the child by innate natural expression-movements which mark avoidance of those around and withdrawal into himself.

The child's earliest bashfulness is generally shown in fear of strange faces; this is sometimes due to unmixed fright, as, for instance, when the child tries to get away from the stranger and begins to cry. But real bashfulness is quite distinct from this. The one-year-old child, brought on its mother's arm up to a stranger, turns away its head and tries to hide in its mother's bosom, but, the moment after, casts shy glances in the other's direction; this glance, however, is barely noticed before the little head is turned away once more. Thus the child endeavours to see the other (curiosity), but wishes to be seen by him as little as possible. Here the child has, as yet, nothing to make him bashful, but soon specific motives of shame begin to make their appearance.

This is shyness before onlookers. In such psychic and bodily performances, which are still something of a novelty for the child, the accomplishment of which has not yet sunk into the "unconscious-matter of course", self-consciousness is increased by the feeling of being observed and controlled by others. But an increase in self-consciousness means in this case a relapse into greater uncertainty; the unconscious simplicity of the action which was already half won, is lost; hesitation and second thoughts intrude between impulse and accomplishment and by robbing the action of its mechanical nature, make it more difficult and more imperfect—indeed under certain circumstances prove an insuperable impediment to its fulfilment.

Gunther (1 ; 3½). The boy is learning to walk. "It has been a somewhat long process between his first efforts and real walking alone. But lately he began, when he thought himself unobserved—i.e. when no one interfered with him—to let go of chairs and tables and to walk straight on."

At 2 ; 2 the boy shows a sort of bashfulness whenever he uses a new word for the first time. Any attempts to get him to repeat it are unsuccessful; he gives the impression of being shy.

This kind of bashfulness is uncommonly like stage-fright in the following instance. "Gunther (3 ; 1½) was acting with his sister as they so often did. On this occasion it was Hansel and Gretel they were performing, and H. always told her brother what he had to say. As a rule they used to play alone, but that day their parents were having breakfast in the same room. Suddenly the boy became conscious of the presence of onlookers, and he struck at once, hiding his face in his hands, a constant expression of bashfulness natural to him. His feeling was not to be overcome; he could not be persuaded to go on playing."

In all these cases the child is not ashamed of any short-coming, but, on the contrary, of some positive power. Closely resembling this is bashfulness caused by praise.

Gunther (4 ; 10½). "When he is praised we really ought to take a cinematographic film, for he then displays an indescribable mixture of pride, joy, shyness, confusion, together with a desire to hide everything. His wish not to show his feelings produces sometimes the most curious grimaces."

Another kind of shame is the exact opposite of that described above; it is the outcome of something that humiliates self-respect. If the child has done something wrong, he tries as far as possible to avoid all intercourse with his fellows or to make them forget, because he sees himself blamed by the judgment of others, and this blame increases his own feeling of unworthiness. This moral shame sometimes leads to an imitation of the ostrich's course of action.

"Gunther (3 ; 3½) was naughty at table, and his mother looks at him severely. Then he shuts his eyes tightly and turns his head away. 'Why are you shutting your eyes?' *Cos I don't want to see you.* 'Why don't you want to see me?'

Cos you are scolding so, I don't want to see you. ('Scolding' was the term he used to apply to reproachful looks, though not a word was spoken.)"

Scupin (2 ; 11). "The boy, although as a rule very particular in personal habits, sometimes had relapses for which he was punished. On every occasion he was terribly ashamed of his fault, dropped his head and played in confusion with his fingers, scarcely venturing to raise his eyes." (I, 193.) Also at the age of 3 ; 3 there were isolated instances of something similar; how strong his expression of shame then was is shown in the following report: "If in the morning he is scolded for it, he drops his head and gives himself up to his mother to be dressed quite without any sign of will-power, his limbs slack and heavy; he lies like a sack on her arm, the image of an utterly resigned, apathetic creature. Only a slight, sad twitching of the corners of his mouth betrays how the child's self-respect has suffered." (II, 43.) Since it is no great step from this kind of shame to contrition and self-reproach, its appearance is of undoubted importance for the growth of the child's moral sense.

But shame is not only felt for faults, but also for other things that tend to lower the feeling of self-respect, such as feelings of weakness or sentiment. Thus Scupin's son (5 ; 1) was ashamed of being moved by his mother's exhortations, ashamed too of the disappointed tears he could not repress when he did not find the little playmate he had gone to visit. (II, 163.)

Shame in a psychic sense, then, has reached a comparatively high development before any signs of spontaneous physical shame appear. In healthy children—with healthy training—this does not seem to be the case before the end of the fifth year. Scupin reports (5 ; 1): "If the boy sees a nude marble statue or an angel in a picture, he finds nothing remarkable in their nudity, at very most only expressing a fear lest the angel should catch cold. Nakedness is a matter of no importance, of no weight to him, nor has he ever yet been ashamed of his own naked body; he has kept, up to the present, the same innocent unconstraint with which, at the sea, he used to jump about in nature's garb or with little bathing-drawers as his only garment. He always looks forward to the moment when as a 'naked frog' he may jump into the big bath; and, if relatives or friends happen to come into the bathroom, his merriment knows no bounds as he jumps about in the water like a mad thing, slaps himself with both hands, splashes the onlookers and proudly shows them that he can swim. It never occurs to him to feel the slightest shame. Nevertheless, on certain occasions he shows modesty and tries to get out of sight. But this is no inborn feeling of shame, but the result of having been taught that it is more seemly to do so." (II, pp. 162 seq.)

Of our own children, Gunther was the first to show any spontaneous signs of a sense of modesty, and even he not till his sixth year. Then he began to avoid undressing in the neighbourhood of the window, for fear anyone should be able to see in from the opposite house.

In conclusion we will give an example of a complicated feeling in which there is a direct union of pretence (pose) and shame of this pretence. It is certainly true that the example is one of an adult's recollections, but it bears (if allowance is made for possible embellishments) the stamp of truth in the main. Albert Schweitzer writes in his autobiography[1]:—

"Further I remember from very early childhood the first time I felt the sensation of conscious and unprompted shame." Whilst his father was working at a beehive the child sat close by and was suddenly stung by a bee. "At my scream, the whole household ran up, everyone pitied me. . . . As I had become so interesting through my misfortune, I wept with satisfaction until all at once I noticed that I was shedding tears without feeling any more pain. My conscience told me then to stop, but to remain the object of interest I went on with my wails and accepted further comfort which I did not really need. How often has this experience proved a warning to me when in adult life I have been tempted to allow some misfortune to keep me in the limelight."

[1] Quoted from Reinhardt, p. 334.

CHAPTER XXXV

FEAR AND NERVOUSNESS (ANXIETY)

THE words fear and nervousness (anxiety) designate two mental conditions so much akin to each other that perhaps we should more rightly say that they represented two different sides of but one attitude of mind. The predominant feature in "fear" is the thought of the object that is the cause of the emotion, whilst nervousness is of a more subjective nature, and exists already before its conscious connection with certain external conditions; sometimes, indeed, even exists quite without an object. Hence we say: I fear "something", but I "am" nervous (anxious).

1. Fear[1]

Fear is referred to objective circumstances: things, people, occurrences, conditions which an effort is made to avoid. In the adult this fear-reaction is, as a rule, confined to circumstances which they feel provide some imperative cause for fear, i.e. when they are conscious of a threatened danger or unpleasantness. This consciousness is the result of experience, whether direct (as fear of a second visit to the dentist) or indirect, through report or reading (as fear of a fire or cholera). So that, at first sight, we might think that consciousness of approaching danger must be a necessary condition of every feeling of fear. The little child, however, shows us that such a supposition is wrong, for most of its fear is not caused by direct or indirect experiences, but by other circumstances. The two- or three-year-old child has scarcely had opportunity to become acquainted with threatened dangers and, on that account, to fear them, yet this age is not entirely, nor even mostly, free from fears, rather, on the other hand, much troubled by such feelings.

We can only explain these by accepting the theory of an inborn fear-tendency which finds expression under certain circumstances, quite apart from any knowledge of their threat-

---

[1] The most important psychological investigation is that by Karl Groos in *Seelenleben des Kindes*, 5th ed., pp. 268 sqq. Mention must also be made of Preyer, Chap. VII, Sully, Chap. VI, Major, Chap. IV, Compayré, Chap. V. Hirschlaff, *Weitere Literatur*, pp. 445 seq.

ening character. We are compelled then to confront fear arising from experience with instinctive fear (each of which has two subsidiary forms) and state their mutual relation as follows: instinctive fear preponderates in childhood's earliest years. The older the child grows, the wider the circle of his experience becomes. Consequently, on the one hand, the cases of fear from experience increase; on the other, instinctive fear decreases, since objects, hitherto feared, are recognized as harmless in the light of experience.

1. Real acquired fear is a favourite stock example in psychological textbooks to explain the formation of association between perceptions and emotions. If any experience has been accompanied once or several times with a strong affective-tone of displeasure, later any further perception of the object or occurrence will be connected with a reminiscence of that displeasure. This anticipation of future displeasure does not remain a mere perception, but already has a present effect on the mind as a feeling of fear. Popular wisdom has compressed the action of this psychic mechanism into a well-known proverb derived from child-psychology: "A burnt child dreads the fire." The following is an illustration of this proverb:—

Scupin (1 ; 5). "In spite of warning, the child took hold of the stove door and burnt his fingers. He ran crying to his mother, who explained to him that the door was hot as she blew on the smarting fingers. At first, Bubi kept at a respectful distance from the stove and blew at the fire, but in a few minutes a second cry of pain arose; he had again taken hold of the stove door, since his first experience had not been painful enough to overcome the child's curiosity and desire for experiment. Since then, however, he makes a wide détour in front of the stove and says nervously: *hot*." (I, 70.)

Watson made experiments with a much younger child to test the development of this fear resulting from experience. A lighted candle was slowly brought within the reach of a little girl at the age; 5 to; 7. At first, this always produced a grasping reaction, although the child drew back her hand each time she had taken hold of the flame. Later on she always made grasping movements at the beginning of the experiment, but afterwards, as a result of the painful sensation of heat just experienced, she ceased taking hold or suppressed the movements in its initial stages. It needed, however, on the whole about 150 repetitions

of the experiment to effect even such imperfect functioning—
as a result of experience—of this avoiding-reaction.

Fear from suggestion may be called fear from indirect experience. In the Chapter on "Suggestion" we have already
discussed how it may produce fear in the child and the mischief
resulting from it.

2. INSTINCTIVE FEAR.—Until the present time only the first
of its two possible forms has been considered, and, as is now
apparent, the importance of this form has been greatly over-
rated. This form is (a) DISTINCT INHERITED FEAR. This is shown
when an object or occurrence of definite character causes fear,
not because the individual himself, but his ancestors have learnt
its danger and handed on the fear of it as an inheritance to their
descendants.

The assumption of such a special fear-reaction as the result
of heredity is founded chiefly upon observation of animals,
New-born animals are said to evince an innate antipathy to the
sworn enemy of their own particular species (e.g. young doves
to a hawk), so that at its approach they fly with every sign of
terror, although they can have had no experience of its dangerous character. It is true, as Groos and Bühler point out,[1] that
later research has thrown doubt upon these suppositions, so
that they cannot in any way furnish ground for assertions in
child-psychology.

The existence of a special inherited fear in man is affirmed by
Preyer, Darwin above all, by Stanley Hall. The latter is not
content to refer the child's fear-tendency to its immediate
ancestors only, but, in accordance with the biogenetic principle,
derives it from remote stages of the long succession of ancestry,
from the times of primeval man, even indeed from the animal
life before man came into being. According to him, the child's
instinctive fear is pure atavism.

Thus Stanley Hall seriously discusses the possibility of the
fear of water being an inheritance from those primeval ages
when animal life was passing from the stage of purely water-
creatures to land-dwellers, that had to avoid and fear the
element they had till then known and trusted. He also assumes
(although with reserve) that the child's instinctive fear, so
widely spread, of animals dates from the time when our ancestors—as primitive man or even earlier—had to be continually

[1] Groos, I, pp. 293 seq. Bühler, I, p. 50.

on their guard against certain animals, and when the present domestic creatures, in a wild state, were a constant menace to life. In the same way he sees in fear of the dark, of thunder, etc., traces of feelings that long, long generations before were of great value as protection to life.

Before we decide to agree to such a measure of heredity in psychic qualities, all other possible explanations must be exhausted and very positive arguments be forthcoming in its favour. But neither of these reasons exists in this case.

We should expect such innate qualities, inherited from those earliest periods of human or pre-human existence, to be effective in every child. There is, however, no proof of such universal results of this alleged heredity. We give examples from our own children and others to show the absence of these forms of fear.

Fearlessness in the Dark.

Hilde (1 ; 6). "In the evening when she has been put to bed and the gas turned out with the usual '1, 2, 3, off', she laughs as a rule at the 'off', or, at the worst, utters a little indignant sound as she hears me go out of the room. But the door is barely shut behind me before everything is and remains quiet."—(1 ; 7.) "H. ran this afternoon several times from the bright gaslight of the bedroom to the dark dining-room, quite fearlessly, of course, as it was her own choice to do so."—(1 ; 7.) "H. yesterday, contrary to her usual custom, was very lively long after she had gone to bed. She had been there three-quarters of an hour, when we heard her babbling and chirruping in the happiest way. Nobody was with her in the pitch dark-room, and yet this extreme content!"

This disregard of the dark continued too and was repeated in the other children. Eva had a slight, quite transitory fear stage at a much later age, but it gave distinct proof of a non instinctive origin.

Eva (4 ; 2½). "I noticed in Eva something I never saw in the other children. She has an undefined fear of the dark, especially if left alone, and of unusual noises. Lately she was with me in the brightly lit kitchen, the passage gas was not lit, and it was but poorly lighted from the staircase gas. I sent her on an errand to the nursery; she refused from fear of the dark passage, and besides she heard on the stairs the loud voices of children coming home; although she knew the children, the babel of voices evidently upset her, and she said she would not go as long as the noise could be heard. I demanded obedience in a serious tone and she conquered her fear. In the same way, she would never go alone into the bathroom, When I noticed it I used to ask her to go, in daylight and in the evening—with success. I teased her a little: 'Are you a baby then?'—she thinks she has long since left babyhood behind—and roused her ambition. I watched her for a few days only, then the cure was complete, and she always went alone, even in the dark. The first few times I went in with her to show her there was nothing to fear, and then left her.''

This attack of fear was doubtless caused by some acquired perceptions of undefined dangers or annoyances; besides, she was just reaching the age when she had a greater number of ideas in her mind and could to a certain degree picture possible dangers, etc. Here, therefore, we should not be justified in considering this a case of an inherited fear-reflex.

FEARLESSNESS AS REGARDS WILD ANIMALS.

Scupin's son, in his second year, was often taken to the Zoological Gardens, and soon showed a very lively interest in the animals and no fear to begin with. Even the elephant only made him (1 ; 2) curious, and it was not until the keeper gave the creature a trumpet to blow that Bubi was frightened at the unexpected noise. (I, 59.)—(1 ; 5.) He showed fear of the camels and goats that probably came too near to him, but none of the lions and bears. (I, 71.)—(1 ; 10.) He was only frightened by the sudden approach of a camel and a harsh-voiced condor, but not at the sight of the creatures themselves. Nor in his later visits to the Zoological Gardens was there any sign of fear; only his awe of the camel—which probably originated in the accident of that one sudden approach—lasted for some time.

Hilde (2 ; 1) paid her first visit to the Zoological Gardens. She delighted in the monkeys' gambols, was enchanted by the kangaroo, and recognized the elephant. But there was none of the amazement we had expected and not a trace of fear of any of the animals. On her second visit (3 ; 2) she acted somewhat differently. The lions, tigers, bears and monkeys she looked at unmoved, but, on the other hand, the visit to the bird-house upset her so that she wanted to go

home, and she got a terrible fright at the sight of the hippopotamus opening his enormous mouth.

Again, we see that it was not the sight of the animals
in itself that aroused instinctive fear, but isolated, definite,
uncanny occurrences associated with them. The parrots outside delighted her, but the same creatures frightened her
when their screams in the confined space of the aviary almost
deafened her. And the hippopotamus's gigantic open mouth
makes even grown-ups shudder, although this mouth, which
only consumes vegetable food, can never have been a danger
to any one of the whole ancestral line.[1]

FEARLESSNESS IN THUNDERSTORMS.

The following notice, written when Gunther was 4 ; 11,
applies equally well to our three children at all ages: "In
several thunderstorms our children have not shown a single
sign of fear; on the contrary, they shared our admiration of
the lightning, the raging storm, the rustling of the trees, so
that there is certainly no reason for assuming the presence
of an innate fear of storms in them. G.'s attitude to the storm
is absolutely that of a love of nature."

Scupin (1 ; 2). "This was the boy's first violent thunder-
storm and he was not in the least frightened, although he
was alone in the room. When it thundered, he called out *huh !*
and apparently thought the noise was made entirely for his
amusement." (I, 59.)

(3 ; 0.) "A storm to-day greatly excited the boy; he ran
first to one window, then to another, bubbled over with
animated questions, scarcely waiting for our answers. When
it lightened, he asked: *Where does the glitter come from?* and
said of the thunder: *And when thunder comes, it's over*

---

[1] Watson describes experimental tests which he made on an infant (; 5– ; 6)
to prove the possible existence of inherited fear-reactions with regard to
animals. Different animals (dog, cat, rabbit, rat, dove) were brought up to
the child, who showed grasping and attraction reactions, sometimes, too,
no reactions, but never fear or aversion. Even when the dove fluttered wildly
against restraint, and touched the child's head, or when the dog came up
barking to her when alone, there was no sign of fear. Nor was there any in
the Zoological Gardens even when several animals put their heads quite close
to her.

She was also entirely without any fear of fire; when a newspaper was set
alight close to the child she only looked at the spectacle with interest until
it went out, without grasping, it is true, but also without any aversion-
reaction.

Mummy's head, and then it goes bum-bum, and Mummy claps her hands on her head. This excitement then was caused by the charm of novelty and had nothing to do with any fear of the storm." (II, 3.)

If the children, mentioned in the above reports were free from inherited fear of darkness, wild animals and thunderstorms, the universality at least of those instinctive fears is contradicted. But we have gained more than this. For in the passing attacks of fear that did occur explanations could be given that have nothing to do with heredity, and we may assume that the same explanations will hold good for those cases in which children show very intensive reactions of fear of the dark, etc. On one hand they are the result of the well-known experience- and suggestion-fear, on the other a form of fear that is also of an instinctive nature, referring, however, not to a fixed definite feature, but to a formal connection of stimuli.

(b) FEAR OF THE MYSTERIOUS.

The special significance of this form of fear, particularly in early childhood, has escaped the notice of the older school of child-psychologists; it has lately been established by Groos and by us.[1] "Fear of the unaccustomed seems to be more a part of primitive nature than fear of a known danger." (Groos, 5th edition, p. 284.) If the child meets with anything that does not fit in with the familiar course of his perception, three things are possible. Either the impression is so alien that it is simply rejected as a foreign body, and consciousness takes no notice of it. Or the interruption of the usual course

---

[1] By Groos, 1911, in the third edition of his *Psychic Life of the Child*. By us as early as 1903 in our notes concerning Hilde. Since these are still unpublished, it is permissible to reproduce certain parts literally to show how the same train of thought can arise quite independently in two different places.

My wife wrote, June 23, 1903: "It is more difficult to explain and place fear of things which are not terrifying to the senses, and whose ultimate danger cannot yet be known either." (Examples follow.) "Perhaps this, with other cases of fear that have been noticed, may be classified as fear of the mysterious, the uncanny. Although H.'s attitude to what is entirely strange is one of indifference or innocent curiosity, and always quite fearless (e.g. of fire, sharp tools, like knives and scissors, strange animals, as bears and lions), she is frightened when she sees familiar persons or things in any unusual connection or situation. The natural associative sequence receives a shock and generates fear. On the other hand, we notice no sign of an acquired fear in the sense of inheritance from experience of bygone times." With this compare the train of thought as expressed in the text by Groos.

of perception is pronounced enough to attract attention but not so violent as to effect disturbance; it is rather surprise, desire for knowledge, the beginning of all thought, judgment, enquiry. Or, lastly, the new suddenly breaks in upon the old with violent intensity, throws familiar ideas into unexpected confusion without a possibility of an immediate practical adjustment; then follows a shock with a strong affective-tone of displeasure, the fear of the mysterious (uncanny).

Groos now has pointed out with keen insight that this fear of the uncanny is also distinctly founded on instinctive fear; it corresponds to a biological necessity which works from one generation to the next. Just because novelty so strongly attracts man's desire and striving for knowledge, the tendency at first is to give himself up to all that is new without enquiry or caution. He therefore needs as self-defence an opposite tendency, a negative attitude to novelty, which is just as certainly inborn as the positive attitude of desire for knowledge and curiosity. Fear of the unaccustomed has to act as this self-defence.

It is further easily understood that anything new may have an uncanny and unattractive effect when presented under certain formal conditions; we mentioned above as such: the sudden action and great intensity of the new impression. To these must be added an unexpectedly close coherence of the new with the elements of the familiar perception, because it is here that the interruption is most keenly felt. We find similar results from the isolated appearance of impressions which, as a rule, only occur as parts of a whole, but cannot now be so placed mentally by the child. Lastly, any strange object which, at first, causes no fear, may at once have this effect when it is seen quickly approaching the child, for, by so doing, it passes from the sphere of what is simply looked at into the practical life of the individual; it seems to demand a certain attitude which the child cannot at the moment assume; hence the shock.

A number of typical examples follow.[1]

---

[1] Groos more than anyone has laid stress on the terrifying effect of close proximity, but here again we find duplicity of trains of thought. My wife in her notes (August 31, 1906) mentions that Eva (1 ; 8) is afraid of fowls and rabbits when they are close to her. "From a distance she will throw food to the fowls, but close by they frighten her. I could see the explanation of this 'inherited' fear. A definite fear of this or that dangerous animal has not been

Examples of the terror caused by proximity or approach: Gunther (1 ; $5\frac{1}{2}$). "A new umbrella was suddenly opened in the room, quite close to him. Then the boy, with a scream of fear, ran away from us to the window, where he stood with his back to us and the umbrella. Some time later the same occurrence had a like result."

Gunther (1 ; 8). "The boy, as he sat happily in the children's bath-tub, began to scream terribly when Hilde was placed beside him, nor could we pacify him. The sister he loved so well, as a rule, became an object of terror to him, first by the absence of her usual clothing, and above all by her unaccustomed and inevitable proximity."

EXAMPLES OF FEAR CAUSED BY ISOLATED SENSE-IMPRESSIONS which the child cannot place in the accustomed perceptive-association:

Scupin (2 ; $8\frac{1}{2}$). "A plaster cast of the boy's hand was to be made, but the soft plaster-mixture so horrified him that the child put his hands behind him and took refuge in the farthest corner." (I, 157.)

Eve (4 ; $2\frac{1}{2}$). "The flat above ours was being done up, and for several days we heard continual knocking and hammering. These mysterious noises for which there was no visible cause so frightened Eva, that she would not go to bed in daylight. But when I quietly insisted that she must go to bed and explained the harmless cause of the knocking, she got over her fear."

It seems very probable that the fear of long-drawn-out tones which we observed during the first year (Chapter VII (a)) may be traced, in part at least, to this isolation of the impression. As a rule the separate note heard has its own place in a melody, in some speech-association, or in a technical activity, but now the long note stands alone and unconnected with all familiar impressions. Thus Eva (2 ; 8) was terribly frightened at the sound of a steamer's foghorn, although here there is a purely displeasing sense-impression as well.

But also objects, which are well known as component parts of a whole, may, when dissociated from this whole, cause fright by the UNFAMILIAR ISOLATION.

stored up through successive generations; man's memory works in a larger and more general scale; it has inherited relative fear. The closer men and beasts come to each other, the more likely is the conflict."

"Hilde (2 ; 7) started back in fear from her toy drawer with the words: '*Got a fright.*' What was the reason? A couple of doll's eyes joined by a wire that had dropped out of a broken doll! I took the eyes out of the drawer, examined them closely with the child looking on, and even spoke to them to calm H.'s fear. But she would not hold them, and knocked them out of my hand on to the floor. I told her to pick them up, and when she refused, threatened the loss of her doll's perambulator. Hesitating and afraid, she obediently went up to the eyes, but retreated again, always saying, '*Got a fright,*' went up again, then back several times, until, at last, she plucked up courage and took hold of them. That broke the spell; as soon as she had them in her own hand and saw that they were quite harmless, she lost all fear, brought them to me with a laugh, begged for them again and called them *pretty peepies.*"

A familiar object may cause fear, by some attribute not really inherent or suitable to it. Under this heading we may place first of all the frequent fear of mechanical toys. The child very soon learns to understand the difference between living things that move and inanimate objects; his usual toys belong to the second group; they are passive recipients of the child's attentions, and only move when he sets them in motion. And then such a toy suddenly begins of its own accord to walk, to rattle, to ring, to twist; there cannot be anything more uncanny for a child.

"Gunther (1 ; 10) was given a little metal dog that ran about gaily when wound up. The boy set up a terrible cry and ran away from the animal; on the other hand, when it was still he liked to pick it up. A mechanical top that played a hymn-tune excited and terrified him much more. He could not think how to escape from the dread object, and even in my arms cried bitterly."

Scupin's son (2 ; 10) found a cuckoo-clock—although its mechanism attracted and delighted him—an object of terror as well. He dared not stay in the room by himself when it began to sing. (I, 186.)

There are, however, other examples to show that the association of inappropriate elements to form an unfamiliar connection produces violent fear.

Hilde (3 ; 3). "Her parents for fun were making an elephant

by covering themselves with a big rug and moving one arm from side to side like a trunk. Although the child had been told beforehand that they would make an elephant, at the sight of it she burst into frightened tears, so that we showed ourselves at once. H. got somewhat calmer as we explained our make-up to her, but later on asked several times: *But not make another elephant, no!* As we knew she had never shown any fear of a real elephant, it was therefore its mysterious character and that alone which frightened her."

We shall meet with fear of the mysterious again when we have to discuss fear for others (Chapter XXXVI, 4).

2. Nervous Fears

If we now turn from the consideration of objects causing fear to an enquiry into the feeling of fear experienced by human beings, we discover several remarkable and fresh points of view. In this enquiry we shall use and modify the suggestions put forward by psychoanalysis.

As already mentioned, we speak of nervousness—in contradistinction to fear—when we wish to express a general mental condition of diminished self-confidence. This condition need not necessarily be connected with a definite object of fear, and under certain circumstances may occur without any object. This mental condition is especially marked in early childhood, when we need look no farther for its explanation than to that feeling of weakness and inferiority which can rarely be entirely conquered. At this period of life the feeling is even prone to grow into a chronic disposition of that nervous timidity which is considered as a quality specially belonging to early childhood.

But the simple and direct reference to this quality of the general feeling of inferiority is not a sufficient explanation of all its manifestations; this nervous fear shows many variations (ambivalence) which tend to great confusion of the picture. We have already referred to the endeavour to make an inner protest against this nervous weakness, and we met with the pose of courage as the first and most apparent form of this "manly protest".

But it is not always possible to dispel the nervous fear in this simple fashion, so another ambivalence makes its appearance, and nervousness itself is pressed into the service of conscious self-assertion by using imagination to increase the dangers; it is especially when threatened with ghosts, phantoms, uncanny beasts, etc., that the child feels his imaginary ego bears a burden touched with special importance, so that when he takes refuge in tears with his mother from such respectable dangers he no longer needs to feel so terribly small in his helplessness. It is very probable that such trains of thought are frequently component parts of feelings of nervous fear.[1]

Wexberg also calls attention to a further connection of nervous fear with conscious desire of self-assertion; by his timidity the child manages to become the tyrant of those around him. For an attack of nervousness is sufficient to turn a child, unheeded hitherto, into the centre of attention and care, and if a child awakes at night in a fright and rouses his mother with cries of terror that bring her to his cot, his feeling of safety may be not quite unmixed with a sense of power at having his mother at his disposal. These factors are liable to grow in magnitude in children of nervous fears, who, by degrees, learn to make use of their states of excitement to subjugate others, until they always have the requisite means at hand whenever they desire to hold the stage.[2]

From other sides we come also to the apparently paradoxical idea of nervous fear as pleasure. That fear need not always be unmixed pain we know from the "creepy" feeling and the mixed sensations with which we listen to ghost-tales or enter uncanny places. Many people actually run after situations where they can experience this pleasurable fear: climbing giddy heights, crossing thin ice, playing with fire, etc. Even in young children we find a similar attitude which it is not enough, from a psychological point of view, to characterize with such terms as imprudence or foolhardiness.

Rosegger gives a very vivid picture of a child's pleasure in fear and his longing for its repetition in a sketch called " The Father's Word", which I quote from von Hattingberg. (II, p. 252.)

R. tells how, in his childish years, his father only had any

---

[1] *Nervous Children*, p. 270. Wexberg, who was the first to call attention to them, seems to me to go too far when he announces as universally true; "Imaginary nervousness stands in necessary correlation to the imaginary self-glorification ot childhood."

[2] Wexberg's analysis is concerned with children of such nervous fears.

dealings with him when he had been troublesome. "Then I felt a curious trembling inside, a feeling not without its charm and pleasure when the thunders of his wrath rolled above me. Tears filled my eyes, trickled down my cheeks, but I stood firm as a little rock, looking at my father with a feeling of inexplicable well-being that grew and grew the longer my father stormed." Then when a few weeks passed with no mis-behaviour, so that his father again ignored him, "gradually a desire began to awaken and grow in me to do something to rouse my father's wrath again. This was not from any wish to annoy him, for I had an especial affection for him, and it certainly was not from malice, but for some other reason of which I was not then conscious."

Now, what is the cause of this admixture of pleasure in what is, in itself, painful? The feelings of enjoyment derived from a sense of power, already mentioned, no doubt have something to do with it, but are not, in themselves, enough, because the pleasure is not only of a mental nature, but of a physical as well. We must go back to the physical accompani-ments of nervous fear, which indeed are varied enough. The most striking are changes in circulation, shown in a stronger and quicker pulse; it is quite possible that such conditions of excitement, if not too intense, may produce a feeling of pleasure. And the snuggling up to someone else so almost universal with children in a nervous state, the gentle caresses and demonstrations of affection, cannot fail to provide a strongly marked factor of pleasure in the sum-total of feeling. But psychoanalysis thinks sensual feelings may be remarked in all this, and von Hattingberg ascribes all "fear-pleasure" to them alone. These pleasurable feelings are said to be especially connected with the anal zone, but also with the genital zone as well. Sometimes it is the forcible continence, sometimes incontinence (e.g. bed-wetting), which is the cause of the excited feeling of mingled fear and sensual pleasure. Now, it has been certainly proved that in later childhood nervous feelings are sometimes accompanied by precocious sexual excitement, but I cannot think there is sufficient evidence to assume a corresponding state in the little child.

In conclusion, a word as to the significance of the radiation of nervous fear in various directions. The real cause of fear and the object producing its manifestation are by no means

necessarily identical. The real cause may be found in physical
conditions (e.g. heart troubles, digestive disturbances); it may
also originate in psychic depths, whilst the perceptions appertaining to it, may have no conscious persistence. For example,
at a later age, anxiety for a relative, fear of an illness, shrinking
from some active responsibility or from some impending change,
may work in this way. But once a condition of nervous fear
has arisen from such a source, it takes possession of the whole
being and radiates into other psychic regions which originally
may have nothing at all to do with it. And, in the end, the
diffused feeling becomes attached to some concrete perception
or other which then becomes the object of fear. Here the
nervous fear takes root, and tries to give its indefinite nature
a definite shape, if only in self-justification. This, then, is the
origin of those numerous apparently meaningless or even
absurd fears that make a transitory appearance in every
normal life (e.g. many children's fear of dogs), and which
may, under certain circumstances, show a pathological
degeneration and as "phobias" cause considerable psychic
disturbance.

Psychoanalysis has been quite right in seeing through this
fixing of a feeling to a secondary object, but has, in my
opinion, brought the occurrence into too close a connection
with "repression"; it assumes, namely, that the secondary
object of the fear must necessarily be a substitute for another
repressed cause, i.e. must symbolically take its place. But in
the young child, especially, it is very possible that a general
feeling—originally attached to no object, but arising from the
feeling of inferiority or from physiological conditions—is
looking for an object; there is therefore no need for another
object to be first repressed to radiate its phobic feeling-tone
on to the "dog" or "horse". For instance, a child may wake
from a terrifying dream of being chased by a horse. It is then
conceivable that the dream-idea of a horse—in itself free of
any feeling-tone—may have derived its fear-tone from some
other unpresented source (possibly digestive trouble), and
from the same cause, also, the further manifestation of terrifying
incidents in the dream (chasing). And as in dreams, so in
waking hours, the fear of a dog may only be the concrete
form of an indefinite mental feeling of nervous fear. Indeed,
even in cases where a feeling of fear has been caused by a

concrete present single experience[1] but has later been associated with quite a different object, a repression of the first need not have taken place. More probably the actual cause of that "trauma" may have faded from memory and been actually forgotten, whilst its emotional effect, in the shape of a general nervousness, is more persistent, and may attach itself when occasion arises to a fresh object. There would therefore, then, be no necessity for the secondary object of fear to stand in any secret symbolic relation to the primary cause.[2]

We will mention the case given by Jung of a four-year-old girl as an instance of the psychoanalytic method of interpreting these occurrences. The child had just gone through the experience of a little brother being born into the family; questions and remarks of various kinds proved, directly and indirectly, that she was greatly occupied with the problem as to where children came from. Jung now assumes that the inward unrest into which the child had been thrown by the questions arising from the event—(also with regard to having children herself, later on)[3]—was much greater than outwardly appeared, for there occurred simultaneously a phobia of an entirely different content, but, as Jung believes, connected by the same causes with those psychic "conflicts". The little girl had, namely, heard of an earthquake that had just taken place in Messina, and from this moment was, for a considerable time, tormented by an earthquake fear, especially violent in the evening and at night, so that her mother had continually to stay by her bed to pacify her. In the daytime she tried to work off her fear by a nervous desire to know, to hear a great deal about earthquakes and to see pictures of them.

Jung now does not assume that the experience "earthquake" in itself formed the real cause of fear—(although a sensitive child might very easily be affected by the strong impression made by the catastrophe on those amongst whom she lived)—but he sees in her fear a compensating occurrence. The child feels the non-explanation of the problem as to the origin of children as a hostile expression of secrecy and sets up her own opposition in the shape of forcing her parents'

---

[1] A "trauma" is the psychoanalytic appellation. Trauma = psychic injury.
[2] Freud, Bernfeld and others go so far to derive all nervous states in man from the fundamental trauma of birth and the fundamental nervousness then experienced.
[3] Cf. Chapter XXVIII, 2 of this book.

love in another quarter (i.e. through her state of fear at night). At the same time the anxious wish to know about earthquakes is a "converted libido", i.e. the desire to know the origin of children with its sexual feeling-tone in another shape and form.

After some time the earthquake fear died away. But neither is this simply explained by Jung as the natural overcoming of the feeling by the child's healthy nature, but is again brought into union with that other percept-complex. The cessation of the phobia was noticed just at the time when, in reply to her continued questions, the explanation was given that the little brother had grown in her mother and come from her. According to Jung's interpretation the sexual desire for knowledge was satisfied and no longer required the disguise of the earthquake fear. To my mind there is another and more obvious explanation of the simultaneous occurrence of both motives, the child had got in the explanation of birth a new source of interest which, as Jung reports, greatly occupied her mind; no wonder then that the older earthquake interest, which, in any case, was no longer working with the original force of novelty, fell into the background.[1]

---

[1] The celebrated phobia-psychoanalysis made by Freud of a five-year-old boy would require too elaborate consideration to be included in this book. I must therefore refer the reader to its detailed critical discussion given by me elsewhere (V). Cf. also Chapter XX in this book.

CHAPTER XXXVI

THE CHILD AND OTHERS

1. General Considerations

THE previous chapters have dealt with the child's striving in a very abstract manner, such abstract treatment being almost inevitable from reasons of method. They have therefore only dealt with those impulses and desires directed by the child to his own ego, which has to be affirmed, enjoyed, asserted and assured. In this treatment, then, it was taken for granted that there was such a thing as an existence referred by the individual solely and entirely to his own ego ; it is well known that this supposition has been magnified by many into the statement that this attitude to the ego is the only elementary one, and that all other desires are, at root, of an egoistic nature or origin. Such a construction is far from reality. From the very first day a fundamental fact of life is the passive participation of a common life, and "the other" belongs as much to the child's existence as does his own self. And the stirrings and desires centred on these others as their goal may possibly be inferior in intensity and extent to "self" aims and strivings, but certainly not as regards their fundamental and direct nature.[1]

In preceding chapters we made frequent mention of the part played by other people, but there they chiefly interested us as the means—positive or negative—for egoistic aims ; as factors of that derogation against which self-assertion rebels, or as points of help or refuge when the child fears for his ego. The rôle of others already became more involved with psychic considerations in the phenomenon of ambition, of pose and shame ; here fellow-man had a significance as the public, i.e. the

---

[1] A. A. Grünbaum has recently narrowed down this thought by stating that boundaries between the individual and his environment are to begin with very indistinct and intermingled. "The child has no idea of the world as categorically separate from his own ego, no idea of it as something unfamiliar, makes as yet no distinction between it and the ego . . . but feels at first only a kind of 'we' within which I and the other have the same structure and mutually carry each other" (pp. 457 seq.). Again: "It seems as if the child in the very beginning did not stand in any mutual action and reaction with the inanimate world of external stimuli, but through these attains a much more intimate, even if primitive companionship with his personal environment" (p. 449).

Cf. also Grünbaum's attitude to the problem of imitation in this book, Chapter V, 2, 3.

individual ego needs for consciousness and affirmation of itself at the same time consciousness that others know of and assent to his existence.

But now we come to those wishes and endeavours whose direct objects are other people, or, to speak more generally, other living creatures, since animals are also included. In short, we now consider the little child as a social unit.

We may understand the expression "social relation" in one of two ways. First as the "syntelic" relation,[1] which is concerned with certain definite fellow-men, then as the "hypertelic", concerned with a whole society of which the individual forms a part. In later years, both social attitudes may be present plainly differentiated; on the other hand, it is characteristic of the young child that the second form almost entirely disappears in the first. He loves or hates, pities or ill-treats this or that concrete individual, has a feeling of familiarity for one or several separate persons or things, but has as yet no abstract idea of a "society" as such. Even those little societies to which he already belongs—family, playfellows—have more significance for the child through their separate personal relationships than they have in their collective character. Probably hypertelic aims, in the narrower sense, become more strongly marked shortly after the age limit fixed in this book; school, which then begins, is, after all, such a social unit where the child enters into a continuous relation of membership and subordination of self to the whole.

Erich Stern has lately given special consideration to group-feeling as shown by the child, and he, too, emphasizes the utter want in the very young child of the group-consciousness so strongly marked in older children. The little child does not feel—as older children do—united with his playfellows so strongly as to make a firm corporate whole, having its own laws, rights, secrets, by whom another child is considered as an outsider and stranger.

After the fourth year group-ideas begin to appear, but remain in a very rudimentary condition.

A general need of comradeship drives the child to a group of playfellows, but his attitude is still distinctly influenced by liking for, aversion from, confidence in, or shyness of individuals. In the first six years there are scarcely any traces of the feeling

[1] Cf. W. Stern, X, p. 45.

that, later on, plays such an important part as class-feeling, "penalism", sense of group solidarity or social duty.

As a positive influence, we must mention the dislike of group-exclusion; the child who has been put in the corner for this reason tries by all kinds of grimaces and noises to arouse the others' attention, and thus, indirectly, to satisfy his desire for comradeship.[1]

The first stirrings of group-consciousness are of course dependent in large measure on the influences of the environment. If the family in which the child grows up is lacking in corporate feeling or even given to disputes, there will be a lack of one of the most suggestive influences for the awaking social feeling and in such cases, under certain conditions, the child's social-ethical development may suffer irreparable injury.

Very remarkable too is the diversity in the social-psychic influence exercised on the individual child by the Froebel kindergarten on the one hand and the Montessori school on the other. Martha Muchow calls attention to this in her comparative study (IV).

The children in the Montessori school are not arranged in groups. As each child in reality is concerned only with himself as the object of his mental and physical exercises the children are only NEAR and BESIDE, but not as a fact WITH each other. Even in the general movement-exercises (e.g. walking carefully along a chalked line, holding a glass full of water) there is only simultaneous movement, but no joint effort of all for a common aim as in the kindergarten action songs and games. Social action in the Montessori system means nothing more than accustoming the child to consideration of its comrades and the practice of certain community tasks, such as laying the table, pouring out milk, etc. Such habits are certainly valuable, but real social feeling cannot yet in early childhood be connected with common service of so abstract a nature. The Montessori class therefore remains a loosely connected and comparatively indifferent life beside one another of children intent on individual aims in the presence of a teacher who intentionally avoids the assumption of the character of a social leader.

The Froebel kindergarten attacks the problem in a quite different and doubtless more correct way. As the little child with his social feelings at their very first beginnings can only

[1] Cf. Chap. XXXVII for group-exclusion as a means of punishment.

grasp the idea of quite small groups, the whole number in the kindergarten is divided into a number of such very closely connected units.

Each of these units has a family character and by really common activity promotes a union of interests and feeling of the strongest kind. The individual group too has its own range and sphere of action, its own little corner, its cupboard, flowers, etc. At the same time the kindergarten teacher acts the part of mother in this would-be family group and on her side contributes greatly to the strengthening of the affective relations of the group members with one another.[1]

The feeling of intimacy with individuals is simpler than group-relationship; but even this seldom appears in an unmixed form in the young child, but generally is intimately connected with the self-feeling. For this reason it is not possible to draw such fine distinctions between altruism and egoism, devotion and self-love in the little child as in the adult. We shall soon see the appearance of strange limitations. Sometimes the feeling of affection to another contributes directly to an increase of egoistic feelings, sometimes the strong attraction of love produces an even stronger reactive aversion due to more narrow self-assertion. But even in this last case (e.g. hate, jealousy) the hostility itself is, after all, only possible as the result of the original feeling of devotion, and has no primary character.

The admixture of egoistic feeling in the child's attitude to other people does not therefore justify us in looking upon him as a pure egoist, or considering him, by nature, "asocial" and "anti-social". The old doctrine of original sin is, from a psychological point of view, as untenable as the opposite theory held by Rousseau that man was born "good", and only corrupted by civilization. The dogma of man's innate corruption has been renewed in a modern form by many psychoanalysts, who, not content with establishing self-love as the sole reason of the child's attitude, even speak of his "criminal" nature (Stekel). This is only possible by looking upon the child's transitory feelings and fantastic wishes expressed in play[2] as its normal aims proceeding from a definite disposition of character. There is in this an entire forgetfulness of the diffused nature of

---

[1] Cf. also the different social attitude of the children in two Ukranian kindergartens described by Dorschenko. (This book, Chapter XXII, 2.)
[2] We shall meet with instances later on.

childish desires and aims, to which an unwarranted definite character is given by the application to them of adults' expressions, such as "criminality"; forgetfulness, too, of the indefinite nature of childish tendencies, which need many years of the constant co-operation of surrounding influences before they develop into firm characteristics. A more detailed treatment of this point follows in Section 3 of this chapter.

2. Affection

Even in the discussion of infancy it was possible to call attention to the child's awaking manifestations of affection (Chapter VII, c). These increase with years in strength and variety. The chief object of the child's love and tenderness is and remains its mother, but the circle grows wider, until it includes the father, brothers and sisters, near relatives, or nursemaid, later also the kindergarten teacher and playfellows.

It may indeed be said that, in general, people with whom the child is connected by frequent association are all regarded by him with feelings of liking, however much these may vary in strength and tone. Affection is therefore greatly dependent—in quite other degree and fashion than in later years—upon habit, intimacy and the self-evident nature of the connection.[1] There exist barely any hints of the characteristic features, in later years, of affection with an erotic feeling-tone, viz. the singling out of one object of affection to the exclusion of all others, the ardent desire for the perfecting of the self in and by another being, hitherto unknown, and the constancy and fidelity which maintains the emotion even during long absence. How quickly the little child gets used to a new nurse, even when it had great affection for her predecessor; how little the child misses—perhaps after short pain at parting—its parents when they leave home, or a favourite animal, etc.[2]

The close connection between affection and habit points, of course, to a certain admixture of egoism; the objects of the child's affection are those who satisfy his need of protection and help, of tenderness and care. His affection and sense of need blend here into one united feeling—and there is no need for us

---

[1] D. and R. Katz give a vivid description of the different shade of the child's love for its father and for its mother.
[2] Instances of this in Chapter XVII, 2.

to draw the conclusion that another's power to satisfy the child's selfish pleasure is the only reason of the latter's love. If, for instance, a great pleasure provided by the mother evokes especially ardent demonstrations of affection, this has the appearance of pure egoism; the child, however, in these demonstrations not only greets his mother as the continual giver, but has a feeling, too, for her generous love and her sympathy with his pleasure, hence, at that moment, a keener appreciation too of his own loving recognition of her affection; here we come to the first beginnings of a feeling of gratitude.

Another proof of the non-egoistic character of childish tenderness is its expression on occasions when the child has least cause to expect anything for himself—or to such individuals as the child feels on a lower level than himself. Tenderness to housepets, to quite tiny babies (and love of dolls, etc., mentioned earlier), has its origin much more in the joy of being able to give rather than to receive. And, lastly, the child's love reaches its highest degree of unselfishness in those cases—not frequent certainly, but still existent—where he acts with the most pronounced self-denial and altruism—but more of these later.

The love and tenderness of the young child is not purely mental action, but closely connected with bodily action as well. Human love is love from the whole being, from the psychophysical neutral person, and for the little child in particular, mental and physical are so intermingled that for him to love and to caress are literally the same thing.[1] Thus the child's love is interwoven with physical movements of attraction; the child tries always to get as near as possible to the person loved; he wants to be taken up on his mother's arm or lap, snuggles up to her, presses his face against hers, strokes her hands and cheeks,[2] or lets his own be so caressed. Thus the embrace takes on a sense-attraction which, in certain cases, may become the principal factor; the child then enjoys the physical contact as a pleasure

---

[1] Cf. Chap. XXVII.

[2] Only one active expression—the kiss—has not the innate character of the others mentioned. It has to be learnt, and everyone knows how long it takes to master its difficult technique; for a considerable time the child makes clumsy efforts with wide-opened mouth to copy and return another's kiss.

Psychological research amongst different peoples has shown that the kiss as a sign of affection is only of late development; it is by no means universal, whilst the other signs of love mentioned above as shown in close physical touch (stroking, etc.) seem to exist wherever human beings do.

through a bodily organ, and endeavours to secure its continuance for that reason alone.

Psychoanalysis has called our attention to the significance of this sense-factor in the little child's affection; but are we to designate as "sexuality" every expression of affection that is connected with a desire for physical proximity and pleasure in touching and being touched? Such an extension of the first idea would entirely obliterate the fundamental difference between affection in early childhood and the growing emotion of love which appears in its new form from the age of puberty onwards.

This seems to me clearly the case in the incest-theory of psychoanalysis. Childish sexuality—according to psychoanalysis —soon leaves the auto-erotic phase behind, and seeks an object of love in another person. The mother naturally becomes this object, and is the child's first "love", providing him with help, food, games, and with pleasurable bodily feelings, not only by her caresses, but also by her tendance, which necessitates continual touching of the "erogenous" zones, genital organs, anus, etc. The mother, too, makes it possible for the child to satisfy his sexual curiosity by touching her body (e.g. when she takes him into her own bed) and looking at her (when she undresses or washes in his presence).

There may be much truth in these statements until it comes to summarizing childish signs of affection under the heading of sexuality. It is not only a question of an unsuitable classification but also of the fatal results it may bring in its train. For it is now assumed that the child becomes conscious of the unnatural and forbidden character of such feelings, and therefore suppresses them. He puts up such an "incest-barrier", and becomes in his Unconscious so much the more the prey of these emotions, which then appear in his surface-consciousness only in the shape of apparently innocent symbolic manifestations.

After the critical discussion of the psychoanalytic theories of symbolic interpretation and suppression to be found in earlier chapters, we need not here dwell especially on this "incest-theory". But it again shows us the need of discriminating in the theses of psychoanalysis between statements of actual facts— in themselves very valuable and until now too greatly neglected—and the interpretations put upon them.

Many similar statements may be made concerning the emotional relations existing between the little child and his brothers and sisters or playmates. For here, too, there are ties of affection varying greatly in strength and desire to give and receive demonstrations of love with bodily contact of many kinds. But some new factors make their appearance.

Consider first their play together. The child can make a plaything of whatever he chooses, therefore, too, of his own body or his playfellow's. If brothers and sisters share the same bed, or romp with one another when only wearing one small nightgarment, it is absolutely impossible to avoid the occurrence of much physical contact which makes the child familiar with the sexual organs touched, for, since natural things are not yet base to children of that age, they see no reason in their play to avoid these parts of the body. The fact that these body zones are kept covered as a rule, and not considered by grown-ups as suitable subjects of conversation or enquiry, may even increase their power of attraction with the child. He has no idea of the why and wherefore of this taboo; the charm of the mysterious and forbidden, however, may well be calculated to strengthen his interest in such games, even without any trace of sexual feeling-tone. And thus the phenomena arise which doctors especially often report: the pleasure that is found in looking at the sex-organs in another child—especially one of a different sex—games with one another's sex-organs (mutual onanie), even, indeed, imitation of the coitus. It is true we know nothing about the prevalence of such abnormalities in early childhood, for the reports to be found in psychoanalytic literature always refer to quite isolated observations—which are at once made into the general rule—or to the very untrustworthy memories of neurotic adults. As regards the period when such actions begin, a neurotic disposition may lead to a certain precocity of instincts that, in normal healthy human beings, certainly do not appear spontaneously as a rule before the end of the sixth year.

In any case, certain outward influences seem also to be contributory factors, and this is the point that demands the attention, from an educational point of view, of parents and guardians. How fond children are of playing father and mother; to be big and able to act as his parents do is indeed a silent longing of every child. Consequently, their impulse of imitation includes everything that they have noticed in their parents. Unfortunately, many parents allow their children opportunities to notice what should be kept from them. It is little children particularly who generally sleep with their parents, but they are not always so fast asleep as their parents think, and what happens in the darkness, from its very obscurity and mystery, rouses in the child's imagination the desire to imitate. Then real misconduct may take place: older children misuse those smaller than themselves to awaken their own sensations of a feeling-tone much akin to sexual emotions, and the unsuspecting little children become familiar with a premature over-stimulation of the genital zone.[1]

The following quotation shows these influences at work. It comes from "The Confessions of a Woman Patient", given by W. Liepmann in his book *The Psychology of Woman.* "My first experience in sexual matters occurred at the age of six. My six-year-old brother used to take a neighbour's six-year-old daughter in the evening dusk, unfasten her underclothes and finger her sexual organs as many of the other children did in secret. The little girl made no objection, but lay on her back apparently enjoying herself immensely. . . . Some days ago at noon I came across a seven-year-old boy and a five-year-old girl on the garret stairs who were doing the same thing. In answer to my question as to what they were doing, they laughed and said: 'We are having a game'. When I said that was not allowed, and if their parents knew they would get a whipping, the boy answered with an impudent look: 'Why, my father does it with my mother.'"

3. Hate, Envy, Cruelty

Greatly as the child desires to love and be loved, he has a good knowledge too of the opposite feelings. It is true, however, that these do not seem to possess the strength and distinctly primitive nature of love. The attempts of modern schools of psychology (especially again of psychoanalysis) to reveal these negative emotions more particularly, and give full weight to their significance was perhaps necessary, in view of the far too rosy picture of perfect innocence and spotless charm drawn in earlier days of the little child; but they went to the other extreme, and now it is again necessary to correct representations

[1] Unfortunately, it is often the case that nursemaids—older as well as young girls—misuse their little charges in such a way.

that aim at making a soured criminal misanthrope out of every child.

The emotion of hatred of certain individuals is in the child as a rule not a primary feeling, but one derived from emotions of another kind.[1] And first amongst these other emotions stands love.

We have already seen (Chapter XXXIV, 2) that the ebullition of angry defiance is really against the dependent position in which the child is placed by its very affection. The ambivalence of the feelings is never so markedly seen as here—and, indeed, not only in the little child. Even in the adult hate is, in great measure, suppressed, disappointed love. The proverb "Only love will drive out hate" is continually justified in the child especially, who after a stormy scene turns again to his mother with redoubled caresses and devotion.

Whilst defiance has no definite motive, the desire for retaliation is always determined by a known cause. Some decided interference on the part of an adult—a punishment, the removal of a toy, a prohibition—meets with the response of the child's momentary resistance, not always of a purely mental nature, but finding vent in a literal attack on the "enemy's" person. These are spontaneous expressions of the revenge-instinct, and are by no means contradictory of the love felt as a rule. The direct declaration of war actually accompanying such attacks: "I don't love you a bit any more," must not be taken too literally; in this we often find only the imitation of an uneducational expression used by grown-ups to a refractory child—not, it is true, an educational method to be highly recommended. Fortunately, the child is so much a creature of the present that he does not bear malice long; his ebullition of wrath does not generally outlast its cause, and the enduring foundations of tender affection remain unshaken. There are only rare exceptions in which this natural affection is permanently injured by neglect or bad treatment and the feeling of hostility becomes chronic. But even in this case it is more the result of the child's sensitive instinct that his affection is not returned than the effect of the pain imposed upon him, for really loving parents—and teachers also—often enough have to cause children pain, punish them, withhold some pleasure from them, yet the child's

[1] We find, at most, exceptions to this in certain idiosyncrasies towards individual people which, so far, still remain unexplained.

affection is not lessened in any way by this treatment. This feeling of revenge is not only directed against people, but may also include anything whatever that annoys the child, even the table-leg he has bumped against, pet animals, etc.

Scupin (4 ; 1). "Bubi is very angry with a 'naughty flea' that worried him in bed. We have to rub his back, but still it tickles. Then Bubi suddenly drags the quilt over his head, rolls a pillow on the top, and when asked why he is doing all this he cries out revengefully from a fold of the quilt: *So that the flea may get no air to breathe.*" (II, 93.)

Other forms of childish antipathy arise from the fact that the child feels an advantage enjoyed by another as a direct slight to his own person. We may here distinguish (1) envy, (2) a grudging spirit, and (3) jealousy. Envy occurs when an advantage possessed by another is striven for by ourselves but not obtained.

Whether it is a question of a toy with which he sees someone else playing, or a caress his mother gives to a little sister and not to him, or the fact that his elder brother is taken on some expedition whilst he has to stay at home—every case soon awakens a spirit of rivalry with the privileged person.

The child may show a grudging spirit even when the other's advantage does not clash with his own striving. It is possible to grudge a thing to someone else, even when we have no wish for it ourselves, even, indeed, when it could not in any way be the object of our aim; the simple fact that another has it is felt as a slight to one's own self-regard. This grudging spirit forms at the same time one root—although a very selfish one—of the sense of justice, for any turning of the scale in another's favour will be felt as unendurable: an equal footing at least is desired as regards all advantages, and also as regards recognition by others of one's worth.

Gunther (5 ; 6½). Before he could skate Hilde was to go on the ice one Sunday with her father. "G. was terribly upset, even to tears, that H. should have such a treat and he not. I comforted him by promising to show him the big illustrated Bible in the afternoon. Much relieved and somewhat triumphant, he told his sister, adding that, of course, H. wouldn't see them too. When I explained to him that, after all, it couldn't hurt him if H. looked at them with us, he exclaimed between his sobs: *Then, after all, Hilde will have two treats and me only one!*

Children, on such occasions, can count well. I tried to make him understand how wrong it was not to be willing to share, and since similar situations often arise and I always treat them in the same way, I hope to get some result. I even fancy he does try to fight against this fault, so natural to children, but wrong."

But these signs of a grudging spirit are in a normal child and under favourable circumstances only momentary ebullitions in no way detrimental, as a rule, to the usual feeling of harmony with the same person. But there is great danger of the feeling becoming permanent. A child who is plainer, more stupid, or weaker than his brothers and sisters or playmates becomes hypersensitive as regards their powers and position, and, in his helplessness, can react only by such a grudging spirit. Even without such evident inferiorities there are cases where mothers or teachers by an unfair division of their sympathies always put one child behind others. Such action may bring about a comparatively early feeling of chronic hate of the more fortunate rivals, and the grudge is then very nearly related to jealousy.

Real jealousy is always accompanied by a monopolizing claim on the affection of another person. The rival is considered and treated as an enemy because he too shares the love (e.g. the mother's) of which the jealous child wishes to have sole enjoyment. For instance, he will not suffer his mother to take his sister on her lap at the same time as him and to lavish caresses on both.

Psychoanalysis has again dealt in its well-known manner with the incontestable truth that jealousy exists even in early childhood, but, in so doing, has overlooked the fact that typical childish jealousy differs most strongly from the erotic jealousy of a later age. The latter is an emotion entirely independent of the presence of the persons loved, indeed all the stronger in their absence. The bare thought that the object of affection can either give or receive love in any other direction is simply unbearable for the monopolizing attitude of the lover. Under normal conditions none of this is to be found in the little child. His claim of monopoly has reference, practically always, only to individual demonstrations of affection, whether it be one present or hoped-for later. Thus he pushes away his little brother who, in his desire for love, has secured the place nearest his mother. Thus, too, he is pleased when his father goes away, because he can then be the sole object of his mother's attention.

But that he should harbour this desire of sole possession when away from her and constantly feed his imagination on such an idea is entirely improbable.

We have thus laid the foundations for a criticism of the psychoanalysts' Œdipus-theory.[1] Just as the child's love for his mother is considered to have a sexual feeling-tone, so too his jealousy of his father. This is not considered in its character of passing emotion, but as a form of striving which exercises a far-reaching influence on the life of the child's personality. It is a fatal primal enmity of the child against his father, for the latter is from the first his rival for his mother's favour, receives from her proofs of love which—as the child dimly suspects—are of quite another nature than the marks of affection which the mother gives to him. It is true this hostility does not generally make its appearance in a manifestly conscious form; it but rarely finds direct expression in utterances of hatred of his father and wishes for his death. But generally the feeling which the child very early knows to be a forbidden one is suppressed into the Unconscious, and it is only possible to gather from its symbolic disguises its strength and persistence. This is the fundamental idea of the psychoanalytic teaching.

The Œdipus-theory is most intimately connected with the incest-theory we lately discussed. As in that, so here we must refer to our earlier critical arguments as to the value or worthlessness of the symbolic interpretations employed, the inadmissibility of giving such a wide application of the principles of suppression in early childhood, and the unconscious memory-falsifications of neurotic adults. What then remains we find in the jealousy-emotions discussed above, which may be manifested in lesser or greater degrees of strength, but need not, necessarily, have anything to do with sexuality, nor possess that persistent subconscious significance ascribed to them by psychoanalysis. A striking example has been given me from a reliable source to prove that a child's action may very easily be interpreted as erotic jealousy and yet be nothing of the kind.

It is early morning and the father, already dressed, brings the boy out of the nursery to the mother, who is still in bed. The child lies down by his mother prepared to sleep (with his finger in his mouth), says "bye-bye" and then commands: "Daddy go out."

[1] See also Chap. XIX, 4.

Explanation: The parents had often said when the boy was put to bed: "There, now we are going out and Bubi must go bye-bye." He had picked up this expression and had the habit, if he was sleepy and anyone was still busy in the room, of ordering him out; as soon as he was in bed, all who were still up must "out". "Mummy out, Herta out" (the nursemaid) were his commands.

Exactly the same thing occurred now; it was only by chance that the order fell on his father, as he was standing there dressed, since he would not think of giving it to his mother, who was still lying in bed.

This is a fitting point at which to glance once more at the theory of every child's original criminality. If we believe with the psychoanalysts that feelings of hate and jealousy, instincts of revenge and envy, continuously play the most important part in the hidden depths of the child's psychic nature, then, of course, we have to accept the fact that they must also give to the will a proportionate anti-social bias; then the child must consider every means justifiable to injure, maltreat, even to do away with his hated fellow-men. The advocates of this opinion are not content with pointing out those evident childish actions which are usually accounted immoral, such as falsehood, deceit, cruelty, but over and above these they make an arch mental-sinner of the child. If he speaks or dreams—or symbolizes under some disguise—that he would like to get rid of his father, boil and eat his little brother,[1] he is supposed to betray thereby his original nature of murderer and cannibal.[2] In reality, such childish expressions are of the nature of chance playful remarks, whose meaning they scarcely understand themselves, or they are the interjectional discharge of a momentary excitement; but they cannot be regarded as expressions of a real desire even, much less, then, as the permanent intention of their will. It is only possible by loading the long-suffering Unconscious with those hypothetical hate and destruction ideas to construct the criminal feature as a general trait of early childhood.

Of course, it is a different matter when the question is put from the point of view of DIFFERENTIAL psychology. That there are isolated cases of children in whom, at a comparatively early

[1] Cf. Chapter XIX, 3.
[2] As a matter of fact, genetic conclusions are drawn between those utterances of the child and the cannibalism of primitive peoples.

age, special tendencies to moral degeneracy can be noted, cannot of course be disputed. The problems here arising—the psychic and psychopathic structure of moral degeneracy, the biological and social conditions of its occurrence—are important enough, but do not come within the scope of this book.

By a concrete group of qualities we will now briefly show that closer psychological analysis can put a very different complexion on what at first bears a very evil appearance.

Heartlessness and cruelty are often laid to the charge of the little child. What truth is there in this criticism?

At first, indeed, our attention is attracted by cases of an unexpected want of sympathy; just in those cases where the adult is overcome by some painful occurrence, and not only hopes but looks for sympathy from the child (e.g. in cases of family bereavement, severe illness, or violent pain of relatives, etc.), we are often painfully surprised by the child's total lack of emotional response. Moreover, the indifference with which he sometimes treats living animals, crushing flies, stamping on beetles, tearing butterflies to pieces, seems to point to the very opposite of sympathy, rather to a cruel delight in another creature's agony. And not only animals but human beings as well (e.g. younger brothers and sisters) are not infrequently teased, pinched, or otherwise persecuted by the small tormentor.

In many cases this want of sympathy is nothing else but lack of understanding. The mystery of death is a closed door for early childhood; the child, living as he does only in the present, cannot yet grasp what it means to be parted for ever from some dear presence. Then, too, we must reckon with the small child's power of concentration and his great forgetfulness; unlike the adult, he is unable to allow himself to be dominated for hours or days at a time by one idea or one emotion. Hence it happens that the child, even in a sick-room or house of mourning, is so much more taken up with the play of his fleeting attention that he actually forgets what is filling others' minds; his want of sympathy therefore does not necessarily proceed from lack of feeling. Of course, though, there are cases of real lack—or late development—of sympathy.

But if want of sympathy appears more as a gap in the child's emotional life, cruelty is surely a positive fault. Yet even here outward appearance must not be hastily accepted as psychological reality. Most of the so called "cruel" deeds rest on other well-known motives, not unmoral in themselves, and only having that effect through association with childish want of apprehension (cf. Chapter VII, Section 2, c). The child's boundless desire of movement, his love of destruction, his curiosity as to the inside of everything, are all brought into play with his characteristic disregard of consequences, whether to some toy or to a living creature; and in such perfect moments of full experience there can be no question of any conscious realization of the possible agony they may have caused. The fact that it is possible to cure this trait of apparent cruelty by educational influences is the best proof that, in normal children, it is not an inborn characteristic, but due to want of thought. Serious teaching and warning, the example of teachers who most carefully avoid all forms of cruelty to animals and all unnecessary taking of life, and—should these prove ineffectual—a slight demonstration on the child's own body of how it hurts to be pinched or have one's leg dragged, may prove a most effectual cure.

In this connection it is perhaps not superfluous to point out that to teach very young children to begin zoological collections (of butterflies, beetles, etc.), in spite of its educative value, is not without drawbacks as moral training. In these early years, at least, the child is still too young to distinguish between justifiable and unjustifiable taking of life, and, moreover, his ideas are still so unfixed that it would be very easy to diminish or destroy feelings of kindness to animals.

In addition to apparent cases of cruelty arising from lack of understanding, there are such cases of tormenting man and beast as originate in a certain delight in teasing. Pleasure in teasing, which is nothing but a kind of tournament (tilting-match), is of very early growth; the teaser enjoys, in his game, his sense of power, his superiority to his victim. It is true, as we know, that in the child the line between play and earnest is not sharply defined, so that teasing may easily degenerate into something worse. The playful delight in another's disadvantage may become actual joy, the enjoyment of power may destroy the power of sympathy in another's pain, and teasing—innocent in itself—turns into something very like actual cruelty and spite.[1] A teacher then should be on the watch to check in time

[1] Erich Stern gives examples of this.

any excessive delight in teasing and so prevent the development of a heartless characteristic.

To the above-mentioned sources of cruel acts—want of understanding, lack of motor control. depraved pleasure in teasing and tormenting—may be added the social influence. For children of neglectful or criminal parents, whose fathers ill-treat their wives, are only too liable to imitate what they see daily. On the other hand, it seems doubtful whether a motive of psychic sexual cruelty upon which psychoanalysis lays great stress plays any part at this early period. It is well known that by "sadism" we understand the tendency to derive personal pleasure from the ill-treatment of another. But the little boy who, in his rage, strikes a playfellow with a whip is not therefore a sadist already, simply because in sexually depraved adults a whip often acts as a means of incitement.

4. Sympathy and Altruism

If analysis only of the inferior qualities shown in childhood forces us to reject the theory of the absolutely egoistic, even criminal nature of the little child, our position is made even stronger by the evidence of the positive part played at this early age by the non-egoistic feelings and desires. We have already spoken of affection; we will therefore now turn our attention to sympathy and altruism. The evidence of these feelings is perhaps not so conspicuous as that of the opposite qualities just mentioned, but none the less significant on that account.

And, in truth, even the two- or three-year-old child has the power of feeling another's sorrow, not only in the sense that, infected by the other's feelings, he grows sad and anxious with him and cries in response to the other's tears—that would only be suggested emotion; but in the higher sense of putting himself in the other's place, identifying himself with his sorrow, pain or fear, and trying to comfort, help, or even avenge him.

W. Boeck has published the results of an enquiry as to sympathy which he held amongst large numbers of children; the method employed is in no way to be compared, as far as accuracy goes, with the observation of individual children.   B. sent out a question-paper to a considerable number of parents requesting: "Cases of plainly marked sympathy in children," if possible accompanied by details of the object of the sympathy, its occasion and expression. In such a method of procedure it is not possible to form any judgment of the psychological competence of the coadjutors, or to have any control as to whether the cases reported are those recently observed or vaguely remembered. Nevertheless, the enquiry can, at least, give an approximate idea of the variety in the phenomena of children's sympathy and of their statistic classification.

Boeck's statistics in the years from 1 ; 0 to 6 ; 0 include 408 cases, which are divided according to years as follows:—

Year of age ..	2nd	3rd	4th	5th	6th
Cases	66	95	94	93	60

We feel a little sceptical of the reliability of the observations as we notice the improbably high number of cases amongst the two-year-olds.

The classification as to the object of the sympathy is of greater interest. Thus sympathy was expended on:—

	Cases of Sympathy.	Percentage of All Cases.
Members of family	145	$35\frac{1}{2}$
Other people	59	$14\frac{1}{2}$
Animals	88	21
Lifeless objects, dolls, plants ..	56	14
People or animals in pictures or tales	60	$14\frac{1}{2}$

So that exactly half the cases recorded refer to living human beings, and amongst these members of their own family head the list; but with increasing years more and more people enter the scope of the child's vision or, more correctly, of his emotion. From year to year, sympathy with lifeless objects diminishes, but increases with animals.

The child's power of sharing another's sorrow originally depends chiefly on the other emotions binding him to that other. The feeling towards anyone is a determining factor of the feeling with him; that instinctive movement of his own emotion with another's comes to pass most easily on the responsive ground of love and tenderness, and thus it is easy to understand that the strongest feelings of sympathy, in early years, are shown towards the mother.

Gunther (3 ; 0). "His mother slipped down some steps, leading from one room to another, and G. at once tries to help her up again, puffing and panting as if to cure her, and continually asking in anxious tones: *Getting well again?* To hide her pain from the children, their mother went into another room. Then G. fetches a footstool, climbs on to it by the door, turns the handle, and continues his tender cry: *Getting well again?* Then he returns to the scene of the fall and carries away the bucket, which he considers the cause of the stumble, at the same time asserting his intention of preventing any more such accidents."

But sympathy and love may exist in opposite relationship, so that sympathy increases affection.

Hilde (4 ; 7). "When her mother was not well, Hilde's tenderness was redoubled; she continually pitied the invalid, asked *poor mother* if she could bring her a drink, fondled and kissed her oftener than usual."

Hilde (5 ; 7). "Lately her mother did not feel well and said she would have to lie down. In a moment Hilde was tender and demonstrative as she uttered the significant words: *Mummy, when you are ill, I love you much more.*"[1]

A curious complication of feeling is the cause of this increased tenderness, the result of altruistic emotion limited by egoistic feelings—more or less unconscious.

If the mother's illness is not too serious, then the child knows that there will be quiet, cosy hours when it can sit at its mother's bedside and listen to her reading or telling tales. Its own good health and power to help increases the child's sense of self-importance; the rôles of helper and helped are indeed suddenly reversed. To all this is added the attractive sensation arising from illness and the unusual nature of the conditions it brings with it.

Two examples show how expression is sometimes given with all simplicity to these motives hidden as a rule. "On the occasion of the first named illness of her mother's, Hilde (4 ; 7) said one evening in a tone expressive of pleasure and joyful hope: *Mummy, if you're ill to-morrow too, I'll cut your bread and butter.*"

"Shortly before this we had been to the Zoological Gardens with Hilde. She had heard that a monkey was ill, and took us aback by suddenly observing: *I want to see how nice and ill the monkey is.* Here sympathy was entirely swallowed up in desire for sensation."

[1] This remark is also of interest as showing that, in exceptional cases, a child of only five and a half years is capable of spontaneous self-observation.

Sympathy with those related to the child is, besides, not only expressed when the suffering is actually present, but even if it is only possible or hypothetical, and then, too, the child's feelings of fear are not always tinged with egoism. The first traces of this fear for others have a strong likeness to that fear of the uncanny described in an earlier chapter, but in this case the child's fear is not concerned with himself.

Hilde (2 ; 3) saw for the first time how the new-born little brother was put to her mother's breast; then she grew nervous, said *nearly done now* (the business was to be finished at once), and began to cry. We get a similar report of other children who thought the baby was biting their mother.

Hilde (2 ; 5). When an aunt sat down on a rocking-seat and rocked up and down the child called out in fear: *Leave off, leave off!* Another time she was anxious for her father when he balanced himself on a fallen tree, and again when he climbed a high bank overhanging the road. Compare also Gunther's fear for his sister in the circus (Chapter XVII). This more familiar form of sympathy is soon joined by a second. The foundation of practically all social and charitable effort is a sympathy with the need and suffering of our fellow-creatures, without seeing them individually and apart from all other sentiments, hence it is surely noteworthy to find this social sympathy already budding forth in childhood's early years.

Hilde (3 ; 6½). "We happened to mention when talking one day that many poor children had no shoes or stockings. Then said H.: *Oh, then their feet will be cold;* (adding joyfully) *then we must buy the children shoes and stockings and gloves too.* And she added several other things we were to buy."

In answer to his general enquiry, Boeck received eleven examples of little children's sympathy with cripples, twenty-two examples of sympathy with social distress. In these cases, as in the one we have quoted, the wish was expressed to relieve the sufferings by gifts.

Such feelings, of course, are not uninfluenced by the parents' teaching. When they call their children's attention to signs of poverty and need, and express their own pity, whilst correcting ridicule on the child's part, and encouraging him to give present and thoughtful help, the feeling of social sympathy is greatly strengthened (cf. ex. of Scupin's son, Chapter XXXII, 3).

The spontaneity of the child's sympathy is especially marked where there is no adult example to influence him. This is true of many cases of feeling for animals—which, according to Boeck's statistics, formed one-fifth of all cases of sympathy. Sometimes the child, by erroneous analogy with man, assumes in the animal a suffering and want that it does not feel; sometimes, however, in his artless way the child is still sensitive where we adults are hardened (e.g. as regards animals used for food).

Scupin's son (2 ; 8½) happened to see the plucking of a turkey-cock when its breast was already half-bare. Then the boy said reproachfully to the cook: *O, Anna, you mustn't tear off poor turkey-cock's little shirt—he will be so cold* (I, 161).— (5 ; 11.) He carefully carried a crippled butterfly lying on the ground to a tree-stump, saying: *Come, poor nun, so that the hares may not eat you* (II, 173.)

Similar cases, such as are to be found in all children, prove at the same time what a mistake it is to account cruelty to animals as a general and constant feature of early childhood.

Boeck's last-named group of sympathetic feelings had reference to non-real beings, i.e. to people and animals in pictures and stories. It is just because the boundaries between appearance and reality are so easily obliterated in the child that his feelings for such imaginary creations are often but little inferior in intensity to his sympathy with real sorrow. Fear and sympathy, the two emotions necessary, as even Aristotle found, to all poetic creation, are then existent in the little child; the tale of Red Riding-Hood awakens in him feelings almost as keen as if it were the recital of some real misfortune that had happened near by.

One of Boeck's cases[1] runs thus: "Every time a boy of five and a half years hears the tale in his picture-book about King Nut-Cracker and poor Reinhold, in which Reinhold's father is dead, and the mother has, all by herself, to care for the sick child, he hides his tears, always pretending he has got something in his eye, as he hugs his parents; when looking at the picture-book, he always tries to pass over that page."

A special emotion resulting from sympathy must be mentioned; viz. those cases in which sympathy with the sufferer leads to antipathy against the originator of the suffering. The same instinct of defence which a child feels when threatened with

[1] P. 89.

injury himself fills him with regard to the oppressor—real or
supposed—of others; thus the tender emotion of sympathy and
the hard feelings of hatred and revenge are found in strangely
close juxtaposition. It is evident how deeply rooted must be
the human instinct for expiation when it shows itself so early,
on occasions too when the avenger's own weal or woe do not
come into question at all.

Boeck gives a number of cases where a brother or sister
comes to the help of another who is being beaten, and even
attacks the chastiser.

Scupin (3 ; 11½). "Bubi always gets very angry when his
father pretends in fun to hurt his mother; he stands there like
a fierce little bulldog, and at the fitting moment throws himself
on his father and uses all possible means to keep him back."
(II, 88.)

The other forms of sympathy, too (with animals or imaginary
beings), may be associated with a thirst for revenge; here,
sometimes — as some of the Scupins' examples show — the
hatred passes all bounds and loses all connection with the
object of sympathy as the boy becomes possessed with his own
lust of battle.

Scupin (3 ; 11). He saw some Kiel sprats, and when he was
told how they were caught, "their sad fate so touched his
heart that, in greatest anger, he poured forth abuse of the
wicked men who caught such dear little fish, abuse mingled
with a truly cruel fantasy: *But they are naughty men to kill the
poor little fish—but I'll beat them and saw them to bits, cut off
their heads, their breasts and arms, and I'll poke out their eyes,
and chuck the little bits into the water, and then the swans will
come and eat them up.*" (II, 84.)

Scupin (4 ; 7). "To-day, as he was looking at a picture of a
battle-scene, where one soldier has just shot another, he was so
upset that he immediately fetched his gun, put the barrel-
mouth exactly on the enemy's head, pulled the trigger—and
drew a sigh of relief: *There, now I've shot him dead for shooting
the other soldier.*" (II, 126.)

It is certain that children feel for others; but are they also
capable of altruistic action?

Here, again, we must distinguish between the different kinds
of altruistic action.

Certain acts are nothing more than direct instinctive expressions of strong emotion, and since, on an average, there is far less restraint of expression-movements in a child than in an adult, we must expect a greater number of such acts from him. And, as a fact, the direct result of sympathy is an attempt to comfort, an endeavour to help, or an attack on the other's oppressor. Of all these we have already given examples.

But this is not yet altruism in its highest sense, for there is still wanting a sense of conflict between one's own and another's interests, and a conscious decision in favour of the latter. The very help rendered is a proof of this; the pleasure in independent activity and the gay consciousness of power are often no less powerful factors in such help than is sympathy with the sufferer (see examples recently given).

Another form of the budding altruism is the "sharing" that is practised after the first year of age. The child's desire to let others share in an enjoyment he has himself is evidently quite elementary. Thus, Hilde (1 ; 2) said after each spoonful of soup her mother gave her: *Mummy eat*, and would not open her lips for the next spoonful until her mother too had pretended to take some. And we all know how children like to hand some of their cake or rolls to other people. They already feel therefore that a pleasure shared is thereby doubled.

It is possible that in its "sharing of pleasures" there may be also at a very early age a touch of primitive justice which feels wounded when another does not get the same as the child himself. For instance, when brothers and sisters are accustomed to do and share everything in common, the child who receives anything, as a matter of course, asks for the same for the others.[1] That is why "only" children are far less favourably placed for the development of altruism than are members of a larger family.

Gunther (1 ; 10½). "If he is given a piece of cake or chocolate, in a moment out rings his enquiring *Hildae?* and the second piece then forthcoming, he never dreams of keeping for himself, but takes straightway to his sister."

---

[1] The question is sometimes asked whether there is an innate sense of justice; child-psychology seems to show that this sentiment arises from several sources. We might name the instinct of one's own worth (Chapter XXXVI, 3), the demand for equal recognition with others (Chapter XXXVI, 3), the instinct to make amends (Chapter XXXVII, 2), the understanding of the immanent logic of punishment (Chapter XXXVII, 2, beginning), and lastly, the recognition of others' equal claims mentioned above.

But it is not long before these preparatory stages develop into true altruism, and the emotional act for others becomes deliberate. The child gains the power to set aside his own interest, although he is quite conscious of it, to give pleasure to another, or to spare him pain. It is, of course, not a question of hard self-denial and great sacrifice; everything shares in the small proportions natural to the child's early life, and this altruism, moreover, is but ill-equipped for a contest with egoistic attacks—especially if these are of some duration—of this we see a striking instance in Chapter XXXI, last two pars. Yet the chief point remains in the proof given that conscious active altruism does exist from the third year on.

Gunther (2 ; 6) often showed unselfishness in the following way. "At dinner some delicacy had been helped round, and Gunther began to eat. Then someone complained: 'I haven't a spoon', and in a trice, quite of his own accord, Gunther stopped feasting and handed over his own spoon. He had for some moments to sit and watch the others enjoying the treat, which he did with patience, never asking for a spoon, but waiting quite contentedly until one was brought to him."

Hilde (3 ; 11). "Her mother ladled all the carrots out of the soup tureen and put them on Hilde's plate. Then H. said: *But Gunther must have some carrots as well, Hilde must not have them all:* and she willingly let some of her carrots be taken away again for her brother."

Her mother said she would use Hilde's glass when she had finished with it, but did not ask the child to make haste. Then Hilde immediately emptied her glass at one draught, and said: *Now Mummy can drink, that's why I drank so quick.*

When once the child has arrived at the general idea that it must, for the sake of others, put aside its own wishes, or do without something nice it possesses, then of course a little care in education will help the child to persevere in altruistic action.

"Hilde (4 ; 8½) began to cry in the night about some trifling trouble. I had already got out of bed several times to go to her in the next room. H. kept on groaning and sighing and calling for me. At last, as I stood by her bed, I said: 'Very well, I will stay here now, although I am very tired and very cold myself, until Hilde herself says that mother can go to bed.' In two or three minutes a voice came from the pillows: *Mummy, you can go to bed now, I will be good.* And she fell quietly to sleep."

Scupin (5 ; 2½). "Bubi often went with us to take cast-off clothes to a very poor family. Before the first visit he was asked to take some of his toys to the three children of the family. But he objected at first, saying they were his own toys and he needed them, only going at last so far as to look out some damaged or old toys, long since put on one side. But when he saw how they delighted the children, he himself began to take pleasure in giving. The very next time he was much more generous, looked out toys of his own accord, and jumped about gaily, in anticipation of giving and seeing the poor children's joy. Yesterday he reminded us on his own initiative that it was time to take the poor children something again, and we even succeeded in persuading him to give them a toy from which at first he would not hear of parting." (II 170 seq.)

We will here as a kind of supplement touch on a subject which has been introduced by Herr and Frau Katz in their new book on *Conversations with Children*. It deals with the problem of confession in childhood. Psychology asks: Are children capable of rendering account to themselves or others of actions good or bad, that lie behind them? Do they feel the need of doing so? What is the effect of such "confession" upon the children themselves? Pedagogy asks: Ought parents to bring about such confessions even in young children and to encourage their feeling of the need of them?

D. and R. Katz answer both sets of questions in the affirmative and amongst the published "conversations" there are whole series of such confessional talks, which generally took place in the evening, just before the children went to sleep. Stress is laid on the points (*a*) that the children should remember not only their small faults but their good deeds as well, in order not to provoke a one-sided sense of sin, and also (*b*) that no punishments should follow such confessions. The smaller boy (3 ; 5) only showed some understanding of these conversations by slow degrees, but his elder brother who was in his sixth year, in his parents' opinion, perfectly understood their meaning and felt the full psychic effect of the mental relief resulting from confession. We will begin by giving a specimen.

T (5 ; 1).   J (3 ; 5).
Mother: "Have you done anything naughty?"
T.: *"I hit Aunt O."*

M.: "Why did you hit Aunt O."

T.: *"Because she broke our railway station. Then she had to build it up again just as it was before."*

M.: "Were you nasty to grandmother too?"

T.: (A silent pause, then:) *"I don't know."*

M.: "Did you do anything naughty? Perhaps you were disobedient."

T.: *"What is 'disobedient' then?"*

M.: "Disobedient is, for example, if Aunt O. calls you and you do not go."

T.: *"Mummy, I ran away from Aunt O. and then Daddy sent me off and I ran to you."*

M.: "Were you disobedient this morning?"

T.: (after long silence:) *"No."*

M.: "Did you finish the work you began, to-day?"

T.: *"Yes, I made the house."*

M.: "Did you put away everything?"

T.: *"Yes, I packed them all nicely into the brick box."*

M.: "Did you clear your plate at meals?"

T.: *"Not quite, but I ate up all the food."*

The mother then turns to J.

M.: "Were you naughty to-day?"

J.: *"No."*

M.: "Would you let yourself be washed?"

J.: (embarrassed laughter:) *"No."*

M.: "Did you empty your plate?"

J.: *"Yes."*

T.: (comes creeping up and with a twinkle in his eyes:) *"He didn't clear his plate. Mummy, to-day I hit grandmother with the stick."*

M.: "That is bad, you mustn't do it."

T.: *"But grandmother was cheeky too: she broke the board of the toy arch."*

M.: "You mustn't speak like that of grandmother; she didn't break the wood on purpose." (Somewhat lengthy silence.)

T.: *"Mummy, why do you ask us then?"*

M.: "So that you may see what you have done wrong and not do it again."

T.: *"But Mummy, let's not ask one day and then see how we do."*

M.: "I don't ask you every day either; often I have to go away and then of course I don't ask you."

As I myself have no opportunity of such confessional talks,
I cannot pronounce any final judgment on the value of this
method. But some considerations might be suggested. It cannot
be doubted that confession for children—as for everyone—
may mean a happy liberation from a mental burden; and where
children feel a spontaneous need of the abreaction of a smaller
or greater fault or disobedience by confession, then the adult
guardians should do everything to ease this process, Indeed,
they should even take careful measures to bring about confession,
if they think they notice that the child is mentally oppressed
but cannot yet find the courage or means to a spontaneous
utterance. It is a long step however from such educational
measures to regular evening confessional talks.

Three chief doubts force themselves on our attention:

1. The confession is generally called forth in a situation when
the child's mind is no longer in the least occupied with the
action—bad or good—that he is to name. He often requires long
deliberation, which shows that he is dealing with things already
dismissed from the mind.[1] Confession is therefore inorganic.

2. The confessional talk may very easily give the impression
of a dominie's examination. For the parents ask for the most
part about occurrences which are already known to them, and
concerning which they only wish to find out if the children
still remember them and think of them in the right light. Little
T. was not so very far wrong in putting to his mother the
astonished query: *Mummy, why do you ask us then?* The answer
given by his mother leads now to the following scruples.

3. Confession produces a self-consciousness not yet suitable
for this period of age. Even if here and there little children have
a feeling of permissibility or wrong-doing in close connection
with some action and show signs of self-complacency or pricks
of conscience, we should let these germs of self-knowledge and
self-criticism slowly develop, but not force them to hothouse
growth by recalling them to consciousness several hours later.
This leads to premature brooding and reflection, may induce
in many children too much regret for their little errors, and
make pharisees of others as they conscientiously register their
good deeds—in short it may prematurely rob them of simplicity
as regards their moral attitude.

[1] Repression could only very seldom occur in these cases of early childish sins.

The force of these doubts evidently in great measure depends on the nature of the children and on the way in which the parents carry on the conversation. D. and R. Katz hold the conviction that the confessional talk proves an excellent means of education with children like theirs; but the general use of this pedagogic method on all kinds of children and its application by parents and teachers without any special psychological acumen might easily have the very opposite effect.

CHAPTER XXXVII

NECESSITY AND EFFECTS OF PUNISHMENT

IF our book was intended to deal only with education in early childhood, this chapter would have to be one of the most detailed. But in a book of psychology we may be brief. For the psychological facts which are concerned in the educational treatment of punishment have, in their various aspects, been brought to the reader's notice in very many parts of this book; we need only arrange them in a somewhat new light and add a little supplementary matter.

Schleiermacher's wise saying, "Punishment must be an ever-diminishing factor in education", is true, both as regards the individual and the race. In the life of the individual child, punishment, the negative factor of education, has with increasing age to give place more and more to the positive factors of example, suggestion, training of will-power, instruction, and help in forming independent judgments. That being so, early education is the least able to dispense with certain forms of punishment. But in human history the limitation of punishment is an exact index of the degree of moral culture reached, so that punishments are less frequent and more reasonable now than in past centuries; this is the case also in the more highly educated classes than in the lower. Let us briefly consider under what circumstances punishments are necessary in early childhood, and in what form they best fulfil the demands of psychology and of educational authority.

1. Necessity of Punishment in Early Childhood

First of all, punishment is indispensable in dealing with unprofitable action whose foolishness the child can neither understand nor appreciate. Reasons of safety to life, health, cleanliness, order, economy, domestic and social regulations all demand that many things, which the child, knowing no better, in its simplicity, is inclined to do, must be marked "not allowed". The child must not suck his finger, make ugly faces, dirty a room just cleaned, not take as toys, throw down or pull to pieces articles of value, such as watches and glass ornaments, etc., nor must he walk on the grass or lean out of a window. And since a simple "no", however often repeated, is sometimes not sufficient to outweigh childish forgetfulness and susceptibility to every passing desire, a stronger preventive measure in the form of some painful association must be taken. Punishment here then has no moral significance, but is simply a deterrent, an artifice designed to have the same effect as described in the proverb, "A burnt child dreads the fire." This deterrent effect may very easily lose its force, unless punishment is dealt out very sparingly. If a child is entirely surrounded by a code of prohibitions, so numerous as to make transgression well-nigh inevitable, and is severely punished for each lapse, he is no longer able to associate the pain of the penalty with definite actions, and so learn to avoid them. He only becomes hardened instead of showing the hoped-for reaction to the deterrent. The action of many teachers in an indiscriminate dealing-out of sharp penalties for every slip, however innocent the child may be of wrong intention, has but very little to do with punishment; often enough it is only an unrestrained explosion of anger at the mischief caused by the child, or a lust of power exercised on a defenceless object.

A second reason for punishment is the conflict of the child's will with that of his teacher (or parent). Childish wilfulness and defiance has to be overcome (Chapter XXXIV, 2), not only because, as a rule, the adult's wish is the wiser, and therefore essential in the child's own interest, but also because he must be trained in self-control and submission to authority. So that here, too, punishment is unavoidable.

It should not of course be forgotten that self-will and rebellion are but the reverse side of that valuable quality in a child of a desire for independence, and since education does not aim at obedience as an end in itself, but only as a preparation for and condition of higher ends, care should be taken when attempting to conquer self-will not to crush the child's strength of character. Even for early childhood slavish obedience and mechanical compliance with orders must not be looked upon as the sum-total of educational aims.[1]

Lastly, the third reason for punishment is such action as may point to undesirable traits of character, e.g. greed, untruth, cruelty, etc. Here, indeed, punishment as a means of

[1] D. and R. Katz also protest against the over-estimation of obedience as a cardinal virtue (I, pp. 96 seq.).

education has to be dealt out with most careful consideration. To begin with, it is, in itself, misleading to speak of "traits" of character in the little child.

It is true the child brings with it certain predispositions, but, at the very first, these are not irrevocably fixed, but only develop later—under continual influence of the environment—in one diretcion or another, into permanent qualities. BUT PUNISHMENT ITSELF IS ONE OF THE MOST IMPORTANT INFLUENCES OF THE CHILD'S ENVIRONMENT. If too frequent and too severe, it may drive the child to his only means of defence, viz. slyness and falsehood, and thus awaken or, at the least, strengthen a tendency to secrecy and obstinacy. Unwise punishment then, under certain circumstances, may even promote the very faults it is seeking to cure. Not that we would advocate a *laissez-faire* policy, but only urge that more use should be made of the higher positive means of education, and that punishment, when indispensable, should not be allowed to lose its CHARACTER OF EXPIATION, not too severe to be comprehensible even to the child. Examples will shortly be given to show that children have a finer feeling for this than most of their elders believe.

Another difficulty in the punishment of offences against morality lies in the adult's interpretation of them. For we are only too apt to judge the child's conduct from our own moral standpoint, i.e. to stigmatize as a lie what may be so in appearance only, entirely forgetting that in the child the psychological conditions of this action may be far otherwise than in the adult's psychic nature. Here, then, insufficient psychological knowledge is the cause of injudicious severity that demands virtues of which the child is utterly incapable, and not only accuses but blames him for crimes—whose all-too-early acquaintance he first makes only through these very reproaches. How many children would long remain in blissful ignorance of the nature of untruth if a condemnatory "you lie" had not forced upon them a premature knowledge of its existence!

2. Appropriate Forms of Punishment

We have already mentioned and refuted the common opinion that in the case of the tiny child corporal punishment must be generally used, since he understands no other. Really, sharp corporal punishment seems justifiable only when used to deter the child from the repetition of dangerous action, e.g. climbing out of an open window.

But in every case where punishment is to have not only a deterrent but also an educational effect, it is of first importance that the child should understand this. This understanding develops from the realization that the punishment follows as the natural consequence of the deed; we might indeed speak of the necessary logic of punishment.

In this sense a tap on the hand may seem justifiable when —as indeed so often happens—the hand is the offending member, but then it is no longer a question of the physical pain inflicted, but only of the symbolic retribution of the trespass of which the hand has been guilty.[1] The example in Chapter XXXIV, 3 shows how soon the child understands this; we give the following instance from a somewhat later period:—

Eva (2 ; 8). "Eva, who has a special liking for butter, put out her finger to-day to take the butter from my roll. I said 'No', but she did it again, so I gave the naughty hand a slight tap. She began to cry, cowered down on the couch, and would for a time have nothing to do with me."

The child too sees the natural result of a fault in its social effect; whoever will not accommodate himself to life in common with others, is excluded from this society. And for that reason, a penalty of banishment is one of the most successful forms of punishment; for years it had the best effect on our children, and just in those very cases where other parents think blows indispensable.

Hilde (1 ; 8½). "When the child is fractious and not to be coaxed into good temper, I put her by herself in the next room to have her cry out. In a very short time I go to the door and ask: 'Will Hilde be good now and come to father and mother?' The answer is a never-failing yes; then I take her back with me and, as a rule, the fractious fit has gone. (1 ; 9.) Twice to-day I only had to point, without a threat of any sort, to the door of the next room, to which H. had often

[1] D. and R. Katz express exactly the same view of the symbolic tap which lies far below the possibility of physical pain and yet may make a deep impression on the child.

been banished, to stop her crying in a moment and start her play once more.''

At a somewhat older age much slighter social consequences of any action are felt as enough punishment by the child. The consciousness that a shadow has fallen upon the happy harmony of love between him and his parents is enough in the fourth year to cause real pain to the child. But such effect, of course, can only be expected where the more sensitive shades of feeling between parent and child have not been dulled by frequent and severe punishment.

Hilde (3 ; 9). "When she is disobedient, the threat of the other room, or even the way I reprove her either with a word or in silence, is always effective. Nothing is more terrible to her than to see me look 'sad'. She begs almost with tears: *But you look so sad, do, do be happy again !* And when I lose the 'sad' look, the joyful cry comes: *You're not sad any more ?* and H. quickly forgets her own troubles. For a few days now, she asks whenever she has been naughty: *But I may still love you, Mummy ?* Often I do not even scold the children when they are tiresome, only look at them reproachfully or sadly, and the transformation is complete. Neither of them can bear to see their mother sad for two minutes: *I'll be good,* they sob, so that there is never any lasting discord, and sunshine follows the shower.''

Punishment as a natural consequence of the fault may assume quite other forms than those we have mentioned; it rests with the teacher's discretion and tact so to adapt the punishment to the special fault, that it may appeal to the child's feeling and understanding. Even apparently paradoxical measures may sometimes work marvels. The variety of possible punishments with purely psychical effects is infinitely greater than can be imagined by those who depend on beating alone with its mechanical results.

Hilde (3 ; 11). "Hilde had seen her mother put cakes aside for the maid, and when after some time these were still on the table, Hilde, in uncontrolled greed, took a cake before our very eyes and bit off a piece. I scolded her and said in stern reproof: 'As a punishment you will now eat all Bertha's cake that you have bitten; be quick and eat it up.' For one second she was quite taken aback (I was anxiously waiting myself to see if the penalty would have the desired result), then came a great outburst of grief and tears: *No, I won't eat it, it's Bertha's cake*, and she held it out at arm's-length, not daring to throw it away. I did not force her to eat it—for the punishment had done its work."

As a rule, however, a punishment will consist not in forcing something good upon the child, but rather in withholding it. In earliest years, one of the most impressive penalties is the deprivation of dainties or certain dishes at meal-times (cf. Chapter XXXIV, 3). Later on, the deprivation not only of dainty food but of other pleasures makes a deep impression on the child (e.g. to stay at home instead of taking a hoped-for walk, to lose a toy for a time, etc.). Nor need it always be a pleasure of which it is deprived; any other ordinary every-day occurrence which the child, from long habit, looks upon as a familiar matter of course will have the same effect.

Gunther (4 ; 7). "Yesterday evening I let him run about without his clothes in the bedroom. 'But not to go in the cold drawing-room,' I warned him. It was a great temptation, as his father was just playing some nursery songs there; no doubt, too, G. had forgotten my warning—in a twinkling he was in the drawing-room. I caught him, threw him into bed, saying: 'As a punishment, you will not be washed to-day.' That was a terrible blow, and again and again G. assured me he would be good; but I did not yield, and he had to put up with it. A blow would soon have been forgotten, but not to be washed was a great trouble."

To bring the punishment down to the childish understanding is not always so easy. In the above examples the child under-stood the connection between fault and penalty, but there are other cases when we rate the child's understanding too highly, and then the punishment may fail in its effect. In the following instance the child's unconscious simplicity is very amusing:—

Gunther (2 ; 6½). "To-day when I was feeding Eva, and thus helpless to control fat Gunther, he climbed on a chair, in spite of my 'No' and got from the sideboard an apple, out of which, after a little hesitation, heedless of my warning, he took a bite. His father, whom I called to my help, dealt the offending hand a sound slap, and Gunther gave a short scream; then his father ordered him—by way of undoing his fault—at once to put the piece of apple out of his mouth.

With a little assistance a portion was produced, but the rest Gunther ate comfortably, saying seriously as he chewed: *good.* When he had finished his meal, his left hand stroked the injured right with an emphatic *ow !* And yet we have to keep a straight face!"

It is particularly difficult for the child to understand a punishment that is not only an immediate effect of the fault but lasts a little time, even after the child has got over his momentary naughtiness.

Hilde (3 ; 3). "At dinner she was told not to take hold of her plate of stewed bilberries, but, in spite of that, she greedily pulled her plate to her. Penalty: 'Hilde gets no bilberries for dinner.' Violent screams follow, she is put in the next room, and soon calls out: *good now,* and expects her stewed fruit. 'No, if you are good, you will get it for supper.' *But I am good, quite good again !* She could not understand that there were two punishments: loss of her fruit because she took hold of the plate, banishment to the next room because she had screamed. The second punishment was settled by being good again, but that the first must still continue she was not yet able to grasp."

The child's sensibility to punishment shows decided development even in early childhood. The first stage is purely one of association, the effect of punishment is simply a pain associated with a certain action, and therefore likely to prevent its repetition. The second stage is a logical one: punishment is understood as a natural consequence, arising from the wrong deed. The third—a moral stage—is reached when there is conscious recognition of punishment as expiation; then the child's attitude to the penalty is no longer one of passive endurance, but his own will is evidenced by his acknowledgment of the justice of penalty, even indeed by a desire for expiation.[1] This highest form of consciousness of guilt is, of

---

[1] The positive attitude to punishment in a child may indeed have its foundation in quite another psychological reason, viz. in a perverted feeling of pleasure in the pain inflicted. That chastisement of a certain nature may lead to premature excitation of sexual impulses, and at the same time divert future sexual action into unnatural channels, is shown indeed in Rousseau's *Confessions.* It is true he had passed the stage of early childhood when he first felt the pleasurable sensation of such corporal punishment, nevertheless those who have the control of little children should be mindful of the possible results, in this direction, of corporal punishment and exercise due caution in its administration.

course, only to be found as a mere germ in the first six years of life. But these germs even are important enough, for they show how erroneous is that point of view in school or state which can only use punishment as a forcible means of compulsion and a deterrent, not as a means of moral self-education.

We gave (in Chapter XXXI, 3) an instance of the acknowledgment of the justice of punishment as shown by Hilde (4 ; 3); as a parallel we mention here an example taken (as an exception) from the seventh year.

Gunther (6 ; 9). "The children had been invited out: Gunther was not to go, because the day before he had been up to all sorts of mischief. Hilde was begging me to let him go, when Gunther said: *No, I mustn't go, some punishment I've got to have.* He didn't say this in any way to win praise but with sorrowful conviction. He had often before said much the same thing."

But this spontaneous desire to expiate a fault is even more marked when a child, here and there, gives proof of the will and power to undertake its own punishment. We have met with this self-inflicted punishment in several forms.

With regard to the "banishment" penalty the report of Hilde (1 ; 10) runs:—

"H. was naughty to-day. Both parents had reproved her with a stern 'Hilde' and returned her glance for several seconds with serious, reproachful looks. Then without a word the child went into the next room, as if she had read the order in our eyes or as if she realized her wrong-doing."

"When H. (2 ; 2½) is defiant and cries or screams she is always put in the next room or in the corner. But sometimes it happens that at such times she herself asks: *put in the corner.* Lately as she expressed this wish and really went of her own accord into the corner, I asked: 'Is Hilde naughty then?' Back came the answer: *yes.* After a little time she called as usual in a gentle voice: *Mummy, Mummy,* I asked, 'Will Hilde be good?' Answer: *yes.* I allowed her to come out: and she gaily trotted up with the words: *Here comes good Hilde !*"

In her fourth year we were able to let the same child punish herself with a slap:—

(3 ; 5). "Hilde now often punishes her little naughtinesses at our request, either spoken or expressed by a reproachful

look, with a slap on her fingers. This began with my once saying to her: 'Mother does not want to whip you, give yourself a slap.' She quickly adopted this kind of punishment; indeed, she often anticipates our penal intentions by saying: *I'll beat myself without you*, and takes up the matter seriously, putting considerable energy into it. Thus she herself makes expiation for her own fault and so restores her psychic equilibrium. In younger days, she often asked me to give her a slap when she considered it deserved."

CHAPTER XXXVIII

CONSIDERATIONS ON THE QUESTION OF LIES

WITHIN the scope of this book we must content ourselves with only a few suggestions on this subject of "lies", since we have treated it very fully in another place, to which we would refer the reader.[1]

Although the discussion of children's occasional and habitual lies takes so important a place in practical pedagogy (even of early years), yet closer analysis reveals the remarkable fact that this subject of untruth in early years belongs quite as much to adult psychology as to children's. For a large number of so-called children's lies are in truth only misconceptions on the part of their adult judges; other real untruths on childish lips are but the product of their teacher's influence; and only a comparatively small remainder really originate in the child's own soul.

Lies are consciously false statements whose purpose is to achieve certain results by the deception of others. An actual lie therefore has three features which distinguish it from other kinds of false statement: (1) consciousness of falsity, (2) intentional deception, (3) a distinct purpose in view. The first two clearly differentiate a lie from a lapse of memory, the third distinguishes it from an imaginative invention.

The presence of all three features already presupposes a comparatively high stage of psychic development. Judgment must have achieved the stage of being able to draw a sharp distinction between true and false, and to give what is false the stamp of apparent truth, and the will-power must have developed enough resolution to arrange and subordinate the different actions necessary for the deception with due regard to the intention to deceive, and this intention again to the purpose in view. This reason alone forbids our belief in the

[1] In the monograph by C. and W. Stern: *Memory, Statement and Falsehood in Early Childhood.* In the present chapter there are literal extracts from this monograph. We may mention, amongst later writings, Franziska Baumgarten's (statistics and psychological analysis of the falsehoods of school-children, founded on the personal declarations of the children themselves); Otto Kaus (a psychoanalytic study of the origin of falsehood in children from the point of view of Adler's theory, viz. lying as an attempt to compensate for the feeling of inferiority). Reiningen's contribution in the compilation (*Die Lüge*), a report founded on examples and statistics of school-children.

possibility of "lies" at a very early age. In the earliest years, statements which seem to deserve that name are for the most part either apparent falsehoods (i.e. statements which only have the outward appearance of untruth) or germs of falsehoods (i.e. momentary tendencies to lies which, in the next moment, give way to another determining tendency).

We have already mentioned what a mistake it is to brand purely imaginative false statements as lies. On the other hand we were obliged to point out (Chapter XIX, 5) that if too much licence be permitted to the child's fantasy it may blunt the essential distinction between appearance and reality, and thus indirectly pave the way for future untruth.

A considerable number of apparent lies owe their origin to the fact that the child's speech and thought still hover midway between an affective-volitional and an actual-factitive condition, a condition we grown-ups can only realize with difficulty. Those terms of speech which we use to affirm or deny facts are often used by the child solely to express his affective attitude, and so what is only a wish sounds like assertion, self-defence like denial.

Cases are often reported of one- or two-year-old children pretending to have a requirement in order to be taken down from their chair or out of bed. The reason of this is that the special word used has by no means been grasped in its strictly limited meaning, but from constant association has assumed the character of a signal which never fails to effect the desired change, thus a wish for change, from pure association, calls forth the word.

The apparent pretence of pain may be explained in a similar way. The following example, therefore, classified by Ament[1] as a lie, was really no such thing:—

A little girl (1 ; 9) with chicken-pox had answered every painful touch with *hurts*, and had then been left in peace. Consequently afterwards she often used to utter an indignant *no hurt*, if very busily occupied with her game she did not wish to be touched. Her *hurts* did not mean: "It hurts me," but only a self-defensive: "Leave me in peace."

The endeavour to get rid of something painful especially often appears in the word "no", which stands out like a clear-cut denial without necessarily having that force.

[1] Ament, II, p. 82.

Hilde (2 ; 6) had given her brother a painful pinch. When, later, she was reminded: "You really hurt your little brother," with an indignant expression she cried out, *no, no*, which did not mean denial of having caused her brother pain, but only expressed a wish to hear no more about it, not to be reminded of it.[1]

From such self-defence there may develop in later years behaviour that might be called "embryo-untruth". Every human being, when confronted with a situation whose consequences he fears, has, at first, an impulse simply to put away all thought of the unpleasantness as completely as if it did not exist. As a rule, an adult can conquer this wish by inner strength, but not so the growing—and as yet undeveloped— human being. He projects his effort at self-defence outwards, sometimes in expression-movements, sometimes in words of denial, and as he does so, subsequently, at any rate, he is conscious that they are not in accordance with fact. Here therefore we find the germ of a lie, and now it depends greatly on the teacher whether he kills these germs or aids their growth by unwise procedure. For, as soon as the child's reaction to the impulse of self-defence has occurred, he is very susceptible to correction and self-correction; this tendency to immediate retraction can be encouraged and the development of nervous lying prevented.

Gunther (3 ; 4½). "I noticed that a piece of the wallpaper had been torn and was hanging down—the chairs in front of it were pushed just as Gunther always put them when playing, so that there was no mistaking the culprit. I asked Hilde and Gunther: 'Who tore the wallpaper?' H. answered firmly: *I didn't.* G. kept his face turned away and also said: *I didn't.* I said to him quietly: 'Come here a minute.' G. hid his hands behind him, saying: *But don't hit me.* Of course that was, in itself, a confession, for he had never once had a slap that was not richly deserved. I answered: 'No, I will not hit you. Now come, my boy, tell me, did you tear it?' G. *Yes.* I seized the opportunity to explain to him that good children always say at once what is true. The fear of punishment, however small, had at first caused Gunther to put up a self-defence. When he saw there was nothing to fear he gave a quite correct statement instead of trying to ward off danger.

[1] The Scupins' recount an instructive parallel case (II, p. 72).

With such young children, where the chief aim should be to give them good principles, it is of the first importance to make it easy for them to get away from the self-defensive denial. At that age, it is out of the question to expect the child to show such self-conquest without help and encouragement."

We come now to real lies, where, over and above the momentary impulse of self-defence, a serious endeavour is made to deceive. This earnest desire is shown either by the child's persistence in false statement, or by the deliberation with which he plans and carries out his deception, or possibly by both. We may not disguise the fact that lies of this nature do exist in early childhood, in one child maybe only in one solitary instance, in another more frequently, in a few—probably always as a consequence of abnormal psychic or educational conditions—as a usual occurrence.

As we examine the instances given of such serious untruth in children, we notice—however much details may vary—a great similarity in type, for they are almost without exception the result of fear. This circumstance itself proves the causal relation between severe punishment and a lie. We give three instances:—

Scupin (1 ; 10). "His father heard to-day how the child in the next room was playing with a glass. He called: 'Bubi.' No answer. At other times the boy always used to run up gaily, but this time he was afraid for his glass. The father now emphatically ordered: 'Bring the glass here at once.' *No*, contradicted Bubi, but very softly. The command being repeated with more emphasis, the child came up with a wooden toy. *Da* (there), he said. He wanted to give his father visible proof that he had not been playing with the forbidden glass, but with a wooden toy. This was indeed the first more serious act of dishonesty of which he had been guilty. The glass stood there right enough on a chair, and, in compliance with another very emphatic command, he at last unwillingly brought it up." (I, p. 89.)

The next case is remarkable from the spontaneous use of the lie; the child tried to anticipate the expected punishment or whipping by a false statement:—

Scupin (2 ; 5½). "To-day, contrary to his usual custom, he tried to deceive. He called from his cot to his mother: *Bubi was good—has gone to sleep nicely: Bubi has not wetted his napkin . . . Bubi was good.* This over-zealous self-praise and his big frightened eyes made his mother at once suspicious, and her suspicions were well founded." (I. p. 139.)

The worst forms of childish lies of fear are to be found where there is not only a lie or deceit, as far as a child himself is concerned, but where other innocent people are dragged in by false accusations.[1] It is perhaps doubtful whether the following example is not over the normal boundary; later on strong hysterical features developed in the child.

A girl Z. (4 ; 6). "Once when Z. was alone in the kitchen she broke a glass. She was seen to hide the pieces in the ash-pan under the stove and then go out. After some time the servants came into the kitchen; Z. followed them, scraped the fragments of glass out from under the stove, and asked: *Now, which of you did that?* The maids told her straight to the face that she had done it herself; she denied it, and even said she had seen which of them broke the glass. Only after much persuasion from the lady acting as her guardian did she own to her lie with great shame."[2]

As we have said, it is quite exceptional to meet with untruths arising from any other cause than fear of punishment. The following, however, is an example of such: Marconowski reports of his daughter, who had an aversion for all rice dishes, as follows: She gets stomach pains with unfailing regularity whilst she is eating different preparations of rice, and with the same unfailing regularity she is entirely free from these notable pains during the consumption of chocolate, rich pudding and similar things, although they are generally followed by diarrhœa and colic.

An occasional lapse from truth is not, however, proof of a lying disposition, and psychological analysis proves the assertion that lies are usual and normal in childhood to be erroneous.

---

[1] There is, it is true, besides this a kind of quite harmless false accusation in which the child's own interest plays no part. It is the result of the logical desire to find a cause for something that has happened, and this desire is projected on to the most likely person. "Eva (3 ; 6) found her broken alpenstock lying close to the cook. Who else, then, could have broken it? The child complained to me: *Tony has broken my stick.* This was not a fact, and I asked Eva seriously: 'Did you see Tony break your stick?' Somewhat ashamed, she said *no*, and I told her always only to tell what she had really seen. The good effect of this warning was shown at once, for she said to the nurse who came in at the moment: *Look, Else, my stick has broken itself.*"

[2] For more details of this case, see C. and W. Stern, *Monagraph* II, pp. 120 sqq.

As Lowinsky rightly points out, the habit of lying has a certain correlation with "incompatibility" (unsuitable surroundings); i.e. it is a weapon and defence, when the individual is oppressed by an uncertain, wavering, too complicated and difficult environment. Thus we understand why children, under especially stern treatment, are disposed to untruth, and also that the child exposed at school to so many difficulties and repressive measures is more prone to lies than the little child growing up in the simple transparent atmosphere of its home.

Nevertheless, the child's natural disposition is of course not without weight; circumstances that might cause untruth in a weak child, with little power of self-control, might prove no temptation to another of different disposition. Yet those cases that may be spoken of as showing an inborn disposition to untruth are much less common than is generally believed, and seem to point almost to a pathological reason; they are counterbalanced by not infrequent cases of perfect or almost perfect freedom from lapse from truthfulness, to which we can happily testify from personal experience. In our own children, with the exception of very rare and instantly conquered cases of "embryo-untruth" (see examples above), we have never noticed anything that could be called a lie. And the Scupins, who had to report isolated cases of untruth in their son during his first three years, have had next to nothing to report from his fourth to his sixth year.

Hilde (4 ; 0). "H. never attempts by deception to get others blamed in her stead, to escape punishment, or to place herself in a more and others in a less favourable light; in these early years she has no idea of the existence of anything else but the simplest sincerity. More than that, she does not wait to be asked before owning to any little slip or naughtiness, e.g. when her father comes home she runs to tell him what trouble she has given her mother, or comes to confess to her mother that she has slapped her little brother."

The desire shown here for truthfulness is doubtless to the normal, unfrightened child, between four and six years of age, much more natural than the habit of falsehood; indeed, when the child first begins to have a general idea of a lie, but does not clearly grasp its exact nature, he may even develop a fanaticism for truth and a fear of lying, which again calls for careful treatment at the hands of his guardians and teachers.

Gunther (5 ; 4). "At the moment G. is so strict with himself that he often supplements his statements with: *at least, I think so.* Any statement he has made, in all good faith, may torment him afterwards—e.g. he once told an uncle he had two boxes of coloured pencils, and several hours later he was tormented by self-reproach because he had only one with coloured pencils and the other was full of chalks."

The following example taken from the same period shows too broad a conception of the meaning of an untruth:[1] "G. called to me one evening: *Mummy, in Berlin at Aunt W.'s, I said once I meant to be a doctor. But now I don't mean to at all, so that is a lie.* I calmed him by explaining that he had not told an untruth, because, at that time, he really did want to be a doctor, but now he had changed his mind, and I would write to Aunt W. that he was not going to be one."[2]

From what has been shown above, we seem able to draw a deduction not without weight in the problem of education, viz. prevention, not cure, of falsehood must be its chief aim in early childhood; not to use punishments and reproaches when the failing already exists, but to see that it never has an opportunity to begin. These preventive measures, treated in detail in our monograph, can only be summarized here in shortened form: Parents and teachers must be truthful with children even in trifles. Favourite deceptions such as: "If you are good, you will get some chocolate" (a promise that is not kept); or, "Look, there's a cat" (to distract a crying child's attention), seem indeed very harmless; but it is just such statements as these that show the child the possibility of intentional deceit, and his strong imitative impulse urges him to the same sort of action. They also plant the first germs of mistrust of his elders in the child's soul.

It is a special sin against the child to train him expressly in lying, for example, by sending him, when undesired visitors call, to say that his parents are not at home.

Over-severity in punishment should be avoided, for it is

[1] Again the Scupins make parallel observations, II, pp. 75 and 97.
[2] Hug-Hellmuth tries to give a psychoanalytic explanation of our son's fanaticism for truth by putting it down as a kind of over-compensation to this child's very strong inclination to imaginative fantasy. No doubt there may be some truth in this. But since there must be some touch of sexual psychology in it, a second motive is dragged in, viz. "the childish desire by his own perfect candour to induce the same in his surroundings, of course with reference to sexual matters".

nothing but systematic training in deceit; in momentary yielding to untruth even, kindness should make it very easy for the child to retrace his steps to self-correction and sincerity. On the other hand, it is essential to avoid over-anxiety and indulgence of the child, for this only prompts him to obtain his every wish by the pretext of some imaginary pain.

Avoid, too, unnecessary inquisition, for continual cross-questioning not only leads to unconscious slips of memory, but, in the end, to conscious untruths. The questioner seems determined to have an answer, so the child obliges him by saying something that will put an end to the uncomfortable examination.

Nor should we prematurely force upon the child the idea of a lie and underline it in our moralizings. Or brand every harmless slip of memory, imagination or deviation from exactitude with: "You are telling a lie." Isolated cases of even distinct untruth should not be over-magnified and treated as if of national importance—as, indeed, in all early training, care must be taken not to impress little faults on the childish souls by emphasizing them unduly.

The child's active co-operation against untruth should be enlisted by the development of a sense of personal responsibility and of simple sincerity. Life, even in the most sheltered environment, does not spare the child an acquaintance with untruth nor the temptation to succumb to it himself. A child who has been taught by his parents the meaning of self-conquest in everything, who has learnt to control his anger, to give up a pleasure for the sake of others, to own to a fault, even indeed to find a certain satisfaction in self-conquest, will master, too, any temptation to deviate from the truth.

INTRODUCTORY OBSERVATIONS
TO CHAPTER XXX

THE VARIOUS FORMS OF ENDEAVOUR

ALL subjects hitherto discussed—perception, memory, imagination, thought—deal with separate parts and fragments of the child's psychic life. But we must now turn our attention to what constitutes the actual entity and vital sense of each human individuality, that to which all else is but subordinate and auxiliary.

We will start from our root idea of personality. Personality is a life unity influenced by various aims, a whole whose forces work in definite directions. We will designate the whole of this activity directed to certain aims by the term "effort" (endeavour). This word, with all its derivatives, must be understood in its widest sense, i.e. as belonging to the entire personality, not only as purely conscious effort. It is a question not only of man's conscious feelings when he is intent on some aim, but of the effort itself. The endeavour to reach some aim is a primitive fact which forms part of the psychologically neutral personality.

The importance and difficulty of the subject make it imperative that we should first show the most important features of the development of effort as it presents itself to the personal conviction, that we should further discuss the chief qualities of effort in early childhood, and, when that is done, pass on to the various concrete divisions and directions of these childish endeavours. In the last-mentioned subject we shall have to confine our treatment to a selection only.

EXPRESSION-MOVEMENTS IN CHILDREN

EXPLANATIONS OF THE FILM-PHOTOGRAPHS ON PLATES VIII TO XI

BY KURT LEWIN

THE pictures on Plates VIII to XI are a condensed selection taken from some few phases of the child's expression during the first six years of life. The pictures are from my own film photos.

The bodily expression at a definite point of time has nothing static about it, but always forms a factor which is only part of a whole happening. It must therefore be understood as a part only of this whole and not as an independent happening.

For example, the significance of the physical bearing at any definite point of time shows most variation if twenty successive pictures on the film roll are almost identical (e.g. in the screaming expression, picture 1, or if each successive picture shows an essential change from the one preceding it (see 13a, b). If a single picture is shown without its context the expression is often misunderstood.

The attitude of the child in question is moreover only to be explained by the whole of the existing situation, in which it must be remembered that the child's body forms only one part of the total "psychic field".[1]

In so far as more detailed explanations are given to the pictures they are comprised under the following points of view:

1. Here we do not ask as to the significance of the expression, nor its adequacy or inadequacy as a sign or symbol of something expressed in it, but we consider it as a psychophysical occurrence like any other, and therefore enquire as to the powers and factors of the whole which is the cause of this particular phenomenon.

2. We will not attempt to build a bridge between the expression in question and any habits, whether inherited or acquired, but we will indicate the connection between the expression under consideration and the forces of the situation existing at the moment.

[1] S. Lewin, Preface, *Wille und Bedürfnis*, Berlin, 1926, pp. 24 seq.

For the investigations of perceptual and will psychology alike have shown that the forces of the *acute* inner and outer situation are at least very much more effective than very many previous repetitions.

3. The composition of an individual as a whole shows a definite structure of psychic strata and systems. It is in conformity with this that a concrete psycho-motor occurrence, especially an expression, is in the main it is true the offspring of ONE system, but that a certain communication is kept up with other psychic regions. If the expression is understood the ultimate meaning is perceived "through the surface" so to speak (cf. Grünbaum, p. 446). In a similar way a definite expression is as a rule an effect of several psychic strata, and this is true even in the young child. In individual cases and different persons there are great divergencies in the nature and extent of this "stratification" (*Geschichtetheit*).

I. Crying, and Some Varieties of Turning or Creeping Away. (Plate VIII)

1. Hanna (1 ; 8) on the shore. The mother has gone to bathe, and as the child's maid also goes away for a short distance, Hanna, feeling quite deserted, begins to scream in a real whole-hearted child's howl. (Unhappy, somewhat cramped attitude, cf. later 7a.[1])

This attitude is maintained almost without any change whatever for a considerable time (over four seconds), not even the mouth being shut.

2a. Bummi (2 ; 6). His elder sister will not give him a watering-can full of water. He has run after her for a long time and now stops, resigned to his fate. As in Hanna's case (1) Bummi's bodily attitude scarcely shows any change through a series of pictures (16 = one second).

2b. His sister has teased him again with the watering-can without giving it to him. He crouches down in despair with his head right on the ground and remains fixed in this position during a considerable time (three seconds).

Here we are face to face with a typical case of "beating a retreat". In a somewhat different situation or in the case of

---

[1] Pictures belonging to the same occurrence are distinguished by the same numbers, with different letter indices, e.g.: 2a, 2b.

another, e.g. an older child, flight would have been the result (cf. 7a). Here the retreat consists—ostrich-wise—(1) in hiding the eyes and the head with his arms and (2), since the child does not literally go away, he draws himself together into the smallest space possible, away from the overpowering unpleasant situation. There is a great abundance of very different types of beating a retreat from the literal physical going elsewhere to the simple occupying oneself with something else. The common feature in the phenomenon is the passing out of one situation (in the psychological sense of the word) and over to a second which is separated from the first as extensively as possible. The following pictures show the expression in some few cases of turning away from unpleasant situations.

3. Fritz (2 ; 8). (The child had been lying several months in a plaster-of-Paris bandage and for that reason could not yet get out of a chair without help.) He wishes to be taken from the chair but his mother does not do it. At first he had stretched out his arms to his mother, then he grew sad, and several times beat restlessly with his right hand on the arm of the chair and began to kick his legs about. At last he ended by turning away in resignation (the position of the left leg is not due to the kicking but to the action of pushing back).

The retreat here then consists, since further movement is impossible, in twisting round the upper part of the body and turning his head away from his mother.

4a. Wawi (4 ; 4) in the scene "Surprise and Disappointment".[1] The child gets an envelope which contains a piece of chocolate; then a second in which there is nothing but a piece of crumpled paper; lastly a third with something nice inside. The picture shows Wawi after her disappointment with the second envelope. She had had a long search in the paper and envelope in the hope of finding something after all. At last she turns away in a similar expressive attitude of resignation as may be noticed in picture 3. Tears are not far off.

In 4b the turning away from the experimenter is complete (cf. 3). Her hands are placed at the back of her neck and the arms encircle her head. The meaning of this very characteristic gesture needs some explanation. It might be looked upon as an emphatic retreat in the sense of a pronounced withdrawal of

[1] Cf. the film photos of impulse- and emotion-expressions in psychopathic children, *Zeitschrift für Kinderforschung*, 32, 4. pp. 414–47.

herself and at the same time there may be in it a holding herself
firm against the danger of tears and finally a hiding of the
emotional outburst.

5. Marianne (5 ; 8). At the same stage in the test there is a
striking resemblance to Wawi (4*b*) in the same attitude of the
arms. But in this case the turning away from the experimenter
is confined to a confused dropping of the eyes. The child, who
throughout the whole performance had acted with great self-
control (cf. later on, No. 14), here too gives a defensive smile.
The limp abandonment of despair is also wanting. In the putting
of the hands behind the head, there is possibly also one of those
cases of "partial" bodily retreat where there is certainly a
general resistance to the pressure of the situation but a yielding
in individual parts of the body. It is often noticed, in embarrassment for instance, that the hands are put behind the back.
In the same way the small child in particular, when faced with
things of which he is afraid, will put one or both hands behind
him on the side away from the object of his fear. Another kind
of "imperfect" retreat is simply turning round (4*b*), casting
down the eyes, or putting the hands before the face (12*b*).

6*a*. Wawi (4 ; 5) at a first balancing test. In an uncertain
attitude (bent knees) she tries to find a support with her right
arm and at the same time uses the arms to keep her balance.

6*b*. The balancing failed, and now Wawi goes through the
drawing herself together into the very smallest space, bending
down her head, covering her face with her arms in exactly the
same way as the very much younger Bummi (2*b*). This picture
too represents a phase altering but very little during a considerable period (five seconds).

7*a*. Agnes (5 ; 10), who is a fanatical "doll mother", does not
get her doll-child given up to her by an older friend. There is a
short tussle for the doll, then Agnes runs away quite broken
down with despair. The picture shows the "quite broken"
attitude (see the knees!), an attitude therefore pointing to
similar dejection as is shown in 2*b* and 6*b*. As a matter of fact,
Agnes after she has run a few steps further in this dejected way
throws herself straightway down on the grass.

7*b*. On her way Agnes inadvertently runs over her little
brother. The picture shows a typical attitude of regret, fright
and excuse; the hand is put over the mouth.

The fact that this misfortune could happen is evidence that

Agnes whilst running was already so far removed psychologically from her environment that she could not even see it.

The faces of the other two children in the picture are turned
to the point of chief interest—for the moment—in the situation.

In concluding this group of pictures we will briefly call
attention to the position of the eyelids. The eyelids in all
pictures representing a position of retreat are cast down, sometimes tightly closed (1, 2a, 3, 4a, 5, 7a). In cases of crying we
might think of special psychological stimuli (possibly tears) as
a direct cause of the closing of the eyes. But the other cases
might suggest that the lowering of the eyelids shows direct
connection with those forces that prompt retreat. The cast-down
eyes are a sign of the simultaneous withdrawal, at any rate to
a certain degree, of the ego from the momentary environment.
The slight motion of the eyelids might in this case be of essential
significance (cf. 11[4] Marianne[1]).

II. WORK AND WORKING GAMES. Plate IX

8. Hans Heinz (0 ; 6) trying to sit up. With his right hand
he is holding tight to his mother's fingers, and she is helping a
little with his left hand.

8a. The mouth opened from exertion.

8b. Heinz ¼ of a second later, half sitting up. His mouth is
still open, though not so wide. Note the typical wobbling
bearing of the head.

8c. Heinz is sitting upright. His mouth is almost shut. The
expression of the eyes is somewhat impaired by the glare of
the sun.

9. Marianne (5 ; 5) on the left. Constance (4 ; 1) in the centre.
Agnes (6 ; 0) to the right, sewing a button on to a piece of
material. The sewing on of a button is for all three children an
unaccustomed, difficult task, which they face, however, with
complete readiness and interest. It amuses them to be working
in competition.

9a. Button, thread and a piece of material lie before each
child. The picture shows the eager delight and expectation in
their start on a piece of work whose difficulty is unknown to
them. Marianne has put out her tongue, a movement frequently

---

[1] But there is no idea of stating that every case of retreat is accompanied by a
lowering of the eyelids (cf. II, 10-11, 15, Constance).

noticed in such critical work in other children too. The two
children have their mouths open. (A couple of later pictures on
the film moreover show the same position of the mouth in
Marianne as well.)

9*b*. Serious industrious face at the difficult task; the faces
look almost a little angry in their strenuous exertion, the
mouths shut and the lips somewhat protruding in their industrious zeal. Marianne in the decisive act of pushing her needle
through a hole in the button wears an anxious frown, Agnes in
the last stage of pulling through the thread is in a somewhat
less strained and more contemplative attitude.

9*c*. Marianne and Agnes are critically examining Constance's
work, having left their own sphere of activity for a moment.
Their heads are sharply turned to the piece of work that is now
the standard and centre of interest. The work of their hands is
thus left to itself and stopped; in Agnes's case already somewhat loosened.

10 (Plate X).[1] The same children a quarter of an hour afterwards, busy building simple towers with narrow buildnig
blocks. A very much gayer, less restrained attitude in this
much more recreative work. (Note the contrast between 10
and 9*b*.)

III. The Whole Course of a Fright whilst Building a Tower. Plates X and XI

11. The children still at the work of 10. The blocks must
only be placed on their narrow end on one another, for the
object was to build as high a tower as possible.

Constance (in centre)

11[1]. Constance has just placed a block with her right hand
on the top of the tower—already fairly high—and is now
carefully taking up another block. As she does so the upper
half of the tower suddenly collapses before Constance has
noticed the threatened danger. (Cf. 12*a* where the threatened
collapse of the tower is noticed.) It might be thought that
Constance had taken the last block with her left hand. The
position of this hand has, however, a longer preliminary history

----

[1] Pictures 13–15 on Plate IX will be described later.

which is specially recounted here because it forms a character-istic example of a certain type of expression-attitudes.

When Constance has put three blocks one on top of the other, at the sight of the slanting unsteady tower she puts both hands over her face as in pictures 12*b* and *c*, except that the hands are stretched out in a direct line with the arms, forming two flat surfaces between which Constance, as from behind a pro-tecting wall, peeps in joyous excitement not unmixed with a little anxiety at her high building.

Whilst she continues to build with her right hand, her left arm has stayed in much the same upright position and only the position of the hand has gradually changed a little, being laid on her hair and somewhat more contracted. The position of the left arm on picture 11 thus represents one of those typical cases where a gesture of an earlier stage in the expression-movement has remained stationary. It has dissociated itself from the active movement of the moment, changed its character a little—so that the original meaning of the expression is often un-recognizable by the observer—and remains fixed then for a long time. Sixteen seconds(!) lie between putting both hands over the face and picture 11, during which period Constance has with her right hand put on three more blocks. In this example it is, however, probably not a case of a simple fixation of the gesture, but the continued fear of the downfall of the tower is an essential contributory factor in the continuation of this remnant of a former attitude.

11². The right arm is a little further on in the grasping move-ment. The eyelids are quite lowered, but not until 11³ does the face assume the real expression of fright, viz. closing the eyes, deep lines to the right and left of the mouth—somewhat broad-ened with the lips apart and slightly turned up at corners. The separate film photos follow at almost exact intervals of $\frac{1}{16}$ of a second, so that $\frac{1}{8}$ of a second elapses between 11¹ and 11³.

11⁴. The face is no longer so convulsively contracted, the mouth is a little more open, the corners not so turned up, and the expression is a transition to

11⁵, where the child looks with shocked regret at what has happened. The first shrinking back in fright thus passes again into a feeling directed rather to the outer happening.[1]

[1] Cf. Giessler, DER BLICK DES MENSCHEN ALS AUSDRUCK SEINES SEELEN-LEBENS 1913.

The position of the arms and of the body has remained unchanged from picture 11^2; the child has a "fright fixation", and this general fixation of the body and arms now remains for a long time, i.e. up to 11^{15} (almost a whole second), without any appreciable change. Only the facial expression alters.

11^6—11^9. Slow unwrinkling of the face and relaxation of the fixation.

11^{10}—11^{15}. Constance lifts her eyes towards the camera. Thus inwardly she is, to a certain degree, escaping from the unpleasant situation of the downfall of her tower. It is distinctly typical that such a turning in the camera direction begins just when the original situation no longer consists in a strongly marked happening but, as in this case for instance, has become so far resolved that for the moment there exist no pronounced powers in that definite direction.

11^{16}—11^{21}. The fixation and stupefaction of the face which had continued in all the preceding pictures completely vanishes and changes into a cheerful acceptance of the situation. (The previous "retreat" from the situation may have eased the way for this acceptance of it.)

In a gay, playful, somewhat emphasized feeling that now appears for the first time when the fixation is over, the left arm is thrown up a little whilst the movement of the body as a whole at the same time tends to a bending forward. (Picking up bricks.)

AGNES (on the right)

11^1. Agnes is just in the act of carefully adding a fresh brick (mouth open).

11^2—11^7. No doubt influenced by the downfall of her neighbour's tower, she continues to hold the bricks with great care (shutting of the mouth).

11^8 shows the beginning of a cautious letting go of the top brick, in which the first finger of the left hand relaxes a little and then

11^9—11^{11} the other fingers of this hand, and at the same time the right hand, tends more and more to leave hold of the bricks.

11^{12}—11^{21}. Even after the hands no longer touch the bricks their further removal continues slow and cautious. The hands —speaking psychologically—still hold the bricks to a certain extent. And with the opening of both hands from one another, the mouth also opens (a so-called "sympathetic movement" *Mitbewegung*).

MARIANNE (on the left)

Marianne's tower is already a good height. After the fall of her neighbour's tower.

11^4, she first turns her eyes,

11^5, then her face in the direction of the occurrence.

11^6—11^7. A serious, somewhat disapproving expression,

11^8—11^{21}, which changes into a more cheerful, indeed distinctly frolicsome, expression at the funny events which do not hurt her own tower. Her own work only stopped from 11^5 to 11^{11}. In 11^{12} her right hand has already begun to pick up a fresh brick.

12. Three pictures of a second fall of Constance's tower.

12a. An angry face at the threatened fall.

12b—12c. The climax of the fright-movement in the facial expression is again reached about $\frac{1}{8}$ to $\frac{3}{16}$ of a second after the actual downfall.

Again closing the eyes, widening of the mouth, corners sideways, and at the same time hands put over the face, an action which emphasizes still more the withdrawal character of the movement shown in the closing of the eyes.

The further pictures of the film show marked agreement with the progress of the former example, (11), in so far as that there is again a fixation-attitude which lasts during the eleven following pictures. Only the facial expression brightens again very quickly, i.e. no later than the very next picture. And whilst Constance's face grows pleasanter and pleasanter she herself creeps out quite slowly from behind the stationary hands. Again as in 11, the eyes look first away from the downfall and towards the camera.

IV. UNCONTROLLED RESTLESSNESS, EXPRESSION OF DISGUISED FEELING AND ONE OF UNCONTROLLED EXAGGERATION
(Plate IX lower part)

13a. Bummi (2 ; 0) is waiting for the plum which his mother is stoning far too slowly for him. His body is on full stretch to the point of attraction, both arms raised, standing on tiptoe.

13*b*. Of course the child cannot keep long in this position, but consequent on the keen suspense, Bummi fidgets, especially with his legs, very restlessly to and fro. The separate successive pictures in contrast to 2*b*,.6*b*, 11, each show a very marked change of position.

14. Marianne in the scene "Surprise and Disappointment" (see 5) has several times examined the second envelope and paper and is now in the act of tearing the paper. Her eyes—although this is not evident on the picture—are full of rage. Nevertheless her attitude shows considerable self-control and the facial expression is inclined to a smile. The tearing-up is not wild either, but slow. Her rage is controlled and disguised. The picture shown is selected so that the rage may, however, be recognizable. But in many other pictures of this series it is so disguised as to be barely visible and the smile in different representations frequently appears quite genuine. (No. 14 thus occurs some time before No. 5.)

15. Constance's tower (cf. 11 and 12) has again fallen down. By now the downfall amuses her and in a playful, distinctly exaggerated manner she throws up both arms and opens her mouth beyond all reason, apparently without uttering a sound.

CONCERNING THE VARIOUS MAGIC ATTITUDES IN EARLY CHILDHOOD

By HEINZ WERNER

I

IN speaking of the child's behaviour in conformity with or resembling magic, we must—in accord with the present day stage of research—not begin with a quite precise idea of magic. On the contrary, it is better to label the whole collection of the very varied psychological ways of thought and action with the term of magic when we have to do with influences on nature and persons which are non-technical, not founded on insight into a natural-scientific-causal connection. Magic action lies between two opposite poles, viz. a more or less playful attitude on the one hand and on the other one that is really religious; we find in the child, even at an early age, all stages between these two extremes. Nevertheless it should be noted that distinction must be made between an early form of magic which is scarcely to be differentiated from the natural childish way of thought and action and a late form at a more advanced age which is in strong contrast to the "natural" way of looking at one's environment. But this progression from purely child-like behaviour in the early form of magic on to the late form is of the greatest significance for development-psychology which has to deal with genetic stages.

If we find that the early form of the magical varies but little from the true primitive attitude—in fact in individual cases it is difficult to distinguish whether the action is still only primitive or already magical—we are at once brought to the fact that the magical can only develop in a definite psychic structure, which we designate as primitive or elementary and which is found in different variety in the child and uncivilized man.

A chief distinguishing feature of such a primitive structure, the essential preliminary condition of every magic attitude and action, is the lesser degree of differentiation in the psychic expressions in childhood. This lack of differentiation shows itself fundamentally: (1) in the lack of differentiation, the diffuse nature, of perception and action; actions in childhood are more generally less distinct in their component parts than are those of the adult; (2) in the less clear separation of the ego from its environment, in the greater part played by the subjective, affective reactions in the idea formed of the world of persons and things by which it is surrounded.

II

One result of the "diffuse", i.e. the undifferentiated, indissoluble, totality of the child's form of action is that the customary succession—no matter how accidental it may be—of the details of an action is often maintained by the child with the most meticulous exactitude. For instance, we know that children when still in their infancy persist in being dressed, fed, put to bed in the way to which they are accustomed. In this we come upon the root of those remarkable child-actions which we might call "ritual" or "ceremonial". The further development of such habitual proceedings leads to the RITE as soon as every omission or change in their form is resented as disturbing and to the MAGIC RITE as soon as the omission of customary reactions is considered as disastrous but their performance as in some way beneficial. The rite-like actions of early childhood form a lower stage of magical performances; in individual cases it will always be difficult to decide whether we are dealing with a simple ceremonial desire or with an influence of magical tendency.

A few examples will now be given: A three-year old child always holds a corner of the pillow in its hand before going to sleep; another four-year-old girl held a piece of a certain garment, a boy from three to five years old puts a handkerchief under his cheek, a three-year-old girl puts her handkerchief over the edge of the bed. "When I was five years old", writes a children's nurse, "every evening my mother had to give me a bright ribbon to hold in bed, but it had to be gaily coloured or I did not go to sleep." "I know", says another lady, "that as a child I could not go to sleep unless my father or my mother came to tuck me up in the blanket." A direct observation of a nurse runs as follows: "Five-year-old Ilse does not go to sleep until she has torn out her hair-ribbon two or three times. She screams until someone comes and ties up the ribbon again, but it must be a certain red ribbon. Ursula is not satisfied until she has rolled up her handkerchief into a tight ball in her little fist. If she loses it at night she sets up a great roaring." In addition to these actions according to a set rule, we often find a spoken formula playing its part before the child goes to sleep. "My little daughter, four years old, has never failed to say every evening since the end of her second year: *Good-night, sleep well, sweet dreams and of a pickled cucumber. Mummy, you must buy me another pickled cucumber.*" Another six-year-old child held every evening a little speech: *I've got a pocket-handkerchief and Pucky* (a little teddy-bear), *so it's all right; the girls are in their room, good-night, good-night.* This custom the child kept up to his tenth year. Formulæ in the form of a dialogue are typical and common too before going to sleep. Two little girls indulged for years in a peculiar speech-ceremony with words of their own invention. The last word was "Bogosho", meaning "good-night", and after that not another word must be spoken or the whole ceremony began again. The use of similar set formulæ appears when saying good-bye, sneezing, etc.; e.g. a five-year-old boy insisted with peculiar pedantry that after a quarrel the lads should shake hands and each of the combatants should say "all right".

III

Much deeper preliminary conditions of magic performances lie in the unity with but slight differentiation between the ego and its environment, which is practically little separated from the ego, but rather takes its form from the ego, its emotions and efforts. But also the reverse is true that the ego is in the highest degree open to moulding influences of its environment.

The result of the "egoistic" character of the environment is the "spiritualizing" of things to such an extent that they cease to be stiff and dead objects but become living realities. Thus there comes to pass a personification of the world of things; under certain circumstances a "demonification" as well, if the experience of inner fear turns objects into terrifying, mysterious phantoms. As to personification of a comparatively innocent nature, the Scupins relate of their son (3 ; o)[1] as follows: *and then the canal will come upstairs and bring Bubi many little stones and then the canal screams out: here's little stones for you, so throw them into me.* Real demonic conceptions make their

[1] I, p. 208.

appearance by means of such anthropomorphic views as soon as feelings of fear try to embody the uncanny atmosphere in their surroundings. The Scupins relate of this same child:[1] "To-day we found the child sitting up in bed in the half-dark room, staring fixedly at the stove: *There, stove does beh: puts out his tongue!*" D. and R. Katz in their book *Conversations with Children* give an example of the demonic views of their little four-year-old son: "His father is sitting by Julius, who in an affectionate, demonstrative mood is stroking his hand. During this operation one little finger curls up and gives the father's hand a slight scratch. Julius is quite frightened at this and asks if it has hurt his father. Then he explains that it was the air and not he himself who had scratched with his finger. Julius: *Is the air angry?* Father: 'No the air is not angry.' Julius: *'But why then did it scratch with the finger?'* . . . ." Mysterious experiences that take on solid shape sometimes occur, naturally enough, most often in the darkness of the night. The following is a typical instance: "Then it was night, and every night I had always to go to the lavatory. My grandmother used regularly to leave all the room doors open. Then I passed five different doors and was not frightened, until I had to pass the red room; the moon was shining, the curtains are patterned and a big palm stands in the corner. I saw the palm coming towards me and I was not able to go on or to scream. This happened a few times one after another and during the day I was dull and disinclined to speak until I became ill, overcome by my fancies. The palm had to be given away."

Objects, situations and connections that are not under-stood or only half-understood may easily magnify what is harmless into something uncanny. "As I was three and a half years old", a children's nurse relates, "I once visited my grandmother. She was just eating some toast and told my mother something which I did not understand, but in which the word 'dead' occurred. From that time on I was afraid of toast. If anyone offered me a piece, I never took it but said: 'No, then death comes'."

The demonification of the outside world is only the simplest and most palpable expression of a feeling that in a higher form, reaching beyond early childhood, appears as a fateful connection of the ego with nature and gives the impulse to

[1] I, p. 116.

real magic actions. For this or that half-muffled feeling of the connection of the personal ego with a mighty world around, causes a sense of man's dependence on that surrounding world, which often cannot be ruled or even influenced by technical-natural means, but only by those of a magical nature. Not very many of all the magical practices in recent times are to be found in early childhood, and even these for the most part only in the period bordering on the school age.

Thus the following example shows the close connection existing between the sense of the mysterious and the so-called "oracles". "I was entered from my fourth year as a pupil in the ballet school of the Court Theatre in H. and was used for children's parts. So as a little girl I had after the performance to go home alone, and I cannot describe the terror that over-came me every time. In anticipation of this nightly horror I used to stand in the evening on the stage or in the wings and think to myself, for instance: If Fräulein X appears to-day in a fair wig, no drunk man will cross my path to-day. Often I used to try to coax some dog or other to follow me; if he went right up to the house door with me, I was again safe for the coming evening. But if the chosen miracle did not happen I was a tormented quarry and I felt every hair stand on end in unutterable terror."

The kinds of oracle that try to unveil fate seldom occur before school age; for them general psychic and intellectual capabilities are requisite (e.g. prudence) which are not often forthcoming in the early periods. At this time we more frequently find a second variety of magic attitude whose intention it is to influence fate by some partly ceremonial proceeding or other. Such attempts at magical influence we find as direct wish- and prayer-magic. We know that it is a most essential feature of a child's nature to confuse his wishes with reality; hence, it is very easy for him to develop the conviction of that almost magic power of his own wishes which Freud had designated as "the omnipotence of thought". When Bubi Scupin (4 ; 7) was looking at a war picture where one soldier killed another, the boy was much affected by the deed; he pulled the trigger of his gun after placing the barrel on the enemy soldier's head and said with a sigh of relief: *There, now I've shot him dead too, because he shot the other soldier.*[1]

[1] Scupin, II, p. 126.

A special form of wish-magic is the utterance of the wish in the form of a prayer. That prayer in early childhood is often enough more or less magical compulsion is shown by the ceremonial nature of the attitude, the necessity of a definite formula upon which fulfilment depends. By prayer everything that is desired can be attained; prayer is a "worker of miracles", a lady writes in a memoir of her childhood. Thus a certain prayer attitude cannot be wanting in children at as early an age as from three to six years; for instance, one must go to sleep with folded hands in order to prolong to a certain degree the power of the prayer into one's sleep, and at the end say three "amens", etc. The following note stands on the border line between a magic and a mystic- religious attitude of prayer. "At the age of four to six years I have always shut my eyelids tight during my evening prayer and pressed my ears so closely in some way that I made them roar; that was connected in my mind with the idea that God was hovering in a perpendicularly upright position over my head. And it was only so long as I kept this thought that I felt devout and certain that my prayer was heard." Prayer as a magical means against ghosts is reported of a six-year-old child. The child was frightened of a little man who was said to haunt the house. The child used to sing a hymn and make three crosses before he went into the cellar. And prayers are often used by little children as magic against thunderstorms. "If I (between three and six years of age) had angered my foster-mother, I had first to go to the garret and say three prayers before I was sure that she would be appeased with an apology."

A negative method of influencing fate is shown in the so-called "crying-down" (*verrufen*), i.e. the opposite must be wished to attain the happy issue of a definite matter. A child of from four to five years of age, when he wants to eat some nice dish or other, thinks all the time that the dinner is pig's pudding, which he absolutely detests.

A lady reports: "In the course of a walk my five-year-old granddaughter brought me a raspberry, which she had gathered, with the words: *It is sure to be wormy!* Then she bent down and whispered in my ear, *My love, Granny, I only say it, so that it may not be wormy.*"

The indirect magic influence, an actual charm, is founded on the magic working power of ceremonial actions and "effective" objects. A preliminary condition in this is non-technical relations between the ego and the outside world, between me and you. Some examples are here given: "At the age of five I believed, that if anyone squinted and the church clock just happened to strike, the squint would never go again. I thought that a neighbour who had a squint had ignored the prohibition as a child." A five-year-old child firmly believes that if he gets out of the window he cannot grow any bigger. According to Sully[1] a girl of three and a half begs her mother to put a big stone by her head because she does not want to die, for she hopes this means will keep her from growing and thereby from getting old as well.

Corresponding to such magical customs there are on the other hand magically effective things—names, places, etc., so called amulets and talismans. In childhood certain garments are at a very early age bringers of happiness, others of unhappiness. For instance: "I had when five years old a dress that always awoke peculiar memories. At the recollection of it I still feel in all their strength the sensations I experienced if I was allowed to put on this frock. For me it betokened great happiness; in my opinion the day must be one of unclouded joy; if I was not allowed to put it on in the morning, the day for me was one of unhappiness, full of disappointment, for the pain was too great to be conquered."

[1] P, 112.

BIBLIOGRAPHY

ABBREVIATIONS:

ZAngPs = Zeitschr. f. angewandte Psychol. Hrsg.: Stern und
      Lipmann, Lpzg. Barth.
Bhft ZAngPs = Beiheft zu obiger Zeitschrift.
ZPdPs = Zeitschr. f. pädagogische Psychol. Hrsg.: Scheibner,
      Stern, Fischer. Lpzg., Quelle & Meyer.
ZPs = Zeitschr. f. Psychologie. Hrsg.: Schumann. Lpzg.
      Barth.

*In the case of periodicals, heavy-type figures signify the number of
the volume.*

ADLER, A., Siehe auch "Heilen und Bilden" und "Handbuch."
  I. Das Zärtlichkeitsbedürfnis des Kindes. In: Heilen und Bilden.
  II. Trotz und Gehorsam.
  III. Praxis und Theorie der Individualpsychologie. München und
     Wiesbaden, Bergmann. 1920.
AMENT, W.
  I. Fortschritte der Kindesseelenkunde. 1895–1903. **2**(4), Literatur.
  II. Die Entwicklung von Sprechen und Denken beim Kinde.
     Lpz. 1899.
  III. Die Seele des Kindes. Eine vergleichende Lebensgesch. Stuttg.,
     Kosmos, o. J.

BASSOW, M. J. Typen vorschulpflichtiger Kinder. ZPdPS **29**. 1928.

BÄUMER, Gertrud und Droescher, Lili. Von der Kindesseele. Beiträge
    z. Kinderps. aus Dichtung und Biographie. Lpzg., Voigt-
    länder. 1908.

BAKER, H. J., and Kaufmann, H. J. Detroit Kindergarten Test.
    Yonkers-on-Hudson (New York). World Book Co. 1922.
BALDWIN.

BALDWIN, Bird J. and Stecher, Lorle J. The Psychology of the Pre-
    school Child. New York and London, Appleton. 1925.

BAUMGARTEN, Franziska. Die Lüge bei Kindern und Jugendlichen.
    Bhft ZAngPs **15**. 2. Ed. 1926.

BECKMANN, H. Die Entwicklung der Zahlleistung bei 2–6 jährigen
    Kindern. ZAngPs 1923.

BELAIEW-EXEMPLARSKY. Das musikalische Empfinden im Vorschulalter.
    ZAngPs **27**. 1926.

BERGEMANN-KÖNITZER, Martha. Das plastische Gestalten des Klein-
    kindes. ZAngPs **31**. 1928.

BERGER, Thea. Der Einfluss der Krankheit auf das Verhalten des
    Kleinkindes. ZAngPs **32**. 1928.

BERNFELD, S. Psychologie des Säuglings. Wien, J. Springer. 1925.

BEYRL, F. Die Grössenauffassung bei Kindern. ZPs **100**. 1926.
Konzentration und Ausdauer im frühen Kindesalter. ZPs **107**.

BINET.

BOECK, W. Das Mitleid bei Kindern. Ergebnisse einer Umfrage. Giessen. 1909.

BUCHHOLZ, Frieda. Versuch einer kritischen Betrachtung des Montessori-Systems. ZPdPs **26**. 1925.

BUCHNER, M. Die Entwicklung der Gemütsbewegungen im ersten Lebensjahre. Beitr. z. Kinderforschung u. Heilerziehung. Heft 60. 1900. (Mit Abbildungen.)

BÜHLER, Charlotte.
I. Das Märchen und die Phantasie des Kindes. 3. Aufl. mit Nachtrag. Bhft ZAngPs **17**. Leipzig, Barth. 1929.
II. Die ersten sozialen Verhaltungsweisen des Kindes. (Enthalten in: Bühler u. Hetzer, Tudor-Hart.) 1926.
III. Der Sechsjährige in psychologischer Beleuchtung. In: Handb. f. d. Anfangsunterricht. Wien. 1926.
IV. Kindheit und Jugend. Genese des Bewusstseins. Leipzig, Hirzel. 1928.
V. (Herausgegeben von Ch. B.) Zur Psychologie des Kleinkindes. Exp.-psychol. Arbeiten. ZPs **107**. 1928.

BÜHLER, Charlotte; Hetzer, Hildegard; Tudor-Hart, Beatrix. Soziologische und psychologische Studien über das erste Lebensjahr. Heft 5 der: Quellen und Studien zur Jugendkunde. Jena, Fischer. 1926.

BÜHLER, Charlotte. Kindheit und Jugend. Leipzig. Hirzel. 1928.
Die seelische Entwicklung des Kindes und der Jugendlichen. Handbuch der Pädagogik. Herausg. v. Nohl und Pallat. 1929.
Zwei Grundtypen von Lebensprozessen. ZPs **108**. 1928.
und Hetzer, Hildegard. Zur Geschichte der Kinderpsychologie. Beitr. z. Problemgesch. d. Psychol.; Festschr. zu Karl Bühlers 50. Geburtstag. Jena. Fischer. 1929.

BÜHLER, Karl.
I. Die geistige Entwicklung des Kindes. Jena, G. Fischer. 4. Aufl. 1924.
II. Abriss der geistigen Entwicklung des Kindes. 2. Aufl. Leipzig, Quelle & Meyer. (Wissenschaft u. Bildung Nr. 156.)

BURKHARDT, H. Veränderungen der Raumlage in Kinderzeichnungen. ZPdPs **26**.

BUSEMANN, A. Über das sogenannte "erste Trotzalter" des Kindes. ZPdPs. **29**. 1926.
Über die Ursachen des ersten "Trotzalters" und der Erregungsphasen überhaupt. ZPdPs. **30**. 1929.

CANESTRINI. Über das Sinnesleben des Neugeborenen. Monographien a. d. Gesamtgebiet der Neurol. u. Psychiatrie. Heft 5. 1913.

CARUS.

CLAPARÈDE, E.
I. Psychologie de l'enfant et pédagogie expérimentale. 5. Aufl. Genf. 1916.
II. La conscience de la ressemblance et de la différence chez l'enfant. Archives de Psychol. 17 (Nr. 65). 1918.

COMPAYRÉ, G. Die Entwicklung der Kindesseele. Dtsch. v. Ufer. Altenburg, Bonde. 1900.

CRAMAUSSEL, E. Le premier éveil intellectuel de l'infant. 2. éd. Paris, Alcan. 1911.

CUNEO.

CZERNY.

DECROLY, O. et Degand, J. Observations relatives au développement de la notion du temps chez une petite fille. Archives de Psychol. 13, Nr. 50. 1913.

DELACROIX, H. Le langage et la pensée. Paris, Alcan. 1924.

DESCOEUDRES, Alice. Le développement de l'enfant de deux à sept ans. Recherches de psychologie expérimentale. Éditions Delachaux et Niestle, Neuchatel et Paris. Ohne Jahr (1921).

DEVILLE, G. Notes sur le développement du langage. Rev. de linguistique et de philol. comparée 23 und 24. 1890/91.

DIX, K. W. Körperliche und geistige Entwicklung eines Kindes. Leipzig, Wunderlich.
I. Instinktbewegungen. 1911.
II. Die Sinne. 1912.
III. Vorstellen und Handeln. 1914.

DÖRING, M.

DOROSCHENKO, Olga. Der Einfluss des Milieus auf den Inhalt und Aufbau frei entstehender Kollektive im vorschulpflichtigen Alter. ZAngPs 30. 1928.

DYROFF, A. Über das Seelenleben des Kindes. 2. Aufl. Bonn, Hanstein. 1911.

EGGER.

EHRLICH, Toni. Vom Erwachsen des ästhetischen Empfindens. Der Säemann. 1912.

ELIASBERG, W. Psychologie und Pathologie der Abstraktion. Eine exper. Untersuchung über aufgabefreie Beachtungsvorgänge. Bhft ZAngPs. 35. Leipzig, Barth. 1925.

ELJASCH, Minna. Neue Abstraktionsversuche bei vorschulpflichtigen Kindern. ZPs 105. 1927.

ENG, Helga. Kinderzeichnen. Vom ersten Strich bis zu den Farben-
    zeichnungen des Achtjährigen. Bhft ZAngPs **39**. 1927.

ERISMANN, Th. Der Trotz. (Eine psychol.-pädag. Studie.) Verstehen
    und Bilden **1**. 1926.

FAULWASSER, A. Der pädagogische Gehalt früher Kindheitserin-
    nerungen. ZPdPs **28**. 1927.

FILBIG, J. Untersuchungen über die Entwicklung von Zahlvorstel-
    lungen. ZPdPs **24**. 1923.

FISHER, Dorothea C. Eine Montessori-Mutter. J. Hoffmann, Stuttgart.
    1927.

FLECHSIG.

FOUQUÉ.

FRANK, H. Untersuchung über Sehgrössenkonstanz bei Kindern.
    Psychol. Forschg. **7**. 1925.

FRANKE, E. Die geistige Entwicklung der Negerkinder. Beitr. z.
    Kultur- u. Universalgesch. Heft 35. Leipzig, Voigtländer.
    1915.

FREUD, S.
    I. Vorlesungen zur Einführung in die Psychoanalyse. Lpzg. u.
        Wien, Heller. 1916.
    II. 3 Abhandlungen zur Sexualtheorie. 4. Aufl. Leipzig und Wien,
        F. Deuticke. 1920.
    III. Über infantile Sexualtheorien. In: "Sammlung kleiner Schriften
        zur Neurosenlehre."
    IV. Eine Kindheitserinnerung des Leonardo da Vinci. 2. Aufl.
        Leipzig und Wien. Deuticke. 1919.
    V. Analyse der Phobie eines 5 jährigen Knaben. Jahrbuch f.
        psychoanal. Forschg. **1**.

FRÖBEL.

FURTMÜLLER siehe "Heilen und Bilden."

GAUPP, R. Psychologie des Kindes. (Aus Natur und Geisteswelt 213.)
    4. Aufl. Lpzg., Teubner. 1918.

GENNEP, A. van. Dessins d'enfant et dessin préhistorique. Archives de
    Psychol. **10**. Nr. 40. 1911.

GERHARDS, K. Zur Beurteilung der Montessori-Pädagogik. E.
    Auseinandersetzung mit ihren heutigen Kritikern (Stern,
    Hessen, Spranger, Muchow). Leipzig, Quelle & Meyer.1928.

GESELL, A. The Mental Growth of the Pre-school Child. 447 S. New
    York. The Macmillan Co. 1925.
    Infancy and Human Growth. The Macmillan Co., New York.
    418 S.

GHEORGOV.

GIESE, F. Kinderpsychologie. (Handb. d. vergleich. Psychologie, hrsg. v.
    Kafka, Bd. I, Abt. 3.) Reinhardt, München. Ohne Jahr.
    1922.

GOETHE.

GOODENOUGH, Florence L. The Kuhlman-Binet Tests for Children of Pre-school Age. The University of Minnesota Press. Minneapolis. 1928.

GROOS, K.
I. Das Seelenleben des Kindes. Vorlesungen. Berlin, Reuther and Reichard. 5. Aufl. 1921.
II. Die Spiele der Menschen. Jena, Fischer. 1899.
III. Der Lebenswert des Spieles. Jena, Fischer. 1910.
IV. Die seelische Entwicklung des Kleinkindes; in:"Kinderfürsorge." Leipzig, Teubner.

GROSSE.

GRÜNBAUM, A. A. Die Struktur der Kinderpsyche. ZPdPs 28. 1927.

GUILLAUME, P. L'Imitation chez l'enfant. Bibliothèque de Psychol. de l'Enfant et de Pédagogie. Paris. Alcan. 1925.
Les débuts de la phrase dans le langage de l'enfant. Journal de Psychol. 24. 1927.
Le développement des éléments formels dans le langage de l'enfant. Journal de Psychol. 24. 1927.

HALL, Stanley. Ausgew. Beitr. z. Kindespsychol. u. Pädag. Altenburg. 1902.

HANDBUCH DER INDIVIDUALPSYCHOLOGIE, in Gemeinschaft mit Alfred Adler, etc., herausg. von E. Wexberg I/II. München, Bergmann. 1926.

HARTLAUB, G. F. Der Genius im Kinde. Zeichnungen und Malversuche begabter Kinder. Breslau, Hirt. 1922.

HATTINGBERG, H. v.
I. Zur Psychologie des kindlichen Eigensinns. Zeitschr. f. Pathopsychol. Ergänzungsband I. 1913.
II. Analerotik, Angstlust und Eigensinn. Internat. Ztschr. f. Psychoanalyse 2. 1914.

HEBBEL.

HEILEN und Bilden. Ärztl.-päd. Arb. des Vereins f. Individualpsychol. hrsg. v. Adler und Furtmüller. München. 1913.

HERBART.

HESSEN, S. Fröbel und Montessori. Die Erziehung 1. Heft 2. 1925 and 1927.

HETZER, Hildegard. Die symbolische Darstellung in der frühen Kindheit. (Wiener Arbeiten z. päd. Psychol. Hrsg. v. Charlotte Bühler und V. Fadrus, 3.) Wien, Lpzg., New York. Deutscher Verlag f. Jugend und Volk. 1926.

HETZER, Hildegard u. Reindorf B. Sprachentwicklung und soziales Milieu. ZAngPs 29. 1928.

HETZER, Hildegard. Entwicklungsbedingte Erziehungsschwierigkeiten. ZPdPs **30.** 1929.

HIRSCHLAFF, L. Über die Furcht der Kinder. ZPdPs. 1901/02.

HOGAN, Louise E. A Study of a Child. New York and London. 1900 Harper and Brothers.

HOYER, Arnulf u. Galina. Über die Lallsprache eines Kindes. ZAngPs **24.** 1924.

HUG-HELLMUTH, H. von.
  I. Aus dem Seelenleben des Kindes. Eine psychoanalyt. Studie (Heft 15 der Schriften z. angew. Seelenkunde. Hrsg. v. Freud.) Lpzg. und Wien, Deuticke. 2. Aufl. 1921.
  II. Analyse eines Traumes eines 5½ jährigen Knaben. Zentralbl. für Psychoanalyse **2.**
  III. Kinderträume. Ztschr. f. Psychoanalyse I.
  IV. Vom wahren Wesen der Kinderseele. (Kleine Beiträge), Imago, Zeitschr. f. Anwendung der Psychoanalyse **2** (1913). **5** (1917).

HUNE.

HUTH. A.
  I. Formauffassung und Schreibversuch im Kindergartenalter. ZPdPs **15.** 1914.
  II. Beiträge zur Untersuchung der seelischen Geschlechtsunterschiede im vorschulpflichtigen Alter. (Pädag. Magazin, Heft 1060). Langensalza, H. Beyer und Söhne. 1926.

IDELBERGER, H. Hauptprobleme der kindlichen Sprachentwicklung. ZPdPs **5.** 1903.

JAENSCH, E. R. Die Eidetik und die typologische Forschungsmethode. ZPdPs **26.** 1925. Lpzg. Quelle & Meyer. 1925.

JESPERSEN, O. Die Sprache, ihre Natur, Entwicklung und Entstehung. Heidelberg, Winter. 1925. Buch II. Das Kind.

JUNG, C. G. Über Konflikte der kindlichen Seele. Jahrbuch f. psychoanal. Forschg. **2.** 1910.

KATZ, D.
  I. Studien zur Kinderpsychologie Wiss. Beitr. z. Päd. u. Psychol. (hrsg. v. Deuchler u. Katz), Heft 4. Lpzg. 1913.
  II. Ein Beitrag zur Kenntnis der Kinderzeichnungen. ZPs **41.** 1906. Neue Gespräche mit Kindern. Bericht üb. d. 4. Kongr. f. Heilpädagogik. (11.–15. April 1928.) Berlin. Springer. 1929.

KATZ, David u. Rosa.
  I. Die Erziehung im vorschulpflichtigen Alter. (Wissenschaft u. Bildung 217.) Lpzg. Quelle & Meyer. 1925.
  II. Gespräche mit Kindern. Untersuch. 2. Sozialpsychol. u. Pädagogik Berlin, Springer. 1928.

KAUS, O. Über Lügenhaftigkeit beim Kinde. In: Adler und Furtmüller, Heilen u. Bilden.

KAUS, Gina. Die seelische Entwicklung des Kindes. In: Handbuch der Individualpsychologie, hrsg. von Wexberg. I. 1926.

KELLER, Helen.

KERN-HALLOWELL, Dorothy. Mental Tests for Pre-School Children. Psychol. Clinic **16.** 1928.

KERSCHENSTEINER.

KIK, C. Die übernormale Zeichenbegabung bei Kindern. ZAngPs **2,** hrsg. von Grosser und Stern, Leipzig. 1913.

KÖHLER, Elsa. Die Persönlichkeit des dreijährigen Kindes. Lpzg. Hirzel. 1926.
Kindersprache und Begriffsbildung. In: Beiträge zur Problemgeschichte der Psychol. Festschrift zu K. Bühlers 50. Geburtstag. Jena. 1929.

KÖHLER, W. Intelligenzprüfungen an Anthropoiden I.—Abhdlg. d. Pr. Akad. d. Wiss. in Berlin. Jhrg. 1917. Physikal.-Math. Kl. Nr. 1.

KÖNIG, A. Die Entwicklung des musikalischen Sinnes bei Kindern. Die Kinderfehler 8. 1903.

KOFFKA, K. Die Grundlagen der psychischen Entwicklung. Eine Einführung in die Kinderpsychologie. Osterwiek, Zickfeld. 2. Aufl. 1925.

KRAUSE, P. Entwicklung eines Kindes von der Geburt bis zum Eintritt in die Schule. Leipzig. 1914.

KRÖTZSCH, W. Rhythmus und Form in der freien Kinderzeichnung. Leipzig. Haase. 1917.

KROH, O. Subjektive Anschauungsbilder bei Jugendlichen. Göttingen, Vandenhoek u. Rupprecht.

KUENBERG, M. v. Über Abstraktionsfähigkeit und die Entstehung von Relationen beim vorschulpflichtigen Kinde. ZAngPs **17.** 1920.

KUSSMAUL.

LEWIN, K. Kindlicher Ausdruck. ZPdPs **28.** 1927.

LICHTENSTEIN, Judith. Fragebogen zu psychol. Ermittlungen im Kindergarten. ZPdPs **20.** 1919.

LINDNER, G. Beobachtungen und Bemerkungen über die Entwicklung der Sprache des Kindes. Kosmos **6.** 1882.

LIEPMANN, W.

LIPMANN, Otto, u. Wendriner, Emmi. Aussageexperimente im Kindergarten. Beitr. z. Psychol. d. Auss. (Stern). Bd. II. Heft 3.

LOEWENFELD, B. Systematisches Studium der Reaktionen der Säuglinge auf Klänge und Geräusche. ZPs **104.** 1927.

MAJOR, D. R. First Steps in Mental Growth. New York, Macmillan. 1906.

MARCINOWSKI. Zur Frage der "Lüge der Kinder unter vier Jahren."
ZPdPs 7. 1905.

MEUMANN, E.
I. Die Entstehung der ersten Wortbedeutungen beim Kinde.
Wundts Philos.-Stud. 20. Lpzg. 1902.
II. Vorl. z. Einf. in d. exp. Pädagogik. 2. Aufl. I. 1911.

(MEYER, Toni.) Aus einer Kinderstube. Tagebuchblätter von Clara
Stern. Bearbeitet von Toni Meyer. 2. Aufl. Lpzg. 1921.

MOLL, A. Das Sexualleben des Kindes. Hermann Walter. Berlin. 1909.

MONTESSORI, Maria. Selbsttätige Erziehung im frühen Kindesalter.
Stuttgart. J. Hoffmann. 1913.

MOORE, K. L. The Mental Development of a Child. Psychol. Review,
Monogr. Suppl. Nr. 3. 1896.

MUCHOW, Martha.
I. Pädag.-psychologische und entwicklungspsychologische Be-
trachtungsweise in der Psychologie der Kindheit. ZPdPs
26. 1925.
II. Kindespsychologische Studien im Kindergarten. Kindergarten
66 (11) Nov. 1925; 67 (4) April 1926; 67 (10) Okt.
1926.
III. Beiträge zur psychol. Charakteristik des Kindergarten- und
Grundschulalters. (Päd.-psychol. Schriftenreihe des Allg.
Deutschen Lehrerinnenvereins, Heft 3.) Berlin. Herbig.
1926.
IV. Das Montessori-System und die Erziehungsgedanken Friedrich
Fröbels (in: Hecker und Muchow: Friedrich Fröbel und
Maria Montessori, Bücherreihe d. Deutschen Fröbelver-
bandes. Reihe B, Bd. II.) Leipzig. Quelle & Meyer. 1926.
Psychol. Probleme der frühen Erziehung. Veröffentlichungen der
Akademie in Erfurt Nr. 19. Erfurt. 1929.

NETSCHAJEFF, A. Psychol. Untersuchungen an Kindern im Alter von
4–8 Jahren, ZAngPs 29. 1927.

NEUGEBAUER.
I. Über die Entwicklung der Frage in der frühen Kindheit.
ZAngPs 8. 1913.
II. Aus der Sprachentwicklung meines Sohnes. ZAngPs 9. 1914.
III. Sprachliche Eigenbildungen meines Sohnes. Ztschr. f. Kinder-
forschg. 1913 (3), 1914 (4/5).

NEUGEBAUER, Hanna. Materialien zur Kindespsychologie. (Traum,
Humor.) ZAngPs. 32. 1928.
Gefühl und Wille meines Sohnes. Materialien zur Kindespsychologie.
ZAngPs. 34. 1929.

OAKDEN, E. C., and Mary Sturt. The Development of the Knowledge
of Time in Children. British Journal of Psychology.
12, Part 4. 1922.

BIBLIOGRAPHY 599

OTTO, B. Von der Helga. Grosslichterfelde. 1910.

PAVLOVITCH, Milivoie. Le langage enfantin. Acquisition du Serbe et du Français par un enfant Serbe. (Paris, Champion. 1920.)

PEISER, J. Prüfung höherer Gehirnfunktionen bei Kleinkindern. Jhrb. f. Kinderheilk. 91 (III. Folge Bd. 41). 1920.

PÉREZ, B. La psychologie de l'enfant. Les trois premières années de l'enfant. 1878. 6. Aufl. 1902.

PFEIFER, S. Äusserungen infantil-erotischer Triebe im Spiele. (Psychoanalyt. Stellungnahme zu den wichtigsten Spieltheorien.) Imago, Ztschr. f. Anwendung der Psychoanalyse 5. 1917.

PFISTER, O.
  I. Das Kinderspiel als Frühsymptom krankhafter Entwicklung. Abgedruckt in: Zum Kampf um die Psychoanalyse. (Intern. psychoanalyt. Bibliothek 8.) Wien. 1920.
  II. Die psychoanalyt. Methode. Pädagogium Bd. I. Lpzg. u. Berlin. Klindkardt. 1913.

PIAGET, Jean.
  I. Le langage et la pensée chez l'enfant. Neuchatel et Paris. 1923.
  II. Le jugement et le raisonnement chez l'enfant. Neuchatel et Paris. 1924.
  III. La représentation du monde chez l'enfant. Paris. Alcan. 1926. La première année de l'enfant. British Journ. of Psychol. 18. 1927/28. La causalité de l'infant. British Journ. of Psychol. 18. 1927/28.

PINTNER, R., and Cunningham, B. V. The Problem of Group Intelligence. Tests for Very Young Children. Journal of Educational Psychol. 13. 1922.

PLATT, William. Child-Music. A Book of Children's Own Tunes. London.

PREYER, W.
  I. Die Seele des Kindes. 1882. 6. Aufl., bearb. v. Schäfer. Lpzg. 1905.
  II. Die geist. Entwicklung in der ersten Kindheit. 1893.

PRÜFER, J. Kleinkinderpädagogik. (Die Pädagogik der Gegenwart VIII.) Lpzg. Nemnich. 1913.

RANK, O. Das Trauma der Geburt und seine Bedeutung für die Psychoanalyse. 1924.

RASMUSSEN, W.
  I. Die seel. Entwicklung des Kindes in den ersten vier Lebensjahren. A. d. Dänischen übersetzt v. Albert Rohrberg. Essen.
  II. Psychologie des Kindes zwischen vier und sieben Jahren. A. d. Dänischen übersetzt von A. Rohrberg. Lpzg. F. Meiner. 1925.

READ MUMFORD, Edith. The Dawn of Character in the Mind of the Child. London. 1925.

REICHARDT, H. Die Früherinnerung als Trägerin kindlicher Selbstbeobachtungen in den ersten Lebensjahren. Halle. Marhold. 1926.

REININGER, K. Die Lüge beim Kind und beim Jugendlichen als psychol. u. pädag. Problem. In dem Sammelband "Die Lüge," hrsg. v. Lipmann u. Plaut. Lpzg. Barth. 1927.

REUTER, Gabriele.

RÉVÉSZ, Géza.
  I. Üb. spontane u. systematische Selbstbeobachtung bei Kindern. ZAngPs 21. 1923.
  II. Ordnung und Reihenbildung. The Call of Education 2 (3). 1925.

RICCI, C. L'Arte dei Bambini. Lpzg. Vogtländer. 1906.

RICHTER, Fr. Die Entwicklung der psychologischen Kindersprachforschung bis zum Beginn des 20. Jahrhunderts. Münster. 1927.

RONJAT, J. Le développement du langage observé chez un enfant bilingue. Paris. 1913. Champion.

ROSEGGER.

ROUSSEAU.

RÜHLE. Die Seele des proletarischen Kindes. Dresden. 1925.

RUPP, H. Über die Prüfung musikal. Fähigkeiten. ZAngPs 9. 1915.

RUSSELL, B. On Education, especially in Early Childhood. London. Allen and Unwin. 1926.

RUTTMANN. Ergebnisse der bisherigen Untersuchungen zur Psychologie des Zeichnens. Leipzig. Wunderlich. 1911.

SCHÄFER, K. L. Kommen Lügen bei den Kindern vor dem vierten Jahre vor? ZPdPs 7. 1905.

SCHÄFER, P.
  I. Die kindliche Entwicklungsperiode des reinen Sprachverständnisses nach ihrer Abgrenzung. ZPdPs 22. 1921.
  II. Beobachtungen u. Versuche an e. Kind in der Entwicklungsperiode des reinen Sprachverständnisses. ZPdPs 23. 1922.

SCHAM, Max and Grete. The Tired Child. Philadelphia. Lippincott. 1926.

SCHILLER.

SCHOBER, G. und A. Über Bilderkennungs- und Unterscheidungsfähigkeit bei kleinen Kindern. In: Hamb. Arbeiten zur Begabungsforschung 2 (Bhft ZAngPs 19). 1919.

SCHWEITZER.

SCUPIN, E. u. G.
  I. Bubis erste Kindheit. Lpzg. Grieben. 1907.
  II. Bubi im 4.–6. Lebensjahre. Ebda. 1910.

Shinn. M. W.
I. Notes on the Development of a Child. Univ. of California
Publications (Division Education). I. 1893–1899. II.
Development of the Senses. 1907. Berkeley, Univ. Press.
II. The Biography of a Baby. Boston and New York o. J.
Houghton, Mifflin Comp.

Sigismund, R. Kind und Welt. 1856. Neu hrsg. v. Ufer. Braunschweig.
1897.

Silverstolpe, G. Westin. Zur Frage der "Urmelodie." ZAngPs 27.
1926.

Simoneit, M. Erziehung auf Grund der seelischen Entwicklung des
Menschen. I. B. Erziehung des Kindes im 1., 2., 3. Lebensjahr. Berlin. 1928.

Spencer.

Sperber.

Stekel, W.
I. D. Sprache d. Traumes. Wiesbaden. Bergmann. 1911.
II. Psychosexueller Infantilismus. Urban u. Schwarzenberg. Berlin
und Wien. 1922.

Stern, Erich. Das Verhalten des Kindes in der Gruppe. Beobachtungen
im Kindergarten. ZAngPs 22. 1923.

Stern, Clara, see Meyer.

Stern, Clara u. William.
I. Monographien über die seel. Entwicklg. d. Kindes. Lpzg.
Barth. Erster Band: Die Kindersprache. 4., neubearbeitete
Auflage. 1928.
Zweiter Band: Erinnerung, Aussage u. Lüge in d. frühen
Kindheit. 4. Aufl. 1930.
II. Anleitung zur Beobachtung d. Sprachentwicklg. bei normalen
vollsinnigen Kindern. ZAngPs 2. 1909.
III. Die zeichnerische Entwicklunge e. Knaben vom 4. bis zum
7. Jahre. ZAngPs 3. 1909. Wiederabgedruckt in: Das
freie Zeichnen und Formen des Kindes. Sammlg. v.
Abhandlungen. Hrsg. v. Grosser u. Stern, Lpzg., Barth.
1913.

Stern, W.
I. Die Aussage als geistige Leistung u. als Verhörsprodukt.
Leipzig. Barth. 1904.
II. Tatachen und Ursachen der seelischen Entwicklung. ZAngPs 1.
1908.
III. Die Entwicklung der Raumwahrnehmung in der ersten
Kindheit. ZAngPs 2. 1909.
IV. Über verlagerte Raumformen. Ein Beitrag z. Psychol. d. kindl.
Raumdarstellung und Auffassung. ZAngPs 2. 1909.

STERN, W.—*continued.*
    V. Die Anwendung der Psychoanalyse auf Kinder und Jugendliche.
        (Nebst einem Anhang: C. u. W. Stern, Kritik einer
        Freudschen Kindes-Psychoanalyse.) ZAngPs **8**. 1913.
    VI. Helen Keller. Die Entwicklung u. Erziehung einer Taubstumm-
        blinden als psychol., pädag. und sprachtheoret. Problem.
        Ziehen-Zieglersche Sammlung 8, Heft 2. Berlin. 1905.
    VII. Die differentielle Psychol. in ihren method. Grundlagen. 3. Aufl.
        Lpzg. Barth. 1921.
    VIII. Die Intelligenz der Kinder und Jugendlichen und die Methoden
        ihrer Untersuchung. 4. Aufl. Lpzg. Barth. 1928.
    IX. Neue Testeichungen für die frühe Kindheit. (Kritische
        Besprechung des Buches von Alice Descoeudres.) ZAngPs
        20. 1922.
    X. Die menschliche Persönlichkeit (Bd. II von "Person und
        Sache"). Lpzg. Barth. 3. Aufl. 1923.
    XI. Jugendliche Zeugen in Sittlichkeitsprozessen. Lpzg. Quelle &
        Meyer. 1926.
    XII. Zur Entwicklungspsychologie der Kindersprache. ZPdPs **29**.
        1928.
    XIII. Über Zweisprachigkeit in der frühen Kindheit. ZAngPs **30**.
        1928.

STERN, W. u. Wiegmann, O. Methodensammlung zur Intelligenzprüfung
        von Kindern und Jugendlichen. 3. Aufl. Lpzg. Barth.
        1926.

STIFTER.

STUMPF, C.
    I. Zur Methodik der Kinderpsychologie. ZPdPs **2**. 1900.
    II. Eigenartige sprachliche Entwicklung eines Kindes. ZPdPs **3**.
        1901.

STUTSMAN, Rachel. Performance Tests for Children of Pre-School Age.
        Genetic Psychology Monographs **1** (1). Clark University.
        Mass. 1926.

SULLY, J. Untersuchungen über d. Kindheit. Lpzg. Wunderlich. 1909.

SUTTNER.

TERMAN LEWIS, M.
    I. The Measurement of Intelligence. Boston. 1916.
    II. The Intelligence of School Children. London. G. Harrap & Co.
        1919. (Especially Chap. III: Individual Differences among
        Kindergarten Children.)

TIEDEMANN, D. Beobachtungen über d. Entwicklung d. Seelenfähig-
        keiten bei Kindern. 1787. Neu hrsg. v. Ufer. Altenburg.
        1897.

TOBIE, D. Die Entwicklung der teilinhaltlichen Beachtung von Farbe
        und Form im vorschulpflichtigen Alter. Bhft ZAngPs **38**.
        Leipzig. Barth. 1926.

VAN DER TORREN, J. Über das Auffassungs- und Unterscheidungsver-
mögen für optische Bilder bei Kindern. ZAngPs 1. 1908.

TRACY, F. u. Stimpfl, J. Psychol. d. Kindheit. 3. Aufl. 1910. Lpzg.
Wunderlich.

VALENTINE, C. W. Reflexes in Early Childhood. Brit. Journal of Med.
Psychol. 1. 1927.

VERWORN.

VOLKELT, H. Fortschritte der experimentellen Kinderpsychologie.
Ber. üb. d. IX. Kongr. f. exp. Ps. in München. Jena.
Fischer. 1926.
Neue Untersuchungen über die kindliche Auffassung und Wieder-
gabe von Formen. Bericht über den 4. Kongress für
Heilpädagogik (11.–15. April 28). Berlin. Springer. 1929.

VOLZ.

WATSON, J. B. Psychology from the Standpoint of a Behaviorist.
Philadelphia and London, J. B. Lippincott Comp. 1919.

WERNER, Heinz.
I. Die melodische Erfindung im frühen Kindesalte. Eine
entwicklungspsychol. Untersuchung. Wien. 1917. A. Hölder.
Wiener Akad.-Berichte. Philos.-Histor. Klasse, 182 Bd.
Nr. 4.
II. Einführung in die Entwicklungspsychologie. Lpzg. Barth. 1926.

WERTHEIMER.

WEXBERG, E. Ängstliche Kinder. In: Adler u. Furtmüller, Heilen und
Bilden.

WINCH, W. H. German Aussage-Experiments with English School-
Children. 1 Congrès intern. de Pédagogie à Bruxelles,
Vol. 2. 1913.

WISLITZKY, Sonja. Beobachtungen über das soziale Verhalten im
Kindergarten. ZPs 107.

INDEX

ABSTRACTION—
in imperfect ideation, 339 *seq.*
in formation of plural ideation, 391
in generalized judgments, 417
experiments in, 424 *sqq.*
experiments with choice of method, 429 *seq.*
ACTION FOR OTHERS (altruism), 543, 548 *sqq.*
ACTIVITY—
infant's feelings of, 134
ÆSTHETIC SENSE, 337 *sqq.*
feeling for optical impressions, 362, 399
AFFECTION—
first signs of, 531 *sqq.*
general consideration of and sympathy, 544 *seq.*
AIMS—
fundamental individual, 450
AMBITION, 504 *seq.*
AMNESIA—
infantile, 485
ANALOGY—
in speech-development, 161
conclusions from, 415
ANIMALS—
compared with children, 62, 71, 87 *seq.*
representations of, 373
cruelty to, 542
fear of, 515
sympathy with, 548
ANTITHESIS, 398, 422
APPETITE, 462
APPROVAL—
need of, 503 *seq.*
• APTITUDES, 53 *seq.*
ARRANGEMENT—
Montessori exercises in, 233
ART—
the child and, 337
ASSOCIATION—
in the infant, 108 *seq.*
in expectation, 112
in remembrance, 242
defective, in fantasy, 294
and causal ideation, 408
in drawing conclusions, 411 *sqq.*
ATAVISM—
theory of, 308, 327, 513
ATTENTION—
in the infant, 104 *seq.*
its importance in aussage, 273
ATTITUDE—
in effort, 451
AUSSAGE—
errors in recollection, 257 *sqq.*

AUSSAGE—
forensic, 262 *sqq.*
experiments in, 266 *sqq.*
with pictures seen only once, 267 *sqq.*
after a continuous impression, 272 *seq.*
educational hints on, 274
fantasy errors in, 349
categories in, 391
AUTOBIOGRAPHIES, 44, 253 *sqq.*
AUTOEROTICISM, 493

BABBLE, 143 *seq.*
BEHAVIORISM, 42
BILINGUAL POWER, 159 *seq.*
BIRTH—
condition at, 65 *seq.*
BROTHERS AND SISTERS—
relation between, 332, 495, 534

CALCULATION, 422
and counting, 431 *sqq.*
CANON (music), 61
CAUSAL LAW—
psychological origin of, 405 *sqq.*
individual and, 409
and anthropomorphism, 409
generality of, 410 *sqq.*
CHANGES OF DEVELOPMENT, 36
CHILDREN, PROLETARIAN, 496
(*See also* Social Differences)
CHOICE—
applications of, 464
COLLECTION—
of investigation data, 46
COLLECTIVE IDEATION, 391
COLOUR—
recognition of, 195 *seq.*
abstraction of, 424 *sqq.*
CONCLUSIONS—
from difference, 314 *seq.*
CONFESSIONAL TALKS, 551 *sqq.*
CONSCIOUSNESS—
in the new-born child, 75 *seq.*
significance of, 447 *seq.*
and unconsciousness, 453, 488 *seq.*
CONTEMPLATIVE ATTITUDE—
to pictures, 19
CONTINUOUS—
fantasy and games, 297 *seq.*
CONTRA-SUGGESTION, 482
CONVERGENCE THEORY, 48 *sqq.*
in regard to perception, 102
in regard to spatial idea, 114
in regard to speech, 150, 155
in regard to play, 315

ILLUSTRATIONS

PLATE I

1. Children
2. Gee-gee
3. Gee-gee
4. Bow-wow
5. Pussy
6. Shoe
7. Stocking
8. Frock
9. Hat
10. Egg Cup
11. Purse
12. Bottle
13. First Chair then Bed
14. Chair
15. Baby's dressing table.
16. First House then la la (piano)
17. Tree

DRAWINGS NAMED IN COURSE OF CONSTRUCTION BY A CHILD AGED 1-YEAR AND 10 MONTHS. (*Cf. p.* 194)

PLATE II

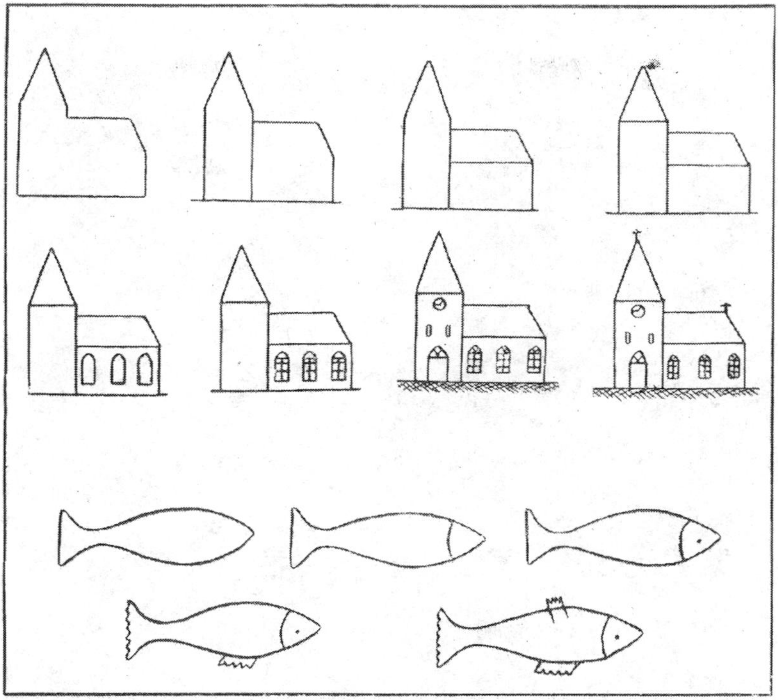

EXAMPLES OF HEILBRONNER'S "PROGRESSIVE METHOD"

CARD OF LOTTO (POSITIONS OF THE BODY) USED BY ALICE
DESCOEUDRES. (*Cf. p.* 205)

PLATE III

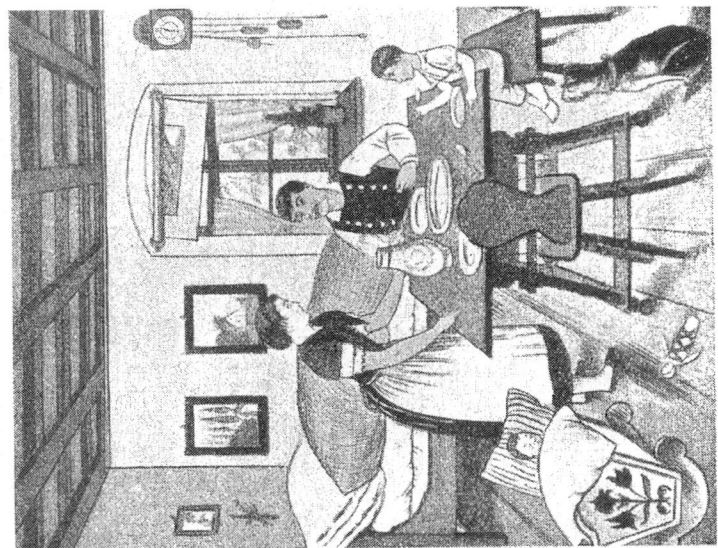

BREAKFAST-ROOM. (*Cf. p. 206 seq.*)

PEASANT'S ROOM. (*Cf. pp. 206, 271, 391*)

Originals larger and coloured

PLATE IV

GOOSE GIRL (PICTURE FOR TEST IN "AUSSAGE"). (Cf. p. 272)

ROOM IN TOWN-HOUSE. (Cf. p. 206)

PLATE V

ORIGINAL BUILDING BY SCULPTOR'S SON (5; 1). (Cf. p. 326)

From G. & E. Scupin's "Bubi from Four to Six"

PLATE VI

Fig.1
3; 2½

Fig.2
3; 11½

Fig 3   *4; 1*

Fig. 4   *4; 8½*

Fig.5
5; 6

Fig 6   *5; 8½*

G St 5; 6½
Sisters Head from life.

Fig.7

BOY R. B. (4; 0).   SUPER NORMAL GIFT OF IMAGINATION
Text referring to Table VI on pp. 374, 376

PLATE VII

STAGES OF DEVOLOPMENT OF MELODY IN EARLY CHILDHOOD,
ACCORDING TO WERNER

The additional lines above or below the notes signify a slightly higher
or lower tone. (*Cf. pp.* 359, 360)

PLATE VIII

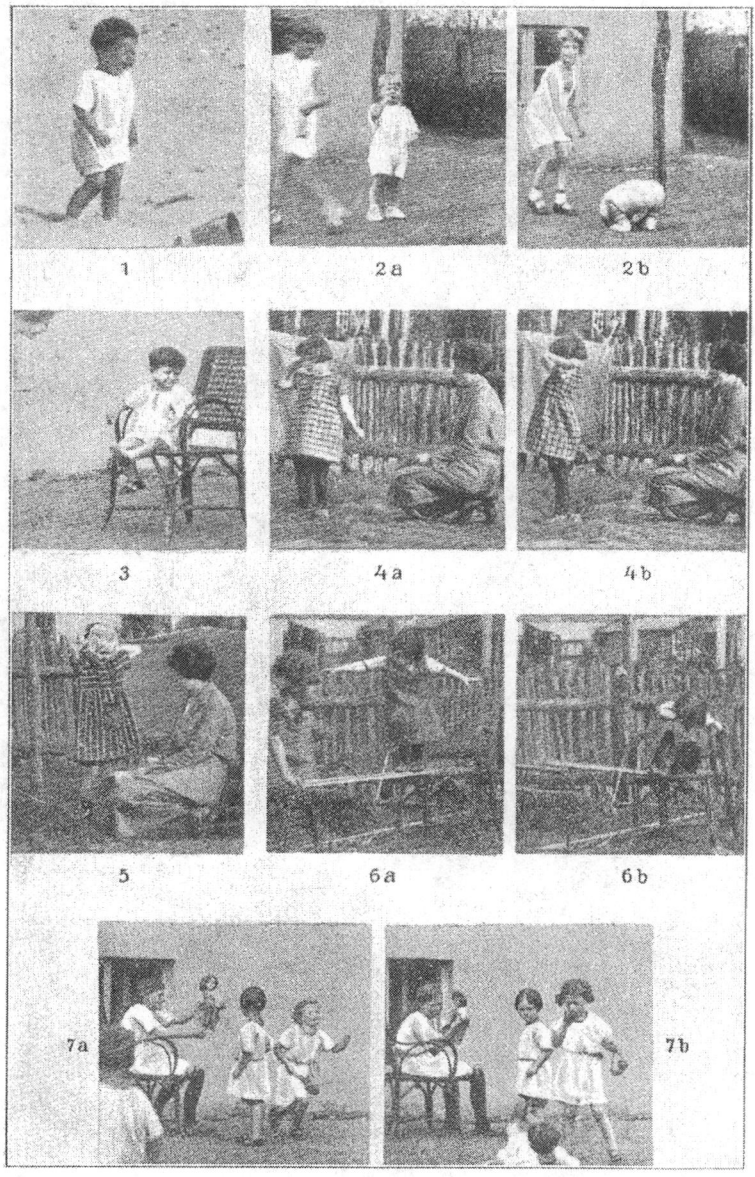

(Cf. pp. 574–577)

PLATE IX

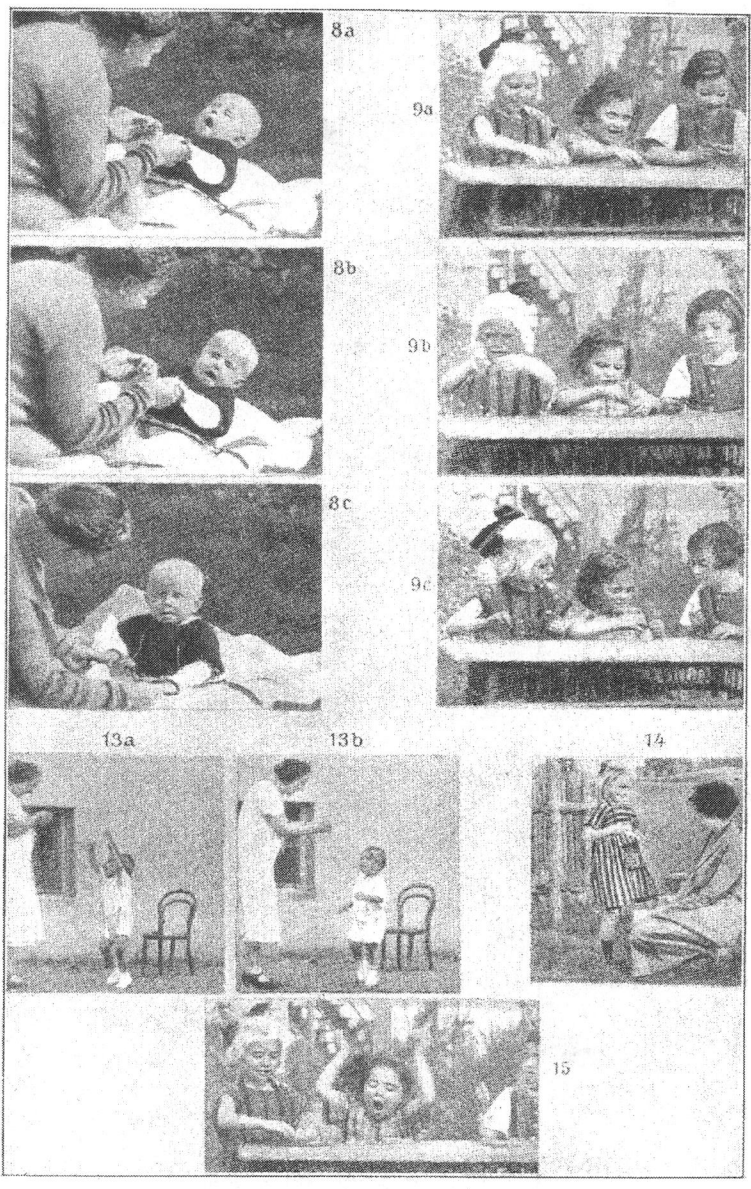

PLATE X

10

11₁

11₂

11₃

11₄

11₅

11₆

11₇

11₈

11₉

11₁₀

11₁₁

(Cf. pp. 578-582)

PLATE XI

11₁₂ 11₁₇ 11₁₃ 11₁₈ 11₁₄ 11₁₉ 11₁₅ 11₂₀ 11₁₆ 11₂₁

12a   12b   12c

(Cf. pp. 578–582)